MW01014765

Additional Praise for

The Risk Management Process

"Risk management is much more than guessing how much an investment can lose. Culp has collected the best thinking on the many dimensions of risk management and presents it in an accessible and thoughtful way. This is valuable reading for corporate treasurers, fund managers, and investors alike."

> Todd E. Petzel
> President and Chief Investment Officer
> Commonfund Asset Management Company

"Culp offers corporate treasurers a number of insights into risk. They can now use explanations in the book to educate nonfinancial executives, from the board level on down, as to what the risks are and how to manage them. His book will elevate discussions far beyond the notion that risk management is simply 'hedging with derivatives.' I only wish this valuable book had been on my shelf while I was treasurer at McDonald's Corporation. I would have drawn from its pages many times."

> Carleton D. Pearl
> President and CEO
> System Capital Corp.
> (a finance company for the McDonald's System)

The Risk Management process

Business Strategy and Tactics

CHRISTOPHER L. CULP

John Wiley & Sons, Inc.

New York • Chichester • Weinheim • Brisbane • Singapore • Toronto

Founded in 1807, John Wiley & Sons is the oldest independent publishing company in the United States. With offices in North America, Europe, Australia and Asia, Wiley is globally committed to developing and marketing print and electronic products and services for our customers' professional and personal knowledge and understanding.

The Wiley Finance series contains books written specifically for finance and investment professionals as well as sophisticated individual investors and their financial advisors. Book topics range from portfolio management to e-commerce, risk management, financial engineering, valuation and financial instrument analysis, as well as much more.

For a list of available titles, please visit our Web site at www.WileyFinance.com.

ISBN 0-471-40554-X

Printed in the United States of America.

10 9 8 7 6 5 4 3 2 1

acknowledgments

My views of risk management have been heavily shaped by my teachers, my colleagues, my friends, and my clients. I have learned much from many—too many to thank here—and so shall adopt the customary academic approach and thank only those by name who commented on this manuscript or whose coauthored work with me appears in some excerpted form within. In that regard, I am grateful to John Cochrane, Chad Coffman, George Constantinides, Kevin Dages, Ken French, Dean Furbush, Steve Hanke, J.B. Heaton, Barb Kavanagh (who deserves special recognition for having helped edit the entire manuscript—brave soul), Laura Kline, Alastair Laurie-Walker, Robert Mackay, Bob MacLaverty, Stuart McCrary, Ron Mensink, Andrea Neves, Mike Onak, Paul Palmer, Todd Petzel, José Scheinkman, Fred Smith, and my Autumn 2000 MBA class at the University of Chicago's Graduate School of Business. Most of the thoughts in this book that you find interesting or original probably belong to these folks, but any remaining errors definitely belong entirely to me.

Special thanks to Bill Falloon at Wiley who shepherded me through my first book project a year ago and was the instigator and faithful editor again of this one. Bill's capabilities as an editor are surpassed only by his knowledge of risk management and his patience for missed deadlines.

At a more personal level, thanks to all in my life who have tolerated what this book has done to my schedule, my personality, my temper, and my ability to honor my outside commitments. Hopefully Mr. Hyde will go back to his closet now that this is done, but for their patience in tolerating my dark and somber disposition and total unreliability these last months, special thanks to all my coworkers at CP Risk Management and Chicago Partners, the Executive Committee of the Governing Members of the Chicago Symphony Orchestra, and my friends and family—especially my parents, Lindalu and Johnny.

Finally, I would like to posthumously thank Professor Merton Miller, who embodied a truly unique combination of tireless energy, intellectual curiosity, creativity, natural intelligence, and insight. Through his unending efforts, Miller became one of the few people whose lasting impact will be felt in both academia and industry. His fingerprints will remain on both the theory and practice of finance, as well as the worthy fight against excessive government intervention in economic regulation.

In addition to his own substantial contributions to corporate finance, Miller also enriched the theory and practice of finance by cultivating the talents of many other innovators of modern financial theory, including Eugene Fama—Miller's first PhD student at the University of Chicago Graduate School of Business and his coauthor on *The Theory of Finance*—and Myron Scholes. Even after officially retiring from the university, Mert continued to teach a symposium for graduate students, supervise dissertations, travel the world delivering speeches, wrestle with heavy-handed financial regulators and the often-archaic laws that empower them, and serve on the boards of the CBOT, the CME, Dimensional Fund Advisors, and several other noteworthy groups.

I had the genuine privilege of working with Mert for the nearly 10 years I spent writing my doctor's thesis, as well as a few years thereafter. Several of those years we spent collaborating on various articles ranging from currency boards in Indonesia to overregulation of financial markets and value at risk. Not a small part of our joint efforts were spent embroiled in the controversy over Metallgesellschaft AG's so-called "derivatives disaster" in 1993. The fruits of our labors in that regard appeared in 1999 in the book we co-edited entitled *Corporate Hedging in Theory and Practice: Lessons from Metallgesellschaft* (London: Risk Books).

In addition to owing Professor Miller much of what I am professionally, I also felt—as did most all of his students—that he was much more than just an advisor. He was a mentor, devoted teacher, innovator, champion of free markets, faithful friend, and father figure—to many of us. Above all, Merton Miller was a gentleman and scholar of the highest order, endowed with prodigious grace and wit, as well as insatiable intellectual curiosity and keen insight. He will be most fondly remembered and greatly missed.

C.L.C.

contents

introduction

Discussions of risk management almost always center more on risk than management. How to measure value at risk is often regarded as more important to risk management, for example, than how conflicts between shareholders, creditors, and managers contribute to the need for risk management and inhibit its effective implementation. In business school programs as in actual practice, risk managers are more often viewed as "finance nerds" than general managers. In corporations, risk managers are usually perceived to be a cost center whose jobs senior managers and directors only sometimes understand and very rarely utilize to productive ends. Risk management, in short, is traditionally viewed as the necessary evil by which firms try to quantify—and, if possible, avoid—financial Armageddon.

To make the risk manager's image problem worse, *financial* risk management is regarded as a relatively new and fad-like phenomenon. Before the great derivatives disasters of the 1990s—Barings, Procter & Gamble, Metallgesellschaft, Orange County, and so forth—risk management was not seen as much more than insurance. Or risk management might have been seen by a trader as, say, how to leg out of one side of a straddle without getting too exposed on the other side. But in general, risk management was *not* seen as a discipline or function by its own right until after a number of mainstream, household corporate giants lost big money on so-called risky derivatives.

But to view *risk management* as novel, independent from, or even secondary to *general management* is to miss the whole point. If anything, risk management is first and foremost about sound general management. In that sense, risk management is an organizational function and business process is hardly new. Principles of sound general management have been around quite a while, and applications of those principles to risk management are not a particularly recent phenomenon—just ask the insurance industry.

Nor is risk management the exclusive playground of financial mathematicians and droll economists. Technical finance problems only enter the picture as distant subordinate issues to the management problems that both necessitate risk management and contribute to the difficulties with its implementation. Even then, the rocket science can usually be done in a back room by a specialist.

This book offers readers an integrated, comprehensive explanation for how a sound risk management process fits into a sound general management framework, whether it be at a bank, a pharmaceutical company, or a pension plan. Risk management as a process is rationalized, investigated, and demystified in terms of the new business strategies and tactics it engenders as well as the old strategies and tactics it impacts. A picture of risk management is painted that strives to *eliminate* thinking of risk management as a separate field. More than anything, a good understanding of risk management requires not an understanding of calculus or value at risk, but rather a solid grasp of the basic tenets of corporate finance and strategy.

WHAT THIS BOOK DOES NOT COVER

This book adds value by bringing together subjects that usually appear in many different places, often without reference to one another. But on any given detailed subject, earlier writings are certainly available.

I deliberately avoid getting into inordinate details about three very well-covered areas in particular, the first of which is asset pricing. Cochrane (2000) provides a serious, complete, and thoroughly current academic treatment of asset pricing, with Campbell, Lo, and MacKinlay (1996) in a distant second place. More narrowly focused and/or dated but nevertheless still solid references include Merton (1992), Duffie (1996), and Ingersoll (1987). For the not-too-faint-at-heart, a more rigorous presentation of asset pricing in a measure-theoretic framework is found in Duffie (1988). And always a classic no matter how old the original text is Fama and Miller (1972).

Risk measurement gets only a few chapters here. Those chapters are reasonably long, granted, but are intended to be broad surveys of methodologies and not toolkits for software programmers. For a deeper look at risk measurement, see Smithson (1998), Jorion (2000), Dowd (1998), and Best (1999). Further, there is no substitute for reading the current academic and trade literature.

A third area that has received enough attention and thus is not dealt with much in this book is financial engineering (e.g., derivatives pricing, hedging, trading strategies, and product design). Essential references in this area include the now-standard text by Hull (2000), as well as Jarrow and Turnbull (1999). For a good mixture of asset pricing and trading strategies, see Petzel (1989).

Two other subjects receive less attention than I would have liked to give them. For lack of space, these subjects—real options and risk-adjusted capital allocation—are given only brief coverage. The stack of books to pull off the shelf is fewer in number in these two areas than the others mentioned. For anyone remotely interested in risk-adjusted capital allocation, the book by Matten (2000) is required reading. For the basics of real options, Dixit and Pindyck (1994) and Trigeorgis (1996) still lead the field. Probably the best collection of actual cases of companies using real options theories in practice is Trigeorgis (1999).

OBJECTS AND CONTENT OF THE BOOK

Most books on risk management and/or financial instruments give very little time and attention to the issue of why corporations—whether trading houses, banks, pharmaceuticals, or windmills—should *care* about risk management. Doherty (2000) is a truly notable exception.

The absence of the treatment of things like expected utility theory and the M&M propositions at the front of many financial instrument and risk management books is not so much the failures of authors, but rather to the unfortunate association that exists between the rise of risk management and the advent of the great derivatives disasters. Risk management gained popularity in the 1990s as a response to large, well-publicized losses—and the regulatory and political scrutiny that followed them. Risk management was around well before Orange County went bust. But the sad linkage often made between risk management and loss avoidance has muddied the waters on why firms manage risk, both in rendering the question unimportant in many people's minds and in severing the link between *why* firms hedge and *how* firms hedge. This book attempts to explore and reestablish that linkage.

Part One begins with a discussion of risk management and corporate finance. Beginning a book on the business strategy and tactics or risk management with a discussion of basic principles of corporate finance may seem strange. But in fact, risk management and corporate finance are inextricably related, with corporate finance being the backbone of the *strategy* of risk management.

In many ways, risk management itself is a substitute for equity capital. Companies that have enough equity, after all, may well prefer to take an occasional loss rather than to spend considerable sums of money managing their risks. Indeed, the first principles of the theory of corporate finance—the Modigliani-Miller capital structure irrelevance propositions—tell us that value-maximizing firms *should not* spend money to manage their risks—at least not under certain assumptions.

For many years, the reasons why firms *should not* manage risk were swept to the side by assumptions that firms behave just like risk-averse individuals. As the modern theory of corporate finance has evolved, however, theories that explain why corporations can sometimes increase their value by pursuing formal risk management initiatives started to appear with increasing frequency. Today, the list of reasons for a corporation to pay serious attention to risk management is impressive.

Nevertheless, without a solid understanding of *why* risk management makes sense, the design of a risk management strategy and the implementation of that strategy can easily fall flat. At best, a failure to connect explanations for why managing risk can add shareholder value with the design of a risk management program will leave some unexploited efficiency gains and opportunities on the table. But at worst, the disconnect between corporate finance and risk management can lead a firm to implement the wrong risk management program altogether, sometimes leaving it exposed to even greater risks than if it had done nothing.

Chapter 1 begins with an introduction to the four-letter word that will reappear hundreds of times in this book—*risk*. This opening chapter offers some context to the definitional conundrum facing us when we use the term risk, and attempts to address some of those ambiguities by classifying risk into different perspectives that will be used throughout the book. In Chapter 2, the effect of risk on individuals is examined—specifically in the context of how risk affects individual behavior and how that behavior can be modeled using expected utility theory. The basic model of portfolio selection by a risk-averse investor—the Markowitz mean-variance portfolio selection model—is developed and extended to the problem of *hedging* by individual traders.

In Chapter 3, the various reasons why models of *individual hedging* do not extend to models of *corporate hedging* are presented, including a basic proof of the M&M capital structure irrelevance propositions. The inability of financial instruments such as derivatives to change the value of the firm in an M&M world is also explained. This then sets the stage for the next four chapters, each of which deal with explanations for why risk management *can* add value to a firm. The explanations include adding value by reducing expected costs, increasing expected cash flows, and decreasing the cost of capital (Chapter 4), reducing conflicts between security holders and managers (Chapter 5), reducing conflicts among different classes of security holders (Chapter 6), and managing or exploiting informational asymmetries (Chapter 7).

Chapters 8 and 9 conclude Part One by raising two strategic risk management issues often neglected in the mainstream theories of why firms hedge. The first issue, discussed in Chapter 8, is that firms can have a risk management focus aimed at any of three measures of financial strength—value, cash flows, and earnings. But these objectives are not always complimentary. An example is provided to illustrate that a firm concentrating on one of these measures for risk management purposes may do so to the exclusion of the others.

The second issue, discussed in Chapter 9 and often disregarded in discussions of corporate hedging, is the distinction between *total* and *selective* risk management. Specifically, some firms are observed actively managing some of their risks while actively bearing—or even loading up on—others. In general, firms focus more closely on managing the risks about which they have relatively less comparative informational advantage. Despite this tendency, however, most classical theories of hedging imply that firms should be indifferent as to which risks they reduce, and some even suggest that firms should strive to reduce *all* their risks. Navigating this minefield of connecting *why* firms manage risk to *how* firms manage risk against a backdrop of ambiguous theories of total risk management is challenging, but necessary if companies want to make the most out of their risk management strategies.

Part Two of the book—Risk Management and Business Strategy—builds on the principles outlined in Part One for how firms can create value by adopting risk management programs and processes and explores how a value-enhancing risk management process can be implemented by a firm. Part Two thus explores the business of risk management, and, in turn, the impact of risk management on business strategy more broadly.

Chapter 10 sets forth three basic business models for how risk management interacts with general business strategy—pure risk control, efficiency enhancement, and risk transformation. At one end of the spectrum, firms manage risks primarily to mitigate the potential for unexpected losses, and this process is usually independent of the rest of the firm's business strategy. Efficiency enhancers, by contrast, attempt to leverage the tools and expertise associated with risk control to exploit efficiencies elsewhere in the company (e.g., through better exposure identification, exploiting real options, and measuring risk-adjusted performance to control costs and improve compensation incentives). Risk transformers, in turn, supply their own expertise on risk management to other firms in the market—usually risk controllers—by integrating risk management into enhanced product and customer management methods.

Chapters 11 through 19 discuss the strategic design of a firm's risk management process, including risk identification, exposure measurement and monitoring, and risk control. In Chapter 11, the basic principles for enterprise-wide risk management are set forth with particular emphasis on people, processes, and technology. Chapters 12 through 14 then discuss exposure identification in more detail—the process by which companies should identify risk exposures and define their risk tolerances (Chapter 12), and the identification of spot, forward, forward-like (Chapter 13), option, option-like, and real option exposures (Chapter 14).

Chapters 15 through 16 address the next aspect of the risk management process: the identification and measurement of risk and the monitoring of risk vis-à-vis tolerances that the firm has defined as part of its business strategy. Chapter 15 presents the basics of market risk measurement and monitoring, ranging from simple parametric measures of risk (e.g., volatility) to more complex summary risk measures like value at risk and shortfall risk. Chapter 16 summarizes the basic principles of credit risk measurement, both for one-sided exposures (i.e., exposures that are always assets, such as purchased securities) and two-sided exposures (e.g., derivatives that can be either assets or liabilities depending on market moves). Chapters 17 through 19 briefly discuss the measurement of liquidity, operational, and legal risk.

Part Three of the book—The Tactics of Risk Control—then discusses how a company can try to ensure that the gaps between the risk tolerances commensurate with its business strategy and its actual risk exposures are kept to a minimum *ex ante* and can be closed *ex post*. Chapter 20 sets forth the basic principles of *ex ante* risk-adjusted capital allocation, both as pre-emptive risk control mechanism and a source of potentially significant security holder efficiency gains. Chapter 21 then explores the related issue of achieving risk control objectives through *ex post* performance evaluation and compensation. Traditional investment management measures of performance are reviewed and are related to corporate applications of risk-adjusted performance, including *ex post* risk-adjusted return on capital (RAROC).

Chapters 22 through 26 discuss various mechanical risk control solutions for firms whose actual risk exposures deviate from their strategically defined risk tolerances. Chapter 22 reviews the principles and practices of sound internal controls. Chapter 23 provides a high-level overview of hedging with derivatives. Chapters 24 to 26 then address how balance sheet and financing vehicles, securitizations, and insurance can be used to close the gap between a firm's actual and expected exposures.

AUDIENCE

The audience of this book is primarily senior managers and directors interested in learning about how risk management fits into the bigger corporate picture and how to figure out what kind of risk management process is the right one for your firm. The book minimizes industry biases. The corporate treasurer of a nonfinancial corporation will find this book as useful as the executive director of a pension plan or the chief financial officer of a bank.

Although some of the examples are industry-specific, they are just *examples*. The general management issues explored here have applications that transcend their industry barriers.

Portions of the book do presuppose some prior training in mathematics and statistics. I have tried to leave these sections general enough, however, that readers less inclined toward technical detail can skip those sections. Nothing in risk management that is truly fundamental requires mathematics or econometrics.

This book can also be used as text for a course on the strategy and tactics of risk management as a business process. The book may also be useful to faculty and students exploring the linkages between financial instruments and corporations. My own course at the University of Chicago's Graduate School of Business, for example, is primarily a course on derivatives, but because it is the second in a sequence of two MBA derivatives courses—the first of which is on pricing and hedging—the topics raised dovetail deeply into how derivatives play a role in corporate finance and strategy. For such a course, I hope this book will be helpful.

Risk Management and Corporate Finance

The Nature of Risk

- A man walks across the street and faces *it:* A car could spin out of control and accidentally run into him.
- A woman sits down in first-class sleeper seat 1A to cross the ocean on Airline FlyByNight and confronts *it:* A flight delay could cause her to be late to the crucial meeting that prompted her to spend $10,000 on her ticket, or the plane could end up in the ocean and she could miss the meeting in a more permanent sense.
- A child plays in its new crib and bears *it:* A design defect could cause the child to trap its head in the bars and get stuck, perhaps causing permanent harm.
- Harrison Ford accepts *it* when he takes a role in a new movie where he plays a drug-dealer cheating on his wife: His wholesome image as Han Solo, Indiana Jones, and Jack Ryan might never be the same.

It of course is *risk*. Risk is everywhere. You do not have to look very hard to find risk. When you want to preoccupy yourself, it is easy to convince yourself that the world is so inherently unsafe that it is better to be the Boy in the Bubble. It is easy to worry about the risks in the food you eat, the machines you operate, the stocks you purchase, and the air you breathe.

Most of us do not opt for the Howard Hughes solution. Instead, we *manage* risks. The man crossing the street at risk from being hit by a car might manage that risk by never crossing the street. Or he might a bit more reasonably adopt intermediate solutions designed to *reduce* his risk without completely eliminating it, such as looking both ways. The woman on Airline FlyByNight can manage risk by checking the frequency of on-time arrivals of her air carrier, calling ahead to see if the flight is on time, and generally avoiding airlines whose planes have a tendency to fall from the sky. Concerned parents can investigate their child's crib manufacturer and look for prior problems or complaints in places like *Consumer Reports*. And Harrison Ford can say no to bad scripts and stick to playing Jack Ryan.

Like it or not, the world is an unpredictable place. And as long as there is some uncertainty about the future that could result in an adverse outcome for individuals, the world is a place in which risk must be managed.

IS THE WORLD A RISKIER PLACE? [1]

Many argue that the world has become "a riskier place." This is certainly what the proponents of health and safety risk management like to argue. As a society, America has become obsessed with risk. Americans are among the healthiest, wealthiest people in history. And yet, we are among the most seemingly risk-averse. We worry about alar in apple juice, cholesterol in red meat, bovine somatotropin in milk, and more.

In finance, as well, many contend that the world has become more dangerous, both for individuals whose wealth is exposed to seemingly larger and larger swings in global equity markets and for corporations whose cash flows seem to depend more and more on unpredictable cross-border variables.

In fact, the evidence that risk is greater today than it was 10, 100, or even 1,000 years ago is hardly compelling—both in health and safety *and* in finance. How many more people are killed today by tainted pharmaceuticals than were killed 100 years ago when home remedies were the only thing available to combat disease? How many more people die from accidental electrocution than froze or starved to death before the advent of alternating current? How many more people threw themselves out of windows after the stock market crash of October 1987 compared to the crash of 1929? The answer to all these questions is not many, *if any*.

The tendency to claim that the world is a riskier place comes not from any real empirical evidence, but rather from the illusory temptation to pursue change without experiencing risk. But as Wildavsky (1988) argues, the effort to experience progress without risk is both paradoxical and futile.[2]

Innovation without risk is paradoxical because the process by which risk is most naturally addressed quite often *is* innovation—replacing the old with the new often makes the world a safer place. Unfortunately, nostalgia makes it all too easy to forget the risks of the old while listening to a news broadcast with sound bites about the risks of the new. Smith (1988) argues, "When we think of travel by horse in the pre-automotive era, we tend to forget the huge disposal problems created by horse wastes and carcasses. When we think of man's effect on nature, we forget nature's often cataclysmic effects, and we underestimate the extent to which material progress has enabled us to temper those effects."

The evolution of financial products in a risk sense has closely paralleled the evolution of health and safety risks. The good old days when the only real financial instruments to understand were stocks and bonds have been replaced by the arrival of new and often more complex financial products like index amortizing swaps, exotic options, finite risk insurance products, and other fancy instruments. But just as society had to take a risk on the canning process in order to reduce the danger of botulism from home canning, financial society has had to risk financial innovation. And that financial innovation has, like canning, led to opportunities to further reduce risk.

True, change often creates new risks. In that, the advent of canning and derivatives are not so different. With the reduced risks of infection that accompanied canning came the increased risks of injury to workers during mechanized processing, lead poisoning, and so on. Likewise, the interest rate, currency, and commodity price risks that derivatives help firms eliminate also pose a greater threat when derivatives are abused or misused.

Progress without risk is not just paradoxical, but also futile. As Wildavsky (1988) says, "Playing it safe, doing nothing, means reducing possible opportunities to benefit from chances taken, and can hurt people." The man who decides to stay at home rather than cross the street may appear to be reducing his risk, but what if staying at home stopped him from inventing penicillin? What if Henry Ford decided safer was better and never took what must have seemed like a *huge* risk of creating dangerous metal objects that roll around and threaten pedestrians? And what if the desire to play it safe had kept the Wright brothers from stepping off Kill Devil Hill in the wind that day in their terrifying artificial birdlike device that paved the way for modern commercial airline travel? How many *other* innovations would be lost without the mobility that air travel has brought us?

THREE COMMON FALLACIES ABOUT RISK

If we recognize that risky changes can be beneficial and choose not to sit idly by while the risky world evolves around us, how can we begin to develop a framework for *managing* risk *responsibly?* The answer to that question, in very broad terms, is that a healthy and responsible risk management framework that neither lends itself to over-caution nor to carelessness is a framework that avoids three basic fallacies. If risk management can be implemented without falling into these three traps, the groundwork for a healthy risk management program has been laid.

Fallacy 1: Risk Is Always Bad

The first important thing to realize about risk is that it can represent either a threat or an opportunity. The most common attitude toward risk is to think of it as a four-letter word—for more reasons than because it *is* a four-letter word. In fact, risk is neither good nor bad. It simply *is*. To a home-owner in coastal South Carolina, the risk of a hurricane is a horrifying one. But to the seller of lumber, sand bags, and weather radios in coastal South Carolina, that very same risk of hurricanes is a livelihood.

A closely related fallacy to "risk is always bad" is a fallacy that labels those who turn risk into opportunity as being insensitive and socially unde-sirable. The construction materials retailer who profits from a hurricane is preying on the suffering of others. Yet, without that construction materials retailer, rebuilding the coastline would be an impossibility. And the retailer is taking risks of his own, moreover. If a hurricane does *not* occur, the de-veloper may find himself with more lumber than he knows what to do with. In return for taking that risk, he charges an appropriately adjusted price when the disaster does occur and the demand for lumber rises. And despite victims' opinions of those retailers at the time, better to have them than not. Despite seemingly high prices, it is those very prices that guide resources to their most highly valued and needed uses. How much better off would we have been, for example, had the price mechanism been allowed to allocate scarcity in the gas crisis of 1979? Examples of turning risk into opportunity abound.

Decrying the role of the construction materials retailer in posthurricane rebuilding for opportunism is to confuse the emotions associated with the risk itself—the hurricane—with those who help provide a buffer against that risk. Even more common will be the tirades and angry accusations of insensitivity leveled at insurance companies that try to limit their payouts on a disaster like a hurricane. But without the insurance company's attention to *its* exposure, insurance would not be available *for anyone*.

Criticisms against those who appear to benefit from risk are nothing new. In his *Wealth of Nations*, Adam Smith reviewed eighteenth-century public attitudes toward *forestalling* and *engrossing*. Forestalling was an ac-tivity in which corn was purchased during times of plenty in hopes it could be resold when prices rose. Engrossing was a similar activity in which corn was purchased in one city and transported to another, hopefully to be sold at a profit greater than the transportation cost (Smith and Culp, 1989).[3]

The antitrade Corn Laws were intended in part to restrict forestalling and engrossing. Smith nonetheless noted the obvious benefits of those ac-tivities: "By making [people] feel the inconveniences of a dearth somewhat earlier than they might otherwise do, [forestallers and engrossers] prevent their feeling them afterwards so severely as they certainly would do, if the cheapness of price encouraged them to consume faster than suited the real scarcity of the season."

Smith went on to call forestalling and engrossing a "most important operation of commerce." He noted, "The popular fear of engrossing and forestalling may be compared to the popular terrors and suspicions of witchcraft. The unfortunate wretches accused of this latter crime were not more innocent of the misfortunes imputed to them, than those who have been accused of the former."

Engrossing and forestalling, too, were risky. If an engrosser guessed incorrectly about the corn price difference between cities in England, the engrosser paid for that mistake. Surely when those losses were incurred, few people were upset. But when some of England's respectable draymen and warehousers lost money engaging in forestalling and engrossing, the outcry against those novel and nontraditional activities must have surged.

Smith's view ultimately prevailed; the Corn Laws were repealed, and England's economy grew to be one of the largest in the world.

Fallacy 2: Some Risks Are So Bad That They Must Be Eliminated at All Costs

Contrary to the assertion of this fallacy, there is no risk so great that it must be eliminated at all costs. To drive home the essential parts of the sentence and avoid confusion, emphasis can be added to the key words and phrases: There is no risk so great that it must be *eliminated* at *all* costs. In other words, the issue is not whether or not bad risks should sometimes be reduced, but whether reduced means *completely eradicated* and whether the cost of that risk reduction comes into play.

Consider the risk that a comet or asteroid could strike the earth and wipe out humanity. As Hollywood has reminded us in *Deep Impact* and *Armageddon,* this is a real risk—there is some positive probability this event will occur. But does that mean everyone is ready to commit all of their personal funds to building self-sustaining caves in the ground below their homes? Hardly. Indeed, when faced with the choice between putting money toward a comet shelter, or, say, keeping the local school open, concern about the risk of an event that could well cause the extinction of humanity becomes greatly reduced.

The first lesson here is that risk must be evaluated in a probabilistic context and not merely in terms of consequences. If a comet hits the earth, the actual loss likely would be the end of the world. But if the probability of a comet hitting the earth is only 1 in 1 billion, then the actual loss must be viewed in that context.

The second lesson this fallacy teaches us is that the management of risk should somehow try to equate the benefit of risk reduction with the cost of risk reduction at the margin. Consider the case of sulfur dioxide pollution, which is a supposed source of such iniquities as ozone depletion and global warming. A factory can install a sulfur dioxide scrubber and *greatly* reduce its emissions. Up to a point, the benefit of reducing those emissions may well exceed the cost of a scrubber. But as emissions are reduced further and further, the cost of further reductions rises *and* the benefits of further decreases become less pronounced. In the extreme, the cost of *eliminating* all sulfur dioxide emissions is virtually unlimited, whereas most of the benefits are achieved early on and not from the reduction of emissions from one to zero parts per million.

Risk management thus must consider not just the benefit of reducing risk—if risk is indeed a thing to be reduced—but also the cost. At the margin, the two should be roughly equal for an optimal level of risk.[4] This leaves us in a politically incorrect position much of the time. We are forced to make statements like the following: The optimal quantity of pollution is not zero; the optimal amount of crime is positive; and the probability the airplane you board will crash *should* be slightly positive. These statements seem unthinkable. Nevertheless, strictly speaking, the statements are all true.

What these statements really mean is *not* that we like pollution, condone crime, or tolerate plane crashes, but rather that the marginal costs of achieving zero pollution, zero crime, and zero plane crashes are higher than the marginal benefits. It may be worth it to move from high risk to low risk, but *rarely* does it make sense to make the final step from low risk to zero risk.

In the end, risk cannot be completely eliminated at a reasonable cost. Instead of being eliminated, *risk thus must be managed.*

Fallacy 3: Playing It Safe Is the Safest Thing to Do

A risk-averse individual is a person who, other things equal, prefers certainty to uncertainty when the uncertainty includes a potential outcome worse than in the certainty case. In statistical terminology, a risk-averse individual will reject a fair bet.

A bet is considered fair if the price to place the bet is the same as the expected (i.e., probability weighted) winnings. Take the case of a lottery ticket that pays zero half of the time and $1,000 the other half of the time. The expected value of the lottery ticket is the probability weighted outcome, or $\frac{1}{2}(\$0) + \frac{1}{2}(\$1,000) = \$500$. A risk-averse individual would not pay $500 for the ticket because the value of $500 *for sure* required to pay for the ticket is higher to that individual than the value of a bet whose expected value is $500 but whose worst-case is zero. The risk-averse individual prefers not to part with the $500 and risk the possibility of having nothing, even if that possibility occurs with an equal probability of doubling his or her money.

A traditional assumption made in microeconomics and financial economics is that investors and individuals are risk averse. This assumption is probably pretty accurate and is *not* the source of this third fallacy. Rather, the third fallacy that playing it safe is the safest thing to do has more to do with the definition of safe than with whether or not people are risk averse.

Especially when dealing with politically sensitive issues like environmental protection or health and safety, the trend toward conservatism in risk management has increased in recent years. The risk that the Food and Drug Administration (FDA) approves a deadly drug to come to market is considered unacceptable. Accordingly, the FDA has an extremely strict and conservative policy about new drug approvals. The FDA thus plays it safe.

But what about the other side of the coin? What happens if the FDA's effort to keep dangerous drugs off the market also keeps *good* drugs off the market? How many people might die from that? Is playing safe in this example really the outcome that leads to the fewest fatalities? *Not necessarily.* And at the extreme, probably/certainly not.

In statistics, this conundrum is known as the Type I/Type II error bias. The following matrix illustrates the problem for some null hypothesis that this drug is not harmful:

		Hypothesis Is	
		True	False
Hypothesis Is	Accepted	Correct decision	Type II error
	Rejected	Type I error	Correct decision

A Type I error occurs when a true hypothesis is rejected, and a Type II error occurs when a false hypothesis is accepted. For the hypothesis "this drug is not harmful," the FDA approval of another killer Thalidomide is a Type II error, whereas the FDA rejecting the approval of the next penicillin would be a Type I error.

Human beings have a natural bias toward avoiding Type II errors. Part of that is just human nature—most risk-averse people err on the side of what they perceive as caution, despite the fact that the *consequences* of caution can sometimes be *worse* than not. In fact, some studies suggest that more people have died from the FDA marooning drugs in the approval process than have *ever* died from an actual bad drug being released.[5] This is not so unreasonable, given that drug companies have a strong desire to stay in business. Killing people is not usually conducive to future profits.

Apart from human nature, the bias toward Type II errors also results from the fact that the consequences of Type II errors are often more obvious than the consequences of Type I errors. *Information* about the consequences of the two types of errors is not always complete. If a bad drug is released, we can count the bodies. But who really knows how many people died from a good drug being withheld, or how many afflicted people the drug would have helped would have died anyway?

The impossibility of knowing the consequences of many Type I errors together with the vivid reality of Type II errors tends to drive people away from making the former in favor of the latter. Despite this tendency, it is important to recognize this might be *the wrong decision*. Playing it safe does not always yield the proper risk management solution, especially when the person making the risk management decision has incomplete information about what "safe" really means.

RISK MANAGEMENT AS A PROCESS FOR INDIVIDUALS AND ORGANIZATIONS

In general terms, risk management is the process by which an individual tries to ensure that the risks to which she *is* exposed are those risks to which she *thinks she is* and *is willing to be* exposed in order to lead the life she wants. This is not necessarily synonymous with risk reduction. As indicated, some risk is simply tolerated, whereas others may be calculatedly reduced. In still other instances, some individuals may conclude that their risk profile is *not risky enough*. A man who is extremely late to an important meeting and about to watch his bus pull away from the curb may not only willingly fail to look both ways at a cross walk, but he might—perhaps quite rationally—conclude that the risk of being late is so much higher than the risk of being hit by a car that bounding across the intersection when the light is green seems like the right judgment call.

The process of risk management can differ based on both the risk(s) being managed and the agent managing them. First and foremost, risk management is a problem faced by individuals. Although organizations, like companies, are just collections of individuals, organizations face a set of risks all their own.

Risk Management for Individuals

Risk management begins at the level of the acting human agent—*homo economicus,* or economic man. The decision to wake up is a type of risk management decision—or, more specifically, the deliberate decision *not* to wake up again represents the most extreme version of unwillingness to manage risk. Once the decision to live another day has been made, nearly each decision that follows has some risk management dimension to it. We manage the risk of not burning our fingers on the toast by using toasters that pop out the bread when it is done at the same time they turn off the heating elements. We manage the risk of not getting sick from spoiled eggs first by buying them from reputable establishments and then again by smelling and cooking them before eating them. We manage the risks of electrocution from the coffee maker by putting covers around wires and over alternating current wall sockets, and so on.

All of these personal risk management issues concern health and safety. But risk of injury or damage to our physical self is certainly not the only risk we face as individuals. We also bear intangible risks that may affect the quality of our life, such as reputation risks. The one homeowner on the street who never mows his lawn runs the risk that the neighbors will ostracize him. Telling too many white lies subjects you to the risk of not being trusted. Blaming the dog for eating the homework once too often makes it harder to miss an assignment when the pooch really *does* get a paper craving.

Reputation risks can also affect individuals through their professional lives. An actor who does a bad job or takes a bad script runs the risk of attracting subsequently fewer fans *and* fewer high-quality scripts. A professor who systematically teaches his students incorrect information will quickly lose his audience. An executive who plays office politics too much rather than earn performance-based promotions will lose the respect of his peers. These sorts of reputation risks cannot only reduce an individual's happiness, but also can reduce the person's *income*.

In broad terms, we refer to any risk as financial if the consequences of that risk come to bear on the cash flows of an individual. Being disliked by your neighbors is a reputation risk that does not necessarily translate into financial trouble, whereas being a dentist known to regularly work on the wrong tooth has direct financial consequences.

Apart from reputation risk, individuals also are subject to a variety of other financial risks: the risk that an increase in interest rates will raise the costs of an adjustable rate mortgage, the risk that a decline in global equity markets adversely impacts the value of retirement assets, the risk that an increase in gasoline prices raises the costs of commuting, and so on.

Risk Management for Organizations

Organizations are collections of individuals. A church is a collection of members and clergy. A golf club is a collection of golfers and the staff that serve them. A financial exchange is a collection of traders and the personnel who manage the exchange's trading infrastructure, and so on.

Fama and Jensen (1983a, 1983b, 1985) define four types of organizations, distinguished principally by the different relationships between stakeholders, managers, and users of the organization. The first type of organization is an *open corporation,* characterized by the almost complete specialization of decision management and residual risk bearing. In other words, management is typically a distinct group from those who have a residual claim on the net cash flows of the company (i.e., what is left after the bills have been paid). The residual claims of open corporations are almost always in the form of unrestricted common stock which can be freely bought and sold in the capital market.

A second type of organization is a *closed corporation* or *proprietorship*. These are organizations in which management and ownership overlap significantly. In other words, the same people that have a residual claim on the value of the firm also do the work.

The third organizational classification is called the *financial mutual*. These types of organizations have residual claimants who are also the *customers* of the organization. When the owner and the customer of the organization are one and the same, the financial mutual can be viewed as a type of club or syndicate. Hedge funds are examples of financial mutuals. Typically set up as limited partnerships, the partners of the hedge fund act as the owners who delegate primary management responsibility to a managing partner and as residual claimants who can withdraw their proceeds from the fund at any time. Spotting a financial mutual is usually easy inasmuch as these organizations have the unique property that a liquidation of shares by all owners *also* shuts down the organization.

Finally, *nonprofits* are organizations whose major goals are not to maximize profits. Instead, the objective of a nonprofit may be to preach the Word of God (e.g., a church or synagogue), feed the poor (e.g., Oxfam), teach the principles of business administration to student customers (e.g., The University of Chicago's Graduate School of Business), and the like. Because generating cash flows is not the primary objective of such organizations, they have no residual claimants per se. The closest thing are the donors and supporters that provide operating cash flows.

Each of the four types of organizations has both stakeholders and customers. A stakeholder in an organization is any individual whose personal welfare is affected by the success of the organization. Primary stakeholders are usually the residual claimants—shareholders or owners—of the enterprise. Creditors can also be stakeholders in these organizations to the extent that the success of the organization determines its ability to pay its bills. Managers are often stakeholders even when they are not also shareholders or creditors. Their jobs, after all, depend on the ongoing viability of the enterprise.

The success of an organization also impacts its beneficiaries or customers. Whether a nonprofit producing education in the classroom or a for-profit corporation producing soda pop, the customers of the organization represent the demand side of the picture, without which the organization could not exist. Customers of an organization may be either other organizations or individuals.

As collections of stakeholders and customers, *every* organization can inevitably be characterized as a group of individuals held together by, as Jensen and Meckling (1976) call it, *a nexus of contracts*. Accordingly, organizations inherit many of the risks to which individual stakeholders and customers are subject. Airline FlyMe runs the risk that all the passengers on a flight purchase refundable tickets and then get caught in a traffic jam and fail to show up. The airline also runs the risk that a disreputable or dishonest employee wrongly but credibly accuses the firm of cutting corners on maintenance, thereby resulting in reduced customer demand and lower revenues.

Apart from the risks an organization inherits from its individual stakeholders and customers, the organization *itself* also bears certain risks arising from the nexus of contracts that keep the organization together. The stakeholders and customers of Airline FlyMe, for example, bear the risk that jet fuel prices increase and adversely impact the net operating margin of the company *or* result in higher ticket prices. Other risks the airline bears include the risk that sales to foreign customers denominated in a foreign currency change in value as exchange rates move, the risk that dividends paid to foreign investors change in value as exchange rates move, the risk that changes in interest rates alters the present value of future investment projects, the risk that changes in interest rates changes the cost of debt capital for the firm, and so on.

The last section argued that individuals are subject to basically two kinds of risk—physical (e.g., health and safety) and financial (e.g., professional reputation or declines in retirement funds). The same grouping of risks is true for organizations. The physical risks borne by a company range from the risks of fire, flood, and theft to the risks of exploding machines and chemical spills. The financial risks include vulnerabilities to changes in market prices, the creditworthiness of contract counterparties, the risk of cash imbalances, and the risk of operational failures. Not to mention risks like reputational risk that can be even *worse* for companies than for people—Tylenol after some tainted capsules were found, Perrier after benzene was discovered, and the epic failure of new Coke that necessitated a name change to Classic Coke.

Unlike individuals whose risk management objectives are clearly defined with respect to personal well being, however, organizations have a muddier risk management mandate. One factor that blurs the clarity of the problem is *whose risks an organization is managing*. Is shareholder welfare the primary issue? Or management welfare? Or creditor repayments? Or employee satisfaction? Or customer retention?

If the interests of all the participants in an organization were perfectly aligned, the risk management objective of an organization would not matter so much. But the interests of various stakeholders in an organization are not only rarely aligned, but often in actual conflict. Managers, for example, might prefer to spend money on a new office coffee maker, whereas the owners of the company would rather see funds invested in a new production technology. Or shareholders of the firm might prefer to take on a risky project with potentially large losses *and* gains because they get to keep the gains and have losses limited on the downside by bankruptcy. The firm's creditors might not like the same project, however, because the higher project risk increases the chances they will not receive their money back without offering them the chance to participate on the upside if the project is a success.

Risk management by organizations thus starts to get tricky. The following questions come to mind:

- What are the risks to which corporations are exposed?
- Should individual stakeholders of the corporation or corporations themselves manage risk?
- What risks should the company manage?
- Is risk management always about risk control and loss avoidance, or can risk be turned into opportunity by the corporation?
- If some risks are to be managed by the company, what are the right tools it needs to engage in risk management most effectively?
- How does a company choose a method of changing the risks to which it is exposed—futures versus forwards, financial instruments vs. insurance?
- How does a company implement its strategic risk management objectives tactically?

The remainder of this book answers these questions.

CLASSIFYING THE RISKS FACING BUSINESSES

Risk can be defined as any source of randomness that may have an adverse impact on a person or corporation. Accordingly, risk management is the reaction to risk by individuals or businesses as they attempt to ensure that the risks to which they *are* exposed are the risks to which they *think they are exposed* and *want to be exposed.*

This book deals with the management of risk as a business process—how risks are managed in the context of broader corporate strategies and financing considerations. Risk management cannot be discussed in isolation from corporate strategy and corporate finance.

Before tackling the strategic and tactical issues of designing a risk management process for a company, agreement must first be reached on what we mean when we say *risk.* What does the risk in risk management really mean?

It is tempting to associate *definitions* of risk with *measures* of risk, such as the variance of returns on some asset. Although risk measurement will be addressed in some detail later, the goal at this stage is an entirely conceptual one. Consequently, this chapter makes use of mathematical formulas only when they make sense for illustrative purposes. Risk is a concept, not a particular statistical construct.

Developing a common understanding of what is meant by the term *risk* at the conceptual level is no trivial task. Some would say that one type of risk is *interest rate risk,* whereas others might break that down by maturity, currency, credit quality, and the like. Neither definition is actually wrong. Rather, it is merely a question of context—What do you plan to *do* with the definition? For a risk manager whose goal is quantifying the precise impact of changes in interest rates on a bond portfolio, the more finely portioned definition makes sense. For a CEO who is merely concerned with broad classifications of her company's exposure, the more generic definition may be adequate.

To most corporate executives, risk is defined in the same manner that U.S. Justice Potter Stewart once defined pornography: "I don't know how to define it, but I'll know it when I see it." Yet, for a risk management process to make sense, the definition of the risks to be managed cannot be left excessively vague. Defining risk in the Potter Stewart manner is a recipe for defining a risk only *after* it has gotten the best of you once.

In general, the conceptual definition of risk varies with the perspective. In this chapter, three different perspectives are offered for how to define risk. After presenting all three, the relations between these three mutually interdependent perspectives are explored.

Note that none of the perspectives of risk discussed next are unique to financial instruments. Whatever risk affects the value of a traded bond will also affect the value of a loan. And even apart from financial exposures, many of these risks affect nonfinancial exposures, as well. When discussing the thing that risk affects, the term *exposure* is used to reinforce the fact that *any* bundle of cash flows whose future value is uncertain is subject to risk.

EVENT-DRIVEN DEFINITIONS OF RISK

The first and probably most common perspective of defining risk is commonly found in risk management functions, corporate treasury functions, and at financial institutions. This perspective defines risk differently based on the type of event that can result in a loss. From this perspective, a potential loss arising from a flood is treated as a different risk than a possible loss tracing to changes in the yen/sterling exchange rate.

The level of detail into which we can go to characterize event-driven risks is practically limitless. Is information technology systems risk a risk, or a part of another, broader risk like operational risk? Is the risk of crop spoilage a risk on its own, or a subset of another? No correct answers to these questions exist. The purpose of classifying risk at all is partly pedagogical and partly analytical, so the level of detail in the classification should be commensurate with the level of detail required in the application.

For the purposes of this book, we will not get into particularly fine distinctions between specific events that give rise to risk. Instead, we use the relatively broader classification system proposed in the Global Derivatives Study Group (1993), often called the Group of Thirty Report after its sponsor.

Market Risk

Market risk arises from the event of a change in some market-determined asset price, reference rate (e.g., LIBOR), or index. The events that define market risk can be separated into two categories. The first type of event that generates market risk defines market risk based on the type of asset class whose price changes are impacting the exposure in question. A common form of asset class-based market risk is known as interest rate risk, or the risk that the balance sheet assets, liabilities, and off-balance sheet items of a firm—including its derivatives—will change in value as interest rates change. Other asset class-driven classifications of market risk include changes in the value of an exposure attributable to fluctuations in exchange rates, commodity prices, and equity values.

Any market-determined price, rate, or index value that impacts the cash flows of an exposure is called a *risk factor*. If we are interested in the present value of an asset, the discount rate also comes into play, although convention does not classify it as a risk factor. We also typically stop short of decomposing risk factors into the nontraded exposures that may underlie them. As will be explained in Chapter 3, Chapter 13, and elsewhere, for example, the common stock issued by a corporation can be viewed as a type of call option on the assets of the corporation. A contract to buy or sell a share of common stock thus has the common stock as its risk factor, which in turn has the assets of the firm determining *its* value. But we usually stop with the fact that common stock is the risk factor underlying a stock purchase or sale.

Apart from the risk factors that influence the value of an exposure, the market risk of an exposure can also be characterized based on *how* those risk factors impact its value. In this context, market risk generally is classified by using a colorful argot known as *fraternity row*. Trade practitioners and academics alike tend to refer to five types of market risk by using Greek or Greek-sounding letters.

Delta is the risk that the value of an exposure will deteriorate as the price or value of some underlying risk factor changes, all else equal. A bond is affected by changes in interest rates, so the interest rate is the risk factor. When interest rates rise, bond prices fall. Similarly, the value of a machine is the discounted NPV of the future cash flows generated by that machine. Because the discounting in the NPV involves interest rates, a rise in rates also puts downward pressure on the present value of the machine.

Gamma is the risk that delta will change when the value of an underlying risk factor changes. It is sometimes referred to as *convexity risk* or *rate of change risk*. Returning to the bond example, bond prices fall as interest rates rise, but the amount of the price change depends on the *level* of interest rates. Large interest rate increases may cause larger bond-price declines than small interest rate increases.

The risk that volatility changes in the underlying risk factor will cause a change in the value of an exposure goes by many names. *Vega, lambda, kappa,* and *tau* are among them. For purchased options (longs), *declines* in volatility pose the risk. Less volatility means there is a smaller chance that the option held will expire profitably. For options written (short), lower volatility increases the odds for profits by reducing the opportunities for unprofitable exercise against the short to occur.

Theta measures the risk to certain exposures due only to the passage of time. Insurance, for example, is an asset that decays or wastes over time. For every day that passes on an unused insurance policy, there is one less day for the insurance contract to become valuable.

Finally, *rho* is the risk that the interest rates, which are used to discount future cash flows in present value calculations, will change and impose unexpected losses on the firm. For many exposures, the discount rate is the borrowing or lending rate that corresponds to the maturity of the contract. For other contracts, such as swaps, a yield curve is used to discount cash flows, and hence any shifts in the level of any of several interest rates may affect cash flows.

Yet another market risk—correlation risk—is the risk of an unexpected change in the correlation of two factors affecting the value of a contract. We must be careful here to distinguish between *basis risk*, or correlation risk arising from the combination of a derivatives contract with another asset or portfolio, and correlation risk affecting a single asset held in isolation *or* in a portfolio.

The term *basis risk* comes from the term *basis*, which is usually defined as the difference in price between a derivatives contract and the current spot price. The oil futures basis, for example, is the difference between the current price of an oil futures contract and the current oil spot price. In equilibrium, a derivatives basis is equal to the marginal *cost of carrying* the asset underlying the derivatives contract to the maturity date of the derivatives transaction. In the oil example, the oil futures basis is thus the marginal expected cost of storing oil and the interest cost of oil storage *less* the marginal expected benefit of holding physical oil, which the holder of a futures contract foregoes. To take another example, the basis of a foreign exchange futures contract reflects the domestic interest rate less the foreign interest rate, because the former would be earned and the latter foregone if the spot currency were stored over time and *then* exchanged for the foreign currency.

Liquidity Risk

Liquidity risk occurs in the event that cash inflows and current balances are insufficient to cover cash outflow requirements, often necessitating costly asset liquidation to generate temporary cash inflows. Most firms, both financial and nonfinancial, have liquidity plans designed to manage funding risks. The well-publicized bankruptcy of Drexel Burnham Lambert Group, Inc., occurred due to a failure in funding risk management and has only increased corporations' attention to this risk.

Liquidity risk also includes a type of risk called *market liquidity risk,* or the risk that volatile markets will inhibit the liquidation of losing transactions and/or the establishment of new transactions to hedge existing market risk exposures. Suppose a firm has a forward contract to purchase British pounds for Deutsche marks three months hence. If the British pound experiences a massive and rapid depreciation vis à vis the Dmark—as happened in September 1992 when the European Monetary System's exchange rate mechanism collapsed—the forward contract will rapidly decline in value. If the forward contract is unhedged or the counterparty to an offsetting contract defaults, volatility may be so high that a new hedge cannot be initiated at a favorable price, even using liquid exchange-traded futures on pounds and Dmarks. The firm's market risk is thus exacerbated by market liquidity risk.

The distinctions between pure funding risk and market risk are reasonably subtle, as the two are clearly related. Market risk can be viewed as the risk of changes in the *value* of a bundle of cash flows when adverse market events occur. But value is just defined as the discounted net present value (NPV) of future *cash flows*. Market risk is thus in some ways inseparable from liquidity risk.

Perhaps a more useful distinction between the two concepts is achieved by noting that liquidity risk is based on the risk of cash flows *when they occur in time*. For the purpose of comparing liquidity risk at one time to liquidity risk at another, discounting to an NPV serves no purpose. On the contrary, all that is relevant is cash balances *per period*. Market risk, by contrast, deals with cash flow risks in *any* period, because *all* future cash flows ultimately affect the current NPV of the asset or liability in question.

Credit Risk

Credit risk is the risk of the actual or possible nonperformance by a firm. Credit risk can be subdivided along a variety of different dimensions, two of which will be summarized briefly here: settlement versus presettlement credit risk, and direct versus indirect credit risk.

Settlement versus Presettlement Credit Risk Presettlement credit exposure arises from the potential for a counterparty to default on a transaction prior to the initiation of the settlement of that transaction, whereas settlement risk is specifically associated with the failure of a firm *during* the settlement window, or the time period between the confirmation of a transaction and the final settlement of that transaction. The transaction may be anything—the initiation of a 10-year interest rate swap, the delivery of funds for securities, the exchange of funds denominated in one currency for funds denominated in another currency, or the transfer of funds in exchange for the acquisition of a real asset (e.g., a machine). *All* transactions take *some* time to settle.

Presettlement credit risk arises from the possibility that a party fails to make good on *future* settlements, or settlements that have not yet been initiated. This exposes counterparties to the risk that valuable assets will have to be unexpectedly replaced at then-current market prices. If Captain Piccard buys a toaster from Commander Riker and the two agree that Piccard will pay Riker $100 in a month at which time Riker will deliver the toaster, the declaration by Riker that he cannot deliver the toaster *before* the month is up constitutes a presettlement default. Assuming Piccard needs the toaster, he will have to find someone else—say, Commander Data— from whom to obtain the toaster. But by the time Riker notifies Piccard of his inability to make good on the deal, the price of toasters may have gone up. If Commander Data wants $110 for the toaster, Captain Piccard has incurred a $10 replacement cost loss (i.e., the difference between the price in the original, defaulted deal and the new price at which the defaulted deal must be replaced).

Now suppose Commander Riker is planning to buy the toaster directly from Counselor Troy for $90 to resell it to Piccard, but a month passes and Commander Riker cannot come up with the $90. This makes sense only if Riker must pay Troy *before* Piccard pays Riker, but assuming that is indeed the case, Riker will have no toaster for Piccard. As long as Riker informs Piccard of this *before* Piccard initiates his payment, the default is still considered a presettlement default.

To take a third case, suppose a month passes and Piccard pays Riker the $100 for the toaster. On the way back to his cabin to get the toaster, Riker is robbed by a Romulan, who steals both the money *and* the toaster. In this case, Captain Piccard will be on the receiving end of a *settlement* default (i.e., a default on one leg of a transaction after settlement on the other leg has been initiated irrevocably). In the case of a presettlement default, Piccard was only out the replacement cost, or the *difference* between the old transaction price and the new one. But in a settlement default, Piccard loses his *principal*, or the whole $100—and no toaster.

Settlement risk is sometimes called *Herstatt risk*, so named from the failure of Bankhaus Herstatt in Germany in 1974. The convention in most foreign currency markets is for settlement two days after a spot transaction is consummated or a forward contract matures. A number of New York banks had initiated payments to Herstatt on their side of a bunch of spot and forward currency trades, and Herstatt failed *after* those payments were initiated from New York but *before* any reciprocal payments were initiated from Germany. The New York banks suffered considerable principal losses.

One means of mitigating settlement risk is by *netting* like cash flows in the same currency whenever possible. Instead of A owes B $10 and B owes A $12, the net payment of $2 from B to A is the only cash flow that occurs at settlement. Although bilateral netting of this sort greatly reduces the settlement risk of many financial transactions, contracts in which funds are exchanged in different currencies or in which funds are exchanged for assets cannot be net and thus are subject to full settlement risk. A toaster cannot be netted for cash.

Direct versus Indirect Credit Risk   A second perspective from which credit risk can be viewed pertains not to the timing of the default as in the prior section, but instead to the source of the risk. Direct credit risk is the risk of a failure by a counterparty to deliver assets or funds when required to do so *or* an increase in the perceived probability that such a failure will occur in the future. The former is typically called *default risk*, and the latter *downgrade risk*. In either case, the direct credit risk borne by a company is limited to the counterparties and security issuers with which that company has direct contractual relations.

Indirect credit risk—sometimes called *credit-dependent market risk* or *spread risk*—is the risk that the value of an asset declines because of a change in the credit risk of some firm with which the enterprise has no direct dealings. For concreteness, consider a swap contract with a notional principal of $1 million in which nonbank Company Ludlum makes a semi-annual payment to nonbank Company LeCarré based on the realization of six-month LIBOR, in return for which Ludlum receives a semi-annual payment from LeCarré based on the six-month Treasury rate. Sometimes called the Treasury-Eurodollar or TED spread, the spread in this swap will be driven in large part by differences in liquidity *and* credit quality in the two markets.

The six-month Treasury rate is the rate on zero-coupon securities issued by the U.S. Treasury and backed by its full faith and credit. If market participants agree that the government has no default risk over the next six months, this rate is determined primarily by the classic equation postulated by Irving Fisher in 1930. According to the Fisher equation, the six-month Treasury rate is approximately equal to the six-month "real" rate of interest—or, as Fisher characterized it, the marginal "rate of time preference" consumers have for consumption today vis-à-vis consumption tomorrow—plus the rate of inflation expected to prevail over the next six months.

Now consider six-month LIBOR, which represents some average of rates at which commercial banks offer to lend money to other commercial banks in the Eurodeposit market. In the absence of any differential liquidity effects, six-month LIBOR is basically the same rate *except* for the important distinction that LIBOR is determined by commercial banks that can, in principle, default on their obligations. Yet, this distinction is enough not only to keep six-month LIBOR at a premium to six-month Treasury rates but also to ensure that premium fluctuates—sometimes quite a lot, as Figure 1.1 shows. Because liquidity effects are not the same in both markets and cannot be assumed away, some of these fluctuations may owe to liquidity and not credit considerations. But at least *some* component of the TED spread reflects changing perceptions of banks about the likelihood of default by their counterparties.

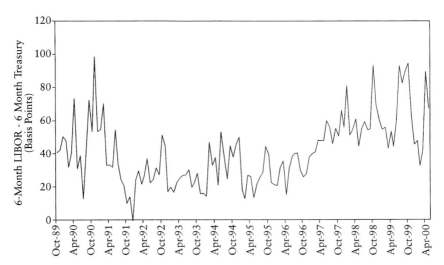

FIGURE 1.1 The TED spread (month-end, Sept. 1989–May 2000). *Sources:* FNMA (LIBOR) and Federal Reserve Board (Treasury).

A bank that borrows from another bank in the form of a six-month term Eurodeposit bears direct default risk and resale risk to the extent the deposit is marked to market. But both of these are clearly *credit* risks. Now return to our basis swap between Companies Ludlum and LeCarré. Because neither firm is a bank, neither firm participates in the determination of LIBOR nor bears any direct default or resale risk *in LIBOR*. The two companies do, however, bear *market risk* that is driven by changes in the TED spread, at least part of which is determined by the credit risk of banks that participate in the Eurodeposit market.

In simple terms, indirect credit risk or credit-dependent market risk is the risk that the present value of a bundle of cash flows can change when the credit quality of a third party (i.e., neither creditor nor debtor in the actual transaction in question) appears to change. Company Ludlum loses money when the banks that determine LIBOR experience an increase in perceived default risk, which places upward pressure on LIBOR relative to the default-free Treasury rate. For Ludlum, this is the *market risk* of the swap, but it is driven in part by the *credit risk* of the participants that determine the reference rate in the swap.

Note that Ludlum and LeCarré also bear direct credit risk in the swap, as well. As the swap moves into-the-money for LeCarré when the TED spread widens, LeCarré now bears the risk that Ludlum will default on its payments to LeCarré. Although the size of the loss to which LeCarré is exposed depends on LIBOR, the risk of a default actually occurring is the credit risk of Company Ludlum. So, the perceived default risk of Ludlum impacts the *direct* credit risk of the swap from LeCarré's perspective, whereas the perceived default risk of participants in the Eurodeposit market impacts the *indirect* credit risk or credit-dependent market risk of the swap.

Operational Risk

Operational risk is the risk that failures in computer systems, internal supervision and control, or events such as natural disasters will impose unexpected losses on a firm's derivatives positions. Consider a firm that enters into a variety of customized transactions—financial and commercial—governed by nonstandard contracts rather than master agreements. If the firm has a fire and its documentation is destroyed, its portfolio might literally become unidentifiable in a matter of minutes.

Other aspects of operational risk relate to personnel quality and internal controls. Fraud or irresponsible trading activities by employees is a type of operational risk. Alternatively, employing personnel whose skills are not adequate to carry out their tasks responsibly is also an operational risk, and can have consequences as significant as fraud.

In the case of operational risk, the problems tend to arise because inadequate attention was paid to some process or system or because personnel either fail to perform their duties or have ill-specified responsibilities. Counterintuitive as it sounds, *people* thus tend to be at the root of most operational risks, which inevitably arise from someone making a questionable decision—either by mistake or on purpose.

Legal Risk

Legal risk is the risk that a firm will incur a loss if a contract it *thought* was enforceable actually is not. The Global Derivatives Study Group (1993) identified several sources of legal risk for innovative financial instruments that are often associated with risk management, including conflicts between oral contract formation and the statutes of frauds in certain countries and jurisdictions, the capacity of certain entities (e.g., municipalities) to enter into certain types of transactions, the enforceability of close-out netting, and the legality of financial instruments. In addition, unexpected changes in laws and regulations can expose firms to potential losses, as well.

Capacity   Some concern remains about the legal authority or capacity of certain entities—most prominently municipalities—to enter into privately negotiated derivatives transactions. In a well-publicized 1991 case before the U.K. House of Lords, it was determined that the Hammersmith borough of London did not have the statutory capacity to enter into the numerous swap transactions that it had been negotiating since 1981. The Law Lords held that "a local authority has no power to enter into a swap transaction," thereby rendering the contracts *ultra vires*. That ruling of the House of Lords invalidated swap agreements between more than 130 councils and 75 major banks, and it reportedly resulted in over $1 billion in total losses to counterparties.[6]

Concern persists in the marketplace that counterparties to certain types of financial transactions, still including many swaps, may not have the legal capacity—or, more recently, the suitability—to enter those transactions, thereby giving rise to fears that the Hammersmith experience could be repeated in the future.

Selective Enforceability   Selectively enforcing or "cherry-picking" only the favorable terms in a contract is another form of legal risk. For example, close-out netting allows two counterparties to net any payment obligations after an event of default by one of the counterparties triggers the early termination of contracts between the two counterparties. Suppose two U.S. nonfinancial corporations, Company Victoria and Company Jungfrau, enter into a simple interest rate swap that stipulates close-out netting. One year before the last settlement date, Company Victoria owes Company Jungfrau $1 million, and Company Jungfrau owes Company Victoria $1.1 million—which means that Jungfrau owes $100,000 to Victoria in the event of default by either firm.[7] But if the netting provision of the swap is unenforceable and Company Jungfrau defaults, it may insist on collecting the *gross* $1 million from Company Victoria *even though it cannot pay the $1.1 million in return.*

Legality The legality of certain transactions like derivatives occasionally is called into question because of broadly or improperly written laws. In the United States, for example, state anti-gambling laws have sometimes inadvertently included certain types of derivatives and rendered them illegal.[8]

Regulatory risk is the related risk that actions taken by regulators constitute events that can unexpectedly raise costs and risks for market participants. Financial instruments can be highly specific, customized products. In contrast, statutory regulations are general and inflexible. Forcing the regulation of financial innovation into an inflexible statutory and administrative law infrastructure in which regulators must operate is rather like instructing a child to insert a square peg into a round hole. Despite the futility, an obedient child will try to make the peg fit, often with disastrous consequences for the peg.

Regulatory risk can take two forms. First, *procedural regulatory risk* is the risk that legal uncertainties and financial losses will result from ill-conceived and costly changes to statutory or administrative regulations. Congressional actions precipitate the first, and unilateral regulatory actions the latter.

The second type of regulatory risk is *judgmental regulatory risk*. This risk stems from inadequately informed examiners and regulatory auditors who attempt to review the derivatives activities of a firm based on incomplete information. Very complex, dynamic trading strategies can be difficult to explain to examiners in a short period of time. Examiners may be likely to draw conclusions based on conservatism, thereby resulting in actions taken to discourage the use of such complex programs. Similarly, examiners and regulatory auditors may not possess the quantitative skills necessary to evaluate the mathematical models used by firms for risk management.

Other Risks

The risks discussed above—market, liquidity, credit, operational, and legal—are the primary risks on which the Global Derivatives Study Group (1993) focused. These risks are called—somewhat misleadingly—financial risks. In addition, there are many other risks with which a firm may need to concern itself, sometimes merely on an ad hoc basis and sometimes through its regular risk management process. These risks will differ in importance from one firm to the next, and the examples that follow are risks that fall outside the classic Group of Thirty taxonomy.

Intellectual Risk   Intellectual risk arises in the event that personnel with specialized knowledge leave a firm and make it difficult for the firm to continue managing the risks of its positions and portfolios. Suppose a firm keeps poor records of derivatives positions, payment schedules, and hedging policies. If key trading personnel leave the firm, the company could miss payments or incur losses on the portfolio as prices change due to a failure of understanding of any dynamic hedging strategies in place.

More realistic examples of intellectual risk occur in large firms with complex bureaucracies. Senior management may fail to realize how important one or two workers are for identifying records, reports, or risk exposures. If those people take ill or leave on vacation, not to mention switch jobs, losses may be incurred in a fast-moving market while important information is located and retrieved.

Customer Loss Risk   At the core of risks facing a business is the risk that the business loses its customers, either because a competitor attracts them away or because they no longer demand the products and services you are selling at the prices you are quoting. Customer loss risk thus encompasses pricing risk, or the risk that firms misestimate either the level or the structure of prices for their customers.

The importance of customer retention has been vividly illustrated by the recent boom in internet commerce. To a start-up Web company, its ability to accurately assess customer value is everything. Only when those values can be compared accurately to the cost of customer acquisition can the business truly be valued. For this reason, attention to customer loss risk and customer valuation has perhaps never been higher.

Nevertheless, customer loss risk is just as important—perhaps *the* real core risk of operating a profitable business—for *all* types of firms. An airline must worry about customer loss just as much as an online bookstore. And a consulting firm must be as attentive as an airline. And so on. If either the demand curve shifts in for exogenous reasons *or* available substitutes for the good or service being sold become relatively more attractive, the business is in trouble.

Supply Chain Risks   Many nonfinancial firms also face risks from adverse events that may occur at any point along a physical supply chain, or the chain that connects inputs to the firm's production process to its outputs. For a typical nonfinancial firm, the physical supply chain and examples of what occurs at each stage are shown in Figure 1.2.

Origination	Transformation	Trading/Execution	Delivery
• Planting	• Milling	• Importing	• Distributing
• Growing	• Processing	• Exporting	• Consuming
• Harvesting	• Storing	• Roasting	
	• Insuring	• Transporting	
	• Refining		
	• Transporting		

FIGURE 1.2   The physical supply chain.

Problems may arise at any juncture in this supply chain. Consider, for example, a firm that grows wheat, mills it into flour, and exports the flour to bread makers around the world. Problems could arise at origination from disease, bad weather, vandalism, or any number of other factors that prevent the crop from being grown and brought in according to schedule (both time and quantity). At the transformation stage, equipment breakdowns could occur, contamination of the grain is a possibility, and losses of product during transportation a consideration, and so on. In short, the firm faces some form of inventory or product risk at every stage here.

DIVERSIFIABILITY

The event-driven taxonomy of risk discussed previously differentiates types of risk based on the type of event that might trigger a loss. Whereas this nomenclature is popular with risk managers and treasurers, an alternative lens through which to view risk is more popular with academics, portfolio managers, and investors. This perspective on risk differentiates between only two types of risk—the risks that a firm can diversify or hedge away, and the risks that it cannot.[9] Diversifiable or idiosyncratic risks in any bundle of cash flows are those risks particular to the bundle of cash flows in question, including the features of the firm holding the bundle of cash flows. *Systematic risk,* by contrast, refers to changes in the values of assets that are driven by movements in some risk factors that affect *all* bundles of cash flows.

To divide the total risk of an exposure into idiosyncratic and systematic components, some set of systematic risk factors must be defined. A systematic risk factor is any economic factor (e.g., aggregate consumption growth) whose changes drive *all* asset prices. The impact of a change in a risk factor on any particular asset price may be different depending on the asset, but if the risk factor is truly *systematic,* it affects *all* asset prices in some way.

The Single-Factor CAPM

The most popular way to decompose risk into idiosyncratic and systematic components is using the single-factor capital asset pricing model (CAPM) of Sharpe, Lintner, Mossin, and Black. In the CAPM, the return on *any* asset *j* is related to a single risk factor, the return on the market portfolio. Specifically, the CAPM implies that the excess return on any asset *j* (i.e., return in excess of the risk-free rate) is proportional to the covariance of the return of that asset with returns on the market portfolio and to the excess return on the market portfolio. Although the model involves the *true* market portfolio of all invested wealth and the *true* risk-free rate, we usually measure these variables using a broad equity index (e.g., the S&P 500) and the U.S. Treasury bill rate, respectively.

Mathematically, the CAPM implies the following for any asset *j*:

$$E(R_j) - R_f = \beta_j \left[E(R_m) - R_f \right] \tag{1.1}$$

where $E(R_j)$ is the expected return on asset *j*; R_f is the risk-free rate (i.e., Treasury bill rate); $E(R_m)$ is the expected return on the market; and:

$$\beta_j = \frac{\text{cov}(R_m, R_j)}{\text{var}(R_m)}$$

The parameter β_j measures the degree to which changes in the systematic risk factor—the market—impacts changes in expected asset returns. In other words, the expected excess return on the market portfolio is the risk factor, and β_j is the "price" of that risk factor *in asset j*. The price of market risk may be different for different assets, because both β_j and $E(R_j)$ differ for different assets and portfolios. Nevertheless, the characterization of expected excess returns on the market as a *systematic* risk factor means that the excess return on the market always affects excess returns on assets *somehow*.

The CAPM is called a single-factor model because excess returns on all assets are systematically affected by only one factor—the excess return on the market portfolio. In the CAPM, all systematic risk thus is reflected in the relation between expected asset returns and expected market returns, and the price of this systematic risk—the degree to which it affects returns on a particular asset—is reflected fully in beta.

Any particular asset also may be affected by idiosyncratic risk, or market risk that is specific to the asset in question. To see the impact of systematic risk on the return on any asset j, we can rewrite the CAPM relation in Equation 1.1 without using expected values as follows:

$$R_j - R_f = \beta_j \left(R_m - R_f \right) + \varepsilon_j \tag{1.2}$$

where ε_j is a term that reflects the idiosyncratic risk of the asset. Equation 1.2 essentially says that the *actual* return on asset j is equal to the risk-free rate plus the asset's beta times the actual excess return on the market *plus a shock that reflects risk specific to asset j*. If the expected value of ε_j is zero, the above equation becomes the CAPM equation in expected value terms. If R_j is the actual return on some well-diversified portfolio j rather than a single asset, the assumption that $E(\varepsilon_j) = 0$ is equivalent to presuming that the diversification effects of the portfolio cause all idiosyncratic risks to net out.

Multifactor Asset Pricing Models

The CAPM has been sharply criticized as an unrealistic representation of systematic risk. Specifically, significant academic work has shown that the excess return on the market is *not* the only factor that significantly affects all asset returns. Other systematic risk factors known to affect all stock returns, for example, include leverage, market capitalization, dividend yields, and the ratio of book to market equity.

Numerous alternatives to the CAPM have been proposed that presume excess returns on any asset are a function of *multiple* systematic risk factors. The particular factors differ depending on the particular model in question, but the basic form of the relation is usually the same:

$$R_j - R_f = \delta_1 \gamma_1 + \delta_2 \gamma_2 + \cdots + \delta_k \gamma_k + \varepsilon_j \tag{1.3}$$

where γ_1 is the first systematic risk factor and δ_1 is the "price" of the first risk factor in asset j. In other words, δ_1 measures the sensitivity of returns on asset or portfolio j to changes in the first systematic risk factor, and so on for the other risk factors through k. The number of risk factors, k, can be small or large depending on the particular model, all of which collectively reflect the systematic risk of asset j's returns. Like the CAPM, the term ε_j reflects the idiosyncratic risk of asset or portfolio j (i.e., that risk which is specific to asset or portfolio j).

Identifying systematic risk factors can be difficult, and the systematic risk factors usually need to have a few important characteristics. The idiosyncratic risk term should be uncorrelated with all the systematic risk factors—$cov(\gamma_m \varepsilon_j) = 0$ for all m. In addition, the systematic risk factors should *exhaustively* span all of the possible sources of systematic risk impacting asset prices. Some factors that fall into these categories are macroeconomic, such as real consumption growth. Other factors cannot be identified directly, so factor-mimicking portfolios—portfolios whose returns are perfectly correlated with the underlying risk factor—must be chosen as substitutes.

FINANCIAL VERSUS BUSINESS RISK

Yet a third perspective on risk attempts to distinguish between financial and business risks.[10] Put most simply, financial risks are those that a firm is not in the business of bearing and business risks are those that the firm must bear in order to operate its primary business.

The distinction between the concepts of business and financial risk was proposed by Frank Knight (1921). Knight defined financial risk as risk, or situations in which the randomness facing a firm can be expressed in terms of specific, numerical probabilities. These probabilities may be objective (as in a lottery) or subjective (as in a horse race), but they must be quantifiable. Because they can be quantified, they can be managed. Financial risk is thus a risk that firms *can* avoid.

Unlike risk, Knight defined *uncertainty* as situations when a firm faces some randomness that *cannot* be expressed in terms of the probabilities of alternative outcomes. This was business risk in Knight's eyes, or the risks about which only the firm in question had some perceived special insight. To Knight, uncertainty was the source of all major profits and losses to businesses. Lord Keynes agreed, choosing the term *animal spirits* to describe essentially the same phenomenon.

In this context, the distinction between business and financial risk—Knightian uncertainty and risk—is driven purely by information. Those factors about which a firm perceives itself as having some comparative informational advantage will be those factors on which the business concentrates for its core business cash flows. Risks about which the firm has comparatively less information will be those risks more likely to be hedged, diversified away, or controlled in some other fashion.

The distinction between business and financial risk clearly rests on a slippery slope. Not only does it vary from one firm to the next, but it also depends not on the quality of information the firm *actually* has, but rather on the firm's *perceived* comparative advantage in digesting that information. Perceptions, of course, can be wrong. Businesses fail, after all, with an almost comforting degree of regularity. Without business failures, one might tend to suspect the market is not working quite right. Accordingly, the preponderance of actual business failures clearly means that some firms *thought* they had a better handle on information than they did, whether that information concerns market demand for their products, their competitors, or their costs.

Despite the vagaries of distinguishing between business and financial risk, the distinction is an important one conceptually and pedagogically for the rest of this book. As will become clearer later, successful business strategy is also in large part about exploiting perceived comparative informational advantages—loading up on the risks the firm is uniquely positioned to handle, and getting rid of the other ones.

RELATIONS BETWEEN THE THREE PERSPECTIVES

As noted at the beginning of this chapter, the three perspectives on risk are not independent. On the contrary, they are *equivalent* ways of looking at the same picture from different angles. Indeed, the primary reason that these three perspectives coexist is the disparity in audiences and in why risks are being examined at all.

The academic perspective of risk is the second one, which views risk as either systematic or idiosyncratic. As noted, the operationalization of this concept is hindered by the dependence of the concept on the "correct" asset pricing model. But as a concept, it is both a perfectly legitimate way to view risk *and* perfectly consistent with the other two. Whatever risk factors are used to characterize systematic risk, the basic principle of portfolio diversification means that *any* event-based risk types are idiosyncratic if they can be diversified away. Accordingly, *all* of the event-based risk types are firm-specific, idiosyncratic, and diversifiable.[11]

Market risk as defined in the event-based risk taxonomy may be either systematic or idiosyncratic from a diversifiability risk perspective. The risk of commodity price changes on a gold mine's cash flows is clearly idiosyncratic, but the risk of marketwide changes in the value-weighted portfolio of world stocks and bonds is clearly systematic, even though *both* are sources of market risk for the gold mine. The particular perspective adopted depends on the business strategy of the firm in the context of its risk management initiatives.

Similarly, gold price fluctuations that represent market risk in the event-based risk nomenclature and idiosyncratic risk in the diversifiability definition of risk can be *either* a business *or* a financial risk. Whether gold price fluctuations represent a source of financial risk that the firm may wish to hedge or represent an opportunity that the firm may wish to exploit is unclear *ex ante*. Indeed, the fact that some gold mining firms hedge and others do not is a strong indication that the distinction between business and financial risk is far from obvious. (For an excellent analysis of hedging in the gold mining industry, see Tuffaro [1996].)

CHAPTER 2

Risk Aversion, Insurance, and Hedging

This chapter presents some of the important linkages between risk and models of individual behavior. The basic goal of the chapter is to explain why *risk-averse individuals* either buy insurance or, in a financial context, engage in hedging and risk management activities. This chapter reviews the basic, classical risk management model applied at the level of the individual. We will see under what circumstances an individual trader might increase her positions in the market, be indifferent to her position, or wish to reduce certain risk exposures by purchasing insurance or hedging.

These issues may seem a bit abstract and far-removed from the subject of corporate risk management, but, in fact, most models of *corporate* hedging and risk management borrow liberally from this benchmark case of *individual* risk management. Yet, as we shall see throughout the rest of Part One of this book, the jump from why *people* manage risk to why *companies* manage risk is a long jump. This jump from individual behavior to corporate behavior often produces models that fall flat empirically and are of little or no use strategically.

RISK AVERSION AND UTILITY THEORY

The notions of risk neutrality and risk aversion were briefly and anecdotically introduced in Chapter 1. Because they are so central to classical hedging and insurance theories, these notions merit further attention. Absorbing, processing, and comprehending all the mathematical details here is unimportant, but the concepts will resurface throughout this book.

A Refresher on Basic Utility Theory

In modern microeconomic theory, individuals are presumed to have a *utility function* that associates wealth or consumption with individuals' degrees of happiness. Although the functional form of this utility function that all individuals are presumed to have is not always specified, most economists agree that it should exhibit several important characteristics for most individuals. The first behavioral feature of a normal utility function is that people prefer more to less. If utility is defined using consumption, more consumption is better than less. You can always give away or burn the excess, after all.

The second, related behavioral axiom is called *nonsatiation*. That simply means that people never reach a point where they have enough. More is *always* better than less. This makes some sense intuitively, because at a minimum it simply means that people derive some happiness from giving away what they themselves do not want or need.

A third important characteristic of the neoclassical utility function is called *diminishing marginal utility*. Although more is preferred to less, people tend to prefer more to less at a decreasing rate. So, the first steak consumed is better than the thousandth steak consumed in a year. Moving from a total wealth of $100,000 to $200,000 is more satisfying than moving from a net worth of $100,000,000 to $100,100,000, and so on.

If a typical individual's utility function is denoted $U(W)$ where W is wealth (or consumption opportunities), then the nonsatiation and diminishing marginal utility behavioral axioms can be expressed mathematically:[1]

$$U(W) > 0 \quad \forall W$$
$$U_W(W) > 0 \quad \forall W$$
$$U_{WW}(W) < 0 \quad \forall W$$

where the upside down A symbol, $\forall$, means "for all" and where subscripts denote partial derivatives—$U_W(W) = \partial U/\partial W$ and $U_{WW}(W) = \partial U^2/\partial W^2$. The first line represents the first assumption. It says that people get more units of happiness when they get more wealth, and that is true for all possible levels of wealth. The second relation (i.e., the first derivative is positive) means that for all levels of wealth people *always* prefer more to less. Finally, the second derivative of the utility function is negative, which means that people prefer more to less at a decreasing rate. In mathematical terms, this function is said to be concave. Economists also like to add some other technical restrictions to this utility function, like continuity and continuous differentiability, which merely guarantee that the above equations exist and are defined at all levels of wealth.

Figure 2.1 depicts a typical utility function. The y-axis reveals the units of happiness associated with the corresponding level of wealth. Note that the function never doubles back on itself, so all levels of wealth are associated with a *unique* level of utility. A wealth of $\$X$ is associated with $U(X)$ units of happiness.

Notice how the mathematical and economic properties of the utility function appear graphically. The assumption that more is better than less is reflected by the fact that the value of the utility function is positive for all positive levels of wealth *and* is increasing in wealth—if $Y > X$, then $U(Y) > U(X)$. The second assumption of nonsatiation is reflected by the fact that the line has a positive *slope* everywhere. For a small increase in wealth, the marginal utility gained is always positive, no matter what the level of

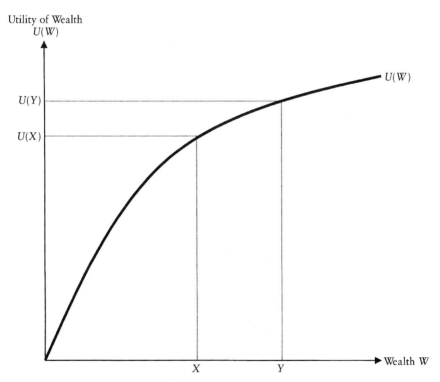

FIGURE 2.1 A typical utility function.

wealth. Finally, the concave shape of the graph means that the slope of the line tangent to the function declines as the level of wealth gets higher. In other words, the marginal utility of an additional unit of wealth declines as the person gets wealthier.

Risk Aversion

The shape of a utility function dictates the degree to which an individual is risk-averse, risk-neutral, or risk-loving. As in Chapter 1, these concepts can perhaps best be understood by considering a lottery ticket that an individual is considering for purchase. Suppose the lottery ticket will award the individual $0 or $1,000,000 with equal probabilities. These payoffs and probabilities are known by all and are not in dispute, and the bet is fair so the price of the ticket is $500,000—½($0) + ½($1,000,000).

Figure 2.2 shows the utility function of a risk-neutral individual. The increase in utility is the same regardless of how wealthy the individual. In

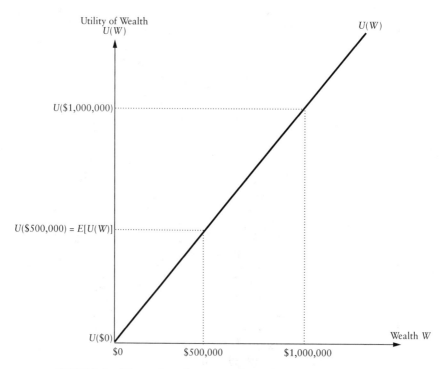

FIGURE 2.2   The utility function of a risk-neutral individual.

other words, this individual has a *constant* marginal utility of wealth. To determine whether or not the individual will buy the lottery ticket at the $500,000 price, a comparison must be drawn of the individual's utility of losing $500,000 for sure (i.e., paying for the ticket) with the individual's gaining $1,000,000 half the time and gaining nothing the other half. This comparison is thus a comparison of the utility of wealth of $500,000 with the *expected* utility of wealth, or the probability weighted utility of nothing and $1 million:

$$E[U(W)] = \tfrac{1}{2}U(\$0) + \tfrac{1}{2}U(\$1,000,000)$$

The comparison is shown graphically in Figure 2.2. The utility of $500,000 for sure is denoted U($500,000). Graphically, the way to find the point in the middle of two other points on a function is to run a straight line between those two points and then bisect the line. The bisection of the line corresponds to the equal-weighted average of the two endpoints. In this example, the utility function *is itself* a straight line, which tells us immediately that

$$U(\$500,000) = E[U(W)] = \tfrac{1}{2}U(\$0) + \tfrac{1}{2}U(\$1,000,000)$$

So, the loss of the utility of $500,000 in buying the lottery ticket is *exactly the same* as the gain in expected utility associated with an even chance of winning $1 million or nothing.

In general terms, a risk-neutral individual will be indifferent to taking a fair bet. The loss of utility paid for the fairly priced bet will always offset the expected utility gain from the lottery itself.

Figure 2.3 shows the contrasting situation of a risk-averse individual, whose utility function is concave rather than linear. In this case, the utility foregone from the lottery ticket purchase is U($500,000). Applying the same method as in the risk-neutral case, the *expected* utility of the lottery can be found by running a line between the two equally likely lottery outcomes, U($0) and U($1,000,000). Because the end points are equally likely to occur, the bisection of that line represents the *expected* utility of the lottery.

Unlike the case of the risk-neutral investor, the line connecting U($0) and U($1,000,000) in Figure 2.3 is no longer the same as the utility function U(W) itself. This time, the line is *below* the utility function. Consequently, E[U(W)] is *less* than U(W) for a W equal to $500,000. In other words, the utility of $500,000 *for sure* is higher than the utility of the *possibility* of $1 million or nothing, even though the expected value of the lottery

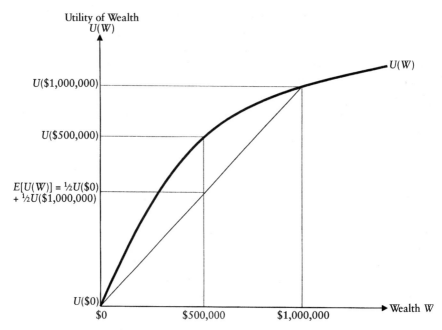

FIGURE 2.3 The utility function of a risk-averse individual.

is $500,000. Because the utility function is concave, the individual will reject a fair bet.

Now consider the final possibility, shown in Figure 2.4, that the individual is risk-loving. In this case, the individual's utility function has two of the same properties as the risk-neutral and risk-averse individuals—more is still preferred to less, and the individual is still never satiated. The risk-loving individual, however, has *increasing* marginal utility of wealth, so that the individual is happier for an incremental increase in wealth when she is already very wealthy than when she is poor. Mathematically, this means that the slope of the function $U(W)$ is increasing over W. The function is convex, so that $U_W > 0$ and now also $U_{WW} > 0$.

As in Figures 2.2 and 2.3, the utility of $500,000 with certainty is indicated as $U($500,000)$. To determine whether or not the individual will pay that price for a fair bet with equal odds at $0 and $1,000,000, a straight line is again drawn between these two extremes and bisected. The point on the y-axis corresponding to this bisection point is the expected utility of the lottery ticket. In this case, $E[U(W)]$ is *above* $U($500,000)$. Not only will the individual buy the lottery ticket, but she will think it's a

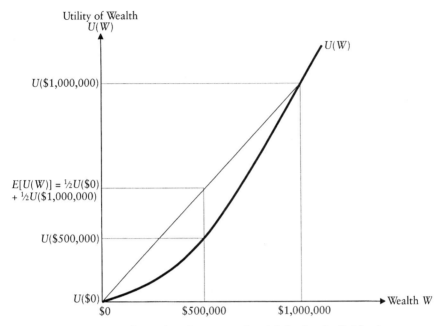

FIGURE 2.4 The utility function of a risk-loving individual.

great deal. The utility foregone from the $500,000 paid is significantly less than the utility gained by the chance at winning a million.

The critical distinction between the three cases lies in the dependency of the individual's marginal utility on her level of wealth. The risk-neutral individual has a constant marginal utility. The units of happiness derived from one more dollar or one more steak do not depend on the number of dollars or steaks she has. For a risk-averse individual, the satisfaction derived from more wealth or consumption declines as the level of wealth or consumption rises. The thousandth steak is still good and still makes the person happier than when she had only 999 steaks, but the jump from 999 steaks to 1,000 steaks yields less incremental happiness than the jump from 0 steaks to 1. Conversely, the risk-loving individual experiences a greater increase in happiness moving from 999 steaks to 1,000 than from 0 to 1.

These differences in marginal utility go a long way toward explaining individual behavior toward risk. Because the risk-averse individual has diminishing marginal utility of wealth, the chance at a big victory is not worth taking the risk of a big loss. Conversely, a risk lover will happily put her whole net worth at risk in order to chance a big win because, unlike the risk-averse individual, she has *increasing* marginal utility.

Gambling and Insurance

For many years, the implications of basic utility analysis posed a problem for economists. The implication of Figure 2.3 is clearly that the individual is risk-averse for *all* levels of wealth, and Figure 2.4 shows that the risk lover is a risk-taker at *all* levels of wealth. What puzzled economists was that people's observed behavior was not entirely consistent with what these nice utility functions predicted. In particular, the tendency for the same people who buy lottery tickets to also purchase health insurance did not make sense. The purchase of lottery tickets would seem to suggest risk-loving behavior, whereas the purchase of insurance implies clear risk aversion—a willingness to pay some amount for certain in order to avoid the risk of a massive decline in wealth.

Friedman and Savage (1948) proposed a solution to this seeming paradox—the now-famous *S-shaped utility function* shown in Figure 2.5.[2] Over low levels of wealth—denoted as the range from 0 to B on the figure—the utility function is concave and demonstrates diminishing marginal utility.

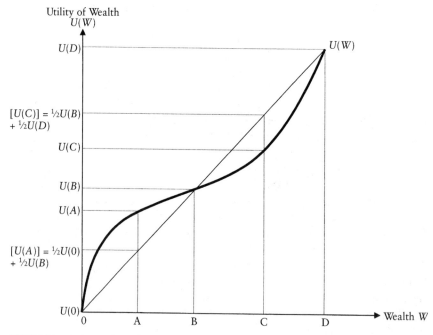

FIGURE 2.5   The utility function of someone who both gambles and insures.

But for levels of wealth above B, the utility function reverses its shape and becomes convex, thus suggesting increasing marginal utility for levels of wealth above B. In other words, this individual is risk-averse at levels of wealth below B and risk-loving at levels of wealth above B.

Consider a person described by the utility function in Figure 2.5 with a current wealth of B. He faces some risk that a tragedy will occur that causes him to lose all of his money, and this tragedy will occur with probability one-half. An insurer approaches him and says he is willing to provide coverage for the individual so that his wealth is guaranteed not to fall below A.

Without insurance, the individual's utility is described by the *expected* utility that he keeps his wealth B half the time and that his wealth declines to \$0 the other half of the time. This expected utility corresponds to the bisection of the line drawn between $U(0)$ and $U(B)$ on the graph, and the utility at this point is equal to

$$E\left[U(A)\right] = \tfrac{1}{2}U(0) + \tfrac{1}{2}U(B)$$

That is the individual's expected utility in the event he does nothing at current wealth level B.

Now consider the purchase of an insurance contract with a coverage level of A. In that case, the individual has a minimum guaranteed *actual* utility of $U(A)$. Clearly, $U(A) > E[U(A)]$. But how much is he willing to *pay* for the insurance? The answer can be seen again from Figure 2.5. As long as the insurance costs no more than the difference between $U(A)$ and $E[U(A)]$, the individual is better off than when he started, and he will indeed purchase insurance. Although the insured level $U(A)$ is below the utility of his current wealth $U(B)$, the current wealth is accompanied by the risk of a catastrophic loss. The individual thus pays a fair price to achieve $U(A)$ and actually improves his situation. In the worst case where the insurance costs exactly $U(A) - E[U(A)]$, he is neither any better nor any worse off, but he has eliminated the stress of worrying about a loss. This is consistent with risk-averse behavior.

Now suppose the same individual is offered a lottery ticket. Half the time the ticket pays nothing, but half the time the ticket will pay $D - B$ dollars, thus increasing his wealth from current level B to new level D. If the lottery ticket is fairly priced at $\tfrac{1}{2}(D - B) = C - B$, he will buy the ticket. Unlike the part of his utility function that exhibits diminishing marginal utility below wealth level B, he is now considering something that puts him in the part of his utility function where the marginal utility of wealth is increasing. He thus pays a fair price for a lottery ticket that has an expected utility of $E[U(C)]$.

UTILITY THEORY AND INVESTMENTS

Things that can cause a *decreased* utility are really what we mean by *risk*. The explicit link between changes in investor utility and probability theory can be seen if an investor who maximizes his expected utility of wealth with a utility function $U(W)$ is considered. Suppose wealth is a random variable drawn from some probability distribution affected by market, credit, liquidity, and all other major forms of risk discussed in Chapter 1.

The investor's utility of wealth can be written as a function of the statistical properties of the random wealth variable using a Taylor series expansion around his utility of *expected* wealth:

$$U(W) = U[E(W)] + U_W[W - E(W)] + \tfrac{1}{2}U_{WW}[W - E(W)]^2$$
$$+ \tfrac{1}{3!}U_{WWW}[W - E(W)]^3 + R \tag{2.1}$$

where R is a remainder term that reflects the fact that the expression could have been expanded further.

With wealth as a random variable, the individual in question maximizes his *expected* utility of wealth. This is slightly different than the utility of *expected wealth* shown in Equation 2.1. Expected wealth is the expected value of wealth given that it is subject to risk and random outcomes. Expected utility is the expected value of utility in the future, which is in turn dependent on expected wealth. But as it is now, Equation 2.1 for *actual* utility of wealth still depends in each term on W, a random variable.

Taking an expectation of Equation 2.1 yields:

$$E[U(W)] = U[E(W)] + U_W E[W - E(W)] + \tfrac{1}{2}U_{WW} E[W - E(W)]^2$$
$$+ \tfrac{1}{3!}U_{WWW} E[W - E(W)]^3 + E[R] \tag{2.2}$$

Applying the properties of the expected value operator gives us a simpler version of Equation 2.2:

$$E[U(W)] = U[E(W)] + \tfrac{1}{2}U_{WW} E[W - E(W)]^2$$
$$+ \tfrac{1}{3!}U_{WWW} E[W - E(W)]^3 + E(R) \tag{2.3}$$

Note also that several of these terms correspond to summary statistics with which we are used to dealing. In particular, recall the following definitions of statistics that summarize the distribution of the random variable wealth:

Definition	Abbreviation	Terminology	Measure of . . .
$E(W)$	μ	Mean	Location of the center of the distribution, or the average value of W
$E[W - E(W)]^2$	σ^2	Variance	Dispersion around the mean
$E[W - E(W)]^3$	γ	Skewness	Tilt of the distribution to one side or the other, or indication of asymmetry of extreme values relative to the mean
$E[W - E(W)]^4$	κ	Kurtosis	Thickness of tails and peakedness of center

In other words, the investor's expected utility of wealth can be written entirely as a function of known summary measures of the shape of the probability distribution from which wealth is drawn:

$$E[U(W)] = U[E(W)] + \tfrac{1}{2}U_{WW}\sigma^2$$
$$+ \tfrac{1}{3!}U_{WWW}\gamma + \tfrac{1}{4!}U_{WWWW}\kappa + E(R) \tag{2.4}$$

Notice from Equation 2.4 that the investor's expected utility depends on *all* the typical summary measures of risk, and that the remainder term R captures an essentially endless sum of other measures of the shape of the distribution of W that do not even have a name. What remains to be seen, however, is *how* these measures impact the investor.

Investor Preferences and Known Statistical Measures

Assume in the spirit of traditional financial economics that investors have utility functions characterized by the three common behavioral axioms discussed earlier: (1) investors prefer more to less; (2) investors are never fully satiated; and (3) investors prefer more to less at a declining rate. For utility function $U(W)$, recall that this means mathematically that $U(W) > 0$, $U_W > 0$, and $U_{WW} < 0$ for all levels of wealth W.

Beginning with the obvious, the first behavioral axiom indicates that investors prefer more expected return to less. A security that has a higher expected return, other things being equal, thus is better.

Now consider variance, or the dispersion of wealth around its average value. Variance itself is always a positive number for risky securities and random variables such as wealth, because it is measured as the *squared* deviation of the variable from its mean. Looking at the second term in Equation 2.4, we also notice that variance enters expected utility as a multiple of U_{WW}. For risk-averse investors, the utility function is concave and U_{WW} is negative. So, the expression tells us that investors *dislike* variance. We can verify this by partially differentiating expected utility of wealth in Equation 2.4 with respect to variance:

$$\frac{\partial E\left[U(W)\right]}{\partial \sigma^2} = \tfrac{1}{2} U_{WW}$$

So, the higher the volatility of wealth or of a security, the less the risk-averse investor likes it—all else being equal. And conversely for the risk-loving investor, who has $U_{WW} > 0$ and thus derives utility from higher volatility.

Skewness and kurtosis are harder to address because no assumptions have been made about U_{WWW} and U_{WWWW}. So, the signs with which these terms enter the expected utility function are unknown. Unlike U_W and U_{WW} which have easy interpretations as marginal utility of wealth and rate of change in marginal utility, the higher ordered derivatives have no natural interpretation in microeconomics. They are basically just statistical constructs to describe how the function U behaves.

Behavioral finance has attempted to shed some light on what investors prefer. Figure 2.6 shows three different probability density functions for the random variable wealth. The distribution labeled A is a *symmetric distribution* because any value above the mean has the same likelihood of occurring

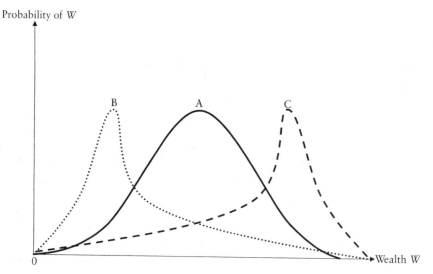

FIGURE 2.6   Symmetric versus asymmetric distributions.

as the same value *below* the mean. This is not true for distributions *B* and *C*. Distributions *B* and *C* are *asymmetric*, so values equivalently far from the mean have different probabilities depending on whether the values are above or below the mean.

In the distribution labeled *B*, a wealth increase of, say, 10% is more likely to occur than a wealth decrease of 10%. There is more probability in the right-hand tail than the left, so that extreme increases in wealth are more likely than extreme declines. This is called a positively skewed distribution, and its coefficient of skewness γ would be a positive number.

The distribution labeled *C*, by contrast, is also asymmetric but is *negatively* skewed. For this distribution, γ would be a negative number, indicating that a large decline in wealth below the mean is more likely than a large increase.

Behavioral finance theorists argue that investors *like* positive skewness, or, more specifically, that expected utility of wealth is increasing in the coefficient of skewness γ. If the expected utility Equation 2.4 is differentiated with respect to γ, the result is

$$\frac{\partial E[U(W)]}{\partial \gamma^2} = \tfrac{1}{3!} U_{WWW}$$

So, for investors to derive units of happiness from skewness, this implies that $U_{WWW} > 0$, as was the case for U_W but not for U_{WW}.[3]

As noted earlier, the third derivative of utility with respect to wealth has no natural interpretation. Nevertheless, Figure 2.6 does suggest why one might be inclined to buy off on the rationale that positive skew is "good" and negative skew is "bad." When focusing *purely* on extreme values, there is some plausibility to the notion that risk-averse investors are more worried about a catastrophic loss than they are thrilled by a correspondingly large gain.

Less well-documented is the impact of kurtosis on investor satisfaction. *Kurtosis* is a measure of the fatness of tails and peakedness of the center of a distribution *relative to* the tails and center of a normal distribution (Figure 2.7). The distribution labeled *A* in Figure 2.7 is a *normal* distribution of *changes* in wealth per period—say, annually. Changes are used here instead of levels to allow the distributions to associate positive probability with negative values.

The normal distribution has several extremely useful statistical properties. First, it is symmetric, like distribution *A* in Figure 2.6 and unlike the other two. Second, it is easy to draw probabilistic inferences from the normal distribution using only mean and variance, which are completely sufficient to

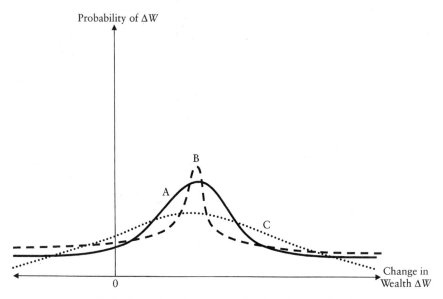

FIGURE 2.7   Leptokurtic versus platykurtic distributions.

characterize the entire distribution. Note in Figure 2.7 that all three distributions are symmetric.

The distribution labeled *B* in Figure 2.7 is *leptokurtic*. This means that the distribution has a coefficient of kurtosis κ above the kurtosis of the normal distribution. More usefully, that distribution *B* is leptokurtic means that it has fatter tails and a more peaked center than the normal distribution. Conversely, distribution *C* is *platykurtic*, or generally flatter than the normal distribution. More probability lies in the middle region of the distribution and less in the tails and center than the normal.

Behavioral finance people argue that investors *dislike* kurtosis, or, more specifically, *excess* kurtosis which measures kurtosis relative to the kurtosis of the normal distribution. Like their arguments in the case of skewness, there is at least some intuition behind this. To see that intuition, imagine that Figure 2.7 is a distribution of returns on a portfolio of securities and not the change in wealth. The returns on the security drawn from distribution *B* would be characterized by long periods of stable, trending markets—the concentrated peak around the mean—followed by periods of extreme volatility and significant price changes—the fat tails. This, behavioral finance tell us, is something we should dislike in an expected utility context.

So, as in the case of skewness, the implication is that U_{WWWW} is negative, which ensures that the partial derivative of expected utility in Equation 2.4 with respect to kurtosis is negative:

$$\frac{\partial E[U(W)]}{\partial \kappa^2} = \tfrac{1}{4!} U_{WWWW}$$

Vanquishing Higher-Ordered Moments

In the 1950s and 1960s when classical finance was being developed, computing power was a legitimate limitation on theoretical and empirical work. Mathematica did not exist to pop out solutions to long differential equations, and SAS was not around to run thousands of regressions. As much for those reasons as any others, the early giants of finance usually made assumptions that eliminated the need to fuss with higher-ordered moments of probability distributions, as skewness and kurtosis are sometimes called. Even Markowitz himself acknowledged the limitations of this in his treatise on portfolio diversification, but he made the assumption anyway for computational simplicity that mean and variance *alone* were important.

Everything except mean and variance can be vanquished from an investor's expected utility function in one of several ways. Perhaps the easiest is to simply assume that all investors have a particular kind of utility function, such as quadratic:

$$U(W) = W - \frac{\theta}{2} W^2 \tag{2.5}$$

where θ is some parameter and $\theta > 0$. Differentiating Equation 2.5 with respect to wealth yields:

$$U_W = 1 - \theta W \qquad U_{WW} = -\theta \qquad U_{WWW} = 0 \qquad U_{WWWW} = 0$$

which can be substituted into expected utility Equation 2.4 and then simplified to get the following relation between investor expected utility and the statistical properties of the distribution of the random variable wealth:

$$E[U(W)] = E(W) - \frac{\theta}{2}\left[E(W)^2 + \sigma^2\right] \tag{2.6}$$

Only the mean and variance of wealth matter to this investor, and he thus will evaluate all assets accordingly.

The problem with making such a specific assumption that *all* investors have this easy utility function is that it is wildly unrealistic. Setting aside even the issue that investors might have different utility functions, the problem here is mainly a problem *with this specific function*. To see this problem clearly, differentiate expected utility in Equation 2.6 with respect to expected wealth:

$$\frac{\partial E[U(W)]}{\partial E(W)} = 1 - \theta E(W)$$

This number is *not* always positive. In fact, for higher levels of expected wealth, the investor actually begins to *dislike* more expected wealth. We saw this as well in the original function, where $U_W = 1 - \theta W$ implies that marginal utility is positive *only* for small levels of wealth! Despite having eliminated higher-ordered moments from the equation, we have also eliminated any link to reality.

Rather than presuming a specific utility function, assumptions can also be made about the distributions of security returns to determine whether investors like or dislike particular moments of a distribution. To see this, suppose the return on some portfolio of securities R is distributed normally with expected value $E(R)$ and variance σ^2. Using the ever-so-statistically-pleasant properties of the normal distribution, we can define a *standard normal* version of R that has a mean of 0 and a variance of 1 as follows:

$$r = \frac{R - E(R)}{\sigma}$$

If we rearrange this, we can rewrite the portfolio return R in terms of its mean and standard deviation and a standard normal variate r:

$$R = E(R) + \sigma r \qquad (2.7)$$

Now suppose the investor lives in a two-period world. At time 1, the investor's wealth is equal to his endowment (i.e., what we pretend he started with), denoted W_0, less what he eats in time 1, which we denote as his time 1 consumption C_1. At the end of period 1, the investor may take whatever he did not eat and invest it in the portfolio of securities. At time 2, the investor thus can eat whatever he had left over from time 1 invested for one period at the rate R. To recap, the investor's wealth/consumption in each period is

$$W_1 = W_0 - C_1$$

$$W_2 = W_1(1 + R)$$

Because the portfolio return is normally distributed, we can rewrite the investor's time 2 wealth using Equation 2.7 more usefully as follows:

$$W_2 = (W_0 - C_1)[1 + E(R) + \sigma r]$$

In this two-period world, the investor's desire is to maximize the expected utility of his wealth in each period, $E[U(W_1, W_2)]$. This expected utility can be expressed using the mathematical definition of expected value for a standard normal density of portfolio returns r, denoted $f(r)$, as follows:

$$
\begin{aligned}
E[U(W_1, W_2)] &= \int_{-\infty}^{\infty} U(W_1, W_2) f(r) dr \\
&= \int_{-\infty}^{\infty} U\{W_1, (W_0 - C_1)[1 + E(R) + \sigma r]\} f(r) dr
\end{aligned}
\tag{2.8}
$$

Equation 2.8 shows that expected utility depends *only* on the mean and variance of the portfolio return, not on any higher ordered moments.

That the investor's expected utility of wealth depends only on mean and variance, however, is not enough. We also need to ensure that mean and variance affect expected utility in the proper manner. To verify that the investor *likes* a higher expected return, differentiate Equation 2.8 with respect to $E(R)$:

$$\frac{\partial E[U(W_1, W_2)]}{\partial E(R)} = \int_{-\infty}^{\infty} U_W (W_0 - C_1) f(r) dr$$

Because the investor is presumed to have a positive marginal utility of wealth for all levels of wealth, U_W is positive and the result is thus positive. More mean is better.

As for variance, we can differentiate Equation 2.8 again, but this time with respect to standard deviation (i.e., the square root of variance):

$$\frac{\partial E[U(W_1, W_2)]}{\partial \sigma} = \int_{-\infty}^{\infty} U_W (W_0 - C_1) r f(r) dr$$

This result is a bit harder to see. We know that U_W is positive, but we also know that a risk-averse investor has a utility function such that $U_{WW} < 0$. This means that U_W is positive but smaller for higher levels of W. Because $f(r)$ is the density for the *standard* normal distribution, it is symmetric around zero. This means that the larger positive U_W's that are multiplied by the 50% of $f(r)$ which is negative are going to exceed in absolute value the smaller positive U_W's that are multiplied by the 50% of $f(r)$ which is positive. The net result is that the whole expression is negative, so investors *dislike* variance.

Variance in Modern Portfolio Theory

Despite the tedious nature of the prior several sections, they were important background to understand why finance is so heavily populated with the assumption that returns on assets are distributed normally. The answer should now be clear. This assumption enables us to keep *everything* in terms of mean and variance.

In the context of the definitions of risk in Chapter 1, the normality assumption saves us from a great deal of statistical headache. In a world where asset returns are jointly distributed multivariate normal, *variance is always a completely sufficient statistic for risk*. Investors like mean and dislike variance, and nothing else enters into the picture. Consequently, most celebrated investment models focus on efforts by investors to maximize expected return and minimize variance. The Markowitz (1959) model for optimal portfolio selection is the perfect example.

The Mean-Variance-Efficient Frontier   The Markowitz model involves the use of linear programming methods to solve the following linear optimization program:

$$\min_{(w_1,\ldots,w_N)} \sum_{i=1}^{N} \sum_{j=1}^{N} w_i w_j \sigma_i \sigma_j \rho$$

$$s.t. \sum_{k=1}^{N} w_k = 1 \qquad\qquad (2.9)$$

$$s.t. \sum_{q=1}^{N} w_q E(R_q) \geq \lambda$$

where w_k is the weight of the kth asset in the portfolio to be chosen. In other words, the investor chooses a set of portfolio weights to minimize the variance of a portfolio of N assets subject to two constraints: full investment (i.e., portfolio weights sum to one); and achieving some target return λ.

When the optimization problem in Equation 2.9 is solved over a *range* of possible λ's, the resulting series of portfolio weights together defines the *minimum-variance frontier*, or the set of portfolios for which no lower volatility asset can be found at a given level of expected returns. A typical mean-variance frontier is shown in Figure 2.8. Portfolios that lie *inside* the frontier, such as portfolio X, are said to be *inefficient* because a portfolio can always be found that has the same expected return for a lower volatility (e.g., portfolio A) or a higher expected return for the same volatility (e.g., portfolio E). Portfolios inside the frontier should never be held by utility maximizing investors. Portfolios *outside* the frontier, like portfolio Z, are not attainable.

Although the whole frontier—the line intersecting portfolio A, B, and C—is the minimum variance frontier, not all of the frontier makes sense for investors. Specifically, the bottom half of the frontier—the line from portfolio A that continues through portfolio C—all contains inefficient portfolios. Portfolio D, for example, is the minimum variance portfolio for that given

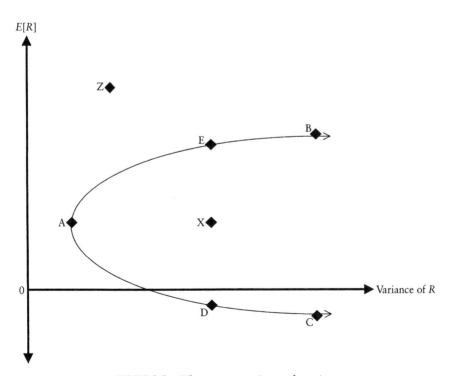

FIGURE 2.8 The mean-variance frontier.

expected return. Portfolio *E,* however, provides the investor with the same variance at a much higher expected return.

A portfolio is said to be *mean-variance efficient* (MVE) if the portfolio lies on the minimum variance frontier *and* there is no other portfolio that would provide the same variance for a higher expected return. The MVE frontier is thus the line beginning with portfolio *A* and continuing through portfolio *B.*

The Optimal Portfolio Choice—Back to the Utility Function Investors maximizing their expected utility of wealth will hold *only* MVE portfolios, *provided* all portfolio and security returns are distributed multivariate normal thus guaranteeing that variance is a sufficient statistic for risk. The actual portfolio held by the investor depends on her precise utility function—the precise way that the utility function generates a tradeoff between expected return and risk. This tradeoff can be depicted graphically for different levels of expected utility by *indifference curves,* shown in Figure 2.9 as U_1, U_2, U_3, and U_4.

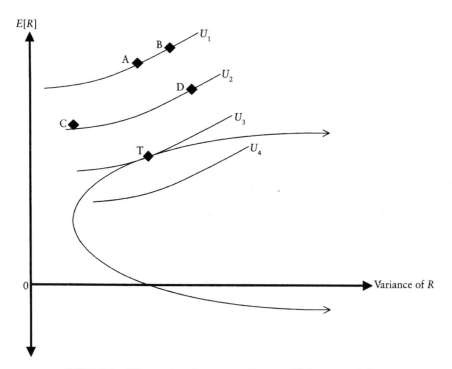

FIGURE 2.9 The optimal mean-variance-efficient portfolio.

Investors are indifferent in an expected utility sense between all portfolios lying on a given indifference curve—say, U_1, where portfolios A and B are *equally* desirable to the investor. Portfolio B has more risk, but also a higher expected return. The shape of the indifference curve reveals the investor's preferences for risk and return at that level of utility.

The indifference curves U_2 and U_3 reveal the same basic tradeoffs between risk and return as U_1, but for *different* levels of utility. The investor prefers to be *anywhere* on curve U_1 than *anywhere* on U_2, and in turn prefers to be anywhere on U_2 than U_3. In each case, the actual expected utility is higher. Sometimes indifference curves are called *iso-elasticity curves* to reinforce the fact that expected utility is the same at all points along the same curve. So, the investor is indifferent between portfolios A and B for given expected utility level U_1 *and* is indifferent between portfolios C and D for given expected utility U_2, but the investor clearly prefers *either* portfolio A or B to portfolios C and D.

Many more than four indifference curves can be drawn, of course, for many additional levels of utility. But only one is relevant. Curves U_1 and U_2 all represent portfolios that are not feasible. The existing set of securities used to generate the MVE frontier simply do not allow for combinations outside the frontier, where indifference curves U_1 and U_2 are located. Similarly, the indifference curve U_4 includes mostly inefficient portfolios. Although feasible, the investor could almost always get a higher expected return for the same level of risk or a lower volatility for the same expected return than portfolios lying on this line.

The investor's optimal portfolio that maximizes expected utility of wealth is located where the investor's marginal utility of wealth is equal to the marginal product of his security portfolio. The marginal utility of any given portfolio is the slope of a line tangent to the indifference curve at that point, and the marginal product of the security portfolio is the slope of the line tangent to the MVE frontier. When these two lines are the same, the investor has found his optimal portfolio, shown in Figure 2.9 as portfolio T and sometimes called the *tangency portfolio* for obvious reasons.

Different investors have different preferences and, hence, different indifference curve maps. The investor whose expected utility is depicted with the iso-elasticity curves in Figure 2.9 is an investor whose indifference curves nice and conveniently exactly hit the MVE frontier at portfolio T. This need not be the case.

Figure 2.10 shows the same MVE frontier with the indifference curve map of a different investor. Also included in this figure on the expected return axis is the risk-free rate, denoted R_f. The line tangent to the MVE frontier whose y-intercept is R_f demonstrates portfolios that the investor can hold by combining the tangency portfolio T with borrowing and lending at

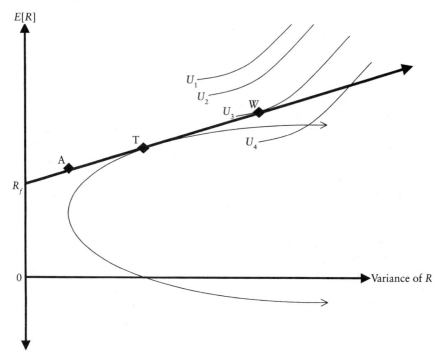

FIGURE 2.10 The optimal mean-variance-efficient portfolio with leverage.

the risk-free rate. To hold portfolio *A*, for example, the investor would hold tangency portfolio *T* and then lend. But as Figure 2.10 shows, this investor clearly prefers to go the other way. The tangency point between the investor's indifference curve map and the *leveraged* MVE— the line tangent to the MVE—occurs at portfolio *W*. So, this investor will hold the tangency portfolio *T* and then lever up by borrowing in order to achieve the higher risk and higher expected return that are consistent with her preferences at expected utility level U_3.

Does Variance Really Matter That Much? What if we had *not* assumed that portfolio returns were distributed multivariate normal? Variance would no longer be an adequate summary measure of risk (assuming we did not replace the normality assumption with an assumption about the utility function that makes variance alone relevant, such as quadratic utility). The efficient frontier would no longer be the mean-*variance*-efficient frontier. The portfolio optimization problem would have to be respecified using some other single measure of risk (e.g., the probability that returns fall below a critical target, or below-target probability) as the thing to be minimized. Although possible, the problem becomes extremely difficult computationally.

Alternatively, investors' iso-utility curves could be drawn in multi-dimensional space to account for the other variables impacting risk, such as perhaps skewness and kurtosis. In turn, the frontier would become a multi-dimensional frontier, also reflecting those multiple factors influencing expected utility. This, too, is computationally extremely difficult.

Even in today's modern computing era, most investment asset allocation decisions are made using the original Markowitz MVE frontier. Variance took root in finance in 1958 as a sufficient measure of portfolio risk, and it has never left us.

CLASSICAL TRADER-BASED HEDGING MODELS

The classical models of hedging and risk management in financial markets presume that the trader is an individual. Specifically, the trader is presumed to be an expected utility maximizer living in a world where returns on all securities and derivatives are distributed multivariate normal. In this world, the hedger as a risk-averse individual basically just uses futures or forwards to solve a Markowitz-style mean-variance portfolio optimization problem.

The Simple Model: Variance-Minimizing Hedge Ratios

In the simplest construct, our investor is assumed to be an expected utility maximizer with a position in some underlying spot market like corn or beans. The investor's spot market holdings are presumed to be *fixed*. In other words, the investor inherits a position in some commodity, such as corn or beans, equal to amount Q_S.

In a world where all asset returns are normally distributed, we have already seen how the trader cares only about two things—expected return, in which her utility is increasing, and variance of return, in which her utility is decreasing. Because fairly priced futures and forwards have zero initial investment costs (see Chapter 3), we can focus for now entirely on the risk side of the picture.

To keep the math simple, suppose there are only two periods in the model, and assume transacting is costless. Let U denote the change in value of the unhedged spot market position, such that

$$U = Q_S\left[S(2) - S(1)\right] = Q_S(\Delta S) \tag{2.10}$$

The delta (Δ) is used to simplify the notation and indicate a *price change*. At time 1, the expected value of the unhedged inventory is thus

$$E(U) = Q_S\{E[S(2)] - S(1)\} = Q_S E(\Delta S) \tag{2.11}$$

where $S(1)$ is the price per unit of the spot commodity at time 1, and similarly for time 2. The variance of the unhedged position can be written as

$$\mathrm{var}(U) = Q_S{}^2 \sigma_S{}^2 \tag{2.12}$$

where $\sigma_S{}^2$ is the variance of the change in the spot price, ΔS.

Now suppose a forward or futures contract exists that is fairly priced at-market. The contract matures at time 2 and calls for delivery of the underlying spot commodity. If Q_F denotes the quantity sold forward to hedge the long inventory position, the expected value and variance of the *hedged* position, H, can be written as

$$\begin{aligned} E(H) &= Q_S\{E[S(2)] - S(1)\} + Q_F\{E[F(2, 2)] - F(1, 2)\} \\ &= Q_S E(\Delta S) + Q_S E(\Delta F) \end{aligned} \tag{2.13}$$

$$\mathrm{var}(H) = Q_S{}^2 \sigma_S{}^2 + Q_F{}^2 \sigma_F{}^2 + 2 Q_S Q_F \sigma_{SF} \tag{2.14}$$

where $F(1, 2)$ and $F(2, 2)$ denote the quoted market prices for a futures contract maturing at time 2 as of times 1 and 2, respectively, and where $\sigma_F{}^2$ is the variance of the one-period change in the futures price ΔF. The covariance of changes in the spot price with changes in the futures price is denoted σ_{SF}.

Now denote the proportion of the spot position hedged with futures as δ, such that

$$\delta = \frac{Q_F}{Q_S}$$

which is often called the *hedge ratio*. We can now use δ to rewrite the expected value and variance of the hedged position from Equations 2.13 and 2.14:

$$E(H) = Q_S[E(\Delta S) + \delta E(\Delta F)] \tag{2.15}$$

$$\text{var}(H) = Q_S^2 \left(\sigma_S^2 + \delta^2 \sigma_F^2 + 2\delta\sigma_{SF} \right) \qquad (2.16)$$

The impact of a change in the proportion hedged on the risk of the position can now be examined by partially differentiating var[H] with respect to the hedge ratio δ:

$$\frac{\partial \text{var}(H)}{\partial \delta} = Q_S^2 \left(2\delta\sigma_F^2 + 2\sigma_{SF} \right)$$

Variance is minimized when δ is chosen to equate the first derivative of variance with respect to δ to zero. Doing this and solving for δ yields the *variance-minimizing hedge ratio*, δ^*:

$$\delta^* = -\frac{\sigma_{SF}}{\sigma_F^2}$$

Note that the sign is negative, which means that the position in the hedge will be the opposite of the position in the spot market as long as the covariance in the two price changes is positive. In other words, a long is typically hedged with a short and vice versa.

Note that this variance-minimizing hedge ratio has an extremely attractive feature. To see this, consider running an ordinary least squares (OLS) regression of spot price changes on futures price changes:

$$\Delta S = \alpha + \beta \Delta F + \varepsilon$$

The OLS estimator for the slope term ß is defined as follows:

$$\beta = \frac{\sigma_{SF}}{\sigma_F^2} = \delta^*$$

which makes sense because the parameter estimate for β is chosen to minimize the variance of the error term ε. So, the variance-minimizing hedge ratio is equivalent to the OLS beta in a regression of changes in the unhedged position on changes in the hedged position.

Heterogeneous Beliefs and Optimal Speculation

To get from the optimal variance-minimizing hedge ratio to a theory of optimal speculation and hedging is not a far jump. We need only assume that the expected change in futures prices is not always zero. The easiest way to do that is to suppose that traders fancy themselves better informed than others in the marketplace. *Their* expectation of a change in futures prices may not be the same as the market's expectation.

The price of a futures contract can always be expressed as a function of the underlying spot price *plus* the net cost of carrying the underlying commodity from the present to the future when the futures contract matures. The difference between the quoted futures price and the spot price—the net cost of carry—is called the *basis*. The time t price of a futures contract maturing at time T thus can be expressed as:

$$F(t, T) = S(t) + b(t, T)$$

where $b(t, T)$ is the basis and is defined as

$$b(t, T) = R(t, T) + W(t, T) - D(t, T)$$

where $R(t, T)$ is the all-in interest cost or capital storage cost based on the interest rate prevailing from t to T, $W(t, T)$ is the lump-sum cost of physical storage from t to T, and $D(t, T)$ is the dividend earned on the physical asset from t to T. For financial futures, the dividend may be explicit (e.g., equity dividends), but for commodity futures the dividend is usually implicit. Called the *convenience yield,* the dividend earned from holding physical commodities is primary driven by the need for some producers to maintain positive inventory at all times rather than risk a production stoppage from a stock-out. We will return to the convenience yield later in Chapter 7. For now, just think of it as a dividend owned for holding a physical asset.

Going long the futures contract at price $F(t, T)$ gives you the obligation to sell the underlying commodity on date T. There is no initial expenditure, and you receive at time T the difference between the then-prevailing spot price and the locked-in futures price:

$$S(T) - F(t, T)$$

Now consider a different set of operations, summarized in the following table: (1) borrow $S(t)$; (2) buy the commodity today at that price; (3) store the commodity through time T, incurring physical storage costs of $W(t, T)$ and earning $D(t, T)$ as a dividend for having the commodity on hand; (4) repay the loan at time T in the amount of principal $S(t)$ plus interest $R(t, T)$; and (5) sell the commodity in the spot market at time T at the then-prevailing spot price.

Action	t	T
1. Borrow	$S(t)$	
2. Buy the commodity	$-S(t)$	
3. Store the commodity—pay storage costs; earn dividend		$-W(t, T) + D(t, T)$
4. Repay loan		$S(t) + R_{t, T}$
5. Sell the commodity		$S(T)$
NET	0	$S(T) - S(t) + R(t, T)$ $- W(t, T) + D(t, T)$

The two strategies are clearly equivalent. Both obligate you to sell one unit of the commodity at date T, and neither involves any up-front cost. With identical risks and identical costs, the two strategies thus must be *priced* equivalently to preclude arbitrage. Setting the terminal payoff of the futures strategy equal to the terminal payoff of the buy-and-storage strategy, we get:

$$S(T) - F(t, T) = S(T) - S(t) + R(t, T) - W(t, T) + D(t, T)$$

so that

$$F(t, T) = S(t) + R(t, T) + W(t, T) - D(t, T)$$

or else arbitrage opportunities will arise.

The change in a futures price is often decomposed into changes in its two components: the spot price, and the basis. We can now write the expected change in the futures price from Equation 2.15 as:

$$E(\Delta F) = E(\Delta S) + E(\Delta B)$$

where

$$E(\Delta B) \equiv E\{F(2, 2) - S(2) - [F(1, 1) - S(1)]\}$$

Differentiating with respect to the hedge ratio then allows us to rewrite the first-order condition for expected value as follows:

$$\frac{\partial E(H)}{\partial \delta} = -Q_S[E(\Delta B) + E(\Delta S)]$$

If this trader believes she has better information than the market—specifically, many traders fancy themselves well-informed about the basis—then the expected value of the hedged position may not be equal to zero *conditional on the information of the trader.* If the trader had any special information about the expected change in spot prices, then the trader could express that view by increasing Q_S and not fussing with the futures. But if the trader's special information pertains to expected changes in the basis, then the only real way to exploit that is through *trading the basis* by hedging some portion of the physical stock and leaving the other portion deliberately unhedged.

Figure 2.11 illustrates the trader's hedging problem graphically. Look familiar? The problem ends up working out just as in the Markowitz portfolio optimization case, which is not all that surprising because we have made essentially the same critical assumptions—that variance is a sufficient statistic for risk, and that all returns are distributed normally.

Notice that in Figure 2.11, the variance-minimizing hedge ratio δ^* is no longer "optimal"—at least not for this particular trader. On the contrary,

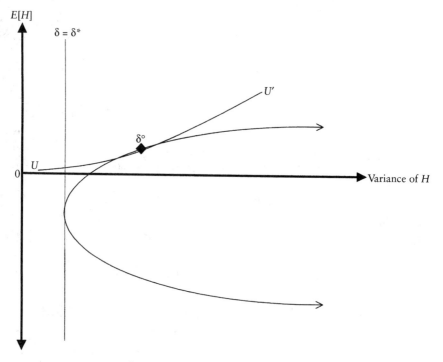

FIGURE 2.11　The optimal hedge ratio.

the *optimal* hedge ratio is now $\delta°$ where the trader's indifference curve UU' is tangent to the MVE frontier.

In this case, moreover, *either parts* of the frontier can be MVE efficient. Whether the efficient frontier is the top as in the normal model or the bottom depends on the sign of $E[\Delta B] + E[\Delta S]$—whether the trader considers futures overpriced or underpriced relative to the spot asset. As δ increases, the trader thus may either move clockwise or counterclockwise around the frontier, depending again entirely on the sign of $E[\Delta B] + E[\Delta S]$.

The last section presented the classical model of hedging, in which traders all have symmetric information and the optimal hedge ratio thus is the variance-minimizing hedge ratio. In this section, the model is the classical model of hedging *and* speculation. The trader's perception that the expected change in the basis might not be zero leads to a hedge ratio that may or may not be the variance-minimizing hedge ratio. In Figure 2.11, it clearly is not.

Note also that there are no real limits on what values δ can assume. If δ is greater than one, for example, that means the trader is taking on a larger futures position than the underlying position. The hedge ratio δ can also be negative, in which case the futures position is on the same side of the market as the underlying position. In general, the *speculative* component of the futures position is quantified as the difference between the optimal hedge ratio $\delta°$ and the variance-minimizing hedge ratio δ^*.

The Irrelevance of Corporate Financing and Risk Management Decisions

The corporate finance industry and academic literature both accepted and practiced the classical trader-based hedging model presented in Chapter 2 for many years. Developed by Johnson (1960) and Stein (1961) and later popularized by Ederington (1979), the theory was boilerplate for corporations until the early 1980s. In other words, *corporate* hedging was treated no differently than *trader* hedging. The company was assumed to behave like a risk-averse investor maximizing expected utility and minimizing variance, and departures from variance-minimizing hedge ratios were defined as *speculation*.

This treatment of corporate hedging, however, is entirely unsatisfactory.[1] At a basic theoretical level, the concept itself is flawed. At one level, organizations are just collections of single individuals, so the temptation to pass through the lenses with which we observe individual behavior to the corporate level is admittedly strong. But it is incorrect.

A firm is a collection of contractual relationships between individuals—between managers and shareholders, shareholders and creditors, managers and input suppliers, and so on. To treat a firm as a monolithic whole is thus to ignore the very reasons that firms exist—to minimize the transaction costs of these multiple contractual relationships, and to exploit joint production opportunities across agents that define this contractual morass.[2]

Analyzing the reasons why a firm might engage in risk management thus requires that we take a view of the firm as, to use Jensen and Meckling's (1976) terminology, a *nexus of contracts*. They offer a sobering admonition that will remain at the center of the analysis of corporate risk management that follows in this chapter and the rest of this book:

Viewing the firm as the nexus of a set of contracting relationships among individuals . . . serves to make it clear that the personalization of the firm implied by asking questions such as "What should be the objective function of the firm?" or "Does the firm have a social responsibility?" is seriously misleading. The firm is not an individual. It is a legal fiction which serves as a focus for a complex process in which the conflicting objectives of individuals (some of whom may "represent" other organizations) are brought into equilibrium within a framework of contractual relations. In this sense the "behavior" of the firm is like the behavior of a market, that is, the outcome of a complex equilibrium process. We seldom fall into the trap of characterizing the wheat or stock market as an individual, but we often make this error by thinking about organizations as if they were persons with motivations or intentions.[3]

Using this view, we explain why the basic state of nature for value-maximizing firms facing equilibrium asset prices is for neither their financial policies nor risk management processes to have any impact on their market values. By starting there, we have a benchmark against which opportunities for risk management to add value can be compared.

The irrelevance of risk management is explored and presented in two ways. The first is the corporate finance perspective of the Modigliani-Miller capital structure irrelevance propositions in which no arbitrage proofs are used to illustrate the independence of firm value from its capital structure and the leverage of its investors. The second perspective shows that fairly priced derivatives—the building blocks of most financial risk management actions and the cousins to insurance contracts—have no impact on the expected value of a firm. In other words, the net present value of an unhedged factory is the same as the net present value of a hedged factory. Unless readers develop a clear understanding of why risk management *cannot* add value to a firm in the basic corporate finance model, exploiting real-world opportunities for risk management to make security holders of companies better off is truly difficult.

THE CORPORATION VERSUS THE INDIVIDUAL

As the quote from Jensen and Meckling reinforced, a corporation is not an individual. It does not have a mind of its own and a utility function that can map the company's wealth into units of happiness. Wealth and assets can be mapped into value, profits, earnings, and cash flows, of course, but where does this leave us with respect to defining a corporate analogue to the individual concept of risk aversion?

To probe the depths of the serious issues raised for hedging by corporate finance, consider asking the CEO of an airline the following question: "Do you hedge the risk that jet fuel prices rise by entering into contracts that lock in the price of your future jet fuel purchases at a price known today?" The CEO of one airline might laugh heartily. Between guffaws, he might mumble something about how his responsibility to his shareholders and creditors obligate him to lock in his fuel purchase prices. Otherwise, the airline would run the risk that fuel price increases destroy the profit margin on a successful franchise and that cash flows and earnings volatility spin wildly out of control, upsetting, among others, the airline stock analysts.

Now ask the same question to the CEO of a different airline. This time, you might get a different answer: "Of course we do not lock in fuel purchase prices! Locking in fuel prices today might protect us from price increases, but my shareholders would be very upset if we could not take advantage of any subsequent fuel price declines!"

Still a third airline CEO might give the most complex answer of all. When asked whether she hedges the risk that jet fuel prices rise, she might look at you with a perfectly straight face and say, "No, because it's irrelevant whether we do or do not hedge that risk ourselves. We let shareholders make decisions on their own. One of our shareholders, Bob Smith, is worried about declining margins from rising fuel prices. If we do not hedge as an airline, then Bob can hedge on his own by buying shares in the oil refinery that sells us the fuel. At the same time, Rachel Jones is a shareholder who is unconcerned about rising fuel prices because she already owns shares in a refinery. If we do not hedge, she doesn't need to do anything. And the reason I say it's irrelevant is that everything works the other way around, too. If the airline *does* hedge, then Bob doesn't need to do anything, but Rachel must sell some of her stock in the refinery to stay neutral with respect to fuel price changes. So you see? *It's irrelevant.*"

So, one airline says that it hedges fuel price risk to avoid eroding profit margins. Another CEO says that hedging is avoided because the risk of price increases that erode margins are offset by the potential cost savings resulting from price declines. And a third CEO claims that it is irrelevant whether or not the airline hedges. Which executive is correct?

The answer, of course, is that *all of these answers* are correct, depending on the characteristics of the airline. To understand why, a closer look at the relations between corporate finance and corporate risk management is necessary.

SOME IMPORTANT IRRELEVANCIES

To understand most clearly why the first CEO said it would be crazy *not* to hedge fuel price risk and the second CEO said it would be nutty *to hedge* that same risk, a good place to start is with the answer from the third CEO, who claimed that hedging is irrelevant. To that end, before the relevance of risk management to certain companies can be fully appreciated, an important starting point is the *irrelevance* of most financial and risk management policies under certain assumptions.

Specifically, financial and risk management policies do not affect the value of a firm whose goal is maximizing the welfare of its security holders when the following four assumptions are true:[4]

1. *Perfect capital markets.* Capital markets are perfect in the sense of no taxes, no transaction costs, no institutional frictions (e.g., short selling restrictions), and no costs of bankruptcy.
2. *Symmetric information.* All investors, firms, and firm managers have the same information *and* have perceptions concerning the impact of new information on security prices that are both true and identical across investors.
3. *Given investment strategies.* Investment decisions by firms are taken as a given and as independent from financing decisions.
4. *Equal access.* Firms and individuals can issue the same securities in the capital markets on exactly the same terms.[5]

Many of the above assumptions are clearly violated in the real world. That the assumptions do not hold, however, does not render them worthless. On the contrary, these tenets of corporate finance orthodoxy provide us with a benchmark against which all *deviations* from the benchmark can be compared. In other words, the third CEO's answer to the hedging question better prepares us to understand the difference between the first and second CEOs' answers.

In the modern theory of corporate finance, that model is the Modigliani-Miller (M&M) model. The above assumptions, sometimes called the M&M assumptions, imply some very strong results for corporate finance and risk management. The three implications most relevant to the development by a corporation of a risk management program are discussed next.

Capital Structure Irrelevance

The first irrelevance proposition of M&M tells us that the value of a company is independent of its capital structure. In other words, leverage does not affect the value of the firm. To illustrate this basic tenet of corporate finance, consider Corporation Superior with \$100 of assets and no liabilities. With no debt, the market value of Corporation Superior at some time t is equal to the market value of its assets at that time t:

$$V(t)^S = A(t)^S = E(t)^S = \$100$$

where superscripts denote the company name—S for Superior—and the t in parenthesis denotes time.

Now consider Corporation Huron whose asset values are drawn from an identical probability distribution as Superiors. The difference between the firms is that Corporation Huron borrows \$50 in debt and Superior does not. The value of Corporation Huron at time t is now equal to the sum of the market values of its debt and equity at time t:

$$V(t)^H = E(t)^H + D(t)^H$$

The essence of M&M Proposition I is that the absence of arbitrage requires the value of Corporation Superior to equal that of Corporation Huron. To see this, consider first an investment strategy in which the arbitrageur Adam Smith buys 10% of the shares of Corporation Huron, which will cost Adam Smith

$$0.10E(t)^H = 0.10\left[V(t)^H - D(t)^H\right]$$

In return for making this investment outlay, Adam Smith earns 10% of the firm's profits each year *after* the interest on the debt is repaid. If the interest rate on the debt at time t is $R(t)^D$, Adam earns the following per year:

$$0.10\left[\text{Profits} - R(t)^D D(t)^H\right]$$

Now consider a second investment strategy in which Adam Smith borrows on his own in order to invest in Corporation Superior. Remember that one assumption of M&M is equal access by individuals and firms to the capital market, which means they have the same borrowing rate. So, supposing Adam Smith borrows an amount exactly equal to the market value of the debt issued by Corporation Huron, $D(t)^H$, to invest in Corporation

The Irrelevance of Corporate Financing and Risk Management Decisions

Superior. Adam Smith then has a net investment outlay of

$$-0.10D(t)^H + 0.10E(t)^S = 0.10\left[V(t)^S - D(t)^H\right]$$

because $E(t)^S$ is the same as $V(t)^S$ for the unlevered firm Superior. Adam Smith then earns gross profits per year on his investment in Corporation Superior:

$$0.10(\text{Profits})$$

where Profits here are the same as for Corporation Huron since the assets underlying the company are identical. But Adam Smith must subtract from this inflow the cost of servicing the debt he borrowed to make the investment. So, Adam Smith's *net* profits per year are

$$0.10\left[\text{Profits} - R(t)^D D(t)^H\right]$$

The following table compares the costs and profits per annum of the two investment strategies:

	Initial Cost	Net Profits per Annum
Invest in Huron	$0.10[V(t)^H - D(t)^H]$	$0.10[\text{Profits} - R(t)^D D(t)^H]$
Borrow to Invest in Superior	$0.10[V(t)^S - D(t)^H]$	$0.10[\text{Profits} - R(t)^D D(t)^H]$

Note that the profits of the two investments are exactly the same. In the first case, the arbitrageur gets 10% of Corporation Huron's profits after debt repayment, or $0.10[\text{Profits} - R(t)^D D(t)^H]$. In the second case, Adam Smith earns 10% of profits from Corporation Superior but then must repay his own debt. Because profits of the two strategies are the same and the borrowing rates are identical, the net profits for Adam Smith are equivalent.

If the profits of the strategies are identical, then *costs* must also be identical, else a riskless arbitrage opportunity will arise. To see why, suppose the value of Corporation Superior exceeds the value of Corporation Huron, $V(t)^S > V(t)^H$. In that case, Adam Smith could invest in Corporation Huron for less than he could invest in Corporation Superior and yet still earn the same return for no risk. Other investors in the same situation would behave likewise. With costless transacting, perfect capital markets, and symmetric information, no one would buy shares in the more expensive Corporation Superior—or, more properly, investors would short the stock of Corporation Superior and buy the stock of Corporation Huron. Eventually, the two values would equalize, so that $V(t)^H = V(t)^S$. This is the import of M&M Proposition I—the value of the firm is independent of its capital structure.

Debt and Leverage Irrelevance

Some might be tempted to argue at this point that the only implication of M&M Proposition I is that it does not matter whether the firm or the individual borrows, but borrowing itself is still a good way to increase value. M&M respond to this in their Proposition II, which holds that leverage itself does not benefit *either* investors *or* the corporation no matter who does it.

A firm's *cost of capital* is the return it must pay to investors in order to induce them to hold its securities. Taking the case of the levered Corporation Huron, we already know the firm had a debt cost of capital of R^D. Now suppose we denote the expected return demanded by investors on Huron's equity as R^E, where this is now the corporation's equity cost of capital.

We can define Corporation's weighted average cost of capital (WACC) as follows:

$$R^{WACC} = \frac{D}{D+E}R^D + \frac{E}{D+E}R^E \qquad (3.1)$$

In other words, the cost of capital for the firm is the interest rate paid on its debt weighted by the proportion of debt in the capital structure plus the expected return demanded by equity holders weighted by the fraction of equity in the firm.

To illustrate M&M Proposition II, we need do little more than rearrange the firm's WACC in terms of its equity cost of capital:

$$R^E = R^{WACC} + \frac{D}{E}\left(R^{WACC} - R^D\right) \qquad (3.2)$$

With no taxes, the WACC is equal to the cost of capital for an all-equity corporation. Recognizing this fact, Equation 3.2 tells us that expected return on equity increases as the leverage of the firm increases.

So, although debt appears to be a cheaper source of financing for a firm, issuing debt increases the risk of holding equity, thereby leading investors to demand a higher expected return on equity. This increase in the cost of equity capital exactly offsets the benefit of the cheaper debt in the firm's capital structure, leaving the overall cost of capital unchanged.

As Merton Miller describes the result, it's as intuitive as the notion that no matter how many ways you slice a pizza, the total size of the pizza remains unchanged. Alternatively, the value of a firm selling whole milk is no different than the value of a firm selling cream and low-fat milk. The higher price at which the cream is sold is offset by the lower price of low-fat milk, leading to the same result as if the whole had never been separated into its parts.

Security Holder Indifference

Saying that the value of a firm is independent of its capital structure is not quite equivalent to saying that the security holders of a firm are unaffected by its financing decisions. To demonstrate this, the model presented in Fama (1976) is reproduced here in which a firm can issue stocks and bonds. At any given time t, the firm cannot do anything with its financial policy to affect the value of stocks and bonds in that period, but the same is not true at the prior time period $t - 1$.

Let $E_{t-1}(t)$ and $D_{t-1}(t)$ denote the market values at time t of stocks and bonds, respectively, that were outstanding in the prior time period $t - 1$. The current value of the firm is thus

$$V(t) = E_{t-1}(t) + D_{t-1}(t)$$

At time t, the firm can issue *new* securities. If the values of new equities and debt issued at time t are denoted $e(t)$ and $d(t)$, respectively, then the value of the firm is now

$$V(t) = E_{t-1}(t) + D_{t-1}(t) + e(t) + d(t) \qquad (3.3)$$

At time t, the firm earns a total net cash inflow of $X(t)$ and invests a total of $I(t)$ in new investment projects, where $I(t)$ is assumed under M&M to be given exogenously. In addition, the firm makes dividend and interest payments at time t on securities that were outstanding from the prior period $t - 1$. The sum of dividends $\delta(t)$ and interest $\rho(t)$ paid at time t must equal the net cash flow of the firm *plus* the proceeds from any new security issues. Called the firm's *cash flow constraint*, this relation can be expressed as

$$\delta(t) + \rho(t) = X(t) - I(t) + e(t) + d(t)$$

Substituting the firm's cash flow constraint into the value of the firm shown in Equation 3.3 allows us to express the *total* wealth of all security holders:

$$\left[E_{t-1}(t) + \delta(t)\right] + \left[D_{t-1}(t) + \rho(t)\right] = X(t) - I(t) + V(t) \qquad (3.4)$$

Under the M&M assumptions of perfect capital markets, symmetric information, given investment strategies, and equal access, the value of the firm $V(t)$ is not affected by the firm's financing decisions. Because $X(t)$ is determined by previous investment decisions and $I(t)$ is assumed given, $X(t)$, $I(t)$, and $V(t)$ are all independent of the firm's financing decisions. We can see from Equation 3.4 that the right-hand side of the equation is thus unaffected by the firm's financing decisions. It follows that the left-hand side is similarly unaffected—combined security holder welfare is *also* independent of financing decisions made by the firm.

Although *combined* security holder wealth cannot be affected by the firm's financing decisions, individual classes of securities may be. Suppose specifically that the debt outstanding at time $t - 1$ was riskless and that the firm issues new debt at time t. The new debt will expose the firm to the risk of default, which will impact the new bondholders *and* the *existing* bondholders. Since the combined value of the securities cannot be affected by this financing decision, the decline in $D_{t-1}(t)$ that accompanies the issuance of new, risky debt results in an increase in $E_{t-1}(t)$. Issuing new risky debt thus reduces the total market value of the firm's debt and increases the value of the firm's equity by the same amount.

Conversely, suppose the debt outstanding at time $t - 1$ was already subject to default risk and that the firm retires a portion of that existing debt at time t. If the firm subsequently goes bankrupt, the bondholders receive a pro rata claim on the firm's remaining assets. With fewer bondholders at time t, each creditor to the firm would retrieve more in bankruptcy than before. The increase in $D_{t-1}(t)$ that results from the debt retirement must come from old equity holders in order to keep *total* security holder wealth constant. So, the rise in $D_{t-1}(t)$ is funded by a decline in $E_{t-1}(t)$.

The four M&M assumptions thus guarantee only that the value of the firm is independent of its financing decisions. To go one step further and say that the firm's financing decisions are irrelevant to the holders of both equity and risky debt, an additional assumption is required. Specifically, we must assume that the bonds issued by the firm contain covenants that preserve what Fama and Miller (1972) call "me-first rules." Such rules would require the firm to assign seniority to existing debt holders so that any new debt is junior in capital structure. This protects current debt holders. In addition, any early retirements of debt would begin with the retirement of the most junior issues and end with the oldest, most senior issues. This protects equity holders. Under this additional assumption, the value of the firm is independent of its financing decisions *and* its security holders are indifferent to those decisions.

The Irrelevance of Hedging and Insurance

The absence of an optimal capital structure for most firms does not obviously imply the absence of any need for hedging by those same firms. Nevertheless, the implication, albeit subtle, is very much there. Under the same four assumptions that guarantee independence between the value of the firm and its capital structure, the value of the firm is also independent of any deliberate actions taken by management to control risks through hedging or insurance purchasing.

As in the illustrative proof of capital structure irrelevance, the key to the logic lies in the portfolio diversification decisions of investors in the company. Suppose our company in question is Airline FlyMe, whose sole business is flying customers between Zürich and Chicago. The revenues of the company that ultimately determine the value of its equity can fluctuate because of changes in customer demand, the quality of service provided vis-à-vis competitors, availability of aircraft, and other business considerations. But equity holders also experience changes in capital value and dividends when jet fuel prices change. As fuel prices rise, the net profit margin of the firm shrinks.

One solution for the company is to hedge its jet fuel purchase costs. If the company uses forward contracts, the treasury department can ensure that the price of all of its anticipated jet fuel purchases is locked in advance. The cost of this hedge is essentially equal to the cost of buying all the jet fuel the firm thinks it will need at today's known price and then storing that fuel until it is consumed.[6] Or if the firm uses call options, it can protect itself against rising jet fuel prices by paying a type of insurance premium that does not force Airline FlyMe to give up the benefits of any price declines.

Now suppose instead that all the shareholders in Airline FlyMe are holding perfectly diversified portfolios. The impact of jet fuel prices on the value of their Airline FlyMe stock *will already have been taken into account* as they constructed their portfolios. If investors need that exposure to jet fuel prices in order to hold the portfolio they want, then hedging by the company will actually mess things up by changing the correlation pattern in FlyMe stock with the other equities the investors chose to hold.

We can also view the problem another way. If investors in Airline FlyMe have no other investments at all and are averse to the impact of jet fuel price changes on the value of their investment, it is still not necessary for the company to hedge. Instead, investors might simply choose to buy stock in, say, an oil refinery that transforms crude oil purchases into refined oil product sales, including jet fuel. When the price of jet fuel rises, the refinery experiences an increase in its profit margin. As long as the investors have been careful to hold the right proportions of refinery and airline stocks, the impact of jet fuel price changes should wash out across the two investments.

This type of diversification argument transcends market risk and can apply to *any* diversifiable risk. Under the M&M assumptions, an investor in Company Duck concerned with the credit risk of Company Goose could simply short the stock of Company Goose. And similarly for other diversifiable event-driven risk types.

Whether or not investors are holding perfectly diversified portfolios, we thus are left with the basic proposition that shareholders should be totally indifferent to the risk management decisions made by corporate managers, provided the assumptions underlying the M&M propositions hold.

Also notice that consistency obligates us to lump *all* risk management solutions into this irrelevancy category. In other words, despite the focus of the example on hedging, the irrelevance of risk management in a M&M world goes beyond hedging and also applies to other risk management structures like insurance. Consequently, a firm that finds hedging unnecessary will also find the purchase of insurance unnecessary, whether property/casualty or financial.

EQUILIBRIUM ASSET PRICES

Any discussion of hedging also must be undertaken in the proper context of equilibrium asset prices. More conventionally, corporations undertaking a hedging program too often forget the basic precept of orthodox finance that you get what you pay for. Sometimes called the Bob Barker Game Show principle, saying that you get what you pay for is the same thing as saying "the price is right."

Specifically, in an economy free from unexploited arbitrage opportunities populated with consumers who prefer more to less, the equilibrium price of *any* asset—stocks, bonds, futures, forwards, options, swaps, insurance policies, refrigerators, beer—already reflects the risk of that asset in equilibrium. If every asset is fairly priced to compensate investors for the risk of holding that asset, the opportunity for risk management to add value to a firm is further cast into doubt.

The Fundamental Valuation Equation

When investors prefer more to less and transaction costs allow for the elimination of violations in the law of one price—that is, all free lunches are risklessly exploited by arbitrage—the price of any asset is equal to the net present value of the cash flows on that asset.

The Fundamental Value Equation—Asset Prices   Written most generally, the fundamental valuation equation (FVE) of finance tells us that the following *must* be true in the absence of arbitrage:

$$P_t = E_t(m_{t+1}X_{t+1}) \tag{3.5}$$

where P_t is the current price of a security, E_t denotes an expected value conditional on the information investors have at time t, m_{t+1} is the discount rate used to discount risky cash flows at time $t + 1$, and X_{t+1} is the risky cash flow on the asset at time $t + 1$. In other words, the price of the asset today must equal the expected present value of the cash flows paid on the asset tomorrow.

Finance theory guarantees us the existence of some discount rate—namely, the rate at which individuals are willing to substitute one unit of consumption tomorrow for a unit of edible consumption today. The trick in finance, of course, is figuring out how to estimate that. And to be sure, there are *many* possibilities. Easily one of the greatest sources of PhD thesis topics at major graduate schools today remains the quest for the Holy Grail of "the right asset pricing model," or, stated differently, the right way to discount risky cash flows in equilibrium and in the absence of arbitrage.

Probably the best-known of all the asset pricing models is the single-factor CAPM of Sharpe, Lintner, Mossin, and Black that was presented in Chapter 1 and expressed formally in Equation (1.1). Multifactor models of those in the form of Equation (1.3) also can be used. The single-factor CAPM and its multifactor cousins share the common feature of expressing the expected return on any asset as a linear combination of risk factors. In the context of Equation 3.5, the CAPM implies that

$$m_{t+1} = a + bR_{m,\,t+1} \tag{3.6}$$

where $R_{m,\,t+1}$ is the return on the market portfolio and a and b are free parameters.[7]

The stochastic discount factor need not be a linear function of the risk factor(s). Much research focuses instead on trying to identify other stochastic discount factors directly. Popular candidates are aggregate consumption and production.[8]

Whatever the asset pricing model used, the basic principle is the same. The price of any asset is equal to the discounted expected present value of future cash flows on the asset. Academics regularly debate the appropriate discount rate, but the debate over *which* discount rate to use does not imply any doubt about *whether* one exists and *whether* to use it. It does, and you should.

The Fundamental Valuation Equation—Asset Returns The FVE can be rewritten in terms of price relatives, or returns. Dividing both sides of Equation 3.5 by P_t, which is known at time t, yields the return version of the FVE:

$$E(m_{t+1} R_{t+1}) = 1 \qquad (3.7)$$

where R_{t+1} is the return on the asset (X_{t+1} divided by P_t) and where the expectation is conditional on time t but the subscript is dropped for simplicity. If the asset is a stock, for example, then $X_{t+1} = P_{t+1} + D_{t+1}$ and R_{t+1} is just the usual expression of an arithmetic return on a dividend-paying asset plus one.

The FVE applies to all assets, including default- and price-risk-free bonds. Consider such a riskless pure discount bond that returns \$1 in one period. Using Equation 3.5, the current price of the bond is thus

$$P_t = E(m_{t+1} 1) = E(m_{t+1})$$

which implies

$$\frac{E(m_{t+1})}{P_t} = 1$$

Because the bond is a pure discount bond, the rate on this riskless bond can be written as a function of the price

$$R_{t+1}^f = \frac{1}{P_t}$$

which gives us a useful correspondence between the risk-free rate and the stochastic discount factor:

$$E(m_{t+1}) = \frac{1}{R_{t+1}^f} \qquad (3.8)$$

Note that R_{t+1}^f is expressed as the inverse of a *factor*, so that

$$R_{t+1}^f = 1 + r_{t+1}^f$$

where r_{t+1}^f is the *rate* we would use if we were discounting.

Using the statistical fact that $E[XY] = E[X]E[Y] + \text{cov}(X, Y)$ for any random variables X and Y, the FVE in term of price (i.e., Equation 3.5) can be rewritten for *any* asset as

$$P_t = E(m_{t+1}X_{t+1}) = E(m_{t+1})E_t(X_{t+1}) + \text{cov}(m_{t+1}, X_{t+1}) \tag{3.9}$$

or, in terms of the risk-free rate,

$$P_t = \frac{E[X_{t+1}]}{R_{t+1}^f} + \text{cov}(m_{t+1}, X_{t+1}) \tag{3.10}$$

Equation 3.10 implies that the price of any asset has two components: a risk-free component and a risk premium. Any bundle of cash flows thus can be priced as the expected future cash flow discounted at the risk-free rate *plus* some risk premium to compensate the investor for the risk of the asset.

As indicated in Chapter 1, asset pricing theory regards risk as either systematic or idiosyncratic. In that terminology, the systematic risk of an asset is reflected fully in the covariance of the cash flows on the asset with the stochastic discount factor. Seemingly more counterintuitive is the fact that the volatility of the cash flows does not enter into the picture. We shall return to one instance when it does in Chapter 7 in particular.

Now let us rewrite the above expression using returns instead of prices using Equations 3.7 and 3.8:

$$1 = E(m_{t+1}R_{t+1}^j) = \frac{E(R_{t+1}^j)}{R_{t+1}^f} + \text{cov}(m_{t+1}, R_{t+1}^j) \tag{3.11}$$

for any asset *j*. Rearranging terms allows us to express this in a more familiar expected return form:

$$E(R_{t+1}^j) = R_{t+1}^f[1 - \text{cov}(m_{t+1}, R_{t+1}^j)] \tag{3.12}$$

Again we see that the expected return on any asset is equal to the risk-free rate plus a risk adjustment. Multiplying and dividing the last term by $\text{var}(m_{t+1})$ yields the familiar beta representation for expected returns:

$$E(R_{t+1}^j) = R_{t+1}^f + \beta_{j,m}\Phi_m \tag{3.13}$$

where

$$\beta_{j,m} = \frac{\text{cov}(R_{t+1}^j, m_{t+1})}{\text{var}(m_{t+1})} \qquad \Phi_m = \frac{-\text{var}(m_{t+1})}{E(m_{t+1})}$$

so that the expected return on an asset is proportional to the OLS beta in a regression of returns on the stochastic discount factor, such as the CAPM where $m_{t+1} = a + bR_{m, t+1}$ as in Equation 3.6.

Utility Theory and Asset Prices   The neoclassical model of risk-averse investors presented in Chapter 2 also has strong implications for asset prices. To see how, suppose the economy is populated with consumers whose utility can be expressed in terms of consumption opportunities today and tomorrow—C_t and C_{t+1}, respectively. Assume that these individuals, in keeping with the neoclassical theory, are never fully satiated and prefer more to less at a diminishing rate. If the investor's utility is denoted $U(C_t, C_{t+1})$, these assumptions imply that U is increasing in both arguments, $U_C > 0$, and $U_{CC} < 0$. (Time subscripts are dropped from the partial derivatives because they are the same for C_t and C_{t+1}.)

Now assume for simplicity that the utility function of our representative investor is also characterized by what we call *additive separability*. This means that we can treat the investor's total utility over consumption in period t and $t + 1$ as the *sum* of the utility received by the investor in the two different periods:

$$U(C_t, C_{t+1}) = U(C_t) + \beta E_t [U(C_{t+1})]$$

where β is the investor's rate for discounting consumption tomorrow back to equivalent terms today. The discount rate β has nothing to do with risk and is sometimes called the investor's *rate of time preference* of consumption today vis-à-vis consumption tomorrow.

Now suppose a single financial asset exists whose price at time t is P_t and whose payoff at time $t + 1$ is X_{t+1}. The payoff could be anything the investor receives from holding the asset. If it is a forward contract for the sale of a commodity at price K, then $X_{t+1} = S_{t+1} - K$, where S_{t+1} is the spot price of the commodity at $t + 1$. If the asset is a stock, then $X_{t+1} = P_{t+1} + D_{t+1}$ where P_{t+1} is the $t + 1$ price at which the stock can be resold and D_{t+1} is the dividend earned over the period.

Suppose the investor can freely buy or sell as much of this asset as she likes at time t. Like the example we explored earlier when we examined the consequences of the normal distribution on the investor's expected utility maximization problem, the investor faces a similar problem here. We have modified the problem slightly—based on Cochrane (2000)—to make the results clearer by expressing utility in terms of consumption directly rather than wealth. In addition, whereas we earlier assumed that the investor put all his residual wealth into the portfolio in question, we now make that a choice variable for the investor, who now solves the following constrained optimization problem:

$$\max_\alpha U(C_t) + E_t[\beta U(C_{t+1})]$$
$$s.t. \quad C_t = e_t - \alpha P_t \qquad (3.14)$$
$$s.t. \quad C_{t+1} = e_{t+1} + \alpha X_{t+1}$$

where e_t and e_{t+1} are just the original consumption levels that would have occurred without the purchase of the asset. Because we have assumed the investor prefers more to less at a decreasing rate, the above problem involves the maximization of a concave function subject to two linear constraints. The problem thus can be reformulated more usefully by substituting the constraints into the objective function:

$$\max_\alpha U(e_t - \alpha P_t) + E_t[\beta U(e_{t+1} + \alpha X_{t+1})] \qquad (3.14a)$$

We now solve the problem in 3.14a by differentiating the objective function with respect to α and setting the resulting first-order condition to zero:

$$P_t U_C(C_t) = E_t[\beta U_C(C_{t+1}) X_{t+1}] \qquad (3.15)$$

In the context of expected utility theory, Equation 3.15 says that the investor will choose the amount of the asset to purchase that exactly equates his marginal cost of investment (i.e., the left-hand side of Equation 3.15) with the marginal benefit of investment (i.e., the right-hand side of Equation 3.15).

We can rewrite Equation 3.15 to characterize the equilibrium price of an asset in an economy where all investors behave as above:

$$P_t = E_t\left[\beta \frac{U_C(C_{t+1})}{U_C(C_t)} X_{t+1}\right] \qquad (3.16)$$

The investor adjusts the amount α of the asset purchased until this equation holds given the equilibrium price P_t.

The first term inside the expected value operator is the *intertemporal marginal rate of substitution* (IMRS) for the investor, or the rate at which one unit of consumption today can be substituted for one unit of discounted consumption tomorrow. In asset pricing, this term is also called a *stochastic discount factor* and may be rewritten as

$$m_{t+1} = \beta \frac{U_C(C_{t+1})}{U_C(C_t)}$$

Equation 3.16 can be rewritten more simply as

$$P_t = E_t(m_{t+1} X_{t+1})$$

which is the FVE was saw in Equation 3.5 earlier. In other words, the current price of an asset is equal to the expected discounted present value of the cash flows on that asset, where the IMRS is the discount rate.

Equation 3.10 earlier showed that the FVE can be reexpressed as

$$P_t = \frac{E(X_{t+1})}{R_{t+1}^f} + \text{cov}(m_{t+1}, X_{t+1})$$

so that the price of any asset depends on its expected cash flow discounted at the risk-free rate and a risk premium to compensate the holder of the asset for its systematic risk.

Using our new definition of the stochastic discount factor as the IMRS, we can rewrite the above as

$$P_t = \frac{E(X_{t+1})}{R_{t+1}^f} + \frac{\text{cov}[\beta U_C(C_{t+1}), X_{t+1}]}{U_C(C_t)} \qquad (3.17)$$

For a typical risk-averse investor, marginal utility of consumption U_C is positive but declines as consumption rises. Consequently, assets whose cash flows are positively correlated with consumption have a lower price.

What is the intuition behind Equation 3.17? Investors in this model prefer a stable stream of lifetime consumption. For this reason, assets that pay off more when consumption is already high are not worth as much to a risk-averse investor as assets whose cash flows are negatively correlated with existing consumption opportunities. This also helps explain why the covariance of an asset's cash flows with consumption is more important than the volatility of the asset's cash flow itself (Cochrane, 2000).

Consider a consumer who adds a small fraction ψ of the asset to her portfolio. Her consumption at time $t + 1$ is now $C_{t+1} + \psi X_{t+1}$. From a volatility standpoint, the investor cares about the variance of *consumption*, not of any single asset. For a small asset purchase, the variance of the investor's new time $t + 1$ consumption is

$$\text{var}(C_{t+1}) + 2\psi \, \text{cov}(C_{t+1}, X_{t+1}) + \psi^2 \, \text{var}(X_{t+1})$$

For a small ψ, the covariance of the cash flows on the asset with consumption is much more important than the volatility of the asset's cash flows. As long as the investor's portfolio is well-diversified, the volatility of any individual asset thus will not really matter.

Derivatives and the FVE

The FVE applies to *all* bundles of cash flows, whether in the form of a factory, a security, or a *derivatives contract*. A derivatives contract is a financial contract whose cash flows depend on one or more underlying asset prices, reference rates, or indexes. Two general types of derivatives can be identified—forward-based and option-based derivatives.[9]

The cash flows on forward-based derivatives at maturity change in a one-to-one manner with changes in their underlyings. Cash flows on option-based contracts, by contrast, can change by more or less than the underlying changes. More formally, option-based derivatives have values that are not linear in the underlying price. The main reason for this distinction is that forward-based derivatives on their own have unlimited liability, whereas option-based derivatives function more like classical insurance and offer their buyers a maximum loss that is known the day the trade is made. Because of this difference, the pricing of the two distinct types of contracts should be discussed separately.

Forward-Based Derivatives   As early as the twelfth century, the medieval fairs of England and France provided opportunities for English, Flemish, Spanish, French, and Italian merchants to gather together and contract for the purchase or sale of a specified amount and quality of a commodity at a specified date in the future. This most basic type of derivatives contract is called a *forward contract*.

A simple forward delivery contract might be a contract to purchase 100 troy ounces of gold one year in the future for a price set equal to the price of gold today (i.e., its *spot* price). If the price of gold is $400/oz when the contract is entered and the price happens to be $450/oz one year from now, the purchaser of this contract makes a profit equal to ($450 – $400) × 100, or $5,000. (To see why, just imagine the forward purchaser buys the gold for the contracted $40,000 and immediately resells it for its market value of $45,000.) Suppose instead the price of gold in a year happened to be $350/oz. Then the purchaser of the forward contract loses $5,000, and she would prefer to have bought the gold at the lower future spot price.

Forward delivery contracts can also be entered to *sell* an asset at a future date. These contracts are popular for numerous underlying assets, including physical commodities and financial assets such as foreign exchange. Forward contracts may also be *cash-settled*. In a cash-settled derivatives transaction, a *cash flow* rather than a physical asset is bought, sold, or exchanged. Cash-settled forwards are based on such underlyings as interest rates or indexes.

The value of a forward contract on one unit of some underlying asset like gold at its maturity date is depicted in Figure 3.1 from the perspective of the forward purchaser, or the long. The value of the contract is represented by the dashed line, and notice that it is a 45° line. Every dollar increase in the maturity price of the underlying S_T above the fixed purchase

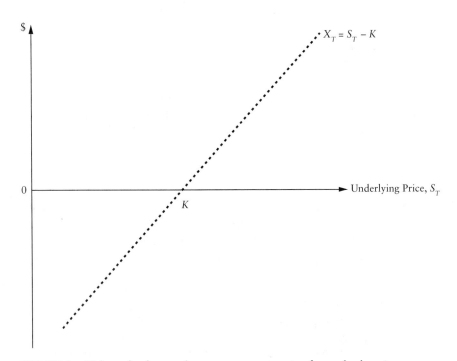

FIGURE 3.1 Value of a forward contract at maturity from the long's perspective.

price K yields a $1 increase in value in the contract at maturity. Every dollar decline causes a loss on the contract. If the contract is our gold forward contract above and the price of gold at maturity is exactly $400/oz—the same as the prenegotiated sale/purchase price—the forward purchaser is no better or worse off than if the contract had not been entered.

As Figure 3.1 suggests, we can express the payoff to the long in a forward contract on one unit of some asset at its maturity date T as follows:

$$X_T = S_T - K \tag{3.18}$$

where S_T is the price per unit of the underlying commodity when the forward contract matures at time T, and K is the fixed price per unit at which the long has negotiated as a forward purchase price. Keeping with the example above, if the contract is based on 100 ounces of gold, the negotiated forward purchase price is $400/oz, and the spot price is $450/oz at maturity date T, the long makes $5,000 [= ($450 − $400) × 100].

Derivatives are bilateral contracts. For every buyer/long, there must be a seller/short standing on the other side of the trade. Not surprisingly, the payoffs to the long and short must net to zero at maturity. Figure 3.2 thus shows the payoff of the above forward contract at maturity from the perspective of the seller or the short.

The term *price* is often misleadingly used to describe the fixed purchase price K, or the prenegotiated price at which the long buys from the short in the future. In fact, the "true price" of the forward contract is the discounted expected present value of the cash flows on that contract, and this true price *must* be zero. Otherwise, either the long or the short is making free money at the expense of the other.

To see this, remember that we are still assuming everyone has the same information and all transacting is costless. Importantly, this means that the expected future asset price $E(S_T)$ is going to be identical for the long and the short in this contract. If this expected future price is $450/oz in the example of a gold forward contract, then a fixed purchase price of $400/oz means the long can expect a profit of $50/oz and the short can expect a loss of $50. The short won't go for this at all unless the long makes an initial payment to the short in an amount equal to the present value of $50. The short can then invest the proceeds of this payment, which will grow to $50 by the time the forward matures and exactly offset the expected loss.

An *at-market* forward contract is a contract that involves no initial purchase price paid by the long to the short (or vice versa). Because neither party makes a payment to the other, the contract is "worthless" to both parties. The price of the forward contract is literally zero.

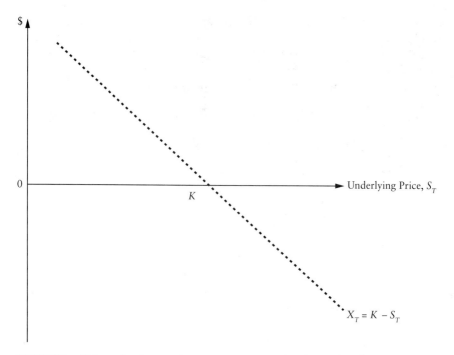

FIGURE 3.2 Value of a forward contract at maturity from the short's perspective.

From this fact, the equilibrium fixed price paid by the buyer in a forward contract is easy to characterize. If the contract calls for delivery of Q units of some asset (e.g., corn or gold or the principal of a certificate of deposit) in month T for a fixed price per unit K, substituting the payoff on the forward in Equation 3.18 into the FVE Equation 3.5 implies that the fixed price K in an at-market contract will satisfy the following equation:

$$E_t(X_T m_T) = E_t[(S_T - K)m_T]Q = P_t = 0$$

which can be rewritten using Equation 3.10 as

$$0 = \frac{E_t(S_T - K)}{R_{t,T}^f} + \text{cov}(m_T, S_T) \tag{3.19}$$

If the covariance between the stochastic discount factor and the future spot price is zero, then

$$K = E_t S_T \qquad (3.20)$$

which says that the fixed rate in the forward contract is an unbiased current predictor of the future spot rate. In other words, the best *forecast* of the future spot price is the current forward fixed purchase price.

The assumption that the spot price and the stochastic discount factor do not covary is a strong one. It essentially means that derivatives are priced *as if* investors are risk neutral. But in fact, this is consistent with the empirical evidence, which tends to support the notion that there is no *risk premium* that shorts demand of longs or vice versa in derivatives—or, if the risk premium does exist, that it switches signs and is too noisy to be statistically different from zero.[10] In that case, the fixed selling price in a forward contract is equal to the conditional expected value as of the trade date of the spot price that will prevail at the contract's settlement. This important result will be presumed to hold for all types of forward-based derivatives (futures, forwards, and swaps) on all underlying assets (e.g., currencies, interest rates, equities).

An *off-market* contract is one in which one party makes an initial payment to the other. Does this mean the price is wrong? Of course not. The price of the forward *plus* the initial payment will still be zero, which is just another way of saying that the price paid initially by one party to the other must exactly equal the discounted expected profits to that party—again, the FVE. Most forwards, however, are at-market, and thus worthless to both investors at their inception.

Notice that because a contract is worthless on the *trade date* does not mean it will be worthless *on the settlement date*. It is certainly plausible that the *actual* time T spot price of the underlying is not equal to its expected value. But that is not the point. The point is that when the two parties agree to this transaction, they are both indifferent to it.

Option-Based Derivatives   An option is a contract giving its holder the *right* but not the obligation to purchase or sell an asset on or before some date in the future. A call option gives its holder the right to buy an asset, and a put option gives its holder the right to sell. When a call or put option is sold, the seller/writer must honor the purchaser's right to buy or sell if the purchaser exercises that right. In exchange for honoring such exercises when they occur, option writers collect option *premiums* from the option purchasers. The use of the term *premium* is not accidental. Whereas forwards give their purchasers unlimited upside and unlimited liability (see Figure 3.1), purchased options are limited-liability assets and thus can act as a form of price insurance for their holders. (See Chapter 26 for discussion on the relations between insurance and derivatives.)

The most common types of options are either European or American. A European-style option is an option that allows its holder to buy or sell only on the option's specified expiration date. An American-style option, by contrast, enables its holder to buy or sell an asset *at any time on or before the option's expiration date.* Options that allow their holders to exercise only a few specific dates prior to expiration rather than at any time or only at expiration are somewhere in between European- and American-style, and thus dubbed Bermuda options.

Options can have a variety of assets, reference rates, or indexes underlying them. In options parlance, we would thus say that options are written on a variety of underlyings. Popular option underlyings include foreign exchange, securities, interest rate indexes (e.g., LIBOR), and commodities. (See Chapter 14 for details.)

The most common way of depicting the value of an option graphically as a function of the price of its underlying is to assume the option is European and look at its value *at expiration.* This graph for the value at maturity of a purchased European call option is shown in Figure 3.3. The point

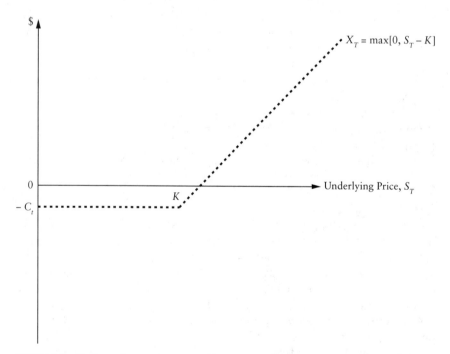

FIGURE 3.3 Value of a European call at maturity from the buyer's perspective.

K denotes the strike price at which the option buyer can purchase the underlying asset at maturity. The option buyer and seller (i.e., writer) agree on the trade date to this price. As in our earlier example, if the option is written on gold, K represents the price per troy ounce of gold at which the option owner may exercise her right to buy gold. If the spot price of gold is above K at expiration, the option owner will exercise her right to buy at K and make a profit of $S_T - K$, where S_T is again the price of gold at expiration date T. If, instead, the price of gold is less than K, the option will expire worthless. It would not pay for the owner of the option to exercise her right to buy gold at the strike price, because the latter is above the price at which she could buy gold in the spot market. When an option has positive exercise (called *intrinsic*) value, it is said to be *in-the-money*—$K < S_T$ in the example above. If the underlying price is less than the exercise price, the call option is *out-of-the-money*.

Notice from Figure 3.3 that the owner of the option has limited liability on the contract. On the option's expiration date, if the price of gold is below the strike price K, the option will be out-of-the-money and will not be exercised. The option purchaser, however, loses nothing due to the decline in the price of gold, *unlike* the owner of the forward purchase (sale) contract depicted in Figure 3.1 (Figure 3.2) who loses dollar-for-dollar as the price falls (rises). Similarly, once the price has risen above K, the option holder gains dollar-for-dollar from the price rise, as the 45°line in Figure 3.3 shows.

Note also in Figure 3.3 that even though the call owner's losses do not increase with decreases in the spot price below K, the flat portion of the terminal payoff on the call is *below* 0 by an amount equal to C_t. This reflects the premium the option owner must pay for the right to purchase the asset at K in the future. The term has a negative sign because the buyer had to pay it, and this term is subscripted by a small t to indicate that the premium of the option is set on the *trade date t*, prior to settlement/expiration date T. Even though a decline in gold prices below K at expiration imposes no additional losses on the option purchaser, the purchaser is out the purchase price of the option paid at the inception of the contract.

Like forward contracts, option contracts are also zero net sum assets. The short or option writer assumes all the liability that the option buyer has limited. Figure 3.4 thus shows the value of a European call option at maturity from the perspective of the seller. Note in Figure 3.4 that the premium C_t is now a positive number. In other words, the seller collects this premium from the option buyer on the trade date to compensate herself for assuming the liability that the option expires in-the-money.

The maturity payoffs for the buyer and seller of a European put are shown in Figures 3.5 and 3.6 on page 86. The put purchaser again faces limited liability that the put seller assumes in exchange for receiving a

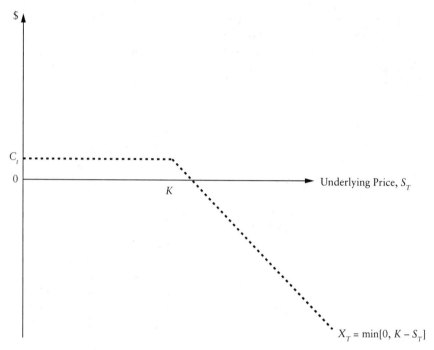

FIGURE 3.4 Value of a European call at maturity from the seller's perspective.

premium payment of P_t. But unlike the call, the put purchaser now has limited liability when prices *rise*. The purchaser makes money as prices fall but does not lose more than the premium paid as prices rise.

Unlike forward contracts, the "price" of an option is not equal to zero on the trade date. Instead, the price is equal to the premium paid by the long to the short. The price of a European call option on its trade date t that expires at time T has a fair price (using FVE 3.5) of

$$C_t = E_t(m_T X_T) = E_t(m_T C_T) = E_t[m_T \times \max(S_T - K, 0)]$$

where C_t is today's call premium paid by the long to the short, and X_T is the maturity payoff on the option, equal to the price of the option at T. And similarly for a put:

$$P_t = E_t(m_T X_T) = E_t(m_T P_T) = E_t[m_T \times \max(K - S_T, 0)]$$

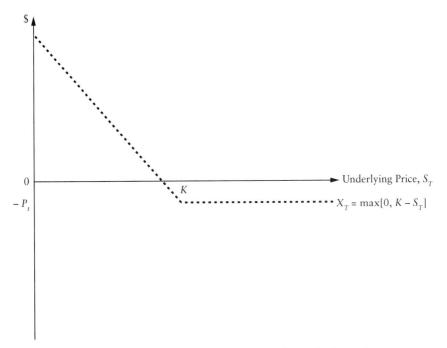

FIGURE 3.5   Value of a European put at maturity from the buyer's perspective.

Like securities, the price of a call or put thus is simply the expected discounted present value of the price of the call or put at expiration. What this tells us is that the price you pay for protection against increases in the spot price when you buy an option is a fair price. That price is exactly equal to what you think the option is worth—the discounted present value of the option expiring in-the-money. Consequently, you are no better or worse off for having paid this price.

To put things in the parlance of the prior section, options are *off-market* because one party expects to benefit more than the other—the long is buying protection from the short. But to compensate for this, the short charges a premium. Just like off-market forwards, then, the *net* price of the whole package is zero.

Corporate Securities as Derivatives

Many textbook discussions of risk management bog down quickly in their definitions of financial instruments by committing the error of *definitional*

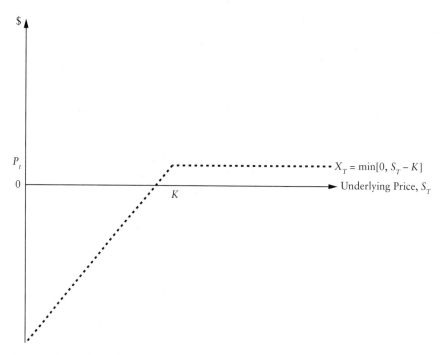

FIGURE 3.6   Value of a European put at maturity from the seller's perspective.

stereotyping. A traditional forward or swap is a derivatives contract, whereas a bond or a share of stock is a security. Another important tenet of corporate finance that bears strongly on risk management involves the recognition that this distinction between securities and derivatives is generally *legal.*

As Fischer Black, Myron Scholes, and Robert Merton recognized and explained in their original treatises on options, corporate securities can always be viewed as types of option contracts.[11] More to the point, as this book will continue to reemphasize, debt and equity *should* be viewed in this manner in order to exploit the strategic opportunities of risk management most effectively.

To see how we can view all corporate securities as options, let us return to Corporation Superior whose capital structure contains no debt. Recall from the earlier discussion of the M&M propositions that the value of the company is equal to the value of its assets, which also determines the value of the total equity issued:

$$V(t)^S = A(t)^S = E(t)^S = \$100$$

Now suppose the company plans to liquidate all of its assets at time period T and that the value of its assets at that time T are unknown as of today's date t. What is the value of the equity issued by Corporation Superior?

To help answer this question, it is useful to graphically depict the payoff to the firm's equity holders at time T for different values of assets at that time. The relation between the value of equity and the value of the assets underlying the firm is shown in Figure 3.7. Note from the figure that we assume equity holders have limited liability in the face of bankruptcy.

Although perhaps not so obvious, the payoff to equity holders in Corporation Superior at time T is identical to the payoff on a call option written on the assets underlying the firm that matures at time T with a striking price of $0.

To see the correspondence between equity and a call option most clearly, now consider Corporation Huron that issued equity *and* debt with a face value of FV. Suppose the debt is payable at liquidation date T, when the firm is divvyed up between debt and equity holders, and suppose debt holders have priority in the firm's capital structure—they get paid first. Figure 3.8 shows the payoffs to the debt and equity holders of Corporation Huron on liquidation date T, as well as the sum of the two—the value of the whole firm.

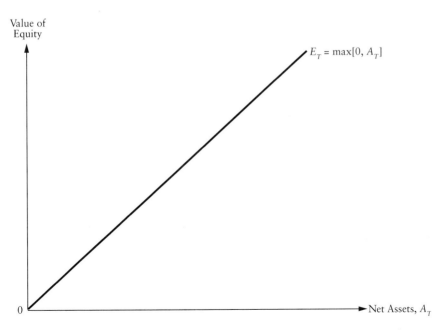

FIGURE 3.7   Market value of equity as a call option on the net assets of the firm.

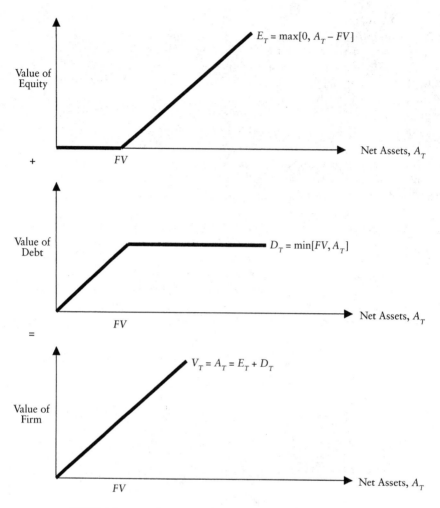

FIGURE 3.8   Market value of a firm viewed as options.

The table below summarizes the value of debt and equity on Corporation Huron's liquidation date T in terms of the value of the assets underlying the firm:

Assets	Debt	Equity
$< FV$	$A(T)^H$	$\$0$
FV	FV	$\$0$
$> FV$	FV	$A(T)^H - FV$

CAPITAL BUDGETING, INVESTMENT, AND THE NET PRESENT VALUE CRITERION

Corporate finance unambiguously tells a firm when to reject certain investments and when to accept other ones, and this criterion by which investments should be evaluated is one of the most important operational considerations facing any firm. The much-vaunted *net present value* (NPV) criterion of corporate finance tells firms to accept only those investments with a nonnegative net present value and to reject all investments with a negative NPV, where the NPV of an investment project with a life of T periods is defined as follows:

$$NPV_t = \sum_{j=1}^{T} \frac{X(t+j)}{R_{t+j}^f} - I(t) \tag{3.21}$$

where $X(t + j)$ denotes a known cash flow at any period $t + j$ between start date t and termination date T, R_{t+j}^f is the risk-free rate plus one, and $I(t)$ is the current investment required to finance the project. If the investment occurs over time, the investment component can be moved into the first term so that it also is appropriately discounted back to time t dollars.

When cash flows on a project are uncertain, the NPV criterion remains the same, but the NPV itself now must reflect the *expected* cash flows on a project discounted at some appropriate risk-adjusted rate. Specifically, the NPV of a T-period project with uncertain future cash flows can be written using Equation 3.5, the FVE, as follows:

$$NPV_t = \sum_{j=1}^{T} E_t \left[m_{t+j} X(t+j) \right] - I(t) \tag{3.22}$$

A more common way to write the NPV in corporate finance is in terms of expected cash flows and the firm's own risk-adjusted discount rate, or

$$NPV_t = \sum_{j=1}^{T} \frac{E_t(X_{t+j})}{1 + \lambda_{t,t+j}} - I(t) \tag{3.23}$$

where $\lambda_{t,t+j}$ is the firm's cost of capital. The unadjusted cost of capital for the firm is the firm's expected return, which is determined by the FVE:

$$\lambda_{t,t+j} = E(R_{t+j}^j) = R_{t+j}^f + \beta_{j,m} \Phi_m \tag{3.24}$$

where $\beta_{j,m}$ and Φ_m are as defined in Equation 3.13. If the firm wants to use a weighted-average cost of capital to reflect leverage, Equation 3.3 gives the proper adjustment.

The NPV criterion is actually one of the most widely misunderstood tenets of corporate finance. True, most managers remember from business school the admonition that negative NPV projects should be rejected and positive NPV projects should be accepted. But managers often fail to recognize that the assumptions under which the NPV criterion holds are generally the same assumptions under which the M&M propositions hold. What that means is that the company is *not* assumed to face any capital constraints arising from the capital market imperfections that have been assumed away.

More specifically, the NPV criterion in corporate finance does not just tell firms to accept *only* projects with nonnegative NPVs. What the criterion actually says under the M&M assumptions is that corporations should accept *all* projects with positive NPVs. The NPV criterion thus provides the necessary condition for undertaking an investment project—a nonnegative NPV—but it does *not* tell a company the *sufficient* conditions for undertaking that project if capital is constrained. We will return to this issue in Chapter 20.

More generally, the optimal investment decisions are governed by the firm's investment *objective function*. Sometimes mistakenly described as maximizing shareholder value, the appropriate objective function for a corporation is actually to maximize *security holder welfare*. From Equation 3.4, we can see that security holder welfare is maximized when the firm maximizes $V(t) + X(t) - I(t)$. Because $X(t)$ was determined by prior investment decisions, this means the firm should maximize $V(t) - I(t)$, the excess of the firm's market value over the investment expenditures required to generate that value, at any time t. Fama (1976) shows how this investment objective strictly dominates either maximizing stockholder wealth or bondholder wealth, unless the firm is all equity in which case maximizing stockholder welfare and security holder welfare are equivalent.

HEDGING AS A CAPITAL BUDGETING PROBLEM

The use of financial instruments to manage the risk of an investment project can be viewed as a capital budgeting problem, where the whole project is now the unhedged project plus the hedge. Alternatively, the acquisition of the financial instruments in isolation can be viewed as a separate project with its own NPV. In either case, the combination of the "price is right" assumption together with the NPV framework illustrates yet again what

M&M already showed us—that risk management does not make a differ-ence in many circumstances. In other words, the addition of financial hedg-ing instruments to an unhedged position does not change the value of the bundle of cash flows.

Suppose a firm considers building a factory that will sell widgets at a constant rate for the next 10 years. Production occurs throughout the month, but the widgets are always sold on the last day of the month. If the current cost of building the factory is $I(t)$, the NPV of the factory is equal to

$$NPV_t = \sum_{j=1}^{120} E_t\left[m_{t+j}X(t+j)\right]Q - I(t) \qquad (3.25)$$

where $E_t[m_{t+j}X(t+j)]$ is the expected value at time t of the cash flow per widget on the factory discounted using FVE Equation 3.5 and where Q is the number of widgets sold per period.

Now suppose the firm considers hedging the production of its widgets against fluctuations in future widget prices. The firm can approach a swap dealer and customize a series of forward contracts—namely, a swap—in which the firm pays an amount at the end of each month equal to the vari-able widget price and receives instead an amount fixed on date t at the in-ception of the life of the swap. To match the factory, assume the swap settles monthly for 120 months and has cash flows based on Q widgets per month.

If the fixed price received by the firm each month per widget is denoted K, the NPV of the swap *in isolation* is

$$NPV^{swap}_t = \sum_{j=1}^{120} E_t\left\{m_{t+j}\left[K - X(t+j)\right]\right\}Q \qquad (3.26)$$

which we know is zero in equilibrium.[12]

If cash flows each period are combined for the swap and the factory, the NPV of the combined project is then

$$NPV^{net}_t = \sum_{j=1}^{120} E_t\left(m_{t+j}K\right)Q - I(t) \qquad (3.27)$$

Because K and Q are both known, the NPV is now known with certainty and riskless. Future cash flows can be discounted at the risk-free rate:

$$NPV^{net}_t = \sum_{j=1}^{120} \frac{KQ}{R^f_{t+j}} - I(t)$$

But now if we substitute back in the equilibrium swap rate K (derived in the Appendix), we can see that the NPV of the *hedged* factory is

$$NPV_t = \sum_{j=1}^{120} E_t \left[m_{t+j} X(t+j) \right] Q - I(t) \qquad (3.28)$$

Equation 3.28 is the same as Equation 3.25. In other words, *the hedged factory has the same NPV as the unhedged factory.* (See the Appendix if you need further convincing.)

This is a powerful result. Basically, this tells us that when derivatives are fairly priced—and under the M&M assumptions, they will *always* be fairly priced—that the NPV of a project is completely unaffected by hedging decisions. If hedging is even slightly costly, then the NPV of the hedged project is actually worth *less* than leaving the project exposed to risk.

Whether using the equilibrium price of financial instruments or the no arbitrage financing proofs of M&M, we have reviewed the major reasons why risk management in a M&M world should not be expected to add value to a firm. In the next several chapters, we thus explore how the real world differs from the M&M world and how those differences may create opportunities for firms to pursue a value-added risk management strategy.

APPENDIX

If the firm discussed in the body of the chapter hedges its Q widgets sold per month by entering into a swap in which it pays the variable widget price each month and receives a fixed payment of K per month, the NPV for the factory will be the same in the hedged and unhedged cases.

In the unhedged case, recall from Equation 3.24 the factory's time t NPV:

$$NPV_t = \sum_{j=1}^{120} E_t \left[m_{t+j} X(t+j) \right] Q - I(t)$$

In any given month $t + j$, the swap results in a cash inflow of K per unit times Q units and a cash outflow of $X(t + j)$ per unit times Q units. Combining that with the cash flows on the factory itself, the NPV of the hedged net project becomes

$$NPV^{net}_t = \sum_{j=1}^{120} E_t \left(m_{t+j} \right) KQ - I(t) \qquad (3.29)$$

To find the equilibrium swap rate, we set Equation 3.26 equal to zero and solve for K:

$$K^* = \frac{\sum_{j=1}^{120} E_t\left[m_{t+j} X(t+j)\right]}{\sum_{j=1}^{120} E_t\left(m_{t+j}\right)} \qquad (3.30)$$

Substituting the swap rate in Equation 3.30 into the hedged NPV in Equation 3.29 yields

$$
\begin{aligned}
NPV^{net}{}_t &= \sum_{j=1}^{120} E_t\left(m_{t+j}\right) \left\{ \frac{\sum_{j=1}^{120} E_t\left[m_{t+j} X(t+j)\right]}{\sum_{j=1}^{120} E_t\left(m_{t+j}\right)} \right\} Q - I(t) \\
&= \sum_{j=1}^{120} E_t\left[m_{t+j} X(t+j)\right] Q - I(t)
\end{aligned}
$$

which is exactly the same as Equation 3.25 and was to be shown.

CHAPTER 4

Increasing Expected Cash Flows or Reducing the Cost of Capital by Managing Risk

In Chapters 2 and 3, we explored the classical hedging and risk management model of Johnson and Stein for single traders and why we cannot immediately extend that model to value-maximizing corporations facing a set of fairly priced financial assets. In this and the next three chapters, we look more closely at corporate hedging and risk management to discover when risk management *can* add value to security holders and to the firm.

As we shall see, violations of certain M&M assumptions resulting in imperfections in the capital market, unequal access of participants to the capital market, and asymmetric information across market participants can all motivate firms to manage risk in a manner that is consistent with value-maximizing behavior of the firm's security holders. But the *implications* of these motivations on the actual strategy and tactics of the risk management program cannot be fully appreciated if the justifications for risk management are used to force the firm into a Johnson-Stein trader hedging model.

The sections that follow and the next three chapters survey the rationales for value-added risk management in the theory of corporate finance. As subsequent chapters will explain, however, some of these rationales have implications that are completely unrealistic. Others have realistic implications but are inconsistent with the actual evidence on how firms manage risk. And still other theories make sense theoretically and practically and are consistent with observed actions by firms.

The theories of value-added risk management explored in this and the next three chapters are separated into four categories, all of which can be associated back to Jensen and Meckling's conception of a firm as a nexus of contracting relationships. The four types of opportunities for risk management to add value to the firm are as follows:

1. Pure frictions in the capital market.
2. Conflicts between managers and stakeholders (i.e., shareholders and/or creditors).
3. Conflicts among stakeholders (i.e., equity and debt holders).
4. Asymmetries in information.

These categories are not unrelated to one another. The second and third categories, for example, both illustrate problems in principal-agent relationships when a principal such as a shareholder engages an agent such as a manager to implement his wishes. Agency problems arise in large part due to frictions in the capital market, such as the cost to principals of monitoring and verifying the actions of their agents. Nevertheless, presenting the various justifications for corporate risk management using the four categories above will make the discussion clearer than trying to define *mutually exclusive* categories of risk management theories.

Also note that there is no clear correspondence between these four categories of risk management models and the M&M assumptions violated to justify risk management. In the category where risk management by firms is justified on the basis of manager-shareholder conflicts, for example, any or all of the M&M assumptions of perfect capital markets, equal access, or symmetric information may be violated depending on the specific nature of the manager-stakeholder conflict. As we will see later, however, the M&M assumption being violated is not the key factor in appreciating how the strategy and tactics of risk management trace back to the rationale for risk management. Again, these four categories will serve us better than others for the purpose of tying the strategy and tactics of risk management to the reason risk management makes sense in the first place.

VALUE-ADDED RISK MANAGEMENT

One of the M&M assumptions is that investment decisions made by the firm are taken as given. But because the firm is a complex set of contractual relations between different types of participants, *who makes* the investment decision is important. *Who makes* the financing and risk management decisions of the firm is equally important, and both of these issues will resurface as a theme throughout this book.

The basic variable underlying all the analysis here is the value of the firm. When the parties comprising the nexus of contracts that is the firm do not take actions that maximize the firm's value, under the M&M assumptions the firm will be taken over and replaced by decision makers who *will* maximize the value of the firm.

From Chapter 3, we know that the investment rule that maximizes the value of a firm is one that maximizes total security holder welfare, or the left-hand side of Equation 3.4:

$$[E_{t-1}(t) + \delta(t)] + [D_{t-1}(t) + \rho(t)] = V(t) + X(t) - I(t) \qquad (4.1)$$

Maximizing security holder welfare is commensurate with maximizing the value of the firm. When this does not happen, the firm becomes a take-over target.

Suppose the managers, shareholders, and creditors of a firm all agree on policies that result in a value of $V^{\circ}(t)$ for their firm at time t. Suppose this value results from the collective decision by all parties to buy a lot of unnecessary corporate jets and wander around the U.S. sightseeing in them at the company's expense. Under the M&M assumption of symmetric information, everyone in the market agrees that the assets of the firm could be deployed without these frivolous expenditures to achieve a true value of $V^*(t) > V^{\circ}(t)$. With equal access and perfect capital markets, other investors will either buy out the existing firm's security holders (and sack the management) for $V^*(t) - V^{\circ}(t)$ or will open a new firm worth $V^*(t)$ that will operate more efficiently and drive the demand for the original firm's securities to zero.

So, the name of the game is *maximizing* the value of the firm in a M&M world, and the way to win the game is by maximizing the value of combined security holder welfare. Risk management, to the extent that it *can be* value enhancing for a firm, thus must somehow help the firm in playing this game.

Four types of value-added risk management are identified and discussed here and in Chapters 5 to 7. Sources of opportunity for value-added risk management can best be seen by remembering that $V(t)$ in Equation 4.1 can be rewritten as follows:

$$V(t) = \sum_{j=1}^{\infty} \frac{E_t[X(t+j) - I(t+j)]}{1 + \lambda_{t,\,t+j}} \qquad (4.2)$$

where the firm's cost of capital is λ. Risk management can add value when *either* it reduces the firm's cost of capital *or* increases its expected future net cash flows. As we will see later, risk management can, in certain circumstances, be a way to do both.

On a more dynamic basis, risk management can also be a source of value added by improving the *process* by which the firm's different participants work together—and sometimes work against one another—in order to maximize $V(t)$ and to maximize combined security holder welfare. To the extent that risk management is a low-cost way to reduce conflicts over policies that affect this value maximization criterion, risk management can be a source of value added, as well.

For the rest of this chapter, we assume that the M&M assumptions regarding symmetric information, equal access, and given investment strategies hold. We focus solely on violations of the assumption that capital markets are perfect. More specifically, we confine our attention here to sources of capital market imperfections that affect a corporation's managers, creditors, and shareholders *in essentially the same way.* In other words, all of the stakeholders in the company consider these imperfections bad, and all would support a means of reducing the costs associated with these imperfections in order to increase the value of the firm (via the increase in expected cash flows accompanying a decline in expected costs).

We can assume in this chapter that the incentives of managers are perfectly aligned with the incentives of all of the firm's security holders. In addition, we assume there are no conflicts between equity and debt holders.

REDUCING EXPECTED TAXES

Suppose we consider an open corporation whose shareholders are capable of fully diversifying away idiosyncratic risks. In this situation, risk management *cannot* affect the firm's cost of capital. The only way that risk management can add value to the firm for a given risk level—or, equivalently, preserve value while reducing risk—is by increasing the expected cash flows to the firm.

Chapter 3 explained that in a M&M world, fairly priced securities and derivatives give corporations exactly what they pay for. As long as that remains true, it is impossible, as shown when we examined hedging as a capital budgeting problem, for hedging tactics *alone* to add value to the firm. Hedging is itself, after all, a zero NPV project.

Much of the literature on corporate finance has attempted to explain risk management by value-maximizing corporations by trying to force corporations into a Johnson-Stein-Ederington-style model. In other words, if we can somehow treat the corporation *as if* it is a risk-averse investor with a concave utility function, then the same mean-variance portfolio framework will lead companies to undertake optimal mean-variance hedging strategies of the kind our traders undertook in Chapter 2.

Merton Miller has referred to this as the process of "concavifying" the firm's value function. Figure 4.1 shows the value of the firm as a function of

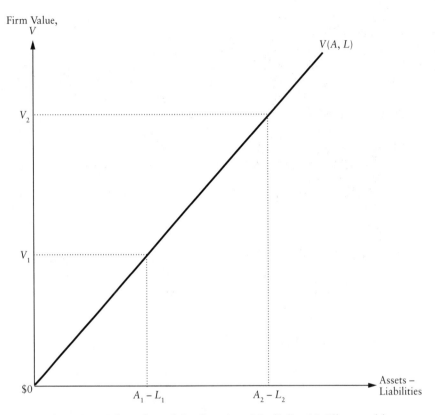

FIGURE 4.1 The value of the firm in a Modigliani-Miller world.

assets and liabilities in a M&M world. As you can see, the function is *linear*. The graph thus compares to Figure 2.2 in Chapter 2—to the utility function of a risk-*neutral* investor who is indifferent to managing risk. Over 20 years of corporate finance research has focused on how to introduce a concavity into this curve that makes it more similar to Figure 2.3.

One of the strong assumptions underlying M&M is perfect capital markets and the absence of institutional frictions, including corporate taxes. If the individual stakeholders that comprise a corporation face positive taxes, their own portfolio optimization decisions will incorporate these taxes. In other words, *personal* taxation is not enough to affect the *firm's* risk management decision. But *corporate* taxes—specifically, a *convex* corporate tax schedule—will concavify the firm's value function and can lead to benefits from managing risk.

A convex tax schedule is one in which a firm's average tax rate rises as pre-tax income rises. Shown in Figure 4.2 as compared to a linear tax schedule, the following factors can contribute to the convexity of a firm's tax schedule:

- Progressivity in the tax rate.
- The alternative minimum tax (AMT).
- Tax carry-forwards and tax credits.
- Other tax shields that defer taxation.

Figure 4.3 shows graphically how the value of the firm *after taxes* can be higher if risk management programs are used to hedge fluctuations in the value of the firm.[1] Suppose V_1 and V_2 denote two possible pre-tax values of the firm. At those levels of pre-tax income or earnings, the firm faces tax liabilities T_1 and T_2, respectively, as shown in the top panel of the figure. If we assume for simplicity that these pairs of pre-tax income levels, firm values, and tax liabilities will occur with equal probability—making a different

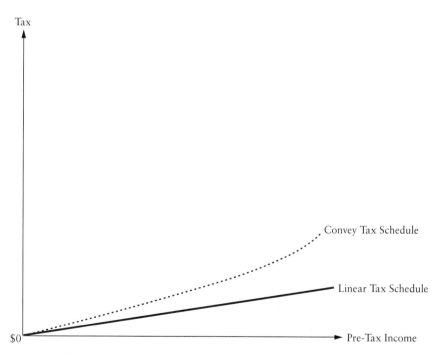

FIGURE 4.2 Corporate tax as a function of pre-tax income.

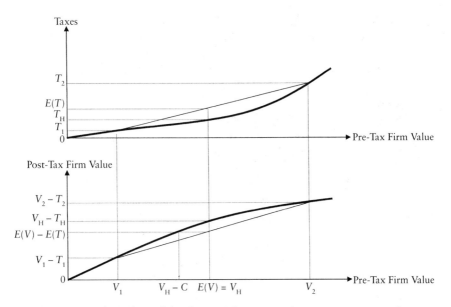

FIGURE 4.3   The value of the firm with progressive corporate taxation.

assumption adds complexity but does not change the results—then the expected pre-tax value of the firm is indicated on the lower panel of the figure as $E(V)$, where

$$E(V) = \tfrac{1}{2}V_1 + \tfrac{1}{2}V_2$$

If the firm does not hedge, the firm's expected tax liability is the probability weighted tax liability corresponding to the two possible firm values and tax liabilities, or

$$E(T) = \tfrac{1}{2}T_1 + \tfrac{1}{2}T_2$$

which implies an expected *post*-tax value of the firm of $E(V) - E(T)$.

Now suppose the firm constructs a *perfect hedge* of its value, so that the value of the firm is *locked in* at $V_H = E(V)$. At this value of the firm, the tax liability is *known* and indicated on the upper panel of Figure 4.3 as T_H. The post-tax value of the firm is then also known and locked in as $V_H - T_H$.

As Figure 4.3 shows, the post-tax known value of the firm is higher than the post-tax *expected* value of the firm. Notice that this would not be true if the firm's tax schedule was linear rather than convex. With a linear tax schedule, the firm's expected tax liability $E(T)$ would equal the known tax liability T_H that the firm could lock in with a perfect hedge of firm value. In this case, the expected post-tax value of the firm without hedging would equal the known value of the firm with hedging.

Because the tax schedule facing the firm is convex, however, the expected tax liability without hedging is higher than the known tax liability with hedging. The probability of the firm's value being high results in a more than proportional increase in taxes than the liability associated with the value of the firm in its low albeit equally likely state.

The lower panel also indicates what the firm is willing to pay for this hedge. Without the hedge, the value of the firm is expected to be $E(V) - E(T)$, whereas the known value of the hedged firm is $V_H - T_H$, or $E(V) - T_H$ because $V_H = E(V)$. The firm's expected *savings* thus *is* $T_H - \frac{1}{2}(T_1 + T_2) = C$. The lower panel indicates graphically that any cost of hedging up to C, the actual value of the firm is no less than the expected post-tax value while remaining unhedged.

This analysis demonstrates plainly that a firm whose objective is maximizing post-tax firm value can benefit from risk management. The M&M assumption of frictionless capital markets was the only such assumption we needed to violate in order to explain why a company might manage risk.

But how should a company manage risk in this situation? Here, theory fails us. Compare Figure 4.3 again to Figure 4.1. The introduction of a convex tax schedule was enough to *concavify* an otherwise linear value function. With a convex tax schedule, the firm now knows that it will pay up to C for a perfect hedge when two values of the firm are equally likely, V_1 and V_2. But what about situations when a whole distribution of outcomes of V is possible?

At this point, corporate finance takes a backward step to the classical model presented in Chapter 3. Assuming that changes in the value of the firm are normally distributed, the *optimal* hedge is the hedge that minimizes the variance of changes in the value of the firm in order to minimize the expected tax liability. True, the rationale for risk management does not immediate imply the need to assume a normal distribution or a variance-minimizing hedge. As long as some criterion is developed to link the distribution of changes in the value of the firm to the expected tax liability minimization, the distribution need not be normal. Nevertheless, in practice, the rationale for hedging presented in Figure 4.3 usually leads straight to a retreat back to the Johnson-Stein variance minimization model.

Also worth noting is that this rationale for hedging has a very specific connection to *accounting earnings,* which determine the tax liability of the firm. An earnings focus will be an important determinant of the firm's risk management strategy and tactics as explored in Parts Two and Three of the book. Chapter 8 provides additional details as to why this makes a difference.

REDUCING EXPECTED EXOGENOUS BANKRUPTCY COSTS

Perhaps the most intuitive reason for firms to manage risk is to avoid financial explosions that result in bankruptcy or financial distress. In a M&M world, however, this would not matter. With no transaction costs, bankruptcy merely results in the prorated redistribution of assets to the firm's liability holders.

In this section and in this chapter, we assume that bankruptcy costs are *exogenous*. In other words, the costs of financial distress may be constant or may vary with the size of the financial disaster—we will explore both cases—but these costs are *not* determined directly or indirectly by any of the *financing* decisions of the firm. If it helps to have an example, suppose in this chapter that we are limiting our discussion of bankruptcy to those situations arising only from natural risk exposures that the firm inherited by virtue of its normal business operations, as discussed in Chapter 1. Assume specifically that we are *not* considering financial distress costs that might somehow be tied to investment decisions in future projects.

Figure 4.4 shows the value of a firm with no liabilities except outstanding debt of face value FV on the date that the firm is presumed to both pay off its debt holders *and* to liquidate its assets and pay equity holders a liquidating dividend. If the firm has assets of A_2, the surplus assets over the face value of the debt—$A_2 - FV$—is the total value of equity, and debt holders receive FV. If instead the value of the firm's assets is below FV—say, A_1—then equity receives nothing. Debt holders each receive a prorated share of the residual assets A_1, and thus lose $FV - A_1$.

With costless bankruptcy, the remaining assets of the firm are distributed to debt holders such that they receive exactly what they are entitled to. Even when the value of the firm's assets declines to zero, the relation between the value of the firm and the value of its assets remains a perfectly linear one. No concavities here, and no need for risk management per se. As in Chapters 2 and 3, the individuals that comprise the corporation's stake holders reap all the rewards and bear all the costs; the distinction between the individuals and the company is immaterial.

But when the costs of bankruptcy are positive and borne by the firm (i.e., taken from the proceeds from the liquidation of its remaining assets), the situation changes. We explore two such situations—constant bankruptcy costs, and costs of financial distress that are proportional to the shortfall of assets below liabilities.

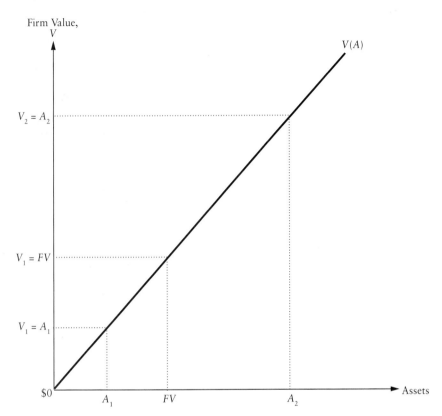

FIGURE 4.4   The value of a firm with debt and no bankruptcy costs.

Constant Bankruptcy Costs

First consider a situation where bankruptcy results in a fixed cost that is borne by the firm (Figure 4.5). This cost might include lawyers and court fees, costs of distributing the remaining assets to debt holders, and the like. Importantly, the fixed cost—denoted B—does not vary based on how bad the situation is. In other words, any situation in which the firm's assets are below the face value of its debt results in bankruptcy, the cost of which does not depend on the amount of the asset shortfall.

For any asset value below FV, the fixed costs of bankruptcy incurred by the firm represent a shift down in the curve that denotes the value of the firm as a function of assets. In Figure 4.4 where bankruptcy was costless, assets of value $A_1 <$ FV resulted in a value of the firm of V_1. Denoted V^*_1 on Figure 4.5, that amount is now *above* the value of the firm when assets are

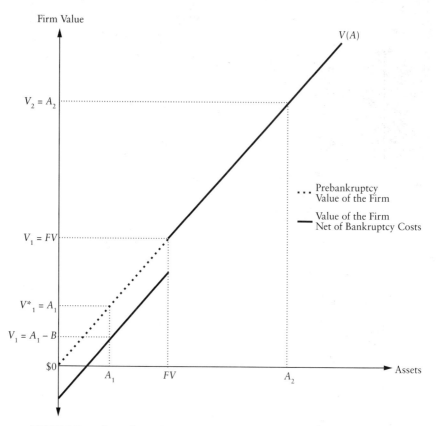

FIGURE 4.5   The value of a firm with debt and no bankruptcy costs.

worth A_1. With bankruptcy costs B, the value of the firm is now $V_1 = A_1 - B < V^*_1$.

Risk management can help reduce the expected costs of bankruptcy in this situation. To see how, consider Figure 4.6, which shows the value of the firm as a function of its assets and fixed bankruptcy costs B on the y-axis just as in Figure 4.5. But in Figure 4.6, the second y-axis now indicates the probability of various asset values on the assumed liquidation date of the firm.

The solid line is the probability distribution for values of the assets underlying the firm given that the firm does not hedge. In this case, the expected value of the firm is the asset value less expected bankruptcy costs:

$$E(V) = E(A) - \Lambda B$$

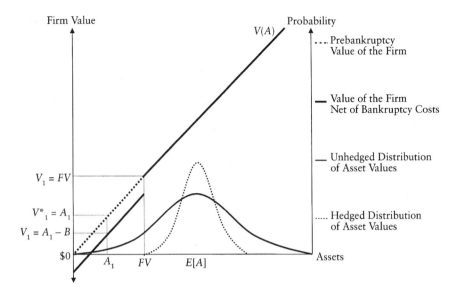

FIGURE 4.6   Hedging with debt and constant bankruptcy costs.

where Λ is the probability that assets are below FV, equal to the area under the solid unhedged distribution of asset values of 0 up to FV.

Now suppose the firm hedges in a manner that reduces the probability of bankruptcy to zero. This requires a new probability distribution where asset values below FV never occur. Such a distribution is shown on Figure 4.6 as a dotted curve. If the hedge is costless, the expected value of the assets does not change because, as we have seen, hedging is a zero NPV project. But the support of the probability distribution—the values on the *x*-axis with positive probability associated with them—is now tighter than before. In other words, the upside has shrunk proportionately to the downside. In our earlier terminology, the hedge has left the expected value of assets the same but has decreased the variance of asset value changes.

What is the expected value of the firm in this situation? Now that bankruptcy costs have been reduced to zero, the expected value of the firm is now $E(A)$, which is higher than $E(A) - \Lambda B$.

Even though the expected value of the firm's assets has not changed, equity holders benefit from an increase in the expected value of the firm when expected bankruptcy costs are reduced to zero. But debt holders do not necessarily enjoy the same windfall. In fact, whether or not debt holders enjoy any gains from the elimination of bankruptcy costs depends on whether or not they knew the firm was going to hedge when they bought the debt. At original issue, the price of the debt and the interest paid by the firm would have reflected some assumption on the part of debt holders about the firm's credit risk. If debt holders knew the firm would hedge, then the debt would have been priced at issue with zero expected bankruptcy costs and no states of default. (See Chapter 16.)

The result of introducing bankruptcy costs even as simple as those constant costs explored in this section has been to concavify the firm's value function. The *optimal* hedge in this case, however, is not necessarily a variance-minimizing hedge because of the nature of the concavity we have introduced. In this example, the value function is concave exclusively because of a discontinuity we introduced at the point the firm reaches bankruptcy. The risk management objective function here is just the reduction of expected bankruptcy costs that occur after that threshold is reached. With no costs of hedging, the optimal hedge is the hedge that reduces bankruptcy costs to zero by eliminating the possibility entirely. This may or may not also be the hedge that reduces variance the most.

Proportionate Bankruptcy Costs

Now consider a slightly different situation in which a corporation incurs costs of bankruptcy that are proportional to the shortfall of assets below liabilities. Denote bankruptcy costs in this case as $B(A)$, and suppose that bankruptcy costs rise *at an increasing rate* as the market value of assets fall. Mathematically,

$$B(A) > 0 \quad \text{where } A < FV$$

$$B_A(A) < 0 \quad \text{where } A < FV$$

$$B_{AA}(A) > 0 \quad \text{where } A < FV$$

Figure 4.7 shows the assumed bankruptcy cost function in the top panel, and the resulting value of the firm in the lower panel. In the lower panel, the solid line represents the value of the firm as a function of its assets and bankruptcy costs. The heavy dashed line represents the value of the firm in the absence of bankruptcy costs—a 45° line. The heavy solid line in the lower panel is essentially the bankruptcy cost function subtracted from the 45° line. When assets are worth A_2, for example, debt holders would still have some small positive prorated distribution to enjoy in the absence of bankruptcy costs. But at asset value A_2, bankruptcy costs are B_2 and the value of the firm is thus $V_2 = A_2 - B_2$. Similarly, when assets are worth A_1, the firm is solvent and its value is $V_1 = A_1$.

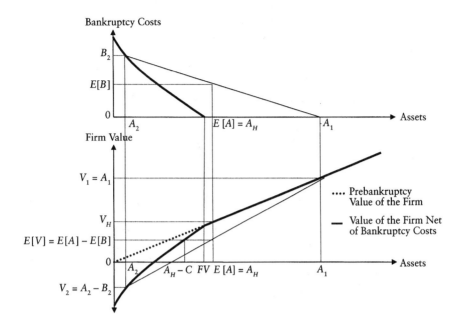

FIGURE 4.7 Hedging with debt and proportionate bankruptcy costs.

The same analysis we used in Chapter 2 to show how insurance makes sense for a risk-averse investor now can be used to illustrate why hedging might make sense for this firm. Specifically, suppose any two asset values—A_1 and A_2—are equally likely to occur. The expected value of assets is the midpoint of A_1 and A_2. If the firm does not hedge, its expected value is just the expected value of its assets, $E(A)$, less expected bankruptcy costs, $E(B)$. Graphically, $E(B)$ is the y-axis value in the top panel that corresponds to the midpoint of the line drawn between where A_1 and A_2 intersect the bankruptcy cost function—0 and B_2, respectively. Similarly, the expected value of the firm in the lower panel is the y-axis value corresponding to the midpoint of the line drawn between where A_1 and A_2 intersect the firm's post-bankruptcy value function—V_1 and V_2, respectively.

Now consider a situation where the firm hedges its assets and locks in an asset value of A_H, which is equal to the expected value of assets. At this known asset level, bankruptcy costs are now zero, and the value of the firm is now $V_H = A_H = E(A)$. This is a higher value of the firm than its expected unhedged value of $E(V)$—higher by exactly the expected cost of bankruptcy. The firm thus would be willing to spend up to C to hedge its assets and lock in value V_H even though it means eliminating the potential for realizing the higher value V_1. *At this level of expenditure on the hedge, the firm is worth the same in known terms that it expected to be worth facing a possibility of bankruptcy, but without that risk of bankruptcy.*

The problem with this particular hedge, however, is that $A_H - C$ is less than FV, which means that the firm *would go bankrupt from the cost of the hedge!* Figure 4.8 makes this point more dramatically. As in Figure 4.6, this figure has two *y* axes—one indicating firm value as a function of bankruptcy costs and asset value, and the second one showing the probability distribution for assets. The distribution $f(A)$ is the unhedged distribution, and $f(A_H)$ is the hedged distribution. The hedged distribution is clearly lower in variance *and* associates a zero probability with all situations that would make it impossible for the firm to repay its debt. But as shown, that particular hedge is simply too expensive.

So how does a firm identify the right hedge? Comparing the analysis in this section with our analysis in Chapter 2 of a risk-averse trader should make it obvious how we have successfully concavified the corporate value function in a manner that allows us to treat *corporate* hedging as indistinct

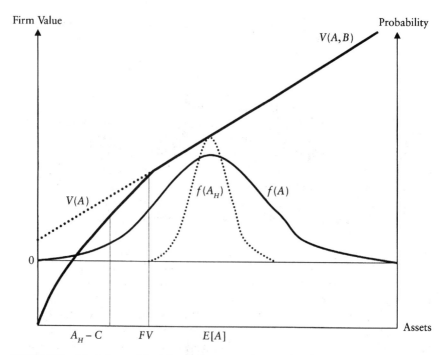

FIGURE 4.8 Hedging with debt and proportionate bankruptcy costs, Part II.

from *trader* hedging. And in fact, many theorists would simply put their pens down here and argue that if we assume normally distributed returns, we could proceed straight to the Johnson-Stein optimal hedge ratio to determine how the firm should manage its risks.

In fact, as in the prior section, the theory itself does not prescribe a variance-minimizing hedge in this situation—at least not necessarily. A properly formatted problem would be to choose the hedge ratio that equates the marginal cost of hedging to the marginal reduction in expected bankruptcy costs subject to the constraint that the hedging cost cannot bankrupt the firm. Indeed, this would be one way for a company to hedge when facing these types of costs. Unfortunately, most theoreticians and practitioners alike stop once the concavity has been identified and simply solve the problem—incorrectly—a la Johnson, Stein, and Ederington.

Note, by the way, that the firm need not begin incurring costs like those discussed here when the company actually goes bust. In fact, this is not very realistic. Instead, one can imagine that a firm begins to incur financial distress costs *before* the exact point at which the current value of assets net of liabilities falls below the face value of outstanding debt. For the moment, we do *not* include in this category the costs of financing continuing operations by issuing new, distressed debt. But even setting aside distressed debt, other costs of financial distress might include, for example, a premium you would need to pay to employees to stop them from leaving, lawyers fees, fees paid to consultants you engage to try to keep you out of bankruptcy, and so on.

If the firm begins to incur distress costs before it reaches bankruptcy, none of the analysis in this section changes materially. On Figures 4.7 and 4.8, the point where bankruptcy costs become positive, now labeled FV to correspond to the face value of debt, is simply shifted somewhere to the right of FV. Alternatively, you could imagine that FV no longer stands for face value and merely indicates the level of assets at which the firm begins encountering distress costs. Whether or not the firm is or is not bankrupt is a legal question. The point at which the firm begins incurring bankruptcy or financial distress *costs* is what drives the analysis, and this may or may not coincide with the firm's level of outstanding liabilities.

REDUCING THE COST OF CAPITAL

From Chapter 3, Equation 3.24, we know we can rewrite the firm's cost of capital as

$$\lambda_{t,\,t+j} = E\!\left(R_{t+j}^{\,j}\right) = R_{t+j}^{\,f} + \beta_{j,\,m}\Phi_m$$

where

$$\beta_{j,\,m} = \frac{\operatorname{cov}\!\left(R_{t+j}^{\,j}, m_{t+j}\right)}{\operatorname{var}\!\left(m_{t+j}\right)} \qquad \Phi_m = \frac{-\operatorname{var}\!\left(m_{t+j}\right)}{E_t\!\left(m_{t+j}\right)}$$

We often write this using a specific asset pricing model like the CAPM, where

$$\lambda_{t,\,t+j} = E\!\left(R_{t+j}^{\,j}\right) = R_{t+j}^{\,f} + \beta_{j,\,m}\!\left[E\!\left(R_{t+j}^{\,m}\right) - R_{t+j}^{\,f}\right]$$

See Cochrane (2000) for an explanation of the correspondence in the two expressions, which is not actually as obvious as would seem from simple substitution.

For risk management to reduce the cost of capital, one of two things would have to be true. First, the risk management program would have to somehow change the way that returns on the firm covary with the stochastic discount factor. This is highly unlikely, as this part of the FVE is based on *systematic risk,* not diversifiable firm-specific risks. As discussed in Chapter 1, all but one dimension of market risk and all the other risks discussed—liquidity, credit, operational, and legal risks—are diversifiable by open corporations. Accordingly, risk management cannot affect the value of the firm through the cost of capital, which remains unaffected by financial policies, including risk management and hedging.

A second case in which hedging can reduce the cost of capital is when the organization is a *closed corporation* whose owners are not well-diversified. Indeed, these shareholders must be *incapable* of holding diversified portfolios because so much of their wealth is tied up in their own firm in order for hedging to reduce the cost of capital. In this case, the idiosyncratic risk of the firm will affect its cost of capital:

$$\lambda_{t,\,t+j} = E\!\left(R_{t+j}^{\,j}\right) = R_{t+j}^{\,f} + \beta_{j,\,m}\Phi_m + \varepsilon$$

where ε is the idiosyncratic risk of the firm that is no longer fully diversified away. If $E(\varepsilon) > 0$, then the idiosyncratic risk of the firm raises the average cost of capital. To the extent that hedging or risk management can reduce $E(\varepsilon)$, the firm's cost of capital will decline and the value of the firm will rise as a result of the risk management program.

Unlike reducing expected taxes and bankruptcy costs, the particular nature of the capital market imperfection that allows firms' risk management initiatives to reduce their cost of capital *also requires* that the M&M assumption of equal access be violated. Otherwise, badly diversified managers of a closed corporation could create securities to reverse out the portion of their portfolios that is disproportionately weighted toward their own closed firm. In fact, existing restrictions on insider purchases and sales of stocks and on the disposition of stock-based compensation lends some plausibility to the assumption that not all small firm managers have the ability to issue securities based on the performance of their own firms costlessly. Without such equal access, risk management may the be the only viable solution.

CHAPTER 5

Reducing Conflicts between Security Holders and Managers by Managing Risk

We now turn our attention to how frictions in the contractual relations between principals and agents can reduce the value of the firm and create opportunities for value-added risk management. To keep separate the conflicts *among* security holders that will be addressed in Chapter 6, in this chapter we focus only on *managers* of the firm as agents of outside equity and debt principals.

We assume in this section that everyone has the same information—managers, shareholders, bondholders, and outside investors. This is an important and a somewhat unusual assumption in *agency theory*. When managers are hired to represent the interests of a firm's shareholders and creditors, the managers are acting as agents for the security holder principals. Many agency models in financial economics assume information is asymmetric—specifically, that the effort of the agent cannot be observed by the principal. In this case, the central challenge is to develop incentive mechanisms such as compensation policies that prod the agent to take the correct actions on behalf of the principal.

Because we assume symmetric information for the time being, we can assume the actions and effort of the agent are *directly* observable. If the agent takes actions counter to the interests of principals, the principals can fix the problem—terminating the agent, publicly chastising him, flogging him, taking away his bonus, and so on. But we do not necessarily assume that it is *costless* for principals to monitor agents *or* to get them to act in the interest of principals rather than in their own interests.

In a world of symmetric information, agency costs typically come in three forms. The first is the cost incurred by principals to monitor the behavior of their agents. These costs include the costs of monitoring and measuring agent behavior, as well as the costs of controlling that behavior through compensation, rules, policies, public humiliations, or what-have-you. A second agency cost is the cost that agents sometimes incur to demonstrate that they will not take certain actions antithetical to principals' interests. Such bonding costs are sometimes incurred either as a substitute for principal monitoring or as a way of paying principals back when actual agent behavior deviates from behavior consistent with stakeholder interests. Finally, a third type of agency cost is the residual loss of firm value that arises when the principal-agent relationship is not managed and controlled.

REDUCING THE AGENCY COST OF OUTSIDE EQUITY

Suppose we enter a world where firms have no debt and are financed solely with equity. That equity either can be held by those who also manage the firm—a closed corporation, as we discussed a bit earlier—or external investors in an open corporation. As we shall see, the very existence of external equity can reduce the value of a firm relative to what it would be worth if it were solely owned by insiders. A solution to that problem would be to have no open corporations, but as we shall see later, this makes little sense. Instead, we shall see that the agency costs of external equity create opportunities for risk management to increase the value of the firm.

Residual Agency Costs without Monitoring

As noted at the beginning of the chapter, Jensen and Meckling (1976) identify three types of agency costs: monitoring costs, bonding costs, and residual costs that manifest themselves as reductions in the values of firms below what they would be if agency costs were zero. In this world, the M&M assumptions of symmetric information, given investment decisions, and equal access remain in force. We assume now, however, that capital markets are imperfect in the sense that agency costs are positive. Shareholders can observe the actions of their manager agents, but managers will not necessarily take actions to maximize security holder welfare unless monitoring and bonding costs are incurred.

The basis of the divergence between the interests of equity principals and manager agents and the source of the aforementioned residual agency costs lies in the ability of managers to accrue nonpecuniary benefits from employment that equity owners cannot enjoy. Such benefits can include things like the quality of a physical office, the pleasure of collegial interaction, the development of personal and professional relationships in the office, and the like. Equity could enjoy these benefits, as well, by also serving as managers or employees. But to make the point of this section most clearly, we consider the case where the firm's equity holders are outsiders that are not also managers or employees. The sole exception is the manager who is assumed to also have an ownership stake in the firm. Assume this manager receives a constant wage rate and makes a single production-financing decision on behalf of all the firm's owners.

Figure 5.1 illustrates the nature of the agency problem and the source of residual agency costs when agency problems are not managed. The y-axis shows the value of the firm, which is maximized at level V^{max} when the marginal cost of producing an incremental unit of output exactly equals the marginal cost of producing that unit. Denote F as the expenditure of the firm on nonpecuniary benefits for the manager, which we assume are achievable only through higher-than-equilibrium output.

Formally, following Jensen and Meckling (1976) let $Y = \{y_1, \ldots, y_n\}$ denote a vector of all outputs and activities of the firm from which the manager also derives nonpecuniary pleasure. If $C(Y)$ is the firm's cost and $P(Y)$ is its productive benefits, equilibrium output occurs at some level Y^* that satisfies

$$\frac{\partial B(Y)}{\partial Y} = \frac{\partial P(Y)}{\partial Y} - \frac{\partial C(Y)}{\partial Y} = 0$$

where $B(Y) = P(Y) - C(Y)$, the net benefit of production. For any vector $Y \geq Y^*$ (i.e., any element of Y is above its optimum), $F \equiv B(Y^*) - B(Y)$ indicates the total cost to the firm of providing $Y - Y^*$ output rather than optimum level Y^*.

The heavy black line between points V^{max} and F^{max} in Figure 5.1 shows the constraints that the manager of a firm in which he also is the sole owner would face in trading off market value of his equity (i.e., value of the firm) against market value of his nonpecuniary benefits from the firm's production. The quantity V^{max} represents the firm at its optimum production level Y^* where zero is spent on nonpecuniary benefits to the manager. This V^{max} assumes some wage rate paid to the manager and some scale of the firm. F^{max} is then the most the manager could ever earn in nonpecuniary benefits from the firm without driving the firm out of business. Note that we could draw many such constraint lines for different values of V^{max} corresponding to different presumed wage rates paid and scales of production for the firm. The constraint line $V^{max}F^{max}$ has a slope of -1 by construction—one dollar spent on making the manager better-off through nonpecuniary avenues reduces the value of the firm by one dollar.

The indifference curves U_1, U_2, and U_3 in Figure 5.1 are isoutility curves that reveal the manager's willingness to trade off a unit of firm value for a

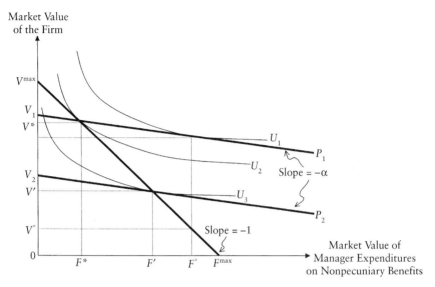

FIGURE 5.1 Manager-shareholder conflict in an all-equity firm without monitoring.

unit of nonpecuniary benefit. From the convex shape of these curves and what we learned in the discussion of the Markowitz model in Chapter 2, you can recognize that we have assumed a diminishing marginal rate of substitution between firm value and nonpecuniary benefits. In other words, the manager values an additional unit of nonpecuniary goods less and less as the actual level of those goods rises.

The point of tangency between indifference curve U_2 and the $V^{max}F^{max}$ constraint line occurs when nonpecuniary benefits to the manager are F^* and the resulting value of the firm is V^*. This is the value of the firm that will prevail if the manager owns 100% of the equity; it entirely reflects his personal tradeoffs between firm value and nonpecuniary benefits. Furthermore, if the manager/owner sells the equity but still acts as manager, he will receive only V^* for the sale. Because he remains manager, the new owner will assume the manager will continue to spend F^* in nonpecuniary benefit expenditures, and the new owner thus will pay no more than the firm is worth at that level of expenditures, which is V^*.

Getting the manager to continue exactly as he did before after he has sold his equity, however, is a problem. The new equity holders will incur significant agency costs in monitoring the manager and forcing him to remain at level F^*. To see this, suppose the manager keeps α% of the firm's equity for himself and sells the remaining $(1 - \alpha)$% to outside equity holders. If the new equity holders believe the manager will continue to consume

F^* in nonpecuniary benefits, the price paid by the new equity holders will be $(1 - \alpha)V^*$.

After the sale of $(1 - \alpha)\%$ of the firm's equity, the manager no longer bears the cost of nonpecuniary expenditures dollar-for-dollar as in the case where he owned the whole firm. The manager alone benefits from the non-pecuniary spending, but each dollar spent now results in $(1 - \alpha)$ dollars being paid by the new equity holders. The slope of the V/F constraint line thus falls from -1 to $-\alpha$. We also know the new constraint line must pass through the original point V^*/F^* at which the new equity holders would wish the manager to remain. Consulting Figure 5.1 again, the new V/F constraint line is thus line V_1P_1—the unique line that passes through point V^*/F^* and has a slope of $-\alpha$.

If the new equity holders spend nothing to force the manager to remain at point V^*/F^*, the manager will not remain there. Now facing constraint line V_1P_1, the optimum choice for the manager occurs at the point of tangency between his indifference curves and line V_1P_1. Notice also that this utility curve U_1 is higher than curve U_2 that intersected point V^*/F^*. In other words, the manager prefers the new outcome.

At this new optimum, the manager increases his nonpecuniary consumption to $F°$. To find the new value of the firm, we still need to return to line $V^{max}F^{max}$ which indicates where the dollar-for-dollar tradeoff between firm value on nonpecuniary expenditure lies. Even though the manager only bears a dollars cost for each dollar spent, the new equity holders bears the other $1 - \alpha$ dollars for a total of a dollar. The new value of the firm thus is $V°$, which is significantly below V^*. Equity holders thus take an immediate hit of $(V^* - V°)(1 - \alpha)$.

In an efficient (as opposed to perfect) capital market where information is symmetric, the new equity holders will realize that the manager will not stay at the V^*/F^* original optimum and will instead seek his new optimum at $F°$. Consequently, the price that new equity holders will pay for their equity is somewhere below V^*.

In fact, we know that the equilibrium price the new equity holders will be willing to pay for $(1 - \alpha)\%$ of the equity of the firm is V' on Figure 5.1. How do we know this? Still following Jensen and Meckling (1976), we know that the total wealth of the manager of the firm after his sale of $(1 - \alpha)\%$ shares of the firm is equal to

$$W = E + \alpha V(\alpha, F)$$

where E is the price paid by the new equity holders and $V(\alpha, F)$ denotes the value of the manager's remaining α shares given his ownership level α and his nonpecuniary consumption level F.

To identify the equilibrium selling price for the $(1 - \alpha)$ proportion of shares sold, first recognize that the manager will choose a level of nonpecuniary consumption so that his indifference curve is tangent to a line with a slope of $-\alpha$. This line represents his cost of trading a dollar of firm value for a cost of α dollars in return for nonpecuniary benefits. Next recognize that the equilibrium also must occur on line $V^{max}F^{max}$ that still represents the total dollar tradeoff between firm value in nonpecuniary expenditures. The unique point where these lines intersect with one another and the manager's indifference curve, U_2, is point V'/F'.

Requiring that the equilibrium lie on the $V^{max}F^{max}$ line is no different than requiring the price paid by outside equity purchasers to be equal to the value of the claim he receives. Similarly, requiring that the equilibrium lies on the V_2P_2 line at its point of tangency with U_2 merely means the manager also gets a fair price for what he sold. The net result of this, however, is that the entire decline in the value of the firm from V^* to V' is borne by the manager. His total wealth after the sale of the firm is equal to

$$W = (1 - \alpha)V' + \alpha V' = V'$$

which, relative to his original wealth V^*, represents a decline of $(V^* - V')$. The decline in the value of the firm $(V^* - V')$ is an approximation of *residual agency costs*.

Monitoring, Bonding, and Risk Management

Now suppose the same basic situation applies as before, except that new equity holders now decide to incur the costs of monitoring required to control the manager's nonpecuniary consumption. Such monitoring could come in the form of auditing, internal controls, policies and procedures, budget restrictions, and the like—all of which can be enforced at some costs given the assumption of symmetric information. See Chapters 20 to 22 for a discussion of risk monitoring methods.

Let $F(M, \alpha)$ denote the maximum nonpecuniary perquisites the manager can consume, given an expenditure M on monitoring by outside equity holders and the manager's ownership share α. Following Jensen and Meckling (1976) still, assume $F_M < 0$ and $F_{MM} > 0$ so that increases in monitoring expenses reduce F at a decreasing rate.

When outside equity acquires its $(1 - \alpha)\%$ of the firm, it considers that it will have to spend M in order to reduce F. The value of the firm with monitoring can be written as

$$V = V^{max} - M - F(M, \alpha)$$

At a given ownership structure α, the values of the firm corresponding to the above are shown on Figure 5.2 as the levels of V corresponding to points on the curve ABC, which comprise the heavy black line. At any point along this line (which reflects a single, given α), the distance between the $V^{max}F^{max}$ line and the ABC line is equal to monitoring cost M.

Indifference curve U_2 is tangent to curve ABC at point B, which means the manager will be satisfied with nonpecuniary consumption $F'' < F'$. In turn, both the manager and external equity holders benefit from the reduction in residual agency costs when the value of the firm rises from V' to V''. The manager will thus freely enter into a contract that gives new equity holders the right to incur monitoring expenses M and ensure that his nonpecuniary consumption is F''. The optimal monitoring costs for outside equity to incur are $M = D - B$, the distance between the $V^{max}F^{max}$ line and the ABC line where $F = F''$. Because the entire decline in the value of the firm was borne by the manager in the first place when F^* increased to F', the entire increase in the value of the firm will be enjoyed by the manager in this case, where that increase is equal to $V''' - V'$.

As we have presented the analysis, the prospective external equity buyers of the $(1 - \alpha)\%$ of the firm for sale should be indifferent between purchasing $(1 - \alpha)\%$ of the firm at total price $(1 - \alpha)V'$ and purchasing

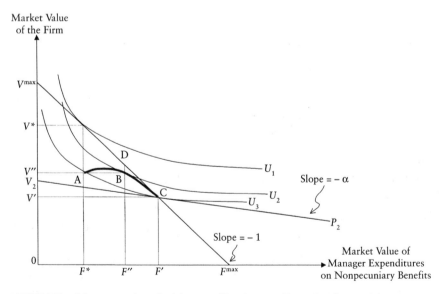

FIGURE 5.2   Manager-shareholder conflict in an all-equity firm with monitoring.

$(1 - \alpha)\%$ of the firm at total price $(1 - \alpha)V''$ with the right to expend resources up to $M = D - B$ to ensure that the manager does not consume more than F'' of perquisites. In other words, as before, the equity holders really do not care what the manager does, provided his actions are priced into the equity. The manager/owner bears all the residual agency costs and all the benefits of monitoring.

Because the manager/owner bears all the residual agency costs, it is of no consequence whether the external equity holders spend $D - B$ monitoring the manager to ensure he consumes only F'' of perquisites or whether the manager/owner spends the same amount to convince shareholders that he will consume no more than F'' of perks. Such bonding activities could include financing and agreeing to external auditing or contractual limitations on his decision-making ability.

Risk management also provides an opportunity for the manager/owner to reduce residual agency costs and increase the value of the firm from V' to V'' so long as the risk management program is aimed at accomplishing the same objective as monitoring or bonding—reducing nonpecuniary consumption from F' to F''. This is entirely plausible, however, when we consider what risk management might do in the context of what you want the manager to avoid. Under the M&M assumptions that still hold, the value of the firm is basically unaffected by the hedging decisions of the manager unless the decision to hedge leads to a decline in nonpecuniary consumption associated with suboptimal levels of production.

Consider a nonfinancial corporation with sales denominated in various foreign currencies. Under the M&M propositions, external equity decides whether or not—and how much—exchange rate risk to bear. But suppose the treasurer, a former trader, genuinely likes to follow the markets. He derives nonpecuniary benefits from trading, or, at a minimum, from behaving like a trader. Despite the irrelevance of exchange rate risk, the manager might spend considerable time and resources monitoring foreign exchange markets—acquiring a costly real-time quotation system; subscribing to numerous newsletters on exchange rates; installing the latest technical analysis software; and spending time on all of the above. If the manager wishes to minimize the residual agency costs associated with these nonpecuniary consumption items, he can simply hedge the company's foreign exchange risk.

Shareholders are indifferent to hedging. To return to our graph, suppose the manager spends F'' on foreign exchange trading-related activities that have no direct effect on the firm except as a cost. The value of the firm declines by $V^* - V'$, but this loss is borne solely by the manager; the shareholders do not care. If the manager uses foreign exchange hedging as a bonding mechanism and spends $D - B$ to hedge the entire company's exchange rate risk, shareholders still do not care. The increase in the value of the firm from

V' to V''' is enjoyed solely by the manager, and the hedging itself either can be reversed by shareholders through portfolio rebalancing if they do not like the diminished foreign exchange risk or can be left alone if they do.

A real challenge with using risk management to increase the value of the firm as a bonding mechanism against agency costs is that the risk management program must be designed very narrowly to reduce nonpecuniary consumption opportunities facing managers. This is not always easy to accomplish. Our example, after all, assumes symmetric information. But when shareholders can no longer perfectly observe the determinants of a manager's nonpecuniary satisfaction, the use of risk management to bond against excess consumption of that nonpecuniary satisfaction becomes more problematic.

REDUCING MANAGERIAL RISK AVERSION

Suppose managers cannot earn nonpecuniary benefits from working that are costly to external equity holders, so there is no *agency cost of outside equity* in the sense of the previous section. This is highly unrealistic, of course, as the examples of nonpecuniary benefits given earlier illustrate— office quality is important to *any* manager, even if only trivially. But the purpose of this section is to demonstrate that *even without* nonpecuniary benefits, managers can still take actions contrary to the maximization of security holder welfare and the value of the firm.

We have already explored a situation where risk management makes sense by helping owners of closed corporations diversify certain risks that are disproportionately high in their portfolios because they own the firm. A related problem arises with *managers,* and this problem is not confined solely to closed corporations. In general, when too much of a manager's wealth is tied up in his compensation package, his expected utility starts to depend on the value of the firm where he works. If the manager faces capital market imperfections or does not have equal access to the market, he may not be able to diversify away enough of these risks.

As discussed in Chapter 1, any firm is subject to both systematic and idiosyncratic risk. Risk-averse managers with too much of their wealth tied to the value of the firm may have the incentive to hedge in order to reduce the idiosyncratic risks of the firm to which they are disproportionately exposed. Even then, the managers may end up bearing too much systematic risk that the managers could not eliminate through hedging; in this case, the firm likely will lose the manager without some adjustment to his compensation package.

The nature of the hedging solution that is appropriate for the managers to pursue in this case depends on two variables: How the manager's own expected utility of wealth is linked to the value of the firm, and how the manager is paid. Smith and Stulz (1985) explore this issue and ascertain that if a manager's expected utility of wealth is a concave function of the value of the firm, the manager's optimal solution is to completely hedge the firm. This is no surprise given the results we saw in Chapter 2, where a risk-averse investor always prefers to avoid bearing risk. Unless the manager is compensated with higher expected income when the firm bears risk, the manager will choose not to bear risk.

Smith and Stulz (1985) explain that this situation is no longer true if the manager's expected utility is a concave function of his wealth *but* his wealth is a *convex* function of firm value. In this case, the expected income of the manager is higher if the firm does not hedge because wealth is a convex function of firm value. But because his utility is a concave function of wealth, he prefers certainty to uncertainty. In this situation, the manager is likely to hedge *some but not all* of the risks facing the firm. The tradeoff between higher expected income from being unhedged and lower volatility from hedging leaves the manager somewhat in the middle.

Finally, if the manager's expected utility is a convex function of the value of the firm, the manager acts like a risk-lover and opts not to hedge at all, just as the risk-lover in Chapter 2 chose to gamble more.

The important insight from the Smith and Stulz model is that the compensation package of the manager can dictate his preference for hedging. By controlling whether or not the manager's expected utility is a concave or convex function of the value of the firm, the security holders of the firm can determine the hedging policy of the firm. Many such compensation packages do not attempt to achieve uniformity across all firm values, moreover, but instead seek to achieve a Friedman-Savage-like result that we saw in Figure 3.5—the S-shaped expected utility function that generates hedging for low values of the firm and more risk-taking for higher firm values!

Recognize, however, that making a manager's expected utility a convex function of the value of the firm can have unintended consequences *on the other side*. Managers may be tempted to over-hedge or reverse-hedge to increase the risks faced by the company. Security holders might not benefit from this, even if they benefit from preventing the manager from hedging.

As an intermediate solution, many firms attempt to tie the compensation packages of their managers to the value of the firm explicitly through the use of options. This *alone* is considered beneficial because it forces managers to focus only on those idiosyncratic risks that are priced into the share value of the firm. Especially if we introduce asymmetric information and assume security holders cannot observe the distinction between systematic and idiosyncratic risk, this is the right way to go; you *want* managers to focus on idiosyncratic risks and ignore systematic risk.

If the firm successfully makes the manager's compensation a slightly concave function of firm value, then over-hedging is discouraged but hedging is then encouraged. As noted, managers will prefer less risky projects, other things being equal. Managers may thus tend to reject positive NPV projects solely on the grounds that they create volatility. We will see a similar problem in the next chapter when we discuss the agency cost of debt and the Myers (1977) underinvestment problem. In this situation, it may make sense to allow managers to hedge in order to manage the volatility of their investments and prevent them from rejecting positive NPV but high variance projects.

Another important issue for the firm's security holders is to ensure that the compensation package of the manager is tied to the appropriate decision variable. Many firms tie management compensation to accounting earnings rather than the value of the firm. But from what we have just seen, suppose the manager's expected utility of wealth is a concave function of accounting earnings and a convex function of firm value. Left alone, the manager would become a risk-lover, because his wages and his long-term employment security depend not on what analysts think but on the viability of the firm as an ongoing, solvent enterprise (i.e., firm value). But if the manager is paid based on accounting earnings, he will respond differently and choose to hedge accounting earnings. As we will see later in the book, a hedge that reduces accounting earnings may *increase* the volatility of the value of the firm, thus making security holders worse off.

The main point of this section is to recognize that when monitoring managers is costly for security holders, managers may make risk management decisions designed to maximize their own expected utility—sometimes at the expense of security holders' welfare. The combination of an appropriately designed compensation package and an appropriate risk management program can prod managers to take actions that are consistent with security holders' wishes.

As noted at the beginning of this section, we have not assumed any differences in information between security holders and managers. If managers have more information about the firm than security holders, the need for a carefully constructed compensation-cum-hedging policy becomes *critical*. But even when security holders can perfectly observe whether the actions of managers are consistent with the maximization of security holder welfare, agency costs are still positive because we have relaxed the M&M perfect capital markets assumption. When monitoring and controlling agents are costly, adopting mechanisms in which the expected utility maximization decision of the manager leads to the same solution as the maximization of security holder welfare clearly is preferable to more expensive, direct monitoring, and disciplining solutions.

REDUCING THE AGENCY COSTS OF FREE CASH FLOW

Many believe that managers have a tendency to grow firms beyond their optimal size. The long-term compensation of the managers, after all, is a function of their employment in the company, including their position. Growth is typically associated with power, the ability to control resources that lead to more growth, the frequency of promotion, and sometimes the bonus (if it is tied to growth in sales or production). Even when managers are investing in projects with negative NPVs, they frequently benefit from the perception that their divisions are expanding.

Managers exhibit the tendency toward unnecessary expansion even when they cannot earn nonpecuniary benefits from working that are costly to external equity holders, so there is no agency cost of outside equity in the sense of the previous section. This is highly unrealistic, of course, as the examples of nonpecuniary benefits given earlier illustrate. But the point remains that agency costs of equity are not strictly necessary for managers to want to grow.

Free Cash Flows, Investment Decisions, and Debt

Jensen (1986) has argued that one major source of conflict between managers and shareholders occurs over *free cash flow*, or cash flow in excess of current investment requirements. In other words, if the firm accepted every positive NPV project and had funds left over, those funds would constitute free cash flow.

Managers like free cash flow. Free cash flow helps finance nonpecuniary expenditures that lead to agency costs of outside equity. But as we said, even ignoring the consumption of such nonpecuniary goods, free cash flows help even a risk-neutral manager by ensuring that funds are always available to finance future growth opportunities. (Strictly speaking, this actually assumes some information asymmetries, as will be discussed in Chapter 7.) In addition, less free cash flow means that the firm must issue new debt or equity more frequently to undertake investments. Each time the firm issues new securities, its activities are scrutinized by capital market participants. Managers *dislike* this—especially managers consuming a lot of nonpecuniary goods or investing heavily in negative NPV projects to flex their growth muscles.

In Chapter 3, we examined the firm's cash flow constraint. We rewrite that constraint here, assuming as we have throughout this section that the firm is financed solely with equity:

$$X(t) - I(t) = \delta(t) - e(t) \tag{5.1}$$

where $\delta(t)$ denotes dividends paid to equity holders at time t and $e(t)$ is new equity issued at t. $X(t)$ represents the cash flows accruing to projects associated with prior investment expenditures and thus is beyond the control of managers at time t.

To analyze the free cash flow problem, let us denote the current free cash flow at time t as

$$\Gamma(t) = X(t) - I^*(t)$$

where $I^*(t)$ denotes expenditures on zero or positive NPV projects. Let $I^\circ(t)$ denote any manager spending in excess of the optimal level on negative NPV growth projects.

Assuming the free cash flows are simply retained by the firm, let us write the value of the firm as follows:

$$E_{t-1}(t) + \delta(t) = V(t) + \Gamma(t) = V^*(t) + X(t) - I^*(t) \tag{5.2}$$

where $V^*(t)$ is the value of the firm that would result if the only investment expenditures were the $I^*(t)$ payouts for positive NPV projects. In this case, the value of equity is unaffected by the excess cash. The only investment expenditures made are those that result in $V^*(t)$, thus guaranteeing that $V^*(t) - I^*(t)$ is positive—or at least not negative.

Now suppose the firms managers decide to invest the free cash flows $\Gamma(t)$ into new investments that are not associated with positive NPV projects. Denote the negative NPV investment expenditures as $I^\circ(t)$ and let $I^\circ(t)$ exactly equal $\Gamma(t)$ so that all the firm's free cash flows are disgorged into negative NPV investments. The value of the firm is now

$$E_{t-1}(t) + \delta(t) = V(t) + \Gamma(t) - I^\circ(t) = V(t) + X(t) - I^*(t) - I^\circ(t) \tag{5.3}$$

Future cash flows are reflected in $V(t)$, which we can also rewrite as

$$V(t) = V^*(t) + V^\circ(t)$$

Equation 5.3 can be expressed as

$$E_{t-1}(t) + \delta(t) = [V*(t) - I*(t)] + [V°(t) - I°(t)] + X(t) \qquad (5.4)$$

Because $I*(t)$ is only associated with projects whose discounted expected cash flows meet or exceed this level of investment expenditure, $V*(t) - I*(t)$ thus is a positive number—or, at worst, zero. $V°(t) - I°(t)$, however, is by definition a negative number because $I°(t)$ is being invested in negative NPV projects.

From Equation 5.4, it is clear that the value of security holder wealth is not being maximized by management. Equity is worth $V°(t) - I°(t)$ less than it would be worth if the firm accepted only positive NPV projects.

Returning to Equation 5.1, it is clear that free cash flow could also have been used to pay a higher dividend to stockholders or to repurchase stock, indicated by the negative sign in front of the $e(t)$ term. In this case, the negative NPV project is avoided *and* the cash is distributed to shareholders. The value of the firm is thus $V*(t)$ and equity holders' welfare is maximized.

When monitoring costs are positive and agency conflicts acute, however, disgorging free cash in the form of dividends and share repurchases will not necessarily satisfy equity holders. Managers are, after all, still in control of any *future* free cash flows. They could announce a permanent dividend increase, but that creates problems of its own because the decision can later be reversed.

Jensen (1986) suggests a solution to the free cash flow problem that *cannot* be reversed by managers—*issuing debt*. Equation 5.1 then can be rewritten as

$$X(t) - I*(t) = \Gamma(t) = \delta(t) - e(t) - d(t) \qquad (5.5)$$

and its value at time $t + 1$ can be written as

$$[E_t(t+1) + \delta(t+1)] + [D_t(t+1) + \rho(t+1)] = V(t+1) + X(t+1) - I(t+1) \qquad (5.6)$$

From Equation 5.6, it is clear that *future* free cash flows will be constrained by the need to service the debt. Equation 5.5 seems to imply, however, that debt should be *retired* rather than issued because $d(t)$ is negative. If the firm did already have debt outstanding, retiring it early would be no different than repurchasing equity or paying a dividend. At best, it would be a temporary solution to a time t cash overage. At worst, it would remove the discipline on future free cash flows created by the debt service requirement.

In this example, the firm began as all equity and thus has no debt to retire. Equation 5.5 thus tells us that what needs to happen is a swap of equity for debt, such that $\Gamma(t) = d(t) - e(t)$, so that

$$X(t) - I^*(t) = \Gamma(t) = \delta(t) - e(t) + d(t) = 0 \qquad (5.7)$$

If Equation 5.7 holds, the mission has been accomplished. Debt has replaced equity in the capital structure and created a disciplining mechanism for managers on their future investment decisions. And in the present time period where the cash surplus occurs, debt and equity have been swapped, thus leaving total security holder welfare unaffected.

Jensen (1986) defines the *control hypothesis for debt creation* as the mechanism for mitigating managers' tendency to pursue negative NPV projects at the expense of current outside equity holders.

Free Cash Flows and Risk Management

If debt issuance is itself a solution to the agency cost of free cash flows, where is the opportunity for risk management to increase firm value? The answer is two-fold.

The first source of opportunity for value-added risk management is indirect. Suppose shareholders do indeed force managers to issue debt in order to control free cash flows. This solves the free cash flow problem, but it creates other problems. In a world of costly monitoring, we can assume other costs are now positive, too—such as bankruptcy costs. We saw earlier that bankruptcy costs create a meaningful incentive to manage risk and a source of opportunity for value-added risk management only when the company has debt in its capital structure. To the extent that an all-equity firm issued debt to address free cash flows, it has traded the free cash flow problem for a positive expected bankruptcy cost.

Value-added risk management can be used in conjunction with the issuance of debt to reduce free cash flows while simultaneously helping ensure that the firm is not exposed to bankruptcy costs. We will explore some examples of this later in the book.

The second source of opportunity for value-added risk management created by the agency costs of free cash flows is the opportunity to use risk management itself as a solution to the free cash flow problem. This does not mean that firms should rush out to spend huge sums of money setting up risk management in order to spend their free cash flows. That might very well end up being just another negative NPV project! But what the firm can do is enter into zero-cost derivatives to lock in cash flows on projects with uncertain NPVs and thus prevent managers from taking on excessively risky projects.

Frankly, this second rationale for value-added risk management is pretty weak. The problem is not that managers take on projects whose cash flow volatility is too high, where risk management and hedging might provide an answer. The problem is instead that managers take on projects that are actually expected to lose money, such as the numerous unnecessary corporate mergers and acquisitions that Jensen (1986) notes. In this sense, derivatives and hedging will not really help.

Nevertheless, as will be discussed in later chapters, an important dimension to the risk management process apart from hedging is monitoring. As discussed in several places in this chapter already, monitoring alone is sometimes the best way to ensure that managers follow policies designed to be consistent with shareholder wealth maximization. We should not diminish its importance.

Can Risk Management Really Work in These Situations?

As a matter of pure theory, risk management can in principle be a solution to the types of agency problems explored here. But in the particular cases of the models of Jensen (1986) and Jensen and Meckling (1976), the empirical support for the suboptimal investment policies that can arise if managers pursue nonpecuniary goods is somewhat lacking. Perhaps more importantly, the examples of managers preferring coffeemakers and plush carpeting to positive NPV investments are often fairly strained and trivial cases of such agency problems.

Nevertheless, if we accept the notion—at least for the purpose of this chapter—that managers can and will shirk and that free cash flows will simply encourage underinvestment in actual projects at the expense of what managers prefer, then examples of value-added risk management can indeed be found.

Consider a large hypothetical company in the business of hotel management that never pays dividends and has substantial retained earnings and free cash flows. The firm has made a few questionable acquisitions in recent years, leading some of its creditors and shareholders to begin worrying. Now suppose the hotel company proposes to take over a chain of theme parks, about which the management company has little or no comparative informational advantage. Quite plausibly, shareholders and creditors might worry that the expenditure is not a positive NPV decision. True, the acquisition does not provide plush carpets for managers, but it does provide an outlet for business expansion using seemingly idle cash resources.

Risk management could help creditors and shareholders address their concerns by essentially eliminating most of the risk of the investment project itself. Creditors, for example, might not agree to provide required bridge financing unless the hotel company agrees to hedge or ensure all of the risks of operating the theme parks. In that case, the NPV of the project becomes easier to observe, and, if it is positive, easier to exploit by avoiding unnecessary risk taking along dimensions that the hotelier is not well qualified to control. In short, risk management can be used to eliminate the influence of variables that the hotel company knows little or nothing about to convince shareholders and creditors that the investment is *genuinely* a positive NPV expenditure.

CHAPTER 6

Reducing Conflicts among Security Holders by Managing Risk

We dealt in Chapter 5 with agency costs and conflicts arising between security holders as a class and managers of the firm. Our discussion ended with a rationale for why debt can serve an important control function on management. Debt, however, creates problems of its own by introducing a second class of security into an otherwise all-equity capital structure.

Just as security holder principals can have conflicts of interest with their manager agents, security holders can also have conflicts with one another. Many of these conflicts arise as a result of questions concerning who runs the firm. If we agree that the value of the firm is maximized when *total security holder wealth* is maximized, then both equity and debt should have something to say about the way the firm operates. At the same time, equity represents a residual claim on the company's assets net of liabilities, where debt is a liability. Because equity is more *at risk* than debt, their control interest in the firm is, expectedly, different.

As we discussed in Chapter 3, even when the four M&M assumptions hold, without the additional assumption of *me-first rules* it is incorrect to say that the irrelevance of the firm's financial policy on its value is synonymous with security holders' indifference to the firm's financial policy. Me-first rules are required to prevent new bonds being issued that decrease the total value of debt for the benefit of existing stockholders, and to prevent old debt from being retired before new debt that would increase the value of the remaining bonds at the expense of old equity holders.

We focus in this chapter on opportunities to implement risk management programs that can add value to firms that conflicts between security holders have taken away. By helping address these conflicts, risk management can increase the value of the firm relative to its value in the presence of monitoring costs without any steps being taken to control such problems.

As noted at the end of Chapter 5, risk management is more than just hedging. It also includes internal controls and monitoring. In some of the cases that we explore in this chapter, these aspects of risk management will be even more important than the hedging decision.

REDUCING UNDER-INVESTMENT

Just as there are agency costs associated with equity, there are also agency costs associated with debt. We saw from the last part of Chapter 5 that there are also *benefits* to debt, but for now we will focus only on its agency costs.

One such agency cost of debt, explored in detail by Myers (1977) and presented here, arises when companies with any debt in their capital structure encounter a loss of value from conflicts between shareholder and debt holder interests that result in under-investment problems. The particular situation that worries Myers also requires no violation of the M&M assumptions except the exogenous nature of investment decisions to financing decisions and vice versa. Information remains symmetric across market participants, all of whom have equal access to the capital market and enjoy the ability to transact in a perfect capital market. But when investment and financing decisions are not independent, the under-investment problem, as its name suggests, can result in equity holders refusing to accept positive NPV projects because the benefits of those projects accrue mainly to creditors.

The critical insight of Myers (1977) model is to recognize that investments fall into two distinct categories. Specifically, suppose $V(t)$ denotes the current time t market value of the firm, and that $V(t)$ can be expressed as the sum of assets already in place and future growth opportunities:

$$V(t) = V_A(t) + V_G(t) = E(t) + D(t) \tag{6.1}$$

where $V_A(t)$ and $V_G(t)$ denote current assets and growth opportunities, respectively, and where the sum of these two assets must equal the sum of the current market values of equity and debt, denoted $E(t)$ and $D(t)$, respectively. The main factor that separates $V_A(t)$ and $V_G(t)$ is that the former market value of current assets depends on either investment expenditures that occurred at some time before t or that occur contemporaneously at time t. Growth opportunities, by contrast, involve an investment expenditure *in the future*. Because the investment expenditure occurs in the future, the firm may or may not actually undertake the project on the decision date. Only on that future date can the NPV of the project be determined.

On current date *t,* the growth opportunity is thus essentially an *option* to invest later. At some time *t* + *k* after time *t,* the firm will have the opportunity to spend *I(t* + *k)* in order to generate cash flows *x(t* + *k* + *q)* where *q* can be zero, some positive integer, or a vector of several integers. In other words, a growth opportunity is an opportunity for the firm to make a subsequent investment in a project that has one or more payoffs either at the time of the investment expenditure or in any periods after that.

In fact, most investment opportunities are growth opportunities *at some point.* Rarely does a firm "happen upon" an investment opportunity that it neither anticipated *nor* had the opportunity to delay. In that sense, most investment opportunities can be viewed as call options on real assets with exercise prices equal to the future investment outlays needed to acquire the assets. $V_G(t)$ is thus not the present value of an asset, but rather the present value of the firm's *options* on assets. Viewing assets as options in this manner—as we will do again in more detail in Chapter 14—is the core distinction between the under-investment problem and the asset substitution problem discussed later in this chapter.

An All Equity Firm

Following Myers (1977), as we shall do throughout this section, begin with a firm that has no current assets, or $V_A(t) = 0$, and one future investment opportunity. The future investment opportunity gives the firm the right at time *t* + 1 to invest *I(t* + 1) and obtain an asset worth $V_G(t + 1, s)$, where *s* is the *state of nature* that occurs at time *t* + 1. The state of nature can be anything that determines the value of the investment project, and can include several different variables. A widget factory that can be built at time *t* + 1, for example, has an NPV at time *t* + 1 that depends on the known investment cost *I(t* + 1) and other factors such as current demand for widgets, future expected widget demand, the price of widgets in foreign currency, the interest rate at which expected cash flows on the factors after time *t* + 1 are discounted, and so on. All these other factors are reflected in the state of nature.

If at time *t* + 1 the firm decides not to accept the project, then the investment opportunity—the call option—expires worthless. The firm did not have to spend *I(t* + 1), but nor does it have the asset worth $V_G(t + 1, s)$. If the firm does accept the project, it invests *I(t* + 1) in one period and receives an asset the same period worth $V_G(t + 1, s)$ given the state of nature *s* at time *t* + 1. Suppose initially that the firm has no debt in its capital structure and is financed with only equity. Suppose, moreover, that no new equity is issued at time *t*—only equity carried forward from the prior period is outstanding.

TABLE 6.1   Balance Sheet at Time t

Assets		Liabilities and Equity	
Value of growth opportunity	$V_G(t)$	0	Value of debt
Value of existing assets	0	$E(t)$	Value of equity
Value of firm	$V(t)$	$V(t)$	

The balance sheet at time t gives the initial market value of the firm and is shown in Table 6.1.

Now suppose time $t + 1$ arrives and the firm can decide whether or not to accept the growth investment opportunity. If no investment is made, the firm acquires no assets *and* loses the growth opportunity. The firm and its existing equity are thus worthless. But if the investment is made, the firm spends $I(t + 1)$ and ends up with an asset worth $V_G(t + 1, s)$. Specifically, the growth opportunity asset declines to zero, but the existing asset assumes a value equal to the value of the asset acquired at $t + 1$ which was a growth opportunity at time t. New equity must be issued to finance the investment expenditure, such that $e(t + 1) = I(t + 1)$. The time $t + 1$ balance sheet of the firm is shown in Table 6.2.

For simplicity of exposition and with no loss of generality, we can define the value of the newly acquired asset—and, from Table 6.2, the value of the firm—as an increasing function of our states of nature. For $s_j < s_k$, this implies that $V(t + 1, s_j) < V(t + 1, s_k)$.[1] If the new asset is a new drug and the states of nature represent the demand for the drug, we are simply *defining* demand s_1 to be lower than demand s_2, so that the value of the drug is correspondingly higher for demand s_2 than demand s_1.

Figure 6.1 shows the investment decision faced by a Myers-like firm at time $t + 1$ graphically. Clearly, the firm invests only if $s \geq s^*$. Remember that $I(t + 1)$ and s are *known* at $t + 1$. For the firm to invest in this project at $s < s^*$ would make no sense, because $V_G(t + 1, s)$ would clearly be less than

TABLE 6.2   Balance Sheet at Time $t + 1$

Assets		Liabilities and Equity	
Value of growth opportunity	0	0	Value of debt
Value of existing assets	$V_G(t + 1, s)$	$E(t + 1)$	Value of equity
Value of firm	$V(t + 1, s)$	$V(t + 1, s)$	

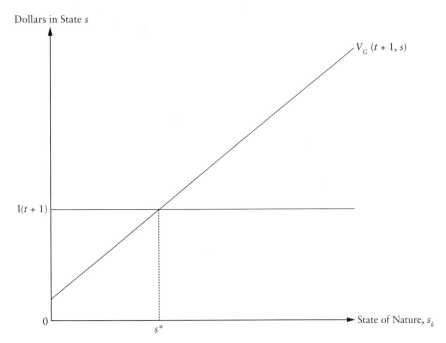

FIGURE 6.1   Investment decision of an all-equity firm at the decision time.

$I(t + 1)$. At $s = s^*$ the firm just breaks even, and for $s > s^*$ the firm acquires an asset with a positive value.

Figure 6.1 is just a restatement of the NPV criterion. We see from the figure that the firm invests only if $V_G(t + 1, s) - I(t + 1) \geq 0$. If the asset has multiple future cash flows that all depend on the value of s realized at $t + 1$ but which are otherwise *known* for the next N periods, then the investment decision of the firm can be rewritten as

$$V_G(t + 1, s) - I(t + 1) = \sum_{j=1}^{N} \frac{X(t + j, s)}{R^f_{t, t+j}} - I(t + 1) \geq 0$$

which is *exactly* the NPV criterion presented in Chapter 3 using our slightly different notation.

Probability theorists and statisticians sometimes find it useful to work with what are called *indicator variables*. An indicator variable is a dummy variable that has either a value of 0 or 1, depending solely on some condition to which the indicator variable is tied. In our example, we can define an indicator variable that lets us know whether or not the firm accepted the investment project, which means the indicator variable has a value tied to the state of nature realized at time $t + 1$. Define the indicator variable, denoted $I_{(s<s^*)}(s)$, as follows:

$$I_{(s<s^*)}(s) = 0 \text{ if } s < s^* \qquad I_{(s<s^*)}(s) = 1 \text{ if } s \geq s^*$$

Using our indicator variable notation, the value of the firm *at time t* now can be expressed using the FVE as follows:

$$V(t) = E_t\{m_{t+1}[V_G(s, t + 1) - I(t + 1)]I_{(s<s^*)}(s)\}$$

If the stochastic discount factor depends solely on the state of the world s, we can rewrite the value of the firm more formally as

$$V(t) = \int_0^\infty m_{t+1}(s)I_{(s<s^*)}(s)[V_G(t + 1, s) - I(t + 1)]ds$$

$$= \int_{s^*}^\infty m_{t+1}(s)[V_G(t + 1, s) - I(t + 1)]ds \tag{6.2}$$

Investment by Equity in a Firm with Risky Debt

Because the firm is worthless when the state of nature is less than s^*, the firm cannot issue debt free from default risk. If the firm issues debt and $s < s^*$, the firm will be unable to pay the debt holders. But the firm can still issue *risky* debt. Let us assume it does so at time t with a face value of FV and a maturity date of $t + 1$. Assume further the debt is used *only* to help fund the investment in the new asset at time $t + 1$—to reduce the amount of new equity that must be issued to finance $I(t + 1)$.

Getting more particular about all the things going on at time $t + 1$, let us now assume that the debt matures *after* the state of nature is realized but *before* the investment expenditure must be incurred at $t + 1$. If $V_G(t + 1, s) - I(t + 1) > FV$, the shareholders of the firm will pay the debtors off. If instead $V_G(t + 1, s) - I(t + 1) < FV$, the bondholders will take over the firm. If $V_G(t + 1, s) - I(t + 1) \geq 0$, the bondholders will spend $I(t + 1)$ and acquire the asset. If not, the firm is worthless and the bonds default.

At time t, the market value of the debt is given by the following expected value, again assuming the stochastic discount factor depends only on realizations of s:

$$D(t) = \int_{s^*}^{\infty} m_{t+1}(s) \min[V_G(t+1, s) - I(t+1), FV] ds$$

If the FV is set high enough that $FV > V_G(t + 1, s) - I(t + 1)$ *for all states of nature* s, then equity is worthless and $D(t) = V(t)$.

Now suppose more interestingly that the debt now matures at $t + 1$ *before* the state of nature is revealed. In other words, the shareholders of the firm now must consider whether or not to pay off the debt *before* the true NPV of the growth opportunity is known—that is, while the growth opportunity is still a call option. In this situation, the time t balance sheet of the firm can be written as in Table 6.3.

If the firm decides not to invest in the project, existing assets are zero and there are no more growth opportunities. Debt and equity again are worthless, as is the firm. But if the firm invests $I(t + 1)$ and acquires the new asset, the balance sheet of the firm at $t + 1$ then looks like Table 6.4.

Table 6.4 clarifies what we have now seen several times, beginning with Chapter 2. Debt is the equivalent of a written put on the firm, and equity is the equivalent of a purchased call—both with striking prices equal to FV, the face value of the debt.

The interesting problem arises when we consider the optimal exercise behavior for these options. As shown in Table 6.4, the equity call option is in-the-money when $V_G(t + 1, s) - FV > 0$. But because shareholders must decide whether or not to pay off debt holders before the state of nature and the value of the growth opportunity is revealed, this is *not* the criterion they use to decide whether or not to exercise their option *on the asset itself*.

TABLE 6.3   Balance Sheet at Time t

Assets		Liabilities and Equity	
Value of growth opportunity	$V_G(t)$	$D(t)$	Value of debt
Value of existing assets	0	$E(t)$	Value of equity
Value of firm	$V(t)$	$V(t)$	

TABLE 6.4   Balance Sheet at Time $t + 1$

Assets		Liabilities and Equity	
Value of growth opportunity	$V_G(t)$	$\min[V_G(t + 1, s), \text{FV}]$	Value of debt
Value of existing assets	0	$\max[0, V_G(t + 1, s) - \text{FV}]$	Value of equity
Value of firm	$V(t)$	$V(t)$	

Consulting Figure 6.2, it is clear that shareholders *do not benefit* from the investment project unless $V_G(t + 1, s) - \text{FV} - I(t + 1) > 0$, or, $V_G(t + 1, s) > \text{FV} + I(t + 1)$. If $V_G(t + 1, s) < \text{FV} + I(t + 1)$ and the investment is made at time $t + 1$, the investment outlay will exceed the market value of the outstanding equity shares *even if the project has a positive NPV*. In other words, shareholders care about whether $V_G(t + 1, s) - \text{FV} - I(t + 1) > 0$ and not whether the project has a positive NPV—that is, $V_G(t + 1, s) - I(t + 1) > 0$.

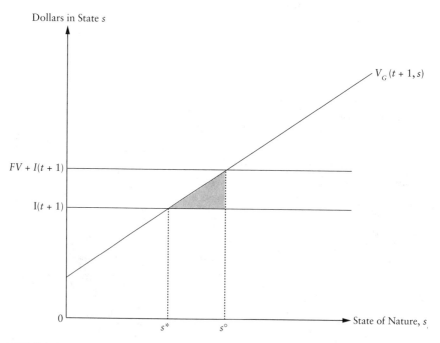

FIGURE 6.2   Investment decision of a firm with debt and equity at the decision time.

The point at which equity holders agree to undertake the investment project is shown in Figure 6.2 as state of nature $s°$, such that $s° > s^*$. At the old breakeven state of nature s^*, equity is worthless. But at values of $s > s°$, equity makes money on the project *and* can pay off debt.

At this new breakeven point that determines shareholders' investment decision, the new market value of the firm is:

$$V°(t) = \int_{s°}^{\infty} m_{t+1}(s)[V_G(t+1, s) - I(t+1)]ds \qquad (6.3)$$

where $s°$ depends on the face value of the debt FV. The value of the firm in Equation 6.3 is strictly less than the value of the firm in Equation 6.2 by the amount

$$V(t) - V°(t) = \int_{s^*}^{s°} m_{t+1}(s)[V_G(t+1, s) - I(t+1)]ds$$

which is equal to the area of the shaded triangle in Figure 6.2. Higher amounts of debt imply a higher hurdle and a larger triangle—hence, a larger loss of value to the firm.

Now that we have determined the optimal exercise behavior for equity, we know that the growth option is never exercised and the firm is worthless when $\min[V_G(t+1, s), FV] = V_G$, which Table 6.4 confirms is the market value of debt. If the new asset is acquired—which occurs only if $s \geq s°$—then $V_G > FV$. So, we know that the time t market value of debt is the expected value of a repayment of principal over those states of the world in which the new asset is acquired, or

$$D(t) = \int_{s°}^{\infty} m_{t+1}(s)FVds \qquad (6.4)$$

As noted in Figure 6.2, the size of the triangle—hence, the value of the firm—depends on the face value of debt outstanding. For any finite FV, $D(t) < V(t)$.

Figure 6.3 shows the relation between debt, equity, and firm values with the size of the total debt issued. At very low levels of debt, the equity holders' investment decision is not affected too significantly, so the value of the firm $V(t)$ is not dramatically below what its value would be in the absence

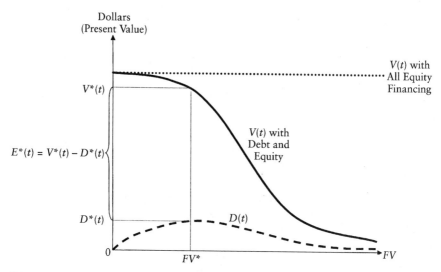

FIGURE 6.3   Value of a firm with a growth opportunity as a function of debt face value.

of any debt—although it *is* strictly lower. As the face value of debt rises, however, the loss in firm value begins to occur more rapidly.

Figure 6.3 also shows that there is a definite maximum amount the firm can borrow, indicated by FV*. At this debt capacity level, the firm is worth $V^*(t)$ and debt achieves its highest value, $D^*(t)$. Equity, however, is worth only $E^*(t) = V^*(t) - D^*(t)$, which is *not* the maximum market value for equity. Shareholder value is maximized only when the firm issues no debt—when FV = 0 and $E(t) = V(t)$. Note that this is also where the *combined* value of debt and equity is maximized.

In other words, a firm facing a growth opportunity achieves maximum security holder welfare when there is *no debt in the capital structure*. Absolutely any promised payment to debt holders will lead equity holders to forego a positive NPV project in at least some states of the world—hence, the term *under-investment*.

Risk Management as a Mitigation Mechanism for Under-Investment

The opportunity for risk management to mitigate the Myers under-investment problem relies on the assumption that the firm is not all equity and does indeed issue risky debt. Indeed, if the firm is all equity, then $V(t)$

is maximized, under-investment does not occur, and risk management provides no source of added firm value—at least, not for *this* reason. But if the firm *does* issue risky debt, risk management can help to close the gap between the curves in Figure 6.3 representing the value of an all-equity firm and a firm with a hybrid debt-and-equity capital structure.

Supposing the firm does issue debt, the central link between risk management and increases in the value of the firm is the firm's presumed sensitivity to certain market price changes.[2] Let us assume this sensitivity is an entirely idiosyncratic risk. Consider a Swiss pharmaceutical company, for example, whose drug sales are denominated entirely in U.S. dollars. Presume that the firm is initially all equity. Figure 6.4 shows the relation between changes in the value of the firm from its current market value $V(t)$, denoted $\Delta V(t)$, associated with changes in the dollar/franc exchange rate from its current level, denoted $\Delta P(t)$. In this example, $P(t)$ is the franc price of dollars.

When one dollar in drug sales in the United States yields more francs, the company's value increases. This is shown in Figure 6.4 as the line between points A and X. Line AX is roughly a 45° line, so that the firm benefits dollar-for-dollar with appreciations in the franc vis-à-vis the dollar and suffers from a depreciation.

Now suppose the firm has both debt and equity and has its investment decisions made by its shareholders. Under-investment is now a problem for the firm. Specifically, declines in the franc price of dollars increase the firm's effective leverage by raising operating costs and reducing firm value. Stated differently, a decline in the value of the firm makes equity viewed as a call option less in-the-money than before, and, in turn, the debt put option moves less out-of-the-money and closer to being in-the-money. As we saw earlier, the higher FV, the larger the under-investment problem. The same is true for *relative* debt in the capital structure. An exogenous decline in $V(t)$ (e.g., as a result of exchange rate changes) increases the relative importance of debt in the capital structure, makes the $I(t + 1) + FV$ hurdle harder to cross for equity holders contemplating growth opportunities, and thus reduces the value of the firm by *more* than in the all-equity case.

Figure 6.5 illustrates the under-investment problem in this context. The line marked AX was the relation between exchange rate changes and changes in the value of the firm with no debt. With debt and the under-investment problem, the line marked BX now shows how the firm's market value is affected by exchange rate shifts. Increases in the franc price of the dollar do not matter, because the firm's effective leverage is declining as equity gets more valuable. But a $1 decline in the franc price of the dollar now exacerbates under-investment and leads to a decline in $V(t)$ of *more* than $1. The total loss to the firm from under-investment is shown as the shaded

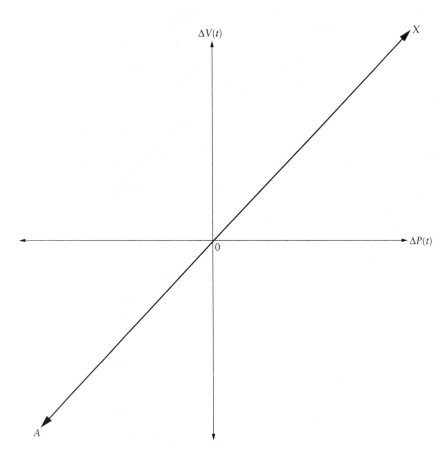

FIGURE 6.4 Relation between the change in value of an all-equity Swiss pharmaceutical firm and the change in the franc/dollar exchange rate.

triangle representing the divergence between curves AX and BX. The larger the exchange rate swing, the more the debt-equity ratio changes and the larger the loss in value to the firm from under-investment.

Figure 6.6 on page 142 illustrates the benefits of hedging. Suppose the firm uses a derivatives contract to partially hedge its exchange rate exposure. (A complete hedge would eliminate all under-investment costs; the firm's value would not fluctuate with exchange rates, and the leverage ratio of the firm would never change.) The hedge is illustrated by curve HH'. The firm's change in value *net* of the hedge is shown as curve $B'X'$. If the firm were financed with only equity, under-investment would not accompany

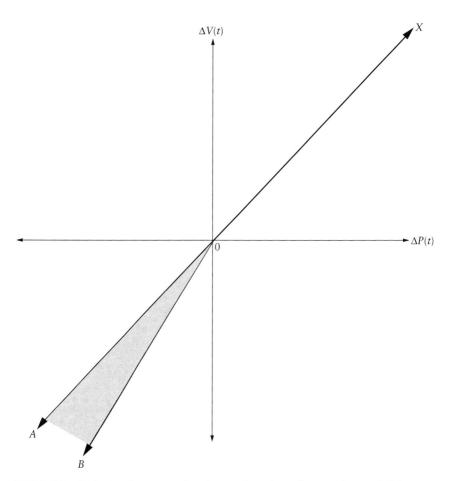

FIGURE 6.5 Relation between the change in value of an equity-and-debt Swiss pharmaceutical firm and the change in the franc/dollar exchange rate.

declines in value associated with exchange rate changes, and the net impact of the hedge is shown by curve $A'X'$. The cross-hatched area between the two curves is now the under-investment loss, or the agency cost of debt.

Because the hedge has reduced the firm's sensitivity to exchange rate fluctuations, the hedged firm experiences a smaller increase in effective leverage than the unhedged firm for a given exchange rate shift. The hedged firm thus suffers less from under-investment. To see this on Figure 6.6, consider any given change in the exchange rate $\Delta P°$. When the firm is not

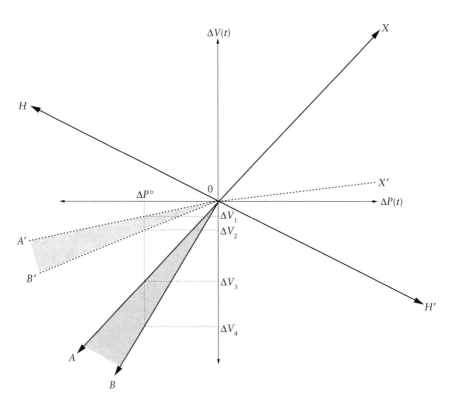

FIGURE 6.6 Exchange rate hedging and the pharmaceutical's under-investment problem.

hedged, the all-equity firm declines in value by ΔV_3 and the pharmaceutical that issues risky debt declines in value by ΔV_4. The difference in these two changes is the under-investment loss or the agency cost of debt. If the firm hedges and the exchange rate declines by $\Delta P°$, the all-equity firm loses ΔV_1 in value and the firm with debt loses ΔV_2. Because the distance between ΔV_1 and ΔV_2 is less than the difference between ΔV_3 and ΔV_4, the under-investment problem has been at least partly addressed.

In this situation, the firm's value is no longer independent of whether the exchange rate hedge is implemented by shareholders or by the firm. If shareholders hedge their personal exchange rate risks and exchange rates decline, the under-investment problem remains unaddressed. The decline in the value of the firm due to exchange rate changes may be hedged at the level of individual shareholders' portfolios, but the increase in the leverage ratio for the firm makes debt harder to pay off *as a whole* and thus affects the firm's investment decisions. The only way to attenuate this cost is if *the firm* hedges.

REDUCING ASSET SUBSTITUTION COSTS

The particular problem discussed in this section is called the *asset substitution* problem, which arises because of the different incentives faced by equity and debt holders to take on certain investment projects. Specifically, we will see that when equity holders control the firm, they may choose to take on riskier projects than debt is comfortable with. And conversely, some of these problems can be solved by risk management techniques, resulting in an increase in the value of the firm by an increase in debt capacity or, equivalently, a decrease in the cost of borrowing for the firm. The model presented in this section to demonstrate the asset substitution problem and potential opportunities for value-added risk management is based on Fama (1976).

Agency Costs and Optimal Investment Policy with Debt and Equity

From Chapter 3, we know that the investment rule that maximizes the value of a firm is one that maximizes total security holder welfare, or the left-hand side of Equation 3.4:

$$\left[E_{t-1}(t) + \delta(t)\right] + \left[D_{t-1}(t) + \rho(t)\right] = V(t) + X(t) - I(t) \qquad (6.5)$$

Because $X(t)$ is based on prior investment decisions, the left-hand side of Equation 6.5 is clearly maximized when $V(t) - I(t)$ is maximized. A firm that does not maximize $V(t) - I(t)$ is thus not maximizing *total* security holder welfare.

Note that there is a direct correspondence between maximizing $V(t) - I(t)$ and adhering to the NPV criterion explored in Chapter 3. To see this, simply recognize that $V(t)$ as defined in Equation 4.1 is precisely the NPV criterion as we characterized it in Chapter 2, except that now we are equating the term *project* to the collection of projects known as the firm. Stating it in terms of $V(t) - I(t)$, however, is more general, whereas the NPV criterion is project specific. Nevertheless, the economics behind the concepts are equivalent. Firms that fail to accept positive NPV projects and fail to reject negative NPV projects are *not* maximizing $V(t) - I(t)$.

To see the consequences of deviating from this optimal policy, suppose stockholders control the firm and decide to pursue an investment strategy that maximizes *equity holder* welfare. This implies the firm is maximizing

$$\left[E_{t-1}(t) + \delta(t)\right] = V(t) + X(t) - I(t) - \left[D_{t-1}(t) + \rho(t)\right] \qquad (6.6)$$

rather than the left-hand side of Equation 6.5. In this situation, the bond-holders will take over the firm. Specifically, bondholders would buy out existing equity holders for the value that equity would have if the rule to maximize $V(t) - I(t)$ were being followed. Comparing Equation 6.6 to 6.5 makes it obvious that the firm value would indeed rise in this situation. In other words, if the rule to maximize the *shareholder* wealth is followed, the bondholders of the firm will buy out the existing shareholders and adopt a rule to maximize *total security holder* welfare, which will raise the value of the firm by exactly the amount the bondholders paid for the buyout.

If we suppose bondholders control the firm and adopt a rule to maximize debt holder value instead of total security holder welfare, the same argument used in the last paragraph can be applied in reverse. The stockholders will buy out the debt holders, change the investment rule to maximizing $V(t) - I(t)$, and recover the costs of their buyout from an increase in the value of the firm exactly equal to the difference between the old and new debt prices.

As Fama (1976) explains, however, there is a dynamic aspect to this line of reasoning that cannot be ignored. The market value of the firm at any time t depends on the distribution of $V(t + 1) + X(t + 1) - I(t + 1)$. $V(t)$ thus depends on the investment policy followed at time $t + 1$. Similarly, the value of the firm at time $t - 1$ depends on the investment policy pursued at time t. This logic can be carried back to the time 0 on which the firm is first set up. A firm's announcement at time 0 that it will pursue an investment policy of maximizing $V(0) - I(0)$ is equivalent to the firm saying it will maximize security holder welfare *in every period subsequent to 0*.

Because of the inherent conflict between stockholders and bondholders, the value of the firm at any point in time t depends not just on the firm's commitment to adhere to the maximize $V(t) - I(t)$ rule in all future periods, but also on the firm's ability to convince stockholders and bondholders that commitment is credible. Fama states the problem succinctly:

> [T]he essence of the potential problems surrounding conflicting stock-holder-bondholder interests is that once time 0 passes it will be difficult for the stockholders to resist the temptation to try to carry out an unexpected shift from a rule to maximize V(t) − I(t) to the rule that maximizes

stockholder wealth. . . . To maximize V(0) – I(0), *the wealth of its organizers, the firm must convince the market that it will always follows the investment strategy maximize* V(t) – I(t). *The market realizes that the firm might later try to shift to another strategy and it will take this into account in setting* V(0). *To get the market to set* V(0) *at the value appropriate to the strategy maximize* V(t) – I(t), *the firm will have to find some way to guarantee it will stay with this strategy.*

The important point is that the onus of providing this guarantee falls on the firm. In pricing a firm's securities, a well-functioning market will, on average, appropriately charge the firm in advance for future departures from currently declared decision rules. The firm can only avoid these discounts in the prices of its securities to the extent that it can provide concrete assurances of its forthrightness.[3]

Note that we have not relaxed the M&M assumption of symmetric information. Everyone still has the same information. But *symmetric* information does not imply *perfect* information, or the absence of uncertainty. Consequently, firms financed with both debt and equity always face this *credibility problem* in convincing even equally well informed investors that their future decision making under uncertainty will not be designed to benefit one class of security holders at the expense of the other.

One major cost to a firm whose stakeholders are concerned might not follow an optimal investment policy is the reduced price—and, consequently, higher interest rate—that the firm's bonds will command. The greater the uncertainty that optimal investment policies will not be followed and the NPV criterion shunned, the greater the discount of the debt in the bond market and the higher the borrowing cost for the firm.

One mechanism the firm can use to provide assurances to investors that the NPV criterion will be taken seriously and that $V(t) - I(t)$ will be maximized is through the use of bond covenants.[4] Such covenants, in addition to guaranteeing me-first rules, could commit the firm to an investment policy that neither expropriates debt nor equity holders. The covenants would compensate bondholders in the event of an attempt by shareholders to deviate from the optimal investment policy. Conversely, the covenants would penalize bondholders should they attempt to force an investment policy shift toward bondholder wealth maximization. The bonds and stocks issued by the firm would then be priced to reflect the presence of those covenants and the protections afforded by them.

As an alternative, the firm could commit to a particular risk management program designed to steer the firm toward an optimal investment policy. To see how risk management could achieve this objective, consider the extreme situation where the firm commits to remain 100% hedged.

The result will be a firm value that no longer varies with the investments made by the firm. Indeed, with all investments perfectly hedged, the value of the firm would be locked in for the future.

The security holders of the firm would be willing to pay for such a hedge in an amount roughly proportional to the costs of ensuring optimal investing over time through other mechanisms, such as covenants. And indeed, hedging may be even more attractive than alternatives like covenants because it avoids the need to specify in great detail what rules the investment policy must obey. Complete hedging, in effect, forces the firm to precommit to an investment policy that is hedgable and, consequently, known *ex ante*.

The extreme situation of complete hedging makes little sense and calls into question why the firm bothered to open its doors for business. In more general terms, however, hedging can still be an effective means of reducing shareholder/bondholder conflicts arising from agency costs. To see why, recall from Chapter 2 that equity and debt can be viewed as derivatives—specifically, calls and puts on the assets net of liabilities (excluding debt) underlying the firm. Figure 6.7 shows the value of equity as a call option written on the market value of the net assets of the firm on some presumed liquidation date T and struck at FV, which indicates the face value of debt outstanding. The y-axis shows the value of the equity, and the second y-axis on the right-hand side shows the probability of a given net asset value being

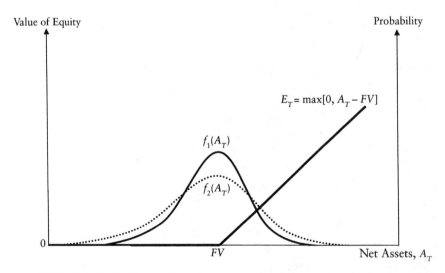

FIGURE 6.7   Volatility and equity as a call on the net assets of a firm.

realized on date T. Two possible probability distributions are shown, $f_1(A_T)$ and $f_2(A_T)$. Both distributions are centered on the face value of the debt, making it essentially equally likely in both cases that the firm goes bankrupt (i.e., net assets fall below the face value of the debt).

When the net assets of the firm exceed the debt liability, equity holders make money—dollar-for-dollar as A_T rises above FV. By contrast, equity has limited liability and thus faces a maximum loss of 0. Whether the firm has net assets of 0 or FV $-$ \$0.01 at time T *does not matter to equity holders,* who receive zero in either case.

The distribution $f_2(A_T)$ has a higher variance than the distribution $f_1(A_T)$—$\sigma_2 > \sigma_1$. The cumulative probability of a given net asset value being realized is the area under the two curves, and you can see that the higher variance distribution has a higher probability of leaving equity holders in-the-money. True, the probability they will end up with nothing is also higher, but the these probabilities do not change the fact that nothing is still nothing. On the upside, however, more probability means a higher expected payoff. Consequently, equity holders will have a strong temptation to deviate from a simple NPV rule and the optimal $V(t) - I(t)$ investment policy in order to pursue higher variance projects.

Debt holders are the opposite. As writers of put options, debt holders benefit from volatility *reductions*. The best case scenario for debt holders is to receive the face value of their loans back. If the firm does better, they do not benefit. But if the firm does worse, they pay the price in the form of a partial—or perhaps total—loss of principal. Because variance is symmetric, higher variance means more probability of *either* a decline *or* a rise in asset values. Because rises cannot help debt and declines only hurt, anything which associates more probability with declines in net asset values is bad (Figure 6.8).

The timing of the investment decision vis-à-vis the financing decision is critical. If the investment decision is made before securities are issued, both debt and equity will simply reflect the distribution of the investment decision actually made. But if bonds can be issued before the investment decision is made, then equity holders have an opportunity to expropriate debt holders. Equity can agree to take the lower variance project, sell bonds on that basis, and then actually pursue the higher variance project, thus transferring wealth from debt to equity.

To see this more clearly, consider another example where the firm has two investment opportunities. The distributions of the cash flows X on the projects, denoted $f_1(X)$ and $f_2(X)$, are shown in Figure 6.9. The expected value of the first project is slightly higher than the expected value of the second project—$\mu_1 > \mu_2$. The variance of the first project, however, is lower than the second—$\sigma_1 < \sigma_2$.

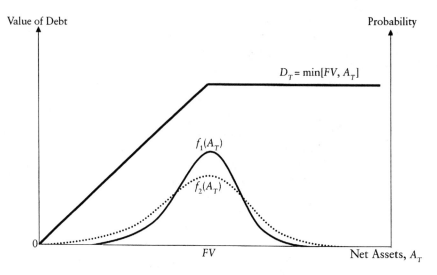

FIGURE 6.8   Volatility and debt as a put on the net assets of a firm.

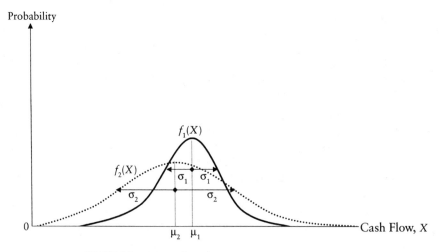

FIGURE 6.9   Two alternative investment projects.

The value of the firm will be lower if the more volatile project is chosen because it has a lower expected value. If we denote the value of the firm given investment project 1 as V_1 and similarly for V_2, then $V_1 > V_2$. Because the project with the lower expected value has a higher volatility, however, the value of equity could be higher if the lower expected value project is chosen. The net impact is not immediately obvious. The difference in the values of the firm for the two investment opportunities can be expressed as

$$V_1 - V_2 = \left(E_1 - E_2\right) + \left(D_1 - D_2\right) \qquad (6.7)$$

where the right-hand side of Equation 6.7 represents the different market values of equity and debt, respectively, given the two possible investment projects.

If the difference in the expected values of projects 1 and 2 is quite small, then the difference between V_1 and V_2 is also quite small in Equation 6.7. In this case, it is quite possible that the value of the equity will increase. Rearranging Equation 6.7 to show the change in the value of equity,

$$E_2 - E_1 = \left(D_1 - D_2\right) - \left(V_1 - V_2\right) \qquad (6.8)$$

The change in the value of equity thus can be expressed as the sum of the amount of wealth transferred from bondholders to stockholders ($D_1 - D_2$) less any reduction in overall firm value ($V_1 - V_2$). Because $\sigma_1 < \sigma_2$, $D_1 > D_2$. And because $\mu_1 > \mu_2$, $V_1 > V_2$. The net impact on equity thus depends on the relative magnitudes. For two projects with extremely different volatilities and small differences in expected value, equity will almost certainly experience a net gain, despite the reduction in the value of the firm as a whole. Debt will lose more value from the increased volatility of the investment than the firm loses in value from the lower mean, resulting in a residual benefit to stockholders. Conversely, if the second project has a much lower expected value and only a trivially higher volatility than the first project, the reduction in the value of the firm will likely exceed the reduction in the value of its debt, so that both equity and debt are net losers.

Debt holders realize that equity may attempt to expropriate them in this manner—called *asset substitution* because equity *says* it will take the lower volatility project but then substitutes the higher volatility project after the debt is issued. Bonds thus are *priced* as if the more volatile project was accepted. Even in the above example, the reduction in bondholder wealth is a fiction. In reality, B_1 would never result as a market price for debt at a firm facing these two projects. Bondholders will always assume equity will pursue the second project and hence always price the debt at B_2. The wealth loss thus ultimately is borne by equity—or, as in Jensen and Meckling (1976), by any *new* outside equity holders to which a manager may sell shares after pursuing the above course of action.

Increasing Debt Capacity and Reducing Borrowing Costs with Risk Management

The stockholder/bondholder conflict can be resolved by managing the risk of changes in the value of the firm. Other things equal, a decision by equity holders to implement a hedge of changes in the firm's value will make debt holders satisfied with less of a discount or risk premium on the price paid for their bonds to address the risk of a deviation from the optimal investment policy of the firm to a higher-variance investment strategy.

Note that once again we encounter our friend variance. And indeed, hedging designed to reduce agency conflicts between stakeholders is very often variance-minimizing hedging. But this need not be the case. Recall from our discussion in Chapter 2 that investors tend to like positive skewness and dislike fat-tailed or leptokurtic distributions. Can anything similar be said for firms?

Figure 6.10 shows the liquidation values of both debt and equity as a function of the time T value of the net assets underlying the firm, where FV

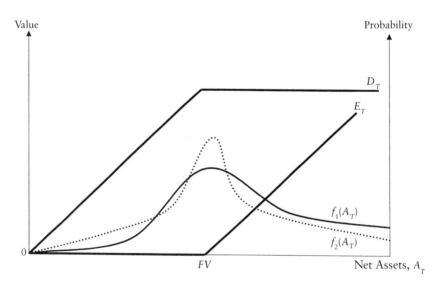

FIGURE 6.10   Skewness, kurtosis, and debt/equity values.

in debt is again outstanding. This time, the distributions $f_1(A_T)$ and $f_2(A_T)$ are not as easily interpreted in the context of what debt and equity might like. The distribution f_1 is pretty clearly positively skewed, and this is something that *both* shareholders *and* creditors would benefit from. The probability of realizing higher net asset values is greater than in the symmetric distributions we saw on Figure 6.9, but unlike the earlier figures, this higher probability of good outcomes is no longer accompanied by correspondingly higher probabilities of bad outcomes. But what about kurtosis? Visually, it is impossible to say whether the reduction in probability in the left-hand tail relative to the symmetric distribution case is greater or less than the increase in the probability of the right-hand tail. Nevertheless, distribution f_1 looks like a distribution that would not necessarily invite equity to make decisions adverse to debt.

The second distribution, $f_2(A_T)$ is a lot more troubling. This distribution has fatter tails and a more peaked center than the symmetric distributions of Figure 6.9—it is leptokurtic—but it does *not* have any apparent skewness. So, the probability of *large* increases in asset values is higher than before, but so is the probability of *large* decreases in asset value. Note, however, that distribution $f_2(A_T)$ does not necessarily have a variance any higher than the distributions shown on Figure 6.9.

Equity holders might be inclined to pursue a project with a distribution like this because of the higher probability of positive outcomes—outcomes that are matched by equally likely bad outcomes that cost equity nothing extra but reduce the value of outstanding bonds. Unfortunately, if the firm has committed to a hedging strategy based solely on *variance*, then a variance-minimizing hedge could well allow equity holders to get away with this. Stated differently, Figure 6.10 shows that equity holders may be tempted to accept projects that increase the value of equity at the expense of bondholders *which would not be precluded by a hedging strategy designed to target variance.*

Ultimately, risk management can be a solution to stockholder/bondholder conflicts, but the particular risk management strategy adopted must be closely tailored to the specific concerns stakeholders have. Arbitrary concerns could encourage arbitrary hedging and risk management objectives that do *not* serve to promote the over-riding goal of ensuring that the firm maximizes $V(t) - I(t)$.

CHAPTER 7

Controlling and Exploiting Informational Asymmetries by Managing Risk

Now we turn to the fourth source of opportunity for firms to add value using properly implemented risk management programs. This set of opportunities arises primarily because the M&M assumption of symmetric information across market participants is violated.

Before getting into the specifics of how risk management can add value when people have different information, a moment should be spent on what we do and do not mean by the term *asymmetric information*. The M&M assumption itself essentially requires that all market participants—shareholders, creditors, managers, other investors, etc.—have access to the same information and accurately perceive the true impact of that information on security prices. The assumption is typically extended to mean that everyone also has the same information about things like investment opportunities— for example, managers and shareholders both accurately perceive whether or not a project is positive NPV.

Symmetric information in the presence of capital market imperfections, however, creates a middle ground that we have already seen in Chapters 5 and 6. Namely, when information is symmetric but costs are positive, some information can only be obtained at a cost. More generally, the true state of nature is sometimes accessible to all, but only at a positive cost of verifying what that state of nature is.

Assuming everyone *can* have access to the same information but that it is costly is not quite the same as *asymmetric* information, where some parties are basically just structurally less-informed than others—that is to say that the costs of obtaining and verifying that information are effectively limitless. A typical principal-agent problem illustrates this important distinction. Suppose first that shareholders, willing to tolerate some mistakes by managers and others that occur for totally exogenous reasons, are primarily interested in the *effort* their manager agents expend. In a world of symmetric information, it may be costly for shareholders to verify that effort, *but it is possible*. More formally, contracts can be written—such as compensation agreements—that depend on a manager's effort, which, if the shareholders are willing to spend the number, is a knowable fact.

Now consider the analogous situation when information is asymmetric. In that case, shareholders simply cannot ever determine how much effort the manager put in at any reasonable cost. In that case, shareholders and managers can only write contracts based on other variables that may be noisy proxies for effort, such as sales or growth.

When we explored the agency costs of equity and free cash flows in Chapter 5, we saw that some believe managers might be inclined to grow their divisions to suboptimal levels. We did *not* assume that shareholders were incapable of recognizing that. All that was required to motivate monitoring, the issuance of debt, or the adoption of risk management is that it is *expensive* for shareholders to know when managers are pursuing excessive growth. In this sense, the agency cost of equity and free cash flow models are not models that rely on asymmetric information.

In this chapter, we review the potential for firms to increase their value by reducing the costs of *or* exploiting the benefits of information that is really and truly asymmetric—known by one party and *both* unknown *and* unobservable to some other party. Having said that, it is appropriate to recognize that many of the models in Chapters 5 and 6 would still imply a source for value-added risk management if we introduced information asymmetries. In the free cash flow model, the notion that something must be done to stop managers from spending excess cash on negative NPV projects *becomes even more compelling* if we assume that shareholders can *never* know the true NPV of the investments managers are accepting, and so on.

To avoid repetition, we do not repeat the agency models discussed in prior chapters here, but we do note that the agency costs of these models not only persist when information is asymmetric, but the costs *grow*. Risk management thus can add *even more value* when information is asymmetric between either security holders and managers or amongst security holders. Although we do not simply repeat the models explored earlier to evaluate the impact of asymmetric information, we do note in some specific instances how the models are relevant and in several cases present new models that are quite similar to some of the ones we have already explored.

REDUCING NOISE FROM "SIGNALS"

In a world where information is not equivalent across all market participants, firms can sometimes have trouble *signaling* the true value of their investment opportunities. Consider, for example, a pharmaceutical company whose scientists have a unique perception of the potential value they could create 10 years down the road with a new drug. In the meantime, the investment expenditures on the drug can be quite high, which can lead to problems if not everyone has the same information about the expected value of the new drug.

Aggravated Agency Costs of Reducing Conflicts

When some stakeholders of the firm have information that other stakeholders do not have, the costs discussed in Chapters 5 and 6, arising from the conflicts between security holders and managers or among security holders, can become quite large. When bondholders, for example, cannot ascertain whether or not the NPV of the projects shareholders are accepting is positive, they cannot tell whether they are being expropriated and whether or not shareholders have deviated from optimal investment policies. At the same time, shareholders may be equally in the dark, to the extent the inside information about the new drug is possessed by managers and not shareholders. In turn, shareholders could become concerned that managers are taking actions inconsistent with optimal investment policies, which could also further exacerbate bondholders concerns with stockholders and vice versa. All in all, when information is asymmetric across stakeholders of the firm—shareholders, creditors, and managers—about investment opportunities, the desire to incur significantly greater costs monitoring those investments becomes significant. In the absence of such monitoring, the securities issued by the firm could trade at a discount, thereby raising the cost of capital for the firm and decreasing the value of the firm.

Risk management can serve as a substitute for monitoring. As will be discussed later, for example, firms may embed derivatives positions into their debt and equity securities in order to signal their confidence in or information about future investment opportunities. To use the pharmaceutical example, the company might choose to issue debt whose coupons are payable in the foreign currency of a country where it expects significant drug sales to occur. By embedding a forward foreign exchange transaction into the debt, the firm is *either* taking a blind exposure to currency fluctuations *or* precommitting itself to a sufficient volume of sales in that currency to offset the new liability incurred through the bond issue.

Bondholders will be indifferent to this currency risk, of course, because they themselves can simply turn around and hedge it. We have not relaxed the equal access or perfect capital market assumptions of M&M, after all, and the informational asymmetry in question has nothing to do with the exchange rate. Nevertheless, hedging the exchange rate risk can *signal* to bondholders the managers' or shareholders' expectations about future drug sales, thus potentially reducing the expropriation premium bondholders might demand as discussed in the previous section. And similarly for equity holders, whose dividends could be paid in foreign currency to achieve the same results.

Analysts and Asset Valuation

In a world of imperfect information, there can be little doubt that investors—rightly or wrongly—pay serious attention to analysts. One of the supposed tasks of analysts is to try and evaluate the quality of the investment decisions made by the firms they follow. When analysts receive poor information, they can easily undervalue a project, especially when the project is intangible like a patentable process or a new drug.

In the same way that hedging and risk management can help better-informed stakeholders signal less-informed stakeholders that investment projects are sensible, a properly designed risk management program can also help send a similar signal to analysts.

DeMarzo and Duffie (1994) and others have explored the use of risk management and hedging to increase the ratio of signal to noise in the informational content of financial variables. Returning to our pharmaceutical firm, suppose the firm is subject to significant risk from foreign exchange fluctuations on the sales of its *existing* drugs, as well as the new one being developed whose value is largely unknown outside the firm. In an M&M world, the firm should be indifferent to hedging its exchange rate risk. But suppose 90% of the firm's earnings volatility comes from exchange rate exposure. The firm might choose to hedge its exchange rate risk and reduce its earnings volatility so that less-informed parties do not *assume* the volatility is due to perceived problems with the drug development.

In this example, the earnings volatility associated with the actual investments of the firm could be considered the true state of the world that only the firm knows. The *total* earnings volatility is all that analysts and others can observe, and if exchange rate fluctuations go unhedged, the noise in the signal sent by earnings will be high relative to the true volatility associated with the firm's actual investments. Hedging to increase this signal-to-noise ratio can help reduce the information asymmetry that might lead to undervaluation of the firm's investment projects, which, in turn, will depress equity and debt prices and increase the firm's cost of capital.

Consider an even more basic but plausible example of a firm whose balance sheet is denominated in U.S. dollars that is building a factory in Malaysia. Under FAS 133, the firm may be able to get hedge accounting treatment if its assets and liabilities are matched (i.e., if the firm funds the Malaysian factory in ringgit, thereby creating a ringgit liability to fund a ringgit asset). Importantly, the firm is *still exposed* to the risk of exchange rate fluctuations between the ringgit and the dollar on both the asset and liability. But suppose the exchange rate vis-à-vis the dollar is reasonably stable except for periodic major devaluations. The firm may actually prefer to run the risk of a major devaluation periodically in exchange for reducing the noise in its earnings that would be created if the ringgit asset were funded with, say, a *dollar* liability. In other words, the firm may be willing to assume a larger risk *that it can explain* than tolerate a smaller one that shows up as unattributable earnings volatility.

MANAGERIAL RISK AVERSION

In Chapter 5, we explained that a risk-averse manager might be tempted to take actions that do not maximize security holder welfare when monitoring is costly. We saw that the degree to which the manager would either fully hedge the firm or simply walk away from risky projects was in large part based on whether or not the expected utility of manager wealth is a convex function of the value of the firm.

Now consider a related situation in which information is asymmetric. Specifically, suppose that a firm is owned by a collection of risk-neutral shareholders that appoint a risk-averse manager to make the financial and investment decisions on behalf of security holders. Managers can tell the difference between idiosyncratic risk and systematic risk, *but shareholders cannot*. In other words, shareholders can only observe the total volatility of the firm's value, not its various component risks.

In this situation, Diamond and Verrechia (1982) have argued that it makes sense for managers to pursue a risk management policy. Specifically, if given the opportunity to hedge, managers will engage in the management of those risks that are under their control and within the purview of their own information. Those risks about which the managers are as ill-informed as shareholders will be left alone. But by reducing risks that are under the manager's control, the temptation for them to walk away from risky projects is reduced. At the same time, the signal sent to equity holders is similar to that explored earlier in the analysts' case. By reducing the noise of the signal, managers can better signal to shareholders that they are taking actions consistent with the NPV criterion.

REDUCING THE COSTS OF EXTERNAL DEBT FINANCING FOR NEW INVESTMENTS

The underinvestment problem of Myers explored in Chapter 6 occurs principally because of the cost to firms of external debt financing of these projects. Because of a debt overhang, new investments made by equity holders may be so heavily weighted to paying off debt holders that equity receives few of the benefits despite bearing most of the costs if the project goes bad. So, firms sometimes reject positive NPV projects because of the cost of external finance.

The basic underinvestment model is driven primarily by the *value* of investment projects, and how the value of those projects comes to bear on the *value* of debt and the *value* of equity. An alternative formulation has been offered by Froot, Scharfstein, and Stein (1993, 1994)—henceforth, FSS—in which the underinvestment problem is recast in terms of *cash flows*.

The FSS Cash Flow Hedging Model

The intuition behind the FSS underinvestment model is that it is costly for firms to finance their projects by issuing new debt. Debt is costly in the FSS model for several reasons. The first is that financial distress is presumed to be costly—a violation of the M&M perfect capital markets assumption. The closer a firm gets to financial distress in the FSS model, the more firms are penalized with higher borrowing costs. This does not require the firm to be near bankruptcy, but can also occur because the firm is experiencing liquidity problems.

A second reason that debt can be costly in a FSS world is also a result of capital market imperfections. Namely, as we have seen in several cases already, it can be costly for principals to monitor their agents.

Finally, debt can be costly when external creditors have less information than internal managers and stakeholders about the quality of the firm's investment projects and growth opportunities—a violation of the symmetric information assumption in M&M. The more intangible a firm's assets, the more trouble outsiders have determining the true value of its assets. And the more trouble the firm has raising money to fund those opportunities.

At the outset, it must be said that the FSS model could have been placed into Chapter 6 instead of this Chapter 7. A sufficient but not necessary condition for underinvestment problems to arise *in a cash flow sense* is that prospective creditors have less information than managers about investment opportunities and thus may charge higher interest rates than if the quality of all investments was observable. But the only necessary *and* sufficient condition for underinvestment problems to occur in a cash flow sense is that the marginal cost of issuing new debt is positive and increasing in the amount of *external* financing required.

We could thus easily get to a cash flow-based version of Myers' underinvestment problem without assuming any differences in information by focusing on one of the two other costs of debt. But the fact is that the FSS theory tends to be much more interesting *and* relevant when information asymmetries exaggerate the costs of external finance.

To see why underinvestment occurs purely because of the costs of external finance, consider the simple model set up by FSS in which a firm's NPV is

$$F(I) = f(I) - I$$

where I is the investment expenditure and $f(I)$ the subsequent level of production output, such that $f_I > 0$ and $f_{II} < 0$. In the normal case where investment and financing decisions are independent of one another, optimal investment occurs where $f_I = 1$—the marginal product of the investment equals its marginal cost. This optimal investment expenditure can be denoted I^*.

To motivate underinvestment, FSS assume that investment expenditures can be financed from internal funds, denoted w, and external funds, denoted e:

$$I = w + e$$

External financing is assumed to be costly for reasons noted. If C denotes these costs, bonds issued by the firm earn C/e over the riskless rate. Internal financing is not presumed to give rise to such "deadweight costs."

The firm now chooses I to maximize $F(I) - C(e)$, where costs depend on the total amount of external financing $e = I - w$. The first-order condition for the firm now says that investment expenditures are optimal when

$$F_I - C_e = f_I - 1 - C_e = 0$$

or when $f_I - C_e = 1$. Because $f_I(I) > 0$ and $C_e(e) = C_e(I - w) > 0$, the optimal investment expenditure I is below the I^* that satisfies the normal first-order condition $f_I = 1$. Thus, the firm invests too little because debt is costly to issue.

Even from this simple model, the direction taken by FSS is a pretty easy one to anticipate. Namely, the more a firm can finance investment from its internal funds w, the less it needs to rely on external funds. The less external funding, the lower C_e and the closer investment comes to its optimal level. In the limiting case where $e = 0$, $f_I - C_e = f_I$ and the original, optimal level of investment I^* occurs.

The intuition behind the FSS cash flow hedging model is best seen from the example offered by FSS in a shortened version of their major article that appeared in the *Harvard Business Review*. (FSS, 1994) Their example is based on a hypothetical pharmaceutical company called "Omega Pharmaceutical" whose revenues are at risk from sales in Japan and Germany—specifically, from fluctuations in the mark/dollar and yen/dollar exchange rates. Omega is dollar-based and expects its net cash flows to be worth about $200 million per annum. Exchange rate swings, however, could change the dollar value of these revenues to either $100 million or $300 million per annum with equal likelihood.

As a pharmaceutical firm, the company's investment expenditures are heavily weighted toward R&D. As part of its normal capital budgeting exercises, Omega has forecast cash flows associated with different investment levels in new drugs. These investment expenditures, cost-of-capital-discounted cash flows, and NPVs are shown in Table 7.1 from FSS (1994). The firm's R&D budget was $180 million last year and will be $200 million next year. FSS (1994) argue that the choice of $200 million is based on the higher NPV at that level of spending as seen from the capital budget shown in Table 7.1. Recall from Chapter 2, however, that corporate finance theory does not tell firms to accept the highest NPV project of several, but rather to take all of them. In truth, the choice of a $200 million investment decision for Omega thus is driven primarily by intuition

FSS (1994) then suppose that Omega does not have the ability to borrow funds to finance its R&D program and is unwilling to issue equity to

TABLE 7.1 Omega Pharmaceutical's Capital Budget (Millions of U.S. Dollars)

R&D Expenditure	Discounted Cash Flows	NPV
100	160	60
200	290	90
300	360	60

do so. Internal cash funding thus is the only option for Omega. In this situation, Omega is quite vulnerable to exchange rate changes that can impact its net cash flows. If the dollar appreciates and Omega's net revenues decline in value to $100 million, only $100 million can be spent on new investment and R&D. By contrast, a dollar depreciation would leave Omega with an extra $100 million above its planned $200 million spending level.

If Omega were to *perfectly* hedge its cash flows against exchange rate risk, the net revenue from its drug sales would be locked in at $200 million per annum. If the dollar appreciates and the dollar value of foreign sales declines from $200 million to $100 million, this means that the hedge will generate a cash inflow of $100 million. Conversely, a depreciation of the dollar that increases the dollar value of foreign sales by $100 million is offset with a $100 million loss on the hedge.

Ignoring the cost of the hedge, Table 7.2 shows the impact of the hedge on the available funds for R&D as compared to the no hedging alternative. For a depreciating dollar, the hedge does not change anything because the cash outflow on the hedge just offsets the cash inflow on the foreign currency-denominated sales. But with an appreciating dollar, the cash inflow on the hedge that offsets the $100 million decline in foreign currency-denominated sales is just enough to finance the additional $100 million in investment that the firm decided to make. Consulting Table 7.2, the increased investment expenditure from $100 million to $200 million increases future expected cash flows by $130 million. Because the $130 million gain exceeds the $100 million loss in a NPV sense, Omega Pharmaceutical can increase the value of the firm from hedging.

The FSS story thus is all about using risk management to match the *demand* for internal funds with the *supply* of external funds in order to avoid the presumed costs of issuing new debt to finance future investment projects. The demand/supply calculus is illustrated in Figure 7.1. The demand for R&D spending is shown at $200 million, the presumed target level. The

TABLE 7.2 The Impact of Hedging on Omega Pharmaceutical's Investments (Millions of U.S. Dollars)

Dollar	Internal Funds	R&D without Hedging	Cash Flows on Hedge	Additional R&D with Hedging	Value from Hedging
Appreciates	100	100	+100	100	+130
Stable	200	200	0	0	0
Depreciates	300	200	−100	0	−100

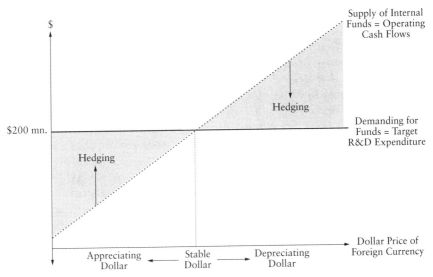

FIGURE 7.1 Using hedging to match the demand for and supply of internal funds at Omega Pharmaceutical.

supply of internal funds is represented by a 45° line that changes in value dollar-for-dollar with appreciations or depreciations in the dollar price of yen and Deutsche marks. The two are equalized at the point where the hedge perfectly locks in the current dollar value of foreign sales. The gain from hedging, in general, is indicated as anything that tilts the supply of internal funds curve close to the demand for those funds.

In this example, the demand for internal funds is presumed to be perfectly elastic with respect to exchange rate changes. In other words, the exchange rate may ultimately affect how the investment expenditure is *financed,* but the exchange rate does not affect the *demand for the investment.*

FSS offer another example to illustrate what happens when the investment itself depends on the value of a diversifiable risk, such as exchange rates. They describe a new company called Omega Oil whose supply of internal funds is clearly affected by oil prices. When prices rise, revenues rise—and conversely. But FSS then assume the demand for investments is also related to the price of oil. When prices are low, they posit that the demand for exploration and new reserves declines and conversely. Unlike revenues which clearly depend on the price of oil in a one-for-one manner, however, investments are a bit less sensitive to oil price changes. Prices could, after all, recover before oil is pumped from the ground. Although the demand for and supply of internal funds both are affected by oil prices, they are not *exactly* matched as Figure 7.2 illustrates.

Comparing Figures 7.1 and 7.2 shows that the gains from hedging are higher for Omega Pharmaceutical than for Omega Oil. In the latter case, the natural exposure of the firm to oil prices exists both in its investments and its sales, thereby providing a bit of a natural hedge. Nevertheless, as Figure 7.2 shows, there is still some room for the firm to protect its investment opportunities by hedging to ensure that cash flows are always adequate to fund new investment opportunities.

So, the FSS model tells us that whenever the marginal cost of *external* finance is increasing in the amount of funds required and the marginal cost of *internal* finance is not, it makes sense for firms to reduce the volatility of their cash flows. Note that this is not the same as saying that firms should hedge their cash flows when external finance is more expensive than internal finance. If the rate a firm pays to bond holders is always 50 bps higher than its shadow price of internal funds, then the FSS model collapses. The firm can in that case always issue debt to finance investments, albeit at a cost of 50 bps. Whether or not external finance makes sense depends on the

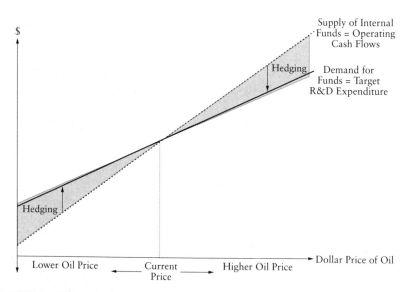

FIGURE 7.2 Using hedging to match the demand for and supply of internal funds at Omega Oil.

comparative cost of hedging and the cost of maintaining free cash flows (as we will discuss several subsections from now).

The FSS justification for risk management adding to firm value really kicks in when the *marginal* cost of external finance is not a constant but the *marginal* cost of internal finance is. In this case, more funds required mean proportionally increasing costs of external funding vis-à-vis internal funding. As noted earlier, asymmetric information is not strictly required to motivate the FSS model, but it helps a lot. Aside from firms that near bankruptcy that encounter distressed debt problems as they lever up, it is hard to imagine how external marginal financing costs can increase with the level of debt *unless* it is because the capital market simply cannot perceive the quality of the firm's investment opportunities. They instead simply observe the increase in leverage and *mistake* this for a distressed debt situation.

CARRYING-CHARGE HEDGING

In the basic trader hedging model of Johnson we examined in Chapter 2, we saw that the variance-minimizing hedge ratio is not necessarily the *optimal* hedge ratio. The optimal hedge ratio was, rather, the tangency point between the trader's mean-variance indifference curve and the frontier of possibilities that a combination of hedged and unhedged positions in the market creates in mean-variance space. Is there an analogous *partial hedging* concept for corporations that can be consistent with the maximization of security holder welfare? In a world where information is asymmetric, the answer can be yes. "Can be" does not always mean "will be," however, as we shall see below.

Types of "Hedging" in the World of Holbrook Working

Any discussion of the important role that asymmetric information can play in theories of corporate risk management must begin with some background on the work of Holbrook Working, an agricultural economist writing from the Food Research Institute at Stanford University in the mid-twentieth century. Working did much to increase our knowledge of the functioning of futures markets, including why people speculate and why people hedge. His work was both theoretically and empirically sound.

Because Working published his work in the agricultural economics journals—really the only place to publish research on futures in the 1940s and 1950s—the corporate finance literature has largely ignored his contributions. Nevertheless, they remain solid contributions to the theory and practice of risk management even today.

The Convenience Yield, the Basis, and the Supply of Storage   As we saw in Chapter 2, the fair quoted price of a futures contract can be expressed using the cost of carry formulation as follows:

$$F(t, T) = S(t) + b(t, T) \qquad (7.1)$$

where $b(t, T)$ is the basis comprised of the capital and physical costs of storing a commodity from time t to time T less the *convenience yield* or implicit dividend earned by the marginal storer of the commodity. We can express the basis as in Chapter 3 as

$$b(t, T) = R(t, T) + W(t, T) - D(t, T) \qquad (7.2)$$

where $R_{t, T}$ is the all-in interest cost prevailing from t to T, $W_{t, T}$ is the lump-sum cost of physical storage from t to T, and $D_{t, T}$ is the dividend earned on the physical asset from t to T.

It is easy to reformulate this expression in any number of ways if you are unhappy with either the presumption of compounding implicit in the above or with the expression of W and D as lump-sum amounts. For example, if $w(t, T)$ and $d(t, T)$ denote the physical storage cost and convenience yield as a function of the spot price and $r(t, T)$ is the interest rate, then Equation 7.2 becomes

$$b(t, T) = r(t, T) + w(t, T) - d(t, T) \qquad (7.3)$$

and Equation 7.1 becomes

$$F(t, T) = S(t)[1 + b(t, T)] \qquad (7.4)$$

Or if you like continuous compounding,

$$F(t, T) = S(t)\exp[b(t, T)] \qquad (7.5)$$

with $b(t, T)$ defined as in Equation 7.3 using continuous rates.

For financial futures and forwards, the cost of carry relation given in Equations 7.1, 7.4, or 7.5 is basic and intuitive. As explained in Chapter 3, the formula is based on the construction of a transaction in the physical market that replicates the forward position and thus, in the absence of arbitrage, allows us to write the quoted forward purchase price as a function of carrying costs. A Treasury security, for example, can be carried over time at its financing rate, the repurchase (repo) rate you get for loaning a Treasury security out. For financial instruments, physical costs are zero. So, you have enough to know the futures price—$S(t)[1 + R(t, T) - d(t, T)]$ where $R(t, T)$ is the rate you earn on the Treasury and $d(t, T)$ is the rate you pay to borrow the Treasury. Foreign currency futures can be priced similarly— $S(t)[1 + R(t, T) - d(t, T)]$ where $R(t, T)$ is the rate you earn on domestic currency and $d(t, T)$ is the rate you are giving up by *not* holding the foreign currency, and so on.

Things get much more interesting when the underlying of the forward contract is a physical commodity. In that case, the physical storage cost $w(t, T)$ has some meaning, but $d(t, T)$—the so-called convenience yield—is a lot more complicated.

The concept of a convenience yield was initially developed by Keynes (1930), with later attention from such well-respected economists as Kaldor (1939), Brennan (1958), Telser (1958, 1960), Williams (1986), and Working (1948, 1949a, 1949b, 1953, 1962). In essence, the convenience yield is the *price of immediacy* in a commodity market.

Let us take a step backward and ask the *reverse* of the question we are considering when we ask why firms hedge: Why might firms *want to hold on to a physical product* rather than a substitute derivatives transaction? The answer lies in the convenience yield.

Working (1962) argued that there are four reasons why people store physical commodities. First, the transactional demand for storage leads some firms to store products to avoid the transaction costs of getting rid of them. People store pennies for this reason—the benefit of getting rid of five pennies for a nickel is surely smaller than waiting until you have 100 or even 1,000 pennies saved up.

Second, firms sometimes have a "pure storage" motive for storage, as Working calls it. This simply means that storage is required for a purely physical reason usually having to do with some production process. Some auto manufacturers let every car leave their assembly lines, for example, with at least *some* gas in the tank. In order for this to be possible, they must store some gas near the assembly lines.

A third motivation for storage is speculative—people store an asset in anticipation of an increase in its value. This is the classical rationale for hiding money under a mattress—or, better still, for buying gold bullion. Gold has virtually no appreciable use in any major production process, but people hold on to it as a store of value and in the hope that its value will rise.

Finally and most importantly, Working characterizes the "precautionary demand" for storage. Firms sometimes have a precautionary demand for storage not because of *current* production needs—that is, the "pure storage" rationale for inventory—but because of *unanticipated shocks* to future production needs. These shocks can come either on the demand side or the supply side. The important thing to motivate the precautionary demand for storage is the cost associated with an inventory *stock out*. How many customers would Bally Switzerland on the Bahnhofstrasse in Zürich lose if it had to announce one day that it was out of shoes? How expensive would it be if an oil refinery had to cease all gasoline and heating oil production because it ran out of crude? How many shareholders of DeBeers would complain if they heard the company telling all of its resellers: "Sorry, but all our diamonds are still in the mines for the next few months."

The distinctions between these four motivations for physical inventory holdings are not always clear. Bally needs *some* shoes on hand to keep its store open. But the company might choose to inventory more than it needs for, say, a week's sales to avoid turning customers away a week later because of a problem with its shipping agent. The shoes it needs to open the store and sell this week is a pure storage motive for inventory, whereas keeping enough shoes to last another week is precautionary.

Or consider a jewelry manufacturer that caters primarily to the Japanese market, where the nonindustrial demand for platinum is extremely high. The jeweler might hold extra stocks of platinum to avoid a cessation in production in the event of a platinum shortage. But the jeweler might fine-tune those inventory holdings based on his beliefs about platinum prices, holding more than needed to satisfy precautionary demand in order to try and make a speculative profit on the actual metal.

The different motives for storage have a close linkage to the forward and futures market, as Keynes and his peer Pierro Sraffa observed in the 1930s. Specifically, the demand for holding physical inventory—or, equivalently, the demand for immediacy—is directly related to the premium placed on selling inventory *in the future* relative to selling into the spot market *today*. In other words, futures and forward markets act as *intertemporal lending markets* to move inventory from the present to the future or vice versa based on relative scarcity.

Figure 7.3 illustrates this demand for immediacy. When inventories are high, the *relative* premium that a commodity commands in the future relative to the present is reasonably small. Plenty of the commodity is on hand to assure producers and intermediaries that a future stock out will not occur given reasonable demand and supply conditions. On the other hand, as inventories start to decline, the spot price rises relative to the futures price in order to give producers an incentive to take physical product *out* of inventory and give it to the current spot market. A high spot price *alone* would not do that. But a high spot price *relative to* the price for the sale of the same commodity in the future is signaling the market that inventories are tight *today* relative to the future.

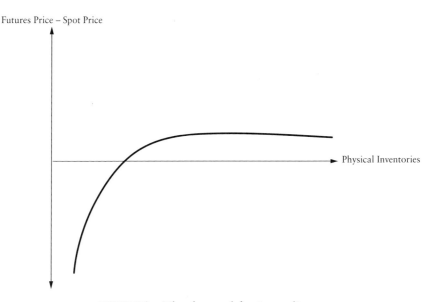

FIGURE 7.3 The demand for immediacy.

The demand for immediacy is sometimes viewed from the opposite perspective and called the *supply of storage,* as shown in Figure 7.4. The basic relations between relative futures/spot prices and inventories is the same as in Figure 7.3, but now the *y*-axis is reversed and is expressed in terms of the spot price premium over the price at some point in the future for subsequent delivery of the commodity. Note in both Figures 7.3 and 7.4 that the sensitivity of the price relation between current and future sale prices for the commodity varies based on the actual amount of the goods in storage. When inventories are high, the price relationship between current and future prices does not change much. But as inventories get tighter and tighter, the spot price becomes more and more responsive to that scarcity relative to the futures price.[1]

Consulting the cost of carry characterization of futures prices is instructive and allows us to assign a good deal more economic interpretation to Figures 7.3 and 7.4 than without it. Rearranging Equation 7.1 tells us the maximum the futures price can ever be relative to the spot price, or

$$F(t, T) - S(t) = R(t, T) + W(t, T) - D(t, T) \tag{7.6}$$

Clearly, the differential between the futures and spot price achieves its maximum when the convenience yield is at its minimum, or zero. Given what we

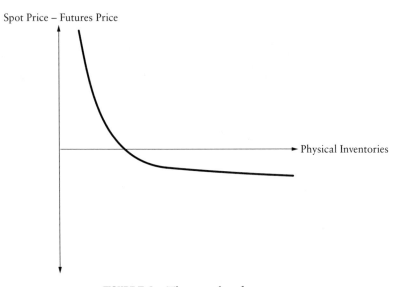

FIGURE 7.4   The supply of storage.

know about the convenience yield, this means that firms essentially place *no value* on having physical inventories on hand during this time period. Accordingly, the futures price is left to drift above the spot price to reflect *only* the pure physical and capital costs of moving a unit of commodity over time. When the convenience yield is zero and futures prices exceed spot prices by exactly the capital and physical cost of storage, a market is said to be *in full carry*.

In most developed countries, physical and capital costs of storage do not fluctuate much and remain below a certain level. Some developing countries can experience hyperinflations that put tremendous upward pressure on rates, but even that does not radically affect the cost of physical storage. Consequently, the quantity $R(t, T) + W(t, T)$ does not fluctuate much *and* does not usually rise above some upper reflecting barrier or boundary. We can denote this *de facto* maximum as $R°(t, T) + W°(t, T)$, the level at which the market is in full carry. Figure 7.5 shows this point graphically. No matter how large inventories grow, at some point they grow large enough to drive the convenience yield to zero, at which point the premium of the futures price over the spot price never really gets any larger than $R°(t, T) + W°(t, T)$.

The convenience yield is overlaid on Figure 7.5 as a dotted line. As inventories shrink, however, the convenience yield becomes positive. And as inventories get lower and lower, the convenience yield rises *at an increasing*

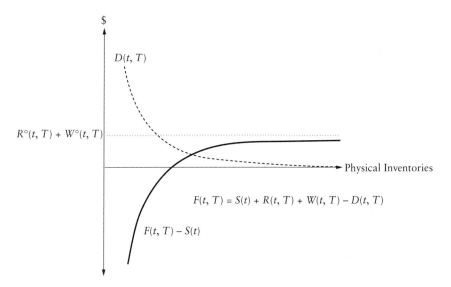

FIGURE 7.5   The demand for immediacy and cost of carry futures pricing.

rate. The less there is available in inventory, the less there is for firms to meet *current* production demands and the more the firms *need* physical inventory, which is the implicit dividend to physical product that the convenience yield is intended to reflect.

Many people become confused when first encountering the convenience yield because of confusions over demand and supply shocks. From Equation 7.1, we know that the futures price is a function of the spot price. In an efficient capital market with rational expectations, we have already seen that the futures price is an unbiased predictor of the future spot price. Consequently, demand and supply shocks *should be reflected in the spot price.* If demand in one year is *known with certainty* to be above average, the price will rise today in anticipation of this. And the futures price *will also rise* because it is a function of the spot price.

French (1986) has carefully studied relations between spot and futures prices and has shown that the impact of supply and demand shocks on spot prices and the spot-futures price relation depends primarily on the level of inventories *when the shock occurs.* If inventories are high, demand and supply shocks tend to impact the spot price and the futures price in much the same way. In other words, because the shock hits the spot price it *also* hits the futures price proportionately. But the convenience yield does not change much, and so the *relation* between the futures and spot price—the basis, as we have called it—remains nearly constant. But as inventories shrink, a shock to supply or demand impacts the spot price much more significantly than the futures price. This is the convenience yield responding to the level of inventories and acting as an adjustment mechanism for moving inventory across time.

The Term Structure of Futures Prices   Our discussion thus far has included nothing about the relationship between prices for the delivery of a commodity at *multiple* points in time. Yet, all of our discussion thus far generalizes for any value of *T* we may consider. As it is, we could simply redraw Figures 7.3 through 7.5 using two different futures prices. When we refer to the *spot-futures basis,* we are referring to what is sometimes known as the *calendar basis,* or the relation between the prices of two identical commodities to be delivered at different calendar times. Just as the spot-futures basis is the difference between the spot price and the futures price observed at the same time, we can define any pairwise basis accordingly. The one-to-three month calendar basis is the difference between the current price of a contract for delivery one month hence and the current price of a contract for delivery three months hence.

The relation between *several* futures or forward prices and the spot price defines the *term structure of futures prices.* Some examples of futures price term structures—all based on futures settlement prices observed on September 6, 2000—are shown in Figures 7.6 to 7.8. Figure 7.6 shows the relation between the price of lumber per thousand board feet and the month in which the lumber will be delivered. The futures price rises steadily each month. The slope of the term structure of futures prices is positive. This tells us that lumber inventories are probably reasonably high and expected to remain high relative to demand through September of 2001. Why? As noted earlier, when inventories are high the difference between any given futures price and the spot price is roughly equal to the cost of storing the commodity over time; the convenience yield is negligible because supply is aplenty. We expect *some* increase in prices over time, of course, because the cost of storage rises—that is, it costs more to store a thousand board feet of lumber for one year than for one month.

The lumber market shown in Figure 7.6 is said to be *in contango* because the slope of the term structure of futures prices is positive throughout. Figure 7.7, by contrast, shows that the world sugar market is in a state of what is called *backwardation* in which futures prices *decline* with successively more distant delivery dates. Sugar is selling for about 10.45 cents per pound today in the spot market, but the exact same quantity and quality and type of sugar to be delivered in the same place(s) in July 2002 is selling for only 8.90 cents per pound today.

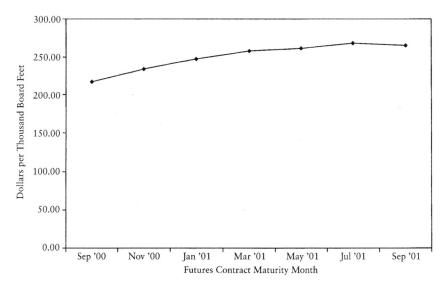

FIGURE 7.6 Term structure of futures prices as of 9/6/00 for lumber (CME).

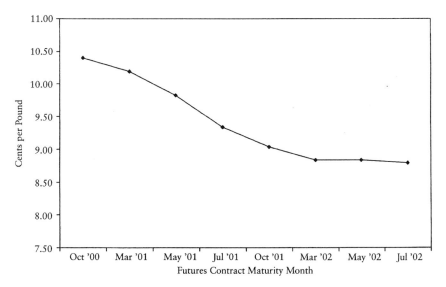

FIGURE 7.7 Term structure of futures prices as of 9/6/00 for sugar (NYBOT).

A market in backwardation has a calendar basis—futures price minus the spot price—that is *negative*. Returning to Figure 7.5, $F(t, T) - S(t)$ becomes negative only when inventories are getting tight and, consequently, the convenience yield associated with physical storage is starting to rise. In fact, we know from Equations 7.1 and 7.2 that the *only* way the spot price can exceed the futures price is if

$$D(t, T) > R(t, T) + W(t, T)$$

so that the convenience yield earned from holding physical product exceeds the capital and physical cost of storing the product. We thus can make a fairly well-educated guess from Figure 7.7 that world sugar inventories are not at their highest levels right now and that demand is high relative to supply in the short run.

The third example, Figure 7.8, shows the term structure of copper futures prices as quoted on the New York Mercantile Exchange on September 6, 2000. The highest price is for copper to be delivered in March 2001

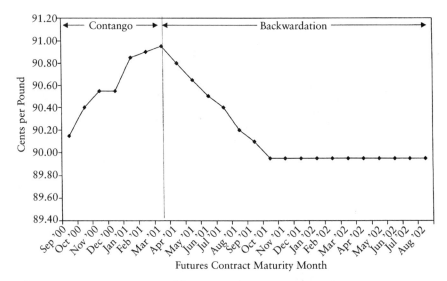

FIGURE 7.8 Term structure of futures prices as of 9/6/00 for copper (NYMEX).

at about 90.90 cents per pound. Copper is currently selling in the spot market for about 90.10 cents per pound. And copper in August 2002 is expected to sell for around 89.90 cents per pound.

Figure 7.8 is instructive because it illustrates that a market can exhibit *both* backwardation *and* contango at the same time. The price of copper to be delivered from now through March 2001 is rising steadily. This contango market reflects a low convenience yield relative to physical storage costs. But in March 2001, the market turns and prices start to decline. By October 2001, the price of copper is below the current spot price and the market is in strong backwardation.

A variety of factors can cause a market to shift from backwardation to contango at some future delivery date. In the case of the copper market, it might be the case that current inventories are enough to meet demand, but a mine could, for example, be going temporarily out of production in March. That would lead to a contraction in supply that would affect *future* inventories, even though inventories are presently reasonably high.

It is important to keep in mind, moreover, that the term structure of futures prices—much like the term structure of interest rates, or *yield curve*—represents a snapshot of the market at a single point in time. The behavior of a market *over time* can be quite different. As new supply and demand shocks occur, the convenience yield can be quite volatile, sending a market from backwardation into contango one week and then back to a negatively sloped term structure the next week.

Petroleum markets tend to exhibit particular volatility in the convenience yield, in large part because OPEC pursues cartel pricing whose stability depends at any given moment on the credibility of its production quotas for member nations. Figure 7.9 shows the impact this can have on the slope of the term structure of futures prices, depicted specifically for the 24-month calendar basis—the price of the futures contract with 24 months to maturity less the spot price. As you can see from Figure 7.9, the market for light, sweet, West Texas Intermediate (WTI) crude was in backwardation for most of the period shown with the notable exception of most of 1998, when the market went as far as $6 per barrel into contango.

To add a different perspective, Figure 7.10 shows the slopes of some *specific* oil price term structures on October 2 for the years 1995 to 1998. The information conveyed by these term structures is quite different from the information we can deduce from the time series graphs in Figure 7.9, which tells us *only* whether the market was in backwardation or contango and by how much. In Figure 7.10, we can see that the driving force appears to be shifts in the spot price and the prices of near-term futures. The long end of the term structures stays relatively stable around $18 to $22 per

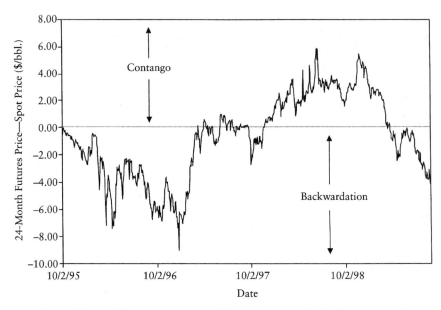

FIGURE 7.9 Slope of term structure of futures prices for light, sweet, west Texas intermediate crude oil (NYMEX), 10/95–8/99.

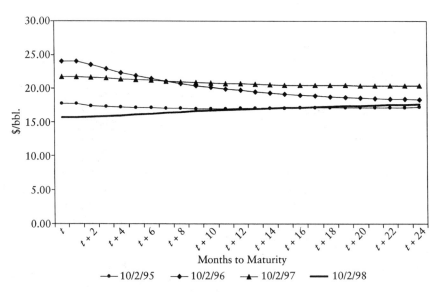

FIGURE 7.10 Term structures of WTI light, sweet crude oil futures prices October 2, 1995–1998.

barrel, whereas the spot price fluctuates from around $15 to almost $25 per barrel.

The phenomenon depicted in Figure 7.10 is not an unusual one. Typically, spot prices and the prices of contracts nearer to delivery are more volatile than the prices of contracts for delivery further in the futures. Sometimes this is called a *horizontal diving board* effect, because the term structures in Figure 7.10 appear to trace the movement of a diving board—bouncing a lot at one end and not much at the other.

This horizontal diving board should not come as a shock, given what we saw in Figure 7.5. As inventories decline further and further, the convenience yield gets higher and higher. And at the same time, the spot price becomes quite sensitive to small changes in anticipated supply and demand. Consequently, it does not take much to move short-term prices in a market like oil, despite the relative stability of the prices of oil to be delivered two years and beyond in the future.

Equilibrium Futures Prices and Convenience Yields   As we discussed earlier in this section and in Chapter 3, the dividend portion of the cost of carry futures pricing formula is not as interesting for financial assets as it is for commodities. For financial assets like foreign currency, equity indices, and Treasuries, the dividend foregone by holding the futures contract is *an explicit dividend* or cash flow. The current time t price of a futures contract on the S&P 500 that matures at time T is just

$$F(t, T) = I(t) + R(t, T) - D(t, T)$$

where $I(t)$ is the current index level, $R(t, T)$ is the all-in cost of borrowing the index value today and financing it through date T, and $D(t, T)$ are the cumulative dividends paid on all the stocks in the index over the time period. By holding a long futures position, you guarantee the purchase of the stocks in the index (or their cash equivalent) at time T, but you forego the dividends. As a benefit, you pay nothing to enter the position today. Buying the stocks now and holding them, by contrast, allows you to earn the dividends, but you must borrow the money to buy the stocks and finance the loan in turn. Any way you cut it, buying and holding the stocks is equivalent to going long the futures.

For commodities, it is not always true that going long the futures is exactly equivalent to buying and storing the physical good. Whereas the dividends paid on the S&P 500 are either known or fairly predictable and do not depend on who holds the stocks, *any given firm* may have a different physical storage cost and convenience yield than the basis reflected in the current futures price. Inventories may be high enough in aggregate that the convenience yield reflected in futures price is negligible, but any particular firm may be in an inventory squeeze.

The cost of carry formula for futures and forwards based on financial assets thus is an *arbitrage* relationship. If the price of S&P 500 futures is above its fair value by more than transaction costs, *any firm* can short the futures and buy the stocks for a riskless profit. At any given time, by contrast, the basis priced into a commodity futures contract is the *marginal* cost of storage less the *marginal* convenience yield for the *marginal entrant into physical storage*. The convenience yield thus is unobservable, different across firms, and not explicitly associated with a cash flow. It serves to establish *equilibrium* between futures and spot prices in order to move inventory across time, but consequently, it cannot be arbitraged easily.

At the same time, the fact that the convenience yield is an unobservable, equilibrium relation rather than an observable quantity means that, as Holbrook Working recognized, it is precisely the place to look for the impact of asymmetric information on trading and risk management activities.

Working describes a type of hedging he calls "carrying-charge hedging" in which the basic intent is to exploit a perceived informational advantage. When a firm believes that one market is mis-priced *relative to another*, the firm can essentially engage in a basis trade to exploit that perceived mis-pricing—until, of course, its own actions reveal its information and drive away the profit opportunity. Why would such a firm not simply sell the over-priced asset *outright?* The answer, for Working, was that firms could not acquire enough information about a financial asset being mis-priced without having a natural exposure in the underlying market. By definition, then, any trading decisions would be *basis* trading decisions. That explanation is not entirely satisfactory, however, because the firm would want to *keep trading* even after its natural exposure had long since been offset with trades attempting to exploit its information about the basis. But, as we shall see in the next two subsections, the minor addition of positive expected bankruptcy costs takes care of this problem.

A Simple Model of Carrying-Charge Hedging

In Chapter 3 we learned that in an efficient capital market, the prices of securities and derivatives preclude riskless arbitrage opportunities. One obvious way that a firm can make money or advantageously avoid losing money in a financial market is if this edict of finance is violated and securities are mis-priced. Can such mis-pricings of securities occur? Indeed, in a world of asymmetric information, they can under one very strong assumption (in addition to the assumption of information asymmetries). Trading is itself informative, so security mis-pricings can persist only when information is asymmetric *and* the actions taken by a firm or a trader to exploit the mis-pricing do not drive the mis-pricing away.

With Holbrook Working's "theory of supply of storage" in hand, we can illustrate the relation between risk management and information asymmetry using a simple model. Our example involves three periods, $t = (0, 1, 2)$. Suppose at time 0 a marketing firm contracts to deliver one barrel of oil at time 1 and time 2 to retail customers for fixed price K (henceforth the *customer swap*). Assume for simplicity there is no demand for the marketer to offer swaps in which it *receives* oil. In addition, the marketing firm is a price taker in all derivatives; its actions cannot influence quoted futures prices or swap rates, and it cannot offer swaps with rates different from dealer-offered fair swap rates.

Assume that the per-period interest rate r is constant but that the net cost of oil storage is not. The net cost of storage from time 0 to 1, denoted $z(0, 1)$, is the difference between the marginal cost of physical storage $w(0, 1)$ and the marginal convenience yield $d(0, 1)$ between time 0 and time 1 expressed as a proportion of the spot price. The net convenience yield from time 0 to time 1 is a random variable realized at time 0.

The expected future spot price one period hence is presumed equal to the current spot price adjusted for the observable basis (i.e., capital and physical storage costs less convenience yield) plus a zero expected value error term:

$$E_0\left[S(1)\right] = S(0)(1+r)\left[1 + w(0, 1)\right]$$

$$E_1\left[S(2)\right] = S(1)(1+r)\left[1 + w(1, 2)\right]$$

where E_0 and E_1 are expected value operators conditional on information available at times 0 and 1, respectively.

The marketing firm perceives itself as having superior information to all external market participants—customers, futures traders, swap dealers, and so on. We do *not* assume the information asymmetry exists vis-à-vis external or internal financing sources, although we must assume the marketing firm's actions do not affect market prices.

To capture the asymmetry of information, we adopt some simple notation. For any random variable X, denote an expected value conditional on time 0 *public* information as $E_0[X]$ and an expectation conditional on *the marketing firm's* information as $E_0^*[X]$.[2] The firm's special information is confined to information about the basis. Consequently, the marketing firm's expectation of future spot prices and subsequent futures price will differ necessarily from the market's. For concreteness, suppose the following is true:

$$E_0{}^* \left[S(1) \right] = E_0 \left[S(1) \right] + \theta$$

$$E_1{}^* \left[S(2) \right] = E_1 \left[S(2) \right] + \theta$$

where $\theta > 0$. Futures and other derivatives are priced as unbiased predictors of expected future spot prices from the public perspective. The quoted price of a contract maturing one period hence thus is

$$F(0, 1) = E_0 \left[S(1) \right] = S(0)(1 + r)\left[1 + w(0, 1) \right]$$

$$F(1, 2) = E_1 \left[S(2) \right] = S(1)(1 + r)\left[1 + w(1, 2) \right]$$

At maturity, the futures price must equal the *realized* spot price—for example, $F(2) = S(2)$. In other words, the expected profit on all futures trades conditional on public information is, as we saw in Chapters 2 and 3, zero.

To express the price of a two-period futures contract quoted at time 0 and maturing at time 2, we assume that futures are marked to market each period. Rational futures pricing as discussed in Chapter 2 then requires that

$$\frac{E_0 \left[F(1, 2) \right] - F(0, 2)}{1 + r} = 0 \tag{7.7}$$

Purely for simplicity, we assume throughout that the spot price is independent of the contemporaneous net storage cost—$E_0[S(1)w(1, 2)] = E_0[S(1)]E_0[w(1, 2)]$ and $E_0{}^*[S(1)w(1, 2)] = E_0{}^*[S(1)]E_0{}^*[w(1, 2)]$. Using this assumption *together with the law of iterated expectations,* we can solve Equation 7.7 for $F(0, 2)$:

$$F(0, 2) = E_0 \left[E_1 S(2) \right] = E_0 \left\{ S(1)(1 + r)\left[1 + w(1, 2) \right] \right\}$$

$$= S(0)(1 + r)^2 \left[1 + w(0, 1) \right]\left[1 + E_0 w(1, 2) \right] \tag{7.8}$$

The arbitrage-free swap rate on a swap dealer-offered commodity swap is just the rate that equates the conditional expected NPV of the commodity swap to zero at its inception, or the K that solves:

$$\frac{K}{1 + r} + \frac{K}{(1 + r)^2} = \frac{E_0 \left[S(1) \right]}{1 + r} + \frac{E_0 \left[S(2) \right]}{(1 + r)^2}$$

which is

$$K = \frac{\dfrac{E_0[S(1)]}{1+r} + \dfrac{E_0[S(2)]}{(1+r)^2}}{\dfrac{1}{1+r} + \dfrac{1}{(1+r)^2}}$$

$$= \frac{S(0)[1+w(0,1)] + S(0)[1+w(0,1)][1+E_0 w(1,2)]}{\dfrac{1}{1+r} + \dfrac{1}{(1+r)^2}}$$

(7.9)

Because the marketer is a price taker in both futures and swaps, the equilibrium quoted futures and swap prices above are unaffected by the firm's private information. In addition, the arbitrage-free swap rate K shown in Equation 7.9 is not only the rate that the marketer would be quoted by a dealer on a hedge, but also the rate that the marketing firm must charge its customers on the customer swaps. Note, however, that from the perspective of the marketing firm, derivatives are no longer unbiased predictors of subsequent spot rates. From the firm's perspective, the information asymmetry results in a mis-pricing of futures and swaps that creates a profit opportunity.

The Unhedged Program   Private information about the basis implies private information about either spot or derivatives prices. If all M&M assumptions are retained except for symmetric information, the marketer has an expected profit function that is linear in firm value. Consequently, there is no reason—at this stage—to assume the firm would need to hedge.

By assumption, the marketing firm may only enter into swaps in which it receives fixed and delivers oil. If the company does not hedge the customer swap, the time 1 and time 2 cash flows on the unhedged position are as follows:

$$\pi_1 = K - S(1) \qquad \pi_2 = K - S(2)$$

The time 0 conditional expected cash flows then can be written using the marketing firm's specific private information as follows:

$$E_0^*(\pi_1) = K - E_0^*[S(1)] = K - E_0[S(1)] - \theta$$

(7.10)

$$E_0{}^*\left(\pi_2\right) = K - E_0{}^*\left[S(2)\right] = K - E_0\left[S(2)\right] - \theta \qquad (7.11)$$

Discounting the expected cash flows in Equations 7.10 and 7.11 and substituting the fair swap rate from Equation 7.9 into the resulting NPV expression yields the following time 0 conditional expected NPV of the program for the marketer:

$$NPV = \frac{-\theta}{1+r} + \frac{-\theta}{\left(1+r\right)^2} \qquad (7.12)$$

Because of the nature of the assumed information asymmetry, the marketer will reject the unhedged program as a negative NPV project. In this stylized example, the private information thus leads the marketing firm not to offer the customer contracts at all.

An Outright Futures Position   The marketer's linear profit function enables it to accept positive NPV profits in an essentially limitless manner. Because the customer swap has a negative NPV and the firm cannot by assumption offer the opposite swap deal, the firm will exploit its private information through futures trading. We consider two such strategies, both of which are intended to function as *synthetic storage* programs—synthetic purchase of oil in each of periods 1 and 2 to mimic the swap or some physical storage program. For now, assume an exogenous one-for-one hedge ratio in both strategies.

The first trading strategy—the multimaturity trade—involves a long one-period contract held from time 0 to 1 and another long contract held from time 0 to time 2. The realized cash flows on the multimaturity strategy are as follows:

$$\pi_1 = \left[F(1,1) - F(0,1)\right] + \left[F(1,2) - F(0,2)\right]$$
$$= S(1) - F(0,1) + F(1,2) - F(0,2)$$
$$\pi_2 = \left[F(2,2) - F(1,2)\right] = S(2) - F(1,2)$$

The time 0 conditional expected cash flows then can be written using the marketing firm's specific private information:

$$E_0{}^*\left(\pi_1\right) = E_0{}^*\left[S(1)\right] - E_0\left[S(1)\right] + E_0\left[S(2)\right] - E_0\left[S(2)\right] = \theta \qquad (7.13)$$

$$E_0{}^*\left(\pi_2\right) = E_0{}^*\left[S(2)\right] - E_0\left[S(2)\right] = \theta \qquad (7.14)$$

The NPV of the strategy is clearly then

$$NPV = \frac{\theta}{1+r} + \frac{\theta}{(1+r)^2} \qquad (7.15)$$

which is positive. The firm accepts the project.

The second strategy is called a *stack-and-roll* trade in which the marketer goes long two one-period contracts from 0 to 1 and a single one-period contract from 1 to 2. Now consider the cash flows on the stack-and-roll trade:

$$\pi_1 = 2[F(1,1) - F(0,1)] = 2[S(1) - F(0,1)]$$

$$\pi_2 = [F(2,2) - F(1,2)] = S(2) - F(1,2)$$

which implies time 0 conditional expected cash flows of

$$E_0^*(\pi_1) = 2E_0^*[S(1)] - 2E_0[S(1)] = 2\theta$$

$$E_0^*(\pi_2) = E_0^*[S(2)] - E_0^*\{E_1[S(2)]\} = E_0^*[S(2)] - E_0[S(2)] = \theta$$

The NPV of the stack-and-roll is

$$NPV = \frac{2\theta}{1+r} + \frac{\theta}{(1+r)^2} \qquad (7.16)$$

which is positive. The firm again accepts the project.

Several important points emerge from the NPVs shown in Equations 7.15 and 7.16. First, the NPV criterion literally states that firms should accept all positive NPV projects. With no assumptions about capital constraints and a linear expected profit function, theory tells us that the firm will accept both of these projects. In the limit, the firm actually will load up on an essentially unlimited number of long futures contracts. Or if not unlimited, the positions the firm will take at least will be enough to make tenuous our assumption that the marketer's trades never reveal its private information.

The other important point to note from Equations 7.15 and 7.16 is that the NPV of the stack-and-roll trade has expected profits that are strictly increasing in the size of the stack. Consequently, if the firm was, say, capital constrained (e.g., by funding requirements), the preferability of the stack-and-roll program over the multimaturity program in terms of expected profit alone would be clear.

The reason that the futures trades allow the firm to exploit its perceived informational advantage arises from the mis-pricing of the futures relative to the expected future spot price. When the futures contract matures, its value to the firm is equal to the then-prevailing spot price. At time 0, this is the firm's expectation of the future spot price. When the futures contracts are either initially quoted or marked to market, their values are based on the public's expectation of future spot prices. Consequently, the firm can appropriate the gain only when a contract actually reaches maturity.

Marking a contract to public information repeatedly yields a gain for the firm only when the contract matures. Rolling over from one maturing contract into a new one, however, enables the firm to earn a private information premium upon each rollover.

Information Acquisition and the Hedged Customer Swap Because the NPV of the customer contracts is negative and the NPV of a futures trade is positive, the firm would never engage in the former without some additional reason for doing so. But in a world of asymmetric information, the customer contracts themselves may be the key mechanisms by which the firm acquires its perceived superior information. By learning its customers' demand functions, some firms can better anticipate calendar and geographical basis shifts. Viewed in this way, the θ paid each period in the swap can be viewed as the marginal cost of information acquisition that enables the firm to profit by combining the futures with the swap.

First suppose the marketing firm offers the customer swap hedged with multimaturity futures. In this case, the realized cash flows each period are

$$\pi_1 = K - S(1) + F(1,1) - F(0,1) + F(1,2) - F(0,2)$$
$$= [K - F(0,1)] + [F(1,2) - F(0,2)]$$
$$\pi_2 = K - S(2) + F(2,2) - F(1,2) = K - F(1,2)$$

The time 0 conditional expected cash flows of the firm are

$$E_0^*(\pi_1) = K - E_0[S(1)]$$
$$E_0^*(\pi_2) = K - E_0[S(2)]$$

When we substitute in the competitive swap rate from Equation 7.9, we see that the NPV of the program is zero. More specifically, the θ earned each period on the hedge is exactly offset by the θ paid each period on the customer marketing contracts. The cost of information acquisition thus is equal to its benefit at the margin, and the firm cannot take advantage of its proprietary information at all.

Now consider the stack-and-roll as a hedge of the marketing contract. The time 1 and 2 realized cash flows are

$$\pi_1 = K - S(1) + 2[F(1,1) - F(0,1)] = K - F(0,1) + S(1) - F(0,1)$$

$$\pi_2 = K - S(2) + F(2,2) - F(1,2) = K - F(1,2)$$

which yields conditional expected cash flows of

$$E_0{}^*(\pi_1) = K - E_0[S(1)] + E_0{}^*[S(0)] - E_0[S(1)] = K - E_0[S(1)] + \theta$$

$$E_0{}^*(\pi_2) = K - E_0[S(2)]$$

When the competitive swap rate is substituted into these expected cash flows, the time 0 conditional expected net present value of the customer contract hedged with the stack-and-roll is

$$NPV = \frac{\theta}{1+r}$$

which is strictly positive. This is not surprising given what we saw earlier in Equation 7.16. Namely, the rollover of two contracts at time 1 nets the firm 2θ at that time. Because only θ is paid in the customer contract for information acquisition costs in that period, the firm earns the residual θ as pure expected profit.

In this example, the asymmetry of information between the marketing firm, its customers, and the general futures market allows the firm to make money on the information it has. This profit is limited, however, by the cost of acquiring its special information, which is the cost of the swap program itself. Nevertheless, in this model the firm makes money and increases its value from exploiting its perceived information advantage in the manner set forth.

The Importance of Financial Distress[3]

The model in the prior section is hardly a justification by itself for "risk management." Even assuming the customer swaps are required to give the firm its private information, which it exploits by hedging those swaps, the particular assumptions we made about the nature of the informational symmetry drive the result. In general terms, if a firm has private information about the relation between a spot and futures price, it must have private information either about the spot price itself or the futures price itself. And if it does, then "hedging" is a stylized excuse for outright position taking. The firm should simply short unlimited quantities of the overpriced security and buy unlimited quantities of the underpriced security.

A more palatable justification for risk management in the world of private information is when we combine our present assumption about asymmetric information with our earlier assumption about exogenous bankruptcy costs to generate a theory of selective hedging à la Working. In this case, a firm with private information could not simply buy or sell unlimited quantities of a mis-priced security—not without greatly increasing its expected bankruptcy costs. Risk management thus enables firms with private information to exploit that information without increasing the risk of bankruptcy.

Recall that we have argued risk management is essentially a substitute for equity capital. Accordingly, the types of firms we might most expect to engage in the sort of *selective* risk management that Working describes as carrying-charge hedging will have capital structures that predispose them to some form of financial distress possibility. To illustrate the link between capital structure and risk management when a firm has the opportunity to exploit a comparative information advantage, let us return to a slightly revised version of Figure 4.6. In Figure 7.11, the value of the firm is depicted in the presence of bankruptcy costs that increase linearly with the shortfall of net assets below the face value of debt outstanding, FV. When assets are equal to A_2, for example, the value of the firm is $V_2 = A_2 - C$, where C is the cost of financial distress that gets larger the lower that assets fall. Unlike Figure 4.6, bankruptcy costs are not constant, but unlike Figure 4.7, nor do they change at an increasing rate. In Figure 7.11, the cost of financial distress increases at a constant rate as assets fall below debt.

Four probability distributions are shown for four different types of firms. The distribution denoted $f_3(A)$ is clearly a well-capitalized, highly rated firm. The probability that its assets will fall below the face value of debt is virtually zero. The opportunities for value-added risk management may not be very pronounced at a firm like this. The firm would likely not encounter distressed debt costs in the cash flow sense of FSS any more than it would run into traditional underinvestment problems. Risk management might well best be undertaken by the shareholders of a firm like this, just as M&M predicts.

As shown, opportunities to exploit asymmetric information also would not necessarily lead to hedging behavior for the firm whose assets have a

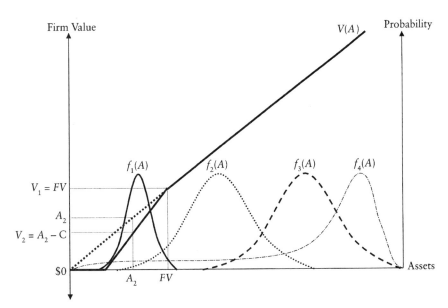

FIGURE 7.11   Capital structure and hedging.

distribution that looks like $f_3(A)$. Especially if that distribution *already re-flects* the trading activities in which it might engage to exploit an informa-tion advantage, the firm simply has no threat of incurring bankruptcy costs. If anything, this is the kind of firm you might well expect *to take outright speculative positions in the market.*

You might also expect the firm whose asset values are drawn from the distribution $f_1(A)$ to undertake speculative trading activities if it has an in-formational advantage, but for entirely different reasons. Clearly, the firm whose asset values are shown in distribution f_1 is in trouble. Debt holders will receive their full face value in almost no scenario, which means the eq-uity of this firm is virtually worthless. You could expect the asset substitu-tion problem at a firm like this to be quite severe. About the only way that equity will extract any value from its shares is to pursue extremely high vari-ance projects. If the firm believes itself better informed about a market or basis relation and covenants or other restrictions are not in place to prevent asset substitution, the firm well might try to exploit its informational ad-vantage through outright position-taking as the proverbial "last punt."

Now consider the firm whose assets are drawn from the distribution $f_2(A)$. Here the firm could appreciably reduce its expected costs of financial distress through hedging. But does that mean the firm should not take a position in the market to exploit its comparative information advantages?

Not necessarily. A firm like this one would have to be careful just how it constructs its hedge, but a well-constructed basis trade could actually involve a *net reduction* in expected bankruptcy costs while at the same time allowing the firm to *trade the basis* and try to exploit a comparative informational advantage.

Consider our earlier simple model of the oil marketing firm. If the firm offers unhedged customer contracts, its NPV is negative. And if the firm offers those contracts with a maturity matched hedge, it breaks even in a NPV sense *and* does not appreciably increase the probability it will run into financial distress. But if the firm tries to exploit its private information with the stack-and-roll hedge, there is almost no way it can generate a positive expected NPV strategy without also *increasing* its expected costs of financial distress. A firm with the distribution $f_2(A)$ is probably not the firm that would adopt this strategy.

Now consider a different example—say, an oil company that owns its own fields and tank farms. Suppose this firm considers its information about the convenience yield better than the rest of the market and believes futures are overpriced. In this case, the firm could short the futures *against the oil field,* simultaneously exploiting its perception that the futures are overpriced *and* reducing its expected bankruptcy costs. A firm with an asset distribution like f_3 might be tempted to *overhedge.* If its trading does not reveal its private information, after all, it will keep selling futures until the market corrects the mis-pricing. Because the firm with asset distribution f_3 has a long way to go before it ever encounters bankruptcy costs, there is no reason for the firm to stop hedging when the size of the hedge reaches the size of the oil field.

If the oil firm has a distribution f_2, however, the firm *would* stop at a 1:1 hedge, where every barrel of the oil field is hedged with a short futures position. The hedge, of course, is really an attempt to exploit its information that futures are mis-priced. The natural long exposure created by the oil field, however, is what makes it possible for the firm to exploit its information advantage through this hedge without increasing its expected bankruptcy costs.

What kind of distribution would our firm need to have to adopt the strategy we discussed earlier for the marketing firm that makes money only on the volatile stack-and-roll hedge? An example of such a firm might be the distribution denoted $f_4(A)$ in Figure 7.11. This distribution has a very high expected value, suggesting a high level of equity capital like the firm in f_3. But unlike the f_3 firm, this firm does face a positive probability, albeit small, of incurring financial distress costs. On the one hand, the high level of equity capital in this firm might lead it to try and exploit its comparative informational advantage through an outright position in the market. On the other hand, an outright position could increase expected bankruptcy costs. But if the firm pursued a stack-and-roll hedge, the net effect is not clear. The distribution f_4 is negatively skewed, but that does *not* mean a strategy that leads to a higher *variance* will necessarily increase the size of the left-hand tail. A firm with asset distribution f_4 thus could very easily pursue a strategy that increased its volatility in order to exploit a comparative informational advantage but did *not* lead to higher expected bankruptcy costs.

The example of the oil field owner with distribution f_2 and the marketing firm with distribution f_4 are classic examples of Working's carrying charge hedger. A perceived informational advantage leads the firm on a NPV basis to an opportunity to exploit a mis-pricing in the security markets. But the threat of bankruptcy prevents the firm from exploiting this information with outright speculation. So, the firm takes a *relative* position of one contract sold or bought against another. This kind of self-hedging transaction is a clear example of how risk management coupled with a trading strategy designed to exploit private information can increase the value of the firm.

CHAPTER 8

Value versus Cash Flow versus Earnings Risk Management

From a practical standpoint, the risk management process of a firm will always be targeted at decision variables (e.g., hedge ratios) that affect at least one dimension of the firm's financial condition: value, cash flows, and/or earnings. The value of the firm—the sum of the market values of its outstanding securities—is equal to the discounted expected net present value of all the future cash flows of the firm on current investment projects *plus* the option value of all future growth opportunities. In that sense, the value of the firm is inextricably linked to its cash flows. And similarly, earnings are basically just cash flows with the appropriate accounting overlay.

Despite the interconnections between a firm's value, earnings, and cash flows, these three alternative measures of a firm's financial condition can be quite different when viewed as strategic variables on which a risk manager is focusing. The distinction between value on the one hand and either earnings or cash flows on the other hand is the difference between a *stock* and a *flow.* The value of the firm is its value *at any specific point in time.* The cash flows or earnings of a firm occur over some *interval* of time. Controlling one of these does not always mean controlling another.

Some of the theories that explain why the value of the firm can be increased by risk management depend on whether the focus of the risk management is on value, cash flows, or earnings. Other theories can hold true for more than one of these financial targets. Knowing what these theories say about the dimensions of the firm's financial condition that should be the focus of the risk management program, however, is half the ball game.

The explanations for how risk management can add value to the firm in Chapters 4 through 7 differ along several broad dimensions, one of which is the financial variable that should be the focus of the risk management process of the firm. Firms can choose between essentially three financial summary measures on which to focus, depending on the sources of value-added for risk management—economic or market value of the firm or changes in that value over some period; net cash flows in some period, or accounting measures like earnings.

VALUE OR ASSET/LIABILITY RISK MANAGEMENT

Several of the theories presented in Chapters 4 through 7 presuppose that the risk management process of the firm is aimed at controlling the value of the firm, or, more specifically, the market value of its assets and liabilities. The firm may focus on value at a specific point in time—for example, the date that a debt issue must be repaid—or may choose to consider changes in the market value of the firm over a given interval of time. In either case, the presumed objective of the risk management process is to take actions that impact the firm's market value.

The most basic value-based explanation for how risk management can add increased security holder welfare is the reduction of expected bankruptcy costs. Unlike the under-investment model of FSS which relies on positive financial distress costs as a motivation for *cash flow* risk management, the classic Smith and Stulz model discussed in Chapter 4 applies only to economic *value*. As is plainly evident in Figures 4.5 to 4.8, a firm is presumed to experience financial distress costs when the market value of the firm's assets net of its non-debt liabilities falls below the face value of its outstanding debt. Firms may increase their value by hedging to reduce the probability of this asset shortfall occurring.

Carrying-charge hedging is also clearly a value-driven rationale for corporate risk management decisions because it is based on the ability of some firms to exploit deviations in expected values conditioned on their private information from observed market prices. In other words, one or more securities or assets must be mis-priced in a value sense in order for carrying-charge hedging to make sense.

As discussed in Chapter 7, asymmetric information *alone* is not enough to explain carrying-charge hedging. If every M&M assumption holds except symmetric information, the firm will simply sell/short the over-priced asset or buy/long the underpriced one. To explain the basis trade rather than an outright position, some form of financial distress costs are also required, and these financial distress costs *need not* pronounce themselves in an asset/liability context but might as easily be incurred through cash flows. A carrying-charge hedger subject to exogenous bankruptcy costs when assets fall below liabilities, however, might exploit its asymmetric information quite differently than a firm with the same comparative informational advantage but cash flow sensitivity. Specifically, the financial instrument choice will be affected—the former type of carrying-charge hedger should be indifferent to futures and forwards, whereas the basis trading activities of the latter will likely involve only OTC derivatives that are not subject to daily variation margin requirements.

CASH FLOW RISK MANAGEMENT

That a firm could increase its *value* by focusing on its *cash flows* might seem at once both completely obvious and completely counterintuitive. On the one hand, the value of the firm *is* its cash flows. On the other hand, cash flow *in any given period* might well have a negligible impact on the firm's financial condition.

Cash flow-based theories of value-enhancing risk management are distinct from value-based theories mainly in the sense of timing. A value risk manager is concerned about the value of the firm, either at a specific point in time (e.g., when debt must be retired) or over regular intervals (e.g., monthly changes in value). A cash flow risk manager, by contrast, is concerned with cash flows *whenever* they might occur. Minimizing the volatility of changes in firm *value* does not necessarily imply the same hedge ratio as minimizing the volatility of *cash flows*.

Apart from different hedge ratios, the basic logic underlying the risk management strategy can differ between value and cash flow risk managers. Note how the motivation for value-added risk management differs, for example, between the under-investment model of FSS in Chapter 7 and the under-investment model of Myers in Chapter 6. In the Myers world, under-investment occurs because the firm has so much debt overhang that the value of new projects is seen to accrue to debt rather than equity. With equity bearing the risk, they simply reject certain projects. In the FSS model, the firm simply does not have the internal funds to make investment decisions without incurring external finance costs. True, Myers-like agency costs of debt can *lead* to external financing costs, but the cash flow model has that type of agency cost one step further removed.

In the Myers under-investment model, the role for value-added risk management was in reducing the effective leverage of the company. Risk management is used to reduce the entire firm's exposure that can eat through equity values and increase the relative proportion of debt in the capital structure. The hedges that make sense are aimed at hedging *value*. In the FSS cash flow model, risk management is not intended to reduce the effective leverage of a company as much as it is designed to reduce the firm's dependence on leverage *to fund certain investments*. Consequently, the appropriate risk management strategy in the FSS world is a hedge aimed at *cash flows*.

Although the cost of external debt is at the root of the two different under-investment models, the implications for risk management actually are extremely different. To a firm whose concern is that its equity holders walk away from positive NPV projects because they will increase the market value of debt and not equity with equity bearing the risk, hedging to reduce effective leverage in a value sense is reasonable. Such a firm could *also* hedge in a cash flow sense, because firm value is just the discounted NPV of cash flows. Lower per-period cash flow volatility means less volatility in firm value. But the converse is not true! A firm whose concern is that external financing costs will rise at the same time funds are needed for new investments but is *not* concerned with equity rejecting those investments due to a debt overhang will focus on cash flow hedging. A value hedge would *not* help a firm in that situation.

In addition to the under-investment theory of FSS, Jensen's agency cost of free cash flow analysis can also explain why some firms engage in cash flow risk management. Jensen proposes the issuance of debt as a solution to the free cash flow problem, but risk management is an equally viable solution. If the issue is reducing the cash flows that might be mis-invested in negative NPV projects, reducing cash flow volatility and reducing free cash flow through hedging can make sense.

Notice that the FSS model and the Jensen free cash flow agency model are inconsistent with one another. FSS argue that firms should hedge to reduce cash flow volatility and help ensure internal funds are available to fund new investments. Jensen argues that firms should issue debt in order to create a mechanism for disgorging those very free cash flows that FSS argue should be maximized. In the FSS model, more free cash flows are good, whereas in the Jensen model they are bad.

Whether or not a firm can engage in cash flow risk management to increase its value thus depends strongly on what the firm is *doing* with its cash flows. Increased internal funds for investment are sensible in the FSS model, but Jensen and Jensen and Meckling warn that managers may well not use those funds for investment purposes and may instead waste them on negative NPV projects.

EARNINGS AND ACCOUNTING RISK MANAGEMENT

Several of the theories explored in the preceding chapters imply that the firm's risk management process should focus on accounting measures of a firm's financial condition, such as earnings or net income. Hedging to reduce expected taxes when the firm faces a convex tax schedule, for example, is clearly risk management driven by accounting considerations. The relation between pre-tax and post-tax income in an accounting sense drives the tax liability of the firm, and hence is the source for risk management value added. Implementing a risk management process aimed at the market value of the firm or its cash flows may well fail to achieve the necessary reduction in *earnings* volatility required to reduce expected taxes.

Managing risk in order to increase the signal-to-noise ratio inherent in some accounting aggregate is also inconsistent with value and cash flow risk management. A firm may successfully reduce the volatility of both its market value and its cash flows, but if it does not simultaneously decrease the volatility of the noisy component of earnings or some other accounting measure of profitability, the signal extraction problem faced by analysts, counterparties, creditors, and the like may not be abrogated at all.

CHOOSING THE RIGHT MEASURE

Several of the theories explaining how the value of the firm can be increased by risk management are not specific in prescribing a value, earnings, or cash flow focus. Reducing managerial risk aversion, for example, requires that the risk management process of the firm target whatever variable is used as the basis for defining manager performance. This will quite plausibly be some accounting aggregate like earnings for formulaic compensation, but when managers are rewarded with financial instruments like stock options, their compensation becomes tied *directly* to the market value of the firm. If risk management is intended to change the actions of managers, a focus on whatever measure defines managerial compensation and risk aversion is appropriate.

Mitigating asset substitution problems also has no clear link to either value or cash flows and could be driven by either. Equity can expropriate debt by pursuing projects that are riskier *in a cash flow sense* if the firm faces external financing costs as in FSS. But equity can also expropriate debt by pursuing projects whose *values* have a higher volatility, even if the *cash flows* on the project are relatively stable over time.

In general, most of the theories explored have either value, cash flows, or earnings as an implied focus for the risk management actions and processes designed to increase firm value. Despite the implicit focus of these theories, however, most of these theories still make sense when value is substituted for cash flows or earnings, and conversely. Distinguishing between these measures of financial strength is not merely a matter of corporate indifference. Indeed, the risk management actions taken pursuant to one objective (e.g., cash flows) can often be inconsistent with actions that would be consistent with an alternative objective (e.g., cash flows), even when the risk management actions trace to a common theory.

To appreciate the importance of distinguishing between these different variables in risk management, consider three firms in the same business with the same financial risk exposures but with different capital structures and access to funding. Suppose all three firms are pharmaceuticals, like Omega Pharmaceutical in Chapter 7, whose revenues are subject to exchange rate risk. The three pharmaceuticals are summarized:

1. *Oak Pharmaceutical* is a German conglomerate financed with both debt and equity. Its primary creditors and equity holders, in typically German fashion, are the largest banks in Germany. Consequently, the firm has no need of obtaining external finance for its R&D activities.
2. *Cedar Pharmaceutical* is a U.S. conglomerate financed with both debt and equity. Its shareholders are mainly pension plans and institutional investors, and its debt is primarily in the form of public bonds.
3. *Elm Pharmaceutical* is a Swiss corporation financed entirely with equity.

Consider first the potential under-investment problem at each firm, with particular attention to the distinctions between Myers-style under-investment problems and Froot-Scharfstein-Stein-style under-investment problems. Oak Pharmaceutical is highly unlikely to need risk management as a way of increasing its debt capacity because it has so little dependence on external financing. Even if external financing is costly as in the FSS model, the firm can fund its R&D activities through borrowing from its existing shareholders and creditors, all of whom are closely held and large banks. Consequently, the firm does not need to worry about the consequences of cash flow volatility *unless* it translates into volatility in the value of the firm.

Notwithstanding the above, Oak Pharmaceutical might very well be concerned about reducing the expected costs of financial distress. If these costs do not accrue from the issuance of new debt, then they must occur more for the reasons outlined in Chapter 4 (i.e., a shortfall of assets below debt liabilities *in a market value sense* is costly). Oak Pharmaceutical thus is most likely to focus on the avenues by which risk exposures impact the market value of the firm rather than its net cash flows in any given period.

Oak Pharmaceutical also might still suffer from under-investment, but again it will be driven by value and not cash flow considerations. Supposing internal financing is available to fund all positive NPV investment projects at their true cost, Myers' agency cost of debt is still a problem even for *internal* financing. In other words, equity may still reject positive NPV projects because the benefits accrue primarily to debt. *This has nothing whatsoever to do with the volatility of the firm's cash flows.* Equity will walk away from the positive NPV projects *solely* because the effective exercise price on their options to invest is too high given the current market value of debt.

Cedar Pharmaceutical, by contrast, is dependent on external financing and may incur significant external financing costs if it attempts to fund new investment projects. In this case, the firm's equity holders will still have the same concerns as Oak about accepting positive NPV projects. But the firm *also* faces a constraint on its capital expenditures arising from its external financing costs. Any increases in cash flow volatility owing to sources other than R&D expenditures and drug production and sales thus unnecessarily jeopardize the firm's ability to accept new projects.

Now consider Elm Pharmaceutical, which experiences no current agency costs of debt or under-investment. Even then, however, the *future* opportunity to issue debt to finance new investment projects creates effects similar to the problems of both firms—Oak and Cedar. Depending on the amount of debt the firm must issue, if the debt is issued before the investment expenditures are made and before the outcome of the investment is known, under-investment might still occur for value-based reasons, as in Myers. If the debt must be issued to fund a project whose outcomes are known and good for both debt and equity, under-investment may occur anyway if cash flows are too volatile to allow the use of any internal funds.

A firm whose sole concern is the external cost of debt required to fund intangible investments is clearly a FSS-style *cash flow risk manager,* whereas a firm with plenty of cash whose equity holders reject positive NPV projects not because of a lack of funds but because the capital structure has too much debt will in turn be a *value risk manager.* And a firm whose primary concern is, say, the failure of analysts to perceive the true value of its investment projects likely will be an *earnings risk manager.*

The decision about whether or not to focus on value, cash flows, or earnings does not mean that risk management should ever be used for a purpose other than maximizing security holder welfare. In other words, a firm that does *not* manage *value risk* is not necessarily failing to maximize security holder welfare. As we have seen already, cash flows and earnings are hardly independent of value. The *value* of the firm, after all, is equal to its discounted future *cash flows.* And the *earnings* of a firm is driven by the accounting treatment of its cash flows and/or changes in value.

Despite the basic interconnections between value, cash flows, and earnings, the tactical implementation of a risk management program can wander badly off in the wrong direction if the objective is not chosen by the firm judiciously. Consider a very basic example of a firm near bankruptcy that encounters distressed debt costs every time it goes to the capital market for external funding. Suppose this firm makes aluminum ladders and sells them on a fixed-price basis—that is, increases in its aluminum purchase prices cannot be passed through to customers. The firm could lock in its effective purchase price for aluminum quite easily by going long aluminum futures. When aluminum prices rise, the gain on the futures will offset the higher purchasing costs and preserve the company's ability to invest.

Suppose, however, that aluminum prices *fall*. In this case, the firm is making a larger profit margin on its ladders sold from decreased input purchasing costs. But its futures contracts are losing money. Because futures are exchange-traded and marked to market at least twice daily, this means the firm has to pay margin to an exchange clearing house or futures commission broker in order to stay in the game. In other words, the firm has achieved a successful *value* hedge at the expense of *heightened cash flow volatility*. For this particular firm, the hedge does not accomplish its objectives. There is a failure in risk management. When aluminum prices are falling, the firm will now be spending its internal funds on margin calls rather than positive NPV investments—a perverse effect quite opposite to the one intended. Consequently, the opportunity for the firm to increase its value through reduced under-investment is eliminated simply by virtue of a poorly designed risk management process whose objectives did not match the firm's rationale for managing risk in the first place.

LINKING STRATEGY TO TACTICS

Part Three of this book deals with the tactics of risk management, but so central is the strategic choice of a financial measure on which to focus in the risk management process that the tactical consequences of this choice are previewed here by way of an example. Consider a commercial bank that funds the acquisition (at a premium) of a portfolio of fixed-rate mortgages with maturity-matched zero-coupon bonds. Figure 8.1 shows the relations between changes in the market values of the issued zeros and the mortgages, as well as the net of the two. When interest rates increase, the value of the bonds declines. Because the bonds are liabilities, the value of the *position* to the bank increases, and the zero-coupon nature of the bonds—implying a constant duration—means that the value of the bonds changes one-for-one with interest rates.

The value of the mortgages declines as rates rise because the mortgages represent a fixed asset to the firm. Unlike the bonds, moreover, the value of the mortgages declines *at a decreasing rate* when rates rise because higher rates cause a decline in prepayments on the mortgages. This reduction in prepayments lengthens the effective maturity of the mortgages. Conversely, a decline in rates leads to a decline in the value of the mortgage assets. For larger rate declines, the decline in value of the mortgages is less because pre-payments increase. In other words, the acceleration of prepayments on the mortgages when rates decline causes the value of the mortgages to rise at a decreasing rate.

Consider Figure 8.1 from a *value* perspective. On the one hand, the mortgage portfolio is being funded *and* pseudo-hedged by the bond. In a *value* sense, the portfolio gains a bit when rates rise, and is exposed to po-tentially major losses when rates fall. But from a *static cash flow* perspec-tive, the prepayments that rise when rates fall generates a *cash inflow* to the bank. In other words, rate declines precipitate a decline in value and an in-crease in cash flows. Conversely, when rates rise and the value of the port-folio rises marginally, prepayments slow and cash inflows are reduced.

A firm concerned with the value of its assets and liabilities might hedge the residual risk of this portfolio by buying a put option on interest rates—provided, of course, that the rate underlying the option is presumed to be reasonably correlated with the prepayment speed on the mortgage

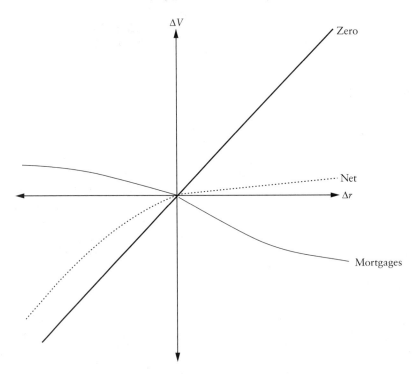

FIGURE 8.1   Relation between changes in interest rates and change in net value of a zero-funded acquired mortgage portfolio.

portfolio. In this case, declines in rates would precipitate a decline in value in the net bond-funded mortgage position that is offset by an increase in the intrinsic value of the put option, as shown in Figure 8.2. The bank now makes money whether rates rise or fall.

From a cash flow perspective, the purchase of this put would not seem to be necessary. A bank concerned with cash flows, in fact, might well consider purchasing *calls* in order to generate additional cash to offset the decline in net interest income associated with a decline in mortgage prepayments. But as Figure 8.3 shows, this doubles the bank's exposure to rate increases, thereby radically increasing its profitability in a rising rate environment, but provides no protection from rate declines. Nevertheless, a firm purely concerned with *cash flow* risk might well choose to adopt this hedge, which has now insured positive net cash flows in either a rising or declining rate environment.

From an earnings perspective, things get even more complex. Because the mortgage portfolio was presumed to be purchased at a premium, SFAS 91 applies. This accounting rule says that if a bank holds a large number

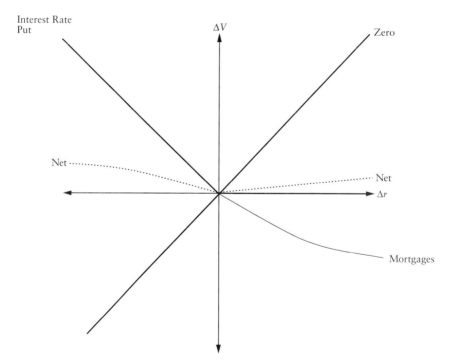

FIGURE 8.2   A value hedge of a zero-funded mortgage portfolio.

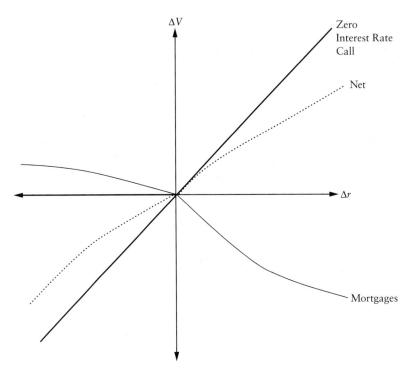

FIGURE 8.3 A cash flow hedge of a zero-funded mortgage portfolio.

of similar loans for which prepayments are probable and the timing and amount of prepayments can be reasonably estimated, the bank may consider those estimates of future prepayments in the calculation of the constant yield necessary to apply the interest income method. In the event of a difference between anticipated and actual prepayment speeds, the effective yield of the portfolio (with acquisition costs) must be recalculated and the portfolio balance adjusted to the level that would have existed had the effective yield been applied since the inception of the loan. The offsetting debit (credit) is applied to interest income, and future interest income is calculated using the new effective yield.

When rates decline, prepayments on the acquired mortgage portfolio increase. The *accounting* impact of this under SFAS 91 is an increase in the rate at which the premium paid for the portfolio can be amortized, resulting in lower portfolio acquisition income and a lower accounting yield on the portfolio. A rate decline thus causes a decline in earnings as the rate paid on the bond exceeds yield on the acquired portfolio.

Conversely, when rates rise and prepayments decline, the rate at which the premium paid for the portfolio can be amortized decreases. This results in higher portfolio acquisition income and an increase in the accounting yield on the portfolio. Rate increases thus imply increases in earnings as the rate paid on the bonds falls below the portfolio yield.

Figure 8.4 depicts the type of hedge that the bank might adopt if it is an earnings risk manager. Because prepayments drive the change in amortization rate of the premium paid for the mortgage portfolio, the hedge adopted will focus more on matching prepayments than value or cash flows. To accomplish this, the bank could enter into an amortizing principal interest rate swap, in which the bank pays a floating rate (e.g., the constant maturity treasury rate matching the bond's maturity) and receives a fixed rate. The amortization schedule of the notional principal used to compute net interest payments on the swap would match as closely as possible the expected prepayment schedule on the mortgage portfolio.

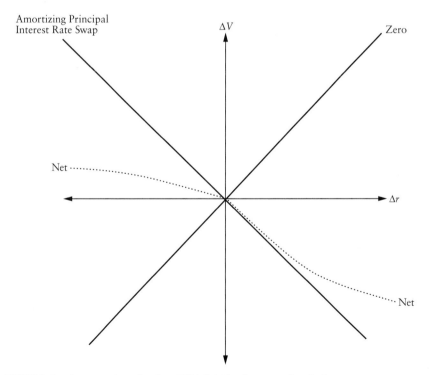

FIGURE 8.4   An earnings hedge (SFAS 91) of a zero-funded mortgage portfolio.

The floating-for-fixed swap generates income when rates fall. As long as the amortization schedule on the swap approximates the prepayments on the mortgage portfolio, the income on the swap can be used to offset the reduced income from the increased prepayments under SFAS 91. The swap thus acts as a hedge of earnings when rates fall. When rates rise, however, the swap offsets the bond liability and leaves the net exposure of the mortgage assets alone, which decline in value as rates rise.

Sometimes it is possible for more than one hedging objective to be accomplished at the same time. As Figure 8.4 shows, the earnings hedge leaves the bank exposed to *value risk* as rates rise. Although the lower prepayments when rates increase lead to higher earnings under SFAS 91, the net risk exposure of the bank leaves it vulnerable to a rate decline *in a market value sense*. The earnings hedge thus leaves the bank exposed to value risk. But in this case, the value risk can be addressed with the addition of a call on interest rates (i.e., cap), as shown in Figure 8.5. Now when rates rise, the value of the mortgage portfolio and the swap decline, but the decline in

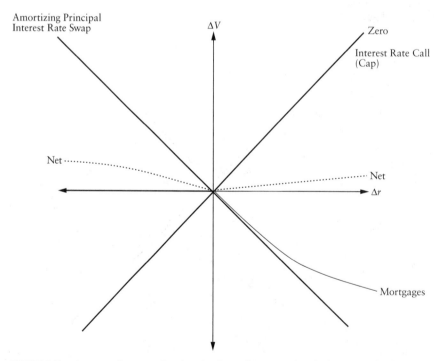

FIGURE 8.5   An earnings and value hedge of a zero-funded mortgage portfolio.

the value of the swap is offset with the cap. The resulting net between the bond and the mortgage portfolio returns the net value exposure to the same one shown in Figure 8.1—the natural exposure of the zero-funded mortgage portfolio. The cap thus *reversed* the effect of the swap for rate increases without interfering with the swap's ability to act as an earnings hedge when rates fall.

Inspecting Figure 8.5, it might appear that the bank could have adopted the same hedge as shown in Figure 8.2 and simply purchased a put or floor on rates. As a theoretical matter, this would work fine as a value *and* earnings hedge, provided the principal underlying the floor could be set to amortize at a rate approximating the expected prepayments on the mortgage portfolio. In practice, caps and floors with flexible amortization rates are extremely rare and quite expensive. Amortizing principal rate swaps, by contrast, are quite common. From a purely practical standpoint then, the non-amortizing principal floor acts as an adequate value hedge, but the amortizing principal swap plus non-amortizing principal cap are required to accomplish both value and earnings risk management.

Note that this value and earnings hedge is *not* a hedge that a cash flow risk manager would necessarily like. The swap completely neutralizes the bond when rates decline, leaving the bank with higher cash flows when rates fall as prepayments rise. When rates increase, however, the cash flow impact is unclear. Because the swap principal amortizes at a rate approximating prepayments, the principal amortization rate declines as rates rise and prepayments fall. This means a relatively higher proportion of cash outflows on the swap than cash inflows on the cap with a non-amortizing principal. If the principal on the cap *exceeds* the principal on the swap, the cash inflows on the cap exceed the cash outflows on the swap and the cash flow risk manager is happy; the net cash inflows on the hedge reduce the reduction in cash inflows on the mortgage portfolio resulting from a decline in prepayments. But if the principal on the cap is *less* than the amortized principal on the swap, the opposite is true and the bank experiences a net cash outflow larger than before.

In this connection, *none* of the hedges explored in Figures 8.2 through 8.5 are *perfect*. As the old saying goes, a perfect hedge can be found only in a Japanese garden. Because caps and floors cannot realistically be acquired with amortizing principals, most of the hedges are subject to basis risk arising from principal mismatches between the hedging instruments and the underlying mortgage portfolio. But even setting aside those basis risks, the example still shows plainly that *why* the bank hedges will affect *how* the bank hedges.

CHAPTER 9

Total versus Selective
Risk Management

All the theories reviewed of how risk management can increase security holder welfare are aimed at diversifiable risks in the equilibrium sense, and diversifiable risks can be separated trivially into more specific event-driven categories as outlined in Chapter 1. But one *problem* with most of the theories presented is that they do not lend themselves to the Knightian perspective of separating risk into *business* and *financial* risk. Specifically, many of the theories explored either say nothing about *which risks* the firm is managing or tell a firm that *all risks are created equal.*

Whether looking at risk through a value, cash flow, or earnings lens, some of the theories of value-added risk management prescribe a *total risk* perspective—the firm should reduce *any* risks that contribute to the problem at hand. If the firm can achieve an increase in value from a reduction in expected taxes, for example, the firm should reduce *any* risks that increase pre-tax earnings volatility. Both Myers' and FSS's under-investment problems imply a similar total risk management perspective—to reduce under-investment, the firm either should hedge *any* risk that allows it to increase its debt capacity (Myers) or should hedge *all risks* that contribute to cash flow volatility (FSS).

Other theories explored are not quite as strong in prescribing a total risk perspective, but nor do they help firms figure out what risks to reduce and what risks to leave alone. Hedging to reduce the exogenous expected costs of bankruptcy, for example, can be accomplished by hedging *anything,* provided the probability of bankruptcy is reduced. Unlike, say, the FSS model which clearly says *all* cash flow volatility should be eradicated, the rationale for risk management of reducing expected financial distress costs only implies that risk must be reduced *just enough* to drive the expected cost of bankruptcy to zero.

Consider the three probability distributions from which asset values are drawn in Figure 9.1, f_1, f_2, and f_3. Each distribution has successively less risk, but also less potential for upside profits. Despite the lower potential for upside profits, the value of the firm is higher for distribution f_3 than for f_2 and higher for f_2 than f_1 because the expected costs of bankruptcy are lower in each case. Consequently, a hedge that reduces volatility and tightens the distribution from f_1 to f_2 is good, and one that reduces volatility to distribution f_3 better still.

Now suppose that the firm in question is English Petroleum (EP), and that distribution f_1 is the distribution of EP's assets when it is exposed to currency and oil price risk. By hedging only currency risk, EP's asset distribution is shifted to f_2. And by hedging both currency and oil price risk, the distribution tightens to f_3.

Purely from an expected bankruptcy cost standpoint, EP might choose to hedge both its currency and its oil price risks, thereby reducing its expected costs of financial distress to zero. But from a Knightian perspective, EP might be reluctant to make the same decision. To hedge against the risk of currency fluctuations might seem to make sense for an oil company with no obvious comparative informational advantage about exchange rates. But

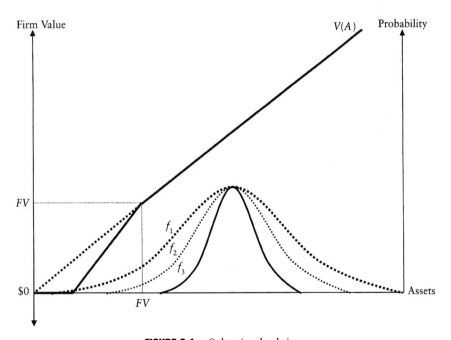

FIGURE 9.1 Selective hedging.

to remove itself from all oil price exposure would be to convert an oil company into an oil *logistics* company. In other words, the hedge of oil price risk that moves EP from f_2 to f_3 might indeed reduce the expected costs of bankruptcy, but it also has the effect of taking the firm out of the oil business and leaving it purely in the logistics business of extracting oil from the ground without bearing any oil price risk.

Some firms do profitably operate logistics companies and bear very little price risk. EP might well be one of those firms. But EP might as easily *not* be one of those firms. After all, what company is likely to know more about oil prices than a large oil producer? And if EP has better information about oil prices than its competitors and other market participants, why should it remove itself from the business by hedging?

As shown in Figure 9.1, if a firm has a choice, it will choose *first* to hedge the risks about which it is relatively less informed and *second* to hedge those risks in which it might possess some comparative informational advantage. In some cases, the firm might opt not to take the second step. In Figure 9.1, the firm *will* take the second step, but this is an artifact of the way the distributions have been drawn.

Consider instead Figure 9.2 in which EP's unhedged asset distribution is f_1, its distribution of assets after hedging FX risk is f_2, and its distribution of assets after hedging oil price risk f_3. Now the choice is not so obvious for EP. Taking the step from f_1 to f_2 reduces the firm's expected bankruptcy costs, but it also reduces the expected *value* of assets from A_1 to A_2. At the same time, however, the hedging of FX risk has shifted the *shape* of the distribution from symmetric to positively skewed, so that EP now has a higher probability of realizing a very high asset value than before.

If EP takes the second step and hedges its oil price risk, its asset distribution shifts from f_2 to f_3. The expected value of assets rises from A_2 back to A_1, and expected bankruptcy costs are now eliminated. But in hedging its oil price risk, the firm has now eliminated the positive skew that arose when it hedged only FX risk, so the firm's opportunity for realizing high net asset values is now greatly reduced.

How far will EP go in its hedging decision in Figure 9.2? Will the firm hedge its FX risk to reduce expected bankruptcy costs and trade the lower expected asset value for the higher probability of big asset value appreciations? If not, why not? And if so, will the firm take the second step and hedge its oil price risk, further reducing expected financial distress costs and increasing expected asset values but totally eliminating the potential for large profits?

Purely from an expected bankruptcy cost standpoint, the firm will hedge all its risks. And therein lies the problem with that and many other *total risk* theories of risk management. Figure 9.2 illustrates why it is not at

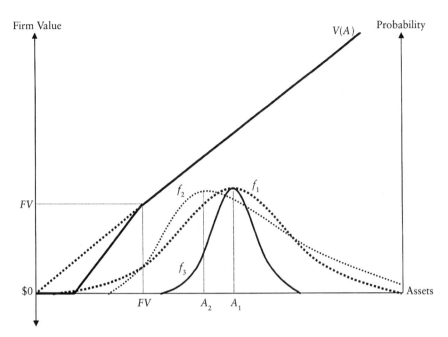

FIGURE 9.2 Selective hedging with asymmetric information.

all obvious the firm would be making the correct decision if it chooses to hedge all the way.

Unfortunately, theories of *selective* risk management are not well-developed. There is really no corporate finance model out there to explain why a firm might choose to hedge from f_1 to f_2 and *not* to hedge from f_2 to f_3, but Figure 9.2 makes it quite clear that in certain circumstances a firm might very well decide not to take this second step.

Risk Management and Business Strategy

CHAPTER 10

Risk Culture and Risk Management Business Models

The lens through which managers and directors of a company view its financial and business risks and organizationally manage those risks define the firm's *risk culture*. In conventional corporate risk cultures, risk management is perceived as a cost center whose primary purpose is the reduction of financial risks that are seen to be undesirable virtually *a priori*. Risk reduction is usually achieved with the aid of expensive analytical systems and costly risk transformation products provided by swap dealers, insurance companies, exchanges, and clearing houses—products that appear to have little or no value to shareholders aside from helping companies avert catastrophic losses. In other words, the classical view of risk management is as a necessary evil.

In this chapter and throughout much of the rest of this book, an alternative risk culture is also explored in which firms leverage their internal risk management processes into potentially significant efficiency gains and new product development opportunities. In this new risk culture, financial risk is not a problem to be solved, but rather a vital component of business and a critical source of innovation and growth. With proper attention to the business processes of governance, product management, customer management, and knowledge management, a well-designed risk management process thus can be viewed not as a cost center, but as a business.

RISK MANAGEMENT AS A BUSINESS PROCESS

Risk management as an organizational process can be separated into five general activities: identify risks and determine tolerances; measure risks;

This chapter is based on Culp and Planchat (2000).

monitor and report risks; control risks; and oversee, audit, tune, and re-align the risk management process (Figure 10.1). Some firms structure this process with more formality and centralization than others, but *all* firms manage risk in this five-step process—whether they realize it or not.

Identify Risk and Determine Tolerances

Risk identification is the process by which a company recognizes and, in some cases, detects the different financial risks to which it is exposed through the normal course of conducting its business. Almost by definition, the risks that are most insidious for a company are those risks to which it is exposed that have *not* been identified.

Risks can be left unidentified for reasons ranging from poor internal controls that allow the unnoticed booking of risky financial transactions to basic oversight of fundamental exposures. The process by which members of a company review, analyze, and discuss their risk profiles is an indispensable means by which risks can be identified, and, hence, managed.

Companies whose risk profiles do not change very frequently often fall prey to thinking that risk identification is not a crucial component of the risk management process. Nevertheless, numerous examples provide strong evidence to the contrary. Had Barings properly identified the huge long position on Japanese equities accumulated in Singapore by rogue trader Nick Leeson, the firm might not have gone bust. Had Procter & Gamble identified the massive interest rate risk affecting its treasury through a naked swap contract, the company might have avoided several hundred million dollars in losses.[1]

To take a simple example of the importance of risk identification, consider a hypothetical company called Airline FlyMe that transports passengers

FIGURE 10.1   The internal risk management process.

from the United States to Switzerland and back. The obvious risks faced by the company include the risk of plane crashes, maintenance-related delays, equipment damage from fire, and a loss of customers. Less obvious but perhaps equally significant are also the financial risks to which Airline FlyMe may be subject, such as the risk of rising jet fuel prices or the risk of fluctuations in the franc/dollar exchange rate. Without a systematic process to analyze these different risk exposures, Airline FlyMe's shareholders may never realize fully the different avenues through which the value of their capital can be adversely affected.[2]

Given the risks a company has identified, senior managers and directors must agree on tolerable levels of those risks required for the operation of the firm's primary business. This determination should be made explicitly by the firm's key stakeholders, including senior managers, the board of directors, and sometimes major creditors.

Measure Risks

Risk measurement involves the quantification of certain risk exposures for the purpose of comparison to company-defined risk tolerances. The process by which different risks are quantified is a critical component in an organization's broad risk management program. Without a good *measure* of risk, a determination can be hard to reach about whether the company is taking too much of some types of risks—or, conversely, not enough of another! Methods of measuring risk are discussed in more detail in Chapter 15.

Monitor and Report Risk

A third component of the risk management process is risk monitoring and reporting. The risks to which a firm is subject can change for two reasons. The first is a change in the composition of a company's assets or liabilities. To monitor changes in risk arising for this reason, firms generally rely on simple tools such as open position reports, statements of current payables and receivables, and the like. But the risks affecting a firm may also change simply because the factors affecting the cash flows on its assets or liabilities (or the discount rates for those cash flows) fluctuate. In Airline FlyMe's case, for example, the jet fuel risk profile could change either because additional fuel must be purchased above the company's baseline natural risk exposure estimate *or* because rising prices increase the cost of existing purchase requirements.

The frequency with which a firm monitors its current risk profile depends on the nature of the risks to which the firm is subject, as well as the ability of the firm to fine-tune its risk-taking activities. A trading firm in the business of selling options, for example, may monitor its market risk as often as intraday using tools like value at risk (VaR) to recalculate potential losses. Airline FlyMe, however, may monitor its jet fuel risks significantly less often. Not only does the risk profile of the airline change more slowly, but the firm may not be willing to incur the costs to control its risks more often than, say, monthly or quarterly.

Control Risks

Closely related to risk monitoring is risk control, or the actions a firm takes to keep its actual risk profile at or below its risk tolerance. Sound risk control decisions are only possible when the measurement and risk monitoring/reporting parts of the process are working properly. In other words, unless a firm can compare its actual risks to its risk tolerances, the firm cannot determine whether actions should be taken to reduce those risks except on a purely ad hoc basis.

In some cases, a company's risk control response to a divergence between actual and desired risk exposures is to take no action. If the cost of closing the gap is larger than the gap, for example, hedging would end up *costing* shareholders. Consequently, a well-functioning risk management process does *not* always yield actions that change the risk profile of the company. But if the risk profile of the company *can* be changed in a manner by which the marginal benefit of the change in exposure is equal to its marginal cost, risk management products are the means by which this is possible.

Risk control can be undertaken *ex ante* or *ex post*. The former usually involves internal controls on risk-taking activities that prevent actions from being taken *ex ante* that would increase the risk of a company beyond its tolerance. Market and credit risk limits are typical such controls, and may require, for example, that traders seek advance approval before executing a contemplated deal that would push the firm's actual risks above its tolerance level. Risk management products like position-keeping and monitoring systems are often essential support systems for a sound system of internal controls on financial risk.

Risk transformation products are also essential components of the risk control process. A company can use trading, clearing, and insurance products to close the gap between actual risk exposures and the target *ex post*. Purchasing fire insurance, for example, is a risk control action taken to address the natural exposure of the firm to the operational risk of fires. Similarly, Airline FlyMe must somehow reduce its annual natural exposure to jet fuel price increases on .5X gallons of its fuel purchases. This exposure reduction can be accomplished by going long .5X gallons of fuel using derivatives such as futures, forwards, options, or swaps.

If Airline FlyMe opted instead to define a loss-based target to ensure that the net margin of its fuel purchases is locked in rather than a quantity of fuel, the risk management products used would still likely consist of futures, forwards, options, and swaps. In that case, however, the tactical implementation of the hedge (i.e., hedge ratio, rebalancing frequency, instrument mix) would differ from the quantity-matched hedging case.

Oversee, Audit, Tune, and Realign

The final component of a properly functioning risk management process is risk audit and oversight and the fine tuning of the risk management process itself. This includes everything from external audits of risk management policies and procedures to internal reviews of quantitative exposure measurement models. In essence, risk audit and oversight is the process by which the firm addresses whether or not its risk management process is working properly and efficiently.

This final step in the risk management process, as Figure 10.1 demonstrates, feeds back into the first step of risk identification and determination of risk tolerances. In other words, the risk management process is a *dynamic* one, with each repeated iteration involving the incorporation of information obtained in previous implementation of the process.

The passage of time throughout the evolution of the risk management process is not instantaneous and can create significant differences between the expectations of senior managers and the actual implementation of the risk management process. Especially if the risk management process is time-consuming to implement initially, this stage of the process provides the critical opportunity for managers and directors to *realign* their goals and try to ensure that the design of the risk management process matches the current needs of the corporation.

THREE BUSINESS MODELS

Corporations can utilize their internal risk management processes in at least three different ways. Some firms rely on their risk management process solely for the purpose of internal risk control and policy compliance. Others leverage their own internal risk management expertise into the supply of risk management products that are demanded by their customers for risk control purposes. And still other firms utilize the risk management process to help identify and achieve efficiency gains in other business processes. How a firm utilizes its risk management process depends on the degree to which they treat risk management as a business, and firms tend to evolve over time from one category to the next, as illustrated in Figure 10.2.

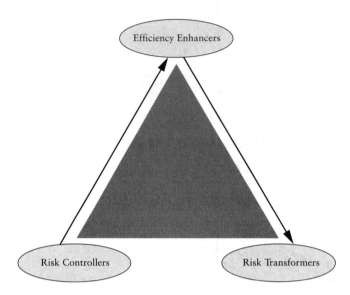

FIGURE 10.2 Three business models for managing risk.

Classical Risk Controllers

Classical Risk Controllers are those firms that allocate resources to a risk management process exclusively in order to avoid losses in excess of shareholders' risk tolerances. Firms of this type do not view risk management as a source of opportunity, but rather as a cost center deemed necessary for the prevention of undesired losses in excess of stakeholder risk preferences.

For firms whose business model is *Risk Control,* gaps between actual risk exposures and target risk exposures often must be closed with risk transformation products. In addition, the internal risk management process at such firms usually involves significant emphasis of concepts like the following: summary risk measures such as VaR policy and procedures reviews; evaluations of the effectiveness of hedging strategies; hedge ratio calculation and rebalancing; credit risk management and monitoring; collateral management; cash management; and the like.

Third parties providing risk management and risk transformation products and services often meet the risk management needs of classical Risk Controllers. On the financial product side, suppliers of risk transformation solutions include swap dealers, exchanges, clearing houses and associations, insurance companies, and other agents. Risk Controllers also often spend significant amounts of money on consulting services provided by accounting firms and a few specialized risk advisory consulting firms, as well as on software applications.

Efficiency Enhancers

Firms that leverage their risk management process into efficiency enhancements in other, nonrisk-related business lines are, like firms that utilize risk management for pure risk control, concerned primarily with managing risk for their own internal purposes and not with providing risk management products to other firms in the marketplace. But the focus of firms with an Efficiency Enhancement business model is on the *strategy* of risk management, rather than on the *tactical* implementation issues raised by firms with a Risk Control business model.

Firms adopting the Efficiency Enhancement model seek to use risk control tools not just for classical risk control, but rather to operate their businesses more effectively. Firms that demand risk management services for efficiency enhancement purposes, moreover, often utilize risk management products that are quite distinct from those used by firms in the Risk Control category. Of paramount importance are strategic consulting services rather than precanned software solutions and over-used policy and procedure templates.

Risk Transformers

Companies that pursue a Risk Transformation business model tend to view risk management primarily as a business opportunity. The design of new financial products was once largely the domain of investment and merchant banks, swap dealers, and insurance companies. An interesting feature of this market segment, however, is that it is increasingly being served by firms that have evolved from being *demanders* of risk management products for Efficiency Enhancement purposes into *suppliers* of financial innovations. Nonfinancial firms like ABB, Siemens, The Andre Group, and Daimler-Chrysler are providing more traditional financial intermediaries with serious competition as they offer their clients more integrated, customer-driven risk management products and solutions.

Although firms with this business model have moved away from using risk management purely for internal purposes, they are still also demanders of other products and services in at least two ways. First, they may continue to require risk management products like systems to conduct their own internal risk management processes. Second, these firms may demand trading, insurance, and clearing products to help offset any new financial risks created by their entrance into financial R&D.

Some firms that supply risk transformation solutions to risk control demanders of risk management products and services do so as their core business. Swap dealers and insurance companies are obvious examples. But for nonfinancial firms that have migrated from the Risk Control and Efficiency Enhancement models to the Risk Transformation business model, an alternative implementation strategy may be required. Specifically, new risk management businesses are often set up on the periphery of a firm's existing business, challenging both the conventional business model *and* the status quo corporate culture. Accordingly, most new businesses should be set up as *incubators* outside the traditional business model and yet still be under the control of the designer.

DETERMINANTS OF THE BUSINESS MODEL

The position of any given firm in Figure 10.2 may well change over time. Firms like Siemens and ABB, for example, once focused more on risk control and efficiency enhancement than financial R&D and the provision of risk transformation products and services.

Where a company lies in this cycle and the degree to which a firm can utilize and leverage that risk management process to exploit commercial business opportunities depends on several key factors. These factors or generalized business processes include governance, product management, customer management, and knowledge management, and how each of these processes interact with the internal risk management process of the firm in question. The interaction between these generalized business processes and a firm's internal risk management process characterizes the company's risk culture.

Governance

The business process of governance is critical at each stage of the internal risk management process. Sound internal risk management, for example, requires independence of risk management decisions from risk-taking activities to preserve the integrity of the risk management process. Apart from the role of governance *in* the risk management process, however, governance as a more general business process also helps characterizes the relation *between* that internal risk management process and new business opportunities.

A sound governance process for a corporation should provide the proper organizational support for the design, implementation, evaluation, and tuning of a company's risk management strategy. For those firms wishing to limit their risk management activities to internal risk management, the key success factors for a sound governance process will include the following: independence between risk-taking and risk-controlling areas of the firm; clear determinations of risk tolerances by senior managers and directors; regular outside reviews of the process; and the like.

A firm that wishes to mobilize its internal risk management expertise into externally offered products, by contrast, faces some additional governance issues. First, the firm must ensure that the risks of supplying risk transformation products is managed in the internal risk management process. Second, governance processes should ensure consistency between the definition and treatment of risk internally and in externally supplied products. Finally, a critical role for governance is ensuring the separation of management responsibilities for the supply of risk management products and the implementation of the internal risk management process.

Whether a firm is restricting its attention to risk control issues or is leveraging its risk management process into efficiency gains and product development, sound governance also should try and ensure that resources are allocated to the risk management process in a responsible fashion— namely, in a fashion that attempts to equate the benefits of risk management to its costs. For firms focused on risk control, governance often means avoiding the temptation to believe that the company has taken all the steps it needs for due diligence by investing a fortune in a piece of risk management software. And conversely, the functionality of the software purchased to assist internal risk managers should be adequate and yet not include too many redundant features, and sound governance processes are necessary to help organizations draw that distinction.

Product Management

Companies that wish to transform internal risk management processes, tools, and expertise into customer-vended products must be extremely attentive to their customer product mix. This mix may include a combination of risk transformation vehicles like insurance solutions, risk advisory services, and systems-based risk management customer solutions.

Financial risk management products come in essentially three varieties. The first is the risk transformation product, or any financial product that allows a firm to alter its financial risk profile. Risk transformation products include trading and clearing products (e.g., securities, futures, and listed options), over-the-counter derivatives (e.g., forwards and swaps), and insurance contracts. Such products are especially important to firms in the risk control component of the risk management process shown in Figure 10.1.

A second type of risk management product is advisory services. Advisory services include consulting services provided concerning any aspect of a risk management process, as well as transaction structuring advisory services that may play a role in selecting any risk transformation products acquired by a company.

Finally, risk management products include decision-support systems that can have a wide range of applications to the risk management process.

Designing Products for Customer   Rarely is the design and marketing of financial products viewed as the same type of problem as the design and marketing of, say, chemicals or razor blades, in which customer demand dictates the nature of the product mix. When the product innovation principles that apply to *physical* products are utilized in the financial engineering process, the outcome is tailored customer financial products and services delivered at a reasonable cost that help the offering firm secure wider market coverage and higher customer retention rates.

One principle of product design often overlooked in the marketing of financial products is the risk profile of the customer and how much the customer is willing to pay for that risk profile. In certain competitive markets, the product mix is essentially given, thus precluding risk-based pricing. Consequently, nonprice mechanisms must be used to try and manage the risks of providing such products.

A means by which companies can leverage their internal risk management expertise into new products for customers is by developing new customer-oriented products that allow customers to price their own risk. When competitive forces dictate the pricing of the basic product, the company must use its own insights into the risk management process to provide *new products* that essentially price risk indirectly through the differences in the product mix, *rather than* observed differences in the pricing of the same product.

Customer Management

A key factor that drives firms to move away from using risk management processes solely for risk control is customer relationship management. Economies of scope are realized when the same input—such as information—can be used multiple times by a firm to reduce total costs. Banks, for example, have always been thought to enjoy economies of scope from their collection and analysis of information about their customers' credit risks.[3] Once that information has been collected for a loan, that same information then reduces the costs to the bank of providing the same customer with other services, such as brokerage or capital markets intermediation.

Increasingly, nonfinancial corporations face similar economies of scope and are enjoying the same informational advantage as banks through their multiproduct dealings with customers. As an example, consider a trade finance provider whose principal business is lending to customers to finance exports and imports. Through knowledge of its customers' total business portfolios, these firms are well-positioned to leverage that customer information into the provision of risk management products and services. The trade financier might provide, for example, outsourced risk measurement to its trade finance clients, thereby both serving its clients's needs *and* helping ensure its customers do not default or fail to hedge the collateral of their trade credits.

Banks can provide that sort of service, as well, and have done so for many years with little competition. But unlike a bank, the trade financier is *also* active in the physical markets in which its customers are operating. Accordingly, they have the same information about their customers as banks and the added knowledge of expertise in the specific product markets in which their clients are active. Not surprisingly, firms like Cargill Investor Services, Cargill Financial Services, and Andre's FinCo. have been extremely successful in making the leap from the Efficiency Enhancement model to the Risk Transformation model, at the expense of their classical bank and investment bank competitors.

Achieving the Balance for Success   Utilizing risk management processes to serve customers requires a balanced alignment of corporate strategy, operations, and culture. On the strategic side, a company must address the following questions:

- To whom do we sell risk management products and services?
- What specific risk management products and services do we sell?
- With whom do we compete?
- How do we win?

Clearly and positively answering these strategic questions, however, is not enough. Equally important is a customer-focused organization and culture. For firms whose past experience with risk management is purely the Risk Control model, some shift in the corporate culture will be essential to leverage the internal risk management process to an external set of products and services. (See the discussion of culture in the Knowledge Management section that follows.) This shift requires the firm to organize itself for success, drive attitudes and behaviors within the firm toward a new strategic customer-centric vision, and fill any critical skill gaps.

Aside from aligning strategic goals with corporate culture, the operational excellence of the risk management process is probably the key ingredient to sound customer management. To ensure excellence in this process, the firm should know those risk management activities in which it excels, how it interacts with customers, and how it leverages its risk technology, systems, and processes for competitive advantage.

Knowledge Management

A final business process that plays a critical role in determining how well a company can leverage its internal risk management process into efficiency gains and externally supplied risk transformation products is knowledge management. Many of the risk management tools, systems, and models used by a firm in its internal risk management can be used to develop financial products, as well as supply advisory services and systems solutions to customers. But this requires careful attention to the management of information and knowledge between the various parts of the company.

Returning to our trade finance company, the firm's internal risk management process will include models used for evaluating customer credit risk, as well as models used to determine the effectiveness of customer hedging strategies. No matter how sound the models used by the internal risk managers for these purposes, they are only as good as the degree to which they are understood and utilized by line credit officers and account managers. The ability of credit officers to achieve maximum productivity gains from models and other tools, moreover, depends not just upon the models themselves, but also upon the extent to which knowledge and information are being effectively communicated by the division of the company that maintains the models to the line credit officers.

A significant part of the challenge in optimizing the personnel-to-tools tradeoff is ensuring that business line account managers and the risk management division are achieving the appropriate level of knowledge sharing. The ideal credit scoring model, for example, will be of limited use if business line managers do not understand its uses and applications. Similarly, a credit scoring model developed by an internal risk manager with no input from business line managers may lack many of the features that would enable the line approval process to become more standardized and automated.

To optimize the knowledge management issues related to risk management, a firm must address four dimensions simultaneously: content, process, culture, and infrastructure.

Content   Any approach to enhancing knowledge management must start by asking which knowledge is relevant for strategy and ongoing operations. Which knowledge will be needed for the firm's activities in 3 to 5 years' time? In what form must lessons learned be documented in order to make an impact on future projects? The goal of knowledge management is not to create an encyclopedia but to determine the critical knowledge requirements for achieving strategic goals and improving operational efficiency. For our trade finance firm, the content might include the relevant models, but also experiences about the different ways of applying those models and the lessons learned by line officers while using the models.

In many cases, the existing sources of knowledge and experience do not provide the quality required in terms of content or form. Then the processes that deliver knowledge (e.g., the risk evaluation processes) have to be considered. Do they really ask the right questions to obtain findings that will ultimately lead to significant and sustainable improvement of the credit approval process? If not, how can they be changed accordingly?

Process Knowledge management must be institutionalized. Processes like defining and redefining objectives, creating and updating knowledge, storing and disseminating knowledge, and applying knowledge thus must become part of the standard operating procedures of the organization. Knowledge management tasks and responsibilities also must be assigned and, if necessary, new roles in the organization must be defined (e.g., Knowledge Sponsor, Knowledge Integrator or Steward, Knowledge Base Architect and Knowledge Base Administrator). Recruitment and training for these new roles must be defined.

Culture The definition and design of a knowledge base in terms of content and technology is often the easiest part in enhancing knowledge management. But how can a company ensure that the corporate culture supports the creation and exchange of knowledge? The barriers that oppose the exchange of knowledge in a company must be assessed, especially in the context of a firm's past experience. The corporate culture must then be evaluated and possibly reframed to ensure the proposed exchange of knowledge can be supported.

In moving from a Risk Control business model to an Efficiency Enhancement or Risk Transformation business model, adopting a risk culture at the corporate level is arguably the most important key success factor for the firm. As noted earlier, the conventional interpretation of a risk culture is a focus on risk avoidance and risk reduction. An essential outcome of the knowledge management process at firms adopting the Efficiency Enhancement or Risk Transformation business models must be to ensure that different parties in the firm recognize this conventional interpretation is *not* the appropriate view of risk. Knowledge management must ingrain into the culture of the firm that risk is vital for business, innovation, and growth, and that risk management is a source of opportunity as well as a means of maintaining the required internal controls.

Infrastructure To facilitate easy access to knowledge, the appropriate media must be chosen, and this choice can differ radically across different companies and different company types. The overall purpose, the intended use, and the contents of the knowledge base define the requirements for the information technology (IT) infrastructure, and the integration of the knowledge management tools into the existing IT infrastructure is crucial. One of the goals of this step thus should be an assessment of the existing IT landscape and of the different technological options for the development of adequate knowledge management applications.

As noted in our discussion of governance, firms should exercise caution when identifying IT packages for support of the risk management process. When the firm is operating in the Risk Control model, the temptation to over-spend on systems with a high degree of functionality is high. But over-investment in the wrong system can have adverse consequences down the line if the firm finds that the high degree of functionality is not aimed at its particular business. An expensive VaR system, for example, may be functional for a swap dealer with a portfolio of exotic options, but, despite the price, may lack basic tools such as industry cost of capital calculations that would be required for use by a nonfinancial corporation. Notwithstanding the appearance that the expensive and sleek solution is better, it often is ill-suited to the actual corporate strategy and thus makes little sense—especially when evaluated on a benefit/cost basis.

Differences across Firms

Depending on the type of firm in question and its business objectives, the four business processes will interact with the internal risk management process of the firm to yield very different risk cultures. How a nonfinancial corporation leverages its risk management process, for example, may differ from how a financial intermediary views risk management as a business.

Consider first a nonfinancial corporation—say, a wholesale manufacturing firm that sells large machines to commercial customers. Figure 10.3 gives some examples of how the four business processes interact with internal risk management if the objective of the company is to leverage its risk management expertise by turning the treasury function into a type of non-bank bank for external customers.

As the examples of the outcomes of each business process illustrate, a key challenge for a corporate treasury that wishes to provide financial management products and services to both internal business lines and external customers is establishing the risk control parameters for how much risk the treasury will take. The role of governance in this case thus is to ensure that by offering a wider range of products and services, the treasury does not assume interest rate risks that the company is unprepared to bear.

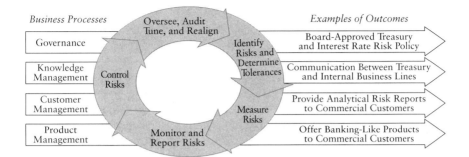

FIGURE 10.3 A nonbank offering banking services to customers.

At the same time, attention to knowledge, customer, and product management are necessary if the treasury is to exploit its knowledge and systems in the risk management area to serve customers through enhanced relationship management and product offerings. In knowledge management, a key issue will be communication between treasury and both internal business line clients and external customers concerning the range of risk management products and services that are available and how those products and services can better help them accomplish their business goals. This is complimented by customer management, in which the treasury must learn enough about customers (e.g., the purchasers of the firm's machines) to provide the services they might need. And product management in turn requires the treasury to alter the financial services provided to commercial clients in a manner that exploits the firm's comparative advantage in risk and financial management by offering products that are tailored to the businesses in which the firm's customers are operating.

Now consider a different example of a financial agent. Although banks and insurance companies are usually considered the prototypical financial agents, consider instead our commodities trade financier from above that offers letters of credit and other structures to help customers finance their imports or exports. Figure 10.4 illustrates examples of the outcomes from interactions between business processes and internal risk management for such a financial agent.

Unlike the case in Figure 10.3 in which the nonfinancial corporate was setting up a nonbank bank, a firm mainly interested in trade finance and related services will have a governance process focus on policies like a clearly articulated *credit* policy. A knowledge management issue in this case, in turn, will involve how the firm manages information flows between line credit approval officers and the centralized credit risk management function. Customer management will likely focus on areas in which the firm can offer its customers new services that exploit economies of scope, such as the

FIGURE 10.4 A trade financier offering new financial products.

offering of cash management services to trade finance borrowers. And product management will involve the careful analysis by the trade financier of opportunities to expand its product mix to include products such as guarantees of performance in the supply chain.

The examples shown in Figures 10.3 and 10.4 illustrate how different the interactions between the four business processes and a firm's internal risk management process may be, depending on the business objectives of the firm *and* its relative sophistication in internal risk management. As Figure 10.5 summarizes more generally, these relations ultimately determine

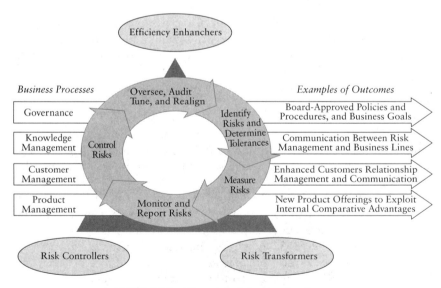

FIGURE 10.5 The risk culture of a firm.

the degree to which a firm is a Risk Controller, Efficiency Enhancer, or Risk Transformer for itself and for its customers.

PUTTING THE PIECES TOGETHER

To view risk management only as the process of reducing risk is to miss potentially significant efficiency enhancements and new business and product development opportunities. The temptation to focus on the negative aspects of risk may be high, but shareholders may end up worse off when risk control is adopted as a business model without consideration of the opportunities the two other business models present.

The appropriate risk management business model for any given firm will clearly depend on the firm and its risk management culture—whether the firm views *risk* as a necessary evil, a way to reduce costs, or an opportunity for new business. In order to identify the most appropriate model and to achieve efficiency gains and begin supplying innovative customer products when possible, the risk management process must be augmented with the business processes of governance, customer management, product management, and knowledge management. In other words, risk management can create a range of opportunities for firms when it is viewed no differently than *sound general management*.

Integrating People, Technology, and Processes through Enterprise-Wide Risk Management

A firm's internal risk management process is the process by which the firm tries to ensure that the risks to which it *is* exposed are the risks to which it *thinks it is* and *needs to be* exposed in order to maximize security holder welfare. In this context, risk management as a process can "fail" for a variety of reasons other than the occurrence of losses. First, risk management can fail to disseminate the right information to the right players. Closing the gap between *actual* risk and *desired* risk means that the right people in the organization are evaluating that gap with the right information. More concretely, many risk management programs fail because they focus on keeping *management* informed rather than *security holders*. But if security holders do not know what the firm is doing in the area of risk management, all the problems discussed in Chapter 4 arise. Risk management then becomes a *cause* of security holder-manager conflict rather than a solution.

Yet another reason that the risk management process can "fail" is if the organization does not make the proper connection between the sources of value added from risk management and the costs incurred to generate those value gains. In other words, companies can fail at risk management, quite simply, by over-investing in it. Even if the marginal benefits of risk management equate nearly to its costs in aggregate, a failure of risk management can occur *internally* if the cost/benefit calculus does not reflect the risk management strategy and risk culture adopted by the firm. If a company realizes a 10% increase in the value of its securities by formalizing risk management and 9% of that is due to increased customer and product offerings based on risk management applications, then a huge investment in risk management tools designed purely for risk control and unusable in customer and production applications would be unwarranted, and, indeed, quite likely a negative NPV proposition for the firm.

A third reason that risk management can fail is by artificially forcing itself into the classical risk control category and thereby leaving potential efficiency gains unexploited across the rest of the company. Closely related to the prior point about the need to associate the costs of risk management with its benefits, this failure of risk management occurs when companies simply *do not see* the benefits of risk management outside the pure risk control box. Economies of scale and economies of scope are left unexploited, real options are left unrecognized, strategic opportunities are missed, positive NPV investments are ignored, and so on.

Although other reasons can be identified for the failure of risk management to achieve its ends, these three reasons—failure to disseminate the right information to the right people, failure to connect the benefits of risk management to its costs, and failure to exploit efficiency gains and strategic opportunities created by risk management—can be addressed in large part through more attention to *integration*.

INTEGRATION AND THE RISE OF ENTERPRISE-WIDE RISK MANAGEMENT

Risk management is fashionable for dressing up old concepts as new hat and then assigning catchy buzzwords to those concepts. One such concept is enterprise-wide risk management or EWRM as it is now known in many circles.[1] EWRM strives to *consolidate* and *integrate* both the process by which a firm manages its risks *and* the risks which are targeted in that process. DeLoach (2000) usefully defines EWRM as

> *a structured and disciplined approach [that] aligns strategy, processes, people, technology and knowledge with the purpose of evaluating and managing the uncertainties the enterprise faces as it creates value. . . . It is a truly holistic, integrated, forward-looking and process-oriented approach managing all key business risks and opportunities—not just financial ones—with the intent of maximizing shareholder value for the enterprise as a whole.[2]*

Despite its rising popularity *and* appropriateness, characterizing EWRM as novel is a bit wrong. Indeed, in the context of the risk classification schemes presented in Chapter 1, the true father figure for EWRM is probably Frank Knight, whose 1935 book *Risk, Uncertainty, and Profit* gave us many of the same concepts as DeLoach (2000) outlines in his quote.

Knight, however, offered an economist's perspective on his version of EWRM. Translating that into a more practical strategic framework for corporations has indeed been a more recent phenomenon.

There are three basic differences between EWRM-based risk management strategies and other, less formal and more ad hoc risk management strategies. First, EWRM seeks to consolidate exposure types, not just across event-driven risk types but also across the Knightian border between risk and uncertainty—between *financial* and *business* risk. Implementing EWRM thus requires an acknowledgment by the corporation and the custodians of its risk management process that a key aspect of risk and exposure management involves what we called selective risk management in Chapter 9. In other words, *EWRM seeks to differentiate those risks in which the firm has some perceived comparative informational advantage from those in which the company perceives itself as no better informed than other market participants.*

A second distinction between EWRM and less systematic approaches to risk management strategy is the attempt to view the risks facing a company through some form of common lens. Often this translates into a common risk measurement framework, but at a more general level EWRM implies the ability for a firm to abandon the terminology of financial instruments. What should matter to a company is *not* whether a risk is best managed through swaps, insurance, or trading limits, but rather the resulting net enterprise-wide risk exposure conforms to the risk tolerances of the firm's security holders. In this sense, what you *call* a financial instrument—or, for that matter, a balance sheet exposure—is irrelevant. What matters is how it affects the net position of the firm relative to its risk tolerances.

A final distinguishing characteristic of EWRM is its aim to consolidate the risk management process organizationally across internal systems, processes, and people. In other words, the "enterprise-wide" in EWRM refers not just to a company's perspective of the risks it is facing, but also the degree of integration and consolidation with which the enterprises manages those risks.

INTEGRATION ACROSS PEOPLE

To design and maintain a sound risk management process consistent with the company's financing and investment strategies, the corporation must first decide who is going to do the designing. More specifically, the company as a collection of different individuals must ascertain where the risk management process will be designed, and, once it is designed, who takes ownership of the process.

Most importantly, the company must decide who the beneficiaries of the risk management program will be, and thus to whom the risk management process should be accountable. At a very basic level, the stakeholders in a risk management process are the principals of a corporation—its equity holders—and their agents.

But defining the beneficiaries of the risk management process is not enough. Because those beneficiaries will almost certainly be principals, the agents of the risk management process that act as its stewards on behalf of stakeholder/owners also must be defined. In other words, who internally will be responsible for ensuring the adequate degree of coordination and integration to achieve the benefits of EWRM? The roles of various parts of the firm's nexus of contracts are discussed below.

Equity Holders and the Board of Directors

For a firm to develop a value-enhancing risk management process, involvement by shareholders as represented by their board of directors is *essential*. Quite a few companies stumble by presuming that shareholders in particular are neither interested in nor capable of articulating the details of a risk management process. Shareholders are thus left out of the process, which is in turn designed mainly by management. This is a mistake.

If the Board of Directors, as the representatives of shareholders, is not aware of the issues confronting the company, it can and should be made aware. Many of the rationales for realizing gains from risk management, after all, trace directly to shareholder welfare.

Apart from rationales for risk management that are based on the protection of equity, the Board of Directors is the custodian of the shareholders—the *owners* or residual claimants—of the firm and its assets. For pure governance reasons, the involvement of the Board as representative of the firm's owners is critical to ensure that the risk management process is appropriately sanctioned, designed, and backed by adequate levels of seniority in the firm.

Shareholder participation is also crucially important as part of the governance process to ensure that the firm fosters an appropriate risk culture, as discussed in Chapter 9. The shift from a pure risk control business model to an efficiency enhancement is often a subtle move, but the leap into the provision of risk transformation products is more substantial. Shareholders should clearly articulate their objectives in this regard and approve all the associated internal policies, procedures, and controls before a company can make this leap from risk controller or efficiency enhancer to risk transformer.

Creditors and Delegated Monitors

Involving representatives of creditors in the design and articulation of a risk management process can also make sense, especially for firms whose risk culture is primarily one of risk control. The number of companies that leave their bankers out of the design of a risk management program is surprisingly high. And yet the behavior of external financiers such as bankers is precisely what motivates EWRM in several instances. Stated differently, if risk management is being implemented as a non-dilutive substitute for equity capital to increase the debt capacity and effective leverage of the firm, existing creditors are likely to need a material say in the structuring of that process. Otherwise, risk management can be used as an excuse for asset substitution. We have already seen in Chapter 6 how risk management can be used by equity to expropriate debt. The involvement of creditors thus is key.

Any given corporation, of course, may have a wide variety of creditors. A creditor, after all, is essentially *anyone* with a fixed claim on the firm. Stretching the definition, this could technically even include salaried employees who are owed a fixed compensation payment by the company. At the more traditional level, debt can include junior and senior bondholders, trade and project financiers, and so forth.

The involvement of representatives of all creditor groups in the design of a risk management process makes little sense. Apart from being unruly and cumbersome, some of the interests represented are simply not on par with others and could abuse the opportunity for involvement as a chance at asset substitution toward their own class of claim on the firm.

Fortunately, there is really no *need* to involve multiple classes or types of creditors in the design of a risk management process. The involvement of one type is typically enough—specifically, the lead banker to the corporation.

Commercial banks provide a number of important functions to the global economy and capital markets. So important are the roles played by banks that these institutions are often regarded as inherently unique or special.[3] The reasons typically cited for the specialness of banks are that they offer transaction accounts, serve as liquidity providers of last resort, and act as transmission mechanisms for monetary policy. But none of these functions are inherently *unique* to banking.[4] None of these roles make banks special.[5]

Academic finance suggests an entirely different reason that banks might be considered special. Specifically, commercial banks serve as *delegated monitors* of the investment activities of their borrowers. By providing borrowers with monitoring and outside discipline, banks encourage their borrowers to undertake only positive NPV projects.[6] In that sense, banks do play a virtually unique role in helping reduce the agency costs of debt, especially for small or growth firms.

To understand delegated monitoring, consider each stage in the commercial lending process. Before extending a bank loan, a bank carefully evaluates the creditworthiness of the customer and signals its assessment by extending or declining the loan.[7] If the loan later must be rolled over, the bank has a subsequent opportunity to *re*evaluate the credit risk of the firm, thus giving the borrower an *ongoing* incentive to undertake only positive net present value projects and investments. Otherwise, the borrower risks the nonrenewal of the loan and the negative signal that nonrenewal would send to other investors.[8] And when a loan *is* rolled over, the *positive* signal sent to the capital market tells other creditors to the firm that they need not undertake the same credit risk evaluations already conducted by the bank.[9] In particular, the scrutiny of the bank over a company's investment decisions abrogates the need for relatively less informed creditors (e.g., public bondholders) to undertake their own costly monitoring of the borrower's investments. In that manner, *informed* bank funds make other sources of *uninformed* funds from public capital markets or venture capitalists viable as additional sources of credit.[10] Not surprisingly, small firms and high-risk start-up ventures in particular build financial market reputation by first acquiring bank-monitored debt and only later move on to acquire arm's-length public or privately placed debt.[11]

The reasons why banks enjoy some comparative advantage in delegated monitoring are not well understood.[12] Perhaps the most compelling argument is that banks are multi-product firms which enjoy large economics of both scope and scale in information acquisition and analysis.[13] This results in a comparative cost advantage for banks in credit risk evaluation relative to firms that have less specialized credit evaluation functions, such as institutional investors and venture capital firms.[14]

The empirical evidence is consistent with the notion that bank debt is "better" than nonbank debt. Cumulative abnormal stock returns are positive following the announcement of a new bank loan. Announcements of new nonbank debt, by contrast, result in *negative* abnormal returns, with privately placed debt typically yielding larger negative stock price responses than public debt offerings.[15] The poor response to public and private debt placements is logical if economies of scope and scale in information acquisition and analysis are the source of banks' comparative advantage—nonbank lenders have less infrastructure and experience in credit evaluations, less specialized attention to credit risk analysis, and less capacity to monitor the investments of individual borrowers. In consequence, the cost of nonbank delegated monitoring is significantly higher than the cost of informed bank monitoring.

A natural question that arises is: Why, if bank debt is so valuable to firms for delegated monitoring purposes, do firms ever seek funds from institutions *other than* banks? Couldn't some of the agency costs we saw in Chapters 5 and 6 be eliminated by replacing less-informed bondholders with more informed bankers?

The answer has two parts. First, delegated monitoring is costly. Obtaining bank finance can yield cost savings to borrowers through reduced agency costs of debt and through lower costs of *non*bank debt finance—the cost of nonbank debt would be higher if other creditors with higher costs of monitoring had to undertake the credit evaluations performed by banks. Nevertheless, firms will borrow from banks only up to the point at which those savings are equal to the marginal costs of delegated monitoring.[16]

Second, although banks help ensure that a borrower undertakes only positive net present value investment projects, the borrower cedes bargaining power to the bank over ongoing projects in the process of purchasing delegated monitoring. That can lead to bank-promulgated decisions that are *too* conservative. A project that *originally* has a positive NPV, for example, might be terminated early at the behest of a bank if the project NPV later becomes negative at some point in the life of the project. In some cases, this is *in*consistent with value maximization by the borrower, as suggested in Culp and Miller (1995a, 1995b). To avoid ceding too much control to conservative bank lenders, firms thus diversify their borrowing sources across nonbanks with less incentive and capacity to monitor ongoing investment projects. In other words, less-desirable forms of debt often are used by borrowers simply to avoid giving a bank total control over investment decisions.[17]

Risk Owners

Every risk taken by a firm can be traced to the decision of one or more individuals. If decisions are traced far enough on an organizational chart, the individuals will ultimately be the board of directors. But somewhere below that level, a decision was made and a risk either taken or avoided. The business unit managers responsible for those decisions that alter the risk of the firm can be called *risk owners.*

Importantly, the ownership of risk is not confined to financial risks. A decision to develop a new drug creates risk ownership for the development team, as well as perhaps the marketing and sales teams. A decision to issue new debt to finance the next month of operations for the company creates risk ownership for treasury.

EWRM relies on the basic principle that risks will be managed in an integrated, consolidated, and comprehensive manner. This means that virtually by definition, the owner of an individual risk is highly unlikely to be the same person as the manager of that risk on an ongoing EWRM basis. But because no one knows better than the risk owner why the risk was taken or avoided, to leave risk owners out of the process would be the equivalent of risk management suicide.

Trading or Trade Execution Areas   Trading or trade execution areas are the financial risk-taking areas of an institution. We refer to them as such not because all transactions increase the firm's risk—quite the contrary—but because the financial risk profile of the institution is ultimately controlled by actions taken in those areas. Thought of another way, although the purpose of these risk-taking areas may well be to reduce risk through hedging or to serve customers by acting as counterparty to risk transformation products, these areas are the ones in which a corporation's entire capital base could be destroyed by a lack of internal risk management controls and oversight.

Large institutions active in derivatives generally have their own trading and capital markets areas. Such trading areas implement the hedging and business strategies within the broad context defined by senior management. Corporations less active in derivatives may execute derivatives contracts through another agent, such as a broker or derivatives dealer. The treasury or finance groups of such institutions then usually have responsibility for interacting with the broker or dealer to adjust the corporation's derivatives exposures, and these groups thus are the gatekeepers of a firm's risk profile.

Business Units   The business units of a company are the risk owners of the institution from a *business risk* perspective. These business units are the profit centers of the firm and are the areas in which the corporation's strategy is implemented in the form of product and customer management. Like trading and trade execution areas, the decisions made in business units directly affect its revenues and the value of the firm.

Participation by business unit managers in a risk management process depends on the scope of the risk management program the firm initiates. If the risk management process is limited to objectives pertaining *only* to financial risk, the input of the business units will necessarily be more limited than in cases where the firm manages risk across both business and financial dimensions. A chemical producer managing its interest rate and FX risk in an active process, for example, requires less input from the line managers of the chemical sales and R&D divisions than a different chemical producer that integrates operational and supply chain risk management into the risk management process.

Even for firms whose risk management processes are limited to the control and management of financial risks, however, some input from business unit line managers is essential. First, these managers must live with the outcomes of the risk management process. To ensure that the company evaluates the benefits and costs of its risk management initiatives properly, the input of business units is required so that hidden adverse consequences of risk management actions are kept at a minimum. Second, business units often end up bearing the resource burdens and costs of the risk management process, thus necessitating input from those units for cost control and process efficiency management standpoints.

For firms whose risk culture and business model is risk transformation (or on the customer service and product development end of efficiency enhancement), the supply of risk transformation products may itself be a business line. In such firms, integrating the business line into the firm's internal risk management process is essential. These customer-oriented structured finance and risk transformation design and supply units regularly develop and enter into contracts that *materially* affect the risk profile of the firm. Their involvement in risk management thus is warranted for the same reasons as the involvement of trade execution areas.

The Chief Risk Officer

All corporations should designate a chief risk officer (CRO). For large financial institutions with active capital market operations, the need for an independent risk management function and senior-level CRO is now accepted as *pro forma* following the 1993 report by the Group of Thirty's Global Derivatives Study Group. For many smaller financial institutions and nonfinancial companies, however, the appointment of a CRO often seems extravagant and expensive. But this need not be the case. The *designation* of a CRO need not mean the construction of a brand-new position in the organizational chart and the hiring of a new salaried employee. Rather, the designation of an *existing* senior manager with the additional responsibilities of a CRO will often serve the purpose.

The need for a chief risk officer at all corporations is entirely prudential. Regardless of the benefit-cost tradeoff the firm faces in implementing a risk management process suited to its own needs and sources of security holder welfare enhancement, the designation of a chief risk officer makes sense *purely to eliminate any ambiguity about who in an organization is vested with the authority to halt transactions that are counter to the interests of security holders.*

If a man experiences a heart attack on a crowded sidewalk, a crowd is likely to gather. A well-known psychological result in such a situation is for *rubber necking* rather than *responding*. In other words, people tend to *watch* rather than *act*, as if almost in paralysis. Consequently, a person helping the heart attack victim should *never* vaguely shout "Someone call a doctor!" Should that occur, it's a safe bet that none of the crowd will move, each expecting another to make the call. By contrast, if the person helping the victim looks up at someone *specific* in the crowd—chosen, say, purely at random—points at that person, and shouts "You there! *You* go call a doctor!" then it's more than likely that the ambulance will be on the way in minutes.

The principle behind the designation of a CRO is the same. The security holders of a corporation appoint this individual to be the one person who is *accountable* for taking actions during periods of crisis. Needless to say, succession planning for this person is equally important, in case the CRO is unavailable. But the point is not necessarily to create a centralized risk dictator in every company. Rather, the point is simply to ensure that accountability for risk control decisions is clearly vested and totally unambiguous.

The CRO should have three characteristics. First, she should be well-informed about the risk tolerances and risk management objectives of the board of directors and any other represented security holders. Her decisions should be made on behalf of the security holders alone. Second, she should have an adequate understanding of the nature of the risk exposures facing the firm to evaluate clearly the implications for changes in those risk exposures on the value of the firm. In short, the CRO must be capable of distinguishing the impact of a 10-basis point move in rates from a 200-basis point move in rates on the security holders' welfare. Finally, the CRO must herself be independent from the areas of the firm that are vested with risk-taking responsibilities.

Nonfinancial corporations often find the temptation irresistible to appoint a CRO who either *is* the chief financial officer (CFO) or who *reports to* the CFO. No matter how small the corporation, this is generally a mistake because the CFO is vested with the responsibility of managing interest rate risk. To the extent any interest rate risk management activities involve authorization to engage in trading products like derivatives, the CFO and her direct reports are thus capable of radically changing the risk profile of the company. Consequently, it is generally a violation of the independence criterion for a CRO to report to a CFO.

A more common and responsible solution is to appoint a CRO that either reports directly to the chief executive or the board of directors. At smaller firms, this designation is often assigned to existing compliance officers, internal auditors, or to the general counsel. The risk in that case, however, is the violation of the second criterion—namely, the general counsel, compliance officer, and/or internal auditor may lack the necessary technical finance acumen to make responsible decisions as a CRO.

Although not a universal rule that all organizations can follow, it is probably better to err on the side of trading skill for independence. Independence can be "simulated" with a rigid set of checks and balances, whereas training, education, and practical time in the trenches cannot.

An Independent Risk Management or Analytics Function

Active financial and corporate derivatives users should measure market and credit risk in independent risk management divisions that support the CRO. The risk management areas may or may not be separate from one another, but they should both be independent of risk-taking area(s) in the firm.

Independent risk management functions serve several purposes. First, they are a catalyst for the development and continuous improvement of models, systems, and procedures used to quantify risks. Vesting risk management responsibilities in independent areas also ensures that risk management policies and principles are consistently applied across all products and risks in the corporation—hence, the importance of integrating derivatives risk management into a risk management area with authority over *all* risk management activities.

Independent risk management areas play the necessary policing role many corporations require to ensure that risk-taking activities do not result in corporate risk exposures significantly different from the risk tolerances defined by managers and directors. This policing function need not be an antagonistic one. Independent risk management areas of many corporations indeed often act simply as intermediaries between traders or trade execution personnel and senior managers and directors. In other words, the necessity of giving independent risk management areas the responsibility and authority to monitor and report excessively risky transactions does not imply that senior management will often have to veto particular transactions.

Risk management areas play the further role of analyzing aggregate information about institutional risk exposures. A bank with both lending and derivatives portfolios, for example, must have an independent credit risk management function so that loans and derivatives transactions with the same counterparty are considered together when the firm's credit exposure to that counterparty is measured. A function of the independent risk management areas, indeed, is to set, monitor, and control limits and the limits administration process—a responsibility for which information on *aggregate* corporate risk exposures is required.

Finally, independent risk management areas are better suited than risk-taking or audit areas to analyze how a corporation's market and credit risk management process works in practice. Typical independent risk management areas may analyze revenue reports, actual and model-predicted historical portfolio values, and any theoretical models developed and used by traders for pricing transactions.

All corporations may not need an independent function with responsibilities *only* over market risk management. If the firm is relatively inactive in derivatives activity or holds derivatives only to directly offset the exposures of balance sheet liabilities or assets, market risk management generally can be done in an existing business area within the firm—such as the treasury function—provided the risk management personnel are not also responsible for risk-taking.

An alternative solution adopted by many smaller firms and institutional investors is to house the support for the CRO in an analytics group responsible for maintaining all the analytical models used by the corporation. A typical pension plan, for example, usually has a functional unit responsible for measuring performance, conducting asset allocation exercises, and maintaining internal asset revaluation models. Vesting the risk management analytical models in this area is perfectly reasonable. Even though the models maintained in such an analytics function support the trading and investment area, the independence *of the* CRO from the trading process ensures that the models housed and maintained in an analytics function need not breach the need for independence between risk-taking and risk management. All that is required is to ensure that the analytics area itself does not have authority to trade.

Back Office and Operational Areas

Every corporation using financial instruments must use a back office to conduct trade reconciliation, bookkeeping, accounting and marking to market, and audits of risk management and trading. Firms active in capital markets activity might choose to spread these back office functions over several areas in the firm, including existing administration, finance, treasury, legal, and audit areas. Smaller institutions often integrate the back office into a single business area.

It is increasingly common for firms to insource or outsource some or all of their back office functions, such as cash management and securities operations. Providers of these services include independent financial institutions such as Jiway Broker Services, Inc., in Stockholm, prime brokers such as Bear Stearns, and asset custodians like Mellon Trust.

Regardless where the back office processes are housed, the participation of the back office in the risk management process—both at the strategic level and the compliance and implementation level—is important to help ensure that the benefit-cost calculus of the risk management process is properly achieved. Chapters 20 and 21 discuss in more detail issues associated with cost allocation and how such issues dovetail with the measurement of the benefits and costs of risk management.

Legal Departments

A corporation should have sufficient in-house legal expertise or retain out-side counsel with specific training in the different bodies of law that affect its business and financial activities. For a risk controller or efficiency en-hancer that is merely a "user" of risk transformation products, the role of legal counsel is primarily limited to issues such as assessing transactional suitability and reviewing documentation. But for a firm actively supplying risk transformation products, access to legal counsel in the areas of com-modity, securities, and perhaps insurance and banking is crucial.

The participation of the legal department in the risk management pro-cess is also important for other reasons apart from evaluating transactions. An additionally important legal function is the enforcement and ultimate administration of policy compliance. Equally crucial is the role of a legal de-partment in liability assessment. Sometimes the risk management process at a firm, for example, can inadvertently *create* liability—"The board knew the risk was $1 million, retained the risk anyway, and lost $1 million!" Statements like that may fly in the face of the goals of putting stakeholder risk tolerances first, but they are nevertheless sometimes made. The man-agement of the liability associated with knowing one's risks and choosing to retain rather than hedge them is an essential part of a smoothly functioning legal support area.

SYSTEMS AND TECHNOLOGY INTEGRATION ISSUES

Achieving the desired degree of cooperation and integration across people within an organization to facilitate EWRM is almost always easier than achieving a comparable level of integration in information technology (IT) systems. But a fragmented IT applications architecture can not only greatly complicate the risk management process, it can also interfere with a com-pany's *traditional* business operations.

Numerous systems and applications interact to collect, analyze, sum-marize, report, and store information that is somehow relevant to the busi-ness strategy and tactics of risk management. Some such systems and applications include the following:

- *External data capture*—systems to capture, disseminate, and perhaps store data including market price data, market information, industry/sector/company information, ratings (counterparties, issuers, and banks), corporate actions, news, and the like;

■ *Research*—systems to capture, store, analyze, and disseminate research—both internal and external—that bears on the firm's assets and liabilities as well as its business decisions;

■ *Trading systems*—trade entry, deal capture, policy compliance, and verification systems for financial transactions;

■ *Portfolio and asset/liability management systems*—portfolio modeling, reporting, performance evaluation, treasury and money market systems, asset/liability management systems, and so on;

■ *General management systems*—production, inventory management, distribution, purchasing, acquisition, sales, and other core systems;

■ *Operational systems*—general ledger, cash management, accounting, financial reporting and disclosure, reconciliation, receivables and payables management, and so on;

■ *Data warehouse or database(s)*—data model, data map, databases, and data interfaces that maintain the storage facilities used by the different applications;

■ *Analytics*—risk measurement, financial instrument valuation, nonfinancial exposure valuation, real options, capital budgeting, strategic decision making, performance evaluation, asset allocation, and other analytical systems and processes; and

■ *External systems and interfaces*—systems and dynamic interfaces with systems of critical external parties (e.g., banks or custodians), including any activities performed by those systems across the interface or bridge and the reconciliations of such systems with internal systems and processes.

Because the IT applications architecture will be different by industry and by firm, a general discussion of how to properly design an IT architecture for optimum efficiency in risk management is well beyond the scope of this book. Nevertheless, some broad guidelines can be sketched so that firms at least can avoid some major pitfalls.[18]

Minimizing Operational Risk in the IT Application Architecture

Operational risk is the main potential problem arising for firms whose IT infrastructures are either inadequate to support the analytical requirements of a sound risk management process or whose application architectures are too fragmented to facilitate appropriate risk measurement, reporting, and oversight. Operational risk in an IT context traces to various administrative or operational problems and is rarely associated with a compensating increase in expected returns. Such risks are commonly caused by systems failures and functional inadequacies. They are especially prevalent in environments in which data and information systems are fragmented or incomplete. Multiple data entry points, excessive manual processing, and onerous or erroneous reconciliation procedures are characteristic of such environments.

Consider some of the problems that may occur when information systems are inadequate: a treasury manager books a leveraged interest rate swap in a money market portfolio that is supposed to contain only money-market instruments or hedges of outstanding bond issues; the exposure of a firm to Company ABC is compliant with investment and risk policies within individual business units (e.g., purchasing, sales, swap deals, securities held in investment portfolios), but a noncompliant excess *aggregate* credit exposure to Company ABC remains undetected *across* business units; or an authorized trader thinks she has bought a simple bond, but the bond has an embedded option that exposes the firm to significant interest rate convexity. In these examples, the firm's inability to measure the risks to which it is exposed traces not to problems with particular software packages, but rather to inadequacies in the relationships between systems and databases. The system *components* may be adequate, but the *architecture* is flawed.

Minimizing operational risk requires sound systems design, proper monitoring and reporting, and well-devised procedures for handling problems. Critical front-office trading and investment and back-office settlement and cash management systems must be integrated and reliable. Minimally, the system as a whole must allow financial risks to be evaluated at the *aggregate firm* (not individual business unit) level. Operationally, clerical or other data handling errors must be minimized. Key transaction verification and confirmation controls must be incorporated into systems design, and activity monitoring and reporting must ensure that transactions, portfolio positions and balances, and aggregate funds are in compliance with investment guidelines.

Specifically, an effective IT operational risk management program must incorporate five critical systems design principles. First, the risk management system must be under the control of, or at least transparent to, the owner of the risk management process. For firms operating in the risk control model, a particular problem in this context may be over-reliance on external systems, such as risk analytics provided through application service providers or through banks. While external systems can provide the vehicle for effective risk management analytics, firms must avoid abdicating responsibility for risk management to a third party.

Second, the architecture must be based upon a central, fully integrated database. A comprehensive view at the firmwide level is essential for

EWRM and aggregate analyses of market risk, credit risk, liquidity risk, and policy compliance, as well as for enterprise-wide revenue and cost optimization, capital allocation, and performance measurement.

Third, data must be entered into the system once at its source to avoid inconsistencies and minimize reconciliations. Multiple entry should occur only where necessary for verification and control purposes. Software packages that do not utilize the firm's central database thus should be avoided. This can present a particular challenge to companies that rely on off-the-shelf accounting and general ledger software such as SAP or PeopleSoft. Costly replication of a data warehouse is often more trouble than it is worth. Nevertheless, firms that conclude such systems are enough to supplant a central data warehouse must recognize that one cost of this is a limitation on the flexibility of risk analytics in which the firm may engage.

Fourth, component systems should be "third-party neutral." Application packages and vendor services may be useful, but firms must avoid *dependence* on any single system or vendor. This includes avoiding excessive technical dependencies, such as proprietary hardware or software, and service dependencies, such as relying exclusively on a bank to provide all cash management solutions. Even if a firm is satisfied with its banker and the risk management applications it offers associated with cash management, the company must still ensure that the efficacy and functionality of its risk management program would *not* be disrupted if the firm adds or changes banks.

Finally, the IT architecture should introduce a plug-and-play approach for all applications. The plug-and-play approach suggests that any functional component—including risk measurement systems, capital allocation engines, capital budgeting applications, real option or financial instrument valuation modules, and the like—can be disconnected and replaced with a minimum of disruption and customization.

Allocating IT Costs for Risk Management

Especially in banking, a new concept of cost allocation for back office and IT processes has begun to emerge in which banks establish service companies charged with the provision of all IT infrastructure and services across the different subsidiaries and business lines of a bank. Some large nonfinancial corporations employ a similar business model. In such hub-and-spoke systems, the costs of IT infrastructure are parked in one division of the firm, and those costs must then be converted into prices that the service company charges business units of the bank in order to recover its expenditures.

Whether in a less centralized environment or in such a service company setting, apportioning the costs of IT infrastructure for risk management purposes is extremely challenging for several reasons. First, IT expenditures are often characterized both by high fixed costs and network externalities. A data warehouse, for example, is extremely expensive to build and maintain, and, once developed, can benefit virtually all aspects of the firm's business operations, only one of which is risk management. Companies frequently do not have the data or methodology in place to *account* for such costs, much less to *allocate* them.

Second, the IT applications architecture is likely to be shared by a number of business units, not all of which will be generating revenues. The risk management function of a firm, for example, is a cost center, just like IT. How IT allocates costs to another cost center like risk management is far from obvious.

Third, the particular benefits from risk management may be difficult to associate with a business line for the purpose of IT cost recovery. If the firm's opportunity for realizing *value added from risk management* (RMVA) is defined at the very broad level of, say, protecting debt holders from asset substitution by equity holders, then the specific business unit that benefits from risk management is completely undefined—and undefineable.

In Chapter 20, issues associated with capital allocation are explored, including the allocation of costs based on some measure of the marginal benefit an activity contributes to the firm. The IT cost allocation conundrum is a similar one to the issues explored in Chapter 20, and the solutions—not surprisingly—are the same. In short, a firm has several alternatives for fair cost allocation in risk management technology, including:

■ Allocate costs based on pro rata shares of revenues and contributions, as in traditional financial and cost account models (i.e., status quo ante accounting policies are used);
■ Allocate costs using activity-based accounting in which intangible costs are shared across business lines and functional units of the firm based on some abstract definition of activity contribution to the firm's value of marginal product;
■ Allocate costs using some economic measure of value added associated with the resource to be costed, including those measures discussed in Chapter 20; or
■ Allocate costs on an ad hoc basis based primarily on the risk management business model adopted by the firm.

As the last point indicates, the risk management business model may have a significant impact on the cost allocation scheme chosen by the company. A pure risk controller will tend to treat IT investments in general as general expenditures and IT investments in highly risk-specific systems (e.g., risk measurement and financial instrument valuation systems) as pure risk management expenditures. An efficiency enhancer, by contrast, may allocate a portion of the costs associated with specific risk analytics systems to product and customer business lines, based on the degree to which those business lines are leveraging the risk management technology.

In the end, there is no right answer to how companies should allocate IT costs for risk management purposes. As with most EWRM issues, the solution is a form of art rather than an artifact of science.

BUSINESS PROCESS INTEGRATION

As discussed in Chapter 10, the risk culture of a firm and its risk management strategy are defined in large part by the interactions between the firm's internal risk management process and four key general management processes: governance; customer management; product management; and knowledge management. Implied in that discussion is the importance of integration across all five of these processes, and, more specifically, integration of the risk management process into the fabric of the other four processes. Risk management for risk control, efficiency enhancement, and risk transformation can become a largely automated process ingrained into the daily operation of a firm through integration of risk management process principles and strategies into appropriate aspects of the other four processes.

Governance

The governance process itself will be characterized by policies, procedures, internal reporting lines and organization charts, and internal controls, checks, and balances on relationships within those reporting lines and organization charts. Work flows and process maps may be adopted at some firms to complement the documentation and definition of the governance process.

Governance processes should integrate principles of risk management strategy at several levels. The primary means by which some degree of risk management can be built in to the governance process is through clear delineation of authorities—including authorities to trade, develop new products, make investment decisions, and the like. When employees are given written authority to engage in decisions that affect the financial or business risk of the firm, they are given authority to become risk owners. At the same time, risk ownership should entail a well-defined set of accountabilities. For example, the governance process should specify that any new product development decisions involve consultation with the CRO and/or some risk management committee. The purpose is not only to ensure that the risks of the new product conform to the risk tolerances of the firm's security holders, but also so that any potential cross-product and cross-exposure synergies with the intended new product can be exploited more efficiently and effectively.

In addition to specifying authorities and accountabilities, the governance process of the firm should also echo the risk management strategy and business model of the firm. If a nonfinancial corporate does *not* wish its treasury department to offer banking services to customers, the policies and procedures of the treasury function should indicate that. Conversely, if the firm sanctions the offering of banking products to commercial customers, the policies and procedures of the firm must allow at least some discretion to managers in their ability to fund the assets they create. The parameters under which risk owners may engage in such activities—for example, engaging in them only after consultation with treasury—should be spelled out in the governance process.

Governance should also clearly indicate the accountabilities of risk owners to various risk management personnel. There should never be any question about whom should be asked if there is any question about the risk impact of a business decision. To continue the previous example, business line managers in a trade finance business unit might be authorized to market and sell banking products to customers, provided those products have been generally approved first by a CRO and risk committee. And even then, the risk owner might be required to seek the counsel of the CRO in structuring the actual deals to avoid inadvertently violating a firmwide credit or market risk limit. None of this changes the fact that the business line manager is the primary risk owner, but the governance process simply sets up the boundaries in which the risk owner can and cannot operate without seeking permission. *And* it unambiguously indicates who that permission must come from when it is required.

Product and Customer Management

As emphasized in Chapter 10, products should be designed to meet the needs of customers, and customers should be managed from a total-relationship perspective. The tools and resources created by the firm's internal risk management process will help the firm redefine its product mix and customer relationship management (CRM) methods on an ongoing basis.

To ensure that the resources of the risk management process are available to and consistent with the product management process of the firm, integration across people and technology as discussed earlier in this chapter is critical. But this alone is not enough. Especially for firms evolving from risk control to efficiency enhancement or from efficiency enhancement to risk transformer, a senior-level policy statement on the need for integration across risk, product, and customer management is absolutely essential. The risk culture of the firm must be institutionalized by a clear statement from managers and directors that a strategic goal of the firm is to leverage its risk management expertise into the product and customer management processes. Otherwise, the firm is likely to remain focused and compartmentalized on its more traditional businesses.

One example of a company that has been very successful in managing the transition from risk controller to efficiency enhancer and on to risk transformer is Cargill whose senior management has always recognized the strategic value of integrating risk management into customer and product offerings. Cargill's participation in financial markets has increased over time, as has its supply of various creative financial solutions to customers. As its CRM methods evolved, so did its innovative development of new products to better serve existing customers. And attention was never lost to the acquisition of *new* customers—again often by offering new and different risk management and risk transformation methods.

Cargill essentially expanded its customer and product offerings well beyond its traditional, original business role as a grain merchant. As CRM and product management evolved, the firm's risk culture evolved. The firm kept its attention strictly focused on risk management, choosing to retain some of the new risks its new products and customer relationships created—presumably those in which it felt it had a comparative informational advantage—while at the same time becoming an expert at transferring other risks to the capital markets. Cargill, in effect, successfully changed its basic, fundamental business strategy over time, and a major reason this worked for Cargill was that risk management was always a fundamental component of customer and product management in the firm's global business strategy.

Knowledge Management

Integrating risk management into customer and product management processes and into corporate governance is absolutely impossible without a very sound knowledge management process. Knowledge management is particularly important when the aspect of the risk management process being integrated through governance and customer and product management process pertains to risk management analytical tools and models. Such models will be discussed in more detail in Chapters 14 to 16 and may include the following:

- Risk measurement systems.
- Financial instrument valuation tools.
- Cash flow simulation and forecasting tools.

- Hedge effectiveness evaluation models.
- Capital budgeting tools.
- Real option and strategic decision making tools.
- Reporting and disclosure methods and modules.

At most firms, models like these that are integral to risk management remain locked away in the "nerds' corner." Very few line business unit managers even know what the firm has bought or developed in the risk management area, much less when and how these models and resources could be used for product development or CRM purposes. The goal of knowledge management is to solve that problem.

Knowledge management as a business process should accomplish the following objectives:

- Indicate what risk management tools are available to business units for their use.
- Clearly demonstrate how these tools can be used to change customer relationship management and to impact the product development process.
- Reveal the people in the company that should be consulted about the use of these risk management resources, as well as those content experts to consult with questions about their usage.
- Suggest specific applications of risk management tools and human expertise to specific industries, client types, or sectors.
- Integrate the flow of common information across different processes.

The specific details of the knowledge management process will depend critically on whether the firm is a risk controller, efficiency enhancer, or risk transformer. Corporations whose risk management strategies are limited to risk control and loss avoidance need to spend less time and money on disseminating the uses of their risk measurement models to business line managers than firms wishing to leverage risk models into customer relationship management. Conversely, the more opportunity a firm perceives in leveraging its risk management expertise to nonrisk business units within the firm or to external customers, the more important it is that knowledge management help achieve a unified awareness of just what the firm's capabilities are.

Sound knowledge management is still relevant even for risk controllers because of the need to integrate risk management into *governance*. As noted at the beginning of this chapter, some firms "fail" in their efforts to manage risk because the right people do not have access to the right information. This is a knowledge management failure much more than a risk management failure. Beneficiaries and owners of the risk management process must strive to implement a sound knowledge management process that keeps risk owners (i.e., trading areas and business units), shareholders, and creditors informed not just about the risks of the firm, but about the risk management *process* of the firm.

A very simple illustrative—and real—example can show how easily a firm can succeed at developing a sound risk management process in its own right but can still experience a risk management failure because of poor knowledge management. Suppose the firm in question is an agricultural farm bank whose directors—and, by extension, asset liability committee (ALCO) members—are basically farmers. Because of their capital and funding profiles, farm banks tend to be active users of derivatives. Consequently, the treasury area of a farm bank is likely to be relatively sophisticated, have a reasonable proportion of derivatives in its book, and have a fairly advanced asset/liability risk measurement system.

No matter how sound the risk management process in place in the treasury of a farm bank, however, the knowledge management problem must be solved of how to educate the directors of the bank in an area that is simply not their field of expertise. The problem would be reversed, of course, if the directors had to present a report on crop rotation to the treasury managers. The backgrounds of the people are simply too far apart to suggest that the quarterly presentation of a report will ever be enough. Instead, the farm bank must strive to close the information gap with knowledge management methods, some of which might include the following:

- Periodic briefing and educational seminars for the ALCO on financial instruments and interest rate risk management.
- Third-party reviews of interest rate risk management activities that are presented to the ALCO in an intelligible form.
- Online or multimedia tools available to bank directors to help them understand the goals and methods of the risk management process.
- One-on-one meetings between ALCO members and treasury personnel to address specific concerns and general questions about risk management methods.[19]

CHAPTER 12

Identifying Market Risk Exposures and Defining Risk Tolerances

A corporation is a bundle of cash flows, including investment expenditures and the revenues generated by prior investment expenditures. The nexus of contracts that is the firm involves security holders, managers and employees, customers, vendors, counterparties, and the like. In the event-driven risk perspective outlined in Chapter 1, all of these contracting dimensions of a corporation are subject to the push and pull of risks like market, credit, liquidity, and operational risk.

In this chapter, we explore the strategic aspect of risk management involving the identification and exposure of market risks facing a firm. As explained in more general terms in Chapter 10, risk identification is the process by which a company recognizes and, in some cases, detects the different risks to which it is exposed through the normal course of conducting its business. Almost by definition, the risks that are most insidious for a company are those risks to which it is exposed that have *not* been identified. The process by which members of a company review, analyze, and discuss their risk profiles is an indispensable means by which risks can be identified, and, hence, managed.

Given the risks a company has identified, senior managers and directors must agree on tolerable levels of those risks required for the operation of the firm's primary business. This determination should be made explicitly by the firm's key stakeholders, including senior managers, the board of directors, and sometimes major creditors.

248

DEVELOPING A RISK ID OR RISK MAP

As noted in Chapter 1, risk can be characterized in different ways, none of which are more correct than any other. Nevertheless, some are more *useful* than others for developing and implementing a risk management strategy. To put it simply, risk should be identified by the corporation at the same level the company wishes to manage and control those risks.

The event-driven risk taxonomy together with a healthy dose of Knightian distinction between financial risk and business risk is the closest match to how most companies will wish to manage risks internally. To adopt the equilibrium asset pricing approach to defining risk would be self-defeating. The world in which diversifiability is the only thing about risk that matters is the same world where shareholders can manage risks through portfolio balancing decisions directly. Accordingly, the company should assume *all* risks it is targeting are diversifiable. The questions then become: Which risks should the company diversify, control, or hedge? How much? and How?

The risk management process at every corporation should include a systematic evaluation and periodic reevaluation of the risks to which the company is exposed. This evaluation should be *exhaustive*. Until a company has identified all of the risks to which it is exposed, the right decisions cannot be made about how much of any given risk the firm's security holders are comfortable bearing.

The first step in the risk identification process can be called *Risk ID*, or the process by which the company systematically associates specific risks with specific business units. The breakdown of risk should not be targeted at individual assets and liabilities, but rather should be aimed to link specific risks with specific managers of the company that own those risks.

The best way to illustrate a typical Risk ID is with a simple example. Every company will be different, after all, and the complexity and style of the Risk ID will vary across firms based not just on the nature of the exposures they face but also on the degree to which the firm wants to control those exposures. Less desire to interfere with certain natural business risks of the firm implies the need for less detail in the Risk ID. But at a broad level, *all* risks should be represented.

Consider a company that produces aluminum foil. The company is based in the United States, purchases aluminum from a variety of producers in the United States and South Africa, and sells foil mainly in the United States, Germany, and Switzerland. Suppose initially that the company engages in no hedging activities. Its capital structure includes both debt and equity, and debt includes bank letters of credit, bank trade financing, bank loans, and bonds. Some bonds are issued in Swiss francs.

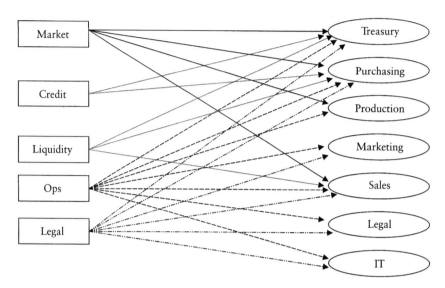

FIGURE 12.1   The Risk ID of an aluminum foil producer.

The First Cut—Event-Driven Risk Factors

Figure 12.1 illustrates a basic risk map or Risk ID for this firm. That Treasury is exposed to all types of risk should not be surprising:

- Market risk includes interest rate risk on outstanding debt and currency risk on foreign exchange-denominated debt, as well as perhaps equity and other price risks on any defined-benefit pension liabilities.
- Credit risk includes the potential for a bank default on a letter of credit or guarantee.
- Liquidity risk includes the risk of cash balance shortfalls.
- Operational risk spans the spectrum from the risk of rogue trading in interest rate derivatives by the treasurer to the failure of disaster recovery systems in the general ledger.
- Legal risk includes documentation problems with trade financing contracts, enforceability of material adverse condition (MAC) clauses in loans, and the like.

Now consider a business line whose risks are slightly less obvious—say, purchasing. In fact, the purchasing division is exposed to every type of risk, as well:

- Market risk includes commodity price risk (the risk of rising aluminum prices), interest rate risk (rising interest rates on trade loans required for input purchases), and exchange rate risk (increases in foreign currency-denominated aluminum purchases).
- Credit risk includes the failure of a vendor to supply aluminum on schedule as agreed and the failure of a trade financier that results in a purchase contract default.
- Liquidity risk arises from the potential for failed trade finance guarantees that might necessitate immediate cash replacements on the spot market.
- Operational risk ranges from poor controls on vendor quality to the risk of unguaranteed inventories being lost at sea.
- Legal risk pertains mainly to documentation risks associated with purchase contracts.

Taking the next business unit, the production area is subject to both market and operational risks. Market risk in this division is interest rate risk, which arises here because of the need to discount future investments at interest-based discount rate. Rises in rates can reduce the profitability of investment and production decisions in present value terms. In addition, production is subject to a variety of operational risks, including the risk of equipment breakdowns and failures.

The marketing business line, on the other hand, is subject to operational and legal risks—the latter due to the usual risk of inadvertent fraud in advertising, compliance with advertising laws, and the like. Operational risks in marketing include, among others, *reputation risk*—the company's brand name and image are valuable assets that could be devalued through poor marketing efforts.

Sales is subject to the same risks as purchasing, albeit perhaps tracing to different specific sources. Market risk still arises from aluminum price risk that could force a change in the customer selling price, as well as from the exchange rate risk associated with European sales. Credit risk is largely absent, *assuming* immediate settlement of sales contracts. If the firm allows large customers to pay after delivery, then sales assumes credit risk, as well. Liquidity risk would arise if the treasury and sales departments are inadequately coordinated on cash funding requirements—say, to service any delayed payables. Operational and legal risks include the usual suspects of failures in processes, controls, or documentation.

Notice that several purely business-related risks were excluded from the analysis, such as customer retention risk. In other words, Figure 12.1 presupposes that the firm has already decided that customer retention risk need not be modeled as part of the risk management process. The only reason for excluding this risk is if the firm *is certain* it is prepared to bear this risk as part of its normal business operations.

The Second Cut—Specific Risk Sources

Figure 12.1 presents a very broad Risk ID for the aluminum foil maker. In the next stage of the analysis, the company drills down to the next level of specificity. This usually will involve associating specific risk factors with specific business units. Figure 12.2 illustrates this time just for market risk to keep the figure legible.

As the figure shows, interest rate risk impacts treasury, purchasing, production, and sales. We might also have broken this interest rate risk down further into specific rate risks, such as debt borrowing costs in the treasury, trade financing costs incurred by purchasing and sales, and discount rate risk in the production area.

A more specific such breakdown has been done for currency risks. As Figure 12.2 illustrates, the Dmark/dollar rate affects the value of the firm through sales made in Germany with revenues denominated in marks. For the Swiss franc/dollar rate, the risk comes *both* through sales in Switzerland *and* in the treasury through franc-denominated bonds. And for the South

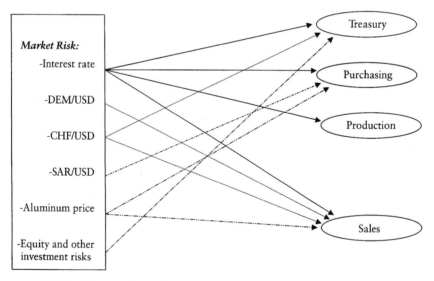

FIGURE 12.2　Risk ID of an aluminum foil producer, second cut.

African rand, the exchange rate risk comes from purchases of aluminum made from South Africa.

Aluminum price risk is apparent in purchases and sales for obvious reasons. Finally, to the extent the treasury funds an investment portfolio and/or defined-benefit pension plan, equity and other investment risks are market risks borne by the treasury.

The Third Cut—Specific Markets and Prices

Again, we might have chosen to get a bit more specific in a third cut and indicate the specific markets and prices that expose the firm to risk. Figure 12.3 shows the Risk ID for the purchasing and sales business units with respect to aluminum price risk only. Market risk can be divided here into three categories: geographical, Greeks, and term structure. Geography can be important because aluminum in one place is not the same as aluminum

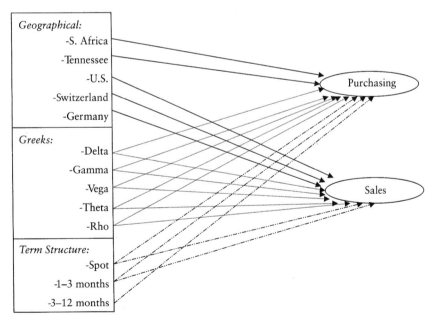

FIGURE 12.3 Aluminum Risk ID of an aluminum foil producer, the third cut (purchasing and sales aluminum price risk).

in another place, both because of transport costs and quality differences. As shown, the two purchased from South Africa are distinguished from aluminum purchased from Tennessee.

The Greeks illustrate the *nature* of the aluminum price risk on the purchase and sales division. Evidently, both purchase and sale contracts contain some feature(s) of optionality because all of the Greeks link to both the purchasing and the sale business lines. This does *not* mean, however, that these risks offset one another. A typical aluminum company might give large customers the right to expand or reduce some quantity of their order at a given price, thus creating an option. A purchasing contract, by contrast, might represent an option of an entirely different nature—different product (i.e., finished foil vs. raw aluminum), different locations (i.e., German foil purchaser vs. South African aluminum seller), different terms (e.g., customer can change quantity within one month of placing order vs. option to buy aluminum over one year), and so forth.

The term structure dimension is also relevant, which indicates the timing of aluminum purchases and sales. From Figure 12.3, the company clearly allows some customers to buy their product spot and others to buy—presumably at a fixed price—up to three months in advance. The purchases the company makes, however, can be done anywhere from today through a year from when the aluminum is needed. As in the case of the Greeks, these risks are not necessarily offsetting. The differences in quality, product, location, and the like create at best an imperfect correlation between the values of purchase and sale contracts. Apart from that, production is time-consuming, so that a spot purchase of aluminum today is associated with a foil sale several months out, thereby creating a calendar basis mismatch between the prices of different aluminum products over time.

The Risk Map

Successive iterations of highly general evaluations like those presented in Figures 12.1 through 12.3 actually can be quite instructive for companies. The goal, however, is to be *systematic* and *exhaustive* in those evaluations. As a basic guideline, companies should get into as much detail on the risk side of the risk map (like those shown in Figures 12.1 to 12.3) to comment on the company's need to bear the particular risks in question. Similarly, business units identified as owners of certain risks may be too generally defined, with the need for a manager- or line-specific designation of risk ownership often better serving corporate needs.

As we shall see later, risk measurement attempts to quantify value, cash flow, or earnings risk across *all* relevant exposures. The Risk ID exercise need *not* be so detailed that it reaches down to the level of specific cash flows. All that must be true is that the risks be defined in enough detail to define tolerances for them.

The outcome of the Risk ID process should be a *risk map*, or a well-defined set of relations between risks to which the firm is exposed and the owners of those risks. With this risk map in hand, the company can then turn to the more important—and harder—question of how much risk it will tolerate of each kind.

Note that any particular company may well choose to adopt some different variant of what has been dubbed here the Risk ID process or Risk Map. In that connection, the *outcome* of this risk identification exercise is usually less important than the *process* of self-examination it creates. In other words, how pretty the Risk Map looks is basically irrelevant if the company has not learned something about distinguishing between its business and financial risks in the process of producing the picture. Conversely, the company may call the picture what it likes and throw it away five minutes after it is completed *provided* the exercise has led the firm to a clear delineation between risks the firm wishes to manage and those to which it is prepared to be exposed through the normal course of its business operations.

DEFINING RISK TOLERANCES

The owners and beneficiaries of a firm's risk management process should work together to establish tolerances for the major risks to which the firm is subject. These risks need not include the risks deemed purely business risks, but rather encompass those risks that the firm may not need to bear fully in order to achieve its primary sales goals.

A firm can express its tolerance for different risks in either absolute or relative terms. For most companies, an absolute tolerance is hard to measure and identify. How does a firm determine, after all, whether $100 million of currency market risk is too much? Some firms thus might tend to prefer relative tolerance measures, where the current risk exposure of the firm is evaluated to some other known benchmark rather than to a psychological comfort level. Nevertheless, both are viable methods for the owners and beneficiaries of the risk management process.

Absolute Risk Tolerances

Firms that take the absolute approach may define risk tolerances based on the type of risk in question or *across all exposures of the firm in aggregate*. In either case, the absolute risk tolerance should satisfy certain criteria:

■ It should be defined in anticipation of the need to monitor, report, and target that tolerance level. Excessively ambiguous or unmeasurable risk tolerances make no sense.

■ It should ideally be comparable across different exposure types. If the beneficiaries and owners of the risk management process decide that aluminum price risk is excessive, that decision should also provide guidance on what amount of currency risk, say, is tolerable.

An easy way to express absolute risk tolerances that satisfies the first but not the second criterion is in terms of nominal capital or quantity at risk. The firm might decide that more than 1 million troy ounces outstanding in aluminum purchase commitments is too much, but this does not facilitate any comparison between aluminum purchase commitments and exchange rate risk.

A better alternative for companies wishing to engage in EWRM using absolute risk tolerances is to specify tolerances in terms of maximum tolerable loss amounts and frequencies of their occurrence. Loss should be defined in terms of value/capital, cash flows, or earnings based on the particular focus of the firm's risk management process. Maximum then might be defined using some statistical criterion, such as the level of a confidence interval—say, 95%. A firm might not wish its aggregate currency capital at risk, for example, to exceed $10 million in more than five of the next 100 months. This $10 million loss tolerance is the firm's value at risk (VaR). Similar measures like earnings at risk (EaR) and cash flows at risk (CfaR) can be defined if appropriate.

For a company to use an enterprise-wide absolute risk tolerance instead of risk-specific absolute tolerances, the firm can still rely on a concept like VaR. But an enterprise-wide VaR may be problematic vis-à-vis the first criterion—measurability. Many firms find this intractable because all the exposures of the firm cannot be reliably aggregated. Most nonfinancial corporations, in particular, thus characterize their risk tolerances either using absolute risk tolerances by major risk factor or asset class *or* use relative risk tolerances instead.

Risk Tolerance Relative to Natural Exposure

A key concept in the definition of relative risk tolerance is the notion of a firm's natural risk exposure, or the risk that the firm must take in order to meet its primary business (e.g., production) goals. The determination of how much of a certain type of risk is too much can then be made relative to the corresponding natural risk exposure. For Airline FlyMe to meet its expected customer transit obligations, for example, the expected jet fuel requirement can be approximated, thereby defining a quantitative estimate of the natural jet fuel exposure the firm must incur in order to fly its planes. If its annual jet fuel requirement is X gallons per year, the airline may choose to be exposed to the risk of rising prices on no more than 50% of those X gallons. The firm then must use risk control mechanisms and risk management products to reduce its natural exposure to rising jet fuel prices in a manner discussed later.

How a firm decides the degree to which it wants to bear the risks of its natural business exposure is a decision that should rest with the beneficiaries and owners of the risk management process. The role of shareholders in defining natural exposure is particularly important, because their diversification decisions have an impact on what can be defined as *natural* for the firm-cum-shareholders combined.

Risk Tolerance Relative to Other Risk Tolerances

For some risks, the concept of a natural exposure is not well-defined, in which case the company's relative risk tolerance must be compared to other yardsticks. Interest rate risk provides a good example. The degree to which a firm is subject to interest rate risk depends crucially on the capital structure of the firm—the amount of debt the firm issues, and the maturities of those debt instruments. Even a violation of the M&M assumptions that creates an opportunity for risk management to add value does not necessarily imply an optimal capital structure. So, determining the amount of debt the firm must issue—and, hence, its natural interest rate risk—is highly subjective.

When natural exposure cannot be easily defined, other candidates for expressing the firm's risk tolerance are usually available. In the case of interest rate risk, for example, the firm may choose to define its tolerance by requiring its interest rate exposure to be no greater than the exposure on its issued debt instruments at any given time. That tolerance says nothing about what the outstanding level of debt should be, but it does preclude *additional* interest rate risk-taking, as in the bet on interest rates made in the early 1990s by Procter & Gamble's treasury.

DYNAMICS

Because risk management is an ongoing process, the risks to which a firm is subject and stakeholders' tolerances for those risks will evolve. Airline FlyMe's jet fuel needs may change as the company grows, for example, thereby prompting a change in the natural exposure of the firm and perhaps in the tolerance of stakeholders for that exposure.

One variable with which risk management process owners must be particularly comfortable is the impact of risk control decisions on the dynamics of exposure. Actions taken to *control* one risk often *create* other ones. Return to our aluminum foil producer for a moment to illustrate the point, and suppose the firm decides that it is prepared to tolerate all of its exposure to aluminum price risk but is unprepared to tolerate the risk that exchange rate swings adversely impact earnings. Over time, at least some exchange rate risk can be managed by not issuing bonds in Swiss francs. But assuming purchases continue to occur from South Africa and sales continue to occur in Germany and Switzerland, the firm must take a proactive tactical measure to close the gap between its actual DEM/USD, SAR/USD, and CHF/USD exposures and the *tolerance* to these exposures of zero.

To make it easy, suppose the company fully hedges its earnings against exchange rate risk using forwards and swaps, all of which are negotiated either with Bank of Chicago or Bank of Brisbaine. Suppose further that these two banks are A-rated and do not have any existing relationship with the firm through a commercial lending, trade finance, or letter or credit program. The banks thus are *new* to the aluminum producer.

Simply assuming the firm tactically constructs its hedges properly (relative to an earnings risk management target), the firm has exchanged *market* risk for *credit* risk. The company is no longer subject to adverse swings in the Swiss franc, Deutsche mark, or South African rand because of its swaps with Bank of Chicago and Bank of Brisbaine. In return for shifting this risk to the two banks (which almost certainly will reshift the risk to other participants), the aluminum company has traded one risk for another—market risk has been replaced with credit risk.

Credit derivatives, insurance, syndication, securitization, or other methods of credit risk management can in turn be used to manage the credit risk the aluminum company has created by hedging all of its market risk with these two banks. But such transactions often lead either to additional credit risk (i.e., the risk of Bank of Chicago is hedged with a credit derivatives transaction done with Bank of Mars) or to some other risk, such as operational risk (e.g., the risk of Bank of Chicago is underwritten by an insurance structure whose details are so complex that the aluminum firm might have been better off retaining its *market* risk).

Tactical management of market, credit, operational, and other risks is left to Part Three of this book. For now, the important point to take away from the discussion is that the exposure identification framework in place at a company must be robust enough to anticipate risks that will be created by the risk management process itself. When the cycle comes full circle, new risks—like the credit risk created when market risk was hedged—will surely be identified in the Risk ID process. But the cycle should not wait that long.

The risk management process itself must have a dynamic element built in that can identify changes in risk exposures *as they occur.*

Dynamic exposure identification may not always be realistic at a reasonable cost, of course, but a company that *tries* to turn exposure identification into a dynamic problem is likely to be better off than one that does not for two reasons. The first is the obvious reason that new, hidden risks can be intercepted as they are created, tolerances for those risks defined, and appropriate responses made. But in addition, dynamic exposure identification greatly facilitates the degree to which a firm can be a selective risk manager. By regularly identifying new risks as they occur, the firm will be forced to regularly assess its tolerances for those risks, including the comparative informational advantage the firm might have in bearing those risks. In our example, trading the market risk of exchange rate changes for the credit risk of Bank of Chicago and Bank of Brisbaine might be a totally legitimate example of selective risk management in which the aluminum firm feels better able to assess the quality of a bank than the future movement in an exchange rate.

CHAPTER 13

Spot, Forward, and Forward-Like Exposures

Chapter 12 outlined the basic principles behind exposure identification and the definition of risk tolerances. In this chapter and in Chapter 14, we examine how a company can decompose its cash flows, value, and/or earnings into elemental building blocks that facilitate the risk manager's job. To implement a risk management process that closes gaps between *actual* and *desired* risk exposures, risk managers must, in accordance with the firm's risk strategy and culture, leverage the risk exposures to other business units and perhaps to external customers. None of this is possible without a basic understanding of what constitutes an exposure.

One of the central challenges to firms wishing to get the most out of risk management is this exposure identification process. To miss an exposure is *either* to miss a potential source of opportunity *or* a potential source of risk—if not both.

In this chapter, the focus is limited to the identification of spot, forward, and forward-like exposures. Specifically, the only exposures discussed in this chapter are those exposures whose values are a linear function of the underlying price, rate, or index on which the exposure is based on its value date.

TRADE VERSUS VALUE VERSUS SETTLEMENT DATES

Before rushing headlong into the exposure identification section, some discussion of terminology (and notation) is important. This terminology concerns the relations between three important dates in the life of a risk exposure—trade date, value date, and settlement date. Underlying the distinction between these three terms is the idea that behind every risk exposure of the firm lies some *contract*. The contract might be a security purchase agreement, an asset purchase or sale agreement, a deal that creates a liability, and the like. For every exposure, there is some specific event that creates that exposure. The distinctions between trade, value, and settlement dates depend on the event in question.

The *trade date* for any exposure is the date on which the contract giving rise to the exposure is initiated. For an asset purchase or sale, the trade date is the date on which the firm and its trading partner agree on the terms of the deal, including the price of the purchase or sale. The value and settlement dates associated with that exposure will generally be defined *relative to* this trade date, often indicated as trade date T.

In organized markets, the terms of a trade are sometimes subject to a confirmation or reconfirmation process in which the trade terms are not considered final until both parties review and authorize a document summarizing those terms of trade. You would expect to encounter this confirmation process in the process of buying or selling securities and futures, but not in most nonlisted assets and liabilities such as payable and receivables. When a transaction does have a confirmation process, the confirmation usually occurs no later than one day following the trade date, or $T + 1$.

The *value date* for a specific transaction is the date on which both parties to the contract know with certainty the value of the exposure. The *settlement date* is the date on which that value is actually realized. These dates need not be the same in calendar time, and one or both may differ from the trade date.

Trading, Clearance, and Settlement

The reason for the difference in *organized* markets between trade, value, and settlement dates arises from the distinctions between three aspects of the trading cycle: trading, clearance, and settlements. Trading is the process by which buyers and sellers agree on the terms of exchanging an asset. Clearance is the process by which some agent calculates the final obligations of buyers and sellers to one another, both in assets (e.g., securities) and in funds. And settlement is the process by which the assets and funds are actually transferred. To achieve what is known as *final settlement,* the transfer must be irrevocable and final. Irrevocability simply implies that the firm initiating the funds or asset transfer cannot revoke the transfer instruction after it has been sent. Finality means that the asset or funds are securely in place in the account of the trading counterparty and can only be taken back from that party through the execution of another transaction.

To illustrate these dating conventions, consider first an example in which Broker Bruckner purchases one share of common stock issued by Company Wagner from Broker Brahms for $10. In this example, the trade date and the value date are the same. Part of the trading process between Brokers Bruckner and Brahms included the determination of the price at which the share of Company Wagner would be transferred—$10 in the example. On trade date T, Broker Bruckner knows it has acquired an asset worth $10, and Broker Brahms knows it has sold an asset in exchange for receiving $10 in cash. The *value* of the trade thus is known at the same time the trade itself occurs on date T—at least assuming for the moment that neither broker defaults.

Because of the *clearing* process for equities, however, it is possible to say that the *value date* for the stock purchase is actually $T + 1$ rather than T because the terms of the deal are not reconfirmed until $T + 1$. Amendments to the trade are not usually allowed between T and $T + 1$, however, so this text will *not* adopt this convention. Instead, trades are assumed to be accurate when initiated and the confirmation date is thus assumed not to impact the value date. This assumption is also made for expositional purposes because many of the *nonfinancial* exposures of interest in this book are not subject to a formal clearance process at all, rendering the confirmation and computation of clearing balances processes further irrelevant.

The *settlement* date for this transaction, however, is three days following the trade date, or $T + 3$. The reason for this delay is that the transfer of securities and funds takes time—in some markets longer than others. Reasons for the delay include the need to allow for reconfirmation of the terms of the trade on date $T + 1$, the lag in achieving "finality" in securities and funds transfers through national central securities depositories and funds transfer mechanisms, respectively, and the operational headaches of securities settlement verifications in general.[1] The settlement dates for several major equities markets around the world and the systems through which these equities are cleared and settled are shown in Table 13.1.

TABLE 13.1   Some Global Securities Settlement Conventions

Regional Equity Market	Settlement System	Settlement Date
France	Sicovam (Relit)	$T + 3$
Germany	Clearstream	$T + 2$
Italy	Monte Titoli	$T + 3$
Netherlands	Necigef	$T + 3$
Sweden	VPC	$T + 3$
Switzerland	SIS SegaInterSettle	$T + 3$
United Kingdom	Crest	$T + 3$
United States	Depository Trust Co.	$T + 3$

Now consider a slightly different example in which Broker Bruckner goes long a forward contract with Broker Brahms—say a gold forward contract—for delivery 180 days hence at the fixed price of $290/oz. For this transaction, the trade date is the date on which Bruckner and Brahms agree on the contract terms and initiate an open forward position. But the *value* of the contract will not be known for another 180 days, as that value depends on the spot price of gold *at maturity*. If the spot price of gold is $300/oz 180 days hence, the long has an asset whose value is $10/oz and short has a $10/oz liability. Conversely, a spot price 180 days hence of $250/oz would translate into a liability for the short with a value on that date of –$40/oz and an asset for the long worth $40/oz. Because the example specifies that gold delivery actually occur 180 days hence, the *settlement* date should be the same as the value date—the maturity date of the contract.

Finality in Funds Transfers and Settlement Lags[2]

The last sentence in the prior section says that the settlement date *should be* the same as the value date for forwards. In practice, that is rarely true—not because of any particular feature of the forward contract, but rather because of the peculiarities associated with achieving irrevocability and finality in *funds* transfers—especially across national borders.

Any funds transfer contains two components—the transfer of information and the final transfer of funds between two banks. For expositional purposes, assume the funds transfer is a simple transfer of money from one commercial bank to another. Even in that simple case, the means by which the transfer is accomplished are not straightforward.

The funds transfer process is initiated when one bank issues a payment order or instruction to the other bank. The transmission of a payment order essentially amounts to an electronic request for payment. The bank that sends the initiating payment request message is called the *payee* and the bank receiving the request for payment is the *payer*.

Most modern payment systems are credit transfer systems. This means that both the payment messages *and* the funds move from the payer to the payee. After the initial request for payment from the payee, all messages thus are sent by the payer and received by the payee. These messages are typically electronic and consist of verifications of the transaction, identification authentications, reconciliations of payment instructions, and so forth.

The information exchange between two banks pertains only to the *instructions* for the funds transfer. The funds transfer itself is usually accomplished electronically and is independent of the information exchanges. As noted earlier, a funds transfer, like an asset transfer, achieves final settlement only when it is irrevocable and final.

In general, finality in a funds transfer is only achieved when "central bank money" has been transferred from the payer to the payee. Commercial banks in virtually all countries around the world maintain balances with the central bank. These balances are held in *nostro* accounts, meaning that the funds are on deposit with the central bank but still belong to the commercial bank. Finality in funds transfers is achieved through debits and credits to banks' nostro accounts with the central bank. Specifically, a funds transfer is final when the nostro account of the payer with the central bank has been debited and the nostro account of the payee with the central bank has been credited. So, finality in a funds transfer occurs when central bank money has been used to settle the transaction.

Large value transfer systems (LVTSs) are used to effect the irrevocable and final transfers of funds in industrialized countries around the world. In the United States, the LVTS for domestic funds transfers is the Fedwire. For transactions involving a foreign party, the transfer also typically involves the participation of the Clearing House Interbank Payment System, or CHIPS. Other countries maintain their own LVTSs, often sponsored by the central bank.

Many different variables differentiate LVTSs from one another, such as the timing of settlements and the netting scheme in place. Notably, the *only* settlement systems that can achieve *real-time* finality are called Real-Time Gross Settlements (RTGS) systems. Fedwire is an example of a RTGS system, although final transfers of funds do not actually occur until the end of the day. The reason the system qualifies as RTGS is that the Federal Reserve guarantees performance on all intraday funds transfers (subject to some limits), thereby making the system operate *as-if* it is RTGS. The only *true* RTGS systems that do *not* involve intraday extensions of central bank credit (called daylight overdrafts) are Austraclear in Australia and SIS SegaInter-Settle in Switzerland. In every other country, the delay in achieving finality necessarily imposes some wedge in most transfers of funds between the trade or value date and the settlement date.

Lags in the finality of funds transfers can account for at most a one-day lag in the settlement cycle behind final clearing. Nevertheless, lags of more than a day are regularly observed in numerous asset markets. Some of these lags are imposed for convenience and to minimize operational risks. When a company sends an invoice for rendering professional services, for example, the value date is the date of invoicing. But the settlement date is not necessarily the date of receipt of the invoice by the client. Quite normal practice is to give the customer, say, 30 days to pay. Among other things, this lag exists to provide the opportunity for the appropriate flows of information and funds to occur. Unlike exchange-executed transactions or bank-to-bank same-currency funds transfers, the communication of payment obligations in this example is most likely done by regular mail, and that takes time. In addition, the customer is likely to pay by check rather than a direct LVTS funds transfer. And checks clear *not* through a LVTS, but rather through a SVTS—small value transfer system—such as Automated Clearing Houses (ACHs) in the United States, through which final settlement can take up to *five* days.

Another major market that experience a routine gap between value and settlement dates—regardless of the transaction type—is foreign exchange. With the exception of the relatively unpopular and unused exchange-traded currency futures, foreign exchange transactions are bilateral—usually inter-bank—transactions that are neither cleared nor settled through an organized clearing house. Instead, the funds transfers between trading parties are effected through a cross-border LVTS, such as CHIPS. Because of the lags associated with confirming transactions and moving multiple currencies across time zones, foreign exchange settlement is virtually always $T + 2$.

Spot versus Forward Exposures

The distinctions between trade, settlement, and value dates are important for a variety of reasons in a risk management context. For the purpose of exposure identification, the differences between these three dates helps characterize the distinction between *spot* and *forward* transactions. If reconfirmations are presumed not to affect the value date, a spot transaction can be defined as any transaction in which the trade date and value date are the same.

A forward or forward-like contract, by contrast, is characterized by two salient features. First, the value of the contract on its value date(s) is a linear function of the value of the asset underlying the forward purchase or sale contract—the value of the forward changes dollar-for-dollar with the value of the asset underlying the forward on the value date, as shown earlier in Figures 3.1 and 3.2. Second, the trade date on a forward contract is earlier than the value date(s) in calendar time. For reasons already explained, virtually *all* transactions have a lag between their value and settlement dates, so this distinction does not enter into the picture.

Using a slightly different taxonomy, the first salient feature of forwards is the characteristic that distinguished forwards and forward-like exposures from options and option-like exposures. Forward exposures have payoffs linear in the value of the underlyings on their value dates, whereas option exposures are a *nonlinear* function of underlying values on their value dates. The second characteristic of forwards is what distinguishes forwards from spot transactions. This distinction is *also* true for options. So, the second characteristic—a trade date occurring before a value date—can be said more generally to be that characteristic that distinguishes *cash market* transactions from *derivatives* transactions.

TRADED FINANCIAL INSTRUMENTS

Probably the easiest forward-like exposures to identify are those exposures arising from financial instruments that were issued or acquired through a formal trading market, whether on an exchange or through the OTC derivatives dealing marketplace. In simple terms, spot and forward-like exposures arising from traded instruments include cash market transactions, forwards, swaps, and futures.

Spot and Cash Transactions

As noted earlier, a spot or cash transaction is a contract whose value and trade date are the same. Settlement usually follows within a few days.

For exposure identification purposes, companies usually will want to identify *market* risk exposures based on the market prices of assets that serve as the underlying for the transactions in question. As noted, the distinguishing feature of spot, forward, and forward-like exposures is a linear payoff in the value of their underlyings.

We have seen several times already that corporate securities can be viewed as options on the net assets of their issuers. That clearly makes the exposure profiles of those securities nonlinear, at least when expressed as a function of the net assets underlying the issuing firm. Consequently, we do not usually drill down to that level of detail for exposure identification purposes. Instead, we treat the exposure of a spot transaction as just that—an immediate purchase or sale of an asset, no more and no less.

Forwards

A plain vanilla forward contract is just a contract for the purchase/sale of some asset or its cash-equivalent on some specific future date for a price agreed to by the long and the short on the trade date. The value date is the maturity date for the contract when its value to the long and short are realized. A foreign exchange forward negotiated on trade date T with six months to maturity, for example, might have a value date of $T + 180$ days. What the transaction is worth is known six months hence when the contract matures based on the realization of the spot exchange rates prevailing on that date.

The settlement date in a forward contract depends on whether or not the transaction is settled in arrears. A traditional forward contract has a value date that corresponds to the maturity of the contract and precedes the settlement date by only a few days. In the above foreign exchange forward contract, for example, the value date occurs on day $T + 180$ and the settlement date is on day $T + 182$ because foreign exchange settlements occur in a rolling two-day cycle.

A transaction that is settled-in-arrears has a value date that occurs well in advance of the settlement date. Sometimes a spot transaction—a transaction in which the trade date and value date are the same—is settled in arrears. A wholesale, interbank, noncallable certificate of deposit (CD), for example, pays the following to the investor when it matures on date $T + m$:

$$Z\left[1 + R_{T,\,T+m}\left(\frac{m}{D}\right)\right] \tag{13.1}$$

where Z is the principal amount deposited and $R_{T,\,T+m}$ is an annualized m-day interest rate prevailing. The terms m and D reflect day counting adjustments to the interest payment, where D is the length of the money market year in the market where R is determined (e.g., 360 days in the United States and 365 days in the United Kingdom). Because both R and D are expressed as annualized rates, m and D are needed to deannualize the rates.

The rate paid on the CD for m days—$R_{T,\,T+m}$—is known on the trade date. Consequently, the value date for the CD is also trade date T. The payment of interest and the return of principal, however, occurs m days later on date $T + m$. So, the CD pays interest in arrears.

A settled-in-arrears forward rate agreement (FRA) is type of settled-in-arrears forward contract that pays the following to the long:

$$Z\left[(R_{T+m,\,T+m+d} - K)\frac{d}{D}\right] \tag{13.2}$$

where Z is the notional principal amount (NPA) of the transaction, K is a fixed rate, $R_{T+m,\,T+m+d}$ is an annualized d-day interest rate paid on the CD referenced by the FRA, as in the CD whose value is shown in Equation 13.1. The principal is called *notional* because the parties never actually exchange it; NPA is for interest calculation purposes only.

In the settled-in-arrears FRA, the trade, value, and settlement dates can all be quite well-spaced in calendar time. The fixed rate K is set *on trade date T*. The value of the FRA is not known to the short and the long, however, until the reference rate $R_{T+m,\,T+m+d}$ is set on date $T + m$. This rate is the rate paid on a CD placed at time $T + m$ with a maturity date of $T + m + d$. Because the FRA is settled in arrears, the settlement date on the FRA is the same as the settlement date for the underlying CD—date $T + m + d$.

Swaps

A single-factor swap is a swap whose cash flows depend on the realized value of a single underlying. A single-factor swap always has two legs: a fixed leg and a floating leg. The fixed payer in a single-factor swap pays a rate or price that is set on trade date T and prevails over the life of the transaction. The floating payer pays an amount that varies over time depending on the realization of the single factor underlying the swap—for example, the price of oil in a pay floating/receive oil swap, the 180-day London Interbank Offer Rate in a pay fixed/received LIBOR swap, the value of the S&P 500 index in a pay fixed/receive an equity cash-equivalent, and so on.

Most single-factor swaps are settled-in-arrears. The cash flow on a pay fixed/receive 180-day LIBOR simple interest rate swap, for example, is as follows on any settlement date S:

$$Z\left[(R_{S-180,\, S} - K)\frac{d}{D}\right] \qquad (13.3)$$

where d is the number of *actual* days that elapse between the setting of the rate $R_{S-180,\, S}$ on the underlying CD and the date that the CD pays interest. D is again the length of the money market year. Because R denotes a LIBOR in this example, $D = 360$ and d therefore may not be exactly 180 days given that the sum of the periods covered by two 180-day CDs must actually cover a 365-day calendar year. The fixed rate K is set on *trade date T*. Any date $S - 180$ is a *value date* corresponding to *settlement date S*. Because the transaction is settled in arrears, the exact amount of a payment on any date S thus is known to both parties on date $S - 180$.

From an exposure standpoint, a single-factor swap is simply a portfolio of forward contracts. Looking at Equations 13.2 and 13.3, the payoffs are evidently the same for a given rate, value date, and settlement date. Accordingly, a single-factor pay fixed/receive 180-day LIBOR swap can be viewed as a portfolio of settled-in-arrears FRAs with a common *notional principal amount* (NPA) of Z and a common fixed rate K. Figure 13.1 illustrates this graphically, where up arrows represent cash inflows and down arrows represent cash payments. The figure is drawn from the perspective of the fixed rate payer and omits both day count adjustments and the NPA for simplicity. The FRAs labeled FRA 1 through FRA N are each single forward rate agreements that settle on successively more distant dates. The swap is easily seen to be a combination of those FRAs. Note also that the settlement of the transactions in arrears is also evident from the figure—for example, the payment at time 2 is based on floating rate $R_{1,\, 2}$. The rate is thus set at

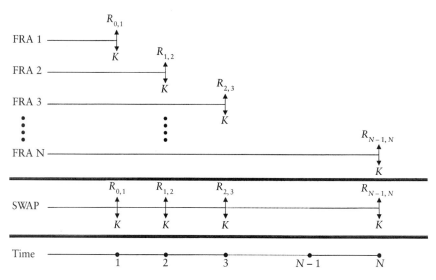

FIGURE 13.1 A swap as a portfolio of forward rate agreements.

time 1—the value date for FRA 2 and for the time 2 settlement on the swap—but corresponds to a cash flow at time 2—the settlement date for both FRA 2 and the swap.

Note also that the transaction labeled FRA is not really a forward rate agreement. Because the *trade date* for FRA 1 is date 0 and the value of the FRA is known on this date, FRA 1 is actually a spot transaction. In fact, FRA 1 can be viewed as two bonds—a purchased fixed-rate bond with coupon rate $R_{0,1}$ and an issued fixed-rate bond with coupon rate K.

A *multifactor* swap is a swap in which both legs are variable. The cash flows of the swap thus depend on more than one underlying market price, reference rate, index level, or risk factor. Recall the TED spread from Chapter 1. A TED swap, for example, is a two-factor swap in which one party pays LIBOR and the other party pays a Treasury rate, for example, 180-day LIBOR for 6-month Treasury.

Like single-factor rate swaps, a multi-factor swap can also be characterized as a portfolio of forward contracts. Unlike the previous case, however, a two-factor basis swap can be viewed as *two* forward contracts on each settlement date—one for each factor. Figure 13.2 provides a simple illustration. Looking only at two settlement dates—2 and N—the figure shows that the swap is equivalent to a long FRA based on one factor and a short FRA based on the other factor, both with a common fixed rate K. In FRA 2a, for example, the payable is K and the receivable is 6-month LIBOR set 6-months prior, denoted $R_{1,2}$. In FRA 2b, the payable is the 6-month Treasury

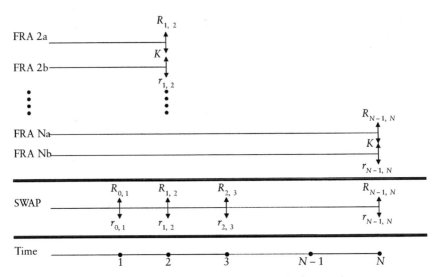

FIGURE 13.2 A basis swap as a portfolio of multiple forward rate agreements.

rate set six months prior, denoted $r_{1,2}$, and the receivable is K. Together, FRA 2a and FRA 2b result in a net exposure of a LIBOR receivable and a Treasury payable, or $(R_{1,2} - r_{1,2})$.

Futures

A third forward-like exposure can arise through a firm's use of futures contracts. To economists, futures are merely exchange-trade forwards. But to regulators and some derivatives users, the two product types are distinct enough to merit some additional discussion.

The Evolution of Futures and Their Distinguishing Characteristics[3] The village of Chicago was incorporated as a city in 1837, and its tremendously rapid growth was due almost entirely to its location and function as a grain terminal for the United States' primary farming region. In the early 1800s, farmers, packers, and millers regularly traveled to Chicago to buy and sell grain and livestock in spot markets (i.e., with no contracting for future delivery). Unfortunately for merchants and producers alike, the weather in Chicago was so volatile that supply and demand conditions changed constantly. By the time a farmer brought his grain to Chicago, he often found no one there willing to buy it. After production gluts, farmers would often dump their grain on the streets of Chicago when they could not find buyers.[4] Forward contracting arose in the Midwest in the 1800s as a means of trying to ensure future purchases and sales after an uncertain harvest period by prearranging buyers and sellers.

Although early forward contracts in the United States addressed merchants' concerns about ensuring that there were buyers and sellers for commodities, credit risk remained a serious problem. Illinois folklore tells the story of a farmer who, before his harvest, sold his crop forward to a grain merchant in Chicago. The entire grain harvest was huge that year. When the time came for the farmer to sell his grain, the price had fallen well below the agreed-upon purchase price in the forward contract. The merchant who had agreed to buy the grain then saw that he could buy it more cheaply elsewhere at current prices and reneged on the forward contract. Legend has it that the farmer walked up to the merchant and said, "I have a wagon of grain and a shotgun with me. Which should I unload?"[5]

To deal with these problems, a group of 82 local businessmen formed the Chicago Board of Trade (CBOT) in 1848 for the purpose of trading commodities in a more centralized and organized arena. The primary intention of the CBOT was to provide a centralized location known in advance for buyers and sellers to negotiate forward contracts. The belief was that merchants who wanted to transact on the CBOT season after season would know the location to which all the merchants were going and would not risk their reputation among those other merchants by failing to perform on forward contracts negotiated on the CBOT.

In 1865, the CBOT went one step further and listed the first futures contracts. They were still bilateral agreements, but the essential difference was that the CBOT listed contracts that had certain standardized elements, thus eliminating the need for buyers and sellers to negotiate *anything* in the contract except the price at which a subsequent exchange would be made.

In 1874, another group of agricultural dealers formed the Chicago Produce Exchange to trade butter, eggs, poultry, and other perishable products. In 1898, the butter and egg dealers split off to form the Chicago Butter and Egg Board, which was again reorganized to allow futures trading in 1919. When it was reorganized, its name was changed to the Chicago Mercantile Exchange (CME).

Although futures trading arose at about the same time throughout the world, the Chicago exchanges are regarded by almost everyone as having set the standards for the trading of these products. The Chicago exchanges sought to offer an attractive product different from off-exchange forward contracts. One way was to exploit the benefits of standardization. The role of an organized exchange was, and still is, primarily to list a contract by predefining its elements of standardization. Those standardized components of a futures contract include the definition of an underlying asset, the amount of the asset to be bought or sold, the date on which the exchange will occur, and the method of delivery and/or payment. The CME currently lists a futures contract on frozen pork bellies, for example, that allows a buyer to purchase 40,000 pounds of cut and trimmed frozen bellies. The pork belly contracts allow buyers to purchase for delivery in February, March, May, July, and August of each calendar year. A contract thus can be entered in September for the purchase of pork bellies the following August.

Organized futures exchanges also maintain a set of rules which buyers and sellers must obey in entering into the derivatives contracts that the exchange lists. Some of these rules address the following issues: trading hours, the particular forum in which trading must occur, price quotation styles, tick sizes, limits on how high or low a price can be quoted, the quality of product that must be accepted by a purchaser and delivered by a seller, the location and time of delivery, and so on. Perhaps the most important rules are those pertaining to the forum of trading. The Chicago exchanges, for example, utilize an *open outcry* trading forum in which buyers and sellers gather together in a pit and literally shout prices at one another. At the other extreme are *electronic* exchanges that require all trading to be done over a set of interlinked computers. Whatever the forum, because it is specified as part of the rules an exchange provides, the forum's details (including any centralized location for trading) are *known* in advance.

The *only* nonstandard component of a futures contract is its price, which is set by buyers and sellers, or *members* of the exchange. In other words, people and corporations pay the exchange for the right to trade the standardized derivatives that the exchange lists within the rules set by the exchange. This system of standardization and rule-setting is regarded by many derivatives users as highly beneficial. It facilitates the speed with which trading occurs by eliminating the need for counterparties to negotiate anything other than price. Standardization thus also lowers transaction costs.

Today, the standardization and low transaction costs of futures markets make them natural arenas for price discovery. As futures markets underwent the process of commodization over time, their liquidity and depth grew, thus making those markets the ones in which most information is first incorporated into observed financial asset prices.

Exchange-traded derivatives have two other features not shared with their off-exchange, customized-contract predecessors. First, *margin* is required by all derivatives exchanges today, which means that a trader must post a performance bond *before* engaging in a transaction. Second, derivatives exchanges utilize what is known as *multilateral clearing and settlement*. Together, these two features help ensure that traders of exchange-traded derivatives *both can and will* honor their contractual obligations.

Wishing to mitigate the potential for farmers to show up with loaded weapons to enforce their contracts, members of the Chicago exchanges began informally collecting performance bonds from one another in the late 1800s. If one party refused to honor his contract, he forfeited his performance bond. This system of margin, as it came to be known, helped mitigate some of the credit risk concerns of buyers and sellers; the exchanges thus attracted merchants who had previously contracted only with forwards.

The farmer/merchant example illustrates what might be called *walkaway* or *don't know* risk—a credit risk relating to the *willingness* of counterparties to honor their commitments. The Chicago traders also perceived another form of credit risk, which pertains to counterparties' *ability* to make good on contracts. Margin arose in large part to manage walkaway risk, but that did not always take care of those situations in which a merchant simply did not *have* the money to pay up. Traders were quick to recognize that the risk of nonpayment on a single, small amount of money was lower than the nonpayment risk on two large sums of money. The risk that one trader, for example, would fail to come up with $1,000 was lower than the risk that either of two traders would fail to come up with $50,000 and $49,000 respectively. Also, it cost less to write one check than two. Pairs of traders on the exchange floors thus began to reach informal agreements whereby *net* rather than gross cash flows were exchanged. This process of reducing the amount of cash flows at risk between individual traders is known as *bilateral netting*.

In the 1860s and 1870s, netting began to occur among more than just two traders *because the contracts traded on the exchanges were standardized*. Groups of traders in the same commodities formed "rings" in which financial obligations were netted *multilaterally* among all ring members. Traders then simplified matters even further by having everyone pay some money into a common ring fund before trading started each day. At the end of the day, traders took back out the net of what was due them.

By the early 1880s, the CBOT rings had grown beyond specific commodities to the whole exchange. Every exchange member paid into a common fund and received his net cash flow at the end of the day. This arrangement was formalized, and the original clearinghouse of the CBOT—now called the Board of Trade Clearing Corporation (BOTCC)—was set up in 1883.

When clearinghouses started to develop in the 1880s, the Chicago exchanges began to merge the settlement risk management function of the clearinghouse with the walkaway risk management function of the margin system. Specifically, clearinghouses began interjecting themselves as the counterparty to all transactions. Previously, if Ms. Woodlawn entered into a futures contract to purchase soybeans from Mr. Midway, her contract would be with Mr. Midway. With the creation of clearinghouses, exchange members recognized the benefit of having the *legal* contract be between each trader and the clearinghouse. Immediately after Ms. Woodlawn negotiates the contract with Mr. Midway and they agree on a price, a legal contract is established that commits Ms. Woodlawn to purchase soybeans *from the clearinghouse* and commits Mr. Midway to sell soybeans *to the clearinghouse*. Ms. Woodlawn and Mr. Midway still set the price in their negotiations, but *after* that their legal obligations are to the clearinghouse.

The clearinghouse system, still in existence today, provides a major attraction for some market participants when compared to off-exchange contracting: Every exchange-traded derivatives contract has the same default and settlement risks, equal to the risk the exchange clearinghouse itself defaults. Exchange-traded derivatives users thus *do not really care who their actual counterparty is.* This benefit of exchange-trading, typically referred to as *trading anonymity,* reduces transaction costs by lowering the costs traders must incur to search for creditworthy counterparties. Not all market participants place a high value on lower search costs. Some firms, for example, might prefer to deal in the off-exchange market with counterparties they have known and trusted in numerous previous relationships. Other market participants, however, who are concerned about search costs and credit risk, often find exchange-traded derivatives appealing.

Standardization coupled with the clearinghouse system makes "offsetting" possible, which greatly enhances the operational efficiency and financial integrity of most futures clearinghouses. Offsetting a position simply entails reversing the purchase of a commodity in the future by selling the same contract. The prices for the purchase and sale may be different, but because the contracts are standardized, the two contracts together remove any obligation of a trader to make (take) delivery to (from) the clearinghouse. In a customized, off-exchange forward contract, by contrast, a counterparty can be released from its obligation only by negotiating an "unwind" of the contract with the *original* counterparty. Because all exchange-traded derivatives are contracts with the clearinghouse, a trader can reverse any obligation to buy by finding any other counterparty on the exchange who is willing to buy. The second transaction need not be negotiated with the same party involved in the first transaction, because both transactions are in fact legal contracts with the clearinghouse.

Offsetting not only improves liquidity on futures exchanges. It also enables an exchange clearinghouse to step in and offset a trader's positions the moment that her creditworthiness is called into question. Over time, futures exchanges have greatly refined the clearinghouse system in order to mitigate credit risk. Instead of merely *allowing* traders to post performance bonds with each other, the exchanges quickly adopted margin as a *requirement* for exchange trading. Today, *initial* or *original* margin is required of *all* traders before any trade is made. If the counterparty to the clearinghouse cannot honor a losing obligation, the posted performance bond is applied to the loss. In the rare event that a loss exceeds the initial margin, the clearinghouse members jointly bear the cost of the default.

Exchanges also now engage in a practice known as *daily settling-up,* or *daily marking-to-market.* At the end of each day, much as they did in the 1800s, the clearinghouses tabulate the net position of all accounts and mark them to current market prices. Net winners may withdraw their profits, which come from the margin posted by the net losers of the day. If losers wish to maintain their positions in the market, the clearinghouse compares the new level in their margin account to a *maintenance* margin level. The maintenance level is often lower than the initial margin level. If a loser has lost so much that the end-of-day value of his performance bond is below that maintenance level, the clearinghouse demands the deposit of *variation* margin to bring the value of his performance bond up to the initial margin level. If the loser fails to meet this *margin call* by the next morning, his position is offset by the clearinghouse.

The effect of this daily settling up is the renegotiation of all futures contracts every day by adjusting margin accounts to reflect *current* prices. This ensures that at the end of every trading day, only those traders who can afford to make additional losses tomorrow are left in the market, and thus the chance of default is reduced significantly. If a default does occur, the loss is limited to a one-day price movement. Some exchanges—notably the CME and CBOT—now even mark to market more than once a day, reducing credit risk even further.

Futures Value and Settlement Dates   The process of marking to market of futures positions at least daily is effectively equivalent to closing out the contract each day and replacing it with a new one at the new market price. Consequently, the value *and* settlement dates for futures are really every mark to market period, and each mark to market period is in turn a new *de facto* trade date.

Consider specifically a futures contract established on trade date T that matures on date $T + 30$. Denote the price at which the long and short agree to open the position as $F_{T, T+30}$. One day later, suppose the settlement price for that contract is $F_{T+1, T+30}$. On that day, the variation margin or mark-to-market cash flow is equal to

$$\left[Z\left(F_{T+1, T+30} - F_{T, T+30} \right) \right]$$

where Z is the NPA of the contract or the number of units of physical asset underlying the contract. If the amount is positive, the variation margin is owed to the long; if negative, the short can collect the proceeds. Either way, the contract with trade date T has a value and settlement date of $T + 1$.

On date $T + 2$, suppose the settlement price is $F_{T+2, T+30}$. Then the positive mark-to-market cash flow either the long or short may collect is

$$\left[Z\left(F_{T+2, T+30} - F_{T+1, T+30} \right) \right]$$

Although the original trade date was T, the settlement and cash flow that occurs at $T + 2$ is based on the $T + 1$ settlement price; the contract was settled up on $T + 1$ already for price changes between T and $T + 1$. So, the *de facto* trade date corresponding to the time $T + 2$ settlement is date $T + 1$.

COMMERCIAL FORWARD-LIKE EXPOSURES

Numerous exposures in a corporation have exposure profiles similar to forward and swap contracts that are nevertheless commercial contracts. This is a terminological distinction. From a risk standpoint, a forward-like exposure is a forward-like exposure regardless what you call it.

Payables and receivables are classic examples of commercial forward-like contracts. When a company receives an invoice from an input supplier that is due 30 days hence, the company books a payable. At a minimum, the value of this payable can change over the 30 day window as interest rates change. If the invoice is for $1 million, a decline in rates over the 30 days the company can take to make the payment changes the terminal value of that cash flow. Conversely, delays in receivables are types of interest rate exposures that can affect the value to the company.

Some types of commercial contracts are more explicit examples of forward-like exposures. Specifically, contracts that call for the firm purchase or sale of something on a specified future date are forward-like exposures. A public utility that agrees for one year to supply 1,000 MW hours of power per day to a commercial customer during peak hours at $40/MWh, for example, has sold a sequence of forward contracts on power to the customer. Each forward has a fixed selling price of $40/MWh, and the maturity dates correspond to the hours occurring during peak demand periods over the year. A car manufacturer that agrees to sell 100 cars to a dealership 60 days hence for a specified price has entered into a forward sale agreement on cars. An airline that buys 1 million gallons of jet fuel over the year either buys it spot or prearranges delivery at fixed prices on specific dates and thus has bought it forward. And so on.

In general, products that take time to design, develop, produce, or otherwise bring to market usually have option-like exposure embedded in them. As will be discussed in more detail in Chapter 14, these types of products are often accompanied by the option for the producer to choose a production or extraction schedule, an investment schedule, and a time to market. Some products, however, have a *fixed* growth cycle or time to market, and those products can be viewed as spot exposures if they are sold at variable prices and forward-like exposures if they are sold at fixed prices.

Consider, for example, pumpkins. The demand for pumpkins is predominantly in the autumn, and the harvest comes in around then, as well. Characterizing a pumpkin farmer as long pumpkins in the autumn thus is fairly obvious, and whether the long is in the spot or forward market depends entirely on whether or not the farmer has pre-sold his pumpkins for a fixed price.

Natural resources subject to some extraction requirement can also be viewed as forward-like exposures. Once an oil field begins producing, for example, it is costly to shut down the pumps and refineries. The minimum amount of oil that must be extracted each month thus can be characterized as a series of forwards or a swap. If oil must be extracted at a rate of 10,000 barrels per month to avoid shutdown costs, then each forward or swap settlement has a principal amount of 10,000 barrels. If the oil is sold at a fixed price, the extracted 10,000 bbls per month define a pay floating (i.e., oil)/receive fixed commodity swap. If the oil is sold in the spot market, by contrast, the difference in the value of the extracted oil sold in the spot market and the oil if left in the ground is proportional to the marginal extraction cost.[6]

FOREIGN-CURRENCY FIXED OBLIGATIONS

Debt issued in a foreign currency represents two types of exposures for the issuing company—the debt instrument, and a spot exposure or forward/swap exposure on exchange rates. Consider, for example, a level-coupon bond issued by a U.S. company in Germany whose interest and principal are Dmark-denominated. Let K_{DM} denote the total interest paid each period in Dmarks and FV denote the face value of the bond. Suppose the issuer is perceived (correctly) as having no risk of default. Figure 13.3 shows the risk exposure to the issuer.

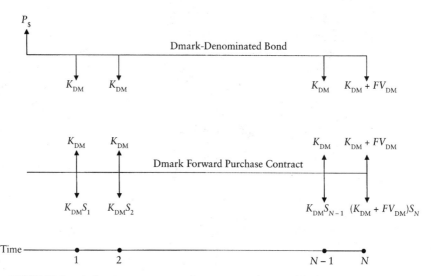

FIGURE 13.3   A foreign currency-denominated issued level-coupon bond.

The top panel of Figure 13.3 shows the debt exposure of issuer. On the trade (i.e., issue) date, the company receives $P_\$$ in proceeds for selling the bond. From the perspective of the *investor,* the bond's trade date is also its value date. The German investors know they will receive K_{DM} each period and $FV_{DM}+K_{DM}$ at maturity. Buying the bond thus is a spot transaction for investors that create a fixed income set of future cash flows.

From the perspective of the *issuer,* however, the trade date and the value date are not the same. As the second panel of Figure 13.3 illustrates, in the absence of any hedging the company must enter the spot currency market at each interest payment date and sell dollars to buy Dmarks. If the time 1 dollar price of Dmarks is S_1, the issuer must sell $K_{DM}S_1$ dollars in order to get K_{DM} Dmarks, and so on for other time periods.

In the absence of any risk management activities, the firm has an unhedged series of spot exchange rate obligations—short dollars and long Dmarks on each debt settlement date. The company can, of course, lock in future exchange rates with a currency swap or a series of forwards, thereby converting their spot exposures into forward-like exposures. Either way, the issuance of Dmark-denominated debt creates a currency exposure for the firm.

This kind of exposure arises for *any* foreign currency-denominated obligations or receivables. The only question is whether the exposure is a spot or forward-like exposure (or, as will be explored in Chapter 14, an option-like exposure). Novartis, for example, sells most of its drugs outside of Switzerland and receives revenues denominated in currencies other than Swiss francs. Most of its expenses, however, are Swiss franc-denominated. Consequently, the firm has a structural currency mismatch that can either be viewed as a series of spot exposures or forward-like exposures, depending on whether or not the receivable assets and payable liabilities are fixed in price.

SUPPLY CHAIN EXPOSURES AND PHYSICAL BASIS RISKS

Financial economics often seek to treat all financial instruments as bundles of cash flows without much attention to the details of the *physical* markets—input, output, and supply chain—in which the firm may be operating. Indeed, many would argue, for example, that the major losses booked by commercial banks in the trade finance area are a result of the lack of exposure at such firms to physical commodity markets. When a bank makes a loan to an exporter to finance, say, the shipment of coffee from Africa to Europe, the bank takes the coffee as collateral for the loan whose cash is used to rent the ship, move the coffee, inspect it, and so forth. If the coffee exporter defaults on the loan, the bank is stuck with the coffee. The inability of most banks to manage physical collateral when repossession occurs has accounted for staggeringly large losses.

Figure 13.4 below shows an example of a supply chain for wheat. Depending on how integrated a processor is, the asset exposure associated with wheat can be viewed as any number of different forward-like positions. For the farmer selling the wheat to an elevator, the farmer is long the wheat itself as a spot asset. For a firm consolidated over both origination and transformation activities, the input exposure might be spot wheat but the output exposure could be milled wheat or milled products such as flour or even bread.

FIGURE 13.4 The physical supply chain: Wheat.

The degree of integration of a producer over different aspects of a physical supply chain determines in large part the degree to which the producer has an outright spot or forward-like asset exposure or whether the producer simply has basis risk—or both. A wheat miller that engages in no origination *and* no delivery activities is principally exposed to basis risk—the risk of rises in wheat prices *relative to* transformed wheat product prices (e.g., flour). A freight and transportation logistic company that picks up flour from a mill and delivers it to a bakery, by contrast, may face no price exposure at all unless the transaction had to be financed with a loan for which the milled flour serves as collateral.

Virtually any product that moves through even part of the supply chain exposes some firm to one or more types of basis risk. A manufacturer of widgets that are ready for sale when they emerge from the factory line still must be transported, distributed, and sold. The price at the point of sale may fluctuate relative to the wholesale price, and the price of transportation—including insurance and quality verification—also could shift.

Vertical integration over all parts of the supply chain is one way to internalize at least some of these risks. In some cases, vertical integration converts an outright asset risk into a basis risk. In the absence of vertical integration, for example, a farmer selling his crop to a mill is long the crop. Price increases benefit the farmer, but hurt the miller. The miller, in turn, is short the crop and long the finished product. By buying the farm, the miller can turn its short crop exposure into a net flat position—the long crop asset exposure is netted against the short crop exposure associated with the production process for transformed goods such as flour. The integrated mill bears the basis risks that the crop supply will not match the output supply one-for-one, that quality differentials will appear, that wheat on the market is cheaper than wheat at the acquired farm, and the like. But these risks are no longer outright asset exposures. They are basis risks that will be addressed through transfer pricing.

CHAPTER 14

Identifying Option, Option-Like, and Real Option Exposures

The basic payoff diagrams for European calls and puts were presented in Chapter 3, and the same chapter demonstrated how the securities issued by a corporation are themselves types of options. Being able to recognize equity and debt as options is an example of how much of the world can be viewed through an options lens.

We have also encountered a "real option" in Chapter 6. Indeed, the term *real option* came from Myers whose under-investment theory is driven *entirely* by the existence of *growth opportunities*, which are classic real options. Of growing interest and popularity in both corporate strategy and financial risk management is the study of and search for such real options— opportunities viewed as options or assets viewed as options. Either way, the real options that a company *owns* are important contributors to the value of the firm, and the real assets that a company *writes* are significant components of the company's risk exposure profile.

Especially noteworthy is that option-like exposures in a corporation may either be sources of financial risk to firms or sources of opportunity. The ability for a firm to integrate options analysis into its exposure identification and decision-making processes thus is often a key distinguishing characteristic from firms whose risk management process follows the pure risk control business model versus those whose risk management process is more aimed at efficiency enhancement in the sense of Chapter 10.

LISTED OR OTC-TRADED OPTIONS ON TRADED ASSETS[1]

The plain vanilla, basic, common, humdrum option is the option that is either negotiated OTC or listed on an exchange based on the value of an underlying asset that is traded, or, at least, has a market-determined price.

Obvious examples are options on common stock, commodities, and foreign exchange. In addition, OTC interest rate options based on market determinations of LIBOR—called caps, collars, and floors—have become increasingly popular over the past decade.

Although options are themselves typically considered derivatives, options based on *other* derivatives can also be negotiated OTC or listed for trading by an exchange. Examples include options on futures, options on forward rate agreements (fraptions), options on swaps (swaptions), and many other creative sounding names.

For many years, the principle distinction between OTC and exchange-listed options was the degree of standardization in the latter compared to the former.[2] Once upon a time, everything in an option contract listed by an exchange was standardized except the premium to be paid by the buyer to the writer. With the advent of FLEX™ options, even many exchange-traded options can now be customized as to the time of delivery and striking price.

Plain vanilla calls and puts can be modified in any number of ways to yield more complex or more specifically tailored payoffs and cash flows for their buyers and writers. Options that deviate from the basic plain vanilla formulation are sometimes called *exotic*. In fact, many such options are not exotic at all, although they may well be a bit nontraditional. Some variations on various themes to the plain vanilla call and put are discussed next, each of which involves changing some aspect of the traditional option structure.

Changing Exerciseability Conventions

Traditional options can be exercised either on their maturity date (European-style options) or on any date prior to maturity (American-style options). Bermuda-style options allow the buyer to exercise on any one of *several* dates before and on the option's expiration date but not on *every* date. Some bond options, for example, only allow exercise on bond coupon payment dates.

Forward-start options also represent a departure from conventional notions of exercise. A forward-start option owner pays the premium on the trade date for an option that does not become live or exerciseable until some future date. A *cliquet* option is a *series* of forward-start options whose strike prices are reset over time so that the option is always at-the-money.

Barrier options also change the exerciseability conventions of traditional options. A *knock-in option* is one that *does not exist* until the price of the underlying has crossed some barrier, whereas a *knock-out option ceases to exist* when some barrier is reached. A down-and-out call, for example, is a traditional call *plus* the additional feature that if prices ever fall below some *outstrike,* the option disappears. If the outstrike is never reached, the terminal payoff on the option is the same as if the call were a traditional European option. But if the outstrike is reached, the option goes away. And similarly for *up-and-in* calls, *down-and-in* puts, and *up-and-out* puts.

Changing Buy or Sell Conventions

A call is an option to buy an asset, whereas a put is an option to sell an asset. A *chooser* or *as-you-like-it* option, by contrast, allows the buyer to decide whether the option is a call or a put after some period of time into the life of the option.

Calls and puts, moreover, are sometimes combined in a single option instrument. A very popular such instrument is called a *range forward,* so named because parts of its payoff diagram look more like a forward than an option. Nevertheless, the instrument is equivalent to a call and a put—one purchased and the other sold. A long range forward with an underlying asset whose maturity date T value is $S(T)$, for example, is a single option-like instrument that is equivalent to selling a put at some strike price K_1 and buying a call at a higher strike price K_2. The payoff to the buyer at maturity is shown in Figure 14.1 as the heavy solid line. Note that K_1 is only slightly below K_2, so that the net position is very nearly equivalent to a forward

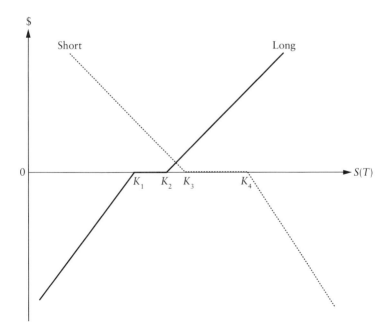

FIGURE 14.1 Value of a range forward contract at maturity.

purchase agreement with a fixed price of K. But instead, the long experiences neither a gain nor loss in the small range between K_1 and K_2.

The heavy dashed line on Figure 14.2 represents another range forward—this time a *short* position equivalent to a purchased put with strike K_3 and a written call with strike K_4. Unlike the long, however, the short has *strike prices far enough away from one another* that the range over which the seller is neither penalized nor rewarded for changes in the maturity spot price $S(T)$ is large. Most range forwards are constructed to be zero-cost instruments for their buyers and sellers.

Changing the Payoff Formula

A basic European call written on some asset with spot price $S(T)$ at maturity date T and striking price K has the following terminal or exercise value:

$$C(T) = \max[0, S(T) - K]$$

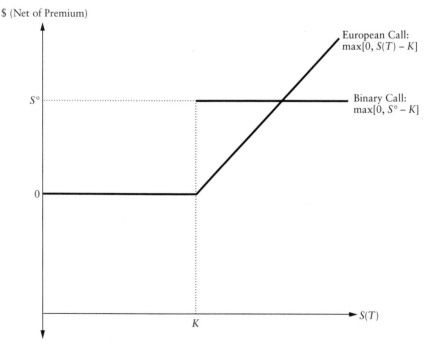

$ (Net of Premium)

European Call:
$\max[0, S(T) - K]$

S°

Binary Call:
$\max[0, S^\circ - K]$

0

K

$S(T)$

FIGURE 14.2 Long European call versus long digital call at maturity.

As $S(T)$ rises above strike price K, the option goes into the money and the buyer benefits dollar for dollar with the increase. This basic option payoff can be changed, however, in several ways. One way to play around with the basic payoff formula is to change the basic definition in a manner where the exercise value of the option depends on some exogenously specified parameter at maturity. Another way is to alter the payoff so that it depends on the *path taken* by one or more underlying prices *before* reaching maturity or being exercised.

Underlying-Independent Payoffs   Consider an option whose payoff does not depend on how deep in the money the option is:

$$C(T) = \max(0, S^\circ - K)$$

where S° is a fixed amount. The buyer either gets zero or $S^\circ - K$, and the latter amount does not vary with the degree to which the option is in-the-money. Called a *binary* or *digital option,* the payoff of this option at maturity (net of premium paid) is shown in Figure 14.2 and is contrasted with the payoff at maturity on a regular European call with the same strike price. Evident is that the binary option gives the long more money for any spot price $S(T) < S^\circ$ but penalizes the holder relative to a European call for $S(T) > S^\circ$.

Note that the underlying price does still affect the welfare of the option buyer by defining when the option is in-the-money. The option's value to its buyer is thus not entirely independent of the price of the underlying at maturity or upon exercise. Only the *payoff* is independent of this price and is dependent instead on the parameter S°.

Indexed Payoffs   Another particularly popular type of nontraditional option is called a *quanto option.* Usually found in equity markets, a quanto option is typically an option on a foreign equity denominated in the local currency, where the currency conversion rate is fixed and embedded in the option payoff formula. At some maturity date T, the exercise value of a quanto option with strike price K (denominated in a foreign currency) on some underlying stock whose foreign currency-denominated value is denoted $S(T)$ is

$$C(T) = \max[0, XS(T) - XK]$$

where X is a fixed exchange conversion factor from the foreign currency into the local currency. The payoff formula thus can be rewritten as:

$$C(T) = X \max[0, S(T) - K]$$

so that the quanto is simply a traditional call with a fixed exchange rate conversion. The fixed exchange conversion factor X is a type of indexing parameter that, together with the traditional definition of intrinsic value, defines the payoff of the option upon exercise or at maturity.

Average Price and Average Strike Options *Path-dependent options* are non-traditional options—usually OTC—whose payoff upon exercise or at maturity depends on not just the underlying asset price at the time of exercise/maturity, but rather on the *path* of underlying prices realized over some dates during the life of the option—perhaps back to the trade date.

One popular type of path-dependent option is called an *Asian* or *average price/strike option*. For an Asian call option with maturity date T, the exercise value is

$$C(T) = \max[0, A(\tau_1, \tau_2) - K]$$

where K is the fixed strike price (as usual) and where $A(\tau_1, \tau_2)$ is the *average* price of the asset underlying the option from date τ_1 through date τ_2. The averaging period from τ_1 through τ_2 may include the trade date through the maturity date or anything in between, and the average itself may either be geometric or average. Puts work the other way around, with the terminal payoff equal to the maximum of zero or the strike less the average price.

A similar type of Asian option is an average *strike* option. For a call with maturity date T, the payoff at expiration on an average strike call is

$$C(T) = \max[0, S(T) - A(\tau_1, \tau_2)]$$

where $S(T)$ is the terminal price of the underlying and $A(\tau_1, \tau_2)$ is the average value of that underlying price over the period from τ_1 to τ_2.

Asian options tend to be quite popular for corporations whose strategic risk management objectives involve smoothing cash flows or earnings over relatively long periods of time. When the objective is to avoid spikes in cash flows or earnings, Asian options can be useful mechanisms for distributing the impact of such spikes over the chosen averaging period. At the same time, because the averaging effect in the payoffs of Asian options reduces the likelihood of extreme price movements, the probability of a large in-the-money move is lower with an Asian option than a traditional call or put. Consequently, Asian options tend to be cheaper—often significantly—than otherwise identical, traditional European calls and puts.

Lookback Options Another popular type of path-dependent option is an option on an extremum, or a *lookback option*. At maturity or upon exercise, a lookback option gives its buyer the right to choose a strike price based on *any* price the underlying has realized either over its life or over some defined interval. A lookback call thus is equivalent to a call whose strike price is the minimum realized price over the indicated interval, whereas a lookback put is an option with a maximum price as strike. Payoffs of lookback calls and puts at maturity are, respectively:

$$C(T) = \max\left[0, S(T) - S^{\min}\right]$$

$$P(T) = \max\left[0, S^{\max} - S(T)\right]$$

Figure 14.3 shows the payoffs at maturity for lookback calls and puts given three different price paths. Path 1 illustrates the most extreme case, where the value of a call at maturity is equal to the terminal price minus the initial price. The put is worthless in that case, but a traditional put also would have been worthless unless it had been struck so deeply in-the-money that the strike price was above S_5.

Ladder Options   A *ladder option* has a strike price that automatically changes when the underlying price moves through some predefined barrier. The

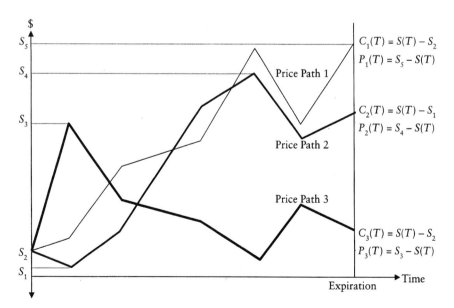

FIGURE 14.3   Payoffs for lookback call and put options at maturity date *T*.

buyer and seller can agree on multiple such *rungs* and a *ladder* of corresponding strike prices. Ladder options are popularly used to lock in some degree of in-the-moneyness of an option so that subsequent reversals before exercise or maturity do not deprive the holder of those gains.

A European ladder call option has the following payoff at maturity date T:

$$C(T) = \max\left[0, S(T) - K, \max\left(0, L_k - K\right)\right]$$

where L_k is the kth rung in the ladder of strike prices specified. The payoffs on a ladder call are shown for three different price paths in Figure 14.4 from Smithson (1998). Price path 1 generates a payoff equivalent to a traditional call because the terminal asset price $S(T)$ is above both ladder rungs. But for price path 2, the price path crossed ladder rungs L_1 and L_2, but the terminal price reversed and ended up below L_2. The ladder payoff thus is $L_2 - S(T)$ larger than it would have been for a traditional call. And for price path 3, the path crosses the first rung of the ladder and then slides downward so that $S(T)$ is well below L_1. Because the option is a ladder, the early appreciation in the underlying price above L_1, however, is locked in.

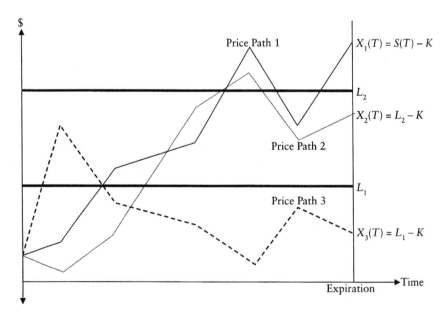

FIGURE 14.4 Payoffs for ladder call option at maturity date T.

Shout Options   A *shout option* is a call or a put where the buyer can "shout" to the seller and define a ladder rung—just as in a ladder option—at one or more times over the life of the option. Usually the buyer can shout only once. In other words, a shout option is a ladder option where the rung is determined over the life of the option rather than in advance. When the buyer shouts to the seller, the intrinsic value of the option is locked in as a minimum terminal payoff. But if only one shout is allowed, the buyer may forego other potentially more profitable shouting opportunities.

The payoff of European shout calls and puts on maturity date T are defined as follows for some buyer-chosen shout level $K°$:

$$C(T) = \max\left[0, S(T) - K, K° - K\right]$$

$$P(T) = \max\left[0, K - S(T), K - K°\right]$$

Figure 14.5 shows price path 2 from Figure 14.4 and the predefined ladder rungs L_1 and L_2. If the buyer of the shout option shouts when prices reach ladder level L_2, the buyer of the shout option receives the same payoff as

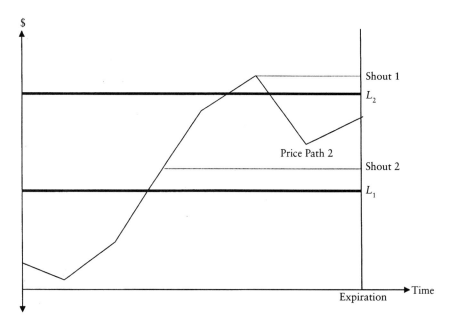

FIGURE 14.5   Payoffs for shout call option at maturity date T.

the buyer of the ladder option. If instead the buyer presciently shouts at Shout 1, the payoff is higher; if the option purchaser shouts at Shout 2, the terminal value of the call is less. The better a shout option buyer is at identifying trends and reversals, the more a shout option will resemble a lookback option.

Changing the Underlying

Yet another way that a simple call or put can be turned into something different involves a change in the underlying asset. Some common examples of options with nontraditional underlyings are summarized next.

Compound Options A *compound option* is an option on an option. Upon exercise, the buyer receives another option rather than an actual physical asset, cash-equivalent, or forward-based derivatives contract. Examples include options on caps, collars, and floors and options on a portfolio of options. Compound options can *be* calls or puts and *can be written on* calls or puts, leading to at least four combinations: a call on a call, a call on a put, a put on a call, and a put on a put.

Exchange, Rainbow, and Basket Options Another type of option where the underlying is not a simple, single asset is an exchange asset, or an option to exchange one asset for another. A European exchange option has the following value at maturity:

$$\max\left[S_1(T) - S_2(T), 0\right]$$

where $S_1(T)$ is the terminal price of asset 1 and $S_2(T)$ is the terminal price of asset 2.

Exchange options are commonly combined with a position in one of the two assets. When this is done, the net result is an option that allows the buyer to obtain the *better* or *worse* of two assets. An option that entitles its holder to obtain the *better* of two assets has a terminal payoff of

$$\max\left[S_1(T), S_2(T)\right] = S_1(T) - \max\left[S_1(T) - S_2(T), 0\right]$$

and an option that entitles is holder to obtain the *worse* of two assets has a terminal payoff of

$$\min\left[S_1(T), S_2(T)\right] = S_2(T) + \max\left[S_1(T) - S_2(T), 0\right]$$

The exchange option is also sometimes called a *relative spread option* or a *rainbow option*. Rainbow options can include two or more assets, and the assets may represent a basket of other assets.

SYNTHETICS

Options can be combined with other options (explicitly traded or otherwise), with assets and liabilities, and with forwards and forward-based derivatives to yield new positions. Sometimes these new positions are identical to products already listed for trading or available OTC on a customized basis.

A *synthetic* position is constructed using financial instrument building blocks. Sometimes options can be combined with options to yield an exposure that looks like a forward or a physical asset, just as we saw in Chapter 3 when we saw that the assets of the firm are equal to a long call plus a short put written on the assets of the firm with a common striking price equal to the face value of the firm's debt. Options can also be recombined to yield other option-like exposures. Although these synthetic options are usually constructed by combining multiple explicitly traded financial products, the same principles apply when the products are not traded. What matters is the *net result*, not what any of the individual instruments are or happen to be called.

A simple and dangerously seductive example comes from the common portfolio management strategy of *writing covered calls*. Suppose you own the stocks in the S&P 500 index. Many managers are tempted to *write* a call against the physical stock. The premium collected enhances income on the portfolio, and managers are too often seduced into thinking the strategy has limited risk because they own the stock that can be used to cover any exercises on the option they have written.

Figure 14.6 shows why this line of reasoning can only lead to trouble from a risk management standpoint. Suppose the current value of the stock portfolio is $S(2)$. To enhance income, the portfolio manager can choose to write a call with a strike price at $S(1)$, where $S(1) < S(2)$ and the option is in-the-money (yielding a higher premium collected). For any price $S > S(1)$ at maturity of the option, the portfolio is neutral. Any gains on the stocks are offset by losses on the option, or, more true to the name of the strategy, the stocks themselves are used to cover exercises against the short call. But for prices $S < S(1)$, the position behaves just like the outright stock portfolio. The *net* position is equivalent to a put written at strike price $S(1)$. In exchange for collecting premium by writing the call, the manager thus has traded all of her upside but has limited none of her downside—hardly a riskless position.

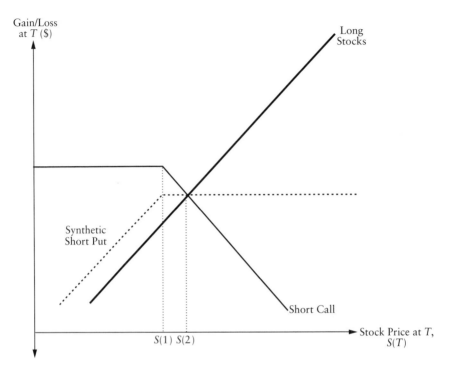

FIGURE 14.6 A covered call as a synthetic short put at maturity.

The opposite of covered call writing is a synthetic known as *protective put purchasing*. Again assume an equity portfolio manager is long a basket of stocks at $S(2)$, but this time has the goal of reducing risk rather than enhancing yield. In this case, suppose the manager purchases a put at strike price $S(1)$. Because $S(1) < S(2)$, the put is out-of-the-money. Although this is cheaper than an at-the-money put, liability is only limited for price declines below $S(1)$. At stock prices above $S(1)$, the position behaves as before (less the premium paid). As Figure 14.7 shows, the net impact of the two positions at the maturity of the put option is a synthetic long call at strike price $S(1)$.

OPTIONS EMBEDDED IN OTHER FINANCIAL INSTRUMENTS

Options and option-like payoffs also often appear in other traded or listed financial instruments, including derivatives and securities. These embedded

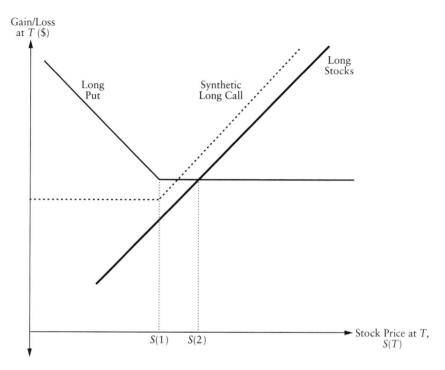

FIGURE 14.7 A protective put as a synthetic long call at maturity.

options may include options that are otherwise available as stand-alone products or implicit options created by virtue of the contract design process.

Embedded Options That Are Sold Separately

A basic and extremely common example of an asset with an embedded option that can be virtually perfectly replicated with a stand-alone purchase or sale is a bond with call and/or put provisions. A callable bond is a bond in which the issuer has the right to call the bond away from the investor in certain circumstances (e.g., if rates rise above a certain threshold during a specified time period). The bond thus includes an embedded call option on interest rates. The underlying of the option depends on how the call provision is structured. If the issuer can call the bond at any time over the bond's life if interest rates fall by more than 100 basis points, for example, then the bond includes an option on interest rates with a tenor equal to the tenor of the bond that the holder has written to the issuer with a strike rate 100 basis points below the current interest rate.

Bonds can also contain numerous other types of embedded options. A putable bond is a bond whose *holder* has the right to redeem the bond for face value prior to maturity in the event certain triggers are hit in the market, such as rate declines that might prompt the investor to want to rebalance her portfolio toward higher-yield securities. Similarly, a convertible bond is similar to a straight bond plus the issuance to the bond holder of warrants. Some bonds even contain options on commodity prices, exchange rates, or equity prices of companies other than the bond issuer.

Embedded Options That Are Not Sold Separately

Apart from bonds, other fixed income assets also often contain various types of embedded options, not all of which have traded or OTC analogues. Mortgages and other loans with prepayment provisions, for example, contain valuable options held by the borrowers to prepay their loans. When interest rates decline, the holder of a fixed-rate mortgage may prepay the mortgage so that she can refinance at a more favorable interest rate. This means that the holder of the mortgage holds a type of option on interest rates written by the lender.

The reason the embedded prepayment option in a mortgage does not have a traded option analogue traces to the imperfect correlation between *any given* individual's prepayment behavior and some interest rate. To take a simple example, suppose Captain Kirk takes out a fixed-rate mortgage loan from a bank. Increases in, say, LIBOR may be indicative of when Captain Kirk will prepay his loan, but imperfectly at best. In addition to LIBOR, Captain Kirk also may have personal liquidity constraints, a variable credit premium that fluctuates vis-à-vis LIBOR, a difficulty parting with his home, and so forth. And even then, perhaps the rate Kirk watches most closely is the Prime rate rather than LIBOR. For any number of reasons, the option that Captain Kirk holds to prepay his mortgage is a nontradeable option that can *at best* be approximated as an option on LIBOR or some other interest rate.

In more general terms, the prepayments on a whole portfolio of mortgages may be correlated very highly with some specific reference rate like LIBOR. But no matter how high the correlation, any given individual borrower holding a mortgage in the portfolio may choose to behave differently at any given time than the LIBOR correlation implies.

Embedded options that have no traded or OTC analogue are common in securitized products, such as asset-backed securities, asset-backed commercial paper programs, and traches of collateralized mortgage/bond/loan obligation structures. The options held by the borrowers are options to be sure, but the embedded option written to the borrowers by the investors in the securitized product vehicle can very rarely be perfectly replicated with traded financial instruments.

Options Created by Standardization in Futures Contracts

Futures contracts also frequently contain numerous types of embedded options, some of which can actually get rather complex. Agricultural futures and other physically settled commodity futures, for example, often contain options on *quality, transportation costs,* and sometimes *timing of delivery.* Consider, for example, the wheat futures contract traded on the Sydney Futures Exchange, that calls for delivery of 50 metric tons of Australian Standard White (ASW) wheat with a minimum protein content of 9% (based on 11% moisture and a 5.7 nitrogen scale). Approved delivery locations include GrainCorp Warehouses at Moree, Parkes, and Junee.

Consider first the quality option. The short can deliver any ASW with the minimum protein content, and the futures contract will be priced by buyers with the expectation that the delivery will involve this quality minimum. If a wheat farmer in Australia has ASW with protein levels of 8%, 9%, and 10%, the farmer will deliver the 9% to the Sydney Futures Exchange clearing house. The wheat with 8% protein is too low to be eligible for delivery, but the 10% protein content is unnecessarily high. The farmer thus exercises his option to deliver *the minimum* and then may try to sell the 10% protein wheat for a higher price on the spot market. This option is equivalent to an exchange option, or, when considered together with a higher protein wheat, an option to deliver the worst of two assets.

Farmers also have a geographical option. If a farmer operates several grain elevators, one of which is discernibly closer to an authorized delivery point in Moree, Parkes, or Junee, the farmer will obviously opt to deliver that wheat before the wheat that is further away. Transportation costs priced into the futures contract, after all, may be inadequate to cover the costs of moving wheat from the more distant elevator, so the farmer's costs are minimized when he selects the cheapest location from which to deliver wheat to the clearing house.

The quality option and the geographical option are sometimes collectively called the "cheapest to deliver" option embedded in futures contracts because together they give the right to the short to select for delivery the cheapest possible physical inventory that still satisfies the contract's minimum requirements for delivery. Note that these options arise because of the need to *standardize* the futures contract for exchange listing. A fully customized contract could specify pricing based on an exact quality and exact location, but in order to generate sufficient liquidity to support an exchange listing a futures contract must be standardized along dimensions like quality and allowed delivery points. Such standardization features inevitably lead to at least some embedded optionality.

Cheapest to deliver options are also not unique to futures on commodities. All that is required is that the contract involve *physical delivery*. The futures contract on the long-term U.S. government bond listed on the Chicago Board of Trade, for example, is a futures contract on a *financial* asset that nevertheless calls for physical delivery. Specifically, the short may deliver any noncallable bond issued by the U.S. Treasury with at least 15 years remaining to maturity (or, if the bond is callable, with at least 15 years remaining to its first call date). The last trading day for a given contract is the eighth to the last business day of the contract month, and delivery can occur any time during the contract month.

When a bond is delivered by the short in the CBOT long bond futures contract, the invoice price paid by the long is equal to the futures price times a "conversion factor" plus accrued interest. Because such a wide range of bonds can be delivered into the CBOT contract, the Board of Trade tries to equalize invoice prices across bonds by adjusting the quoted futures price with a conversion factor calculated as the approximate decimalized price at which the delivered bond would yield 8% to maturity or first call.

Even with the conversion factor applied to the invoice price, the short has at least two valuable options written by the long by virtue of the contract's standardized features—an option on *what* to deliver, and an option on *when* to deliver it. These two broad options can be viewed as a combination of more specific options, some of which can be exercised before the last day of trading and others of which can only be exercised between the last trading day and the last delivery day.

Options embedded in the long bond futures contract that the short can exercise before the contract stops trading collectively define the quality option. [3] Because the short can choose among a variety of deliverable bonds, the short will virtually always select the cheapest to deliver, which is determined largely by the bond's duration, convexity, and changes in rates. Figure 14.8 from Burghardt and Belton (1994) shows the relation between bond prices divided by the futures conversion factor (CF) and yields assuming the only three eligible bonds for delivery have coupon rates of 12%, $9\frac{7}{8}$%, and $8\frac{7}{8}$% with respective maturities of 2014, 2021, and 2023. The 12% 2014 bond has a relatively low duration and the $8\frac{7}{8}$% 2023 bond a relatively high duration.

As Figure 14.8 illustrates, the cheapest to deliver bond depends on the interest rate environment. For yields below Y_1, the 12% 2014 bond has the lowest converted cash price. For yields between Y_1 and Y_2 the $9\frac{7}{8}$% 2021 bond is cheapest to deliver. And for yields above Y_2, the high duration bond has the lowest price adjusted by the conversion factor. If relative yield

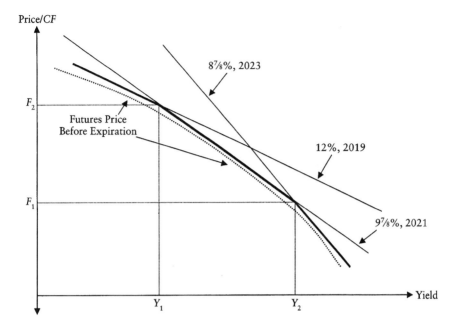

Price/CF

F_2

Futures Price
Before Expiration

$8\frac{7}{8}$%, 2023

12%, 2019

F_1

$9\frac{7}{8}$%, 2021

Y_1 Y_2

Yield

FIGURE 14.8   The cheapest to deliver bond in the CBOT long bond futures contract.

relations behave as expected, the futures price *at expiration* and the yield of the $8\frac{7}{8}$% bond has a relation shown on the graph as the heavy shaded line tracing out the lowest part of each price/yield relation. Prior to maturity, the relation between the futures price and yield follows the smooth, dotted, curved line lying below the heavy shaded line.

The difference between the cash price of the bond adjusted by the conversion factor and the futures price is a version of the *futures quality basis* for the bond in question and indicates the return to holding the bond for delivery against the futures contract. For yields well above Y_2, the high duration ($8\frac{7}{8}$% 2023) bond is cheapest to deliver and has a relatively small chance of becoming more expensive relative to the other two delivery-eligible bonds, especially if the futures contract is close to expiration. As yields fall, the cheapest to deliver bond changes and the premium of the $8\frac{7}{8}$% 2023 bond relative to the futures price—indicated by the dotted line—rises. This relation, shown in Figure 14.9, is the same payoff diagram one would expect to see prior to maturity for a call option on bonds; as yields decline and prices rise, the payoff to the option holder increases. Also shown in Figure 14.9 is the relation between the low and medium duration bond bases and yields. The low duration bondholder has a payoff that resembles

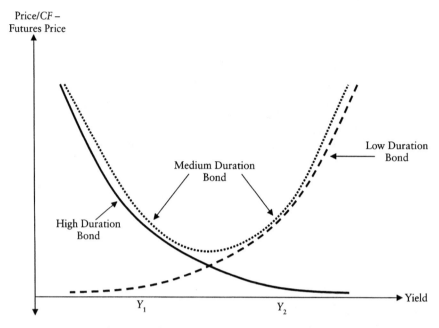

FIGURE 14.9   The bond futures quality basis as an embedded option.

a put option, and the medium duration bond has a payoff that resembles a straddle.

Apart from the quality option embedded in many futures contracts, a related futures-embedded is a timing-driven quality option. Returning to the CBOT long bond futures contract, the short may deliver any time between the close of trading on the last trading day—when the invoice price is fixed—and seven business days later. If the cheapest to deliver bond changes during this time, the short's right to deliver the cheap bond is known as the *switch option*.

In addition to the quality option, the short possesses several additional options, all of which concern the timing of deliveries into the futures contract. These options arise both because of lags in the delivery process itself and the standardized delivery terms of the CBOT long bond contract. The delivery process itself requires three days. On the first day—*Tender* or *Position Day*—the short must give official notice to the clearing broker or exchange that it intends to make delivery. This must occur by 8 P.M. central time, or six hours after the market close. On the second day—*Notice* or *Intention Day*—the short must identify the bond to be delivered by 2 P.M. Chicago time. On the third and final *Delivery Day,* the short (or its clearing member) must deliver the bond to the long's bank by 1 P.M., by which time the short's bank must have received payment. Because deliveries can occur at any time during the contract month and the delivery process takes three days, the first allowed Tender/Position Day is the second business day prior to the contract month's beginning and the last allowed Tender/Position Day is the second business day before the end of the contract month.

One timing option held by the short is a one-day switch option if intent to deliver is given before trading in the contract ends. The invoice price is set from the futures settlement price by 8 P.M. on Notice Day, but the short need not designate the bond to be delivered until 2 P.M. on the next day, the Tender Day. Changes in the cheapest to deliver bond during this time period can be exploited by the short.

Another timing option, called the *wild card option,* arises from the six-hour lag between the 2 P.M. close of trading on the Notice Day and the 8 P.M. deadline for the short to file intent to deliver.[4] Furthermore, trading in the cash market for treasuries continues until 4 P.M. If bond prices decline after 2 P.M., the short can issue a notice of intent to deliver and then buy the cheapest to deliver bonds in anticipation of the delivery, generating a gain vis-à-vis the futures invoice price determined at 2 P.M.

Options Embedded in OTC Contracts   The prior section shows that the standardization of exchange-traded derivatives that settle physically almost always includes embedded options. Does this mean that fully customizable OTC derivatives do not? No.

First of all, even OTC contracts may involve standardization of some kind in order to control the costs of verifying the quality of the underlying or to limit the possibilities for delivery points. Some firms may be willing to trade a little customization in order to gain some efficiencies in pricing and contract design and thus will tolerate standardization along at least some dimensions.

In addition, OTC contracts also often contain embedded options involving early termination. For OTC derivatives negotiated and documented under the ISDA Master Agreements, for example, events of default may occur that allow—if not obligate—one or both parties to terminate the transaction early for a specific payment. This is an option to default, although it can be very difficult to price and manage because the defaulting party is not known *ex ante.*

NONTRADED FINANCIAL OPTIONS

Some options are option-like in every way, down to being written on a financial asset price, except that they *cannot be freely traded, bought,* or *sold.* Stock options are a very common example of such nontraded financial options. Employee stock options can neither be traded nor transferred but are nevertheless contracts in which employees or managers or a firm are compensated with a kind of option-like equity component that allows them to buy some number of shares on or before some specified date at a preagreed price.

The restrictions on trading products like stock options often also imply that such options cannot be viewed as simple calls and puts. Two common features of stock options, for example, are *vesting* and *barriers*. A vesting period is a period of time in which the employee must remain at the company before the option can be exercised, whether or not it is in-the-money. From a risk management perspective, this means that the stock option product is better viewed as a forward-starting option and not merely as an option.

Employee stock options also may contain barrier provisions, especially when granted by high technology or start-up venture firms. Until the stock price of the firm has, say, doubled, the employee options are worthless, *even if they are struck at-the-money*. If an at-the-money option contains a knock-in feature that says the option conveys no rights until the stock price doubles, then the *minimum* payoff on the option *if* it is ever exercised will be the value of the stock grant on the date of issue.[5] This feature transforms the simple employee option into an up-and-in option.

The use of down-and-out provisions in employee stock options is not as common for obvious incentive reasons. Although some companies do not mind rewarding employees for better performance even when that performance is due entirely to correlations of the company' stock price to the broad market (i.e., systematic risk), companies are reluctant to punish employees for broad market corrections that might also pull down their stock prices below the out-strike at which the option grant ceases to exist.

OPTION-LIKE FINANCIAL CONTRACTS

A significant number of financial contracts have option-like features even if they are not themselves called options. One of the most obvious analogues to financial options is the traditional insurance contract. In exchange for paying a premium to an insurance company, the company agrees to make a payment proportional to the damage incurred. If this insurance covers damage from floods, then the insurance policy can be viewed as a type of put option with an underlying of the value of the insured property less any deductible. The difference between the current value of the insured property and the payment guaranteed by the insurer is equal to the deductible, which means the option is out-of-the-money.

The big difference between insurance and a traded financial option is indemnity. Not just anyone can collect flood insurance on *my house,* for example. I must have an interest in the insured asset in order to have an insurance policy written on it. This requirement is intended to control moral hazard problems that might affect my behavior. In other words, if I could insure assets other than my own, I might have the temptation to destroy them and collect the insurance. If my own assets are at risk, I presumably prefer some of my assets to none of my assets and thus will be less inclined to destroy them for insurance value alone.

OPTION-LIKE NONFINANCIAL CONTRACTS

Financial contracts are not the only contracts with optionality in their cash flows and payoffs. Nonfinancial assets frequently contain options and option-like components. Consider a typical capital equipment lease program, in which equipment leased over time may be purchased for a fixed price at the end of the lease. The buy-back option is a call-like contract on the asset being leased.

Commercial contracts also often contain option-like features associated with the timing of deliveries. A take-or-pay contract, for example, is a contract that allows a firm to purchase some amount of a commodity at a fixed price *and at a variable rate* over time. The only requirement is that the entire amount of the commodity must be drawn down by the end of the life of the contract, else the customer pays anyway. Common in the natural gas and oil industries, a typical take-or-pay contract might call for the delivery of one million barrels of WTI crude over two years at the fixed purchase price of $25/barrel. The buyer can choose the schedule for delivery, which can be as flexible as the buyer's needs dictate—ranging from all million barrels in the first month to all million in the last month to equal monthly draw downs.[6]

The take-or-pay contract is essentially a series of long call options spread over time to allow for flexible deliveries *plus* a written call option on the *unpurchased* amount at the end of the life of the contract. Contracts are occasionally offered to retail customers with similar provisions, and one such contract may be easier to understand. The AAirpass™ program of American Airlines allows frequent travelers to purchase 25,000 miles per year for one passenger at a prespecified price of about $0.48 per mile. All the miles have been purchased, but for a customer who flies more than 25,000 miles on American Airlines, the option has value. On any *given* flight, the customer can decide whether or not to take delivery of the option. If a cheaper ticket is available on the market, the customer will buy it. But if a ticket cannot be identified that works out to less than $0.48 per mile, the customer can exercise part of the option—usually for less than the price of a full-fare ticket but for more than a discounted fare. Like a take-or-pay, if you don't use all the miles, they expire at the end of the year *and you've already bought them.*

Contracts like these only give their holders flexibility on the timing of deliveries, not on the actual purchased amount and price. But if the demand for flying greatly exceeds the quantity in the contract, this can be a very valuable option. And similarly for natural gas. In those cases where demand exceeds the fixed amount purchased, the short call will always be left with a zero underlying quantity.

Numerous other option-like nonfinancial contracts can be identified in retail markets. Consider some examples:

- The option to purchase a full tank of gas at a fixed price from a rental car company at the time of the rental.
- The option to make anywhere from a minimum to a full payment on a credit card.
- The option offered by Diner's Club to business travelers to delay payment interest-free for 30 additional days upon giving notice.

ASSETS AS OPTIONS

Recall from Chapter 6 that Myers distinguishes between two types of assets: current assets, and growth opportunities. Both current assets and growth assets can sometimes be viewed as option-like exposures from a risk management perspective.

Current Assets as Options

Current assets are not always options. A receivable from a customer to pay $1 million in 10 days with a negligible probability of default is a forward-like exposure on the $1 million payment. A machine that is always operating at capacity and must be operating all the time in order to facilitate continuous production is a spot or forward-like exposure with little or no optionality.

Current assets sometimes do contain optionality, of course. Perhaps the most obvious example is the option of a counterparty to default. In the prior example of the receivable, a credit-risky counterparty has actually got a $1 million payable *and* the option to default if its net assets are below the amount due on the payable. In that case, net assets would include assets net of all liabilities senior to the payable in the counterparty's capital structure.

If that number is not sufficient to cover the payable, then the payable becomes a type of long put option stuck at the amount of the payable. For net assets less than $1 million, the firm owes only the pro rated amount of its payable out of whatever current net assets remain. This amount is pro rated to reflect the fact that other liabilities of the firm may have the same seniority in capital structure as the payable.

The option of the vendor to default is not a great example of a current asset as an option, however, because the exercise decision is not really under the direct control of the counterparty's stakeholders. Especially if the payable is small in size relative to the firm's capital, the firm would be very unlikely to blow itself out and put itself into default in order *just* to default on the payable. It's possible, but not very likely. And if the firm is unwilling to default itself to default on the payable, then the exercise decision of the payable as a put option is dependent on the firm's normal investment decisions and returns and not so much on a deliberate exploitation of the option to default.

To take a better example of an asset as an option, consider a public utility that has more than enough generation assets to meet both its normal baseload demand and any reasonable demand during peaking periods. The generator owned by a utility in this situation can be viewed as a type of call option on power. Specifically, suppose the generator has no fixed start-up or warm-up costs and can be started with absolutely no delay. Suppose the marginal cost of generating one megawatt of power per hour (MWh) is $15 from this generator.

When the spot price of power *plus* transmission and distribution costs of getting power from the generator to the spot market is below $15/MWh, the generator sits dormant. It would cost the utility more to generate each megawatt than the utility could recover. But when the market price of power plus the price to the utility of getting power from the generator to the market exceeds $15/MWh, the generator becomes profitable. And as Figure 14.10 indicates, this profit opportunity increases dollar-for-dollar with every increase in the spot price above the marginal cost of generation. This exposure is identical to a call on the power. When power prices rise, for example, to $150/MWh, the generator can be turned on and power can be sold for a $135/MWh profit (net of transmission, distribution, and generation costs).

When excess supply is driving the optionality of generation assets, the utility can take advantage of traded financial instruments and optimize its revenues using traded electricity options. The fair value of the generator as an option can be computed using real options valuation methods, such as Monte Carlo simulation or dynamic stochastic programming. This *premium* then can be compared to the *traded* price of comparable options on

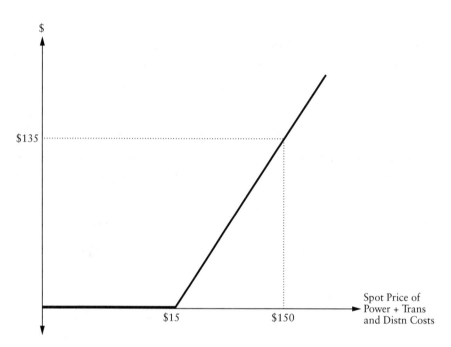

FIGURE 14.10 A power generator with excess capacity as a call option.

power in the market place—plus or minus transmission, distribution, wheeling, and other costs. Especially if the utility is a low-cost producer, the premium for a traded option resembling the power plant—the cost of *synthetic* generation—likely will be higher than the value of the generator. In this case, the utility can *sell* call options in the market and use the generator to cover any exercises.

Note that the generator can be optimized with a covered call sale in a relatively riskless manner *only* when the utility has excess capacity. Otherwise, the generator will be needed to meet peaking or baseload demand. And if a call has been sold against the generator in that case, the utility will have to go into the market and buy the excess power it needs—at possibly huge prices. Selling a call against a generation asset thus makes sense for a utility *if* its own demand area is covered.

Even if the utility has true excess capacity, selling a call against the generator de facto takes the utility out of the market and deprives it of the chance to sell power at spot prices into *other* demand areas should prices rise. Whether or not this makes sense depends on the business and risk management objectives of the utility. On the one hand, selling a call against an unused generator eliminates the time decay problem of the unused generator as a wasting asset. On the other hand, selling the call against the power supply source eliminates the option value of having a generator if prices in other demand areas spike.

Electricity generators, moreover, are not the only assets that can be viewed as options. Unlike electricity generators, however, many other current assets that look like options will not have traded market analogues to facilitate revenue optimization. Just about *any* equipment that is excess capacity is an option. A printing press at a newspaper, for example, is an option if the normal production of the paper is covered by other machines. The unused printing press can be used, say, for special editions or unusually large runs. When the market price of product sales is high enough, it makes sense to turn on this excess capacity asset.

Financial assets also can be viewed as options, and not just in the sense that debt and equity can be seen as options on the net assets of the firm. More concretely, suppose a firm sets aside $10,000 per month in self-insurance to cover potential losses from fire and flood. The resulting *guarantee fund* is basically a put option on property values with a strike price equal to the size of the fund. In the event fire or flood damage causes a loss in property values, the put is exercised and the guarantee fund applied.

Growth Opportunities as Options

In Chapter 6, growth opportunities as options was discussed. On some date t, the growth opportunity is an option to spend some amount of known investment capital $I(t + k)$ on a later date $t + k$ in order to generate cash flows $X(t + k + q)$ where q can be zero, some positive integer, or a vector of several integers. In an all-equity firm, the growth asset is a call option with a strike price equal to the investment cost of the project. In a firm with both debt and equity in which equity makes the investment decision and in the absence of any proactive risk management, the growth asset is a call option with a strike price equal to the investment cost of the project plus the face value of outstanding debt.

REAL OPTIONS

Any option in which managerial flexibility to make decisions conveys value on the firm is called a *real option*. In this section, the main types of real options are summarized and some examples provided.

As the discussion and examples illustrate, many real options are "naturally occurring," that is, a firm has them whether it realizes it or not. Apart from identifying these exposures for risk control, the identification of real options also plays a critical role in corporate strategic planning, capital budgeting, and revenue optimization. To ignore real options from capital investment decisions is quite often to leave money on the table.

Common Types of Real Options

Real options are typically associated with what Myers calls "growth opportunities," or options to spend something later to get investment returns later still. In other words, both the investment expenditure and the cash flows that expenditure may generate occur in the future. In that sense, real options typically involve the exploitation of either the *timing* of investment and production decisions or the *size* of investment and production decisions.

Waiting to Invest   One of the most basic real options is the *waiting-to-invest option* for capital-intensive investment projects. The reason this option is a basic one is that, in its pure form—articulated by Ingersoll and Ross (1992)—the value of the option is based entirely on interest rate uncertainty and not on market price uncertainty. In other words, the option to wait when making an investment decision has value *even when the cash flows on a project are totally known.*

Traditional capital budgeting theory tells us to do a project if the NPV is positive and not to do it otherwise. Ingersoll and Ross (1992) offer an incredibly simple example of why that criterion *alone* is not enough. Suppose the one-year risk free interest rate is 10%, and a capital investment is available that requires a one-time current investment outlay of $100. The investment will return $112 *for certain* in one year. According to the NPV criterion, we accept the project:

$$NPV = \frac{\$112}{1.10} - \$100 = \$1.82$$

Now suppose the yield curve is inverted and the one-year interest rate one year from now is 7%, known today with certainty. Instead of taking the investment now, we could wait a year. If we wait a year, the NPV *today* for the investment taken in a year is

$$NPV = \frac{\dfrac{\$112}{1.07} - \$100}{1.10} = \$4.25$$

By waiting, we are clearly better off.

If interest rates fluctuate, that fact *alone* is enough to give value to the waiting to invest option. Suppose the yield curve is flat at 10% and you consider undertaking a project that yields $109 in a year for sure. Based on the NPV criterion alone, you reject the project:

$$NPV = \frac{\$109}{1.10} - \$100 = -\$0.91$$

And because the yield curve is flat, you will *always* reject this project.

But now suppose there is *some* chance, however small, that the one-year rate will fall below 9% at *some* point in the future, however distant. Because the project *might* be valuable to undertake in the future, it is not worthless today despite what the NPV criterion alone tells us. That means the investment has *some* value today.

Similarly, what if the yield curve is flat at 7% today but interest rates fluctuate? The NPV of the project today is positive at that rate, but the fluctuation of rates means that we should *not* definitely undertake the project today. If the probability is high enough that rates will decline further in the future, it pays to wait.

The Option to Defer   The waiting-to-invest option is a special case of the more general *option-to-defer* an investment expenditure. In the waiting-to-invest case above, the source of only uncertainty was the variability of the interest rate, or the discount rate used to calculate the project's NPV. When input and output price uncertainty and/or market, credit, and other event-driven risks subject the cash flows of the project to uncertainty, the deferment option becomes even more interesting.

Consider the variables that can affect the value of waiting to invest when the cash flows on the underlying project are uncertain. These variables include the following:

- Gross present value of expected future cash flows on the project—other things equal, the higher the gross PV of expected future cash flows on the project, the more valuable the option.
- Investment cost of the project—other things equal, the lower the investment cost, the more valuable the option.
- Time until the opportunity to undertake the project disappears—other things equal, the longer you have to decide whether to undertake the project, the more valuable the option.
- Uncertainty about the value of the project—other things equal, the more uncertain you are about the value of the project, the more likely

it will be that the project *is* valuable and, hence, the more valuable the option.

■ Riskless interest rate—other things equal, the higher the interest rate, the more valuable the option.

To convince yourself that waiting-to-invest is indeed a real option, compare the factors that impact the value of the waiting-to-invest option with the factors that impact the value of a call option on equity (Table 14.1).

As Table 14.1 shows, the deferment option really is an option. The inputs may differ slightly from a common stock option—especially in their observability—and the valuation method may be different, but the option to defer an investment until some sources of uncertainty are realized in the market clearly has value.

Examples of the deferment option abound. The option to postpone investment in tools to extract natural resources, such as oil and gas or forestry products, is a common deferment option. The option to defer investment in new products with cyclical demand is also a common deferment option. The demand for hotel rooms in the Caribbean, for example, tends to be seasonal. The option to defer investment in new vacation resorts so that they are completed when demand is high thus is an example of how deferment can make sense.

Real estate development is also an industry rife with deferment options. Consider, for example, a parcel of land that can be developed into an office complex for a cost that does not depend on the time chosen for the development. If the land is located just outside of a city experiencing urban sprawl, it may pay to wait to develop the land until the sprawl moves further and the demand for office space increases. More sprawl outward will mean more demand for office space and higher rental rates, whereas developing the complex today would yield lower rents.

Figure 14.11 illustrates the value of the deferment option in this real estate development example. The cost to develop the property into a commercial

TABLE 14.1 The Deferment Option versus a Common Stock Option

Call Option on Common Stock	Waiting to Invest Option
Current price of stock	Gross PV of expected project cash flows
Strike price	Investment cost
Time to expiration	Time until opportunity disappears
Stock price volatility	Project value uncertainty
Riskless interest rate	Riskless interest rate

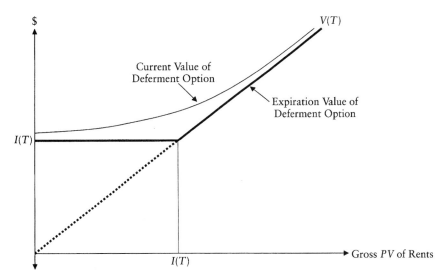

FIGURE 14.11   The option to defer a commercial real estate development venture.

office space at time T is $I(T)$, and the discounted gross present value of rents on the office space from time T onward valued as of time T is denoted $V(T)$. The payoff is clearly similar to that of a call option whose striking price is $I(T)$. When the gross PV of rents exceed the development cost, the developer will commence work. Otherwise, the land is more valuable if left undeveloped.

A well-known result in options theory is that an American call on a nondividend-paying asset should never be exercised prior to maturity.[7] If the deferment option is an American call, does it make sense to *ever* exercise the American call early? It very well might. The traditional result that it makes no sense to exercise early holds because the *sale* of the option always yields more than the present value of the exercise of the option. But if the option cannot be freely traded, this result may not hold. Because the deferment option is a real option and is not explicitly traded, the only way for a holder to realize its value may be to exercise it, and this exercise behavior may not always mimic the exercise behavior of a traded option.

The presumption that the underlying asset pays no dividends is also a strong one. Because deferment options tend to exist for physical assets, the asset will often have a convenience yield associated with it. As discussed in earlier chapters (e.g., Chapter 7), the convenience yield is the return to physical ownership of an asset, which may differ, of course, depending on the condition of the asset (i.e., developed or not). In the real estate example, the owner may be able to profit from temporary inventory shortages either in the undeveloped land (e.g., a nearby farmer must expand) or the developed office building. The presence of a positive convenience yield can affect both the exercise behavior of the owner of the option and the value of the asset underlying that option.[8]

The Option to Abandon a Current Asset   The option to abandon a current asset is the option to terminate all production and operations and sell the current asset for its market value. The abandonment decision thus is permanent unless the company repurchases its assets on the market after liquidating them.

Abandonment options are particularly common in capital-intensive industries, such as transportation and financial services. The capital intensity of investments is sufficiently high that even small declines in demand for the end product may imply a higher liquidation value of investments and assets than they would have if left in development or active production.

Figure 14.12 shows a classical abandonment option for a railcar production facility. Suppose the machines in the railcar production facility can be sold *or* converted into an aircraft production assembly line. The value of the assets as an aircraft assembly line equal their salvage value on the open

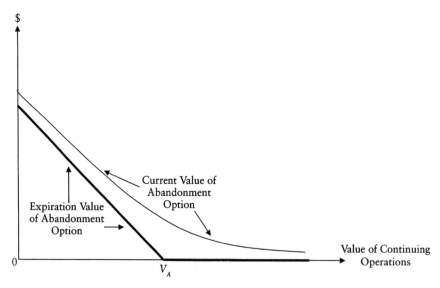

FIGURE 14.12   The option to abandon a railcar production facility.

market, and this value is denoted V_A. The horizontal axis shows the market value of the railcar production line *assuming continuing operations*. The payoff profile of the abandonment option resembles that of a put option on the value of continuing operations. When the gross present value of cash flows from ongoing operations falls below the salvage value V_A, the railcar production facility is liquidated or transferred to an alternative use.

Note that Figure 14.12 shows the values of the abandonment option both before maturity and at expiration. In this example, expiration could be considered the date on which all assets have depreciated to a point that additional investment is required to maintain operations.

Because the value of the abandonment option often depends on the value of the assets in an alternative use, the strike price for the abandonment option is generally an asset value itself. Rather than expressing the option as a put on the underlying of continued operational value, the abandonment option can also be viewed as the combination of an asset in its current use with the option to exchange that asset for its salvage value or alternative use. The two positions thus together constitute an option on the maximum of two asset values, where the two assets are the machines and equipment of the railcar factory under alternative use scenarios.

Abandonment can sometimes be achieved synthetically through the use of derivatives. The example earlier in this chapter of an electric utility that sells calls in the market against a dormant generator is an example of synthetic abandonment. Unlike the actual abandonment or sale of the generator, however, the use of a market-traded call to synthetically abandon the asset *is reversible*. When the call expires, the utility has the option to abandon it again synthetically by selling another call or to put the generator back into production. In this context, the abandonment option thus is a compound option, or an option on the synthetic abandonment of the asset today plus a subsequent series of options to abandon the asset synthetically in the future.

The Time to Build Option The *time-to-build option* combines the deferment option and the abandonment option. In the time-to-build option, capital investment expenditures are staged and coupled with the option to abandon the investment project at any time if new information is obtained that reduces the NPV of the project. The presumption is that information impacting the project's NPV is released gradually over time and that investment decisions can be linked to those information releases.

Each stage of an investment project can be viewed as a compound option, or an option on the project itself *plus* the subsequent options to abandon the project at any stage. Applications include any time-sensitive R&D, such as the pharmaceutical development of new drug products.

Other applications include large-scale construction products and the venture capital financing of start-up industries.

The time-to-build option is more valuable when the assets acquired through staged investment decisions can be resold (as in the regular abandonment option), but this is not a requirement. Abandoning a staged investment project midstream can make sense even when no costs incurred to date can be recovered. Consider the example of the buggy whip industry just after the invention of the automobile. If you were in the middle of staged investment expenditures in a new buggy whip factory when the auto came along, abandonment might make sense even if no recoveries were possible. Any such situation where demand falls *structurally* rather than *cyclically* can give the time-to-build abandonment option value. Considering the option from a different perspective, structuring investment decisions in a staged fashion makes more sense the more variable the demand for the final product at the completion of the investment project.

The Option to Alter Operating Scale   Sometimes the abandonment of an asset or current investment is a bit extreme, even if a contraction in demand for the product produced by an investment-intensive production process suggests a smaller scale than initially thought. Temporary shut-down decisions can even make sense in this situation.

Conversely, suppose demand for the product being produced is much higher than expected. In that case, you might wish to incur additional investment expenditures in order to *expand* your capacity and meet this newly arrived demand.

The option to expand or contract (including temporary shut down and restart decisions) is known as the *option to alter operating scale*. Common applications of the option to alter operating scale include the following:

- Natural resource extraction, where extraction costs vary with extraction rates and where output prices vary significantly over time.
- Facilities planning, construction, and real estate development, especially in cyclical industries such as entertainment.
- Fashion- and fad-sensitive industries, including entertainment, fashion apparel, and food service.

The Switching Option   The *switching option* can refer either to switching inputs or outputs in a production process. Input switching is common in industries where production inputs are flexible, such as electric power and rotated-crop farming. In the former case, for example, power can be generated using natural gas turbines, hydroelectric and pump storage facilities, fossil fuels, nuclear fuels, and the like. If the price of natural gas rises significantly with respect to the price of fossil fuels like coal, the ability to switch generation from gas turbines to coal-fired plants is a valuable option.

Output switching is valuable and common in industries whose outputs are characterized both by volatile demand *and* by small-batch production. An excellent example of the output switching option that is beneficial to the product buyer and easily accommodated by the seller is the option to switch aircraft types provided by Airbus Industrie.[9] When airlines want to purchase aircraft from Airbus, they enter into purchase agreements that obligate them to a *family* of aircraft, but not to a specific type. The purchase agreements may give the airline the option to buy planes for several years. Once exercised, there is still a manufacturing lead time required to produce the aircraft. For example, a purchase agreement might entitle the airline to a four-year option to buy a family of aircraft and an 18-month manufacturing lead time between the airline's decision to exercise its purchase option and the actual delivery.

One family is the Airbus A319/A320/A321 family, which differ primarily based on seat numbers—the A319 and A320 seat 120 and 150 people, respectively, but otherwise do not differ materially. Another aircraft family is the A330/A340 family, which differ mainly based on distance (i.e., the A330 can be used for short-haul or long-haul flights, whereas the A340 is primarily a transcontinental aircraft).

The flexibility afforded the purchaser of Airbus aircraft is the option to defer investment. Not only can the airlines decide not to purchase at all, but they can choose the product they want *after* getting a better sense of their demand curves. This flexibility can be offered by Airbus because of Airbus' own output switching option created by its standardized production processes. Specifically, each family of aircraft *comes off the same assembly line*. Because the A330 and A340 are produced on the same production line, the cost of switching A330 and A340 to meet customer demand is next to zero. This greatly enhances the ability of Airbus to tailor its production decisions to the demands of its customers.

The switching option can be viewed in the two-asset case—the option for airlines to choose between the A319 and A320—as an exchange option or an option on the better of two assets. Recall from earlier in the chapter that an option on the better of two assets has an expiration value of

$$\max[S_1(T), S_2(T)] = S_1(T) - \max[S_1(T) - S_2(T), 0]$$

or the value of one asset (net of its acquisition costs) minus the value of the option to exchange that asset for a second asset. In the Airbus example, $S_1(T)$ and $S_2(T)$ might denote the present values to an airline of an A319 order and an A320 order, respectively, both of which would depend on the demand for travel observed at time T. A higher demand would increase the value of $S_2(T)$.

Figure 14.13 illustrates the value of this option over time for a given demand curve, where demand is shown as average number of passengers expected on short-haul flights. The value of the option depends on the timing of its expiration, or the date on which the airline must tell Airbus which aircraft it wants. For times occurring before T_c, demand is steadily below 120 seats per flight, which makes the cheaper A319 a sensible and more valuable aircraft choice. But choosing the A319 would be the wrong decision, given that demand quickly rises above the capacity of the A319 after time T_c. If the switching option expires after T_c, the airline will see the higher demand and thus will choose the bigger (and more expensive) A320 model.

Option for Interactive Growth   *Interactive growth* is an option where the staged investment in one project opens up opportunities for growth in other areas. Mergers and acquisitions, for example, are obvious examples of transactions with embedded options for interactive growth. When one oil company merges with another, the merger target conveys on the acquiring firm its current assets *and* its own real options. The investment in the merger thus enables the acquiring firm to acquire the target's real options, as well as its current assets.

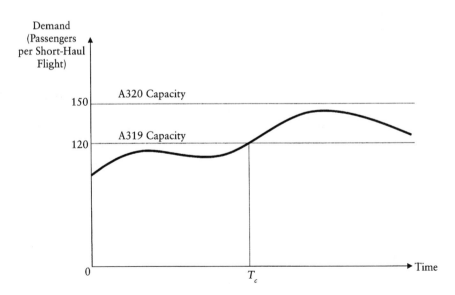

FIGURE 14.13   The value of switching from an A319 to A320.

To consider another example, suppose a minerals exploration firm owns some land that has never been surveyed or explored. The firm can invest in exploration to determine what other real options the firm has. Exploration for oil can identify an oil reserve, for example, which upon discovery then conveys on the firm the asset plus all the real options the asset conveys.

An Oil Field Example

Many assets contain multiple real options, and the value of any one of these options may be correlated with the values and exercise decisions of the other options. An excellent example of this can be found in a typical oil company.[10] Suppose Oil Company Rockefeller has a finite-period lease to begin drilling on unexplored land with potential reserves, and suppose the following investment costs must be incurred for various interrelated activities:

- The land can be explored for cost I_e any time between t_0 and t_1.
- Construction on a processing facility can be commenced at time t_2 for cost I_p in the event that oil reserves are discovered at or before time t_1.
- Management can terminate construction of the processing facility at any time during the construction period, which ends at time t_3.
- During construction between t_2 and t_3, management can reduce the scale of the extraction facility by k percent and recover a portion I_k of its latest outlay if demand is perceived to be weak.
- Once the facility is producing beginning at time t_4, management can expand the scale of the facility by x percent for an additional investment of I_x.
- Once the facility is producing beginning at time t_4, management can temporarily shut down the plant for one period by paying its variable operating costs during that period, I_V.
- Once the facility is producing beginning at time t_4, management can abandon the plant and sell the assets *or* switch the assets to an alternative use for value V_A.
- Management can build a refinery based on alternative energy input sources to refine the crude in the ground into refined products like heating oil.

Consider the real options Oil Company Rockefeller owns.

The Option to Defer Investment The lease on the exploration of the land creates a deferment option for Rockefeller. If the firm perceives a decline in interest rates *or* oil prices as likely, Rockefeller might be inclined to delay its investment expenditure of I_e. At the end of the lease period, the option is worth

$$V(t_1) = \max\left[0, PV(t_4, \ldots) - I_e(t_1)\right]$$

where $PV(t_4, \ldots)$ is the gross present value of the completed plant's expected operating cash flows from time t_4 onward. Exploring the land early in the lease period thus sacrifices the value of waiting to see what interest rates and oil prices will do and thus makes sense only when $PV(t_4, \ldots)$ is very high relative to I_e.

The Time-to-Build Option   Oil Company Rockefeller also owns a time-to-build option because the extraction facility can be abandoned at any time prior to its completion. Even in the simple example, the option to spend I_e at or before t_1 to explore the land is already part of a staged investment decision since the firm can learn the results of the exploration by spending I_e but before spending the I_p required to develop the whole facility at time t_2. Suppose Rockefeller spends I_e at time t_1 and ascertains that there is oil in the ground but that the oil field is a small one. In that case, Rockefeller may wish to abandon the field and not spend I_p at time t_2 to develop it.

The initial investment decision that was modeled before as a deferment option can be modified to take into account the compound option that the time-to-build option conveys. Specifically, the value of the oil reserve can now be written on or before date t_1 as

$$\max\left\{0, \max\left[PV(t_4, \ldots) - I_p, 0\right] - I_e\right\}$$

In other words, the company can choose not to explore the land and incur no costs or can choose to spend I_e at or before time t_1 in order to get the option to spend I_p at time t_2 to build an extraction plant that will be completed at time t_3 and yield a gross present value of oil sold from the extraction plant PV from time t_4 onward. This makes sense if PV exceeds the cost of building the plant incurred at time t_2 *and* exploring the land at or before time t_1.

The Option to Change Scale   Oil Company Rockefeller also owns an option to alter the operating scale of the plant, either by reducing its scale by k percent during construction and recovering I_k in costs or by expanding production by x percent upon spending an additional I_x after production commences.

The option to contract the scale of the plant during construction can be viewed as a type of American *put* option that exists only between time t_2 when construction begins and time t_3 when the plant is finished. The existence of this option is conditional on the firm having spent I_e at or before t_1

to explore the land and having spent I_p at time t_2 to commence construction on the plant. At or before time t_3, the exercise value of the option to contract the scale of the plant is

$$\max\left[0, I_k - kPV(t_4, \ldots)\right]$$

If time t_3 approaches and the demand for oil and oil products is extremely light, for example, Rockefeller may wish to exercise this put option, recovering I_k in investment costs and reducing the gross PV of future cash flows by k percent.

The option to expand, by contrast, can be viewed as a call option on the gross PV of the additional production less the investment cost I_x for realizing that larger scale. Because the expansion option is only alive beginning at time t_4 when the field goes into production, the combination of the plant built to its original design plus the call on the additional capacity can be expressed as $PV(t_4, \ldots) + \max[0, xPV(t_4, \ldots) - I_x(t_4)]$, where the call is American and can be exercised any time after t_4 when production begins. If demand is higher than expected, for example, xPV may exceed I_x by enough to justify the new investment for the additional x percent of capacity.

The option to change operating scale also includes an option for management to temporarily shut down the extraction facility for one period after it begins producing. If demand and prices drop, for example, it might pay for management to take the field off-line and save the oil reserves for a later, higher demand, higher price period.

If the cash revenues for any one period t_m to $t_m + 1$ are denoted $C(t_m, t_m + 1)$, for example, the option to temporarily abandon the field for a time period can be viewed as a call option on the cash revenues of the field during that period with a strike price equal to the variable operating costs Rockefeller incurs during that period, or $\max[0, C(t_m, t_m + 1) - I_V(t_m, t_m + 1)]$.

The Abandonment Option   The abandonment option allows Rockefeller to sell the assets associated with the field or place them into alternative use for V_A at any time following t_4 when the field begins producing. The value of this option is equal to the gross present value of the field if it continues to operate plus a put option on the field struck at V_A. At any time $t_m > t_4$, the combined position in the oil field and the option to abandon the field is

$$PV(t_m, \ldots) + \max[0, V_A - PV(t_m, \ldots)]$$

Recall from the discussion earlier in this chapter on exchange options that this combination of the oil field plus the option to exchange the oil field for its salvage value can be expressed as a single option on the maximum of the field and its salvage value, or

$$\max[V_A, PV(t_m, ...)]$$

The Option for Interactive Growth and the Switching Option The ability of Oil Company Rockefeller to build a refinery to convert the extracted crude into a variety of oil outputs is an option for interactive growth. Without incurring the costs of exploring the field and building the oil extraction facility, the option to build the refinery would not exist.

The option to build the refinery bestows on Rockefeller another potentially valuable asset *and* another set of real options similar to those found in the extraction facility (e.g., time to build, deferment, abandonment). In addition, the refinery and the extraction facility *together* also create new real options for the firm in the form of both input and output switching options. The input switching option is created by the ability of the refinery to utilize a variety of energy sources (e.g., fuel oil, natural gas, or electricity), and the output switching option allows the firm to achieve flexibility in producing the highest-price and most demanded output across the refined crude product spectrum.

Factors Affecting Optionality

Apart from the value of the asset underlying the real option and its volatility, several factors can impact the value of real options. Recognizing these factors as part of the exposure is an important precondition for a firm to truly optimize the value of its real option portfolio.

The first factor that can impact the value of a real option is the degree to which its value is affected by the behavior of competing firms. Specifically, a real option can be classified as rivalrous or non-rivalrous. A *rivalrous option* is a real option whose value to one firm depends on the behavior of other firms. An unexplored and unowned oil field, for example, cannot be owned by everyone. Consequently, the decision of one firm to acquire the land simultaneously deprives its competitors of the same decision. Alternatively, the decision of one oil company to sell a parcel of land that it owns without exercising its exploration option conveys that exploration right on the new buyer.

Not all real options are rivalrous, however. The option of an Airbus customer to switch an A319 order for an A320 order, for example, does not depend on what other airlines do.

A second factor that influences the value of certain real options is the degree to which an exercise decision affects the value of other real options. In other words, the "compoundedness" of real options should be considered carefully by their owners.[11] The decision not to explore the oil field automatically eliminates every other option the firm owns. The interrelatedness of exercise decisions thus must be a part of the exposure identification process.

Finally, the time to maturity of the option should be assessed carefully. For some options, this is obvious enough—the option to explore the oil field between t_0 and t_1 in our oil example. But for many other options, the degree to which the exercise decision can be delayed is not obvious and can be very important.

Recall from basic options theory that options are decaying assets. As time passes, the value of the option declines at an increasing rate. For some real options, time decay can be a real risk to be managed.

Return to the example of the railcar production line that conveys on its owner the option to abandon the facility and sell the assets or transfer them to an alternative use. The value of this option was shown in Figure 14.12. Figure 14.14 now shows the value of continued operations of the railcar production facility as a function of the remaining useful life of the facility's assets.[12] The figure indicates both the value of the assets under an alternative use (i.e., liquidation or salvage value) and the critical value of the railcar production assets at which abandonment makes sense. With many years of

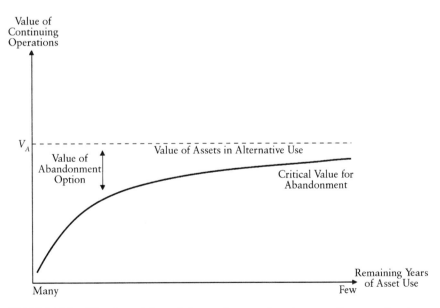

FIGURE 14.14   The time delay of the option to abandon a railcar production facility.

useful life left in the assets, the value of the abandonment option is quite high. Uncertainty about future demand makes the railcar production assets quite valuable in continuing use. In other words, abandonment of the assets early in their useful life makes sense only when the current asset value is *well* below the liquidation or salvage value. But as the number of years of useful life in the assets declines, the value at which those assets will be abandoned begins to rapidly approach their liquidation value. Consequently, the value of abandoning the assets is lower the fewer useful years remaining—the option to abandon has decayed with time.

CHAPTER 15

Measuring and Monitoring Market Risk

Once a company has identified its risk exposures as discussed in Chapters 13 through 14, the risk management process of the firm must include a process by which actual exposures that have been identified can be compared to the tolerances for bearing those risks as defined by the firm's stakeholders. The means by which risk is monitored and compared to tolerances is not independent of the means by which risk is measured. Accordingly, some firms may wish to explore alternative risk measurement methods as a means by which they can better learn how to express their risk tolerances.

In this chapter, the fundamental methods of measuring *market* risk are explored. After these methods have been reviewed, some basic principles of risk monitoring are presented. The measurement and monitoring of credit, liquidity, and other risks are discussed in the next several chapters.

Recall that market risk is the risk that changes in market-determined prices, rates, index values, and other risk factors will result in an expected adverse change in value, cash flows, and/or earnings. For each major risk exposure the firm has identified, the market risk should be summarized and compared to the firm's risk tolerance. Both the measurement of market risks and the comparison of those measures to risk tolerances should be consistent with the firm's strategic risk management targets of value, cash flows, or earnings. In addition, if the firm is engaging in risk management selectively, the firm's attention should be focused on those risks in which the firm has relatively little comparative informational advantage.

NOMINAL EXPOSURE MEASURES

One of the most rudimentary forms of market risk reporting is the *nominal exposure report,* or a report that indicates how much capital is at risk in a given exposure or portfolio of exposures. Consider a pension plan that treats equity and fixed income risk as normal risks it needs in order to fund its liabilities. Suppose that currency exposure, however, is a risk the plan deems unnecessary for liability funding purposes. Currency exposure is thus measured and tracked, perhaps even relative to a policy-defined maximum.

Figure 15.1 shows an example of how a dollar-based pension plan uses a nominal exposure report to measure currency risk.[1] The solid black bars represent total market values of the pension plan's major portfolios. Next to each black bar is a cross-hatched bar that represents the nominal dollars at risk in that portfolio to currency fluctuations. The domestic equity portfolio, for example, has a market value of US$23 billion, of which virtually none is denominated in foreign currency.[2] The international equity portfolio, by contrast, has about $9.5 billion in market value, about $9 billion of which is exposed to currency fluctuations. The remaining $500 million has evidently been hedged, and so on for the other portfolios. Figure 15.2 illustrates an additional nominal exposure monitored by this particular pension plan—the percentages of two of its major portfolios exposed to emerging market risk.

Nominal exposure reports like the examples shown can be invaluable tools for comparing the actual exposure of a firm to its target exposure. For

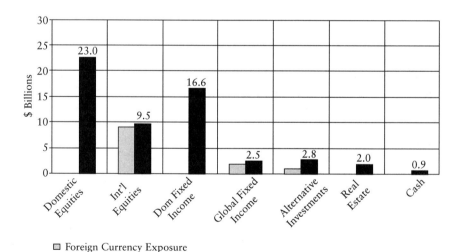

FIGURE 15.1 Nominal exposure chart for the currency risk of a pension plan.

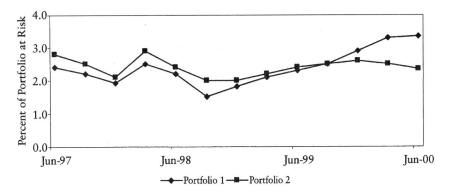

FIGURE 15.2 Nominal exposure chart for the emerging market risk of a pension plan.

many exposures, however, nominal exposure reports will be part of the picture but not the whole picture. Specifically, a nominal exposure report tells a firm how much is *exposed,* but not how much it *could lose.* In the international equity portfolio shown in Figure 15.1, for example, the reported $9 billion in foreign currency-denominated international stocks tells the pension plan sponsor how much capital is exposed to exchange rate risk, but it provides no good indication of how much that exposure might *change* over time.

A nominal exposure thus is a static snapshot of current risks. To get a better handle on how much that exposure might translate into a dollar loss, additional risk measures are required.

SENSITIVITIES

To move toward an estimate of how much the exposures reported in nominal risk reports may change in value, one simple method is to compute the *sensitivity* of an asset or liability's PV to changes in its underlying risk factors. Sensitivity measures of market risk attempt to make no statement about the likelihood of a loss occurring, but they do represent a step beyond the nominal exposure reports by indicating the *speed* with which an exposure could experience a change in value.

The sensitivity of an asset or liability to a change in one or more market risk factors is essentially an asset valuation problem. We start with the current value of the asset, and we want to know the market risk of that asset—the possible *change in value* of that asset. Suppose we consider an asset whose value depends on the Greeks discussed in Chapter 1. If the current asset value is V_0 and this value depends on the current value of underlying risk factors, we can write the current value of the asset as a function of the current values of the underlying risk factors:

$$V_0 = V(S_0, \sigma_0, \tau_0, R_0) = V(z_0)$$

where S_0 is the current spot price of the asset underlying the exposure, σ_0 is the current volatility of that spot price, τ_0 is the time to maturity of the asset from time 0, and R_0 is the risk free rate at time 0. We can also define V as a real-valued function with a vector-valued domain, so that $V(z_0): \Re^4 \rightarrow \Re$ where $z_0^T = (S_0\ \sigma_0\ \tau_0\ R_0)$.

Not all exposures will have all of these risk factors, of course. If V_0 is the value of a contract to buy one share of firm XYZ spot, then $V_0 = V(S_0)$, where S_0 is the price per share of common stock. If V_0 is the value of a zero-coupon bond, then $V_0 = V(y_0)$, where y_0 is the yield.

We can examine the change in value over a small time period for some specific alternative set of risk factors:

$$dV = V_1(z_1) - V_0(z_0)$$

so that dV then depends on the change in the four underlying risk factors from 0 to 1, or

$$dV = dV(\Delta, \Gamma, \text{Vega}, \theta, \rho)$$

In other words, the *change* in the value of the position can be viewed as a function of the option Greeks. Sticking with a share of common stock, we know that

$$dV = V_1(S_1) - V_0(S_0) = V_0 \Delta_s$$

so that the change in the value of the stock is its original value times its delta. Writing the change in this manner helps us avoid the need to actually recompute the price at time 1. All we need is the current asset value and its sensitivity to changes in the underlying stock price, which in this case is dollar-for-dollar.

Sensitivity analysis seeks to compute the risk of assets and liabilities without fully repricing them. Instead, we look at the sensitivity of assets or liabilities to a small change in one or more risk factors and then express the risk of the position accordingly as its potential change based on that sensitivity. The most common such sensitivity measures of market risk are summarized in the next section.

Delta and Related Sensitivity Measures

Perhaps the simplest way to measure the risk of an exposure is to calculate the sensitivity of an asset or liability to a small change in the primary risk factor that influences the value of the position. The primary risk factor would be the value of the position itself for a spot exposure, and the value of the underlying(s) for forward-like exposures and option-like exposures. The most basic family of market risk measures assumes, for the purpose of keeping the calculations simple, that each exposure whose risk is being measured is *linear* in its underlying risk factor(s). Recall from Chapter 13 that is how a forward-like exposure was defined. Accordingly, this first set of market risk measures assumes *every* exposure can be treated as a forward-like exposure or as some forward- or spot-equivalent exposure.

The sensitivity of the value of the position to a small change in the underlying is then just the delta of the position. For exchange-traded contracts, the delta is sometimes called the DV01 or the dollar value of a one tick move, which is defined by the listing exchange. More formally, delta can be expressed as

$$\Delta = \frac{\partial V}{\partial z}$$

where V is the value of the position and z is the value of the primary risk factor. For a share of common stock, V is the price of the common stock. Because the position is a spot exposure, z is also the price per share of the stock, so that delta (Δ) is just $1 per share of exposure. For a foreign currency receivable due in 10 days, the daily delta computed today is the sensitivity of the receivable V to be paid in 10 days to a small daily change in the exchange rate z. As we saw in Chapter 3, this delta is equivalent to the ordinary least squares beta (β) in a regression of daily changes in the present value of a 10-day currency forward on daily changes in the spot exchange rate.

The delta of an asset or liability can be obtained in several ways. For some exposures, delta can be determined analytically by simply examining the payoff formula. A simple forward contract whose cash flow to the long on value/settlement date T is $X(T) = S(T) - K$ per unit of principal, where K is fixed on the trade date, clearly has a delta of one. Returning to the payoff diagram for this forward contract shown in Figure 3.1, the unitary delta should not be surprising. Delta, after all, is the slope of the line tangent to the exposure payoff at any point, and because the payoff function itself is linear with a slope of one, the slope of the line is constant and the slope of the tangent line thus equals one for all values of $S(T)$.

The analytical delta of a futures contract is perhaps the easiest delta to define of any asset or liability because it is quite literally defined by the listing exchange in the terms of the contract. The dollar value of a one tick change in the British pound futures contract, for example, is $6.25. Clearly, delta equals $6.25!

When delta cannot be determined this easily, numerical determinations of delta are still possible. The numerical delta of an asset or liability corresponding to a ε change in the value of the underlying is just

$$\Delta = \frac{V(z + \varepsilon) - V(z)}{\varepsilon}$$

In other words, take a small change in the underlying, reprice the exposure, and calculate the change.[3]

An alternative expression of delta is the elasticity of the value of an exposure with respect to a change in its primary risk factor. The elasticity of an exposure is just its delta scaled by the current level of the risk factor and the current value of the position:

$$\eta_{V \cdot z} = \Delta\left(\frac{z}{V}\right) = \left(\frac{\partial V}{\partial z}\right)\frac{z}{V}$$

where the notation $\eta_{V \cdot z}$ is read "the value elasticity with respect to z."

One of the oldest ways to measure market risk comes from the banking and insurance world and is called the *duration gap* model. Macaulay duration measures the delta sensitivity of the present value of an asset or liability to a small change in interest rates:

$$D = -\left(\frac{\Delta V}{\Delta y}\right)\left(\frac{1 + y}{V}\right)$$

where V is the current value of a position, y is the interest rate, and Δ indicates a change. Duration is the value elasticity of an asset or liability with respect to an interest rate. It is often convenient to define modified duration as

$$MD = -\frac{D}{(1+y)}$$

in which case the risk of a position for a given change in rates is just

$$\Delta V = V \times MD \times \Delta y$$

To measure the value risk of a net asset/liability position using a duration gap model, a firm will calculate the modified duration of all the assets and liabilities in the exposure area it wants to evaluate—a portfolio or business unit. The duration gap for a business unit at any given time is defined as follows:

$$D = D^A - wD^L$$

where D^A is the duration of all assets in the business unit, D^L is the duration of all its liabilities, and w is the proportion of assets funded by liabilities in the business unit at the time of the risk measurement. From this the firm can calculate the business unit's delta-based market risk as in the single-asset case just shown.

Duration gap measures are especially prominent in the management of interest rate risk by banks and insurance companies whose asset/liability mismatch tends to be a structural part of their businesses. Even for interest rate risk, the duration gap, however, is far from perfect. In the simple formulation just shown, a major problem is the assumption that only one rate influences the value of the business unit's assets and liabilities. In reality, rates of different maturities and credit qualities—possibly for different currencies—will be relevant. The same criticism can be leveled at more general measures of delta, such as the foreign exchange delta that may depend on both the exchange rate and the discount rate used to calculate the present value of the position.

The limitation on delta that it is based on only a single underlying can be addressed without abandoning the delta framework by using *multifactor* delta models. Such models express the business unit's market rate risk as a function of a number of different duration measures, each depending on a different interest rate or risk factor. In other words, Δ becomes a *vector* of numbers, defined as $\underline{\Delta} = \delta V/\delta \underline{z}$ where $\underline{z}$ is now a vector including all the relevant risk factors. For the duration gap, the multifactor delta equivalent would be multifactor duration defined as a vector of duration estimates, each calculated with respect to a different maturity on the term structure or a different interest rate.

Expressing delta or the duration gap as a function of multiple risk factors or interest rate indices does not, however, address two other major shortcomings of delta-based analysis. First, the duration gap in particular still depends on strong assumptions about expected repricing speeds for assets and liabilities. Duration as a measure of interest rate risk depends on a *known* maturity date, so assets and liabilities with no maturities (e.g., demand deposit accounts) or with prepayment options (e.g., mortgage loans) have *effective* durations that are based on presumed repricing speeds. If a bank's core deposits reprice at a different speed than expected and loan assets prepay in a manner that deviates from expectations, for example, the *effective* durations of liabilities and assets used may be quite inaccurate.

More importantly, delta and duration itself are measures of risk that are effective only for small changes in the underlying risk factors. In the duration gap model, if the sensitivity of assets or liabilities to changes in interest rates depends on the level of interest rates, the resulting convexity that is not captured by duration can cause the duration gap to seriously understate interest rate risk. This problem is shown graphically in Figure 15.3, which

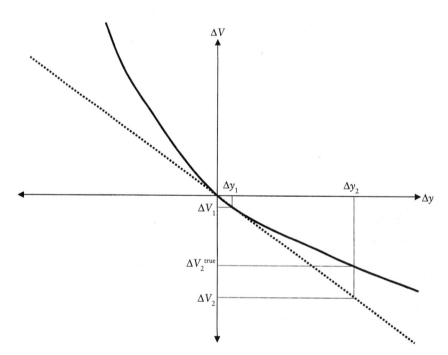

FIGURE 15.3 The inadequacy of delta sensitivity measures of risk.

shows how the value of a level-coupon bond changes (ΔV) for a given change in interest rates (Δy). The dashed straight line tangent to the heavy curved line is the delta of the bond at current rates, or its sensitivity to rates. The heavy curved line is how the bond's price *actually* changes when rates change. For a small change in rates Δy_1, the delta approximation is similar to the true price/yield relation; the change in value is indistinguishable for the two on the figure and is approximately ΔV_1. But for a large change in rates Δy_2, the delta sensitivity overstates the risk of the bond, indicating a potential change of ΔV_2 as compared to the true price change of ΔV_2^{true} that will occur given the bond's convexity.

The delta of the bond is the slope of the line tangent to the true price/yield relation for any given level of interest rates. Because the price/yield relation is convex, the slope of this tangent line will depend on the level of rates. We thus need a *gamma* risk factor in order for sensitivity analysis to paint a more complete picture of the risk of this exposure.

Nonlinearities, Sensitivity Analysis, and Scenario Analysis

If a firm wants to use a delta-like approach without focusing on the impact of only small changes in risk factors, two alternatives are available. First, the firm may simply supplement the delta measure with additional measures of risk that reflect the *convexity* of assets and liabilities but that still adhere to the basic philosophy of sensitivity analysis—namely, avoiding the need for fully recalculating any asset prices. Consequently, this is known as a *partial revaluation* sensitivity analysis. As an example, the change in the value of an asset that has a nonlinear relation to its underlying spot price can be expressed using a Taylor series expansion around current value V_0 as

$$\frac{dV}{V_0} = \Delta dS + \tfrac{1}{2}\Gamma dS^2$$

This is simple enough to estimate if the delta and gamma of the asset are both available. The convexity of the position is captured, and the position did not need to be completely repriced. The same method can be used for bonds in which both duration and convexity are important.

Second, firms can calculate sensitivities of assets and liabilities to rate changes *directly* by using models actually to reprice the assets and liabilities in question. Known as a *full revaluation* sensitivity analysis, one such measure of the sensitivity of assets and liabilities to a change in a risk factor is called the DVx of the asset, where x is the size of the change in the underlying risk factor being considered. DVx in the duration gap, for example, measures the dollar value of a change in interest rates of x basis points on the net asset liability mismatch, where x need *not* be small.

Sensitivity analysis is closely related to another risk measurement concept known as *scenario analysis*. In scenario analysis, the firm considers a specific market price or interest rate scenario (possibly across many prices and rates) and then uses models to reprice the assets and liabilities of an exposure under those scenarios.

The similarity between DVx sensitivity analysis and scenario analysis owes to the fact that some presumed risk factor scenario is required to calculate DVx in the first place. A DV05, for example, is the sensitivity of assets and liabilities to a five basis point change in rates. DV05 thus is the measure of risk resulting from a simple scenario analysis in which rates change by five basis points.

In general, scenario analysis is much more robust than sensitivity analysis. With the latter, the firm may calculate sensitivities for the assets and liabilities of business units periodically and then assume those sensitivities are stable. Scenario analysis, by contrast, often involves the regular full revaluation of all assets and liabilities. This can be significantly more cumbersome computationally, but the results tend to accommodate a wider array of risk scenarios than when sensitivities alone are merely applied to assets and liabilities on an ongoing basis.

Dollar Sensitivities versus Present Values

A cash flow risk manager may be content to examine deltas and $DVxs$ because they are expressed in *nominal* dollars—dollars at the time they are earned or lost. But a value risk manager quite likely will be more focused on translating these sensitivities into their impact on the *present values* of assets and liabilities. And even a cash flow manager may care about the distinction when it comes to translating these measures of market risk into actual hedging rules—much more on this in Part Three.

The present value of a DVx is known as a PVx and is computed as follows:

$$PVx = PV[DVx] = \frac{DVx}{(1+R)^n}$$

where R is the annualized rate at which the firm finances its losses or invests its gains and where n is the number of years (possibly fractional) until the economic change in the value of the asset or liability is realized.

To take a simple example of why this matters, consider a futures contract on the S&P 400 stock index whose DV01 is $500. Because futures are marked to market daily, all the cash flows on the position are realized immediately. In this case, the DV01 is equal to the PV01. But now suppose you consider the sensitivity of a S&P 400 index portfolio to a small change in the index *six months hence*. If the index portfolio has no tracking error to the index, the DV01 is equal to one—one index point change in the S&P 400 *in six months* yields a one dollar change in the portfolio per unit of principal invested. But because the change in value occurs six months hence, the PV01 is equal to today's price of a pure discount bond maturing in six months times the DV01.

The relevance of this distinction depends, of course, on what the firm is *doing* with the risk measure. For pure reporting purposes, a cash flow risk manager might prefer to compare DV01s because they preserve the nominal dollar nature of the cash flows, whereas a value risk manager will want to convert the DV01 into a present value equivalent. But for the purpose of hedge construction, by contrast, the value and cash flow risk managers are *both* likely to opt to choose a hedge that equates the PV01 on the hedge with a PV01 on the portfolio. Otherwise, a hedge that matches DV01s will result in a hedge that is too large. A decline in the futures hedge thus generates margin calls *today* that must be financed *for six months*. Failing to take that into account in the hedge ratio means that cash outflows are larger than need be and that the value of the hedged position will incur slippage equal to the amount of these financing costs. We shall return to this in a later chapter on hedge ratio construction.

Other Risk Factors and Interpretation Problems

All the summary risk measures discussed thus far presuppose that the price of the underlying is the sole risk factor influencing the exposure whose risk is being measured. Delta and gamma capture different sensitivities of the PV to a change in the underlying price, but both depend *only* on the underlying price.

As discussed in Chapter 1, the option Greeks are typically used to summarize other event-driven sources of market risk. Specifically, vega measures the sensitivity of the PV of an exposure to a change in the volatility of the underlying, theta captures the time decay of option-like exposures, and rho reflects the risk of either discount rate or cost of carry changes. All of these sensitivities can, of course, be calculated in the same manner as delta—either analytically or numerically.

One of the major drawbacks to simply measuring and reporting the Greeks is that the resulting numbers may be quite hard to interpret. What does it mean to compare the gamma of a stock option with the vega of a real option to delay the exploration of an oil field? Sensitivity measures of risk may be useful, but they are unlikely to be enough on their own to help a firm truly get its hands around the difference between its actual and its desired market risk. If for no other reason, the number and nature of the different tolerances the firm would have to define explicitly would be just huge if the sole basis for measuring risk relative to tolerance were sensitivity analysis. A Greek *tolerance* would have to be defined for every major group of Greek *exposures* in the firm!

PARAMETRIC SUMMARY MEASURES OF RISK

In Chapter 3, we saw that an investor's expected utility of wealth can be written using a Taylor series expansion in terms of the mean, variance, skewness, and kurtosis of the wealth distribution. These four terms are "parameters" of the probability distribution of wealth. Some of these parameters, when calculated for the right distribution, can serve as useful summary measures of market risk in their own right.

In general, the kth central moment of a probability distribution for the return on some exposure, denoted simply as r, can be defined as follows:

$$m_k(r) = E(r - \mu)^k = \int_{-\infty}^{\infty} (r - \mu)^k f(r)\,dr$$

where μ is the mean or expected value, $E[r]$, of random variable r and where $f(r)$ is the probability density function from which returns of r are drawn. In terms of the parameters we discussed in Chapter 3, the first four moments of the distribution $f(r)$ are summarized in Table 15.1.

TABLE 15.1 First Four Central Moments of Probability Density Function $f(r)$

Parameter	Central Moment $(k =\ )$*	Definition	Notation
Mean	1	$E[r]$	μ
Variance	2	$E[r - \mu]^2$	σ^2
Skewness	3	$E[r - \mu]^3$	γ
Kurtosis	4	$E[r - \mu]^4$	κ

* Strictly speaking, the mean is a moment but not a central moment. The first central moment—the mean minus the mean—is zero. All other moments of interest are central moments.

Volatility

As discussed at length in Part One of this book, variance and volatility are extremely popular measures of market risk all on their own. The volatility of an asset or liability is the degree to which its periodic changes or returns deviate from its expected value. Volatility thus measures the uncertainty associated with the PV of an asset or liability without differentiating between downside and upside uncertainty.

Historical Volatility   Volatility is usually an inherently *historical* measure of risk, based on the estimated sample standard deviation of some time series of observed returns on assets and liabilities. The resulting estimate of the risk of an exposure will reflect any risks that impacted returns in the time series.

Consider, for example, a corporate bond for which you have the last 50 trading days (i.e., 10 weeks) of data. Using all the data available, the volatility of the bond's daily returns calculated on day t will be estimated as[4]

$$s_t = \sqrt{\frac{1}{50} \sum_{j=t-49}^{t} \left(R_{j-1,j} - \overline{R}\right)^2} \tag{15.1}$$

where $\overline{R}$ is the sample mean daily return over the last 50 trading days.

Suppose that during the last 50 trading days the bond experienced absolutely no fluctuations arising from changes in the perceived credit quality of the issuer. Returns varied solely based on nominal interest rate variations. The volatility estimate s_t will thus reflect *only* credit-independent market risk in this case because credit-dependent market risk had no impact on returns over the period used for the calculation. A major drawback of using volatility as an estimate of the sensitivity of an asset or liability to changes in risk factors thus is its neutrality with respect to what risk factors cause the PV of the asset or liability to change. As discussed in Chapters 1 and 2, volatility is a *total* risk measure, capturing both idiosyncratic and systematic risk and not differentiating between market, credit, liquidity, and other risks. *Anything* that causes the asset or liability to change in value over the period used for the sample volatility calculation is reflected in the number. A poor choice of sample period thus can lead to misleading inferences when volatility is used as the basis of risk measurement and reporting.

Numerous statistical methods are available to smooth volatility estimates over actual sample periods, as well as to produce predicted volatility numbers. To appreciate the differences in these methods, suppose a time series of daily bond returns is available going back ten years. Taking the simple standard deviation of the whole series, as in Equation 15.1, yields an unconditional variance.

One of the simplest alternatives to taking the standard deviation of a whole time series is a moving average estimate of volatility, which keeps the number of observations constant for each day. In other words, an unconditional volatility estimate would add a new observation each day when new returns are realized without dropping any old observations, whereas a moving average drops the oldest observation each time a new return is realized. On date t, the moving average volatility over the past N days is

$$s_t = \sqrt{\frac{1}{N} \sum_{j=t-N+1}^{t} R^2_{j-1,j}} \qquad (15.2)$$

where a zero mean daily return is assumed for simplicity. At time $t + 1$, s_{t+1} is computed in the same manner, except the last observation—$R^2_{t-N+1,\,t-N}$— is dropped and replaced with the newest observation, $R^2_{t,\,t+1}$.

If we had chosen a window of the last 50 days, the moving average volatility estimate in Equation 15.2 would be the same as the unconditional variance estimate in Equation 15.1 as long as we assume in both cases that mean returns are equal to zero. Both unconditional volatility and moving average volatility thus *equally weight* all the observations in the calculation. In the unconditional case, because new observations are added without old ones being dropped, all available data is used, and, consequently, relatively less weight is given to more recent data. In the moving average case, recent observations are given more weight by keeping the moving average window (i.e., number of observations) constant each day.

Some firms prefer to give even more weight to recent history than the moving average. This can be done easily enough by using an exponentially weighted moving average, or EWMA. For any day t, the EWMA *variance* is defined (assuming a zero daily mean return) as

$$s_t^2 = \frac{\sum_{j=1}^{t} \lambda^{j-1} R^2_{t-j,\,t-j+1}}{\sum_{j=1}^{t} \lambda^{j-1}} \qquad (15.3)$$

where λ is a smoothing parameter. Using the properties of geometric sequences, this can be rewritten a bit more usefully as

$$s_t^2 = s_{t-1}^2 + (1-\lambda)\left(R^2_{t-1,t} - s_{t-1}^2\right) \qquad (15.4)$$

so that the current EWMA estimate of variance is equal to the prior day's EWMA estimate of variance plus the deviation of *today's* variance from that value weighted by one minus the smoothing parameter.

The summands in Equation 15.3 both begin with $j = 1$ to reflect the fact that the EWMA uses *all* the available data. Nevertheless, much of the data vanishes from the calculation because of the smoothing term λ. In fact, the parameter λ can be chosen so that a desired number of days τ impact the estimate using the following approximate relation between λ and τ:

$$\tau = \left(\frac{2}{1-\lambda} \right) - 1$$

A decay or smoothing factor of $\lambda = 0.9$, for example, means that only the last 19 days of data are being reflected in the EWMA estimate of variance. A higher decay factor implies a higher weight on older observations, and a lower decay factor weights more recent observations relatively more.

A related approach for estimating variance involves the use of *conditional variance* time series methods. Perhaps the most common such conditional variance model is the generalized autoregressive conditional heterskedasticity (GARCH) model.[5] A GARCH(m, n) model expresses the variance of returns at any time t as follows:

$$s_t^2 = \alpha + \sum_{p=1}^{m} \delta_p s_{t-p}^2 + \sum_{q=1}^{n} \gamma_q R_{t-q,\, t-q+1}^2 \tag{15.5}$$

In other words, the current conditional variance of returns is equal to a weighted average of prior conditional variances (the autoregressive component) and prior sample variances (the moving average component). A very popular special case of the GARCH(m, n) model is the GARCH(1, 1) model, or

$$s_t^2 = \alpha + \delta s_{t-1}^2 + \gamma R_{t-1,\, t}^2 \tag{15.6}$$

Note that the EWMA in Equation 15.4 is a special case of the GARCH(1, 1) model in Equation 15.6 when $\alpha = 0$ and $\delta + \gamma = 1$, in which case $\gamma = 1 - \delta = 1 - \lambda$. This is called an Integrated or IGARCH(1, 1) model.

No matter what econometric methods are used to estimate volatility, however, all historical volatility measures are by definition limited by the historical data used to calculate them. One measure of volatility, however, does *not* rely on historical data.

Option-Implied Volatility   Merton (1973) explains that the volatility input into a specific option pricing model, such as the model of Black and Scholes (1973), can be defined as follows:

$$\overline{\sigma_t^2} = \int_t^T \sigma f(\sigma)d\sigma \qquad (15.7)$$

where σ is the instantaneous volatility of the return on the underlying asset, $f(\sigma)$ is the probability density function for σ, and T is the date the option in question expires. In other words, the volatility used to price this option is the conditional expected value at time t of all future instantaneous volatilities from current time t through expiration date T.

Given a particular option pricing model and an observed transaction price, the problem can be reversed to back out an inherently forward-looking measure of volatility, called *option-implied volatility*. Implied volatility can be computed by iteratively substituting different volatilities into a pricing model until the *theoretical* transaction price is equal or very close to the observed *transaction* price. The volatility that equates the theoretical model price to the actual transaction price is the volatility implied by the option pricing model and the observed data.

Because implied volatility is based on actual transaction prices, this measure of risk reflects the best available information of market participants at any given time. By Equation 15.7, this information reveals the volatility of the underlying asset that is expected to prevail *for the remaining life of the option.*

The dependence of the option-implied volatility on a particular pricing model is precisely what makes this measure of risk interesting. By using an option pricing model with known and basic assumptions about the probability distribution of underlying asset returns, we can draw inferences about what market participants think the *true* distribution of returns looks like. To take the obvious case, the Black-Scholes (1973) model allows the theoretical price at any time t of a European call maturing at time T to be expressed as follows:

$$c_t = S_t e^{-q(T-t)} N(d_1) - K e^{-r(T-t)} N(d_2)$$

$$\text{where } d_1 = \frac{\ln\left(\dfrac{S_t}{K}\right) + \left(r - q + \tfrac{1}{2}\sigma^2\right)(T-t)}{\sigma\sqrt{T-t}}$$

$$d_2 = d_1 - \sigma\sqrt{T-t}$$

where S_t is the current price of the asset underlying the option, σ is the volatility of the continuously compounded return on that asset, r is the risk free rate, K is the option's strike price, q is the continuous dividend rate or convenience yield on the asset, and $N(d)$ is the cumulative *normal* distribution function evaluated at d. In the case where the underlying is a futures contract, we can convert the Black-Scholes model into the Black (1976) model by using the same equation and replacing S_t with current futures price F_t, σ with the volatility of the futures price change, and by setting $q = r$.

For any observed transaction price c_t, a unique implied volatility can be computed. In other words, only one number will retrieve the observed option price when that number is substituted in as the volatility input. Conversely, a given volatility input can yield only one theoretical price. Knowing the volatility of the underlying price thus is enough information to compute the theoretical price of a call, and knowing the implied volatility of the underlying price from the option model is enough to compute the actual price at which this option last traded.

The Black-Scholes and Black models assume that the price of the underlying spot asset (Black-Scholes) or futures contract (Black) is distributed lognormally, which implies that returns are distributed normally. Armed with this assumption, the volatilities *implied* by the Black-Scholes or Black models together with observed transaction prices tell us how market participants perceive the underlying probability distribution of returns over the remaining life of the option.

Figure 15.4 shows Black model-implied volatilities on a futures option as a function of the implied percentage change in underlying futures prices over the remaining life of the options. The implied futures price change can be inferred from the relation between the strike prices on the options used to compute the implied volatilities and the current futures price. If only in-the-money options are considered in the analysis, negative implied futures price changes on the x-axis correspond to in-the-money puts and positive implied price changes to in-the-money calls.

The relation between implied volatility and the *moneyness* of the options implied by the Black model is indicated by the heavy black line, flat at 20%. In other words, the Black model predicts *no relation* between the implied volatility of the option and the degree to which it is in-the-money. Because implied volatility is related to the transaction prices of the options, this means that the Black model predicts no relation between an option's *price* and the degree to which it is in-the-money.

Figure 15.4 also shows one possible relation between implied volatility and moneyness using actual transaction prices and the Black model. Clearly, this *volatility smile* does not look like the Black model predicts it should; the implied volatility *does* depend on the moneyness of the option.

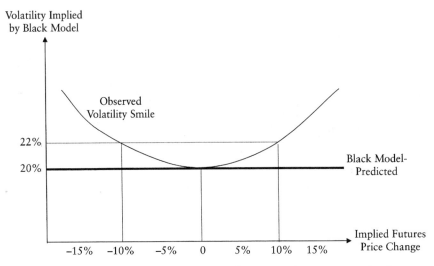

FIGURE 15.4 Black-implied volatility as a function of moneyness (in-the-money options).

For a put option that is 10% in-the-money (corresponding to −10% in the underlying on the *x*-axis), the Black model says that volatility should be equal to the at-the-money volatility of 20% per annum as shown in the figure. But instead, the observed volatility smile associates a 22% annualized implied volatility with that 10% price decline. This means that the Black model *underprices* the observed put transaction.

Because the Black-Scholes and Black models assume a normally distributed return for the asset underlying the option, observed deviations from these models can be used to draw inferences about the probability of price changes in the underlying. If the implied volatility associated with a 10% in-the-money put is 22% as shown, this means that market participants believe there is a higher probability of this return being realized than indicated by the Black model—that is, than indicated by the normal distribution on which the Black model depends. Calls, in this case, are *symmetrically* underpriced by the Black model. A 10% in-the-money option has an implied volatility two percentage points above the volatility that would be associated with a normal distribution. This makes sense only if market participants associate a higher probability with a 10% price increase than the normal distribution.

Figure 15.5 reproduces Figure 15.4 and also adds a second panel that shows the shape of the probability distribution implied by this particular

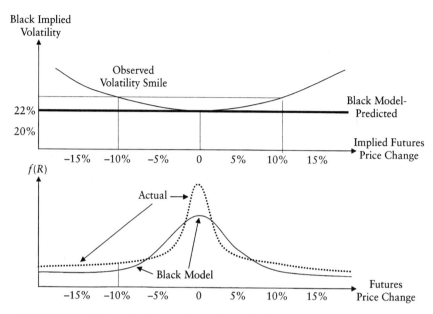

FIGURE 15.5 The volatility smile and implied probability distributions.

volatility smile. Because the volatility smile is indeed a smile, both in-the-money puts and in-the-money calls are underpriced by the Black model roughly symmetrically. For this to be true, market participants that were willing to transact at higher-than-predicted prices must believe that the probability of the option moving into the money is higher than implied by the normal distribution on which the Black model rests. The probability density must still integrate to one, and we might conjecture or deduce that the actual distribution is likely leptokurtic. In that case, the fatter tails in the actual distribution implied by the observed Black-implied volatility smile would be accompanied by a more peaked center, with the reduction in probability relative to the normal distribution occurring in the middle to compensate. In that case, Figure 15.5 might well represent a currency futures market, which is indeed known to exhibit leptokurtic but still roughly symmetric return distributions.

The volatility smile could, of course, exhibit just about any pattern we might imagine. Figure 15.6, for example, shows a volatility *smirk* instead of a smile. In this figure, the implied volatility smile computed from observed transaction prices indicates that the Black model *under*prices in-the-money puts and *over*prices in-the-money calls. In this case, the underlying probability that a put expires in-the-money is higher than implied by the normal

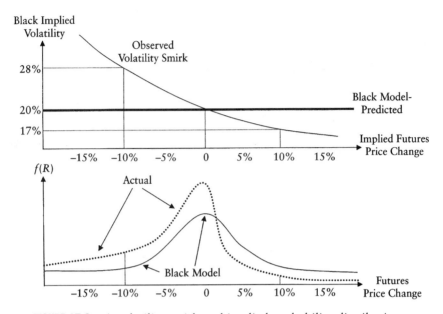

FIGURE 15.6 A volatility smirk and implied probability distributions.

distribution as in Figures 15.4 and 15.5, but now the probability that a call will expire in-the-money is viewed by market participants as *lower* than the normal distribution indicates. The implied distribution of futures price changes thus is negatively skewed with a fat left-hand tail and a right-hand tail that is thinner than the normal.[6] This volatility smile and implied price change distribution is characteristic of large-cap equities—at least since October 1987.

Note that the inferences we can draw from the shape of the volatility smile do not imply that implied volatility *itself* necessarily has a probabilistic interpretation. For now, it is just another sensitivity of the value of the asset to expected changes in risk factors over the remaining life of the asset.[7]

By incorporating market participants' expectations of future price volatility, though, implied volatility does improve on historical measures of volatility in several ways. First, interpreted properly, implied volatility does not force us into the view of the world where all returns are presumed to be symmetric, as is the case when traditional volatility measures are computed and reported. Second, the risks reflected in implied volatility are risks market participants *expect* to experience over the remaining life of the options. In the earlier example of a corporate bond whose historical time series evidenced no credit-dependent market risk, the same need not be true of the implied volatility for that bond. If market participants anticipate a downgrade before the option on the bond expires, the implied volatility will reflect that risk as Equation 15.7 confirms.

Nevertheless, implied volatility does still suffer from one limitation that also plagues traditional historical volatility measures. Namely, implied volatility is still an agglomeration of *all* risk sources. For a selective risk manager more interested in the credit-dependent market risk of an exposure than the credit-independent piece, for example, variance-based risk measures simply do not do the trick.

Downside Semivariance

An alternative measure of market risk that attempts to summarize the sensitivity of an exposure to changes in market prices is *downside risk*. When probability distributions are thought or known to be asymmetric and/or leptokurtic, classical variance measures of risk are not enough. For a firm wishing to stick with historical statistics, in particular, downside risk measures can be easy alternatives to historical variance and other sensitivity measures that assume symmetry in the underlying population data. Perhaps the most popular such measure is called *downside semivariance* (DSV) and may be defined for a time series of N daily returns as follows:

$$DSV_t = \frac{1}{N} \sum_{j=t-N+1}^{t} \left[\max\left(R_{j-1,j} - \overline{R}, 0 \right) \right]^2 \quad (15.8)$$

In other words, Equation 15.8 takes the *negative* squared deviation of returns from the mean, disregards the positive squared deviations, and averages over the whole time series. The resulting risk measure is an indication of the tendency of returns on this asset to deviate from their expected value, but *only* on the downside.

The roots of the DSV trace to a concept in probability theory known as the *lower partial moment* (LPM) of a distribution. The kth LPM of density $f(r)$ can be defined as

$$LPM_k(r) = E(r - T \mid r < T)^k = \int_{-\infty}^{T} (r - T)^k f(r) dr \quad (15.9)$$

where T is some target. Only those returns *below* the target are considered in the definition. When $k = 1$, the LPM measures the *expected loss* relative to target T, and when $k = 2$ the LPM is the downside semivariance, estimated using sample data as shown in Equation 15.8.

PROBABILISTIC MEASURES OF MARKET RISK

Noticeably absent from all the risk measures discussed thus far in this chapter is any attempt to systematically associate the risk exposures these summary measures indicate with the likelihood those exposures will actually translate into losses. To make that leap, we either need a probability distribution or we need to know enough about the data—or be willing to *assume* enough about the data—to draw probabilistic inferences from what we can observe, such as the parameters of a distribution.

Linking a measure of market risk to a probability that the adverse risk exposure will be realized lends realism to the summary risk measure. As an added benefit, probabilistic measures of risk are typically expressed in dollars at risk. This means that market risk exposures measured using one of the probabilistic techniques summarized in this section *can be compared* across exposures. What good is a market risk measure, after all, if it can neither be interpreted nor reported? In addition, by expressing potential losses in dollar terms, the measures of risk discussed in this section are easily comparable to most reasonable ways of expressing risk tolerances as summarized in Chapter 12.

To help ensure that the concepts in this section can be illustrated clearly, we will make two assumptions. First, we assume the exposures we have are sufficiently small in number that any computational or numerical problems with what follows can be ignored. Second, we assume for now that all the exposures are spot, forward, or forward-based.

Value at Risk[8]

Much-vaunted and badly understood, value at risk (VaR) is essentially a more systematic version of DVx/PVx scenario analysis. In a simple scenario analysis, a firm analyzes the consequences of one particular scenario on its assets and liabilities—the scenario in which a change in the underlying risk factor of x occurs. VaR extends this concept by considering how likely that scenario is to occur. And it does so not just for a single change in the market risk factor of x, but rather for an entire range of x's.

After computing a VaR, risk managers can make statements like the following: "I am 95% confident that I will not lose more than X in the next day," where X is the VaR and 95% is the chosen confidence in the statement's accuracy. In other words, the VaR in this example is obtained by solving the following for X:

$$\Pr(x \leq \$X) = 0.05$$

or, more formally, for some distribution of exposures $f(x)$

$$\int_{-\infty}^{\$X} f(x)dx = 0.05$$

Several decisions must be made before the VaR of an exposure or portfolio of exposures can be calculated, some of which are implied by the example statement above. First, the risk manager must choose a *risk horizon,* or the time period with which she is concerned that losses might occur. A one-quarter risk horizon means that the user is concerned with its potential market risk-related losses between now and the end of three months, whereas a one-day horizon implies a shorter window. Typically, this risk horizon will be influenced by several factors:

- Frequency of risk reporting requirements.
- Frequency of comparisons by the firm between actual risk and tolerances.
- Time required to liquidate or hedge huge losing positions.

Second, the risk manager must specify a confidence level. In a Bayesian context, the confidence level is the confidence that a risk manager has in the VaR representing the true worst-case loss in the next period. A 5% confidence level, for example, will result in a calculated loss that the risk manager believes will occur in the next period with 5% likelihood. If the risk manager is willing to assume probability distributions are stable over time, then a Frequentist probability interpretation allows the user to make an even stronger statement about a chosen confidence level of, say, Y%: "I will not lose more than $\$X$ in more than Y of the next hundred periods," where $\$X$ is the VaR.

The confidence level chosen for a VaR calculation will henceforth be denoted $(1 - \alpha)$%, where α% is the amount of probability in the left-hand tail of the risk distribution. We can use the tail parameter α notationally in several equivalent ways:

- Our confidence in the number or "confidence level" is $(1 - \alpha)$%.
- The computed VaR is the α% VaR.
- Our critical probability or VaR level is α%.
- If probability distributions are stable over time, our computed VaR should not be exceeded more than α% of the time or in more than α periods out of the next 100.

Third, a risk manager will need to define a calculation frequency, or the regularity with which a VaR statistic is computed. This is up to the risk manager and depends on the goals of the firm. Worth noting, nevertheless, is that a calculation should occur no less often than the risk horizon, although the converse is not necessarily true. A risk manager, for example, might well want to calculate a one-week VaR every day, whereas calculating a one-day VaR every week would make little sense.

With the definition of VaR as a concept in hand, we turn now to explore several different methods of actually measuring VaR. The summary that follows is far from exhaustive, and interested readers are recommended to turn to Jorion (2000) for a much more complete picture.

Historical Method   One way to measure risk is to assume that the future will behave precisely like the past. Specifically, the *historical method* for VaR measurement assumes that the distribution from which future asset returns will be drawn over the risk horizon is *identical* to the distribution of historical asset returns over some specified historical window of time. Under that assumption, VaR can be calculated using only the sample statistics of the time series of past security returns.

Consider a single asset k whose value is linear in a single underlying risk factor (e.g., a share of common stock, a Eurodeposit, or a pure discount Treasury security). Suppose first that we specify a risk horizon of exactly one month—the user wishes to calculate how much it will lose more than $\alpha\%$ of the time between today and one month hence. If we have a time series of N historical monthly returns on that asset, $(R_{t-N, k}, \cdots, R_{t, k})$, where t denotes current time and $R_{t-N, k}$ denotes the return on asset k realized N months ago, the one-month VaR can be calculated as of current date t as follows:

$$VaR_{t, k}(\alpha) = V_{t, k}\left(1 + R_k^{\alpha}\right)$$

where $V_{t, k}$ equals the current price of asset k and R_k^{α} equals αth percentile return on asset k from $(R_{t-N, k}, \cdots, R_{t, k})$. In principle, returns can be calculated either arithmetically or continuously using this method.

If the user specifies a longer risk horizon, a different set of underlying data is required. Specifically, the frequency with which returns are calculated must conform to the length of the risk horizon so that the return distribution inferred from the histogram spans exactly the period of time of interest. For example, a user concerned with a one-quarter risk horizon would need to generate a simple histogram of quarterly returns using

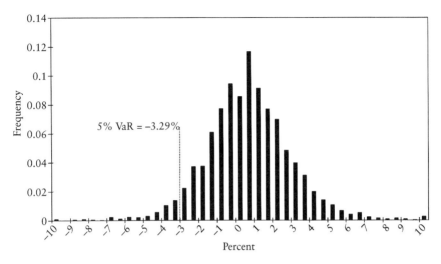

FIGURE 15.7 Historical one-day VaR, Microsoft Corporation (3/86–12/99).

historical quarterly time series data. The αth percentile return of the resulting quarterly return distribution then would serve as the basis for the one-quarter VaR.

Figure 15.7 illustrates the historical method for the calculation of a one-day VaR at the 95% confidence level for the common stock issued by the Microsoft Corporation. Using daily returns from March of 1986 through the end of 1999, the 5% one-day VaR (i.e., 95% confidence daily VaR) is shown in the figure as the line below which 5% of this historical returns on this stock lie. Expressed in returns, the VaR is equal to −3.295%. Translating this into a dollar amount trivially requires the multiplication of one plus the critical return shown by the current price of the stock. At year-end 1999, Microsoft closed at $116.75 per share, so the 5% VaR would have been $113—the price per share which Microsoft stock is not expected to fall more than 5% of the time.

Now suppose we wish to calculate a VaR using the historical method for a *portfolio* of exposures—something we have thus far not been able to do with any of the risk measures explored up to this point in this chapter. Suppose the current portfolio contains K assets with values linear in a single underlying risk factor. Because the current holdings of the portfolio are known, the weights of each asset in the portfolio also are known as of current date t. Define the weight of the kth asset in the portfolio at time t as follows:

$$w_{t,k} = \frac{V_{t,k}}{\sum_{j=1}^{K} V_{t,j}}$$

Calculating a one-month portfolio VaR using the historical method requires time series of monthly returns on all K assets. If the length of the historical window chosen is N, the historical returns collected should include
$[(R_{t-N,\,1}, \ldots, R_{t,\,1}),\ \ (R_{t-N,\,2}, \ldots, R_{t,\,2}), \ldots, (R_{t-N,\,K}, \ldots, R_{t,\,K})]$. These
asset-specific time series then can be used to create a *new* time series of re-
turns for what the current portfolio *would have returned* had the assets in
the current portfolio been held in their current proportions over the last N
months. Denote the return on this portfolio q months ago as $R_{t-q,\,P}$, which
is defined as

$$R_{t-q,P} = \sum_{j=1}^{K} w_{t,j} R_{t-q,j}$$

which is the arithmetic weighted average of all monthly asset returns from
month $t - q - 1$ through month $t - q$ assuming *current* portfolio weights
for each asset. Repeating this calculation for all N months yields a time series of returns the current portfolio would have exhibited if held over the
last N quarters: $(R_{t-N,\,P}, \ldots, R_{t,\,P})$. The one-month portfolio VaR as of time
t then is

$$VaR_{t,\,P}(\alpha) = V_{t,\,P}\left(1 + R_P^{\alpha}\right)$$

where R_P^{α} equals αth percentile return on asset k from $(R_{t-N,\,P}, \ldots, R_{t,\,P})$
and where

$$V_{t,P} = \sum_{j=1}^{K} w_{t,j} V_{t,j}$$

Note that the correlations across assets are naturally embedded in the historical time series and require no separate estimation.

As in the single-asset case, the historical method for computing portfolio VaR can be generalized to a multimonth risk horizon by changing the
sampling frequency of the underlying asset return historical data.

Parametric Normal Method   The parametric normal VaR estimation method
was popularized by J.P. Morgan and Reuters through the distribution of

their RiskMetrics™ data sets and *Technical Document.* So popular is this method of VaR estimation that it is sometimes confused with the concept of VaR itself.

Recall that a sensitivity analysis allows us to express the potential change in the present value of assets net of liabilities (i.e., the net worth) of an exposure as follows:

$$\Delta V = V \times S \times \Delta z$$

where S is the sensitivity of the exposure's present value to risk factor z. If z is a single interest rate and S is modified duration, for example, the above is equivalent to the duration gap model:

$$\Delta V = V \times MD \times \Delta y$$

If some probabilistic interpretation can be assigned to the above duration gap model, we can synthesize duration gap and scenario analysis into VaR. Specifically, suppose the firm is willing to assume that changes in the interest rates are *normally distributed.* In the normal distribution, 5% of the distribution lies 1.65 standard deviations to the left of the mean. Assuming a zero daily mean interest rate change, 1.65 times the standard deviation of interest rate changes can be substituted into Δy above to get

$$\$VaR = V \times MD \times 1.65\sigma_y$$

where σ_y is the standard deviation of daily interest rate changes.

The above one-day VaR is exactly like the change in exposure measured by the duration gap model. The only difference, in fact, is that the following *probabilistic* statement now can be made: This firm expects to lose more than \$VaR from the impact of adverse interest rate changes on this exposure less than 5% of the time.

In more general terms, consider a single asset k whose time t holdings have a market value of $V_{t,k}$. Assume the arithmetic return on the asset in month $t + q$ is drawn from a probability distribution denoted $f_{t+q}(R_{t+q,k})$ whose pdf is known. For simplicity, assume the pdf is normal and intertemporally stable—$f_{t+q}(R_{t+q,k}) = f_t(R_{t+q,k})$ for all q. The VaR for asset k over the next month is then

$$VaR_{t,k}(\alpha) = V_{t,k}[\mu_k - \lambda(\alpha)\sigma_k]$$

where μ_k is the average arithmetic monthly return on asset k, σ_k is the standard deviation of monthly returns on asset k, and $\lambda(\alpha)$ is the confidence interval constant.

The confidence interval constant allows the above expression to be interpreted probabilistically using properties of the normal distribution. If $\alpha = 5\%$, then $\lambda(\alpha) = 1.65$ tells us that the 5% VaR is 1.65 standard deviations below the mean. This 5% VaR corresponds to a statistical confidence level of 95%.

Because we assumed that the distribution for this asset's returns is stable over time, we can calculate a multiperiod extension of the above for users with risk horizons longer than one month. Specifically, the T-month parametric normal VaR for asset k is

$$VaR_{t,k}(\alpha) = V_{t,k}\left[T\mu_k - \lambda(\alpha)\sigma_k\sqrt{T}\right]$$

Note that many short-horizon parametric VaR calculations (e.g., one-day VaR) assume mean returns are zero, in which case the T-period VaR is just the one-period VaR times the square root of the number of periods:

$$VaR_{t,k}(\alpha) = VaR_{t,k}(\alpha)\sqrt{T}$$

Figure 15.8 shows the 5% one-day VaR for Microsoft (returns only) computed using the parametric normal method. This computation *and* the normal distribution corresponding to the sample mean and variance for the stock are overlaid on the frequency distribution and historical VaR from Figure 15.7 for comparative purposes. As Figure 15.8 shows, the normal distribution is not a particularly good representation of Microsoft's daily returns for the past roughly 15 years. Not surprisingly, then, the VaRs are different. The parametric VaR expressed as a percentage is −3.78% as compared to −3.29% in the historical case. Using the year-end closing price per share of $116.75, the parametric VaR is $112. An additional dollar per share is "at risk" when VaR is computed using the parametric normal method vis-à-vis the historical method.

The actual distribution in Figure 15.8 is seen to be extremely leptokurtic relative to the superimposed normal. A significant amount of probability is stacked in the center of the actual distribution rather than in its middle portions. Although the tails are a bit thick—primarily due to some large outliers on both sides—the kurtosis in this case is no doubt coming from a shift in probability from the middle regions toward the center, thus accounting for the lower actual VaR than predicted by the normal. In fact,

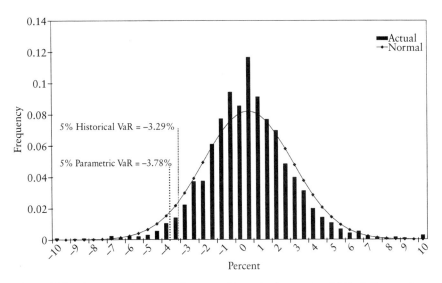

FIGURE 15.8 Parametric normal versus historical one-day VaR, Microsoft (3/86–12/99).

the sample excess kurtosis (i.e., kurtosis above the kurtosis of the normal) for this distribution is about 10.[9]

In practice, any estimate of volatility can be used to compute the parametric normal VaR. The volatility need not be an unconditional estimate, in particular. Using a conditional variance, for example, allows the parametric VaR to better track market movements and changes over time in the underlying probability distribution of returns. The parametric normal methodology itself actually assumes this distribution does *not* change over time, so using a conditional variance estimate—such as a GARCH(1, 1) or EWMA/IGARCH(1, 1) estimate—is a way of "tricking" the methodology to reflect changes in the volatility parameter of the distribution even though the distribution itself is not changing.[10] In fact, following the use by J.P. Morgan of the IGARCH(1, 1) volatility estimate in constructing its RiskMetrics™ data sets, IGARCH(1, 1) is now widely accepted as the standard volatility estimate for parametric normal VaR calculations.

Now suppose the firm has a portfolio of K assets and that the user is willing to assume the returns on all these assets are distributed multivariate normal. The multivariate normal monthly return distribution is assumed stable, as is the covariance matrix between individual asset returns (i.e., no serial correlation or conditional heteroskedasticity).

Suppose the single-asset VaRs have been calculated for each of the K assets, and the single-asset VaR for any asset k is denoted $\text{VaR}_{t,k}$ as above (with the α parameter now dropped from the notation for convenience). Now define a $1 \times K$ column vector denoted $\underline{\text{VaR}}_t$, such that

$$\underline{VaR}_t^T = \left(\underline{VaR}_{t,1}\ \underline{VaR}_{t,2} \ldots \underline{VaR}_{t,K} \right)$$
$$= \left\{ V_{t,1} \times \left[\mu_1 - \lambda(\alpha)\sigma_1 \right] V_{t,2} \times \left[\mu_2 - \lambda(\alpha)\sigma_2 \right] \ldots V_{t,K} \times \left[\mu_K - \lambda(\alpha)\sigma_K \right] \right\}$$

where T denotes a transpose and the underscore denotes a vector or matrix. Now denote the matrix of pairwise correlation coefficients as $\underline{\Sigma}$, where the (i, j)th off-diagonal element of $\underline{\Sigma}$ is $\Sigma_{i,j} = \rho_{ij}$ which denotes the pairwise correlation between returns on assets i and j and where the diagonal elements of $\underline{\Sigma}$ are all unity.

The one-period parametric normal *portfolio* VaR is calculated as follows:

$$VaR_{t,P} = \sqrt{\underline{VaR}_t^T\, \underline{\Sigma}\, \underline{VaR}_t}$$

If a zero mean is assumed for each asset, the T-period portfolio VaR is simply the single-period VaR multiplied by the square root of T. In the more common case of a nonzero mean, however, the multiperiod calculation requires going back to the matrix multiplication stage and redefining the vector of single-asset VaRs using the appropriate time scaling,

$$VaR_t = \left\{ V_{t,1} \times \left[T\mu_1 - \lambda(\alpha)\sigma_1 T^{1/2} \right] V_{t,2} \times \left[T\mu_2 - \lambda(\alpha)\sigma_2 T^{1/2} \right] \right.$$
$$\left. \ldots V_{t,K} \times \left[T\mu_K - \lambda(\alpha)\sigma_K T^{1/2} \right] \right\}$$

and then recalculating the portfolio VaR accordingly.

Historical Sampling with Replacement   A simple type of simulation analysis known as *sampling with replacement* can be used as another method of computing VaR. Consider a single asset k. Suppose we have a time series of N monthly historical returns on that asset $(R_{t-N,k}, \ldots, R_{t,k})$, where t denotes current time t and $R_{t-N,k}$ denotes the one-period return on asset k realized N periods ago.

Now suppose we generate a single sample path where the length of the path is equal to the number of periods in the VaR risk horizon. The next-period VaR requires a sample path with unitary length; the annual VaR requires a sample path with twelve elements if monthly returns are used; and so on. Denote the length of any given sample path T and denote that path $R_k^1 = (R_{t+1, k}^1, \ldots, R_{t+T, k}^1)$. Each return in the sample path is generated by sampling *with replacement* from the historical time series of asset k returns. We then similarly generate m different sample paths $R^1 \ldots R^m$, where m is large (e.g., 10,000). The result is T return distributions, each of which consists of 10,000 returns. The one-month VaR then can be calculated just as was done in the historical method, or, as of current date t, as follows:

$$VaR_{t,k}(\alpha) = V_{t,k} \times \left(1 + R_{t+1,k}^\alpha\right)$$

where $V_{t,k}$ equals current price of asset k, and $R_{t+1, k}^\alpha$ equals αth percentile return on asset k from each of the m returns on all sample paths for month $t + 1$ (i.e., the αth percentile return from the set $(R_{t+1, k}^1, \ldots, R_{t+1, k}^m)$

The calculation of the multiperiod VaR depends on whether continuous or arithmetic returns are used. To see why, consider a single sample path—say, the jth path—of returns over the next T periods and suppose the risk horizon is exactly T periods. Suppose $R_{t+q, k}^j$ denotes an arithmetic return on sample path j from any month $t + q - 1$ to month $t + q$:

$$R_{t+q, k}^j = \frac{V_{t+q, k}^j + D_{t+q, k}^j - V_{t+q-1, k}^j}{V_{t+q-1, k}^j}$$

where $D_{t+q, k}^j$ is the dividend paid (if any) on asset k between months $t + q - 1$ and $t + q$ along sample path j. The *cumulative* return on asset k over the entire sample path then is the product of one plus each monthly return. So, the *value* of the asset at the end of this sample path is

$$V_{t+T, k}^j = V_{t, k} \times \prod_{i=1}^T \left(1 + R_{t+i, k}^j\right)$$

The deviation of the time T value of the asset from its initial value then is

$$dV^j = V_{t, k} \times \left[\prod_{i=1}^T \left(1 + R_{t+i, k}^j\right) - 1\right]$$

For each of the m sample paths, we can calculate T-period changes in asset value, resulting in a distribution of changes in value with m total observations. The αth percentile of this distribution is the T-period VaR.

Now suppose instead that returns were calculated geometrically between months $t + q - 1$ and $t + q$ as follows:

$$r^j_{t+q,\,k} = \ln\left(V^j_{t+q,\,k}\right) - \ln\left(V^j_{t+q-1,\,k}\right)$$

where any dividends are presumed to be continuously reinvested over the period. The T-period VaR then can be calculated in a manner similar to the case in which arithmetic returns were used—cumulate the current value to the end of the sample path, calculate the deviation of the terminal value from the initial value, and repeat until m deviations in value are generated. For any sample path j, the deviation in terminal value from initial value for asset k can be written using the properties of the natural logarithm function as

$$dV^j = V^j_{t+T,\,k} - V^j_{t,\,k} = V_{t,\,k}\left[e^{r^j_{t+1,\,k}+\cdots+r^j_{t+T,\,k}} - 1\right]$$

The αth percentile of this change in value distribution is the T-period VaR.

To generalize this approach to the level of a portfolio, we need only form the portfolio as of current date t. We then calculate m sample paths of *portfolio* returns by sampling with replacement *contemporaneously* from the historical time series. Let

$$w_{t,\,k} = \frac{V_{t,\,k}}{\sum_{j=1}^{K} V_{t,\,j}}$$

denote the weight of asset k in the portfolio p at time t. Denote the return on this portfolio at any time t as $R_{t,\,p}$, which is defined as

$$R_{t,\,p} = \sum_{j=1}^{K} w_{t,\,j} R_{t,\,j}$$

Now, suppose we have a time series of N historical monthly returns on all K assets: $[(R_{t-N,\,1}, \ldots, R_{t,\,1}), (R_{t-N,\,2}, \ldots, R_{t,\,2}), (R_{t-N,\,K}, \ldots, R_{t,\,K})]$. Consider our first sample path of historical portfolio returns, $R_p^1 = (R^1_{t+1,\,p}, \ldots, R^1_{t+T,\,p})$. We can generate any return on this sample path by randomly choosing a historical time increment and then calculating what the return on the *current* portfolio *would have been* on that historical date. If our first sample path return is randomly sampled from the multiple asset returns q months ago, then

$$R^1_{t+1,p} = \sum_{k=1}^{K} w_{t-q,k} R_{t-q,k}$$

By sampling in this manner, the correlations in returns across the multiple assets is *naturally embedded into the sample returns*. It is thus not necessary to separately estimate a correlation matrix using this approach. The VaR thus is just the current value of the asset times the αth percentile return defined by the first step across all sample paths. Multiperiod extensions for the portfolio are analogous to the case of a single asset.

The historical simulation methodology does not add a lot to the historical method. Sampling with replacement many times from a historical time series should—and certainly *will* in the limit—simply retrieve the properties of the historical sample. Nevertheless, for purely operational purposes some firms prefer this method. One particular benefit is that the method allows steps to be generated along a sample path that can be useful to firms interested in interim *cash flows* rather than values, thereby making this method attractive both to value hedgers and cash flow hedgers. Just using a historical histogram, by contrast, leaves most cash flow hedgers unsatisfied.

Monte Carlo Simulation   A more robust form of simulation relies on Monte Carlo sampling but instead of defining the distributions along sample paths using only historical data, this method defines the candidate distribution using a presumed stochastic process.

Consider a single asset k. The parametric normal VaR calculation method forced us to make certain assumptions about the form of the *unconditional* probability distribution. In other words, we assumed that returns were independent and identically distributed and then used a single density function to generate one-step-ahead VaR forecasts *and* multiperiod VaR forecasts. The Monte Carlo simulation method requires only that we make specific assumptions about the *conditional* density, or the transition density that governs movements in a random variable along a stochastic process. Consequently, we need to make an assumption about that stochastic process itself that generates changes in the values of assets and liabilities.

To keep things general, suppose we consider only the simple case of common stock k that pays no dividends and presume the stock price evolves according to an Itô process of the form given in the following *stochastic differential equation* (SDE):

$$dV_k = \mu_k V_k dt + \sigma_k V_k dZ_k$$

where dZ_k is a Gauss-Wiener process and where μ_k and σ_k are parameters. We can think of

$$dZ_k^2 = \varepsilon^2 dt \quad \text{where } \varepsilon \sim NID(0, 1)$$

so that our conditional transition density is conditionally standard normal. The "inputs" to the stochastic simulation are simply the parameters of the presumed stochastic process—for this process, mean and variance. Once we have these, the process can be discretized with time interval length dt set equal to the monthly time step. We then can express the time $t + 1$ price of asset k as

$$V_{t+1, k} = V_{t, k} \exp\left(\mu_k - \tfrac{1}{2}\sigma_k^2 + \sigma_k \varepsilon\right)$$

At time t, we thus can simulate the next value on a sample path by making a draw from a standard normal variate. We can repeat that process to generate a sample path of length T, corresponding to the multiperiod VaR risk horizon. Note that the value of the asset at each point along the sample path is expressed in nominal dollars and not in terms of time t dollars.

We then repeat the above procedure to generate m sample paths for possible future values of asset k, where m is about 10,000. Once we have our m sample paths, calculating VaR is easy for linear instruments whose values depend only on the single stochastic process. For a one-period VaR, we will rely exclusively on the first step in each of the m total sample paths. Specifically, the first step on each of the m simulated paths give us m possible equity prices one month from now ($V_{t+1, k}^1, \ldots, V_{t+1, k}^m$). Using those possible equity values, we want to calculate a VaR *expressed in time t dollars* as all our previous results have been expressed. In order to do that, we need to discount the m possible equity prices back to present value. To do this we use the relevant term structure—interbank for equity products. This yields a distribution of possible changes in equity values, all expressed in time t dollars. The αth percentile of this distribution is the single-asset VaR.

Figure 15.9 illustrates the results of a Monte Carlo simulation of daily returns on Microsoft as compared to the parametric normal and historical VaR calculation methods. The historical mean and variance were used to parameterize a geometric Brownian motion equation, and a single-step sample path was generated 20,000 times (based on 10,000 draws from a standard normal variate and its antithetical variate). The resulting critical

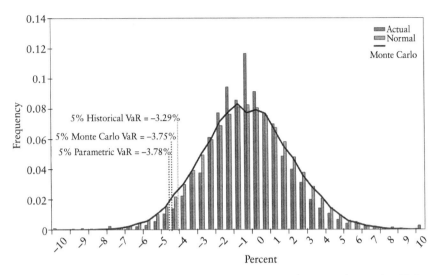

FIGURE 15.9 Monte Carlo versus parametric versus historical one-day VaR, Microsoft (3/86–12/99).

return, representing the 5th percentile of the simulated one-day return distribution, is shown as −3.75%, or just under the parametric normal VaR and just over the historical VaR.

The problem gets more complex with multiple linear instruments whose returns are correlated. In that case, the stochastic simulation requires that we simulate all the relevant stochastic processes *simultaneously*. To take an easy example, suppose we have two assets whose arithmetic returns are correlated that evolve as follows:

$$\frac{dV_1}{V_1} = \mu_1 dt + \sigma_1 dZ_1$$

$$\frac{dV_2}{V_2} = \mu_2 dt + \sigma_2 dZ_2$$

where

$$dZ_1^{\,2} = \varepsilon_1^{\,2} dt$$

$$dZ_2^{\,2} = \varepsilon_2^{\,2} dt$$

and where the two processes exhibit correlation ρ_{12}.

We can rewrite this system in terms of the correlation as follows:

$$\frac{dV_1}{V_1} = \mu_1 dt + \sigma_1 \varepsilon_1 \sqrt{dt}$$

$$\frac{dV_2}{V_2} = \mu_2 dt + \sigma_2 \rho_{12} \varepsilon_1 \sqrt{dt} + \sigma_2 \sqrt{1 - \rho_{12}}\, \varepsilon_2 \sqrt{dt}$$

In this example, the realizations of V_1 and V_2 are not independent at any time increment. In the simple case of two variables, we simulate the realizations for the first stock with independent draws from ε_1, and nothing in the first sample path depends on the second stock. The second stock, however, has realizations that depend *both* on the realized shocks to the first stock return ε_1 *and* on the simulated draws for the second process. Note that the order in which the substitution is made does not impact the results.

The more general case can be reviewed by expressing the system of stochastic differential equations in vector form. Suppose we have K correlated equities whose prices evolve according to geometric Brownian motion. We can express the system of SDEs as follows:

$$\frac{dV_1}{V_1} = \mu_1 dt + \sigma_1 dZ_1$$

$$\vdots$$

$$\frac{dV_K}{V_K} = \mu_K dt + \sigma_K dZ_K$$

or in vector and matrix notation

$$\frac{dV}{V} = \underline{\mu} dt + \underline{X}\underline{\varepsilon}\sqrt{dt}$$

where $\underline{\varepsilon}^T = (\varepsilon_1, \varepsilon_2, \ldots, \varepsilon_K)$, each element of which is standard normal. The $K \times K$ matrix $\underline{X}$ transforms the K independent variables $\underline{\varepsilon}$ drawn from standard normal distributions into correlated changes in the K equity returns.

If the covariance matrix across the K returns is positive definite, matrix $\underline{X}$ can be expressed in the following useful way:

$$\underline{X}\underline{X}^T = \underline{\Sigma}$$

where the covariance matrix $\underline{\Sigma}$ is defined as follows:

$$\underline{\Sigma} = \begin{bmatrix} \sigma_1^2 & \cdots & \sigma_1 \sigma_K \rho_{1K} \\ \vdots & \ddots & \vdots \\ \sigma_K \sigma_1 \rho_{1K} & \cdots & \sigma_K^2 \end{bmatrix}$$

and where

$$\underline{X} = \begin{bmatrix} X_{11} & 0 & \cdots & 0 \\ X_{21} & X_{22} & \cdots & 0 \\ \vdots & \vdots & \ddots & \vdots \\ X_{K1} & X_{K2} & \cdots & X_{KK} \end{bmatrix}$$

Using a Cholesky decomposition, we can solve forward to get a lower-right triangular matrix that makes the simulation fairly straightforward and computationally manageable.[11]

The covariance matrix may not be positive definite, however, in which case $\underline{X}$ cannot be expressed as simply as the above. First, the covariance matrix may have zero eigenvalues if one of the equities is a linear combination of the others—holding components of an index *and* the index. Alternatively, the covariance matrix could have negative eigenvalues if the lengths of the time series used to estimate the volatilities are significantly different. In either case, principal components analysis can be used to analyze the eigenvectors if required so that the problematic ones are dropped, although this process is hard to automate and can be computationally troublesome.

Shortfall Risk

VaR allows the risk manager to specify a risk horizon and confidence level and calculate a potential worst-case loss. But suppose the worst-case loss is *known* in the form of a target, below which the firm *cannot go*. Examples would include the contribution threshold for a defined-benefit pension plan sponsor or the funding threshold for a liability pool at an insurance company. In these cases, the firm may choose a different kind of summary statistic to measure and monitor market risk.

Based on the concept of a LPM discussed earlier, shortfall risk measures are summary statistics that indicate the risk of some asset or liability falling in value below a chosen target level. Like VaR, the risk manager thus specifies a risk horizon, but, unlike VaR, the risk manager now postulates a loss and solves for a type of probability rather than the other way around.

Recall the expression for the LPM of some probability distribution $f(r)$ from Equation 15.9. The parameter that characterizes the risk measure of interest, k, has three commonly defined levels for risk management purposes. When $k = 0$, the resulting summary risk measure is called *below-target probability* (BTP) and literally measures the probability of a loss below the specified target T:

$$BTP = \int_{-\infty}^{T} f(r)dr$$

Unfortunately, this does not tell the user how severe those losses might be.[12]

To get a sense of the size of the loss in a probability-weighted context, the risk manager can choose $k = 1$ and calculate the *conditional expected loss* on a portfolio of exposures whose distribution is given by $f(r)$. *Conditional expected loss* (CEL) is just

$$CEL = \int_{-\infty}^{T} rf(r)dr$$

But this still does not really communicate to the risk manager the *risk* of major shortfalls relative to target T.

With its roots in downside semivariance, the risk manager may wish to compute a measure of risk that penalizes relatively large deviations from the target more than small ones. In this case, the risk manager can select $k = 2$ and compute the *below-target risk* (BTR) of a position, equal to the square root of *below-target variance* (BTV):

$$BTV = \int_{-\infty}^{T} (r - T)^2 f(r)dr$$

which can be estimated from sample data using Equation 15.8 where μ is replaced with T.

These measures of market risk do not really change any of the computational methods discussed earlier. If you are willing to assume the future will behave like the past *or* that returns are normally distributed, you will be able to generate a sample distribution for $f(r)$ relatively easily. But if not, the real work comes into the generation of $f(r)$. Once $f(r)$ has been constructed in sample data for your actual portfolio of exposures, whether to summarize the risk with VaR or with some measure of shortfall risk is really a question of semantics and interpretation.

Some people believe that shortfall risk has an inherent advantage over VaR because it does not assume symmetric probability distributions. In fact, neither does VaR. The parametric normal method is so popular that some people mistake it for VaR itself, when in reality there is no *theoretical* reason that VaR cannot also be calculated for asymmetric or leptokurtic distributions. In that sense, VaR and shortfall risk are different ways of reporting the same basic information. Neither measure is theoretically any better than the other.

VaR with Asymmetric and Leptokurtic Distributions

Saying that fat tails and asymmetric distributions can be accommodated by either VaR or shortfall risk is easier than doing it, of course. The left-hand tail is where large losses will occur in the probability distribution, but it is also in this area where the distribution of losses is most difficult to estimate. In addition, the occurrence of such seemingly catastrophic scenarios could also change the economic definition of a dollar loss—the 95% confidence one-day VaR for Microsoft might be tolerable to a large pension plan but intolerable to those whose entire wealth is invested in Microsoft.[13]

To address the estimation issues concerning large losses in leptokurtic and potentially asymmetric distributions, some have recently advocated the use of *Extreme Value Theory* (EVT). EVT is a subset of statistics that concentrates on values in the tail of a distribution and looks at the rate at which those values approach zero in order to determine how fat the tail is.[14]

Various methods exist for estimating the "tail index," or the rate at which the tail decays—and hence the fatness of that tail. One such method, proposed by Pownall and Koedijk (1999), involves the use of this tail index as the parameter for the number of degrees of freedom in a Student's *t* distribution, which generally has fatter tails than the normal but has the advantage of nesting the normal, as well. They then use the same IGARCH(1, 1) model (i.e., EWMA) used in the traditional parametric normal implementation. Instead of using a normal variate, however, they assume the errors for the estimation are drawn from a Student's *t* distribution with the estimated tail index as the number of degrees of freedom.[15] After making a few additional changes for scale, the authors demonstrate that the tail index-modified VaR estimate—called VaR-*x*—captured significantly more of the extreme downside moves during the Asian currency crisis than the parametric normal VaR.

Other methods have been proposed for incorporating either distributional asymmetries, fat tails, or both into the distributions used for VaR estimation. Some of these include Zangari (1996), Venkataraman (1997), Hull and White (1998), Aït-Sahalia and Lo (2000), and Longin (2000).

A separate set of models that address non-normal VaR distributions include those models that construct an implied distribution designed to fit the observed volatility smile. We discussed in an earlier section how to infer the basic shape of the distribution that option prices suggest is perceived by market participants. Using numerical methods, a lattice can be constructed to generate exact state prices and the terminal risk-neutral distribution of asset values. Some complications can arise in converting these distributions from risk-neutral into more easily interpreted ones, but such conversions are possible. And once done, the VaR can be computed directly as the percentile of interest from the implied distribution.[16]

ACTUAL HOLDINGS VERSUS PRIMITIVES

We assumed in the previous section that the use of actual exposure-level data was feasible. In fact, obtaining exposure-level payoffs and time series data is not always practical for computational, data, and modeling reasons.

The RiskMetrics™ parametric normal method of VaR calculation is popular not just because the computational costs are low, but because the data needs are manageable and do *not* require exposure- or holdings-level time series data. The RiskMetrics™ approach pioneered the use of *primitive securities,* or securities that act as proxies for the actual holdings in a portfolio. In the case of equity, for example, the primitive security is defined as beta units of an index. A U.S. equity like Intel, for example, thus would be treated as β units of the S&P 500, where the S&P 500 is the primitive. The VaR then is calculated using the parametric normal approach as follows:

$$VaR_{t,\,k}(\alpha) = V_{t,\,k} \times \beta_{k,\,z}[\mu_z - \lambda(\alpha)\sigma_z]$$

where $\beta_{k,\,z}$ is the OLS beta from a regression of asset k's returns on the S&P 500 return, μ_z is the average arithmetic return per quarter on primitive security z (i.e., the S&P 500), σ_z is the standard deviation of quarterly returns on primitive z, and $\lambda(\alpha)$ is the confidence interval constant.

For bonds, FX, commodities, and most linear derivatives, the parametric normal VaR calculation method does not rely on empirical estimates of beta. Instead, *cash flows* on the instruments are decomposed into simple spot instruments *and* zero-coupon bonds or deposits. For example, a DEM/USD forward contract is treated as a DEM/USD spot transaction plus two money market deposits, one denominated in DEM and one in USD.

Using primitive securities vastly simplifies the VaR data problem by eliminating the need for parameter data on specific securities *other than* any parameters required to make the transformation from the original asset to its primitive (e.g., beta in the case of stocks). But the mean, variance, correlations, and other parameters used in the VaR calculation itself then are the parameters of the *primitives* rather than the specific securities held in the portfolio. In this manner, the primitives method can greatly reduce data and computational costs.

The RiskMetrics™ approach to mapping securities into primitives depends entirely on the asset class type. For equity, the primitive mapping method is based on delta, or the sensitivity of returns on the stock or index of interest to changes in the return on the primitive. The relation is typically estimated using OLS, where the OLS beta is the conversion factor—one share of actual stock is treated as equivalent to beta shares of the primitive. This can introduce specification problems of several kinds. First, the beta estimate may be subject to significant measurement error, especially if the primitive is poorly correlated with the equity. Second, if the primitive is poorly chosen, the residuals may exhibit conditional heteroskedasticity. Finally, a bad primitive will result in an error term or intercept with a non-zero expected value, so that the idiosyncratic risk of the portfolio is ignored in the primitive mapping.

For interest-sensitive instruments, the primitives in the RiskMetrics™ approach are zero-coupon government bonds and interbank depository instruments. The primitive mapping for debt uses a cash flow mapping approach rather than a delta-return approach. Specifically, the cash flows of all actual holdings are mapped into equivalent notional principal amounts in the corresponding primitives on a dollar-for-dollar basis. For example, consider a corporate bond with a $10 semiannual coupon, $100 face value, and 18 months to maturity. The primitive mapping would treat the corporate credit risk as equivalent to government credit risk and map the level-coupon bond into three primitives: a zero with $10 face value maturing in six months; a zero with $10 face value maturing in a year; and a zero with $110 face value maturing in 18 months.[17]

The two primitive mapping approaches used in the RiskMetrics™ approach are fundamentally different. In the case of equity, the delta of the linear instrument is used to map from the holding to the primitive, which requires historical data to estimate the beta parameter. In the case of debt, the actual cash flows are used. No historical data is required on the actual holding, *but* developing code to map cash flows from holdings into primitives is where most of the leg work lies.

NONLINEAR INSTRUMENTS

Our discussion of VaR has also excluded nonlinear payoffs, such as bonds with convexity, most derivatives, real options, and the like. In this section, the methods for calculating VaR on instruments with multiple underlyings or instruments whose cash flows (and value) are a nonlinear function of underlyings are summarized.

As noted when VaR was introduced, value at risk is conceptually similar to DVx scenario analysis where x is now a distribution of possible values in a risk factor and where a probability is associated with the results. When we discussed DVx calculations earlier, we noted that two methods—partial revaluation and full revaluation—could be used when x is large. The same two such methods can be used to extend VaR to the world of nonlinearity.

Partial Revaluation and Taylor Series

Consider a risk exposure whose present value depends on a single underlying in a nonlinear fashion (e.g., a bond) or whose value depends on the value of multiple underlyings (e.g., derivatives). For asset k, we denote this value at time t as $V_{t,k}$ and can express the value generally as $V_{t,k}(z)$ where z is a Q-dimensional state vector of Q underlying risk factors. Each element of the state vector thus is a factor on which the value of asset k depends—perhaps in a nonlinear fashion.

To take a concrete example, consider a European call option on a dividend-paying common stock whose current price is denoted S_t. The state vector z has five elements, such that z is a 5×1 vector and $z^T = (S_t\ \sigma\ \tau\ r\ \delta)$ where S_t is the current price per share of the common stock underlying the option, σ is the instantaneous volatility of the underlying stock, τ is the time to maturity of the option, r is the riskless interest rate, and δ is the dividend yield (presumed continuous) on the underlying stock. [It is often convenient to let $r - \delta = b$ and write $z^T = (S_t\ \sigma\ \tau\ r\ b)$].

Note also that although the underlying price appears in the state vector only once, the value of the call depends on the value of the underlying stock price in a nonlinear fashion. Accordingly, we have the usual "option Greeks":

$$\Delta = \frac{\partial V}{\partial S} \qquad \Gamma = \frac{\partial V^2}{\partial^2 S} \qquad Vega = \frac{\partial V}{\partial \sigma}$$

$$\Theta = \frac{\partial V}{\partial \tau} \qquad \rho_r = \frac{\partial V}{\partial r} \qquad \rho_b = \frac{\partial V}{\partial (r - \delta)} = \frac{\partial V}{\partial b}$$

Using a Taylor series expansion, we can mathematically approximate the change in value of the option as a function of a small change in the underlying risk factors that comprise the state vector on which the option's price depends:

$$dV = V(\underline{z} + d\underline{z}) - V(\underline{z})$$
$$= V(S + dS, \sigma + d\sigma, \tau + d\tau, r + dr, b + db) - V(S, \sigma, \tau, r, b)$$

where dx indicates a small change in x. This can be expanded and then simplified to yield

$$dV = \Delta dS + \tfrac{1}{2}\Gamma dS^2 + Vega\, d\sigma + \Theta d\tau + \rho_r dr + \rho_b db$$

In other words, a small change in the value of the option around its current price can be expressed using the current values of the underlying spot price, volatility, time to expiration, interest rate, dividend yield, and the five Greek parameters.

The same logic can be applied to *any* position, whether the payoffs are linear in the underlying risk factors or not, as we discussed earlier in the case of sensitivity analysis. Consider, for example, a bond whose value depends on the interest rate in a nonlinear fashion. The option Greeks vega, theta, and rho are equal to zero, delta is the bond's Macaulay duration, and gamma is the bond's convexity. Then,

$$\frac{dV}{V_0} = \Delta dr + \tfrac{1}{2}\Gamma dr^2$$

so that a small change in interest rates causes the bond to change in price by an amount proportional to both the bond's duration (Δ) and convexity (Γ).

The Taylor series expansion holds only for small changes in the underlying risk factors. Nevertheless, it is commonly extended to a VaR measure using an implicit parametric normal approach. By substituting 1.65 times the standard deviation of each *risk factor* into the above (e.g., $dS = 1.65\sigma_s S$ where σ_s is the volatility of the spot price return), the theory is that a multivariate extreme change is captured. Mathematically, it is of course *not true* that the same probabilistic inferences can be drawn. Consequently, people often substitute three standard deviations for the changes in the risk factors and then interpret the result as the three-sigma VaR in the final asset. The results are aggregated across assets using the usual correlation matrix.

From a computational standpoint, this approach is very tractable. Additionally, the data requirements for this approach are relatively minor and not significantly different from the parametric VaR approaches. As long as a correlation matrix is available across instruments, the input requirements are limited to parameter estimates of the option Greeks.

Unfortunately, the major limitation of this approach is a statistical one. The Taylor series is a mathematical approximation to a real-valued vector function based on the assumption that changes in the underlying risk factors are *small*. For large changes, the relation may hold imperfectly, at best. For example, using the Taylor series (i.e., duration and convexity) to analyze the effect of a one basis point change in rates on a bond's price may be a very reasonable and easy approximation. But generalizing the effects of that one basis point change to a 100 or 200 basis point change may be extremely unrealistic. Higher-order terms can be added to reduce the magnitude of this specification error, but the underlying assumption that the expansion holds only for small changes will still be relevant—as will its violation.[18]

Full Revaluation

As discussed earlier in scenario analysis, the Taylor series approach to capturing nonlinearities is a partial revaluation approach because it takes *current values* of the risk factors in state vector z and perturbs those values by a sensitivity, which is then used as the basis for an *extrapolated* perturbation over a larger range of changes in the risk factors. The alternative means by which instruments with nonlinear cash flows can be handled in the VaR calculation is full revaluation.

We begin as before with an instrument whose value depends on the value of a state vector, $V = V(z)$. To keep the discussion concrete, suppose the instrument is an option so that the state vector can be expressed as $z^T = (S \; \sigma \; \tau \; r \; b)$. Earlier we expressed the change in the option price to indicate a *small* change in V and used the Taylor series to avoid recalculating the option price for the new state vector:

$$dV = V(z + dz) - V(z)$$

Now suppose we express the change as follows:

$$V' - V = V'(z') - V(z)$$

where primes indicate the new option price and state vector. The initial option price V and the initial state vector z are *known*. In the full revaluation approach, we compute a new option price given a new possible state vector $\underline{z}'$. This yields a change in the value of the asset that can serve as the basis of a VaR calculation, as long as the new values of the elements of the state vector are sufficiently far from the current values to indicate extreme movements. We can come up with these extreme movements in any way we wish—three sigmas, parametric sigmas, simulation, historical, and the like.

VALUE VERSUS CASH FLOWS VERSUS EARNINGS[19]

As the term *value* at risk implies, organizations for which VaR is best suited are those for which *value* risk management is the goal. VaR, after all, is intended to condense the risk of a stock of assets over a particular risk horizon into a single present value. Those likely to realize the most benefits from VaR thus include clearing houses, securities settlement agents, swap dealers, institutional investors, and other organizations with a common concern about the value of their exposures over a well-defined period of time. In addition, the relatively short risk horizons of these enterprises imply that VaR measurement can be accomplished reliably and with minimal concern about changing portfolio composition over the risk horizon.[20]

Almost all value-based measures of risk can easily be adapted to the goals of an earnings risk manager. Analogous to VaR, EaR—earnings at risk—is essentially equivalent to VaR with the added overlay of the appropriate accounting definitions and rules.

For cash flow risk managers, however, VaR and shortfall risk can be a bit misleading. By distilling all market risk back to a single moment in time—the present—the cash flow consequences of a set of risk exposures may be obfuscated.

For cash flow risk managers, scenario analysis is often adequate to capture potential cash outlays over time. If a firm has more sophisticated risk measurement needs, the Monte Carlo approach to VaR generalizes quite naturally into a cash flow approach. Because a sample path must be generated in order to determine the terminal *value* at risk, the Monte Carlo simulation also produces interim cash flows that can be analyzed on their own. Historical simulation to construct multistep sample paths accomplishes the same objective. Summaries of these time-dependent cash flow risks are usually grouped under the VaR-like name *cash flows at risk* (CfaR).

TOTAL VERSUS SELECTIVE RISK MANAGEMENT

Selective risk managers deliberately choose to manage some risks and not others. Specifically, they seek to manage their exposures to risks in which they have no comparative informational advantage—for the usual financial ruin reasons—while actively exposing themselves, at least to a point, to risks in which they *do* have perceived superior information.

For firms managing total risk, the principal benefit of VaR is facilitating explicit risk control decisions, such as setting and enforcing exposure limits. For firms that selectively manage risk, by contrast, VaR is useful largely for diagnostic monitoring *or* for controlling risk in areas where the firm perceives no comparative informational advantage. An airline, for example, might find VaR helpful in assessing its exposure to jet fuel prices; but for the airline to use VaR to analyze the risk that seats on its aircraft are not all sold makes little sense.

Consider also a hedge fund manager who invests in foreign equity because the risk/return profile of that asset class is desirable. To avoid exposure to the exchange rate risk, the fund could engage an overlay manager to hedge the currency risk of the position. Using VaR on the *whole position* lumps together two separate and distinct sources of risk—the currency risk and the foreign equity price risk. And *reporting* that total VaR without a corresponding expected return could have disastrous consequences. Using VaR to ensure that the currency hedge is accomplishing its intended aims, by contrast, might be perfectly legitimate.

MARKET RISK MONITORING[21]

As discussed in Chapters 10 and 11, risk management in general and market risk measurement and monitoring in particular should *compliment* rather than *compete with* the primary business goals of the firm. Market risk measurement is a tool for helping firms determine whether the risks to which they *are* exposed are those risks to which they *think they are* and *want to be* exposed. Measures like VaR, EaR, and CfaR will *never* tell a company *how much risk to take,* only *how much risk is being taken.* In this sense, market risk *measurement* is little more than an academic exercise unless these market risk measures are *monitored* and compared to the firm's risk tolerances.

Monitoring Risks Taken by Agents

One of the primary benefits of market risk measurement and monitoring is that it facilitates the consistent and regular monitoring by principals of market risk assumed by agents. VaR thus can be a useful control mechanism for resolving the agency conflicts discussed in Chapters 5 and 6.

Firms can calculate and monitor market risk on a variety of different levels. When calculated and monitored at the asset portfolio level, for example, the risks taken by individual portfolio managers—whether internal traders and portfolio managers or external account managers—can be evaluated on an ongoing basis. Market risk also can be tracked and monitored at more aggregated levels, as well as by asset class, by issuer/counterparty, and the like.

Suppose that a nonfinancial corporation calculates the quarterly VaR once a week for all of its treasury positions. If the VaR for treasury account managers is monitored each week, major departures of VaR from either peer risk measures or past history should trigger an enquiry into the treasury area's recent investment activities—transactions that the firm's senior managers and directors might otherwise have no reason to scrutinize.

For VaR to provide a useful monitoring benefit, precision in the measurement of VaR is *not* absolutely essential. In fact, the primary benefit of VaR monitoring comes from examining *relative* VaR, or the VaR of a business unit compared to the VaR of other business units or the same manager *over time*. Even if the actual levels of VaR—$10 million and $50 million above—are imprecisely measured, the same measurement bias may affect other exposures in the same way. The theory is that these measurement errors cancel out when *relative* VaR is the focus instead of the absolute level of the VaR measure in question. Consequently, firms can derive a surprising amount of marginal benefit from monitoring even a simplified parametric VaR.

This monitoring benefit of market risk measurement is not restricted to internal and external trading activities. The same monitoring benefits can help the firm optimize its risk profile when applied to non-trading activities, as well, including certain core business exposures. In addition, outside contractors (e.g., pension plan external asset managers) sometimes engage in activities where they act as agents for the firm as a whole acting as principal. In such cases, the day-to-day business activities of the external contractor may not be transparently available to the firm at all times. But a market risk measure reported to the firm periodically can go a long way toward helping assuage any residual principal/agent concerns about market risk without necessitating disclosure of proprietary activities.

Monitoring to Fine-Tune Financial Decisions

Firms may monitor various measures of market risk in order to help fine-tune certain financial decisions. A very common application of market risk measurement and monitoring, for example, is the tracking of diversified VaR (i.e., VaR aggregated across exposures to reflect cross-exposure correlations) to monitor the extent to which hedging strategies are accomplishing the desired objectives. To take a simple example, consider two nonfinancial corporations with significant exchange rate risks on both the input purchasing and output sales sides of the firm. The CROs of the two firms can evaluate the effectiveness of their corporate hedging decisions and analyze the extent to which returns and risks are affected by currency risk by tracking the diversified VaRs of the business units on hedged and unhedged bases. Such an exercise will also help the firm identify whether or not hedging is worth the cost.

Suppose more specifically that Company Independent specifies in its risk management policy that no more than 1% of the profits *in any given business unit* can be exposed to exchange rate risk. The business unit manager of each input is then left to hedge to ensure compliance with that risk tolerance. The effectiveness of each manager's hedge can be evaluated by examining the diversified VaRs of each portfolio *separately* with and without the inclusion of the hedging contracts.

Now suppose that a different firm—Company Centralized—specifies in its risk policy that no more than 1% of the firm's *total profits* can be exposed to exchange rate risk and that business unit managers do *not* do their own hedging. The firm instead engages in FX hedging through its treasury on a *consolidated* basis. The effectiveness of the consolidated hedging program can be evaluated by comparing the plan's *aggregate* diversified VaR to its risk tolerance with and without the hedging program.

These two companies might *measure* their risks in similar ways, but the monitoring at each must necessarily differ according to the different risk management policies at the two companies. Specifically, suppose Company Independent's commodity purchases are denominated entirely in Dmarks and that its sales are denominated entirely in Swiss francs. These two currencies happen to be *positively correlated* to the dollar. Consequently, if the firm specifies a risk management policy *by business line,* the independent hedging decisions of the purchasing and sales managers may achieve the firm's desired VaR reduction on an individual business line basis but may *increase* the firm's aggregate diversified VaR. By partially hedging two business lines whose currency risks are negatively correlated (i.e., the exchange rates are positively correlated, but one unit is short and the other long), the "natural hedge" is removed and the firm's consolidated diversified VaR rises.

Company Centralized might not have this problem. For a firm interested in hedging its *consolidated* exchange rate risk, the treasury manager thus can achieve the desired VaR reduction. At the same time, evaluating the decisions of each business unit with regard to currency becomes much harder.

The usefulness of VaR in evaluating hedging programs thus depends strongly on the particular hedging objectives specified by the firm in its risk management policy. Some firms may be more concerned about currency risk at the aggregate level than at the business line level. The firm may, for example, want to reduce expected bankruptcy costs. In that case, the company would specify consolidated hedging requirements and then must monitor hedge effectiveness *at the aggregate firmwide level.* Any individual business unit might not appear to be hedged, but the company as a whole is.

By contrast, a firm whose primary concern is monitoring the trading decisions of its agents may find it more useful to measure and monitor risk by business line. In that case, however, natural hedges across business lines may slip through the cracks, resulting in an *increase* in the firm's aggregated diversified VaR. Provided the firm is hedging in order to monitor and bond its agents, this extra risk might be more than compensated by agents whose autonomous risk-taking decisions are under better control.

"What-If" Modeling of Candidate Trading and Business Decisions

Market risk measurement and monitoring also can be beneficial to firms that wish to eliminate transactional scrutiny by senior managers or directors. In this way, measures like VaR can actually help give business unit managers and traders more financial autonomy than they might otherwise have without a formalized, market risk measurement-based risk monitoring process.

After the "great derivatives disasters" of the early 1990s, many corporate directors and trustees of institutional investors became concerned with the risks posed by derivatives transactions. As a result, such transactions were prohibited in numerous investment policies and were subject to board-level approval in many others. Transactional monitoring using measures like VaR can be an effective way of addressing this issue.

Suppose, for example, that the board of a company is concerned about the possibility that its treasurer will engage in leveraged derivatives to augment her returns. Rather than micro-manage the treasury, the board might prohibit the treasurer from such transactions or require their advance authorization. Either way, the treasury will have to bear significantly higher costs associated with any *legitimate* risk management decisions. As a better alternative, the board might simply agree not to engage in any transactions that would, say, increase the firm's VaR by more than X% of capital.

In order to minimize unnecessary scrutiny of particular business decisions, a firm need not require that VaR be calculated and reported *ex ante.* Especially if the cost of a VaR system is an issue, few affordable VaR systems allow for this type of real-time computation. Nevertheless, the requirement could be instituted and enforced *ex post,* with the corresponding requirement that any trades in violation of the "maximum marginal VaR" requirement would be liquidated or hedged within, say, a week of the deal.

As a cautionary note, firms should be attentive to the means by which the VaR of a particular transaction is calculated in order for this application of VaR to make sense. Partial revaluation measures of *marginal* market risk, such as Garman's (1996) "DelVaR," examine the impact of a particular trade on the VaR of a portfolio. Although quite useful in its own right, DelVaR would *not* be appropriate for the application of marginal VaR discussed here. The particular measurement method proposed by Garman is useful for evaluating the impact of a particular security on the VaR of a portfolio *only for small presumed changes in underlying prices.* DelVaR badly underestimates, however, the marginal risk of certain trades for *wide* price swings. In order to apply marginal VaR as a true substitute for an internal control function, the portfolio VaR would have to be calculated using *full revaluation* with and without the candidate trade to compute the true—not approximate—marginal VaR.

Risk Targets and Thresholds

Another potentially valuable application of market risk measures in the risk monitoring process involves measuring and monitoring market risk using a formal system of predefined risk targets or thresholds. In essence, risk thresholds take ad hoc risk monitoring one step further and systematize the process by which market risk is evaluated and discussed for exposures or business unit managers.

A system of risk thresholds is tantamount to setting up a tripwire around a risk *field,* where the field is characterized by a company's risk tolerances. This tripwire is defined in terms of the maximum tolerable market risk like VaR allocated to a business unit or portfolio of exposures and then is monitored regularly (e.g., weekly) comparing actual VaRs to these predefined targets. Managers are permitted to leave the risk field when they wish, but the tripwire signals senior managers and directors that they have done so. When a tripwire is hit (e.g., a VaR threshold is breached), an exception report is generated, and discussions and explanations are required.

Risk targets can be specified in terms of absolute or relative market risk measures. A private bank might conclude, for example, that a particular client's capital should never be placed at risk above a certain amount *regardless* of the risks taken by other clients or managers. In that case, the traders on that client's account could be subject to an absolute VaR or shortfall risk threshold. A mutual fund, by contrast, might prefer to specify its risk targets relative to the VaR of its benchmark portfolio or peer group.

BACK TO THE RISK MANAGEMENT BUSINESS MODEL

The hallmark of a well-functioning market risk measurement and monitoring system is *not* that targets are never breached or that all exceptions are rectified through liquidating or hedging current holdings. Rather, the primary benefit of a risk target system is the formalization of a *process* by which exceptions are discussed, addressed, and analyzed. Risk thresholds thus are a useful means by which asset managers can systematically monitor and control their market risks without attenuating the autonomy of their portfolio managers. Because the primary purpose of risk limits is to systematize discussions about actual market risk exposures relative to defined risk tolerances, huge investments in market risk measurement systems, moreover, typically are not required. Even an imprecise measure of market risk might allow a firm to accomplish its basic risk control needs.

Larger expenditures on market risk measurement systems start to make more sense for firms pursuing Efficiency Enhancement or Risk Transformation business models. The identification and measurement of real options exposures, for example, rarely impact the firm's exposure to unexpected financial losses but *often* impact the firm's ability to exploit efficiency enhancements and streamlined corporate strategy. Firms with large amounts of real option exposures thus may want to consider investing more in market risk measurement so that those potential efficiency gains can be better exploited.

A higher investment expenditure in market risk measurement also makes sense for firms engaged in risk transformation at the customer level. By leveraging internal systems, such firms may be able to enhance their customer and product offerings, thereby recovering a chunk of their investment costs in classical market risk measurement systems and activities.

CHAPTER 16

Identifying, Measuring, and Monitoring Credit Risk

Credit risk is the risk that a firm does not make a required payment or delivery on schedule and thus imposes some form of cost on the party to which the payment or delivery was due. Designing a credit risk management process that is consistent with the strategic business objectives of the firm and with its rationale for managing risk can be a tricky business. All too tempting for many corporations is to ignore it. A distressingly common phrase heard in risk management circles is "that's for banks to deal with, not us." In fact, credit risk management plays a very important part in a well-functioning, comprehensive EWRM process. In addition, credit risk management is often the source for opportunities to move out of a pure risk control model into efficiency enhancement and risk transformation for many firms. But before discussing those opportunities, we first need to understand how credit risk can be identified, monitored, and measured vis-à-vis stakeholders' defined credit risk tolerances.

IDENTIFYING CREDIT RISK AND DEFINING TOLERANCES

A firm bears credit risk only on its assets. A receivable that Company Beethoven is owed from Company Mahler is an asset and thus a credit risk to Beethoven, but *not* to Mahler. A trade credit extended to Company Mahler by Company Beethoven is a credit risk to Beethoven. The risk of a default by the issuer of a security Beethoven holds as an investment is a credit risk. The risk of nonperformance by a bank on a letter of credit, guarantee, project or trade loan, or commercial loan made to Beethoven is yet another credit risk. Even the risk of nonperformance of services contracted from an external vendor is a form of credit risk.

The consequences of a default will lead to the actualization of credit risk for any firm, but the precise nature of those consequences will depend on whether the firm is a value-, cash flow-, or earnings-oriented risk manager. A cash flow risk manager will be concerned with the unexpected disappearance of assets primarily as they occur. Defaults that hit cash balances without warning clearly would be perceived as more adverse from a cash flow risk management standpoint. A value risk manager, by contrast, will tend to focus more on the foregone *present value* of the asset than on the later cash balance impact. And an earnings risk manager will be concerned with charge-offs and recoveries. All three types of firms, however, must measure and monitor their credit risks relative to a well-defined set of tolerances.

There are two general dimensions along which a firm may express its tolerance to credit risk—by category of obligor, or by specific obligor. These dimensions are not mutually exclusive, moreover. A firm can actually express credit risk tolerances along both lines if it so desires. Each type of credit risk tolerance is discussed briefly next, along with how these tolerance definitions impact the management and control of credit risks.

Risk Tolerances Defined by Category

Many companies choose to express their tolerances for credit risk by reference to some category of credit risk into which any given potential obligor to the firm must fall. These categories may be defined either by regulatory agencies or external credit rating agencies, or may include more economically motivated categories such as country of risk.

Published credit ratings are widely utilized by firms as the basis for their expressions of credit risk tolerances. A mutual fund, for example, might prohibit a portfolio manager from having more than 10% of her bond portfolio invested in securities rated A or below. Or a corporation might allow letters of credit to be obtained only from banks rated AAA by Standard & Poors or Aaa by Moody's and so on.

Regulatory categories are also sometimes used to express corporate credit risk tolerances. A nonfinancial corporate, for example, might allow swaps to be done only through a commercial bank or a registered broker/dealer, thereby excluding insurance companies and unregulated derivatives product company subsidiaries of investment banks.[1] Or a pension plan might require that only state-chartered Federal Reserve System member banks be eligible as a custodian.

Other categories may also serve as the basis for credit risk tolerance determinations. Such categories may involve separating obligors based on

- Currency denomination.
- Country of domicile.
- Index of human rights or economic freedom in country of domicile.

- ■ "Greenness" or friendliness toward the environment.
- ■ Political correctness (e.g., "sin" producers).

Risk Tolerances Defined by Specific Obligor

Some firms may choose to define company-specific risk tolerances, either as a supplement to risk tolerances by category or in lieu of them. As an example of the former, a securities exchange clearing house seeking a source of liquidity might use bank letters of credit, all of which must be obtained from AAA-rated banks. To manage *concentration risk*, the clearing house might then specify certain bank-specific maximums for any banks with which the organization is relatively more concerned about credit risk. An example of the latter, by contrast, would be a firm that simply publishes a list of banks from whom letters of credit may be obtained and how large those letters of credit are allowed to be.

Tolerances on exposures to specific obligors can be especially common in several situations. The first is when settlement risk is involved—particularly Herstatt risk. In this situation, firms likely will limit their maximum exposure to a firm over a given settlement cycle. Reducing or managing that exposure may simply mean delaying and spreading out settlements, but the tolerance of some firms to huge exposures may in fact be quite low.

Another situation in which specific obligor risk tolerances are used arises when a firm relies on institutions with correlated performance either for core liquidity provision or core credit protection. Firms tend to diversify their letters of credit and liquidity provision facilities across more than one bank for this reason, and in so doing may try to avoid banks whose ability to provide critical liquidity on short notice is correlated with other liquidity providers. Similarly, a firm in California may choose to spread its earthquake insurance across two insurance companies with different geographical exposure profiles rather than run the risk that correlated exposures across companies make both unable to pay.

SOURCES OF CREDIT RISK

One of the complex aspects of measuring credit risk traces to the fact that a default can sometimes lead to other risks. The default of a swap counterparty midway through the life of a swap being used as a hedge suddenly exposes the nondefaulting firm to market risk until the swap can be replaced. The default of a debtor on a large payable unexpectedly depletes the nondefaulting firm's cash balances, forcing it into the capital market to borrow at distressed debt prices. Or the surprise failure of cash to arrive as planned could trigger defaults by the nondefaulting firm on payments it had been planning to make with the defaulted receivable that has failed to materialize, and so on.

Although these risks related to credit risk are important, we turn now to focus on the sources of credit risk themselves in more detail.

Presettlement Credit Risk

Presettlement credit risk includes default risk, downgrade risk, and indirect credit risk. The first two risks are driven by the possibility that an obligor on an asset held by some firm defaults. Indirect credit risk, by contrast, arises from a change in the probability of default (or a default itself) by some party that does not necessarily have a direct contractual relation with the firm bearing the costs of a change in the party's default probabilities.

Direct Default Risk   Direct default risk is the risk that a firm will not receive cash flows or assets to which it is entitled because a party with which the firm has a bilateral contract defaults on one or more obligations of that contract. A $100 loan made by a bank to a corporation that obligates the borrower to make two annual interest payments of $10 each and to repay the $100 principal in two years exposes a bank to default risk on two cash flows—the first $10 interest payment, and the second payment of $110 (interest plus principal).

One complication in credit risk management is the distinction between true defaults and failed transactions. A fail occurs when a settlement on a transaction of some kind is delayed for operational reasons. The settlement will eventually occur late, but it *will* occur. The problem arises in distinguishing *ex ante* between an obligor that failed to make a payment or delivery for operational reasons and one that *cannot* make the payment or delivery for financial reasons.

Direct Downgrade or Migration Risk   Direct downgrade risk also traces to the possibility of default by an obligor. Unlike default risk, however, the cash flow need not *actually* default in order for a firm to incur downgrade credit losses. More specifically, downgrade risk is the risk that changes in the *possibility* of a future default by an obligor will adversely impact the present value of the bank's contract with the obligor *today*. The risk is called downgrade risk because a downgrade in a company's credit likely will reduce the value of any claims it has issued. For similar reasons, downgrade risk is also often called *migration risk,* indicating the risk of an obligor migrating from one rating to another. Despite the term, however, downgrade risk can have an impact on securities issued by firms that have not experienced a rating downgrade or that are unrated. All that is required is that the market-assessed probability of default goes up.

A value or cash flow risk manager realizes the impact of downgrade risk only in the event that the firm bought the asset before the change in market expectations about the issuer's default probability and then sells the downgraded asset prior to maturity. Consider a zero-coupon, two-year bond with $1 face value issued by Corporation Melville, and suppose at the time of the bond's issue that every market participant agrees that Melville has absolutely no chance of defaulting. Then suppose that one year into the life of the bond, market participants revise their assessments and conclude that Melville could default on the principal repayment with a 10% probability. The market's assessment of Melville's financial condition then does not change again before the bond matures.

Any firm that buys *and* sells Melville bonds within the first year will experience no loss of capital value from downgrade risk. Similarly, any firm that buys Melville bonds after the change in market expectations of its default risk *also* experiences no downgrade-related losses; the price paid for the bonds after the downgrade is a fair price that already reflects the new default probability. Downgrade risk is borne only by those firms that bought Melville bonds before the downgrade and sold them later. The initial price paid reflected no probability of default, whereas the price received for the bonds upon their sale following the downgrade reflects a positive probability of default.

To see the impact of a downgrade loss, recognize that the price paid for the bond upon its issue in year t would have been

$$B(t) = \frac{\Lambda(t) \times 0 + [1 - \Lambda(t)] \times 1}{(1+R)^2} = \frac{1 - \Lambda(t)}{(1+R)^2}$$

where R is the annualized risk free rate and where $\Lambda(t)$ is the probability of a default by Melville assessed by the market at issuance year t on its principal repayment to occur at $t + 2$. Assume no recoveries occur in the event of default. By assumption, $\Lambda(t) = 0$ and thus $[1 - \Lambda(t)] = 1$, so purchasers of the bond in year t paid

$$B(t) = \frac{1}{(1+R)^2}$$

At time $t + 1$, the market's assessment of the probability of a time $t + 2$ default is denoted $\Lambda(t + 1)$. Any firm that sells the Melville-issued bond at year $t + 1$ immediately *after* the value of $\Lambda(t + 1)$ is observed will receive no more than the following for the bond:

$$B(t+1) = \frac{1 - \Lambda(t+1)}{1+R}$$

If $\Lambda(t + 1) = 0$, then the difference in the bond prices at times t and $t + 1$ just represents the riskless one-period return earned by bondholders:

$$\frac{B(t+1) - B(t)}{B(t)} = R$$

But if the market's new assessment of Melville's default likelihood is $\Lambda(t + 1) > 0$, the one-period holding period return for a firm that bought the bond at issuance and sold it right after the downgrade is

$$\frac{B(t+1) - B(t)}{B(t)} = R - \Lambda(t+1)(1+R)$$

Now consider a firm that buys the bond at $t + 1$ *after* the downgrade. If Melville does not in fact default at time $t + 2$, the new bondholders will earn a return of

$$\frac{B(t+2) - B(t+1)}{B(t+1)} = \frac{1+R}{1 - \Lambda(t+1)} - 1$$

which is greater than the risk free rate to compensate bondholders for a possible default.

But now suppose the original bondholders decided *not to sell* at time $t + 1$. In that case, the two-year realized return given that Melville does not default at $t + 2$ is

$$\frac{B(t+2) - B(t)}{B(t)} = (1+R)^2 - 1$$

which is exactly the two-year compounded riskless return. In other words, the original bondholders only experience a downgrade loss *if they sell after the downgrade.* Holding onto the bond exposes them to *actual* default risk, of course, but if Melville does indeed repay its principal at time $t+2$, the original bond holders that stuck it out would not experience any kind of capital loss.

The time $t+1$ price of the bond will adequately compensate its holder for the risk of nonpayment of principle. In other words, a bond holder should be indifferent between selling the bond at its new price or holding it to maturity and bearing the risk of a default. In fact, depending on whether the firm is a value, cash flow, or earnings risk manager, this expected indifference is not always the observed case.

A value-focused firm will take the downgrade risk at face value. Because the firm is concerned with value, the increase in default probability will not change the firm's behavior in deciding whether or not to sell the bond. Either the firm pays for the loss in the resale or in the form of a chance of default, but either way the impact on value is the same and similarly for a cash flow risk manager. In either case, the new bond price is discounted properly by the capital market, making the firm indifferent between selling at $t+1$ and taking its hit or holding the bond to maturity and risking a default.

An earnings risk manager, by contrast, might behave differently. Securities held to maturity can typically be accounted for at cost, whereas securities available for sale must be marked to market. If the earnings hedger has already classified this security as available for sale, the downgrade will not influence its behavior. Whether the firm sells the bond or not, earnings will reflect the repricing of the bond downward at time $t+1$. But if the earnings hedger that bought the bond at issue classified the bond as held to maturity, the firm would almost certainly *not* be indifferent between selling the bond following the downgrade and holding on to it. If a security is sold early that was accounted for at cost, the firm simply marks the sale to market. Because the price of the security is fair, the firm *should be* indifferent between holding onto the bond to maturity and risking a default or selling it and paying the expected loss at year $t+1$. But this is not the case. A firm primarily focused on reducing earnings volatility—say, to reduce expected taxes—will likely prefer to take its chances with a default than to take the mark-to-market loss that it can avoid by keeping the security in the held to maturity category.

Indirect Credit Risk Indirect credit risk is best explained by example. Suppose Company Twain has no contracts at all with Firm Conrad. If an increase in the market's perception that Firm Conrad will default on some of its obligations results in a decline in the value of any of Twain's assets, the mechanism through which that risk is transmitted must be indirect credit risk—also sometimes called spread risk or credit-dependent market risk. Alternatively, if Company Twain *does* have a contract in place with Firm Conrad when Firm Conrad's credit risk increases, the decline in the market value of Twain's contract with Conrad is a form of downgrade risk as discussed in the previous section. Any additional contracts Twain has outstanding with firms other than Conrad that are adversely impacted by Conrad's risk increase would be subject to indirect credit risk.

Indirect credit risk can arise for essentially two reasons. First, Company Twain has some asset or liability whose cash flows depend on a market price that is affected by Firm Conrad's perceived creditworthiness. To take a simple example, suppose Company Twain enters into a 10-year pay fixed/receive floating interest rate swap with Bank Mann as the floating rate payer, and suppose the floating rate paid semiannually is six-month LIBOR. LIBOR is the rate at which banks borrow in the Eurodollar market—often from one another—and thus is influenced by perceived credit quality of the banks that participate in that market. If Firm Conrad is a large bank and its credit risk rises enough, LIBOR could actually reflect that. This would increase Twain's swap payables. The resulting loss is indirect credit risk, or a risk tracing to Firm Conrad but not requiring that Twain and Conrad deal with one another directly.

As discussed in Chapter 1, fluctuations in the TED spread are thought to reflect various factors such as interbank liquidity, the demand for quality, and the creditworthiness of the wholesale banking sector. Provided Company Twain is not a player in the Eurodollar market but nevertheless engages in transactions referencing a Eurodollar or LIBOR rate, Twain will continue to bear indirect credit risk.[2]

A second source of indirect credit risk is an *equilibrium* increase in the spread of credit-sensitive assets over the risk-free rate. Known as the aggregate *default premium,* the spread between high and low quality debt is widely regarded as a proxy for some fundamental factor that affects the *systematic* risk of bonds in particular.[3] In particular, the default premium tends to be strongly counter-cyclical—risky debt becomes riskier relative to less risky debt during business cycle contractions.

Because of the equilibrium systematic risk relation that appears to exist between the aggregate default premium and bond returns, any assets or liabilities are potentially subject to market price fluctuations—*nondiversifiable* fluctuations—purely as a result of capital market equilibrium (i.e., the determination of expected returns that properly reflect systematic risk).

Settlement Risk[4]

Settlement risk arises from the lags between the value date and settlement date that arise in most transactions, whether on- or off-exchange. The *settlement window* for a transaction is the time period between its value date and the final settlement of that transaction. Two types of settlement windows are commonly observed.

First, an *account day settlement system* involves the settlement of transactions on a specific calendar date, called the account day. An account day system, for example, might specify that all trades within a trading week settle at the close of business on Friday, thus indicating Friday as the account day.

Second, settlement may also occur on a *rolling* basis in which trades settle a specific number of days subsequent to the trade date rather than on a particular account day. The number of days by which final settlement follows trading is *fixed*, resulting in settlements occurring on every business day. If a system specifies rolling settlement within $T + 5$, for example, participants will issue securities and funds transfer instructions on date $T + 5$ for the settlement of trades made on date T.

Settlement risk can either take the form of replacement cost risk or principal risk. Suppose, for example, Broker Hemingway buys one share of stock from Broker Forster at the date T spot price of $10 per share for settlement three days later. Suppose further that the price of the stock declines to $7 per share from T to $T + 3$. On date $T + 3$, if Broker Hemingway fails to make payment for the stock but the stock has not been delivered, Broker Forster experiences only a $3 replacement cost loss. The stock sold at $10 can now be sold for only $7, but the stock is still Forster's to sell. If Forster fails to deliver the stock, by contrast, Hemingway loses nothing except the convenience of having the stock. For Hemingway to go back into the market and buy the share from another broker on $T + 3$ actually saves him $3.

Now suppose Forster has irrevocably and finally transferred his share of stock to Hemingway, and *then* Hemingway defaults. In that situation, Foster bears principal or Herstatt risk as explained in Chapter 1. He does not get the $10 he was promised by Hemingway *and* no longer owns the stock. The best Forster could hope for is a pro rata claim on Forster's remaining assets in an insolvency proceeding.

One means by which settlement risk is mitigated in many markets is through the active participation of one or more *settlement agents*. A settlement agent is an enterprise charged with maintaining whatever infrastructure is required to facilitate funds and/or asset transfers. Settlement agents typically operationalize the Delivery-versus-Payment (DVP) principle.[5] Under the DVP principle, some entity—called the DVP agent—acts as a transfer agent and ensures that asset ownership does not change until payment has been made by the buyer of a security. DVP agents bear no principal risk because they have no obligation to honor asset or fund transfers in the event of a default, although firms whose transactions settle through a DVP agent can only incur replacement cost losses. The DVP principle, properly executed, eliminates principal risk.

Another type of settlement agent is a *central counterparty* that steps in after a trade is done and becomes counterparty to all transactions. In such a regime, a default on an asset or funds transfer results in a default *to the settlement agent,* which is still responsible for honoring the other side of the original transaction. Central counterparties thus offer trade guarantees to the original counterparties that eliminate both principal and replacement cost risk.

The type of settlement risk borne by a firm will depend on the type of transaction and the settlement agent—if any—involved in the discharge of obligations arising pursuant to that transaction. Futures contracts are settled by central counterparties in which the trading participants bear essentially no settlement risk. Most securities are settled through a DVP agent, thereby mitigating principal settlement risk but leaving intact the risk of replacement cost losses. Most OTC derivatives and commercial contracts are completely bilateral and thus involve no settlement agent at all, hence subjecting counterparties to all forms of settlement risk.

THE TRADITIONAL CREDIT RISK MEASUREMENT FRAMEWORK

Credit risk is traditionally measured as the *expected loss* on an asset, where expected loss is a function of three variables:

1. The probability(ies) that the counterparty will default today or on some future date before the asset matures;
2. The loss that a creditor incurs in the event that an obligor defaults today; and
3. The potential exposure of the creditor to a default on some future date.

At any given point in time, the credit risk of an asset with a life extending through date N can be expressed as:

$$\Lambda(t)\max\left[V(t)-\chi(t),0\right]+\omega\left[\Lambda(t+1,\ldots,N),V(t+1,\ldots,N),\chi(t+1,\ldots,N)\right] \quad (16.1)$$

where $\Lambda(t)$ is the probability of default at time t, $V(t)$ is the value of the asset at time t, and $\chi(t)$ is the dollar value recovered plus the market value of any collateral or security held against the asset at time t. The reason the expression is a maximum of the asset's value net of collateral and recoveries is to reinforce the fact that liabilities do not expose a firm to credit risk. A swap on which the nondefaulting firm is deeply out-of-the-money, for example, has a negative value and thus imposes no credit risk on the nondefaulting firm in the event of a counterparty default.

The second term in Equation 16.1, ω, is a function that describes the potential exposure of the asset. This term reflects the fact that a default *after* current date t but *before* the asset reaches the end of its life on date N will generate a loss to the firm that depends on *future* default probabilities, asset values, and recovery rates.

Credit risk measurement can become very complicated very quickly. The probability of default can vary conditionally over the remaining life of the asset, and both current losses and potential exposure may be random variables with probability distributions. Especially if these variables are correlated across assets and/or obligors, modeling potential credit losses is no trivial task.

To ensure that the concepts of credit risk measurement are clear, let us begin with the simplest possible scenario—the traditional credit risk framework still used today by many banks in evaluating commercial lending risk. In this approach, we will work only with assets whose exposures are one-sided—assets that are always assets, such as purchased bonds, letters of credit, trade credits, and the like. We thus ignore contracts like swaps whose exposures are two-sided because such contracts can switch from assets to liabilities and conversely.

In the traditional credit risk management framework, Equation 16.1 can be written for any given asset as the expected loss on an asset in the event of default:[6]

$$E(L) = DR \times LIED \times PCE \qquad (16.2)$$

where DR is the average default rate of the obligor, LIED is the expected loss on the asset in the event of default, and PCE is the expected potential credit exposure of the asset. Note that in Equation 16.2, PCE has replaced the function ω and now enters the expected loss calculation multiplicatively rather than additively as in Equation 16.1.

This traditional approach to credit risk measurement is a *transactional* approach, not a *portfolio* approach. Consequently, many of the more complex features of credit risk measurement can be ignored for the moment.

LIED and PCE, for example, are expressed as expected values. Similarly, DR is treated as a constant, and not as a process of conditional probabilities that vary over time *or* that reflect migration from one credit rating to another; DR is literally *just* a default rate.

All three of these variables are much more complicated. But by using a constant DR and expected LIED and PCE, we skirt the complexities of modeling these distributions *and* we eliminate the dynamic nature of the problem and collapse everything into the present. With this basic framework in hand, let us now turn to explore how the traditional credit risk framework goes about measuring these three variables.

Default Rate

The default rate of an obligor depends on factors such as the obligor's credit rating and financial condition, the nature and tenor of the asset, and a good set of historical data. Different firms measure DRs in different ways, ranging from the ridiculously simple to the wildly complex. In general, there are four means by which firms can associate a numerical value with the DR of a specific obligor.

Subjective Judgment The first technique for estimating the DR of an obligor is basically to make an educated guess about how likely it is or how often that the firm will default. This may sound strange, but reliance on personal judgment is still highly prevalent with many loan officers, credit officers, and business managers. Allowing the DR to rest on so much judgment and so little empirical data has the problem that the probability of default likely will be inconsistent across time and firms. Nevertheless, reliance on the judgment of credit officers in DR measurement should not be dismissed. Many financial institutions have managed highly successful credit portfolios through expert systems and relationship management that make a loan officer quite plausibly much better informed about the default risk of her customers than many statistical models ever will be.

External Ratings Some companies rely on published statistics maintained by data vendors and rating agencies to populate DR measures. Included in this group is the set of firms that rely *solely* on default probabilities published by rating agencies. Sometimes called the *external ratings* approach to DR determination, the firm simply takes the probability of default published by a rating agency for a given credit rating and assigns that probability to all obligors with the same rating.

TABLE 16.1 Average Cumulative Default Rates by Holding Period (1920–1999)

Rating	1 Year (%)	10 Years (%)	20 Years (%)
Aaa	0.00	1.09	2.38
Aa	0.08	3.10	6.75
A	0.08	3.61	7.47
Baa	0.30	7.92	13.95
Ba	1.43	19.05	30.82
B	4.48	31.90	43.70
Investment-grade	0.16	4.85	9.24
Speculative-grade	3.35	25.31	37.74
All corporates	1.33	11.49	17.79

Source of data: Keenan (2000), Exhibit 20.

Table 16.1 gives some examples of default rates published by Moody's Investors Service that can be used as DR estimates. The table shows average cumulative default rates over several different time horizons.

Internal Ratings and Credit Scoring Models Increasingly popular is the use of *internal ratings* to assess the default probability of an obligor. This approach has gained in popularity in recent years because, as will be discussed in more detail in Chapter 20, the Bank for International Settlements now allows some commercial banks to calculate their capital requirements using internal credit risk ratings. Internal ratings are a systematic set of ratings by a firm for all its obligors using a consistent methodology and a basic set of risk factors, one of which may include any *external* ratings.

Popular sources of internal ratings are *credit scoring models* that attempt to assign specific numerical scores to specific obligors based on observable variables and historical data.[7] Some firms use these credit scores for purposes other than DR estimation, whereas other credit scoring models are designed to produce both a score and an associated probability of default. One such model that is both is Altman's (1968) famous Z-score model. In his original analysis, the credit score assigned to a publicly held corporate borrower is calculated as follows:

$$Z = 1.2\frac{C}{A} + 1.4\frac{E}{A} + 3.3\frac{EBIT}{A} + 0.6\frac{ME}{BL} + 0.999\frac{S}{A} \qquad (16.3)$$

where C = working capital
           A = total assets
     $EBIT$ = earnings before interest and taxes
      ME = market value of equity
       BL = book value of liabilities
         S = sales

The resulting credit score, Z, then can be used to infer the probability of the firm's default, which in turn can be used as the estimate for the obligor's DR.[8]

Credit scoring models, as with any other empirical structural model of the economy, are highly sensitive to variable choice, the quality of sample data used for parameter estimation, and specification. Variable choice is important both because of the risk of omitting important variables and the potential to include variables that appear statistically significant but actually are not. Related to variable selection are specification issues, or the nature of the precise relation between the postulated variables and the credit score. Altman's model, for example, has a linear specification, despite the fact that, to quote Saunders (1999), "the path to bankruptcy may be highly nonlinear."

Internal Models   The latest in the evolution of credit risk measurement is the *internal models* approach. These models have become particularly popular in recent years because of the increased recognition of the importance of *portfolio effects* across time, exposures, and obligors. In this section where the emphasis remains on the transactional approach, however, we will not address the portfolio benefits of internal models. Nevertheless, part of what *some* of these models deliver is the ability to estimate DFs. Internal models for DF estimation fall into essentially two categories—those based on the market prices of firms' traded securities, and those based on actuarial mortality rates.

Asset-Based Internal Models   Merton (1974) first recognized that default risk can be viewed through an option pricing lens, from which default probabilities about firms can be inferred. Suppose a firm with a current value of $V(t)$ is financed with equity worth $E(t)$ and debt worth $D(t)$. The debt is zero-coupon debt maturing at time T with face value FV.

Suppose the value of the firm evolves according to geometric Brownian motion:

$$\frac{dV_t}{V_t} = \mu dt + \sigma dZ_t$$

where dZ_t is a Gauss-Wiener process such that $dZ_t = \varepsilon_t^2 dt$ and $\varepsilon_t \sim NID(0, 1)$. The value of the firm at time T when the debt matures is thus

$$V(T) = V(t)\exp\left[\left(\mu - \tfrac{1}{2}\sigma^2\right)(T - t) + \sigma\sqrt{T - t}\,\varepsilon_t\right] \qquad (16.4)$$

Figure 16.1 illustrates the distribution of the value of the firm at time T.[9] At time t, the expected value of the firm at time T can be found by taking an expectation of the change in value of the firm to get

$$E[V(T)] = V(t)\exp\left[\left(\mu - \tfrac{1}{2}\sigma^2\right)(T - t)\right]$$

As is shown in Figure 16.1, the line from $V(t)$ to $E[V(T)]$ represents the expected growth rate of the value of the firm. Note that this expectation is *not* taken in the risk-neutral measure and is the *actual* growth rate of the firm from the stochastic process presumed earlier. The gray line shows one possible *actual* price path, ending at $V(T) > E[V(T)]$.

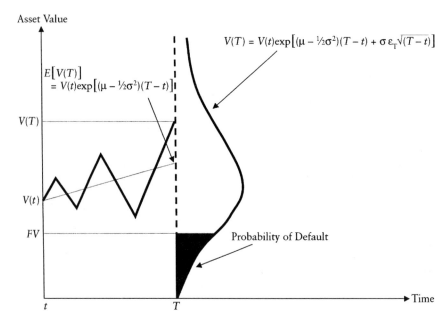

FIGURE 16.1 Probability of default in the Merton (1974) model.

The probability that the firm will default at time T is shown on Figure 16.1 as the gray shaded region of the distribution of the value of the firm $V(T)$ where $V(T) < FV$, the face value of the debt. This probability can be calculated as of time t using the Merton (1974) model as follows:

$$\Pr[V(T) \leq FV] = N\left\{-\frac{\ln\left[\dfrac{V(t)}{FV}\right] + \left(\mu - \tfrac{1}{2}\sigma^2\right)(T-t)}{\sigma\sqrt{T-t}}\right\} = N(-d_2) \qquad (16.5)$$

where $N(\cdot)$ indicates a standard normal cumulative distribution function. The quantity d_2 is sometimes called the *distance to default*.

The practical implementation of the Merton (1974) model follows from our ability to treat the value of the firm's equity as a call option on the assets of the firm:

$$E(t) = C[A(t), \sigma_A(t), FV, r, T-t] \qquad (16.6)$$

where $A(t)$ is the current value of the assets of the firm, $\sigma_A(t)$ is the volatility of assets, and r is the risk-free rate. The variables FV, r, $T-t$, and $E(t)$ are all observed variables, whereas $A(t)$ and $\sigma_A(t)$ are *not* observable. $A(t)$ and $\sigma_A(t)$ are, however, the variables we *need* in order to measure the probability of default for the firm, as Figure 16.1 shows.

We can extract *either* $A(t)$ *or* $\sigma_A(t)$ from Equation 16.6 numerically in much the same manner that we extract an implied volatility from an observed transaction price, as discussed in Chapter 15. But not both. Instead, we can exploit a known relation between the observed (or, at least, measurable) volatility of the firm's *equity* and the volatility of its *assets:*

$$\sigma_E^2 = g\left(\sigma_A^2\right) \qquad (16.7)$$

where g is some function. In fact, under the Merton (1974) model, the function g is known and is:

$$\sigma_E = \eta_{E \times A}\sigma_A$$

where $\eta_{E \times A}$ was defined in Chapter 15 as an elasticity—here, the equity volatility elasticity with respect to asset volatility. Substituting in the definition of an elasticity, we have that

$$\sigma_E = \left[\frac{\partial E(t)}{\partial A(t)}\right]\left[\frac{A(t)}{E(t)}\right]\sigma_A = \Delta\left[\frac{E(t)}{A(t)}\right]\sigma_A \qquad (16.8)$$

where Δ is the delta of the equity call on the firm's assets. Equations 16.6 and 16.8 now give us *two* equations with *two* unknowns—$A(t)$ and $\sigma_A(t)$. From there, we can arrive at Figure 16.1.

The Merton (1974) model has some limitations, however, when it comes to practical implementation. First, the volatility of equity tends to be a very noisy proxy for asset volatility and can be extremely sensitive to asset price changes.[10] Second, the capital structure of a firm is rarely as simple as equity plus zero-coupon debt with a single maturity date.

Perhaps the most popular and successful commercial version of the Merton (1974) approach to estimating probabilities of default is the KMV Corporation's Credit Monitor® model. The output of the model is an expected default frequency (EDF) for any obligor whose equity is publicly traded, and that EDF can be used as an estimate of the obligor's DR.[11]

The KMV model assumes that the obligor whose EDF is to be estimated has a capital structure consisting of equity, short-term cash-equivalent debt, long-term debt treated as a perpetuity, and preferred convertible shares. Like Merton (1974), the KMV model uses Equation 16.6 to relate the observable value of equity to its theoretical call value as a function of, among other things, the unobservable $A(t)$ and $\sigma_A(t)$. From this equation, KMV backs out the implied asset value $A(t)$. KMV then uses an *empirical* relation like Equation 16.7 to solve for $A(t)$ and $\sigma_A(t)$ simultaneously and iteratively.

Distance to default in Figure 16.1 can, in principle, be calculated once $A(t)$ and $\sigma_A(t)$ are known. In practice, KMV argues that an interim step is required to account for the empirical regularity that firms tend to default when asset values reach a level somewhere between the value of all liabilities and the value of short-term debt. In other words, defining default as the value of assets falling below the face value of debt as in Figure 16.1 may understate the probability of default. KMV thus defines its own distance to default based not on $A(t) < FV$, but rather on what the firm calls the *default point*.

The KMV default point is defined as the par value of all current liabilities plus half the long-term debt. Short-term debt to be serviced over the time horizon of interest is included in the par value of current liabilities. The distance to default in, say, one year then is defined as

$$DD = \frac{E[V(1)] - D^{ST}(1) - \frac{1}{2}D^{LT}(1)}{\sigma_A}$$

where $D^{ST}(1)$ and $D^{LT}(1)$ are the values of short-term and long-term debt, respectively, at the end of the risk horizon. We can restate this more simply as

$$DD = \frac{E[V(1)] - \Psi(1)}{\sigma_A} \tag{16.9}$$

where

$$\Psi(1) = D^{ST}(1) + \tfrac{1}{2} D^{LT}(1) \tag{16.10}$$

is the default point.

As in Equation 16.5 from Merton (1974), the probability of moving from current asset and firm value $V(0)$ to the default point in T years can be expressed generally as

$$\Pr[V(T) \leq \Psi(T)] = N\left\{ -\frac{\ln\left[\dfrac{V(0)}{\Psi(T)}\right] + \left(\mu - \tfrac{1}{2}\sigma^2\right)T}{\sigma\sqrt{T}} \right\} = N(-DD) \tag{16.11}$$

The situation is shown graphically in Figure 16.2.

Unlike in the pure Merton (1974) model, the KMV model does *not* treat $N(-DD)$ as the probability of default. True, this is the probability of reaching the default point. But to move from there to an EDF, KMV maps the *DD* from Equation 16.11—*not* $N(-DD)$, but *DD* itself—into a database of actual default frequencies. A firm with a *DD* of 6, for example, would be compared with the database to determine how many firms with a *DD* of 6 in the database *actually defaulted* over horizon *T*. If the proportion is 0.283%, then the EDF assigned to this firm is 0.283%.

Actuarial Internal Models   All internal models used to estimate default probabilities are not driven by option models. Indeed, one common model does not even relate to the capital structure of the would-be defaulting obligor. This model—CreditRisk+™ from Crédit Suisse Financial Products (CSFP)—uses actuarial mortality rates as the sole determinant of default probability.

Specifically, the CSFP model assumes that the probability of an asset default is constant across time—the probability of a loan default next month will be the same as the probability that the loan will default this month

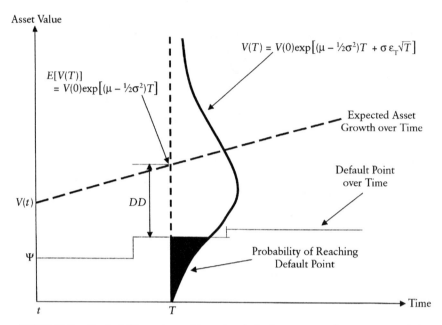

FIGURE 16.2 Probability of reaching the default point in the KMV model.

(assuming the default does not occur *ex post* this month). The model also assumes that the probability of default is independent across obligors. Under these assumptions, the total number of obligor defaults during a given time period is assumed to follow a Poisson distribution and can be described as follows:

$$\Pr(n \le N) = \frac{\mu^N e^{-\mu}}{N!} \tag{16.12}$$

where n is the random number of defaults over the chosen time horizon (one year) and where μ is the average number of defaults per period, where

$$\mu = \sum_{j=1}^{K} \Lambda_j$$

where Λ_j is the probability of default of the jth obligor of K total obligors.

The random variable in this case is the *number* of defaults. Because the arrival rate of these defaults is assumed to be drawn from a Poisson distribution, the average number of defaults per period is μ and the volatility of the number of defaulting obligors per period is $\sqrt{\mu}$. Because the Poisson distribution is a single-parameter distribution, the mean and variance of the number of defaults are based on the same number.

In reality, however, the average number of defaults per year and the volatility of that number varies with business conditions. CSFP thus assumes that μ itself is a random variable drawn from a gamma distribution, such that[12]

$$\Pr(\mu) = \frac{\lambda^r}{\Gamma(r)} \mu^{r-1} e^{-\lambda \mu}$$

where $\lambda > 0$ and $r > 0$. The expected number of average defaults per year is r/λ with variance r/λ^2.

Loss in the Event of Default

The *exposure* of an asset in the event of default is not the same as the *loss* in the event of default. Exposure is the current market value of the asset, or its replacement cost. In other words, the exposure of an asset is what the asset is worth, and, hence, what the nondefaulting creditor has to spend to replace the asset when a default occurs. LIED is then defined as current exposure *minus* recoveries, the market value of collateral held, and the costs of recovery.

Most defaults involve at least *some* recoveries. Even unsecured, uncollateralized obligations still entitle creditors to a pro rata claim on the remaining assets of the defaulting firm. In addition, any collateral held by the creditor can be applied to and offset at least some portion of the loss, assuming the legal documentation is secure. Finally, LIED reflects the costs of collateral application and recovery, including purely administrative costs such as legal fees as well as the interest foregone on recoveries that occur with a substantial delay.

Recovery rates are strongly influenced by three factors. The first is the quality of the collateral and the security of the issue. The second is the seniority of the defaulted claim in the capital structure of the obligor.[13] Table 16.2 shows the median and average price paid for defaulted bonds from 1970 to 1998 and in 1999 reflecting both of these variables.

In addition, recovery rates also tend to be strongly cyclical, thereby leading to a third influence—economic growth. Recovery rates since 1980 have tended to bottom out near the beginning of business cycle contractions and to peak during the height of expansions.[14]

TABLE 16.2   Defaulted Bond Prices, 1970–1999

	1970–1998		1999	
	Median ($)	Average ($)	Median ($)	Average ($)
Senior/secured	53.00	52.31	33.00	43.08
Senior/unsecured	48.00	48.84	42.00	46.72
Subordinated	30.00	33.17	21.00	30.34
Preferred stock	9.13	11.06	4.19	10.92

Source of data: Keenan (2000), Exhibit 21.

Potential Credit Exposure

LIED is a measure of the *current* exposure of an asset net of recoveries, collateral, and costs, whereas PCE is a measure of the potential exposure an asset *might* have if a default occurs in the future. The potential exposure of fixed income assets is fairly straightforward in the traditional credit risk measurement framework for one-sided exposures because the exposure is *known* for each future period. Lines of credit that have not been drawn become more complicated, but are usually treated as fully drawn prior to default as the obligor is presumed to scramble for liquidity.[15] Conditional credits, such as contingent guarantees, are more difficult and must be analyzed using more advanced modeling techniques and/or historical data.

    Amortizing principle loans or bonds with sinking fund provisions are also not particularly hard to accommodate in a PCE context. Despite the change in the amount of the principal over the life of the loan, the manner in which the principal changes is generally *known*. And if the cash flows are known—even if the *value* of those cash flows is not—modeling the PCE is straightforward.

Problems with the Traditional Approach

In most of the discussion thus far, the traditional approach has rested on the assumption that credit risk is the expected default rate times the LIED and PCE. But we have retained the assumption that the probability of default by an obligor is just some constant. In fact, average default rates can be quite volatile.

    The standard deviations of one-year default rates on Moody's rated debt are shown for two time periods in Table 16.3. Although the DRs are stable for highly rated bonds, Ba- and B-rated debt tend to exhibit pronounced volatility around expected values.

TABLE 16.3 One-Year Default Rate Volatilities, Moody's

Moody's Debt Rating	1920–1999 (%)	1970–1999 (%)
Aaa	0	0
Aa	0.2	0.1
A	0.3	0.1
Baa	0.5	0.3
Ba	1.7	1.4
B	4.5	4.8

Source of data: Keenan (2000).

In addition, the distribution of default rates is highly asymmetric, suggesting that volatility alone does not capture the uncertainty associated with expected default frequencies. Figure 16.3 shows the extrema and interquartile ranges of one-year percentage DRs grouped by Moody's rating. The lower the quality of the obligor, the more variability is associated with the DR.

Apart from the volatility of DRs that can make them less than reliable as estimates of default probabilities, the use of a single DR for every time period prevents us from examining any form of credit risk other than *default* risk. Most importantly, downgrade or migration risk is ignored. Nevertheless, changes in ratings occur reasonably often—certainly often enough to be important. Table 16.4 indicates the corporate debt rating

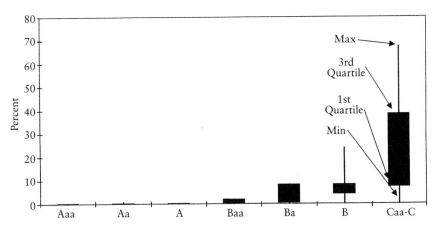

FIGURE 16.3 Variability of Moody's one-year default rates, 1970–1999.
Source: Keenan (2000).

TABLE 16.4   1999 Moody's Rating Transition Frequency Matrix

	Aaa (%)	Aa (%)	A (%)	Baa (%)	Ba (%)	B (%)	Caa-C (%)	Default (%)	Withdrawn (%)
Aaa	95.41	2.75	0.00	0.00	0.00	0.00	0.00	0.00	1.83
Aa	1.99	88.05	5.38	0.00	0.00	0.00	0.00	0.00	4.58
A	0.00	2.28	89.02	5.87	0.11	0.33	0.00	0.00	2.39
Baa	0.12	0.36	4.79	86.11	5.27	1.08	0.00	0.12	2.16
Ba	0.00	0.14	0.29	7.07	74.46	9.38	0.87	1.01	6.78
B	0.00	0.00	0.23	0.35	3.95	77.24	6.50	5.46	6.27
C*	0.00	0.00	0.00	0.00	0.00	5.26	70.33	18.66	5.74

Source of data: Keenan (2000).
* Includes C, Ca, and Caa.

transition frequency matrix published by Moody's for 1999. Each cell in the table represents the frequency of jumping from the rating in the left-most column to the rating across the top row or to a rating withdrawal or default. Using the 1999 numbers as the basis for transition probability inferences, an Aa-rated firm, for example, has a 1.99% chance of being upgraded to Aaa, an 88.05% likelihood of remaining Aa, a 5.38% chance of being downgraded to A, and so on.

The traditional framework can be modified, of course, *at least* to take into account changes in the probability of default over time. Instead of using an average DR, we simply replace that with a time-specific default probability. But even then, a major missing piece of the puzzle in the traditional framework is the need to account for *portfolio effects*. Portfolio effects within exposures to a single obligor are dealt with mainly through giving netting its proper treatment, but portfolio effects can also be pronounced *across obligors*—for example, correlations in default probabilities, diversification across time, correlations across obligor exposures, and so forth. To explicitly address these effects—as well as to address downgrade risk—we need to move beyond the traditional approach into the portfolio approach for credit risk analysis.

THE PORTFOLIO-BASED INTERNAL MODELS APPROACH

A number of alternative methods of measuring credit risk have surfaced over the past few years, both in the academic literature and in industry.[16] Space precludes discussing the more recent developments, or even the mainstream models in any great detail. Apart from going to the sources directly (e.g., software user manuals), several good third-party references outline the major approaches in more detail.[17]

In general, portfolio models come in two varieties (Bank for International Settlements, 1999). The first, called *mark-to-market* models, are those that take into account both default and downgrade risk. *Default mode* models, by contrast, focus only on realized default risk.

In this section, four types of portfolio-based internal models are reviewed: J.P. Morgan's CreditMetrics, KMV's Portfolio Manager, CSFP's CreditRisk+, and McKinsey's CreditPortfolioView. CreditRisk+ is a default mode model. CreditMetrics, Portfolio Manager, and CreditPortfolioView can produce both mark-to-market and default mode analyses.

Default Mode Models

The major model that addresses default risk in a portfolio context without addressing downgrade risk is the CSFP actuarial model CreditRisk+. Recall from the prior section that CreditRisk+ is used to estimate DRs that are based on actuarial assumptions and a presumed Poisson arrival rate for the number of defaults per year. Based on the predicted number of defaults in a given time horizon, CreditRisk+ calculates credit risk by associating LIEDs with potential defaults. In CreditRisk+, LIEDs are exogenous to the model and depend only on actual exposure estimates plus expected recovery rates.

To generate a distribution of losses on a portfolio of assets across obligors, the LIED for each asset is first converted into a bucket or band number equal to the LIED rounded to the nearest $100,000 and then divided by $100,000. An asset with a current LIED of $200,000 thus is classified in band 2, whereas an asset whose LIED is $350,000 is a member of Band 4 (i.e., $350,000 rounded to $400,000 and divided by $100,000). All assets in a given band are then presumed to have the same exposure, equal to the band number times $100,000. The asset above with a $350,000 LIED thus is treated as if the LIED is $400,000 because the asset is classified as Band 4.

Each band is treated in CreditRisk+ as an independent portfolio of asset exposures. The expected loss for any asset in the jth band per $100,000 is calculated as:

$$E(L_j) = X_j x \mu_j$$

where μ_j is the expected number of defaults in band j and X_j is the common exposure for the jth band per $100,000. If $j = 3$, for example, $X_j = 3$. The probability generating process for default losses per $100,000 in a given time period for the jth band can be written as:

$$F_j(L) = \sum_{j=0}^{\infty} \Pr(n) L^{nX_j}$$

where n is the number of defaults per period as in Equation 16.12 and L is the realized loss per \$100,000 of exposure. From Equation 16.12 that describes the probability of n defaults per period as being drawn from a Poisson distribution, we can rewrite the probability generating model for losses in band j as

$$F_j(L) = \sum_{j=0}^{\infty} \frac{\mu_j^n e^{-\mu_j}}{n!} L^{nX_j} = \exp\left(-\mu_j + \mu_j L^{X_j}\right) \qquad (16.13)$$

Because each band is an independent portfolio of exposures, the *joint* probability distribution for losses on the whole portfolio is just the product of the m marginal probability distributions from Equation 16.13 for each band, or

$$F(L) = \prod_{j=1}^{m} \exp\left(-\mu_j + \mu_j L^{X_j}\right) = \exp\left(-\sum_{j=1}^{m} \mu_j + \sum_{j=1}^{m} \mu_j L^{X_j}\right) \qquad (16.14)$$

The probability density function for a loss of $N = \$100,000n$ for some n then is

$$f(N) = \frac{1}{n!} \frac{d^n F(L)}{dL^n} \Big|_{L=0} \qquad n = 1, 2, 3, \ldots \qquad (16.15)$$

This probability of loss is actually fairly easy to implement. The result from Equation 16.15 depends only on estimates of $E(L_j)$ and the LIED for the assets in the jth band for all j. Closed-form probability expressions are available for this approximation.

Because the CSFP model does not measure migration or downgrade risk, the model does not provide a good measure of the value of assets at risk from adverse credit events. Value-based risk managers thus may prefer to avoid this model. For earnings risk managers, however, the CSFP model may be more than adequate. The resulting loss distribution in Equation 16.15 essentially measures a loss of earnings or *book* capital at risk from default events. For earnings risk managers, this measure of credit risk and other default mode models thus may be more than enough.

Mark-to-Market Models

For a value risk manager, changes in the present values of assets arising from credit quality migration or downgrades is an important consideration. Models that either measure this risk alone or this risk together with default risk thus may be preferred to a pure default mode model like the CSFP model examined in the previous section. Three such models, summarized below, demonstrate the range of methodologies that can be employed to incorporate migration risk into summary measures of portfolio credit risk.

CreditMetrics™ J.P. Morgan, together with Bank of America, KMV, Union Bank of Switzerland, and a few others introduced CreditMetrics in 1997 as a credit version of VaR. The primary focus of the model is analyzing potential worst-case changes in the present values of assets resulting from credit migration risk over a chosen risk horizon—usually one year. Default risk can in principle be addressed as a special case of a downgrade.

In CreditMetrics, the probability of default by an obligor is an exogenous input to the model. The risk manager inputs a transition density matrix of the type shown in Table 16.4, and all obligors within a rating class are assigned the same transition probability of migrating from one rating to another or into default.

The value of a one-sided asset exposure one year hence (i.e., at the end of the risk horizon) is calculated in CreditMetrics using one of several static forward curves, each of which reflects different credit spreads over Treasuries. A distribution of potential values of the asset exposure in one year then is generated based on the transition probabilities of exposures migrating from one curve of credit risk-adjusted discount rates to a different one, and the αth percentile of that distribution is the credit-VaR or credit at risk.

The probability of a default or downgrade can be inferred using the Merton (1974) model. Figure 16.4 shows the standard normalized asset distribution for the value of a firm rated BB.[18] Various standardized asset levels denoted Z correspond to migrations through different ratings, where, in the extreme, values below Z_{CCC} indicate default. The probability of default at time T evaluated as of time t is just

$$\Pr(Z \le Z_{CCC}) = N(-Z_{CCC}) = N\left\{-\frac{\ln\left[\dfrac{V(t)}{V*}\right] + \left(\mu - \frac{1}{2}\sigma^2\right)(T - t)}{\sigma\sqrt{T - t}}\right\} \quad (16.16)$$

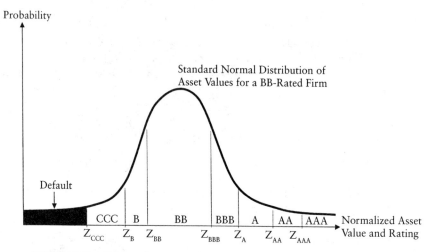

FIGURE 16.4   Generalization of Merton (1974) to rating changes.

where V^* is the value at which the firm's assets fall below its liabilities as a function of μ and σ in a Merton (1974) context.

The Merton (1974) framework can also be used to infer migration probabilities. The probability of a BBB-rated firm having assets that migrate the firm into a BB rating, for example, is the difference in the cumulative probability that the firm will be rated at least BBB and the cumulative probability that the firm will be rated BB.

For a portfolio of one-sided asset exposures, correlations across transition densities associated with different assets and obligors must be taken into account. As discussed in the previous section, the KMV model estimates the volatility and value of the assets underlying an obligor using an iterative method together with the Merton (1974) model. CreditMetrics makes the much simpler—and less realistic—assumption that the asset volatility of an obligor is reflected completely in the volatility of its common stock returns. Correlations embedded in a joint distribution of equity returns for all obligors in a portfolio thus become the basis for correlations across transition densities. Once these correlations are estimated, the single-asset case above generalizes to a portfolio basis, where the probability distribution used for default probability inference is *multivariate* normal.

KMV   The means by which the KMV model estimates default probabilities for obligors has been discussed earlier. Once the EDF has been computed, transition probabilities can also be estimated in the KMV model to facilitate downgrade risk measurement.

Unlike the simplistic static forward-curve based valuation model used to compute downgrade losses in CreditMetrics, the KMV model uses a more complex and robust valuation method based on the financial principles of risk-neutral valuation. As discussed in Chapter 3, some adjustment for risk, such as a stochastic discount factor based on the intertemporal marginal rate of substitution, must be made to compute the *NPV* of a risky cash flow.

As an alternative to using a risk-adjusted discount factor applied to a risky cash flow, the expected cash flow itself can be modeled in what is known as the risk-neutral measure, or a probability measure in which all agents in the economy are presumed to act as if they are risk-neutral in the sense of Chapter 2.[19] When an expected cash flow is expressed with respect to a risk-neutral measure, the discount rate used to compute the *NPV* is then the risk free rate. Alternatively, all risky assets have an expected return equal to the risk free rate if the expectation is taken with respect to the risk-neutral measure.[20]

Denote the recovery rate for measuring LIED as θ, where $0 \leq \theta \leq 1$. A bond or loan can be separated into two portfolios of cash flows for valuation purposes—the cash flows that are not de facto subject to default risk because they are recovered in the event of default, and those that are subject to default risk and thus remain unrecovered. The default risk-free cash flows (i.e., recoveries) can be treated as riskless and thus discounted at the risk-free rate, whereas the expected loss subject to default risk must either be discounted at a risk-adjusted discount rate or expressed as a risk-neutral expectation and discounted at the risk-free rate. Adopting the latter approach, a bond or loan with N remaining cash flows has a present value of

$$PV = (1-\theta)\sum_{j=1}^{N} CF_j e^{-r_j T_j} + \theta\sum_{j=1}^{N}(1-\pi_j)CF_j e^{-r_j T_j} \qquad (16.17)$$

where CF_j is the cash flow to occur at time j, r_j is the continuously compounded risk-free rate for a time j cash flow, T_j is the time from the present to the cash flow occurring at j, and π_j is the risk-neutral probability of default at horizon T_j. The probability π can be viewed as a risk-neutral EDF in KMV parlance.

Valuing one-sided asset exposures using Equation 16.17 is straightforward if the risk-neutral probabilities are known. This risk-neutral EDF for any risk horizon T can be defined as follows:

$$\pi_T = \Pr[V(T) \le \Psi(T)]$$

where $\Psi(T)$ is the default point for an obligor at horizon T, as shown in Figure 16.2.

In a risk-neutral valuation world, the expected return on all assets relative to a risk-neutral probability measure must equal the risk-free rate. So, the stochastic process for the evolution of the value of the firm given earlier can be rewritten in a risk-neutral economy as follows:

$$\frac{dV^*(t)}{V^*(t)} = rdt + \sigma dZ(t)$$

where r is the riskless rate and $dZ(t) = \varepsilon(t)^2 dt$ is a Gauss-Wiener process such that $\varepsilon(t) \sim N(0, 1)$. The difference in this stochastic process and the one given earlier in the discussion of the original Merton (1974) model is the expected return—μ in the Merton (1974) model and r here. From this stochastic process, we can write the risk-neutral probability of covering the distance to default as

$$
\begin{aligned}
\pi_T &= \Pr[V^*(T) \le \Psi(T)] \\
&= \Pr\left\{\ln[V(0)] + \left(r - \tfrac{1}{2}\sigma^2\right)T + \sigma\sqrt{T}\varepsilon(T) \le \ln[\Psi(T)]\right\} \\
&= \Pr\left\{\varepsilon(T) \le -\frac{\ln\left[\dfrac{V(0)}{\psi(T)}\right] + \left(r - \tfrac{1}{2}\sigma^2\right)T}{\sigma\sqrt{T}}\right\} = N(-DD^*)
\end{aligned}
\tag{16.18}
$$

The *actual* probability of covering the distance to default—the shaded tail of the distribution in Figure 16.2—was given by Equation 16.12. The risk-neutral distance to default can be expressed as a function of the actual distance to default as follows:

$$-DD^* = -DD + \frac{(\mu - r)\sqrt{T}}{\sigma} \tag{16.19}$$

Recall from Chapter 1 that the single-factor CAPM allows us to write the expected excess return on any firm or security as

$$\mu - r = \beta(\mu_M - r)$$

where μ_M is the expected return on the market and

$$\beta = \frac{\mathrm{cov}(R, R_M)}{\mathrm{var}(R_M)} = \rho\frac{\mu_M - r}{\sigma_M} = \rho SR_M$$

where ρ is the correlation between returns on the firm and the market portfolio and SR_M denotes the market Sharpe ratio. Equation 16.19 then can be rewritten as

$$-DD^* = -DD + \rho SR_M \sqrt{T} \qquad (16.20)$$

so that the risk-neutral probability of default is then

$$\pi_T = N(-DD^*) = N\left(-DD + \rho SR_M \sqrt{T}\right) \qquad (16.21)$$

Note that because SR_M is positive and ρ will be positive for most assets, $\pi_T > N(-DD)$—the risk-neutral probability of default exceeds the actual probability of default.

KMV estimates risk-neutral default probabilities by estimating the parameters in Equation 16.21. The parameter ρ is the square root of the coefficient of determination (R^2) in an OLS linear regression of the firm's asset returns on the market return. The market Sharpe ratio in Equation 16.21 is calibrated to actual bond data. Specifically, the continuously compounded return R_j for an obligor's cash flow at time j can be written from Equation 16.17 as

$$e^{-R_j T_j} = \left[(1-\theta) + (1 - \pi_j)\theta\right]e^{-r_j T_j}$$

or, rearranging terms and using Equation 16.21,

$$R_j - r_j = -\frac{1}{T_j}\ln(1 - \pi_j\theta) = -\frac{1}{T_j}\ln\left[1 - N\left(-DD + \rho SR_M \sqrt{T}\right)\theta\right] \qquad (16.22)$$

The expression in Equation 16.22 is the corporate credit spread of an obligor over the risk-free rate. This spread can be observed from bond data, and KMV uses the observed spread to calibrate SR_M and verify that the parametric root of T is indeed one-half.[21]

The valuation methodology outlined above is used by KMV to estimate portfolio credit risk, including downgrade risk. Correlations across multiple obligors are obtained in KMV by assuming each obligor's returns are generated by a multifactor model like the one discussed in Chapter 1. The factors include a composite company-specific factor, country and industry exposures, and global and sector exposures. The factor-generated obligor returns then enable KMV to generate a correlation structure that, when combined with the valuation methodology outlined, results in a measure of portfolio-level downgrade and default risk. For more details on the factor construction method, see Crouhy, Galai, and Mark (2000).

CreditPortfolioView   CreditMetrics relies on static forward curves by credit spread as a driver for estimating downgrade risk, whereas KMV relies on risk-neutral valuation methods to reprice a portfolio of assets from a given obligor. Yet a third approach, embodied in CreditPortfolioView developed by Wilson and used by McKinsey, quantifies default and downgrade risk as a function of macroeconomic risk factors.

The Wilson (1997a,b) model contains three basic ingredients. The first is a structural relation between some macroeconomic index defined for different segments of the market. Only speculative grade obligors are considered. The relation between this index and a set of K macroeconomic risk factors is presumed to be linear and can be expressed as follows:

$$y(j,t) = \beta_{j,0} + \beta_{j,1} X(j,1,t) + \beta_{j,2} X(j,2,t)$$
$$+ \cdots + \beta_{j,K} X(j,K,t) + v(j,t) \tag{16.23}$$

where $y(j, t)$ is the time t index value for segment j, $X(j, k, t)$ is the time t value of macroeconomic factor k in segment j, and $v(j, t)$ is an independent and identically distributed normal variate. The macroeconomic risk factors can include any variables presumed to be correlated with defaults, such as GDP growth or unemployment. Any macoreconomic factor k is presumed to follow an AR(2) process, such that

$$X(j,K,t) = \varphi_{k,0} + \varphi_{k,1} X(j,K,t-1) + \varphi_{k,2} X(j,K,t-2) + \upsilon(j,K,t) \tag{16.24}$$

where $\upsilon(j, k, t)$ is a normal variate.

The probability of default of a speculative-grade obligor in segment j at time t is expressed by Wilson as a logit function:

$$p(j,t) = \frac{1}{1 + \exp[y(j,t)]} \tag{16.25}$$

where Equation 16.25 is determined simultaneously with Equations 16.23 and 16.24, where

$$\begin{bmatrix} v(t) \\ \upsilon(t) \end{bmatrix} \sim N(0, \Sigma) \quad \Sigma = \begin{bmatrix} \Sigma_v & \Sigma_{v\upsilon} \\ \Sigma_{\upsilon v} & \Sigma_\upsilon \end{bmatrix}$$

The stacked covariance matrix can be written using a Cholesky decomposition—which we encountered in Chapter 15—as:

$$\Sigma = AA'$$

The speculative default probability $p(j, t)$ then can be simulated by defining a vector of random numbers $Z(t)$ such that each element is distributed standard normal. The residuals from the regressions in Equations 16.23 and 16.24 then can be simulated as:

$$\begin{bmatrix} v(t) \\ \upsilon(t) \end{bmatrix} = A' \underline{Z}(t)$$

That is enough to determine $y(j, t)$ and $p(j, t)$, given estimates of the parameters in Equations 16.23 and 16.24 (which can be obtained from OLS). In the Wilson model, the *unconditional* transition densities are defined exogenously from a rating agency, prior beliefs, or any other source. The time t element of the *conditional* transition density matrix then can be defined as:

$$M(t) = M\left[\frac{p(j, t)}{M^U} \right]$$

where M^u is the unconditional transition density matrix. This can easily be extended to multistep time horizons by multiplying the relevant one-period transition matrices.

The result of repeated simulations is a full-conditional transition probability matrix that then can be used to calculate asset values under the assumptions of either migration or default.

TWO-SIDED CREDIT EXPOSURE MEASUREMENT

All of the models surveyed in the prior section were presumed to apply only to one-sided exposures. A contract is said to have two-sided exposure if it can be either an asset or a liability. Forward-like derivatives, unlike lines of credit or bonds, may be either assets or liabilities depending on market price movements.

The main implication of the introduction of two-sided exposures into the picture is on the potential exposure of the position. Recall that in moving from Equation 16.1 to Equation 16.2, we dropped the potential exposure function $\omega[\Lambda(t + 1, N), V(t + 1, N), \chi(t + 1, N)]$ and replaced that with a multiplicative PCE in Equation 16.2. This was possible because for one-sided exposures, the PCE is *known* as of date t based on the drawdown schedule of the asset. Because that is unknown for forward-based derivatives, we now must return to the more general structure of Equation 16.2.

The potential exposure of some forward-like derivatives with multiple cash flows—chiefly swaps and nonfinancial contracts with swap-like exposures—is driven primarily by the change in the risk factor(s) or underlying(s) of the position. In addition, the combination of market price changes with the passage of time itself. The impact of these two variables on the potential exposure of a derivatives transaction are explored below.

Potential Price Changes and Two-Sided Potential Exposure

Consider a simple spot transaction—say, the purchase of a single share of common stock.[22] On trade date T the price of the stock is agreed by buyer and seller to be $S(T)$ per share. Further suppose that the transaction is negotiated on a market where the settlement agent acts as a DVP agent but not a trade guarantor and that settlement occurs at $T + 2$. The potential exposure of the buyer is shown in Figure 16.5. If the stock price $S(T + 2)$ rises above $S(T)$ and the seller fails to deliver the stock, the buyer is deprived of any capital gains associated with the stock price run-up during the settlement window. For stock prices above $S(T)$, the buyer's credit exposure thus rises dollar-for-dollar with the stock price. If the stock price declines below $S(T)$, by contrast, the buyer has *no* credit exposure. The asset has declined in value, but a failure of the seller to deliver stock means that the buyer can replace the purchase in the market at the new lower price.

The heavy line in Figure 16.5 representing the stock purchaser's credit exposure at settlement looks exactly like the payoff diagram for an expiring European call option. Accordingly, the *potential* exposure of the transaction can be viewed as a call option *two days prior to maturity*, whose value is shown on Figure 16.5 as a dashed line. Because the option is so close to maturity, the dashed line is very close to the solid line and nearly perfectly tracks the maturity payoff.

But suppose instead this contract was a *one-year* forward contract for the purchase of the same share of stock one year hence. To keep things

Exposure

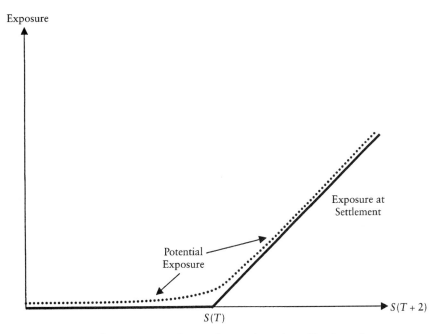

FIGURE 16.5 Credit exposure of a stock purchase in a $T + 2$ settlement system.

simple, suppose the fixed purchase price for the stock K is set on trade date T, the value date is $T + 250$ business days, and the settlement date is $T + 252$ days. Buyer and seller thus agree to initiate settlement so that settlement achieves finality one year hence, on which date the buyer has irrevocably remitted a K dollar payment and will receive a stock worth $S(T + 252)$.

For this transaction, the exposure at settlement is similar to Figure 16.6 except that the exposure threshold is now determined by $S(T + 252)$ relative to K. The potential exposure vis-à-vis the settlement day exposure is shown in Figure 16.6. Unlike Figure 16.6, the *time value* of the exposure now has a fairly pronounced component, indicated by the vertical distance of the dashed line above the solid settlement exposure line. In the two-day stock purchase case, the time value was only two days, so most of the potential exposure was the intrinsic value of the option-like exposure. Now in the $T + 252$ day case, the potential exposure includes a lot of time value, as well.

An option has time value because, *ceteris paribus*, the longer the option has before it expires, the more time can elapse during which the price of the underlying might move into the money or deeper in-the-money. And we

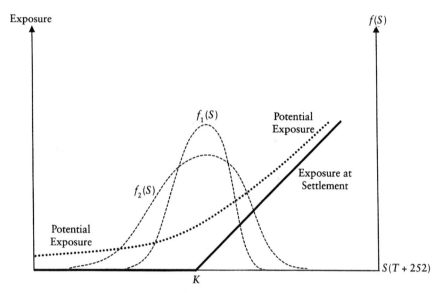

FIGURE 16.6 Potential exposure of forward stock purchase and volatility.

know from vega that the higher the volatility of the underlying, the more pronounced this effect. Figure 16.6 illustrates the impact of vega on potential exposure. Two probability distributions of possible values of the stock price at $T + 252$ are shown. Distribution $f_1(S)$ and $f_2(S)$ have roughly the same expected value, both of which are approximately equal to K. But distribution $f_2(S)$ has significantly higher volatility than distribution $f_1(S)$. Figure 16.6 illustrates that the probability the potential exposure on the transaction is positive is clearly higher with distribution $f_2(S)$ than with distribution $f_1(S)$.

Suppose, as in the seminal paper by Black and Scholes (1973), we assume that stock prices evolve over time according to geometric Brownian motion. Over an infinitesimally small increment of time, the evolution of the stock price can be described according to the following stochastic differential equation:

$$\frac{dS}{S} = \mu dt + \sigma dz \qquad (16.26)$$

where dz is a Gauss-Wiener process, such that $dz^2 = \varepsilon^2 dt$ where ε is a standard normal variate. Equation 16.26 can be discretized into any given time change Δt, such that the stock price change is just

$$\frac{\Delta S}{S} = \mu \Delta t + \sigma \varepsilon \sqrt{\Delta t} \qquad (16.27)$$

In the last term of Equation 16.27, the variable σ is the instantaneous volatility of the stock return, and the whole quantity $\sigma \sqrt{\Delta t}$ is called the *diffusion coefficient*. This diffusion coefficient embodies the interaction of the passage of time with the volatility of the underlying in an options context. The degree to which the stock price on date $T + 252$ has moved away from its starting value depends not only on the volatility σ of *per-period* stock returns, but also on the amount of time remaining. The more time remaining, the higher the diffusion coefficient.

This particular terminology has led some to describe the impact of potential price changes on the potential exposure of a forward-like exposure as "the diffusion effect."[23] For the price process shown in Equation 16.27, the more time between the trade and settlement date on any given forward-like exposure, the higher the diffusion coefficient—by an amount proportional to the square root of the number of time periods remaining. So, the potential exposure of a forward-like exposure is an increasing function of time to maturity.

For stochastic processes other than Equation 16.27, the diffusion effect can be less pronounced—especially over long periods of time. Consider, for example, the following process describing the evolution of interest rates over a small time increment:

$$dr = \alpha(\mu - r)dt + \sigma \sqrt{r}\, dz \qquad (16.28)$$

where dz is a Gauss-Wiener process. Equation 16.28 is a mean-reverting process, where the interest rate r reverts to mean μ at speed α. In addition, the diffusion coefficient is now proportional to the square root of the level of the interest rate, implying a lower diffusion effect for lower rates. In a high interest rate environment, the interest rate thus tends to drift further away from its initial value, although the rate itself is pulled back to the long-run average as time passes. In markets better described by Equation 16.28 than Equation 16.27, the diffusion effect thus will be less pronounced.

The Passage of Time and Two-Sided Potential Exposure

In the example of a forward purchase of a share of stock, the amount of time between trade date and settlement date does not affect the portion of the transaction at risk from credit defaults. If the transaction was marked to market half-way through, his would no longer be true. In that case, the successful payment by the stock seller to the buyer of an amount equal to the replacement cost of the stock up to the date in the transaction where the payment occurs would *reduce* the potential exposure on the remaining part of the transaction.

To take a better example, suppose on trade date T that Company Haydn enters into an interest rate swap with Firm Bach that calls for semi-annual settlements for the next five years. Being a typical rate swap, principal is notional and is not exchanged. Accordingly, the potential exposure of the swap will fall as time passes, all else equal, because each successful payment means one less cash flow at risk from a credit default to the in-the-money party. *Any* marking to market of a position has the effect of forcing periodic settling up so that a subsequent default will affect only cash flows that have not been marked to market. The reduction in potential exposure as time passes and cash flows occur is called the *amortization effect*.

The Net of the Diffusion and Amortization Effects

The amortization and diffusion effects pull the potential exposure of a two-sided exposure in different directions. For an exposure representing a swap-like series of cash flows with no exchange of principal at inception or final settlement, the amortization effect tends to decrease the potential exposure as time passes and the contract is settled up, whereas the diffusion effect puts upward pressure on the potential exposure as rates/prices drift further away from their initial values.

For a given stochastic process such as the ones shown in Equations 16.27 and 16.28, a distribution of possible values of the underlying risk factor can be generated for each year in the swap—for example, using Monte Carlo simulation, as outlined in Chapter 15. Once this distribution is generated for each period, the diffusion and amortization effects can be translated into simulated potential exposure estimates.

Figure 16.7 illustrates the simulated diffusion and amortization effects for a simple, plain vanilla interest rate swap with 10 years to maturity.[24] The potential exposure shown is based on the *expected* interest rate change each period. The resulting expected potential exposure peaks around 3.5 years to maturity with an expected replacement cost of around 4% of the notional principal underlying the swap.

If the exposure involves a very large cash flow or asset exchange toward the end of the life of the exposure, the expected potential exposure profile of the exposure over time looks quite different. Consider, for example, a cross-currency swap, which is synthetically equivalent to an interest rate swap plus a portfolio of currency forward contracts to convert one leg of the swap—both interest payments *and* a terminal principal exchange—into a

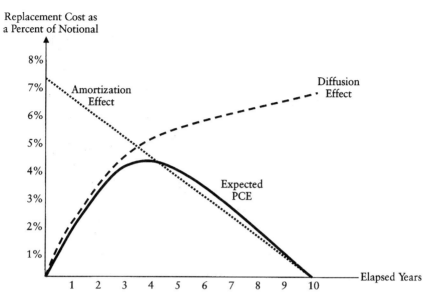

Replacement Cost as a Percent of Notional

FIGURE 16.7 Diffusion and amortization effects on the expected potential exposure of an interest rate swap.

different currency. Because principal is exchanged at the end of the transaction, the amortization effect is negligible and the diffusion effect dominates. The net result is shown in Figure 16.8. In addition to having an expected potential exposure profile that is now strictly increasing with the passage of time, the size of the expected exposure—replacement cost as a percentage of principal—is higher than in the case of the rate swap. The single large asset exchange at the end of the life of the transaction thus both raises the potential exposure at *all* times and results in a potential exposure that is strictly increasing with time elapsed in the swap.

Figures 16.9 and 16.10 illustrate the difference between the *expected* potential exposures plotted in Figures 16.7 and 16.8 and more conservative worst-case potential exposure estimates. To generate these worst-case profiles, we choose in this case a 95th percentile confidence level and use the 95th percentile price change from the simulated distribution each period rather than simply the expected value. This worst-case estimate of potential exposure, given some confidence level α, is sometimes called the credit at risk of the exposure at the $\alpha\%$ confidence level because of its similarity to the VaR concept discussed in Chapter 15. Not surprisingly, credit at risk has many of the same theoretical and practical advantages *and* limitations as VaR.

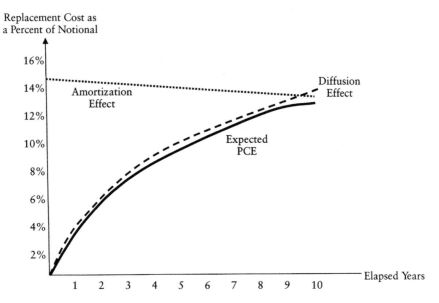

FIGURE 16.8   Diffusion and amortization effects on the expected potential exposure of a cross-currency swap.

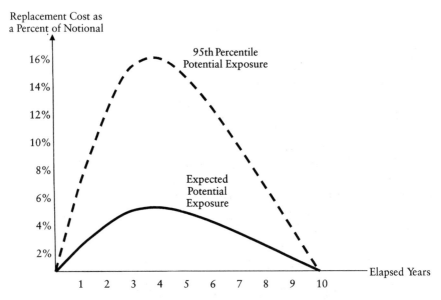

FIGURE 16.9   Expected versus worst-case potential exposure of an interest rate swap.

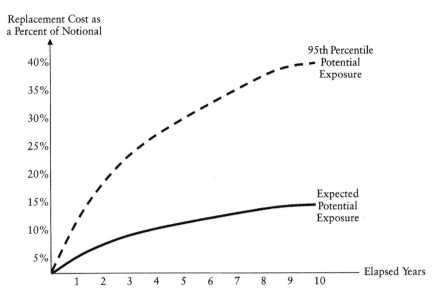

Replacement Cost as
a Percent of Notional

FIGURE 16.10 Expected versus worst-case potential exposure of a cross-currency swap.

Cross-Asset Single Obligor Portfolio Effects and Default Credit Mitigation

When an institution has exposures to a single obligor that include both one- and two-sided assets, credit risk mitigation mechanisms can be used to reduce that exposure. This effect is easiest to see if we work only with *current* exposure. So, potential exposure is ignored for the time being.

If an institution has M total exposures to an obligor, the *current* exposure of the institution to that obligor, from Equation 16.1, is just

$$\sum_{j=1}^{M} \max\left[V_j(t) - \chi_j(t), 0\right] \qquad (16.29)$$

where $V_j(t)$ and $\chi_j(t)$ are the current value and market value of collateral plus recoveries of the jth exposure to the obligor, respectively.

The use of collateral to reduce LIED was discussed earlier. In addition to collateral, OTC derivatives participants in particular make use of several other credit exposure mitigation mechanisms as a matter of course. One such mechanism, mentioned in Chapter 1, is the use of close-out netting arrangements together with full two-way payments. This is a standard choice under the ISDA Master Agreements—pro forma documentation used to document most OTC derivatives transactions—and the enforceability of close-out bilateral netting is widely regarded as secure in most significant legal jurisdictions. In addition, swap participants often include nonswap transactions under a master netting agreement that subsumes all individual contracts so that close-out netting can be applied to as many transactions between a defaulting firm and its counterparties as possible.

The implication of bilateral netting is to change the last term in Equation 16.29 from the sum of a series of maximums—each of which reflects whether or not *any single* transaction is in-the-money—into a maximum of a sum, so that assets and liabilities are netted *before* looking at whether or not there is a net payable on the part of a defaulting obligor. In addition, one-sided exposures can be included in this calculation, as well, so that *with enforceable bilateral close-out netting,* the credit risk to a firm of the default of a single counterparty can be rewritten as follows:

$$\max\left[\sum_{j=1}^{M} V_j(t) - \chi_j(t), 0\right] \tag{16.30}$$

In the prior case of Equation 16.29, the absence of netting implied that the gross portfolio credit risk to a counterparty default was the sum of all current and potential exposures on all assets with the counterparty. In Equation 16.30, the benefits of netting are reflected by allowing the assets to be summed with any liabilities *before* taking the maximum. In the extreme, if liabilities exceed assets, the maximum will be zero and the firm has no net credit risk.

Another benefit of master netting agreements, depending on how they are structured, can be application of collateral *to the net exposure* rather than to the LIED of a specific transaction. For secured bonds and loans, the collateral is usually tied to the instrument and thus must be left in the LIED calculation for that particular instrument. But for unsecured exposures, collateral usually can be applied across the net of all exposures, thus allowing us to rewrite Equation 16.30 as:

$$\max\left\{\left[\sum_{j=1}^{M} V_j(t) - \chi_j(t)\right] - CV(t), 0\right\} \tag{16.31}$$

where $CV(t)$ is the value of collateral at the time of default that a defaulting obligor has pledged to the firm *on its unsecured assets.* If lien has been perfected to tie specific collateral to a specific instrument as security for just that instrument, the collateral is still presumed to be a component of the LIED and is included in $\chi(t)$.

The portfolio effects of two-sided exposures become much more complex when potential exposure is reintroduced *and* when portfolio effects are taken into consideration *across obligors*. Most of the models discussed earlier do not handle two-sided exposures, or, in the case of CreditMetrics, handle them in an unsatisfactory and oversimplified manner.[25]

EXPECTED VERSUS UNEXPECTED LOSS

Except for some brief attention to worse-case exposures in a couple of places, the outcome of the credit risk measurement process on which we have focused all of our attention thus far is expected loss. As a management device, expected loss plays an important role. But so does *unexpected* loss.

Expected Loss as a Cost of Doing Business

Financial institutions typically treat expected credit losses as a normal cost of doing business. The *unexpected* loss is the credit *risk,* whereas the *expected* loss is the credit *cost.* How the institution accounts for and manages that cost, however, depends on the structure of the firm.

In one business model, the actual performance of the asset is left in the business unit that originates the asset. When the asset (e.g., a loan) is booked, the expected loss is deducted as a cost. If the asset later turns out to be nonperforming, the *actual* loss net of collateral and recoveries is treated as a mark-down for that business unit. In most companies with this business model, *managing* the credit exposure is left to the business unit that bears the exposure.

Larger banks in particular tend to adhere to an alternative business model in which the expected loss on an asset is charged to the asset originator, but the *actual* performance on the asset is not. Upon origination, the credit risk of the asset is transferred to a credit risk management group that then manages the bank's total portfolio of credit exposures using credit derivatives, securitizations, and the like. Any losses below expected losses are credited to this credit risk management group, and any unexpected excess losses are charged to the group. In either case, the originator of the asset bears *only* the expected loss as a *cost.*

For a nonfinancial corporation, this approach may seem somewhat counterintuitive: If the loss is *expected* then why is the asset originated in the first place? The answer depends, of course, on whether or not the credit exposures are an inseparable part of the normal business of the firm. For a railcar producer, the credit risk of nonpayment following delivery is indeed unavoidable unless the firm switches to prepayment. The competitive business environment in which the firm is operating thus will dictate whether or not credit losses are avoidable. If not, then treating expected losses as a cost of doing business is reasonable.

Treating expected credit losses as a cost of doing business is becoming increasingly common for *any* type of firm engaged in numerous credit-sensitive relations. In Chapter 20 when capital allocation is explored, the treatment of expected loss as a cost of normal business will be particularly important.

Unexpected Losses

Returning to the simple case of Equation 16.2, assume LIED and PCE are fixed factors, and further assume PCE is unitary (e.g., all exposures are one-sided and all lines are presumed fully drawn).[26] In this case, expected loss is just

$$E(L) = DR \times LIED$$

The variance of expected loss then can be expressed as [27]

$$\sigma^2 = E(L)^2 - [E(L)]^2 = E(L)[LIED - E(L)]$$

The unexpected loss is often expressed as the volatility of the expected loss, or the square root of the above:

$$\sigma = \sqrt{E(L)[LIED - E(L)]} \qquad (16.32)$$

If we relax the assumption that LIED is fixed, then the unexpected loss in Equation 16.32 can be rewritten for the jth asset exposure as:

$$\sigma = \sqrt{DR_j(1 - DR_j)\overline{LIED}_j + DR_j\sigma^2_{LIED,\,j}} \qquad (16.33)$$

where $\sigma^2_{LIED,\,j}$ is the volatility of the LIED.

The unexpected losses in Equations 16.32 and 16.33 are the variables that most financial institutions manage when they say they are managing credit risk. Two-sided exposures and correlations in DR, LIED, and PCE—as well as correlations across obligors—render this approach oversimplistic very quickly, however.

As a more general matter, unexpected loss can be defined by examining the distribution of losses on the whole credit portfolio—including one- and two-sided exposures and all assets across all obligors. A typical such distribution is shown in Figure 16.11. *Expected* losses are illustrated as those losses from zero up to the mean of the distribution. *Unexpected* losses in this case are represented by the shaded area, where the confidence level α dictates the distance of unexpected losses from the expected loss. As drawn, unexpected losses represent about 5% of the distribution.

The primary rationale for the calculation of unexpected losses is the determination of appropriate capital reserves required to allocate against credit-sensitive assets. Unexpected loss can also play a role in systems where credit risk is monitored mainly through the pricing of credit risk. These are issues that will be explored in more detail in Chapter 20.

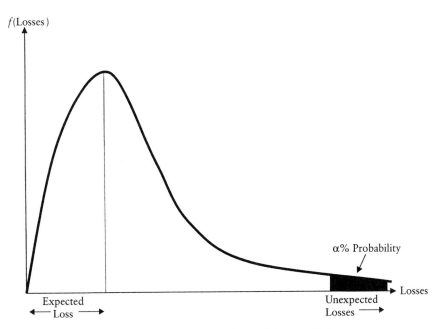

FIGURE 16.11 Distribution of portfolio credit losses.

RECONCILING CREDIT RISK MEASURES TO RISK TOLERANCES

Three distinct management philosophies are regularly observed at companies that seek to monitor whether their actual exposures match their firm-specific tolerances. The first philosophy rests on the use of explicit credit approvals on a deal-by-deal basis. This credit risk management philosophy is a bit like Visa and MasterCard—before a transaction can be charged, the merchant is required to obtain an approval code that the transaction will not over-extend the buyer's credit. Under this management philosophy, risk takers and business units within a firm thus are required to seek approval *in advance* for at least some of the transactions that increase the firm's credit exposures.[28]

The second credit risk management philosophy is fairly similar to the first and echoes the distinction between market risk thresholds and limits as discussed in Chapter 15. Namely, business managers authorized to engage in transactions that change the credit exposure of the firm are allowed discretion in how they do so up to a predefined credit line that is specific to the counterparty or security issuer in question. Counterparties whose credit line utilization is below the maximum are typically considered authorized counterparties, at least for deals up to a certain size. If during the course of the day the decisions of multiple managers to spend more of a counterparty's credit line than is available in aggregate, corrective actions are typically required *ex post*.

To take an example, suppose Company Spielberg defines a maximum credit exposure to Bank Lucas as $1,000,000 based solely on the principal outstanding in credit-sensitive assets. At the start of a trading day, suppose only $500,000 of that line is being utilized with existing open transactions. Under this type of credit risk tolerance and control system, it is entirely plausible that multiple business managers acting independently of one another could burn through *more* than $500,000 in credit in a day—for example, the treasurer obtains a new $500,000 letter of credit, and the export division secures $500,000 in trade financing. Under this second management style, both transactions would be permitted *ex ante*. When the overutilization of the credit line to Bank Lucas by Company Spielberg is detected through the monitoring process, either the line will be raised if appropriate to accommodate both transactions or some action will have to be taken to reduce the credit exposure (e.g., collateral requested from Bank Lucas or the early termination of one of the credit-sensitive transactions).

A fundamentally different credit risk management philosophy involves the extension of *internal* credit lines. A firm extends internal credit lines to business managers whose actions impact the firm's credit exposures, and managers are allowed to spend that credit line however they see fit *subject to* a charge of some kind. This capital charge may be a flat charge defined by firm or by category, or may be based on some form of internal ratings-based approach in which the firm defines the price of risk for specific firms or types of firms. Some relatively more sophisticated companies rely on internal models in which exposure is measured and compared to tolerances not just based on the credit quality of the counterparty, but also on the total portfolio of exposures the firm has with that counterparty over some period of time.

For firms adopting either a credit limit or credit line perspective, credit risk management means comparing actual exposures to risk tolerances either *ex ante* or *ex post*. For firms that define an internal line and *price of credit*, credit risk management is inextricably tied to capital allocation—a subject to which we return in Chapter 20.

CHAPTER 17

Identifying, Measuring, and Monitoring Liquidity Risk

In this and the next two chapters, the identification, measurement, and monitoring of several other important financial risks are briefly discussed—liquidity risk, operational risk, and legal risk. The absence of any explicit discussion of risks like customer loss risk, strategic risk, supply chain risk, and reputational risk is not meant to minimize their importance. Those risks are not discussed formally here because they represent *business* risks, not purely *financial* risks.

One reason for the brevity of this chapter and the next two is the state of flux and progress on the risks discussed here. Operational risk, in particular, is presently being examined by industry and regulatory organizations alike. Measuring operational risk is quite fashionable at the moment, and by the time this book is at press any serious discussion here would already be outdated.

Similarly, legal and regulatory risk depends so strongly on the current legal and regulatory environments and the country of focus that any detailed discussion here is simply not practical. Not only is law and regulation constantly changing as it pertains to financial instruments in particular, but the geographical disparities in even the most stable financial regulations provide enough material for a book of its own.

Accordingly, Chapters 17 through 19 are attempts to raise only the highest level issues pertaining to how companies should integrate liquidity, operational, and legal/regulatory risk into their EWRM processes.

Liquidity risk means very different things to different people. To a banker or traditional corporate CFO, liquidity risk is likely synonymous with the risk that cash balances unexpectedly fall and jeopardize the sustained payment of current operating expenses and liabilities. To a capital markets participant or trader, liquidity risk more likely means the problems associated with liquidating or hedging a position that is losing value rapidly. When we wish to distinguish between them, we shall refer to the former as *funding risk* and the latter as *market liquidity risk*.

Both perspectives are correct. In fact, funding risk is determined in large part by market liquidity risk. So, although some specific types of firms might separate out the management of funding and market liquidity risk, we treat the two as interrelated here, as they often should be treated in an EWRM framework.

IDENTIFYING LIQUIDITY RISK

Liquidity typically means access to sufficient cash to fund normal business operations without having to incur the distressed debt costs of raising additional monies at a disadvantageous time. In essence, as Uyemura and Van Deventer (1993) put it, "Liquidity buys time to work out problems."

For financial and nonfinancial institutions alike, funding risk arises both from the balance sheet and from off-balance-sheet activities. Specifically, the *net liquid assets* of a firm can be defined as the difference between its *liquid assets* and *volatile liabilities*.[1]

Liquid assets typically include cash, money market accounts, demand deposits, and term deposits or placements with short maturities (e.g., six months). Other liquid assets include any contracts that are callable on short notice for cash, such as callable or short-term reverse repurchase agreements in which the firm has borrowed a security in exchange for liquid collateral or cash. By returning the security, the liquid collateral or cash can usually be retrieved quickly.

The treatment of securities may depend both on the nature of the securities and the accounting treatment accorded those securities if the firm is concerned with earnings as well as cash flows. Securities classified as *held to maturity* can only be liquidated at a fairly substantial penalty to earnings and thus are not considered liquid assets unless they are close to maturity. Securities *available for sale* may be liquid assets, especially if they are eligible to be pledged in a repurchase agreement. In other words, if the firm can lend the security for cash, the security is typically considered relatively liquid.

Liabilities are usually classified as either *stable* or *volatile*, where stable liabilities involve fairly predictable and/or manageable cash flows.[2] Short-term fixed liabilities like commercial paper and maturing long-term debt are considered fairly stable. Call provisions can be used to convert long-term debt into stable liabilities, as well. And, of course, equity and equity-like exposures are stable. By contrast, noncallable long-term debt, debt that requires repo-eligible collateral, and long-term purchase agreements are examples of liabilities with relatively higher volatilities.

Off-balance-sheet exposures with two-sided credit risk—forwards, futures, and swaps—also exhibit two-sided funding risk because they may be current assets or liabilities. The degree to which these exposures can be converted into cash thus dictates both their liquidity and their potential volatility. A futures contract, for example, can usually be offset almost immediately, and positive cash balances can be withdrawn each day. But if the position is losing money, margin deposits are required to service the position each day. Culp and Miller (1995a) refer to the "hedger's ruin" problem as arising when futures are used as a *value* hedge of a long-term asset or liability that is not marked to market. Although the position may be hedged in a value sense, the cash required to meet margin calls in the event the futures take a hit early on can be so large that the entire position must be prematurely liquidated.

Credit risk can also precipitate funding problems. The default of a counterparty on an in-the-money transaction may deprive a firm of badly needed cash. This, in turn, could cause the firm to default on obligations of its own. And if the firm has contracts with cross-default provisions, its default on one obligation could be a trigger for the selective or automatic early termination of still additional contracts on which the firm owes money. In this sense, even failed trades that will be eventually settled in full can lead to serious funding problems.

MEASURING LIQUIDITY RISK

Liquidity risk can and should be measured and monitored by *all* firms with a comprehensive risk management process—not just cash flow hedgers. To the extent a firm has a lot of equity capital and a high level of net liquid assets, however, the firm may be able to avoid truly complex modeling of liquidity risks; simple, static measures may be enough. But the lower a firm's net liquid assets and the more the firm is strategically motivated to manage cash flow risk, the more attention must be paid to liquidity risk measurement issues. The strategic rationale for a firm's decision to manage its risks also may affect the degree to which liquidity risk management is important. In particular, any theory of value-added risk management based on the firm's internal funding situation may create a role for liquidity risk management and monitoring. FSS-style cash flow hedgers will measure and monitor liquidity risks, as noted, to avoid excessive cash flow volatility. But firms concerned that *too much* internal cash may lead to suboptimal investment decisions—as in the models of Jensen and Meckling and Jensen—may also need to use liquidity risk measures to ensure that cash flows are not reduced *too much* to inhibit the normal operation of the business. Even then, liquidity risk monitoring can itself be a useful check and balance on how the managers of the firm are utilizing its liquidity balances.

The Liquidity Gap

The banking industry suggests several static measures of liquidity risk that nevertheless can be very revealing about the vulnerability of a firm's cash balances to market and credit risk. Perhaps the most basic measure of liquidity risk is just the net liquid assets of a firm on its own—sometimes called the *liquidity gap* because of its similarity to the traditional interest income gap presented in Chapter 15.[3] When the number is a negative, the firm's liquid assets exceed its volatile liabilities. A company with a negative net liquid asset number thus should be extremely attentive to cash balances and potential unexpected changes in those cash balances.

Liquidity Risk Elasticity

An alternative measure of liquidity risk, similar to the use of duration as a measure of interest rate risk, is the *liquidity risk elasticity* (LRE) of a portfolio of exposures.[4] The LRE for a set of exposures is the change in the net of assets over funded liabilities that occurs when the liquidity premium on the bank's marginal funding cost rises by a small amount:

$$\frac{\partial NA(t)}{\partial \Xi} = \frac{\partial A(t)}{\partial \Xi} - w \frac{\partial L(t)}{\partial \Xi} \tag{17.1}$$

where $A(t)$ and $L(t)$ are current values of assets and liabilities—often *liquid* assets and *volatile* liabilities—w is the proportion of liabilities funded with the assets, and Ξ is the liquidity premium on the firm's funding cost. The liquidity premium Ξ may be expressed as a spread over LIBOR or Fed Funds if the institution is a bank or a spread over the commercial paper rate if the firm is a nonfinancial.

The LRE of the firm can be calculated for the firm or a set of exposures numerically in a manner similar to what we called *full revaluation* in Chapter 15. First, the firm computes the present value of its liquidity-sensitive assets net of liabilities for a given term structure of interest rates presumed to reflect the firm's normal funding costs. Next, the firm recomputes the PV of its net assets for a small increase in its funding spread over Treasuries that can be viewed as the liquidity premium the firm will have to pay if it must incur new debt on distressed financing terms in order to sustain its short-run operations. The sensitivity of the firm's net assets to a change in its funding liquidity premium then can be expressed as an elasticity:

$$LRE = \eta_{A(t) \bullet \Xi} = \left[\frac{\partial NA(t)}{\partial \Xi} \right] \frac{\Xi}{NA(t)}$$

Like duration, the LRE suffers from several limitations. First, this measure of liquidity risk is effective only for small changes in funding costs. Second, the embedded presupposition in the above expression is that the firm experiences a *parallel* shift in its funding costs across all maturities.

Asset Liquidation Cost

At the core of the liquidity risk management problem is the time it takes to liquidate assets for cash. This cost will be impacted by the time period over which the asset must be sold, the type of asset, the fungibility of an asset, and the market microstructure in which the asset trades. With these sources of impact in hand, the firm can try to measure its liquidity risks as a function of asset liquidation costs.

Liquidation Time Horizon All else equal, the faster an asset must be sold, the higher its liquidation costs. Not only will the firm not have time to pursue all cost-minimizing alternative sale mechanisms, but the firm also runs the risk of being perceived as having a *fire sale*—that is, everyone knows the firm needs cash, making it less likely that the firm will get fair prices for its assets, just as a store will take whatever it can get to sell goods damaged following a fire. Even in the absence of the appearance of a fire sale, the optimal liquidation time horizon is not always immediate. Large sales of assets at the same time, after all, will tend to depress prices purely for supply reasons, thereby suggesting that a slower sell-off—especially of very large positions—can make some sense.

The speed of liquidation of assets for cash thus involves a delicate trade-off. On the one hand, a faster asset sale may be warranted to rectify a cash balance deficit and/or to hedge or liquidate positions exposed to significant amounts of market risk. On the other hand, selling too fast can both create the appearance of a panic sell-off and an adverse market impact on realized sale prices for large orders.

Asset Type   The type of asset affects its liquidation cost through several avenues. The most obvious is the degree of complexity of the asset. Simple assets like short-term Treasuries are easier to liquidate because the number of counterparties that *already understand* the risk/return characteristics of the asset likely will be reasonably high. A complex structured note, by contrast, make be harder for potential buyers to analyze, thereby creating a hesitancy to buy the asset from the selling firm quickly and at a fair price. A related liquidation cost associated with asset type is the complexity of the pricing model required to determine theoretical values and hedge ratios. Other things equal, the harder an asset is to price, the harder it will be for firms to hedge and the less a counterparty will pay for it.

Asset Fungibility   The degree to which an asset is fungible also affects its liquidation cost. Futures are contracts with a clearing house central counterparty and thus can be liquidated by offset. Securities are also fungible, although they cannot simply be offset. A buyer—often in a decentralized market—must be identified. And assets like certificates of deposit and in-the-money swaps are *not* fungible. They must be unwound by negotiation with the counterparty.

Nonfungible assets that must be unwound rather than offset or sold are subject to potential bilateral monopoly bargaining problems. If Firm Zermatterhof *knows* its counterparty Firm Baur Au Lac is experiencing a liquidity crisis, for example, Zermatterhof may not release Baur Au Lac from its obligations at a fair price. Zermatterhof may be forced to take a discount on the replacement cost of the asset.

Drexel Burnham Lambert Group, Inc. (DBL Group) filed for chapter 11 status on February 13, 1990, but did *not* require many of its capital market subsidiaries to file for bankruptcy at the same time. DBL Trading Corporation, for example, was left to resolve over $50 billion in foreign exchange, oil, and precious metals contracts, and began a massive liquidation of its entire portfolio immediately after DBL Group filed its bankruptcy petition. By the end of February 1990, most of its positions had been closed out. Although many counterparties that owed money to DBL Trading willingly paid their obligated cash flows in an effort to end their relationship with a failing institution, other counterparties attempted to take advantage of DBL Trading by charging excessive prices and spreads to close out positions—to take advantage of the bilateral monopoly bargaining problem created by the fact that the counterparty's consent is required to get out of an OTC derivatives position.[5]

Similarly, at least a year prior to the failure of the Bank of New England (BNE)—which finally occurred on January 6, 1991—traders had been attempting to unwind BNE's portfolio of about $36 billion in OTC derivatives. Traders reported numerous counterparties attempting to extract nuisance fees from BNE to close out their positions. This reportedly resulted in millions of dollars in losses for BNE.[6]

Market Microstructure   The microstructure of a market is the set of rules—explicit and implicit—that determine the process and outcomes of asset trading and exchange decisions.[7] Two major determinants of a market's microstructure are its temporal aggregation mechanism and its dealership structure.[8] Temporal aggregation refers to the timing of trading decisions. In a *call market,* trading occurs synchronously at preestablished times, whereas *continuous markets* involve asynchronous trading during long intervals of time. The auction of U.S. Treasury securities is an example of a call market, whereas the 24-hour market for trading foreign exchange is an example of a continuous market. Futures and securities listed and traded on organized exchanges fall in between.

The dealership structure of a market relates to the provision of immediacy in a market—namely, who provides such immediacy.[9] In a decentralized market, buyers and sellers come together, identify one another, and trade with one another. Any agent can be a buyer or a seller, and no agent has the responsibility to maintain a continuous presence in the market to facilitate buying and selling. The Chicago Mercantile Exchange and Chicago Board of Trade are classic decentralized markets in this sense.

At the other extreme, a market maker may be designated as the official supplier of liquidity. The market maker is charged with maintaining continuous two-sided markets—a market to buy *and* to sell. Specialists on the New York Stock Exchange (NYSE) are examples of designated market makers.

In between the two extremes, dealers in foreign exchange and swaps may function much of the time like market makers, providing immediacy and quoting two-sided prices. Unlike NYSE specialists, however, dealers are not *obligated* to maintain a continuous market presence, and, especially in periods of market instability, often do not.

Liquidation costs can be significantly impacted by the microstructure of the market in which an asset is being liquidated. During times of crisis, a continuous market likely will be preferred to a call market. Although prices could be more favorable in the latter because the firm's desperation will not be as evident, the delay in trading between call periods could be longer than the firm can bear. The dealership structure of a market may be less important, provided the depth of the market is adequate to support the liquidating firm's asset sales. In other words, an informal market with a large number of dealers might be preferable to a formal market maker system because the number of potential buyers is greater.[10]

A crude measure of the liquidity of a market is the bid-ask spread, or the difference in the price at which market participants are willing to buy and sell the same asset at the same point in time. The bid-ask spread is explicit and observable in dealer markets where a market maker maintains two-way quotes. Liquidity can be inferred under certain assumptions about this spread. First, we must assume that trades can be simultaneously crossed at this spread—both a buy and a sell occur at the prevailing spread either instantaneously or without any change in the spread. This is quite unrealistic, of course, and has been cited as a major limitation on the use of spreads as a measure of market liquidity.[11]

Second, the spread is presumed to reflect a stable market impact function that relates the cost of transacting to order size. In other words, a *given* spread likely will be valid only for orders up to a certain size. Larger sale (purchase) orders will put downward (upward) pressure on prices to clear the market. Endogenizing this market impact into any particular observation of the spread is empirically challenging but critical if the spread is to be used as a measure of liquidation costs.

A third problem with using the bid-ask spread as a measure of liquidation cost is knowing which spread to use. In a dealership market that allows both market and limit orders, transactions within the spread often occur, which means the *effective* spread—deviation of actual transaction prices from the midpoint of the bid and the offer—can differ dramatically from the *quoted* spread.[12] And in a completely decentralized market like a futures market, the spread is defined simply as the bounce between bids and offers that are shouted or placed into the system consecutively until a transaction occurs.[13]

Whether suppliers of immediacy are all market participants collectively in a decentralized market or one or more dealers in a more organized market, the supply of immediacy—the provision of order execution on demand—is costly. If we are willing to accept the above assumptions about the spread, the quoted or effective bid-ask spread becomes one possible measure of those costs of supplying liquidity, including operational or administrative costs associated with processing order flow, inventory carrying costs, hedging costs, and the costs of any asymmetric information that may lead dealers to believe they have inferior information to some of the firms with which they are transacting.[14] Consequently, the bid-ask spread is perhaps the most commonly used quantitative measure of the cost of asset liquidation in a given market. This measure is traditionally defined relative to the mid-point between the bid and offer to convert the dollar spread into a type of percentage. For some asset j at time t whose bid and offer prices are $P_{t,j}^b$ and $P_{t,j}^a$, respectively, the bid-ask spread $S_{t,j}$ can be defined as

$$S_{t,\,j} = \frac{P^a_{t,\,j} - P^b_{t,\,j}}{\frac{1}{2}\left(P^a_{t,\,j} + P^b_{t,\,j}\right)} = \frac{P^a_{t,\,j} - P^b_{t,\,j}}{P^{mid}_{t,\,j}} \tag{17.2}$$

Cash Flows at Risk and Scenario Analysis

As discussed in Chapter 15, a summary risk measure analogous to VaR exists for use by cash flow risk managers or firms concerned about the funding risk of a position or portfolio of positions. Cash flows at risk (CfaR) is calculated in much the same manner as VaR except that present values are not taken. Instead, cash flows are left in *nominal* dollars when they are due to occur. The result is a *series* of CfaR estimates, each of which represent some tail of a cash flow distribution at a specific point in time.

As noted in Chapter 15, Monte Carlo and historical simulation are often useful methods of cash flow risk measurement because they depend on a sample path of cash flows being generated from the risk measurement date across every period of interest to the end of the risk horizon. Whereas a value risk manager will focus only on the present value of the terminal distribution, a funding risk manager looks at *all* periods.

Another method of funding risk measurement that can prove quite useful to firms is scenario analysis. Particularly important in conducting a scenario analysis of cash balances is to examine situations in which adverse liquidity shocks occur at the same time. A scenario spanning several adverse liquidity shocks might include the following:

- Securities held stop paying interest and dividends.
- Letters of credit and short-term funding guarantees are revoked.
- Putable debt is redeemed.
- Reverse repos, repos, and derivatives counterparties calls for additional collateral.
- Swaps, forwards, and futures require substantial margin or mark-to-market cash flows to keep the positions open, and so on.

LVaR

CfaR is a sensible summary risk measure for firms whose risk management process is focused on cash flow risk. As noted earlier, however, earnings and value risk managers also must be attentive to liquidity risk. Fire-sale losses on assets sold at below their present values to generate cash, after all, affect shareholder value and earnings as much as cash flows.

For a value risk manager concerned with liquidity risk, Jorion (2000) proposes a summary risk measure called *liquidity-adjusted* VaR (LVaR). If the bid-ask spread is constant at $S_{t,j}$ for some asset j, the parametric normal LVaR for that asset then can be computed as follows:

$$LVaR_j(\alpha) = V_{t,j}\left[\mu_j - \lambda(\alpha)\sigma_j + \tfrac{1}{2}S_{t,j}\right] \qquad (17.3)$$

where $V_{t,j}$ is the value of the asset, μ_j and σ_j are its mean and standard deviation of returns, $\lambda(\alpha)$ is the confidence parameter, and $(1 - \alpha)$ is the confidence level of the estimate. Notice that the spread is multiplied by one-half to reflect the fact that a liquidation would constitute only a sale and not a round turn, whereas the actual spread measures the cost of supplying immediacy for a round trip.

When the spread varies over time, LVaR can be modified to take into consideration the worst-case execution spread.[15] Just as VaR is a worst-case estimate of market risk at confidence level $(1 - \alpha)$, the worst-case spread can be defined for some confidence level $(1 - \alpha^*)$ as

$$\tfrac{1}{2}\left\{V_{t,j}\left[\mu_S + \lambda(\alpha^*)\sigma_S\right]\right\}$$

where μ_j and σ_j are the mean and volatility *of the spread.* LVaR is then defined as

$$LVaR_j(\alpha, \alpha^*) = V_{t,j}\left\{\mu_j - \lambda(\alpha)\sigma_j + \tfrac{1}{2}\left[\mu_S + \lambda(\alpha^*)\sigma_S\right]\right\} \qquad (17.4)$$

As in the parametric normal approach, correlations across *spreads* over different assets can also be taken into account.

If a firm prefers not to adopt the parametric normal approach to VaR measurement, spread risk as a measure of asset liquidation costs can be incorporated into the other approaches, as well. In Monte Carlo, the spread can be presumed to evolve according to a stochastic process of its own that is correlated with the evolution of the asset itself. Bivariate Monte Carlo then yields the single-asset LVaR. Similarly, historical spreads can be used to reflect liquidity costs in either historical or historical simulation LVaR estimates.

The above liquidity-risk-adjusted measures of market risk are *static* because they assume no change in the composition of the portfolio over the VaR horizon. Consequently, the market impact is ignored, or, equivalently, is presumed not to impact the spread in any predictable manner. As noted, moreover, the time horizon of the liquidation also affects the risk of the asset sale. A slower liquidation implies better pricing and less market impact, but leaves the firm exposed to market risk for a longer period of time.

For a more detailed discussion of how trading strategies designed to address the tradeoff between price impact and market risk of timed liquidations, see Jorion (2000) and the references therein.

MONITORING LIQUIDITY RISK

As with the other risks we have discussed in this book, stakeholders of the company and the owners of the risk management process should work together to define liquidity risk tolerances. How these tolerances are expressed likely will depend on how liquidity risk is measured.

Apart from sound liquidity risk measurement and monitoring relative to pre-defined tolerances, companies can also take several basic steps to minimize their undesired liquidity risk exposures from the outset. One such step is for companies to diversify their liquidity risks across sources of liquidity. Provided funding is available to a firm on comparable terms by several providers, the company should consider defining tolerances on a firm-specific basis and then spreading its liquidity sources around. Standby liquidity provision facilities obtained from several banks, for example, are usually recommendable vis-à-vis the single-bank solution, provided any difference in the marginal funding cost across the banks does not exceed the liquidity premium the firm would have to pay to issue distressed debt.

Sound scenario analysis-based contingency planning will also help firms manage their liquidity risks. Return, for example, to the hedger's ruin example mentioned earlier in which a lack of margin financing forces a firm to prematurely terminate an otherwise hedged position.[16] Firms hoping to initiate potentially cash-intensive financial or business programs might be well advised, for example, to do an unsecured borrowing *up front* equal to the initial face value of the total hedge/futures position—a so-called *pure synthetic* strategy. Rather than depositing only the required minimum initial margin with a futures exchange clearinghouse, such firms could give this *total amount* to the clearinghouse in T-bills thus ensuring that no further cash outlays would be required over the life of the hedge, regardless of price movements.

It can be argued that no lender could have assurance that the unsecured loan would in fact be used to purchase T-bills and posted as margin. But this potential agency problem could be solved by requiring the borrower to keep the funds on deposit at the lender bank. The lender bank would then pay all variation margin calls of the borrower by drawing down its margin-equivalent deposit account.[17]

LIQUIDITY RISK AND CRISIS MANAGEMENT

Despite all good intentions and best laid risk management plans, problems may still arise. What should a firm do if it *does* find itself in a liquidity crunch?

First and foremost, the firm should try at all costs to avoid the appearance to the market of a fire sale. Otherwise, a classic "bank run" problem can result in which a solvent firm is forced to sell assets at below-market prices to generate cash, but the losses on the asset sales as market participants circle the wagons become so large that a liquidity crisis *becomes* a solvency crisis. To combat this, firms should communicate with the market about the sources of its liquidity problems and should avoid panic selling.

An excellent illustration of how *not* to manage liquidity risk when it becomes reality is provided by the case of the U.S. firm Metallgesellschaft Refining & Marketing, Inc. (MGRM).[18] MGRM undertook in the early 1990s a marketing program under which it offered long-term customers fixed-price guarantees for up to 10 years on crude oil products purchased from MGRM. By December 1993, MGRM had sold over 150 million bbls. of oil in its creative marketing program. To avoid speculating on the future direction of oil prices, MGRM hedged its entire future delivery obligations using mainly short-dated futures contracts and commodity swaps. As Culp and Miller have argued extensively, the particular hedging strategy MGRM used successfully insulated the firm from the risk of rising spot prices.[19] But when oil prices plummeted in 1993, cash payments were required to meet margin calls on the losing futures leg and collateral calls on MGRM's swaps.

In December 1993 after a year of falling prices and rising margin calls, the supervisory board of Metallgesellschaft AG—parent company of MGRM—ordered the liquidation of substantial portions of MGRM's futures hedge and subsequently canceled up to 40 million bbls. of its customer contracts.

By tabulating MGRM's cash drains on its hedge transactions, the special auditors of MGRM estimated MGRM's total *gross* derivatives-related loss from June 1, 1992, through December 31, 1993, as $1.277 billion.[20] What matters to stockholders, however, are the *net* losses after allowing for gains on the other leg. To arrive at their *net* loss estimate, the auditors subtracted $233 million for the positive value of MGRM's various fixed-price delivery contracts on the other leg of the hedge. Adding another $16 million for interest and other costs, the auditors arrive at a net loss of $1.06 billion.

Just how the auditors arrived at their estimate of the value of MGRM's contracts on the other leg is far from clear. And without access to the company books or to the precise valuation formulas the auditors used but did not present, outsiders have no way to verify the calculations. Culp and

Miller (1995a,b) argue that the auditors' estimate for the value of MGRM's customer contracts was far too low, and their net loss estimate thus was far too high. They contend that the firm's net 1993 loss was about $200 million—a far cry from the auditors' $1.06 billion.

Losing even $200 million is hardly pleasant, but even a $200 million net loss for 1993 does not justify the supervisory board's decision to wind down the program by liquidating part of the futures/swaps hedge and canceling some of the customer contracts *with no compensation required from customers*. First, MG AG might have used MGRM's positively-valued hedged customer contracts as security for loans to finance the continuation of the combined marketing/hedging program after 1993. Culp and Miller's (1995a) $200 million estimated 1993 net loss, after all, was simply the cumulated loss through the first year of the program's operation. That loss was *not* guaranteed to persist for the remaining nine years. Had the program continued, in fact, it would likely have shown a *profit* in 1994 and thereafter. Assuming MGRM set the fixed-selling prices in its contracts above the spot price when the program was started, as Culp and Miller (1995c) argue, it would have locked in a gross profit margin on its hedged contracts sufficient to provide security for at least some form of bridge loan.

Second, if MGRM's major creditors and shareholders—including Deutsche Bank and Dresdner Bank—had been unwilling to continue funding the program, the supervisory board might have directed that MGRM's hedged customer contracts be sold to another firm. Culp and Miller (1995a) estimate that if MGRM had been able to sell the combined program for its year-end 1993 capital asset value, it would have received nearly $800 million from the sale. MGRM's *net* 1993 loss would still have been about $200 million, or roughly the same as if the program had been continued. But the sale would at least have halted the cash drains with which the supervisory board had become so concerned.

Third, the supervisory board could have instructed MGRM to buy back its customer contracts by unwinding them. When the market smells trouble, unwinding bilateral contracts rarely nets the unwinding firm a cash flow equal to the actual capital value of the contract. (See Chapter 19 for a further discussion of this issue.) That MGRM might not have collected from its customers the same $800 million it could have made by selling the program to another firm is thus plausible. But between the time MGRM negotiated the fixed prices on its customer contracts and year-end 1993, the oil spot price had fallen by nearly $5.75/bbl. Unless MGRM negotiated its contracts at a *massive* initial loss, customers should have been willing to pay *something* to get out of their contracts.

A former MGRM employee explained that on December 22, 1993, one of MGRM's biggest customers paid MGRM $2 million to unwind its fixed-price contracts. Two months later when many of MGRM's similar contracts were canceled with no compensation required from customers, MG *refunded* the $2 million it had been paid earlier. Although it is not clear whether the $2 million paid was a reasonable estimate of that customer's actual contract value, much less what other customers would have paid, it is likely that if one of them was willing to pay, so were others.

In sum, MG AG's supervisory board had at least three viable alternatives in December 1993: secure additional financing and continue the program intact, sell the program to another firm, or unwind the contracts with the original customers. Instead, the supervisory board chose the profit *minimizing* solution of liquidating much of the hedging program and then letting its customers off the hook. The supervisory board thus pursued the *worst possible course of action* in December 1993 and increased, perhaps dramatically, the price tag paid by shareholders for MGRM's ultimate bailout.

CHAPTER 18

Identifying, Measuring, and Monitoring Operational Risk

Operational risk has been defined by the International Swaps and Derivatives Association, British Bankers' Association, and RMA as "the risk of loss resulting from inadequate or failed internal processes, people, and systems or from external events."[1] Examples of losses that can be attributed to operational risk include failed securities trades, settlement errors in funds transfers, stolen or damaged physical assets, damages awarded in court proceedings, penalties and fines assessed by member associations or regulators, irrecoverable or erroneous funds and asset transfers, unbudgeted personnel costs, and negligence or fraud.[2]

Developments in operational risk (op risk) management are occurring extremely rapidly, both on the risk measurement side and the risk management side. Even the definition of operational risk is under debate.[3] Needless to say, this makes the subject quite difficult to write about. Nevertheless, the basic principles associated with defining and identifying operational risk, developing some form of quantitative framework for operationalizing op risk, and comparing the outcomes from that framework to the strategic and tactical risk management objectives of a company are fairly well-defined. Those basic principles are reviewed briefly in this chapter.

IDENTIFYING SOURCES OF OPERATIONAL RISK

Risks like market and credit risk can often lurk undetected in hidden exposures of a company. Operational risk seems to suffer the reverse malady—the concept itself is so broad that operational risk can be found in just about *everything*. For this reason, identifying op risk in general should not be the goal of the firm. Rather, identifying *meaningful* operational risks that can have a significant impact on the value of the firm is the task at hand, and it is not an easy one.

Operational risk identification is more art than science and can get sticky for several reasons. First, the definition of operational risk and its distinction from *business risk* at any particular firm depends strongly on the risk management *and* business strategies of the firm. A company in the commodity export business, for example, bears a number of supply chain and logistic risks—crop spoilage, processing plant malfunctions, quality verification problems, truck breakdowns, worker strikes. As an expert on supply chain issues, the firm may well consider all those risks as normal business risks well within the purview of its expertise. If those same risks faced a bank, it might be tempting to call them op risks. But when facing the commodity exporter whose main business is dealing with those aspects of supply chain management, differentiating between business risk and op risk is tough.

A second complication to operational risk identification arises from the linkage between the risk and loss. Operational risk-related losses are quite often driven by market, credit, or liquidity risks. The failure of Barings to catch the huge position build-up by rogue trader Nick Leeson was in some sense an operational risk management failure. It was a failure of processes (i.e., internal audit and control), people (i.e., Leeson was defrauding the firm and others), and systems (i.e., a consolidated global position-keeping system would have revealed Leeson's rogue positions). But in the end, Barings went bust because Leeson's positions went underwater as a result of their market risk. Operational risk management may have failed to catch the process, personnel, and systems problem, but market risk sank the firm.

Most operational risks ultimately translate into potential losses for a firm because the operational risks expose the firm to market, credit, or liquidity risk. Separating op risk-driven market risk losses from normal business-related market risk losses, for example, is complicated to be sure.

Yet a third reason that op risk is a slippery thing to identify is driven by the different organizational processes that firms use to address operational risk. Some firms address op risk on an ad hoc basis, whereas others have appointed Heads of Operational Risk Management. Similarly, banks and nonfinancial corporations tend to view op risk through different lenses. For banks, op risk is an internal risk that is only recently being addressed in any formal context. But for nonfinancial firms like Schindler Elevator or Boeing, the operational risks associated with product management and potential product liability captured the undivided attention of risk management personnel long before market and credit risk did at many firms.

The wide gulf that separates one firm from the next in its degree of op risk management preparedness and awareness is in large part *cultural*. Firms like Schindler have a risk culture that leads to zero tolerance for operational faults on its elevators, but its risk culture may not have absorbed the same philosophy for interest rate and exchange rate risk. Conversely, banks like Barings may claim to have little tolerance for naked market risk exposures, but their cultural disposition to risks like internal control failures and fragmented IT systems obviously was *not* one of low tolerance.

Stages of Evolution in Op Risk Management

The BBA/ISDA/RMA (1999) survey notes that companies typically evolve through five stages of operational risk management maturity. Any given company may have a very different conception of op risk depending on the stage at which they are and thus may tend to define its tolerance for operational risk accordingly.

The first stage of op risk management is called the traditional baseline stage. This is the most informal treatment of op risk that a firm can exhibit. The firm has no processes or personnel dedicated to op risk in particular, but rather manages op risks on an ad hoc basis through other business processes like internal audit. Tolerance for operational risks likely will be determined at such firms on an entirely *reactive* basis—once encountered, managers will make a case-by-case determination of whether the uncovered op risk is a risk with which the firm can live.

In the second evolutionary stage of op risk management, firms enter into awareness that op risk must be explicitly addressed. Personnel are appointed with op risk-specific responsibilities, and senior managers and directors begin to craft policies and procedures for the systematic identification, measurement, monitoring, and control of op risks. The ownership of op risk management is clearly defined in this stage to be at the level of individual business units, and op risk exposure tolerances—albeit still vague and ad hoc—will start to be defined at the business unit level.

The third stage in the evolution of op risk management is the monitoring stage. At this stage, the notion of explicit and formal risk tolerances for op risk first begins to emerge, albeit on a largely *qualitative* basis. The business begins to focus on tracking internal risk indicators, op risk scoring systems, and business unit performance measurement adjusted for op risk. Senior managers and directors define and express their tolerances for op risks based on these qualitative and pseudo-quantitative criteria *and* in the context of the business and risk management strategies of the firm.

In the fourth stage of op risk management evolution, a firm finally develops a quantitative system of some kind for the formal measurement of op risks on a business unit basis. Only at this stage can senior managers and directors begin to articulate their tolerances for operational risk along a dimension that can be consistently and regularly compared to an actual *measure* of current op risk exposure. Also at this stage, a firm is presumed to have developed an operational risk management function, either independent or within an EWRM unit under the CRO.

Finally, a firm matures into the integration stage where op risk becomes a fully integrated part of a comprehensive EWRM process. Quantitative op risk measures are then integrated into other risk measures and reports, and the risk tolerances of the firm become defined at much more general levels—for example, firmwide VaR inclusive of integrated market, credit, liquidity, and operational risk sources.

In all five of the above stages, the company's risk culture and risk management strategy will play a paramount role in helping the firm understand and articulate its risk tolerances. As noted, nonfinancials used to operational risk management in product line areas will find the progression in many ways much easier than financial institutions whose business is more directly tied to financial risk. But despite the difficulty of shepherding the evolution of op risk management through these five stages, it *is* an important risk, and stakeholder tolerances thus *must* be defined as a precursor to any effective risk management process.

MEASURING OPERATIONAL RISK

Very few firms have evolved to the full maturity end of the op risk management spectrum. Consequently, op risk measurement methods and their integration to a broader op risk management process are diverse and vary widely across firms and industries.

One major reason for the huge disparity in op risk measurement methods is the lack of data on operational losses at many firms. Experience with large losses owing to operational risks may be infrequent, and the firm may not have tracked those losses that did occur. Because op risks are inherently firm-specific, the absence of such data is a real obstacle in sound op risk measurement.[4]

ISDA (2000) characterizes four basic types of op risk measurement regimes, each of which is summarized next.

The "Basic Indicator" Regime

A basic indicator op risk measurement regime typically relies on one or two risk indicators that are coarsely defined. A basic indicator risk measurement regime is usually accompanied by a reasonably decentralized and ad hoc op risk management process that emphasizes existing control structures like internal audit to facilitate op risk management.

Several basic indicators may be used for op risk measurement in this kind of regime. An industry or regulatory measure of op risk, for example, can allow the firm to incur essentially no effort to measure its *own, unique* op risks but instead at least to rely on standardized operational loss information about broad classifications of firms, industries, and sectors.

One type of basic indicator that firms should *not* adopt is a residual earnings volatility approach. This method of op risk measurement entails calculating a firmwide EaR and then *subtracting* risks otherwise attributable. The residual EaR after subtracting earnings at risk due to market, credit, and liquidity risk, for example, would be a basic indicator of the firm's op risk.

The residual earnings volatility approach is fundamentally flawed for several reasons. Most importantly, residual earnings op risk measures presuppose that every other risk facing the firm is measurable and has been measured properly, including the strategic and business risks that are not included in op risk. Yet, for reasons discussed in Part One of the book, many firms have no reason to quantify and manage their *business* risks. Consequently, the residual EaR likely will lump together op risk with any number of other risks that a selective risk manager has chosen to tolerate rather than measure and manage.

Residual earnings-based op risk measures also de facto assume independence between market, credit, and op risk. But as noted earlier with the example of Barings, these risks clearly are *not* independent.

Finally, residual earnings volatility is inherently historical in nature, so that op risks to which the firm is exposed that have never impacted earnings will also be omitted. Just because a massive flood or fire has never destroyed the firm's assets and systems does not mean that op risk can be ignored, although in fact it *would be* ignored in a historically calculated residual earnings basic indicator of op risk.

The "Standard Lines of Business" Regime

The second op risk measurement regime identified by ISDA (2000) is accompanied by more structure along all dimensions. The op risk management process is more clearly defined and less ad hoc, and the firm is presumed to have articulated some basic set of op risk tolerances at the business unit level. Accordingly, op risk can be measured at the business unit level in this regime.

Common forms of op risk measurement within this regime include industry-level indices of risk categorized by business line type, as well as self-assessments of business-unit-specific op risks. Surveys and other techniques may be used to help the firm develop a Risk Map of op risks at the business unit level. Online risk measurement facilities like Measurisk.com often provide standardized op risk surveys to help firms give more structure to these self-assessments.

The "Internal Ratings" Regime

Called the internal risk regime by ISDA (2000), internal ratings better conveys the intent behind this type of op risk measure given our discussion of such internal ratings methods for credit risk measurement in Chapter 16. In a manner similar to the use of internal ratings for credit risk, op risk internal ratings are subjectively determined quantitative ratings that are assigned to specific op risk factors in individual business units.

An internal ratings based approach may or may not be dependent on historical operational risk and loss data. Even firms with sound and well-defined, comprehensive op risk management processes may not have a decent time series of historical loss data from which to draw probabilistic inferences about future op risk-related losses. Consequently, expert systems like those found in credit risk management are common sources of internal op risk ratings.

The "Internal Models" Regime

Again akin to the use of the term in Chapter 16, the internal models approach to op risk measurement typically represents the most advanced available op risk management tool. Such systems are usually based on institution-specific loss data and may rely either on structural econometric models (like credit scoring models) or analytical- and simulation-based *VaR*-like constructs.

Most op risk measurement models bear great similarity to some of the models discussed in Chapter 16 for credit risk measurement. Indeed, a goal of op risk measurement is to generate a figure essentially similar to Figure 16.11 except for *operational risk* losses instead of *credit* losses. As in the cases of market, credit, and liquidity risk, the objective then is yet again to come up with an estimable probability distribution.

Like downgrade or migration risk, operational risk often has two distinctly different sources of randomness—the random arrival of events that lead to losses, and the random size of the loss. As discussed already, the latter is usually dependent on market, credit, or operational risk.

In general terms, suppose the density function for the arrival rate of operational risk loss events is denoted $f(n)$ where n is the number of loss events. Suppose further that the amount of any given loss assuming it occurs only once is denoted $g(x)$. We can then define the total loss as the sum of losses over a random number of loss events:[5]

$$S_n = \sum_{j=1}^{n} x_j$$

So, we are generally left with the need to generate a probability density function for S_n given n, or

$$h(S_n) = \int_{-\infty}^{\infty} g(s \mid n)f(n)dn = \int_{-\infty}^{\infty} g(s, n)dn$$

In other words, the probability density function for total loss S_n is the integral of the *joint* distribution of the size of losses with the occurrence of losses, or, equivalently, the conditional density of loss size given occurrence of losses times the marginal density for the probability of n losses occurring.[6]

Depending on the structure of the distributions involved, the probability densities for loss magnitude and frequency sometimes can be combined into named distributions. Jorion (2000) shows, for example, that if the frequency of losses is geometrically distributed and the severity of losses exponentially distributed, the total loss is also exponentially distributed. If the resulting distribution is not named, then parametric statistical inference may not be possible and simulation methods may have to be used.

One source of op risk noted in Chapter 11 is fragmented IT systems and excessively decentralized IT application and data architectures. Ironically, to achieve an internal model level of sophistication in op risk measurement, this particular source of op risk arising from systems must be virtually negligible *already*. In other words, if the op risks typically associated with fragmented IT infrastructure are a real problem for a company, then that company almost by definition will not be able to implement an effective internal models-based op risk measurement system.

OPERATIONAL RISK MONITORING

ISDA (2000) has set forth six fundamental principles to which any institution should adhere in developing an operational risk management process. The monitoring of op risks vis-à-vis the firm's tolerances for those risks should occur against the firm backdrop of these six principles.

First, ultimate accountability for the management of op risk should lie with the board of directors or the security holders whose welfare is being enhanced by the risk management process. The degree to which op risk is tolerated should be defined on a top-down basis, and business units should accept whatever tolerances and guidelines are articulated by senior managers, directors, and other key risk management process stakeholders.

Second, senior managers and directors should ensure that operational risk management moves out of the traditional baseline stage and evolves into a formal process and framework as quickly as possible. Even if the op risk management process at the firm is relatively immature, organizational responsibilities and lines of reporting concerning op risk should be well-defined and known throughout the organization.

Third, senior managers and directors should ensure that the op risk management process includes an exhaustive internal classification of all types of op risk facing the firm. A catalogue or Risk ID/Risk Map of internal processes, people, and systems and external factors that can create operational risks must be developed and serve as the backbone for the administration of the op risk management process.

Fourth, the firm should produce a set of written policies and procedures that outline the operational risks facing the firm, the tolerances of stakeholders for those risks, and the suggested means by which those risks will be managed. These policies and procedures should be consistent with the risk management strategy of the firm, as well as its overall business strategy.

Fifth, business units and back office support areas should be represented and have a voice in the op risk management process, in a manner reflective of any sound EWRM process as discussed in Chapter 11.

Finally, line management should develop a tactical implementation plan for the day-to-day management of operational risks in a manner consistent with the overall risk management process of the firm. In other words, op risk management should involve identification, measurement, control, and realignment phases just like the comprehensive EWRM. As firms evolve from earlier stages of op risk management maturity to later ones as discussed in the prior section, the op risk management process will simply fold into to the firm's EWRM process.

Ironically, the Bank for International Settlements (1998) reports that as of today, more banks *monitor* operational risk than *measure* it—at least not in the sense of using internal ratings or models. Banks regularly monitor indicators like business unit volume and turnover, settlement fails, delays, errors, and the like. In this sense, operational risk is being *managed* even without the usual processes of op risk identification, measurement, and comparison to tolerances. As the rest of the discussion in this chapter has suggested, however, adding even a degree of formality to ad hoc monitoring processes could provide significant marginal benefits to financial and nonfinancial institutions alike.

CHAPTER 19

Identifying and Managing Legal Risk

The nature of the legal risks that firms can face in their risk management process depends on whether the firm is a risk controller, efficiency enhancer, or risk transformer. Many sources of legal risk are transactional—arising from legal and/or regulatory issues concerning specific transactions. Risk controllers can face such risks through their use of financial instruments, while risk transformers face such risks through their supply of financial instruments. Apart from transactional legal risks, firms also can face legal and regulatory risks at a broader firmwide or strategic level.

Legal risk has so many different dimensions that it is difficult even to *categorize,* much less discuss. This chapter considers risks that arise primarily because of the actions of the firm engaged in risk management or one of its counterparties. We then summarize how the interaction between laws, regulators, and market participants can exacerbate certain uncertainties in the risk management process.

Although firms must strive to *manage* legal risk, it is perhaps the one risk in the risk management process where risk tolerances and the measurement and monitoring of risks relative to those tolerances is not practical. Firms should strive to minimize legal risks on an ongoing basis, but quantifying and systematizing that process is a nearly insurmountable task. Unlike the other risks discussed in Part Two of this book, this is the one risk that probably can be managed as well as possible *without* the aid of formal quantitative risk measurement and monitoring vis-à-vis explicit tolerance levels.

DOCUMENTATION RISK[1]

Documentation risk is the transactional risk that a firm will incur a loss if a contract contains terms in its documentation that are either unenforceable or enforceable in a different manner than the firm had in mind. Examples include the lack of written confirmations for OTC derivatives, ambiguous language or misunderstandings regarding the treatment of holidays in OTC derivatives or other commercial contracts, the enforceability of close-out bilateral netting, the enforceability of multiproduct netting, and the like. All of these documentation risks share the common feature that they are *transactional* risks—risks arising from one or several specific deals, rather than the broad positioning of either the firm or a body of law.

A number of industry associations around the world have sought to bring a level of operational uniformity to documentation in OTC derivatives transactions. The International Swap Dealers Association was formed in 1984 as a trade association designed to provide a forum for the pursuit of issues of common interest to all swap participants. Although ISDA is neither a regulatory nor a self-regulatory body, it exercises a significant amount of influence over the practices of industry participants, both domestically and internationally. In 1993, ISDA changed its name to the International Swaps and Derivatives Association, Inc.

For some years, derivatives transactions were legally governed almost entirely by disparate contracts that were bilaterally negotiated on a product-by-product basis between counterparties. For a number of reasons, this heterogeneity of contracts led to a considerable amount of uncertainty regarding the enforceability of the various provisions in those contracts. Of particular concern was the ability of counterparties to enforce close-out netting provisions, introduced in Chapter 1.

To moderate uncertainty surrounding enforceability, as well as to lower transaction costs for participants in derivatives activity, standardized forms of documentation for OTC derivatives transactions began to evolve. Such documentation is generally offered by ISDA and other industry associations, including the British Bankers Association, the Australian Financial Markets Association, a loose confederation of German bankers, and the Association Francaise des Banques.

In 1987, ISDA formulated its first set of standardized contracts, known as the ISDA Master Agreements, which were substantively revised in 1992. Although the development—and exhaustive legal review—of these pro forma documentation templates has greatly reduced documentation risk for derivatives, misunderstandings still occur. Consider the following examples.

Delays in Obtaining Written Transaction Confirmations

When OTC derivatives like interest rate swaps first became popular, oral confirmations tended to precede written confirmations by a surprisingly long interval of time in quite a few transactions. A survey by the Global Drivatives Study Group (1993) of market practices indicated, for example, that only 39% of respondents normally received a trade confirmation (confirm) from a dealer on the day of the transaction, and only 36% normally received a confirm on the next day. Even fewer reported normally receiving same- or next-day confirms from end users.

Failure to obtain a written confirm expeditiously exposes the firm to the risk that the counterparty has a different understanding of the deal than the firm. Such misunderstandings are often small but important. Interest payments in rate swaps, for example, are calculated on settlement dates based on some "day counting" convention to determine the size of the payment. Popular day counting conventions include Actual/360 Actual/365, Actual/Actual, and 30/360 where Actual denotes the actual number of days between settlements and where the denominator references the number of days in the money market year underlying the reference interest rate. A U.S. dollar swap whose floating leg settles to six-month LIBOR, for example, likely will have interest payments calculated on an Actual/360 basis because the U.S. money market year contains 360 days rather than 365. If a counterparty mistakenly—or deliberately—marks the trade confirm as Actual/365 days, the firm will not know this until the confirm is received.

In recent times, the time gap between oral and written confirms of OTC derivatives has narrowed.[2] Nevertheless, especially for nonfinancial transactions like commercial purchase and sale agreements, documentation backlog remains an issue to which attention must be paid.

Holiday and Weekend Payment or Exercise Conventions

When counterparties in different legal jurisdictions negotiate contracts with one another that involve optional delivery or payment dates, ambiguous documentation can lead to serious problems. Consider a forward purchased by European Firm Rousseau from U.S. Dealer Paine. The documentation must clearly delineate one of three business day conventions: preceding, following, or modified following, all of which relate to the possibility that the value and/or settlement date occurs on a holiday in one jurisdiction—say, Thanksgiving in the United States. "Modified following" means, for example, that if the date of maturity is not a business day, payment of principal and interest required to be made on such date will be made on the next business day with the same impact as if made on such date. No additional interest shall accrue as a result of such delayed payment. Misunderstandings or ambiguities about these business day conventions can lead to serious disagreements on swap and OTC option transactions, in particular.

Even when a transaction is well-documented and clearly specifies a mutually satisfactory business day convention for normal settlements, further problems can arise if *abnormal* activities occur on holidays. Suppose that Broker Burke is clearing futures trades for a wealthy Chinese private banking client, Mr. Fang, who is located in Hong Kong. At the peak of Chinese New Year, Mr. Fang's positions take a radical turn for the worse and a request for margin is sent to his office. Because he is celebrating the holiday, he neither receives the margin call *nor* the notice that Broker Burke is blowing him out—liquidating his positions at the market. Even with clear documentation allowing Broker Burke to take such an action, Mr. Fang likely will be not be happy, especially if prices reversed after the blow out and moved in his favor.

CAPACITY AND SUITABILITY RISKS

Some concern remains about the legal authority or capacity of certain entities—most prominently municipalities—to enter into OTC derivatives transactions. In a well-publicized 1991 case before the U.K. House of Lords, it was determined that the Hammersmith borough of London did not have the statutory capacity to enter into the numerous swap transactions that it had been negotiating since 1981. The Law Lords held that a local borough of London had no power to enter into a swap transaction, thereby rendering the contracts *ultra vires.* That ruling of the House of Lords invalidated swap agreements between more than 130 councils and 75 major banks, and it reportedly resulted in over $1 billion in total losses to counterparties.[3]

Some concern persists in the marketplace that counterparties to certain types of financial transactions, still including many swaps, may not have the legal capacity to enter those transactions, thereby giving rise to fears that the Hammersmith experience could be repeated in the future.

These days, a bigger concern than the *capacity* of firms to enter into certain transactions is the *suitability* of certain types of firms to do so. Especially following on the heels of the highly publicized so-called risk management failures at the Orange County Investment Pool (OCIP) and Procter & Gamble (P&G), some politicians and regulators have attempted to promulgate regulations regarding a swap dealer's obligation to assess the suitability of their counterparties. Institutions like OCIP and P&G, some contend, are just not capable of assessing the risks of derivatives on their own, and implementing requirements for suitability assessments like those that exist under U.S. securities laws, liability for failing to assess suitability, and/or a formal industry "code of conduct" was proposed as the solution.[4]

The OTC derivatives industry, in particular, however, has done a good job over time policing itself, leading others to conclude that calls for regulation are both precipitous and unnecessarily costly.[5] As an example, the

ISDA promulgated in 1996 an addendum to its master agreements that attempts to deal with "Representation of Relationship Between Parties"—the suitability issue—by explicitly requiring each counterparty to attest that it is "capable of assessing the merits of and understanding (on its own behalf or through independent professional advice), and understands and accepts, the terms, conditions, and risks of [the transaction]. It is also capable of assuming, and assumes, the risk of [the transaction]."

RISKS ARISING FROM INSOLVENCY

A variety of legal concerns remain concerning how insolvency law affects existing commercial transactions and risk management transactions such as derivatives. These risks range from the enforceability of contracts under local insolvency laws to the impact of particular contract provisions on their participants in the event of a failure.

Close-Out Netting and Cherry Picking

A particular problem is the lack of enforceability of bilateral netting under certain local insolvency laws, which can lead to "cherry picking." This is a notorious form of risk vexing companies that rely on close-out bilateral single- and multiproduct netting clauses in their master swap agreements, some of which include regular commercial transactions as well as derivatives. When netting is not enforceable under the law, stipulating it in a contract may not be enough.

If a Malaysian bank negotiates a simple interest rate swap under London law with a British bank, for example, the insolvency of the Malaysian bank may create a situation where local insolvency law supercedes the London law governing the open contract. If the Malay bank owes the British bank a payment of $100,000 and the British bank owes the Malay bank a payment of $50,000, unenforceable netting and cherry picking could occur if Malay law allows the receiver for the failed Malay bank to demand the $50,000 payment *even if it cannot make the $100,000 payment that it owes under the same transaction.*

Liquidity Risks

Chapter 17 discussed the risks associated with unexpected shocks to cash balances. Liquidity risk includes both the risk of cash flow problems and the risk that forced asset liquidation will be costly. The nature of a counterparty's problems and the options selected in master agreements with that counterparty can exacerbate these liquidity risks.

Under the 1992 ISDA Master Agreements, the obligation to make or receive payments for the life of the contract is terminated if a counterparty experiences an "Event of Default" or a "Termination Event." Events of Default under the ISDA Master Agreements include failure to make payment or delivery on a settlement date, counterparty bankruptcy (including the appointment of a conservator or receiver), or "cross-default," wherein the default-based termination of *any* specified contract between two counterparties constitutes an Event of Default for *all* transactions between those counterparties.[6] Termination Events are events *not* based on default that result in early termination of the contract. They include changes in the law governing the contract, tax code changes, changes in counterparty credit resulting from a merger, and so forth.

An "Early Termination Date" may be designated by the nondefaulting party under the ISDA Master Agreements, so that some time after the occurrence of an Event of Default, no further scheduled payments or deliveries between counterparties are made. For default-based termination events, cross-default provisions of the Master also apply, resulting in early terminations of *all* transactions. Even though an Early Termination Date can be specified as early as the date of the Event of Default, the nondefaulting counterparty can wait up to 20 days to give notice of early termination. If the counterparty waits, however, the notice of early termination only may be given if the Event of Default is still continuing at that later date.

Alternatively, counterparties may opt at the time of the contract's inception for "Automatic Early Termination." If this option is chosen, any Event of Default will result in the automatic specification of an immediate Early Termination Date upon the occurrence of the Event of Default.

Liquidity risk in swaps can manifest itself when Automatic Early Terminations occur unexpectedly on out-of-the-money transactions, thus necessitating an immediate payment to the counterparty of the replacement cost of the transaction. If the firm planned only for the next net cash payment in its cash balance forecasts, funds may not be on hand to honor the replacement cost payment associated with an Automatic Early Termination.

This problem can become particularly acute when a company is relying on "cross-default" provisions in its master agreements. Such provisions can result in Early Terminations when a firm defaults on *any* of its outstanding swap obligations. In the extreme, an operational failure that leads to a cash imbalance and a skipped swap payment can trigger an Automatic Early Termination. This in turn can trigger *other* Automatic Early Terminations, and a liquidity crunch can rapidly move from bad to worse.

Walkaway Clauses

Once a default-based termination has occurred and an Early Termination Date has been set, the ISDA Master Agreements stipulate that counterparties engage in close-out netting as of the Early Termination Date.[7] The Master Agreements require, moreover, that counterparties *choose* at the time of the contract's inception a method by which close-out net values are calculated. Under what is now known as the First Method, the nondefaulting party may terminate a contract with no payment obligation to the defaulting party, *regardless* of the market value of the transaction. In other words, under the First Method, a defaulting party has no right to receive payment from a nondefaulting counterparty when the contract represents a net entitlement to the defaulting party. This payment provision is often also referred to as a limited two-way payments (LTP), or walkaway clause.[8] In November 1992, a New York federal court upheld the legality of LTP clauses in *Drexel Burnham Lambert Products v. Midland Bank PLC.*[9]

Under the Second Method of calculating net payments following a default-based termination, the net value of all transactions between the parties is exchanged. So, under this method—sometimes referred to as full two-way payments (FTP)—if the defaulting party owes a positive lump-sum termination net payment, then that party must pay it to the nondefaulting party. Conversely—and unlike the First Method—if the close-out lump-sum payment is owed to the defaulting party, then the defaulting party *is* entitled to payment by the nondefaulting party.

The 1987 ISDA Master Agreements specified the First Method, or limited two-way payments, as the contractual default, thereby requiring an addendum to the contract for full two-way payments. As such, a number of outstanding swap transactions, especially long-term transactions entered into prior to 1992 that were not renegotiated after the introduction of the revised 1992 agreements, still contain LTP clauses.

The presence of LTP clauses does not always lead to problems, but it can. Consider, for example, the insolvency of the Development Finance Corporation (DFC) of New Zealand. At the time of its failure, the DFC derivatives portfolio consisted primarily of swaps and had approximately NZ$4 billion in notional value. It consisted of 108 swap transactions with over 60 counterparties, most of which were foreign and most of which had relatively high credit quality.[10] Though most of the DFC portfolio had not been negotiated under ISDA Master Agreements, many of the contracts included a form of LTP provision.[11]

Most of the counterparties which chose to avail themselves of LTP provisions after DFC's failure did so immediately. Within the first few days after DFC went into statutory management, several counterparties gave notice of early swap termination—despite claims by the statutory managers that DFC could meet its off-balance sheet obligations. A few more counterparties followed suit within the next several weeks.

Largely to preserve the value of the combined DFC portfolio for sale *en masse*, DFC strongly resisted overtures by counterparties to terminate their contracts and enforce their rights to limited two-way payments. Indeed, DFC continued to make payments on all its interest rate swaps and foreign exchange agreements. Many counterparties that acted on the LTP provision were persuaded either to reinstate some type of relationship with DFC or to settle with DFC for some cash payment. In a few cases, the contracts were not reinstated due to impending maturity. In only one case did the counterparty insist on full application of the LTP.

LIABILITY FOR STRATEGIC RISK MANAGEMENT FAILURES

Another type of legal risk can arise when inadequate attention is paid to the liability implications of the risk management strategy adopted by the firm. A firm runs the risk of lawsuit, for example, whenever it measures market risk reasonably accurately, concludes that its exposures are above its tolerances, and takes no corrective action.

At a more subtle level, U.S. case law provides some reasons to believe that broader strategic risk management decisions can also expose the firm to legal risk. Specifically, if directors err in their articulation of the firm's risk tolerances, liability can result.

The Indiana Court of Appeals ruled in 1992 that the failure of a grain elevator to hedge its exposure to declining grain prices constituted a breach of the fiduciary duty of the elevator's directors to the cooperative shareholders.[12] The grain elevator received 90% of its operating income from the sale of grain. Typically, a corporate director can avoid such liability in acting as a fiduciary to shareholders by exercising good faith and honest judgment. But in this case, the court argued that the directors had no such protection because they did not take reasonable steps to identify hedging opportunities that could have mitigated their losses.

A similar case arose a year earlier when the shareholders of Compaq Computer Corporation filed suit against the company's chief executive officer and chairman of the Board of Directors for alleged violations of securities laws concerning representations about future company performance.[13] The plaintiffs alleged that the president's comments about the firm's growth prospects were materially misleading because he omitted to disclose a lack of hedging against foreign exchange risk, despite the fact that Compaq then derived 54% of its revenues from foreign markets.[14]

REGULATORY RISK[15]

Regulatory risk can take three forms. First, *procedural* regulatory risk is the risk that legal uncertainties and financial losses will result from ill-conceived and costly changes to statutory or administrative regulations. Congressional actions precipitate the first, and unilateral regulatory actions the latter.

The second type of regulatory risk is *judgmental* regulatory risk. This risk stems from inadequately informed examiners and regulatory auditors who attempt to review the risk management activities of a firm based on incomplete information. Very complex, dynamic trading strategies can be difficult to explain to examiners in a short period of time. Examiners may be likely to draw conclusions based on conservatism, thereby resulting in actions taken to discourage the use of such complex programs. Similarly, examiners and regulatory auditors may not possess the quantitative skills necessary to evaluate the mathematical models used by firms for risk management.

Third, unexpected changes in regulation also may account for legal risk if such regulatory changes affect the legality of certain transactions. This can arise in part because no single corpus of law defines the regulation of financial products and their users. Instead, financial product regulation in most countries—especially the United States—is comprised of a mixture of other legal fields, including banking, securities, commodities, and bankruptcy law. And any time multiple areas of law and regulation come together, complexities arise.

The regulation of risk transformation products is also troublesome because significant jurisdictional ambiguities arise on a very regular basis both regarding financial products and the *users* of financial products. Certain types of financial products are subject to stringent regulations, whereas others fall outside the jurisdiction of any regulatory agency. Similarly, some participants in financial markets are subject to duplicative and costly supervision by three or four different agencies, while others are not regulated at all. Infighting between agencies vying for ill-defined and constantly changing regulatory turf further exacerbates these jurisdictional uncertainties.

Further adding to complexity and reinforcing the need for sound counsel—especially for suppliers of risk transformation products—some financial products such as derivatives are not specifically regulated per se— no Federal Derivatives Commission or comparable body is charged with the supervision and regulation of derivatives. That does *not* mean that derivatives and their users are unregulated. On the contrary, derivatives are regulated in essentially two distinct ways. First, certain institutions that are already subject to government regulation (e.g., banks and thrifts) may have their derivatives activities scrutinized by their institutional supervisors as part of the broader institution-specific regulations. Second, specific types of derivatives—namely, futures and certain options—are federally regulated as financial products.

The model for the regulation of derivatives as a hodgepodge of financial *instrument* regulation and financial *market participant* regulation serves as a useful framework for the prospective regulation of *all* risk management and risk transformation financial products. Some regulation is based on who the user or supplier is, and other regulations are contract or instrument specific. To develop a better understanding of the role of the legal counsel in the risk management process, a deeper look at this regulatory distinction is warranted with an admittedly U.S. bias.

Institutional Regulation of Risk Management Activities

Certain institutions are regulated because they are perceived as special. Banks, for example, are regulated because they take deposits that are federally insured and because they often are perceived as being systemically important. The risk management activities of such special firms may be subject to specific regulations promulgated by their institutional supervisors. Institutions that are regulated in this manner include nationally chartered and state-chartered commercial banks, bank holding companies, thrifts, insurance companies, and some pension plans.

Because institutions are regulated—or not, as the case may be—based on their type of corporate charter or firm classification, a user or supplier of risk transformation products can be subject to multiple institutional regulators, most of which oversee derivatives activities in slightly different ways. Regulators that have issued supervisory guidance on derivatives usage by their constituent firms include the Federal Reserve, the Office of the Comptroller of the Currency (OCC), the Federal Deposit Insurance Corporation (FDIC), and the Office of Thrift Supervision (OTS). So, a national bank affiliate of a bank holding company, for example, might have to comply with both OCC and Federal Reserve regulatory guidance on derivatives activities.

Risk management activities that are scrutinized by institutional regulators typically are subject to three types of supervision. First, regulators of these institutions often specify permissible activities for the institution. This allows some firms to engage in derivatives while prohibiting others from doing so. In addition, some agencies allow risk management products to be used only in certain circumstances. Thrifts, for example, may engage in interest rate swaps, but *only* for the purpose of hedging or reducing their overall interest rate risk.[16]

Second, risk management activities are subject to prudential oversight. This oversight usually includes examinations of derivatives portfolios, risk management policies and procedures, risk limits administration and compliance, derivatives position and risk reporting, and related back-office activities. Institutional regulators typically give their constituents a significant degree of autonomy in whatever transactions they are permitted to engage—institutional regulators tend to monitor more than regulate once an activity has been deemed permissible.

Finally, institutional regulators may adopt special provisions for financial instruments in any capital adequacy requirements imposed on their constituent institutions. Specifically, to the extent that the use or supply of risk transformation products are deemed to expose an institution to additional credit or market risk, the institution's regulator likely will demand additional capital to cover those risks.

Product-Based Regulation

Unlike the regulation of risk management activities at firms already subject to institutional government regulation, product-based financial instrument regulations are targeted at the financial products themselves and, hence, *any* institution that uses them. Three types of financial products are separately regulated in the United States, for example, as distinct financial products—futures, options, and securities.

Futures In 1936, Congress amended the Grain Futures Act of 1922 and adopted the Commodity Exchange Act (CEA), which remains the primary statute underlying U.S. futures regulation today. The legislators' primary objective was protecting the integrity of markets whose main perceived functions were risk shifting and price discovery. The initial focus of futures regulation thus was on deterring fraud and market manipulation. Congress created the Commodity Exchange Commission to fulfill this legislative mandate. That commission delegated day-to-day regulatory authority to the Secretary of Agriculture who, in turn, formed the Commodity Exchange Administration (later renamed the Commodity Exchange Authority).[17]

To promote the integrity of futures markets in practice, Congress relied heavily on a provision of the CEA known as the "exchange trading requirement."[18] This clause of the CEA provides that unless specifically exempted by the CFTC, a futures contract is illegal unless it is traded on a *board of trade.*[19] The term *futures contract,* however, is never explicitly defined by the CEA. Instead, futures contracts are *implicitly* defined as "any transaction in, or in connection with, a contract for the purchase or sale of a commodity for future delivery."[20] The statute thus rests heavily on terms like *commodity* and *future delivery,* but those definitions, too, are far from straightforward in the CEA.

In 1974, Congress significantly revised the CEA in the Commodity Futures Trading Commission Act (CFTC Act). Among other things, the Act moved responsibility for futures regulation from the Secretary of Agriculture to the Commodity Futures Trading Commission (CFTC), which was created in the 1974 act. The CFTC Act also expanded the definition of the term *commodity.* Previously, commodities were limited to specific agricultural products, but the CFTC Act broadened the list to include a variety of unspecified financial assets. The resulting definitional ambiguity simultaneously broadened the jurisdiction of the CFTC *and* muddied the water concerning exactly what products fall under the purview of the CFTC.[21]

CFTC regulations now include significantly more than the antifraud and antimanipulation rules Congress originally envisioned. Today, the CFTC regulates almost everything having to do with futures and options on futures. CFTC regulations now cover a wide spectrum, ranging from delivery requirements for commodity futures to audit trail requirements on trading. One of the most notorious regulations obligates futures exchanges to obtain the approval of the CFTC *in advance* of listing a new futures contract. The approval process can take as long as two years, during which time privately negotiated derivatives dealers may offer a nearly identical product subject to no approval process.

Although CFTC regulations are all based on *products,* those product-based regulations also affect institutions. Unlike institutional regulation, which targets only those institutions deemed "special," CFTC product-based regulations affect *all* institutions using "futures contracts" and options on "futures contracts."[22] Product-based regulations aimed at institutions include registration and capital requirements for futures commission merchants, registration and permissible activity requirements on Commodity Trading Advisors (CTAs), and risk management standards for exchange members.

Because all CFTC regulations ultimately trace to the definition of a futures contract and because that definition is itself ambiguous in the CEA, numerous institutions that are not actually CFTC-regulated live with the *threat of possible* CFTC regulation. A nonfinancial corporation that renders advisory services to its customers about privately negotiated derivatives along the lines of either the efficiency enhancement or risk transformation risk management business models, for example, may be called a CTA if the CFTC subsequently determines that the products in question actually were futures contracts. And sometimes it is not at all obvious just when the CFTC will make such a determination. So, ambiguity about the legal status of a particular financial *product* also translates into ambiguity about the regulatory status of certain *institutions*.

Securities Various laws establish the regulatory framework for securities.[23] The Securities Act of 1933 (33 Act) regulates the public offering of securities, ostensibly because Congress deemed necessary the protection of capital formation in public markets. Unlike the CEA which never explicitly defines futures, however, the 33 Act *does* explicitly define securities, including those securities exempt from the Act.[24] The 33 Act also prohibits fraud in the public sale of securities and requires that any public offering of a nonexempt security be conducted through a firm registered with and regulated by the appropriate federal agency.

The Securities Exchange Act of 1934 (34 Act) elaborated on and broadened much of what was behind the 33 Act. The 34 Act accomplished three primary objectives in securities regulation. First, it established the Securities and Exchange Commission (SEC) as a formal regulator of securities, securities markets, and security market participants. Second, the 34 Act established new regulations on the trading of securities in secondary markets. Third, the 34 Act expanded on the 33 Act by promulgating such regulations as prohibitions on market manipulation and fraud, registration requirements for broker/dealers, and permissible activities for broker/dealers. The 34 Act also established registration requirements and regulations for securities exchanges, clearing associations, and transfer agents.

Apart from regulating securities, the SEC also regulates certain types of derivatives—listed options on nonexempt securities, to be precise. This jurisdictional oddity traces to a long-standing dispute between the SEC and CFTC over financial products that have attributes of *both* a security *and* a futures contract.[25]

An "exclusivity clause" granting the CFTC *exclusive* jurisdiction over futures was adopted in the CFTC Act of 1974. Because the 1974 Act also widened and muddied CFTC jurisdiction by broadening the definition of commodities, the SEC demanded that Congress preserve its jurisdiction over securities that might *also* be deemed futures contracts or options on futures contracts. Accordingly, a SEC "savings clause" was included in the CFTC Act providing that

> . . . *nothing in this section shall (I) supersede or limit the jurisdiction at any time conferred on the Securities and Exchange Commission or other regulatory authorities under the laws of the United States or of any State, or (II) restrict the Securities and Exchange Commission and other such authorities from carrying out their duties and responsibilities in accordance with such laws.*[26]

Among other things, the inclusion of the savings clause was intended to secure the SEC's jurisdiction over options on securities, such as options on common stock.

A year after the CFTC Act was adopted, the scope of the SEC savings clause was tested. Based on a CFTC determination that Government National Mortgage Association (GNMA) certificates were "commodities" under the amended CEA, that agency approved the listing of futures on GNMAs for trading at the Chicago Board of Trade. The SEC, however, argued that "GNMA certificates . . . are securities, as that term is defined in the federal securities laws. [The SEC] also believe[s] it to be quite clear that contracts for future delivery of those securities are also 'securities.' "[27] The CFTC rejected the SEC's argument, and GNMA futures continued to trade on the CBOT.

The SEC took its jurisdictional grievance to Congress in hearings regarding the Futures Trading Act of 1978. The agency argued that futures contracts on securities and options on securities were functionally indistinguishable. The SEC further maintained that because the SEC savings clause gave it jurisdiction over securities options, it should *also* have jurisdiction over futures on securities. Congress disagreed and left the CFTC's exclusive jurisdiction intact over *all* types of futures.

The burgeoning jurisdictional dispute was finally litigated in *Board of Trade of the City of Chicago v. SEC* (hereinafter *GNMA Options*).[28] This case arose after the SEC approved, in February 1981, a proposal by the CBOE to trade options on GNMA certificates. The SEC claimed that the products were options on securities and hence were securities, protected under the SEC savings clause. The CFTC and the CBOT, on the other hand, claimed that because GNMA futures had already been deemed futures by the CFTC, GNMA certificates had implicitly been deemed commodities, which made GNMA options equivalent to futures options under the CEA. In November 1981, the Seventh Circuit Court of Appeals agreed with the line of reasoning presented by the CFTC and CBOT and granted a motion by the CBOT for a stay pending review, thereby blocking the CBOE from listing GNMA options on the grounds that GNMA options were futures options under the CEA.

Still unhappy with the jurisdictional uncertainty surrounding products with attributes of both futures and securities, the SEC and CFTC took matters in their own hands in December 1981 while *GNMA Options* was still pending. They reached an agreement called the "Shad-Johnson Accord" that provided four basic ground rules: (1) the CFTC would regulate *all* futures and options on futures, even if the futures are based on securities; (2) the SEC would regulate all options on securities; (3) futures on individual securities, such as stocks, were prohibited; and (4) the SEC would play a formal role in the CFTC's approval of then-evolving stock index futures contracts.

Shortly after the Shad-Johnson Accord, the *GNMA Options* decision called the Accord into question, specifically noting that "the CFTC and SEC [cannot be allowed] to reapportion their jurisdiction[s] in the face of a clear, contrary statutory mandate."[29] Congress subsequently decided to give force to the Accord, however, and enacted it into law almost verbatim in 1982.

The statutory adoption of the Shad-Johnson Accord left in place the central premise on which the Seventh Circuit based its final decision in *GNMA Options:* the CFTC has exclusive jurisdiction over any transaction that is *both* a security *and* a futures contract, unless that contract is an option on a security in which case it is regulated by the SEC. Judge Frank Easterbrook of the Seventh Circuit Court describes the result:

> *[T]he question a court must decide is the same as in* GNMA Options: *is the instrument a futures contract? If yes, then the CFTC's jurisdiction is exclusive, unless it is an option on a security, in which case the SEC's jurisdiction is exclusive. So long as an instrument is a futures contract (and not an option), whether it is also a "security" is neither here nor there.*[30]

The Tactics of Risk Control

CHAPTER 20

Ex Ante Capital Allocation

O nce a company has identified and measured its risks and monitored deviations between risk tolerances and actual risk exposures, the firm must develop mechanisms by which those deviations are managed and reduced. Perhaps the most basic such method is the use of internal capital allocation.[1] This control mechanism is not particularly useful for correcting deviations between actual and desired risk exposures, but rather to ensure that enough equity capital is allocated out of the firm's capital structure to *avoid* those deviations *ex ante*.

Chapter 3 set forth the assumptions under which the capital structure of a firm is irrelevant to the market value of that firm and its security holders. Chapters 4 to 7 then outlined a series of rationales for why risk management in many ways can simply be viewed as a substitute for equity capital. In the context of the risk control business model outlined in Chapter 10, capital allocation thus can serve as a substitute for risk reduction using financial instruments or changes to the balance sheet. When the actual risk profile of a firm departs from its risk tolerance, allocating more capital to the exposure can fix the deviation as surely as hedging—*provided* that the capital is allocated on a basis that makes economic sense. The remainder of this chapter outlines some of the principles under which those capital allocation decisions can make sense.

THE RELEVANCE OF CAPITAL

Before tackling the mechanics of capital allocation, the rationales for capital allocation are summarized. A pure risk controller might allocate capital using all the right methods and tools but might do so purely because it views equity capital allocation as a buffer against losses. In fact, capital allocation using all the right models and tools can be much, much more than a buffer against unexpected losses. Capital allocation also plays a very important role in distinguishing between risk controllers and efficiency enhancers in the sense of Chapter 10.

Capital as a Loss Buffer

Banks can use the liability side of the balance sheet as a source of often-considerable profits. In traditional nonfinancial corporations, the liability side of the balance sheet was only used to fund the asset side of the balance sheet. Increasingly, however, efficiency enhancement-oriented or risk transformation-minded nonfinancial corporates are following in the footsteps of banks, often leading both types of firms to manage the liability side of the balance sheet for business reasons *other than* simply financing asset acquisitions. And it can lead firms to be extremely leveraged institutions.

Part One presented several theories that explain why risk management can be viewed as a substitute for equity capital. Alternatively, risk management increases debt capacity. Taken hand in hand with risk-adjusted capital allocation, the two together can enable financial and nonfinancial firms alike to lever up as much as they need to in order to fully exploit their business and strategic product and customer growth opportunities.

Capital as an Investment Mechanism

Recall from Chapter 3 that corporate finance tells value-maximizing firms to accept *all* projects with nonnegative NPV and reject only those projects with negative NPVs. If only projects with nonnegative NPVs should be accepted, that implies a *hurdle rate* for new investment opportunities. Specifically,

$$(R - K) \times CC \geq 0$$

where R is the return on an investment activity, K is the capital investment required for that activity, and CC is the firm's cost of capital.

Unfortunately, the NPV criterion—even when modified to take into account all the possible real options that can impact investment decisions as outlined in Chapter 14—does not help firms when capital is scarce choose between several competing projects. Consider, for example, a capital constrained Swiss multinational facing two potential investment opportunities—financing new commercial construction locally, or financing cocoa bean imports and processing the beans for use in its top-selling cocoa and chocolate products.[2] Suppose both projects involve investment expenditures of CHF500 million and that the firm has only CHF500 million to spend.

Now suppose that the construction project is financed with CHF100 million in equity and has discounted expected net revenues of CHF520 million.

The NPV of the project is positive and equal to $20 million, and the project has a return on assets (ROA) of 4% and a return on equity (ROE) of 20%.

The cocoa trade finance project, by contrast, is less equity intensive and thus is financed with only CHF40 million in equity capital. The present value of discounted expected net revenues is CHF510 million, so that the project has a positive NPV of CHF10 million. The project's ROA is 2% and its ROE is 25%. The details of these two projects are summarized in Table 20.1.

The traditional NPV criterion tells the firm to accept *both* projects, but a scarcity of investment capital prevents the firm from doing that. So, the company must choose which project to undertake. On a ROE basis, the firm's shareholders are better off undertaking the cocoa trade finance project. On a ROA and NPV basis, the firm seems to be better served by accepting the real estate construction project. How does the firm decide?

ROA ROA starts with the basic measure of an activity's unadjusted, gross contribution to a firm's income statement—gross yield, or the rate and/or fees earned by the firm on the activity. The costs of the activity (e.g., funding costs and expected credit losses) are then subtracted form gross product yield to get the activity's margin, and deducting expenses (e.g., tax provisions and operating expenses) from margin gives the net spread. ROA is the margin or net spread—generally, net income—divided by the book value of assets, usually measured end-of-period or as a period average.

Corporate capital allocation decisions were once tantamount to chasing margins and ROAs. Despite its popularity even today at some banks, however, allocating capital based on raw ROA can lead to serious problems. In particular, ROA does not tell the bank whether capital is being deployed *in the best possible manner*. ROA does tell the bank what activities to *avoid* much of the time, but the activity with the highest ROA is not necessarily the activity with the highest return for shareholders.

TABLE 20.1 Capital Budgeting at a Swiss Multinational (CHF Millions)

	Real Estate Project	Trade Finance Project
Investment expenditure	500	500
Equity financing	100	40
PV of discounted revenues	520	510
NPV	20	10
ROE	20%	25%
ROA	4%	2%

The inability of ROA to guide capital to its most efficient applications is especially evident when one realizes that ROA does not take into consideration off balance sheet exposures and business lines, such as derivatives. Increasingly, however, banks and nonfinancial corporations alike rely very heavily on off balance sheet activities to remain competitive. A capital allocation scheme based on ROA thus does not take into consideration opportunities the firm may have in its nontraditional activities and thus may prompt the company to over-invest in traditional balance sheet businesses. This can devastate a firm competitively. For this and the other two aforementioned reasons, the days of capital allocation based on ROA are—or certainly *should be*—gone.

Finally, the most important drawback of ROA as an investment criterion is the almost complete lack of attention to risk. Some risk is reflected in the subtraction of expected losses from gross yields to calculate margins, but these are the losses that are *known* and treated as a cost of doing business rather than a source of uncertainty to the revenues of the firm. Consequently, ROA is completely unrevealing in indicating the degree to which shareholder wealth has been bet on a particular business activity.

ROE   ROE is calculated as net income divided by average or end-of-period equity (i.e., equity capital plus retained earnings) rather than assets. A closely related concept is return on capital (ROC), which is just ROE multiplied by equity and divided by capital (again measured as a period average or end-of-period).

Investing in activities with high ROEs or ROCs rather than ROAs solves some of the problems endemic to ROA-based capital investments. Most importantly, ROE and ROC allows off-balance sheet activities to be compared to more traditional activities. Unlike the asset denominator in the ROA measure, the equity or capital denominators of the ROE and ROC investment measures can act as a buffer against *all* losses, including those incurred on off-balance sheet activities. But like ROA, ROE and ROC are still at face value accounting aggregates that include no adjustments for risk.

In other words, the information provided in Table 20.1 is *not sufficient* to ascertain which investment the firm should accept. Until we have factored the importance of risk into the picture, the means by which the firm can allocate its capital to the best project remains indeterminate.

Economic versus Regulatory Capital

Economic capital can be viewed as the long-term economic liabilities of a firm such as long-term debt and equity. But for *banks* in particular, *regulatory* capital also plays a crucial role.

The Basel Accord   Regulatory capital is a subset of economic capital that includes only those liabilities recognized as capital under the Basel Accord (hereinafter, the Accord) of 1988. Under the Accord, regulatory capital includes the following: equity and disclosed reserves (Tier I); medium- and long-term subordinated debt, unrealized investment gains, and hidden reserves (Tier II); and short-term subordinated debt (Tier III). The Accord requires banks to hold a minimum amount of Tier I and Tier II capital against credit risk, and Tier I, II, or III capital against certain market risks, subject to a number of constraints and requirements. Tier II capital, for example, can be no greater than 100% of Tier I capital, and subordinated debt can be no more than 50% of Tier I capital.

Even for huge money center banks with virtually unlimited access to global capital markets, capital allocation may be important because of distortions created by *regulatory* capital requirements. Under the Accord, banks must perform capital adequacy calculations based on all bank assets, as well as certain off-balance-sheet items such as swaps. One requirement is that the sum of Tier I and Tier II capital be greater or equal to 8% of all bank assets measured on a risk-weighted basis. Risk weights in the Accord adjust asset sizes for the credit risk (as defined by the Bank for International Settlements) of the claimant.

Although risk weights and capital charges are asset-specific, the requirement that Tier I and Tier II capital be at least as great as 8% of risk-weighted assets can distort relative investment decisions even for a bank with plenty of economic capital. By forcing banks to allocate or pledge capital to cover unexpected losses on risky assets, the Accord essentially presupposes the need for the allocation of capital as a loss buffer as discussed in the last section. Importantly, however, the loss buffers (i.e., risk weights) specified in the Accord for different assets may be quite different from the capital a bank would allocate as loss buffers on its own.

Consider an example of a bank that makes two $1 million loans, one to a AAA-rated nonfinancial corporation and the other is to a BBB-rated OECD bank. The nonbank loan gets a 100% risk weight under the Accord, whereas the claim on the bank gets a 20% risk weight. This means that every dollar of the claim on the bank is treated as $0.20 in risk-adjusted assets, whereas the corporate loan is treated at face value. The bank must allocate $80,000 in regulatory capital to the corporate loan asset and $16,000 to the claim on the bank.

That the claim on the bank has a greater risk of default than the claim on the nonfinancial corporation is more than plausible. Nevertheless, under the current rules, a bank might be constrained in its ability to make nonbank loans because of the regulatory capital they tie up. The claims on the OECD are still presumably positive NPV projects else the bank would not make them, but they might not be *the best* use of capital.

Recent Developments in the Basel Accord[3]   The BIS announced last June a plan to revise the Accord. The concept release contemplates tightening the link between the credit risk of bank assets and the capital regulators require internationally active banks to hold against those assets. Acknowledging the limitations of the Accord, the BIS considered three alternative capital adequacy schemes in its concept release. The first, ultimately embraced by the BIS, ties capital requirements when possible to ratings published by external credit assessment institutions or bodies like export insurance agencies. Transactions with relatively good credits will generally require less capital than before, and conversely for high-risk borrowers. Loans to corporations, for example, have a lower capital charge if the borrower is rated AAA to AA– and a higher charge if the borrower is rated below B–.

As a part of this change, the BIS proposes to add a capital charge for operational risk. The current 8% flat charge is presumed adequate to include operational risk, but the new external ratings-based approach would not. At present, the BIS is considering alternative methods for the calculation of the required capital charge for operational risk.

Worth noting is that the external ratings approach itself could have undesirable competitive consequences for countries like Switzerland, where, like most of Europe, markets for rated domestic corporate debt are practically nonexistent. The new capital charge for unrated firms is the same as the capital charge for all corporate loans under the original Accord. Internationally active Swiss banks with significant exposures to unrated firms thus will enjoy no capital relief from the new proposal even if their credit portfolio is very high quality. Banks with highly rated borrowers in countries like the United States, on the other hand, would benefit even if their borrowers are actually riskier than high-quality yet unrated Swiss firms. Swiss corporate borrowers also could suffer if the capital penalty on banks for lending to high-quality yet unrated firms leads to higher borrowing rates.

Acknowledging some of these problems, the BIS is developing as a second alternative a proposal that links capital charges to banks' internal credit ratings as discussed in Chapter 16. Although no details are provided in the concept release, a capital scheme based on banks' internal ratings would rely on information that banks themselves collect about borrower credit risk. Relying on internal ratings for capital charge calculations would not penalize banks for dealing with firms that have chosen to remain unrated by external credit assessment institutions.

As Chapter 16 explained, however, internal ratings do not allow banks to take into consideration portfolio effects arising from multiple credit exposures. This omission could discourage the use of credit derivatives that often facilitate portfolio credit risk reduction. A third alternative thus was explored by the BIS that would allow banks to use internal portfolio-based credit evaluation models for capital measurement. Although only a handful of sophisticated banks would find this alternative palatable in the short-run, those banks could benefit greatly from an internal model-driven approach. Unfortunately, the BIS rejected it, citing difficulties such as "data availability and model validation."

Capital charges based on internal risk measurement models are not unprecedented. In 1995, the BIS amended the Accord to require capital charges for the *market risk* that financial instruments will lose value as market prices change. Banks may allocate capital to market risk using either a standardized approach similar to the standard credit model *or* using internal models. In 1995, the U.S. Federal Reserve proposed to simplify the model-based alternative with a precommitment approach in which banks internally assess their maximum loss potential over a certain time horizon. The maximum loss estimate becomes the capital requirement, and any actual losses in excess of this precommitted capital would result in stiff penalties.

A precommitment approach for *credit* risk would work in much the same way. Such an initiative would recognize that bankers have better information than regulators about individual borrowers and loan portfolios. Banks would have a strong incentive to use the best information possible about credit risk in their capital allocation decisions, and regulators would be able to limit their unnecessary and costly examinations of internal risk models. Banks without the necessary internal capabilities, moreover, likely would begin developing systems so they too might enjoy the benefits of a precommitment capital adequacy scheme, thereby promoting a safer and sounder financial system in the process through enhancements to bank-level internal risk management.

CAPITAL ALLOCATION STYLES

For the reasons just outlined, all firms must allocate capital. The issue is not *whether*, but *how*. The simplest capital allocation scheme for financial institutions followed by a surprisingly large number of banks in particular relies *solely* on the Basel Accord of 1988. Some nonfinancial corporates even follow the Accord for guidance on flat-charge capital allocation. Such firms essentially equate risk capital to regulatory capital as defined in the Accord.

Because the asset risk weights defined in the Accord are woefully imprecise and increasingly outdated, however, regulatory capital allocation can seriously distort investment decisions. Some banks may over-invest in excessively risky activities that the Accord defines as safe (e.g., lending to Russia), and others may underinvest in relatively low-risk activities for which the Accord provides no capital relief (e.g., eliminating credit risk with credit derivatives).

Firms that rely instead on internal measures of risk capital may allocate that capital in a manner that spans a spectrum ranging from totally decentralized to fully centralized. In decentralized capital allocation, capital is allocated on an ad hoc basis—business unit managers and senior managers mutually consider investment and performance objectives and determine unit-specific capital allocations independently of enterprise-wide considerations. At the other extreme, senior management defines an enterprise-wide capital at risk number that is consistent with the firm's enterprise-wide risk tolerance and apportions it across business units using some systematic allocation mechanism or rule. In between these extremes lie any number of variations on these two themes.

Risk-adjusted return on capital (RAROC) can serve as the basis for risk capital allocation decisions at firms with virtually any capital allocation style. More often that not, however, RAROC-based capital allocation is used by (and tends to work better at) firms with centralized, top-down EWRM functions, of which capital allocation is only a part.

RAROC is defined as the net economic income of a business line scaled by its economic capital at risk:[4]

$$RAROC = \frac{\text{Net economic income}}{\text{Capital at risk}}$$

The numerator and denominator of this measure will be defined in more detail shortly.

As a measure of risk-adjusted return, RAROC is appealing because it can be consistently applied to and compared across business units, regardless of the nature of the businesses. RAROC provides a common yardstick, for example, to compare a derivatives desk with a trade finance or construction project. RAROC also has some very intuitive interpretations as the basis for measuring shareholder value added that will be discussed later.

MEASURING RAROC FOR INDIVIDUAL BUSINESS UNITS: BOTTOM-UP

The dominant use of RAROC is to serve as the basis for systematic, enterprise-wide allocations of risk capital. RAROC used as the basis for capital allocation decisions is called *ex ante* RAROC. Because the application of RAROC can significantly affect how it is measured at the business unit level, some discussion of both the numerator and the denominator is warranted.

Net Economic Income

Net economic income is the period revenue on an activity less the economic costs of that activity, where the period is based on the frequency of capital allocations and rebalancing. Costs may include funding costs, operating costs, bonuses, salaries, and other costs of doing business for the unit. Depending on the intended application of RAROC, costs may be measured on either a total (i.e., period average or period-ending) or marginal basis. Net income may also be adjusted to reflect the opportunity cost of regulatory capital tied up in a business line.

Net economic income should include a subtraction of *expected losses* as a cost to the business unit of normal operations. These expected losses should include expected losses arising from credit, liquidity, and operational risk and should be calculated in the manner prescribed in Chapters 16 through18.

Capital at Risk

The other component of RAROC is capital at risk (CaR), or the capital a firm allocates to a business unit to cover all losses the firm desires to avoid over its risk horizon. For a value-based risk manager, the appropriate measure of CaR is VaR or LVaR.[5] In addition, some attempt should be made to consider *un*expected credit and operational risk losses, as well.

Firms focused instead on earnings risk management may prefer to define CaR in terms of EaR or LEaR. Because RAROC expresses returns relative to *capital* at risk and not ear*nings* at risk, however, EaR must be converted to an equivalent amount of CaR for use in RAROC. One such conversion relies on the definition of CaR as the smallest amount of economic capital that a firm must invest at the risk free rate to ensure that an intolerably low earnings level is avoided.[6] The CaR in the RAROC measure then can be expressed in terms of EaR as follows:

$$RAROC = \frac{\text{Net income}}{\dfrac{EaR}{r}} = \frac{\text{Net income} \times r}{EaR}$$

where EaR is the unit's earnings at risk and r is the risk-free rate.

For capital allocation purposes, the firm should adopt the most forward-looking measurement methodology available. In particular, firms should avoid any historical risk measurement methods that rely on *actual exposures* the firm may have had in the past. Relevant to *ex ante* capital allocation decisions are the *current* exposures of the firm, perhaps even modified in a manner to take into account *future* exposure changes in a manner suggested by Dembo et al. (2000).

DEFINING ENTERPRISE-WIDE "ALLOCATABLE" CAPITAL AT RISK

Before a company can actually define a RAROC allocation rule, the firm must decide what kind of CaR it plans to allocate to business units in the allocation process—specifically, how business unit CaRs are related to the CaR for the whole firm.

Enterprise-Wide Capital at Risk

The main distinction between different measures of *aggregate* capital at risk is how correlations are taken into account *across* business units. If correlations across business units are not taken into account, the business-unit-level CaR is called its stand-alone or undiversified CaR, denoted CaR_j^U for any business unit j. The sum of the stand-alone CaRs for all K business units in a firm is called its *undiversified total* CaR:

$$CaR^U = \sum_{j=1}^{K} CaR_j^U$$

The aggregate CaR of the firm inclusive of cross-business-line correlations, by contrast, is called the *enterprise-wide* CaR, or CaR^E. Undiversified total CaR is not equal to enterprise-wide CaR unless the returns on different business units are perfectly correlated. Otherwise, enterprise-wide CaR is less than undiversified total CaR.

Undiversified and enterprise-wide CaR are both measures of *total* capital at risk. Alternatively, a corporation can measure the *marginal* contribution of a business to enterprise-wide VaR. The marginal CaR of a business line is the difference between enterprise-wide CaR with and without that business line, or CaR_j^M.

Interactions between business units can impact enterprise-wide CaR differently depending on the specific combination of businesses in the total firm. Consequently, the sum of marginal CaRs is less than enterprise-wide CaR if changes in *net asset value* (NAV) or earnings are imperfectly correlated across business lines. The following relation thus generally holds:

$$\sum_{j=1}^{K} CaR_j^M \leq CaR^E \leq CaR^U$$

Allocatable Risk Capital Measures

Firms may define allocate enterprise-wide CaR using any of four different methods, each of which define an allocatable CaR. Method I for capital allocation allocates undiversified total CaR pro rata across business units. Each unit receives an allocation of undiversified total CaR based on the share of its stand-alone CaR in the total amount. If the allocation of capital to business unit j is denoted δ_j, Method I defines that proportion as:

$$\delta_j = \frac{CaR_j^U}{CaR^U}$$

Method I thus evaluates each business in isolation and takes into consideration no interactions between business units.

Method II for capital allocation incorporates cross-business correlations by allocating enterprise-wide CaR. Called the *Splitting Method,* this approach allocates each business unit a proportion of its stand-alone CaR, where the proportion is equal to the ratio of enterprise-wide CaR to total undiversified CaR:[7]

$$\delta = \frac{CaR^E}{CaR^U}$$

The resulting allocation is called the diversified CaR for business unit j and is:

$$CaR_j^D = \delta CaR_j^U$$

If enterprise-wide CaR is 20% less than undiversified CaR, for example, Method II will allocate each business unit 20% of its stand-alone CaR. This method thus assumes—incorrectly—that each business unit contributes equally to enterprise-wide risk diversification.

Return to our Swiss multinational, and suppose the firm has three existing business units: chocolate sales, cocoa sales, and espresso/coffee machine sales. Table 20.2 shows the correlations in returns across these business units and how Method II would be used to apportion capital across them.

The total undiversified CaR is CHF1,600 mn (CHF500 mn + CHF400 mn + CHF700 mn), and the total diversified CaR taking correlations into account is CHF1,230 mn. The resulting adjustment factor is the ratio of the latter to the former, or 0.769. That adjustment factor applied to each unit's undiversified CaR yields the diversified CaR for each unit. Notice in Table 20.2 that the

TABLE 20.2   Allocating Capital in a Swiss Multinational—Method II

	1—Chocolate Sales	2—Cocoa Sales	3—Machines Sales
Correlation with 1	1	0.8	−0.1
Correlation with 2	0.8	1	0.65
Correlation with 3	−0.1	0.65	1
CaR_j^U	CHF500 mn.	CHF400 mn.	CHF700 mn.
δ	76.9%	76.9%	76.9%
CaR_j^D	CHF384 mn.	CHF308 mn.	CHF538 mn.

sum of the diversified CaRs equals the enterprise-wide diversified CaR. In other words, Method II allocates the risk capital of the firm fully.

Because the sum of *marginal* CaRs does not equal enterprise-wide CaR, however, Method II allocates risk capital in a manner that does not reflect the true marginal contribution of each business to the total risk of the firm. In extreme cases, the overinvestment of risk capital to some businesses—which, as will be discussed later, is costly for the businesses—can cause new investment opportunities to be rejected when they should actually be accepted.

Method III allocates capital based on the marginal CaR of a business unit. This method takes into account the specific contribution of each business unit to firmwide CaR in the allocation scheme and has the added benefit of being naturally comparable to the standard investment criterion of investing capital up to the point where its marginal benefit equals its marginal cost.

Table 20.3 shows how Method III would be implemented at the Swiss multinational. The first row shows the enterprise-wide diversified CaR for only two business units—assuming the omitted unit does not exist. The marginal CaR allocated to a given business unit is then the *total* enterprise-wide diversified CaR of CHF1,230 mn minus the diversified CaR of the two remaining units. In the case of unit 1, for example, the marginal CaR of chocolate sales is CHF223 mn, or CHF1,230 minus the CHF1,007 CaR that results when only cocoa and espresso machine sales are considered.

TABLE 20.3   Allocating Capital in a Swiss Multinational—Method III

	Unit 2 + 3	Unit 1 + 2	Unit 1 + 3
CaR^D for given units (CHF mn.)	1,007	819	854
Excluded unit	1	3	2
CaR_j^M of excluded unit	223	411	376
CaR_j^M / CaR_j^U	0.45	1.03	0.54

Note from Table 20.3 that the sum of the marginal CaRs is CHF1,011 mn., or about CHF200 mn less than total enterprise-wide diversified CaR. Method III thus does not fully allocate enterprise-wide capital as long as business line returns are imperfectly correlated. Merton and Perold (1993) characterize this implication of Method III as a type of "positive intra-firm externality" in which different businesses *de facto* insure one another and, in the process, reduce the total economic risk of the firm.

Finally, Method IV allocates enterprise-wide CaR based on the *internal beta* of each business unit. Internal beta is defined for any business line as the covariance of its returns with the returns on the whole firm scaled by the variance of firmwide returns. Each business line is assigned such a beta and then allocated a fraction of diversified enterprise-wide CaR based on that beta in a manner similar to the capital budgeting rule of thumb in which positive NPV projects competing for scarce funding capital are selected based on their internal beta ranks.

Unlike Method III, Method IV fully allocates enterprise-wide capital. The weighted average of all internal betas is equal to one, which means that the sum of the weighted CaR allocations to each business unit will exactly equal enterprise-wide CaR.

Methods I and II can clearly lead to inappropriate capital allocation decisions, whereas Methods III and IV can both be appropriate. Differentiating between Methods III and IV, however, is no easy task. Both have economic intuition behind them, as well as practical appeal. For those who believe the Merton and Perold (1993) story that risk capital diversification effects create a firmwide externality, unallocated enterprise-wide CaR should not be a concern. But for those who believe unallocated risk capital is a wasting asset, the internal beta approach likely will be preferred to the marginal CaR allocation rule.

IMPLEMENTING RAROC-BASED CAPITAL ALLOCATION

RAROC is of limited use unless it can be linked to decisions about whether business units deserve allocations of scarce economic capital. To accomplish this, the firm takes its definition of allocatable capital, measures that allocatable CaR for business units and the enterprise as a whole, and then allocates capital using a RAROC rule. The mechanics of this process vary widely from firm to firm. In general, two types of allocation rules are utilized. The first is the comparison of RAROC to hurdle rates for unit-by-unit allocation decisions. The second allocation rule treats the problem at a much broader level and allocates CaR using mathematical optimization.

Hurdle Rates

The comparison of RAROC to a hurdle rate enables a firm to determine whether a business is viable and thus entitled to new capital (or to keep its existing risk capital). One such hurdle rate is the requirement that risk-adjusted returns on a business be at least as high as the risk-adjusted returns required as compensation for the systematic risk of the business.

Suppose RAROC is measured as revenue-equivalent returns relative to stand-alone VaR assuming normally distributed zero-mean returns. The RAROC for a business unit is:

$$RAROC = \frac{R_B}{VaR} = \frac{R_B}{\alpha \sigma_B}$$

where α defines the level of conservatism for the calculation, σ_B is the volatility of business unit returns, and R_B is return-equivalent business unit net income. A related measure is the *net* RAROC for the business, or the *excess* return of the business unit over the risk free rate R_f divided by VaR:

$$RAROC_{net} = \frac{R_B - R_f}{VaR}$$

Now suppose the Capital Asset Pricing Model (CAPM) is a true description of how returns are generated. The excess return on business unit can be expressed as:

$$R_B - R_f = \beta(R_m - R_f)$$

where R_m is the return on the market portfolio and β is the covariance of business unit returns with the market returns scaled by the variance of market returns. The β here should not be confused with the internal β used for CaR allocation in Method IV; this β reflects the component of returns owing to *market-wide* risk rather than business-specific risk.

RAROC can be compared to CAPM-predicted excess returns to determine whether the business unit is generating enough value to compensate the firm for the systematic risk of its activities. Specifically, the business is adding value to the firm if:

$$RAROC_{net} > \frac{\beta}{\alpha \sigma_B}(R_m - R_f)$$

Similar hurdle rates can be expressed in which the business line is viable if its RAROC exceeds the return that would compensate the firm for bearing systematic risk defined using a more general asset pricing model than the CAPM.[8]

Another popular hurdle rate is based on Economic value added (EVA™).[9] The traditional formulation for EVA™ is that a business adds economic value to the firm if:

$$\left(\text{Net income} - CaR\right) \times CC > 0$$

where CaR is the risk capital allocated to the business, CC is the cost of that risk capital, and net income is realized end-of-period. The EVA™ criterion can be rewritten in terms of RAROC so that a business line adds value to the firm if:

$$RAROC > CC$$

Imputing the proper shadow price to CaR is a tricky business. For *ex ante* decision making, the marginal cost of capital (or the cost of marginal CaR) should be taken into consideration. One school of thought argues that the marginal cost of risk capital is the cost of the provision of "insurance" to the business unit. In that sense, option pricing models can provide the basis for calculating the cost of CaR.

Other firms prefer to rely on more traditional measures for the cost of capital. The cost of capital in an EVA™ framework, for example, is often approximated with the firm's weighted average cost of capital (WACC). A problem with using such measures for cost of risk capital comparisons to RAROC, however, is that WACC is constant and independent of the business line's performance.

Optimizing the RAROC-Based Allocation

Many firms utilize many or all of the pieces of the RAROC puzzle discussed so far in some way. Only a small handful, however, pull all these pieces together to answer systematically the question posed at the beginning of this article: How do firms allocate risk capital across existing and new businesses when all of the prospects have positive expected economic profits? The solution to this problem lies in the application of mathematical programming techniques to RAROC concepts for the purpose of optimizing the firm's risk-adjusted capital allocation.

Optimization is the process by which a firm chooses the allocation of marginal CaR or internal beta-adjusted enterprise-wide CaR to maximize business unit RAROCs less their costs of risk capital and subject to certain constraints. If regulatory capital has not been included as an opportunity cost in RAROC net income estimates, BIS capital requirements should be represented as a set of constraints on the optimization problem. In addition, allocations of capital to every business unit should satisfy the proper hurdle rate constraints and guarantee that only positive NPV projects are allocated positive CaR.

Treating the RAROC problem as an optimization problem has a number of advantages over using case-by-case hurdle rates or ad hoc economic profit calculations. Chiefly, hurdle rates and economic profits tell a company specific information about each business unit's value added, but these measures in the absence of a firmwide CaR optimization do *not* tell the firm how to choose among multiple value-added projects all competing for scarce economic CaR. Optimizing the firmwide allocation of marginal or internal beta-adjusted enterprise-wide CaR with the proper constraints and a well-defined optimization objective can take managers a long way toward solving that problem.

FROM RISK CONTROLLER TO EFFICIENCY ENHANCER

Especially for firms that have invested large amounts of money in risk measurement systems for risk control purposes, implementing a sound risk-adjusted capital allocation framework can provide a mechanism by which the firm recoups some of those costs and, in the process, identifies new efficiencies.

Yet, risk-adjusted capital allocation is also a type of *ex ante* risk control. One specific application of RAROC, hinted at in Chapters 15 and 16, is as a transfer pricing mechanism for risk. RAROC measures can be used, for example, to price credit risk so that external lines and limits are supplanted with internal credit lines. A trader might be given $1 million in risk-adjusted capital to spend on credit decisions based on the firm's risk tolerances. The marginal contribution of that trader to the firm's capital at risk due to credit then could serve as the basis for evaluating whether or not the trader is compliant with the firm's risk tolerances. In other words, RAROC-based internal transfer prices for market and credit risk can, in the extreme, eliminate the need for explicit risk limits or transaction-based risk evaluations.

At the same time, institutions should not place more faith in *ex ante* RAROC measures than the measurement models used to populate the numerator and the denominator warrant. If CaR cannot be measured in a reasonably precise way *or* does not include *all* the firm's business line exposures and products, then adhering too literally to a RAROC or risk "budget" can *mis*allocate resources.[10]

In addition, implementing an enterprise RAROC-based capital allocation system requires that a number of building blocks be in good enough shape to accommodate this versatile but complex task. These prerequisites include the following:

- Consolidated IT applications and data architectures.
- Robust risk measurement models across all major products and exposure for market, credit, liquidity, and operational risk measurement.
- Internal transfer pricing methodology.
- Transactional customer data warehouse.
- Cost/economic accounting systems.
- Sound management reporting systems.

Consider, for example, the questions raised about the accounting system alone:

- Does the firm's cost accounting system capture sufficient detail for revenue and cost allocations down to the business unit or product level?
- Does it allocate overhead between divisions?
- Does it accommodate transfer pricing of interdepartmental products and services?
- Does it provide marginal transaction information?
- Is it process/activity-based?
- Does it cross legal entities within the consolidated corporate structure?
- Is the allocation methodology for expenses consistent with the approach for the denominator (e.g., marginal vs. full cost)?

Implementing RAROC-based *ex ante* capital allocation clearly is no easy task. But especially for firms that have sunk tremendous costs into risk measurement systems for risk control purposes, the efficiency gains and opportunities that can arise from a working, functional RAROC-based capital allocation system may justify the additional marginal cost of getting there.

CHAPTER 21

Ex Post Performance Measurement and Compensation

Risk-adjusted capital allocation as explored in Chapter 20 is the process by which firms try *ex ante* to price their internal risk-taking decisions. Risk control is achieved passively by matching allocated capital to measures of risk vis-à-vis stakeholder risk tolerances. Risk control can also be facilitated analogously by linking *ex post* performance evaluation and compensation to similar concepts.

This chapter outlines *ex post* risk-adjusted performance measures (RAPM) and their uses in the tactics of implementing risk control decisions. Most of the measures discussed are basically similar to the RAROC-like measures presented in Chapter 20, with the notable exception that the *data* and *measurement methods* can differ dramatically.

CLASSICAL PERFORMANCE EVALUATION[1]

When a business unit manager's performance is evaluated, some measure of risk must be used to characterize and quantify the *risk-adjusted* returns of that manager—namely, how much risk was taken to generate some level of returns. In that connection, performance evaluation is inherently *backward-looking* and *ex post* in nature. All measures of risk-adjusted performance are based on business managers' past actual performance. True, inferences are sometimes drawn about how managers may perform in the future based on how they have performed in the past. But at its core, performance measurement relies solely on returns that have *actually been realized* in the past.

One important aspect of performance measurement involves the choice of an appropriate time series of historical return data—namely, the frequency and sample period. To the extent that the choice of a time period over which to evaluate historical performance is left to the evaluator, there are no hard and fast rules except to choose a period that is both long enough to yield good *statistical* estimates (e.g., at least three years of monthly data, or at least 30 observations) and to choose a period that corresponds with any strategic directives the manager has been given. For example, a manager mandate to maximize the long-run value of a production line would suggest a longer evaluation time horizon, whereas a trader arbitraging swaps and Eurodollar futures might have a shorter sample data period for performance analysis purposes.

Classical measures of performance fall into two major categories—returns relative to *total risk* or returns relative to *systematic and/or idiosyncratic risk*.

Total Risk Measures of Performance

Recall from Chapters 1 and 9 that total risk is a measure of the risk of an exposure or business line owing *either* to systematic risk *or* to idiosyncratic risk, or both. From the standpoint of the line manager, both of these risks are important. Both affect compensation, peer evaluation, and other qualitative assessments of performance. But from the standpoint of *shareholders*, what is of concern is how the risk of the portfolio impacts the firm's total invested wealth at risk. Specifically, measures of risk-adjusted performance based on total risk are most appropriate when the firm has most of its wealth invested in the portfolio in question or when the portfolio in question is sufficiently diversified that it exhibits virtually no idiosyncratic risk on its own.

Return to Risk Ratio The Return to Risk Ratio is the ratio of average historical returns to the standard deviation of that manager's returns:[2]

$$\frac{\overline{R}_j}{s_j}$$

where an overbar represents the sample average of the return on portfolio j and where s_j is the *sample* standard deviation of business unit j's returns over the chosen sample period. This is perhaps the simplest measure of return per unit of *risk*, where risk is defined as the standard deviation of actual returns. The Return to Risk Ratio thus quantifies return per unit of total risk, where portfolio risk is presumed to be reflected entirely in the sample variance of the actual returns examined.

Sharpe Ratio The Sharpe Ratio is quite similar to the Return to Risk Ratio and reveals a manager's *excess* returns per unit of risk, where risk is again defined as the historical standard deviation of returns. Specifically, the Sharpe Ratio is the ratio of the manager's average historical return minus the average T-bill (i.e., risk-free) rate to the standard deviation of historical manager returns:[3]

$$\frac{\overline{R}_j - \overline{R}_F}{s_j}$$

This measure can be viewed as the risk-adjusted return of assets acquired hypothetically, assuming that Treasuries were used to finance the acquisition—that is, the bang for the Treasury buck per unit of portfolio variability. Alternatively, by focusing on the *out-performance* of the actual manager vis-à-vis T-bills, the measure can be viewed as the benefit to holding risky assets relative to the opportunity cost of *not* holding riskless Treasuries.

Sharpe Ratios provide a way to compare and rank exposures on a risk-adjusted basis, with higher Sharpe Ratios being more desirable. The Sharpe Ratio of a particular business line can be compared to the Sharpe Ratios of other benchmarks or peer groups for risk-adjusted, comparative performance analysis. Sharpe Ratios thus can be used *either* to evaluate performance relative to the performance of other business units *or* to evaluate the return/risk profile of a line manager in isolation as "excess return per unit of risk."

Like the Return to Risk Ratio, the Sharpe Ratio is a performance measure based on the total risk of the portfolio. Variance, moreover, is presumed to be the only relevant summary statistic for capturing total risk. The Sharpe Ratio thus makes two important implicit assumptions. First, because the measure is based on total risk and thus aggregates systematic and idiosyncratic risk, this measure of performance is most appropriate *when the firm has all or most of its capital in the business line being evaluated.* In other words, the Sharpe Ratio does not take into consideration that the firm may be holding other portfolios that result in the diversification of idiosyncratic risk *across exposures.*[4] Second, because standard deviation is used as a proxy for risk, the Sharpe Ratio *assumes* that the assets in the portfolio have return distributions that can be completely characterized by mean and variance. For portfolios including assets whose returns are not well-described by a symmetric distribution, the Sharpe Ratio will reveal only part of the risk/return picture.

Tracking Error Tracking error is the standard deviation of excess returns, defined as business line returns *less* the returns on a benchmark or comparison business unit. The resulting statistic reveals the total risk of the business line in question, *controlling for common factors influencing* *both the actual business line and its benchmark.* In other words, the tracking error of a portfolio reveals the total risk in excess of the risk of the benchmark.

Consider the Sharpe Ratios for two business units—*j* and *m*. The total risk of the two lines, which serves as the denominator for each Sharpe Ratio, is defined using the sample standard deviation of returns over some sample period—s_j and s_m. Now suppose one wishes to compare the total risk of business unit *j in excess of business unit m.* In this case, total risk is the tracking error of business unit *j* with respect to business unit *m.* Using variance instead of standard deviation, the tracking error is defined as follows:

$$s_{j-m}^2 = Var(R_j - R_m) = Var(R_j) + Var(R_m) - 2Cov(R_j, R_m)$$

Note that tracking error takes into consideration the total risk of each business line *and* the comovements between returns in the two businesses.

Although Sharpe Ratios can be compared across managers to gain insight into *relative* risk-adjusted performance, a simple comparison does not take into consideration the common factors that might be influencing *both* portfolios.

Modified Sharpe Ratio   The Modified Sharpe Ratio (Sharpe, 1994) is a measure of excess business unit returns to risk where both excess returns and risk are defined relative to a benchmark portfolio. Specifically, the Modified Sharpe Ratio measures average business unit returns less average benchmark returns *per unit of tracking error:*

$$\frac{\overline{R}_j - \overline{R}_m}{s_{j-m}}$$

This measure of risk thus offers a reasonably complete picture of average benchmark-relative returns per unit of benchmark-relative total risk. It can be interpreted as the reward per unit of risk of investing in the actual portfolio rather than in the benchmark. Indeed, the traditional Sharpe Ratio is actually a special case of the Modified Sharpe Ratio where the benchmark portfolio is just a Treasury bill portfolio.

The Modified Sharpe Ratio can be extremely useful in comparing the performance of alternative business lines. Unlike a simple comparison of two actual Sharpe Ratios, the Modified Sharpe Ratio takes into consideration the common factors that may be influencing risk and return in *both* exposures. Like the Sharpe Ratio, however, the Modified Sharpe Ratio is a total risk performance measure. Because total risk includes both systematic

and idiosyncratic risk, the Modified Sharpe Ratio thus can be less appropriate for firms that measure performance across a large number of different,
diversified business units. Also like the Sharpe Ratio, variance remains the
sole statistical summary of risk; asymmetric distributions and fat tails thus
are ignored.

Sortino Ratio   The Sortino Ratio is the average excess manager return per
unit of downside risk—specifically, BTR or downside semi-standard deviation for a given return target T:

$$\frac{\overline{R_j} - \overline{R_F}}{\sqrt{BTV_j}}$$

As with the Sharpe Ratio, higher Sortino Ratios indicate more favorable
risk/return relations, and the Sortino ratio of a particular business line is most
useful when compared to Sortino ratios of comparable business activities.

The Sortino Ratio is essentially the same as the traditional Sharpe Ratio
with one important difference—namely, total risk is defined as downside
risk rather than portfolio variance. For this reason, the Sortino Ratio
is more attractive than the Sharpe Ratio when measuring the performance
of businesses whose returns are asymmetric. Like the Sharpe and Modified
Sharpe Ratios, however, the Sortino Ratio is still a measure of total risk and
thus is still inappropriate for firms whose activities are diversified and reflect no real idiosyncratic risks.

Measures of Idiosyncratic and Systematic Performance

The particular means by which performance (i.e., returns) is adjusted for
risk depends, of course, on the specific assumptions made about how risk
is defined. Apart from total risk performance measures, some firms may
also wish to distinguish between systematic and idiosyncratic risks. In that
case, some asset pricing model must be assumed to hold in order to separate risk into its systematic and idiosyncratic components. Despite its lack
of realism, the most common model used for such purposes is the CAPM.
In addition, several performance measures based on multifactor risk also
are available.

Jensen's Alpha   One performance measure implied by the CAPM is Jensen's
alpha, which measures the average excess return on a portfolio relative to
the excess return predicted by the CAPM. To estimate this measure of performance, we need to run the following linear regression:

$$R_j - R_F = \alpha + \beta(R_m - R_F) + \varepsilon_j$$

where R_j is the time series of returns on the jth business unit and where β is the covariance of business unit returns and market returns divided by the variance of market returns.

If the CAPM holds, the estimated regression intercept should equal zero. We assume, moreover, that idiosyncratic risk is diversified away so that $E(\varepsilon_j) = 0$. As a result, the CAPM implies that the excess return on the business line *exactly* compensates shareholders for the systematic risk of the business unit.

The estimated intercept α indicates any positive excess returns above and beyond returns that are commensurate with the systematic risk of the position. In other words, Jensen's α measures the business manager-specific returns in excess of those returns that are no more than a compensation for the systematic risk of the unit. A positive α indicates value added by the manager.

If the CAPM is *not* the appropriate asset pricing model, however, Jensen's α can be a very biased measure of risk. Consider, for example, an investment portfolio of small-cap equities. One reason the CAPM may not be the best asset pricing model is that firm size is known to explain expected excess returns beyond those predicted by the CAPM relation. Specifically, small-cap firms tend to be riskier and have higher expected returns than large-cap firms. Consequently, the Jensen's α for a small-cap portfolio might be positive, suggesting at face value that returns to active management are positive. In reality, however, the positive estimate of α might simply reflect the greater systematic risk of the portfolio due to its small-cap concentration *which is not reflected in the CAPM*.

Treynor Ratio   The Treynor Ratio is another measure of performance that assumes that the CAPM is the relevant means by which risk can be decomposed into systematic and idiosyncratic components. The Treynor Ratio is the analogue of the Sharpe Ratio when only the price of systematic risk in the portfolio (i.e., the β of the portfolio) is deemed relevant to the firm. Specifically, the Treynor Ratio measures average excess returns over the chosen sample period relative to the portfolio's CAPM beta:

$$\frac{\overline{R_j} - \overline{R_F}}{\beta}$$

This summary measure of risk-adjusted performance yields an estimate of average excess returns per unit of systematic risk for business j.

Appraisal Ratio   The Appraisal Ratio is the third CAPM-based performance measure. The Appraisal Ratio is defined as α/s_ε, where α is Jensen's α and where s_ε is the sample volatility of the residuals from the CAPM regression. The former is an estimate of the average excess return on a portfolio over and above the excess return that exactly compensates investors for the systematic risk of the portfolio, and the latter is a proxy for the idiosyncratic risk of the portfolio. The Appraisal Ratio thus reveals the average value added by managers (above the systematic risk-based excess return) per unit of idiosyncratic risk.

BEYOND CLASSICAL PERFORMANCE MEASURES: EX POST RAPM

Most of the traditional measures of performance reviewed in the last section were developed for use in comparing alternative *investments*. To make risk-adjusted performance measurement tie in with business line-specific risk and return issues that may slip through the cracks in classical performance measurement, RAROC-like measures are again desired.

Ex post RAROC has the same basic structure has *ex ante* RAROC:

$$RAROC = \frac{\text{Actual net income}}{\text{Actual capital at risk}}$$

When used for performance measurement rather than capital allocation, however, some serious issues—both conceptual and technical—arise.

Net Economic Income

Actual net economic income is the period revenue on an activity less the economic costs of that activity. As in Chapter 20, costs may include funding costs, operating costs, bonuses, salaries, and other costs of doing business for the unit.

For *ex post* performance measurement purposes, net economic income may reflect either *expected* or *actual* quantities. The importance of distinguishing between expected and actual net income is nowhere better illustrated than in the treatment of credit losses. As noted in Chapter 16, some banks debit the loan desk for *expected* losses at the time of loan origination. In exchange for that debit, resembling a payment by the desk of an insurance premium, actual losses relative to expected losses are managed in another part of the bank. At other banks, however, the loan desk may be accountable for actual losses.

For capital allocation decisions, firms should use expected net income in RAROC inclusive of expected losses. If a bank treats expected loss as an explicit cost, it should be subtracted from revenues as just another cost of doing business. If a bank allocates actual losses to the desk, expected loss is still an expected cost of doing business—it is the best estimate *ex ante* of future actual losses. In either case, expected losses should be subtracted from expected revenues in the RAROC used for capital allocation.

But RAROC calculated to measure actual desk performance *ex post,* however, should attribute losses in a manner that is consistent with the internal loss allocation mechanism of the bank. If a firm books expected losses as a debit to the desk at loan origination and never goes back to credit or debit the difference between actual and expected losses, RAROC should treat expected loss as a known operating cost. If a firm attributes actual losses to the loan desk, however, RAROC net income measured *ex post* should reflect actual losses, even though the RAROC for the same desk used to determine its CaR allocation *ex ante* would treat losses on an expected value basis.

Depending on the compensation scheme, a lending officer compensated based on revenues less actual losses could have an incentive to take greater risks because she has a finite downside in income and a potentially unlimited upside. Yet, the risk capital allocated to that manager *ex ante* will reflect her *un*expected loss potential, unlike the risk capital allocated to the manager whose performance is independent of actual losses. As is desired, the manager of the desk that reaps the rewards of riskier lending is allocated less capital. This might not be true if the company is inattentive to the distinction between *ex ante* and *ex post* RAROC.

Capital at Risk

When measuring CaR for capital allocation purposes, the individual risks of the assets and liabilities of a business unit at the time risk is measured are calculated and then aggregated up to the business unit level using appropriate within-desk correlations to get a business-unit-level CaR. This CaR estimate is both forward-looking and independent of past management style. For *ex post* performance evaluation purposes, however, *historical* earnings or changes in net asset value serve as a better basis for the VaR or EaR estimate. Because the future is assumed to behave just like the past, this measure of CaR is backward-looking and depends critically on past performance of the business unit—namely, this measure of CaR depends on the style of the manager running the business line over the evaluation period.[5]

The means by which CaR is measured can significantly impact the incentives of business unit managers. If managers are compensated with a RAROC whose CaR is forward-looking, her compensation would be based on the composition of assets and liabilities in the business unit at the time RAROC is calculated. Managers could thus raise their compensation by delaying asset and liability management decisions, resulting in suboptimal investments.

If a business manager is instead compensated using *ex post* RAROC but is allocated risk capital historically and backward-looking, the manager will receive a risk capital allocation based solely on past performance of the desk rather than the current risk of the business unit. Especially if the tactics or management of the business unit have changed, *ex post* measures of CaR can badly understate or overstate the true risk of a business line, again resulting in suboptimal investments.

ALLOCATABLE CaR AND EX POST PERFORMANCE EVALUATION

How to measure CaR for *ex post* performance evaluation is a fundamentally different problem from how to allocate risk capital *ex ante*. The manager of a given business unit, after all, can control only the risks that the activities and investments of that business unit create; the interaction of those risks with the rest of the firm is not under control of the business line manager. Ultimately, whether or not to reward line managers for how their businesses interact with the risks of the whole bank is a decision every firm must make for itself.

A related problem in using RAROC for the basis of *ex post* performance measurement is whether performance should be evaluated based on *allocated* CaR or *utilized* CaR.[6] Allocated risk capital is the CaR actually assigned to each business unit. Because this capital is intended to provide a buffer against significant losses, however, the risk capital actually used by the desk to generate its realized net income in any period will almost always be less than risk capital allocated.

On the one hand, measuring *ex post* RAROC with utilized capital is appealing because the risk capital utilized is the risk capital that led to the actual revenue stream. If allocated capital exceeds utilized capital, compensating managers relative to the former would create an incentive for managers to use *all* of their allocation, which might not make sense. On the other hand, if managers are compensated based on *ex post* RAROC measured with utilized capital, they will have no incentive to use allocated capital efficiently. This is thought to lock up capital—much like regulatory capital requirements—and prevent the bank from reallocating risk capital toward higher valued uses.

As a solution, some advocate performance evaluation based on utilized risk capital plus a penalty for unutilized risk capital.[7] The lower the penalty rate, the closer solution to utilized CaR, and the higher the penalty rate, the closer the solution to an allocated CaR regime. This solution has the advantage of giving the bank the flexibility to let its approach evolve over time by changing the penalty rate rather than changing the entire basis for performance evaluation.

INTEGRATING PERFORMANCE MEASUREMENT, COMPENSATION, AND CAPITAL ALLOCATION

Beyond indicating whether a project is viable *ex ante* as discussed in Chapter 20, EVA™ and RAROC can also serve as the basis for a measure of how much value the business added to the firm *ex post*. Economic profit can be defined using RAROC and EVA™ as follows:

$$\text{Economic profit} = RAROC - CC$$

This measure of value added is used, for example, by Bank of America is its RAROC implementation.[8] *Ex post* performance measurement should account for the all-in cost of capital for the allocated or utilized CaR.

When hurdle rates or mathematical optimization is employed to allocate risk capital, the capital allocation decision is essentially independent of the performance evaluation decision. Because past performance is no guarantee of future performance, allocating capital without biases from past performance is intuitively appealing. But *total* independence is not always necessary, or even desirable.

One means by which a bank may integrate performance evaluation with the capital allocation process is to incorporate past performance through the constraints to an optimization problem. Capital is allocated based on *ex ante* RAROC, but the optimization can be steered toward desired outcomes through *ex post* RAROC-based constraints so that particularly bad managers never receive too much capital and particularly good managers receive some minimum amount. Modeling the constraints in this manner is, of course, completely subjective, and it can lead to problems if the bank relies so heavily on past performance that *ex ante* measures of risk and return are neglected.

An alternatively means by which performance measurement and capital allocation can be integrated would require managers to precommit to maximum levels of utilized capital. If actual risk capital exceeds their precommitment levels, the managers would be penalized in their compensation. And conversely.

CHAPTER 22

Internal Controls

Chapters 20 and 21 reviewed methods companies can use to help auto-mate keeping actual risk exposures in line with desired risk exposures. Capital allocation tries to price risk *ex ante* in order to impact the behavior of the firm's risk takers, and risk-adjusted performance measurement and compensation imposes a penalty-and-reward structure on managers for *ex post* deviations from the firm's risk tolerance. Both are examples of indirect controls on risk-taking—they attempt to define a set of incentives to prod risk takers in the direction of making the right decisions.

In this chapter, we explore the tactics of *direct* risk control. These are the *explicit* sets of rules, policies, and procedures that a firm can establish to help ensure that actual risks taken remain within the risk tolerances de-fined by the firm's stakeholders.

ENSURING TACTICS ARE CONSISTENT WITH STRATEGY

The system of internal controls adopted by a firm as a tactical means for pre-venting actual risks from deviating too far from risk tolerances should remain consistent with the risk management strategy of the firm. This means that in-ternal controls should control only those risks that a selective risk manager has determined should be actively managed rather than tolerated. Keeping in-ternal control tactics consistent with strategy also means that careful atten-tion must be paid to the design of the internal control process itself.

To develop a sound internal control infrastructure that supports the risk management strategy of the firm, the following basic principles should be adopted and closely followed.[1]

Avoid Fads and Fashions

Perhaps the hardest part of establishing an internal control infrastructure is for the owners of the risk management process and the stakeholders of the firm to keep their eyes on the right risk management ball. It is tempting to focus on the risk *de jour,* as defined by the press, the firm's short-run financial performance, analyst reports, and the like. Although important, these short-run considerations should not alter the fundamental premises on which a set of internal controls are defined.

The so-called great derivatives disasters of the mid-1990s drew a large—arguably highly disproportionate—amount of attention toward those financial instruments, often in a negative light.[2] But for many firms where derivatives usage was either reasonably limited or confined to plain vanilla hedging, this attention was probably more a distraction than a sound reaction of a robust EWRM process. In some cases, excessive attention drawn to the risks of derivatives may even have discouraged companies from adopting otherwise sensible hedging solutions.

Why was the attention paid to derivatives in the 1990s a distraction? Was it not true that firms like Procter & Gamble and Barings really *did* take major losses on derivatives? Yes, they did. But in most of these derivatives loss cases, the problem was not so much *caused* by derivatives as by a *general* failure in internal controls and sound management.[3] To the extent firms pointed a finger at derivatives, they were blaming the messenger without necessarily getting the message.

A major objective of any internal control system thus should be to try and insulate the system from short-term distractions, reprioritizations, and refocusing. The internal control process should be dynamic and flexible, but it should also be sufficiently *general* that particular business decisions, exposures, and financial products are not given a biased or disproportionate emphasis.

Keep the Focus of Internal Controls Enterprise-Wide

As discussed in Chapter 11, the risk management process should view *all* financial risks comprehensively. Sound risk management distills market, credit, liquidity, and operational risk into information that is comparable across all business lines. Only then can a risk management function ascertain whether the company *on the whole* is taking the risks it wants to be taking.

Ensuring that internal controls reflect the enterprise-wide scope of the risk management process can be challenging. By their very nature, internal controls are narrowly defined and specific. Nevertheless, the backdrop against which any system of internal controls should be constructed must be the risk management strategy of the firm and its business model. A classical risk controller, for example, may exhibit more conservatism regarding the use of new financial instruments with commercial customers than a risk transformer. A system of internal controls designed to catch rogue derivatives traders might be suitable for the former type of firm but might simultaneously put the latter into a product innovation straitjacket.

Specifically Delineate the Risks to Be Controlled

The risks on which internal controls focus should be chosen to ensure consistency with the risk management strategy of the firm. If the company is a total risk manager concerned with reducing expected taxes, for example, all risks that contribute to earnings volatility should be included in the risk management process. If instead the firm is a selective risk manager, only those risks about which the company is concerned should be the focus of the risk management initiative.

Respect Business Unit Autonomy

The ultimate objective of risk management should be a diagnostic one and should complement rather than compete with the primary business objectives of the firm established by stakeholders. Risk management thus should take shareholders' risk/return preferences—where clear articulation is an absolute prerequisite to value-added risk management—*as given*.

If a firm is a risk transformer, this means that internal controls should avoid—to the extent possible—second-guessing the business decisions of product designers. To the extent possible, the firm should rely instead on more indirect control mechanisms like capital allocation, risk-adjusted compensation, and measurement and monitoring. Explicit transaction approvals for each deal would unduly limit a risk transformer.

Segregate Risk Taking and Risk Control

The risk management function of the firm should be *independent* from risk-taking activities. This need not imply a separate risk management division. But at least one individual in any corporation should be charged with monitoring risk-taking activities who is not also empowered to make risk-taking decisions for the firm.

The importance of ensuring adequate segregation and independence between risk taking, risk monitoring, and risk reconciliation cannot be understated. Just ask Barings.

Focus on Exposures, Not Products

Many firms find it tempting to focus their internal controls on specific types of products, such as derivatives. As earlier chapters in the book have indicated—especially Chapters 12 to 14—commercial contracts can generate risk and return exposures that are identical to derivatives without actually *being* derivatives. A real option is an option, but because it has no traded market analog it is unlikely to be deemed a derivatives transaction per se.

The internal control infrastructure of a company should strive to control *exposures*. Products are unstable. The names change, the purposes of the deals vary, and the net impact on the firm's value, cash flows, and earnings is hard to infer from a terminological stereotype. A contract may be called a swap, but its main risks may come from an embedded option, for example. Aiming internal controls at catching the exposure would intercept this, whereas a system of internal controls that allows swaps but not options might never identify the relevant risk.

Separate the Risk Policy and Risk Management Policy

Written policies and procedures serve as the backbone for a sound internal control process. Firms should distinguish between two general types of written documents in this regard. First, firms should have a *risk policy*. A risk policy is a document that outlines the risk management *strategy* of the firm. This document should be approved by the Board and other key stakeholders of the firm and should address the following issues:

- If the firm is a selective risk manager, the risk policy should articulate those risks that the firm wants to actively control versus those risks in which the firm perceives itself as having a comparative informational advantage. If the firm is a total risk manager, the written risk policy should clearly articulate that.
- The risk policy should define the risk management strategy of the firm in broad terms—specifically, whether the firm is a risk controller, efficiency enhancer, or risk transformer.
- The risk policy of a firm should provide detail on the risk tolerances of the firm's stakeholders.
- The risk policy should specify whether its primary focus is on value, cash flows, or earnings, if the rationale for the firm's risk management process is predicated on any such distinction in the sense of Part One of the book.

Separate and apart from a *risk policy*, firms should adopt a *risk management policy* that is approved by key stakeholders but that is crafted by and designed for the internal risk management function. The risk management policy essentially outlines the internal controls that will be used to help the firm enforce its risk policy. Details on the specific aspects of risk management and internal controls used by the firm should appear in the risk management policy and not the risk policy.

In other words, the risk policy is a written statement by the firm about its attitude toward risk, whereas the risk management policy is a detailed document that outlines the means by which the firm's risk management process will tactically accomplish the strategic risk management objectives set forth in the risk policy.

Eliminate Any Ambiguity in Risk Reporting Lines

The risk management policy of the firm should define reporting lines in a completely unambiguous manner in the area of risk management. The independent risk management function should have a reporting line directly to the firm's stakeholder representatives; the independent risk management function should not report to a risk-taking area within the firm. In addition, the risk management policy should clearly define (a) who has the authority to engage in transactions that materially change the risk of the firm, *and* (b) who has the authority to veto such transactions.

INTERNAL CONTROLS AND THE RISK MANAGEMENT INFRASTRUCTURE[4]

A well-designed system of internal controls will focus on three areas of any firm—the "front lines" where risks are taken or hedged, the independent risk management function and/or committee, and the internal audit function. Next some of the different types of internal controls—not exhaustive by any means—are discussed for each part of the business.

Front-Line Risk Management

The goal of front-line risk management is the maintenance of a risk management infrastructure which simultaneously preserves management and risk takers' desire to maximize profits while preserving incentives to avoid irresponsible risk taking.[5] Front-line risk management is a filtration process that helps ensure that transactions conducted that affect the focus risks of the firm are consistent with the risk tolerances of the firm. Chapters 20 and 21 already outlined how capital allocation and performance evaluation can help ensure that front-line risk managers remain attentive to these issues. In addition, internal controls can play an important role in this process.

Trading and Hedging Policies   A firm must explicitly determine its policy toward risk-taking in the context of its primary business activities. Part of the front-line risk management process includes expressing to risk owners and risk takers the firm's tolerance toward risk types. This requires an explicit dissemination of the corporate risk policy *and* the risk management policy. In addition, whether traders or senior management have authority to assume new risks must also be explicitly defined in any separate trading and hedging policies. Such additional policies should strive where possible to adhere to the focus on exposures rather than specific financial products.

Limits and Limits Administration The independent risk management function should define a comprehensive set of global limits on various types of market, credit and settlement, liquidity, and operational risk so that the institution remains within the risk tolerance levels desired by the company's stakeholders and risk management process owners. As noted earlier, only those risks with which the firm is explicitly concerned should be subject to limits. A risk that the firm has strategically determined to be a business risk rather than a financial risk should not be subject to limits.

Firms may still find it advantageous to measure and monitor their business risks. That does not necessarily imply the need to *limit* those risks. Rather, measuring and monitoring business risks can be a source of efficiency enhancement to the extent that such activities help a firm optimize their performance or identify new product or customer development opportunities.

A risk limit system is more than a set of quantitative limits. It also includes guidelines that influence the nature and type of risk that the firm takes. The purpose of such a system is twofold: (1) to set boundaries for reasonable risk-taking in the normal course of business, thus providing risk takers sufficient flexibility to make the kind of rapid decisions required by a market environment; and (2) to trigger discussion between management and risk takers when the assumption of unusually large risks is being considered. The hallmark of an effective system of limits and guidelines is not that limits are never violated, but rather that dialogue occurs among senior management, business areas, and traders about the risk positions of the firm relative to the firm's financial condition, its business strategy, and its risk tolerance.

A firm's risk limits should satisfy three criteria. First, firms should have some form of limit system targeted to each risk with which the firm is strategically concerned to ensure that risk owners and risk takers cannot engage in transactions that threaten to undermine the strategic objectives of the firm. If the limits are based on maximum tolerable losses, these losses should be reasonably defined and not be triggered after capital has been significantly depleted. If the limits are based on probabilistic risk measures like VaR or portfolio measures of credit risk, statistical methods should be appropriate to the exposures involved. Any exogenously specified parameters, such as confidence levels and risk horizons, should be defined reasonably.

Second, risk owners should not persistently violate limits in the extreme. If a firm does exhibit persistent and large limit violations, they should be reported to senior management and perhaps to key corporate stakeholders. Discussions should follow, and the reasons for persistent limit violations should be clearly understood by all participants in the market risk management process.

Third, a corporation's policy on limits administration and enforcement should be included in the risk management policy and available to all risk takers and risk owners, and these employees should be thoroughly familiar with the policy.

Suitability Legal evaluations of suitability and customer sophistication should be undertaken when new relationships and new transactions are initiated. For reasons outlined in Chapter 19, front-line risk management should include a process by which customer suitability is evaluated, at least to a first approximation. If appropriate, unauthorized customer or counterparty lists should be defined as a type of limit on unsuitable firms.

Controls on Risk Measurement Systems

There are two general approaches to measuring financial risk. The first is a centralized approach depicted in Figure 22.1. In this approach, each business unit maintains data on its risk exposures that are periodically transferred to and/or reconciled against a data warehouse or central database of position exposures. (Recall the issues concerning IT fragmentation raised in Chapter 11.) This data is then accessed by an independent risk management function that maintains all of the market, credit, and other risk measurement models. The risk management function also maintains databases to track market information (e.g., prices to calculate current mark-to-market values of securities and replacement costs) and risk parameters (e.g., inputs to parametric normal VaR calculations, Greeks for pricing traded and real options, and the like).

In a centralized risk measurement regime, information flows upstream to the risk management function. Models and input data are maintained there, and positions are *uploaded*. The risk management function then performs the calculations, analyzes the output, and distributes risk reports. For example, suppose a Swiss multinational has a business line dedicated to coffee sales and a different business line dedicated to coffee purchasing. The purchasing and sales units would quantify their expected volumes, the prices in their purchase or sale contracts, and other such information gathered as discussed in Chapters 12 and 13. The business lines would then download this data to the risk management function, which would calculate

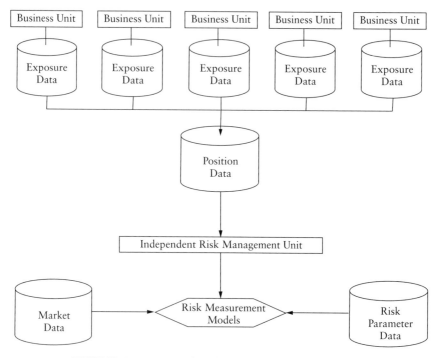

FIGURE 22.1 A centralized risk measurement system.

market, credit, liquidity, and operational risks arising from coffee purchases and sales. Market risk, for example, might be calculated using a parametric normal VaR, where the primary inputs are current coffee prices and the volatilities of forward coffee prices.

An alternative risk measurement system, depicted in Figure 22.2, is much more decentralized. In this type of regime, each business unit maintains their own risk measurement models *and* exposure data. The independent risk management unit *downloads* risk parameter and market data to each business unit. The business units perform the requisite risk calculations and upload the risk reports to the independent risk management function. To continue with the example, in this situation each business unit would have models capable of repricing their purchase and sale contracts for a given shock to coffee prices, given current prices. The risk measurement unit would download a vector of current coffee prices *and* the coffee volatilities the risk measurement group wants to use as the basis for a VaR. The business units would reprice their exposures and then upload them to the risk management group, which would then use correlation data to aggregate the exposures, analyze the results, and distribute reports.

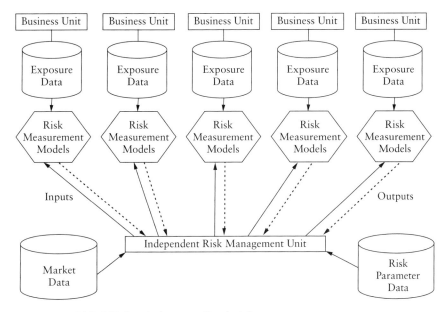

FIGURE 22.2 A decentralized risk measurement system.

Either type of risk measurement system can be perfectly acceptable, but the internal controls warranted to ensure that the process retains its integrity differ significantly depending on the system. Some of the differences in internal controls are discussed next.

The Use and Evaluation of Mathematical Models To generate risk measures, both theoretical valuation models and risk measurement models must be used for repricing the assets and liabilities given some assumed risk parameters. In centralized risk measurement systems, the valuation and risk measurement models are maintained by the risk management function and generally are models unique to that function. In decentralized risk measurement systems, the same models are often used to reprice exposures that are used by business managers themselves—for example, trading models used by traders for pricing.

In both systems, the models should be independently verified on a regular basis by internal audit or risk management areas and perhaps also by outside parties, including consultants, external auditors, and rating agencies. Model verification consists of two parts: (1) an independent determination that the theory underlying quantitative models is sound, and (2) an independent verification of the method by which the theory is implemented. Internal model verification generally requires frequent reviews of theory and computer code by internal risk managers or auditors, and external model verification should involve independent reconstruction of the valuation models to spot check their accurate implementation of sound theory.

Decentralized risk measurement systems will involve the review of a much larger universe of models at any given time. In addition to reviewing those models for their appropriateness, the models should also be reviewed for consistency. Real options, for example, can be valued using several different option pricing approaches. If two different business lines regularly encounter real options, the models used to value similar exposures in different business lines *should not be materially different.*

In addition, decentralized risk measurement systems will necessitate a higher level of security in an IT context on source code. If the risk management unit is separate from the risk-taking areas of the firm and maintains its own models, protecting the code from changes by risk takers is fairly straightforward. If risk takers' own models are used as the basis for revaluations in a decentralized system, however, safeguards must be in place to ensure that traders or risk takers cannot alter the code to mis-state the values of their exposures.

Data and Prices   Data used for the measurement of risk should be high quality, and firms should be familiar with all the important defining attributes of the data set, such as the precise mathematical definitions of any variables. Where prices are required as inputs for revaluation, firms should always use market prices if they are available rather than transaction prices or model prices. If a market price is unavailable for a particular product due to illiquidity, firms should use a model price rather than a transaction price; even imprecise theoretical prices are preferable to transaction prices, as the latter may either be stale, a prevailing bid or an offer rather than a transaction price, or a product-specific price based on market conditions that do not prevail for the valuation of the product for risk management purposes.

If transaction prices must be used, appropriate adjustments for mid-market pricing should be made so that positions are not repriced at bids or offers. If adjustments need to be made for liquidity risk, these bid-offer-based adjustments should be made subsequent to mid-market revaluations.

Either in a centralized or decentralized risk measurement regime, primary responsibility for maintaining, scrubbing, and checking market information and risk parameter data should lie with the risk management function. Traders, for example, should never be allowed to pick their own volatilities for calculating the current mark-to-market values of options. This volatility should be an input dispatched from the risk management function. In a decentralized risk measurement system, however, the risk management function must still verify the quality and accuracy of the data managed and housed within each business unit.

Internal and External Audit

A key component of the internal control process is the periodic internal review of the risk management process by auditors. The basic principles of internal audit are set forth here, although in actual practice the guidelines followed by auditors likely will be significantly more comprehensive than those set forth next.

Management and Policies Internal audit typically reviews each of the firm's management and operational processes on a periodic basis to identify key risks and vulnerability points. The internal review process should also include periodic evaluations of different valuation models used by the front and back office for similar products to ensure that the results of the models are consistent with one another.

Risk management staff, as well as senior management and important stakeholders, should regularly reevaluate any relevant written policies and procedures to ensure their continued reasonableness vis-à-vis the firm's risk profile and risk tolerance.

Evaluations of Risk Measurement The firm should regularly reevaluate its risk measurement procedures. Risk management models and the underlying modeling methodologies should be reviewed at least annually, and more often as market conditions dictate, for their appropriateness and consistency across products. Internal evaluations of models in many cases should be supplemented by external auditing and review. In addition, outside consultants should sometimes be retained to ensure that highly technical models or processes remain consistent with known risk management technologies, both theoretical and computational.

In decentralized risk measurement systems, the risk management function will undertake these model reviews regularly. But even these should be supplemented by periodic internal audit reviews or outside reviews. In a centralized risk measurement system, the models maintained by internal risk managers should be reviewed by a different party.

As part of the model review process, reviews should be undertaken at least quarterly to ensure the reasonableness of assumptions and parameter values used in modeling. Because conditions can rapidly change in most financial markets, the risk management division should be responsible for evaluations of the reasonableness of assumptions. Assumptions that are especially sensitive to current market conditions should be reevaluated as often as market conditions significantly change.

Back-Testing and Revenue Attribution Firms should regularly review the performance of their risk measurement systems in light of actual exposure gains and losses. The ability to evaluate theoretical prices against actual prices daily necessitates saving historical data to facilitate such *ex post* performance evaluations. For less active participants in capital markets, monthly or quarterly evaluations and data may suffice. The frequency of such reevaluations should be based on the firm's strategic risk management goals.

The back-testing of models also should include periodic reviews of any capital allocation and performance measurement models used, as outlined in Chapters 20 and 21. Apart from back-testing performance evaluation models, firms should also regularly undertake revenue attribution analyses to ascertain how business units are making their money. This is *especially* critical if a firm does not utilize RAROC-like measures of *ex post* performance.

Audit Follow-Ups   The scope, depth, and effectiveness of internal and external audits should be reviewed regularly by the Board of Directors, including ascertaining whether the audit staff has the requisite technical background to perform effective audits. In addition, the stakeholders in the risk management process should ascertain the extent to which management follows up audit recommendations, including making any recommended policy changes or justifying its decision not to make recommended changes.

The Role of Checklists in Internal Audit   The concept of a Risk ID or Risk Map as a risk identification aid was developed in Chapter 12. This can be used as a basic guideline for the development of a questionnaire or checklist that can be used to assist firms in their internal audit processes for evaluating the effectiveness of their risk management processes. And indeed, such checklists are good ideas in internal audit. They can also serve as helpful starting points for the development of policies and procedures.

Many people like the safety and security of a checklist. There is a natural appeal to resting a risk management process on a foundation of checklists. Unfortunately, there are several problems with lists of questions.

First, checklists create a false sense of security. If every question can be answered favorably, some will be inclined to assume that everything is fine. Yet, a checklist can *never* be exhaustive. It can never anticipate every corporate nuance, every situation, every twist in the tale.

Second, a checklist can create a sense of boundaries. Whether an auditor following a checklist, an examiner following an examination guide, or a risk manager following a crisis management action plan, a checklist should never create limitations on the natural intuition, creativity, and curiosity of the questioner. Otherwise, the examiner is only as good as the checklist, and, as said a moment ago, the checklist can *never* be good enough.

Third, a checklist can convey an implicit set of necessary and sufficient conditions for sound risk management. Yet, a reason that best practices documents are often criticized in the financial industry is that they *rarely* keep pace with financial innovation and thus rarely present both the necessary and sufficient conditions for a firm's truly best practices. But if a checklist does not embody those principles that *should be* both necessary and sufficient for a sound risk management process, it may lead to a self-fulfilling prophecy in which the checklist items *become* necessary and sufficient.

The biggest problem with a checklist is that it reveals everything the *writer of the list* knows. From a purely cynical standpoint, knowing what an examiner or auditor is looking for simply makes it easier for those being examined to appear compliant. If you know what's on the checklist, then you find it that much easier to navigate your way *around* the checklist.

Having said all this, there is still an appropriate role for checklists. Perhaps the best analogy is the checklists that airline pilots use before take off or landing. The checklist serves as a systematic and formal set of guidelines that impose some discipline on those normal flight processes. At the same time, the checklists—self-assessed by the pilots—in no way diminish the importance of the role played by the *judgment* of the pilots. Risk management process auditors should face the same types of tradeoffs between the judgment of well-trained professionals and the rigor of well-crafted audit guidance.

OTHER INTERNAL CONTROL ACTIVITIES

The previous section discussed the organizational infrastructure on which a sound system of internal controls should rest. Apart from infrastructure issues, internal controls also involve the risk management process and its participants regularly undertaking certain prudential activities. Some of the more important internal control-related activities are summarized next.

Specific Controls on Operational Risk

The measurement of operational risk was discussed in Chapter 18. Apart from measuring and monitoring operational risk relative to risk tolerances, the firm should adopt a clear and unambiguous set of internal controls on operational risk. The full aspects of operational risk should be considered by management and directors, including the following:

- *Adequate Resources for Risk Management.* The firm should have adequate staff and resources relative to the extent of its strategic risk management needs. This not only requires that management and directors dedicate adequate resources to ensuring that quality personnel staff the risk management areas and business units, but also the back-office areas responsible for internal management and control.

■ *Segregation of Front and Back Offices.* Sufficient segregation of duties should exist between front-office and back-office activities, and also within the front office and back office. Similarly, the independent risk management functions of a firm should be sufficiently segregated to ensure that all risks are adequately measured, monitored, controlled, and reported.

■ *Reliance on Personnel.* The firm should ascertain whether it has become over-reliant on individual staff members who might be difficult to replace in the event of a sudden departure, especially if integral trading or risk management staff depart the organization in the event of a serious deterioration in the firm's financial condition, the firm should attempt to structure its staff so that the departure of no particular individual would impede its ability to continue managing its risks or, in the event of a serious problem, to unwind a derivatives portfolio.

■ *Systems Disaster Planning.* A corporation's policy on disaster planning should include contingency plans in the event of the failure of any computer system required for the measurement, management, or reporting of risks. The firm should utilize back-up systems to address the potential for a system crash that could hinder its ability to manage risk on an ongoing basis.

■ *Systems Documentation.* The operation of all computer systems used for trading, risk measurement, risk management, and reporting should be fully documented, especially if the systems are internally-developed, proprietary products.

New Product Review

All firms should have a new product review process. Consumer-oriented products should be reviewed from a business process standpoint as discussed in Chapter 10. Part of this process, however, should include a tactical assessment of how the new products will impact the risk exposure of the firm, as well as its ability to manage risk in a process context.

Financial products that are either new to the firm or new to the marketplace and of potential interest to the firm should receive attention by management. A firm should not begin using a financial product until senior management and all relevant risk management and internal control personnel have a thorough understanding of the product and the firm's ability to integrate it into existing risk measurement and control systems.

Although important, the new product review process also should remain consistent with the broader principle of internal controls that emphasizes exposures rather than particular products. In other words, products subject to advance review should really represent new *classes* of products. Where possible, specific financial instruments or transactions should be evaluated through exposure management and not necessarily subject to senior management approvals.

Reserves

Especially for firms that do not engage in enterprise-wide risk-adjusted capital allocation in the sense of Chapter 20, companies should apportion reserves to market risk, credit risk, and other types of risks. Capital reserves might be set aside, for example, to cover the risk of early terminations of hedges that result in temporary exposures to market risk while the underlying transaction is unwound or rehedged. Capital allocated to specific risks should be reevaluated based on the information produced in the risk measurement process as frequently as required.

Capital also should be allocated against hedging costs. Mark-to-market valuation, for example, is typically done at the mid-market price level between bid and offer prices. If a contract must be liquidated, however, it is unwound either at the bid or offer. Capital should be allocated to cover this difference between mid-market prices and the average bid or offer. Capital should also be allocated against any unearned credit spread, potential close-out costs, portfolio rebalancing costs, and administrative costs of trading.[6]

Oversee, Tune, and Realign

As discussed in Chapter 10, the last step in the dynamic risk management process involves the oversight, tuning, and realignment of the risk management process. To accomplish that, regular general briefings of the risk management stakeholders on risk taking, risk management, and capital markets activities are an important part of the risk management process. A management plan should also be in place for the management of risks to be reviewed and updated by the Board regularly.

Realignment refers to the need for the risk management process to accommodate changes in expectations relative to actual performance. At all times, the stakeholders of the risk management process should ensure that what is expected of the risk management function in light of the firm's strategic objectives is well-known by participants in the risk management process. There is no substitute for regular interplay between front-line risk managers, independent risk managers, and the firm's senior managers and stakeholders.

CHAPTER 23

Tactical Risk Control
with Derivatives

We have now discussed three *ex ante* means by which firms can try and tactically control their actual risks vis-à-vis their risk tolerances—capital, incentives, and internal controls. In this and the next several chapters, we review several types of risk control solutions in which the firm may engage to close these gaps between actual and desired exposures when they do emerge. We begin with a discussion of *why* such gaps may emerge. We then turn to discuss the use of financial instruments—derivatives, in particular—as mechanisms for addressing divergences between actual and tolerable risks at a corporation. Chapters 24 through 26 discuss the use of other risk control mechanisms.

EXPLANATIONS FOR GAPS BETWEEN ACTUAL AND DESIRED RISK EXPOSURES

Why might a company find itself in a situation where, despite all the preventive measures discussed thus far, its actual risk exposures suddenly badly exceed its risk tolerances? Actually, there are quite a few reasons this can happen. One reason is that the firm's actual risk exposures *do not* exceed tolerable risk exposures, but the firm becomes concerned that they *might* in the future. That alone is enough to prod a firm toward risk control solutions, including financial instruments, that can protect the firm *ex ante* from subsequent risk changes *ex post*.

In some cases, however, the firm's actual risk *does* deviate from its risk tolerance. Several common situations that account for this are summarized next.

Failures in the Risk Management Process[1]

When one or more of the *ex ante* risk management mechanisms discussed thus far fail, the firm will find itself with a gap between its actual and desired risk exposures. To take a concrete example, during 1993 Procter & Gamble (P&G) undertook derivatives transactions with Bankers Trust that resulted in over $150 million in losses. Those losses traced essentially to P&G's writing of a put option on interest rates to Bankers Trust. Writers of put options suffer losses, of course, whenever the underlying security declines in price, which in this instance meant whenever interest rates rose. And rise they did in the summer and autumn of 1993.

The put option actually was only one component of the whole deal. The deal, with a notional principal of $200 million, was a fixed-for-floating rate swap in which Bankers Trust offered P&G 10 years of floating rate financing at 75 basis points below the commercial paper rate in exchange for the put and fixed interest payments of 5.3% annually. That huge financing advantage of 75 basis points apparently was too much for P&G's treasurer to resist, particularly because the put was well out-of-the-money when the deal was struck in May 1993. But the low financing rate, of course, was just premium collected for writing the put. When the put went in-the-money for Bankers Trust, what once seemed like a good deal to P&G ended up costing millions of dollars.

Some form of systematic risk monitoring and control program likely would have helped P&G. Most obviously, senior managers at P&G would surely have been reluctant to approve the original swap deal had its exposure been subject to a market risk measurement. But that presupposes a lot. Although market risk measures like VaR would have helped P&G's senior management measure its exposure to the apparent speculative punt by its treasurer, the internal controls at P&G would also have to have been in place to provide managers with an opportunity to pull the plug on the deal. In fact, the lack of risk *measurement* at P&G was probably a minor failure of risk management when compared to its lack of internal controls.

No case illustrates an internal control failure, however, better than Barings PLC, which failed in February 1995 after rogue trader Nick Leeson's bets on the Japanese stock market went sour and turned into over $1 billion in trading losses.[2] To be sure, some form of market risk measure like VaR would have led Barings senior management to shut down Leeson's trading operation in time to save the firm—*if they knew about it*. If P&G's sin was a lack of internal management and control over its treasurer, then Barings was guilty of an even more cardinal sin. The top officers of Barings lost control over the trading operation *not* because no market risk measurement system was in place, but because they let the same individual making the trades also serve as the recorder of those trades—violating one of the most elementary principles of good management.

The more interesting question emerging from Barings is why top management seems to have taken so long to recognize that a rogue trader was at work. In the case of Barings, however, a variety of risk management tools would have enabled management to spot Leeson's run-up in positions in his so-called arbitrage and error accounts—revenue attribution, risk-adjusted performance measurement, and even basic consolidated account monitoring and nominal exposure reports.

Serious market risk measurements at Barings, on the other hand, would have been impossible to implement, given the deficiencies in the *overall* information technology (IT) systems in place at the firm. At any point in time, Barings' top managers knew only what Leeson was telling them. If Barings' systems were incapable of reconciling the position build-up in Leeson's accounts with the huge wire transfers being made by London to support Leeson's trading in Singapore, no risk measure would have included a complete picture of Leeson's positions. And without that, no warning flag would have been raised. In the end, perhaps the biggest reason for Barings failure—other than Leeson himself—thus was a failure to achieve a de-fragmented IT architecture, as noted in Chapter 11.

In the case of Barings, the risk management failure was discovered after the damage was done. But this is not always the case. When problems are uncovered that have resulted in large unintended exposures for the firm and the company is *not* too far down the road to ruin when those exposures come to light, derivatives and other financial instruments can provide a means by which actual risk exposures are brought back into line with risk tolerances.

Strategic Risk Management Failures

The risk management process can also fail if there is a lack of mutual understanding between stakeholders of the firm, the owners of the risk management process, and risk owners themselves. Consider, for example, a firm that has senior managers' and directors' approval to engage in a long-term commodity sales project and uses futures to hedge its major exposure to financial catastrophe—in this example, spot price risk. At the same time, suppose the firm—again with the approval of senior managers and directors—attempts to exploit a perceived comparative informational advantage in the basis and thus opts for a hedge that is designed to maximize the gains from basis trading while simultaneously protecting the project from spot price risk. The managers of the commodity program may believe they have the commitment of managers and directors to fund all the margin calls that might occur on the hedge in the short run.

If large margin calls occur early in the life of the program *and* are accompanied with basis trading losses, management may fail to produce the funds required to sustain the program and pull the plug on the hedge. Such a situation could arise either because senior managers thought they understood the risks and business objectives of the program but did not *or* because the managers of the commodity program failed to articulate all the dimensions of the risk of the program to managers *ex ante*. Either way, the result of the premature hedge liquidation is a major unexpected unhedged long-term commodity price exposure.[3]

The risk management process can also fail when a company has paid inadequate attention to the consequences of its strategic risk management objectives. Barrick Gold is a gold mining company that hedged a good portion of its gold price risk using *spot deferred* contracts to borrow gold from central banks, which it then sold and invested in Treasuries. A spot deferred contract (SDC) is a contract for the sale of gold in the future in which the seller can choose at the end of each year whether or not to deliver into the contract (i.e., return the gold to the bank) *or* to wait another year. If the firm chooses to wait, a new delivery price is established that reflects the new price for future delivery. In addition, any losses that the firm would have incurred had it delivered gold in the current year must be paid to the gold lender. The firm must eventually return the gold to the bank, but only after about 15 years. Up to that point, when the firm delivers the gold is up to the firm. SDCs are synthetically equivalent to a rollover strategy involving the one-year forward sale of gold, but whereas firms are required to account for losses on forward contract rollovers when the rollovers occur, losses on the SDCs may be deferred until final delivery occurs.

Figure 23.1 shows a graph of gold prices from 1999 to late 2000, along with Barrick's stock price. As is evident from the figure, gold prices increased by about $75 per ounce in late 1999, and Barrick's stock price fell about $10 per share over the ensuing several months. That a gold mining company could experience a *decline* in share prices as the price of gold *rises* may seem odd. But consider again the SDC program, in which Barrick was apparently attempting to hedge its *earnings* using contracts where losses could be deferred for accounting purposes. Stockholders evidently disagreed with the company's strategic risk management objective, however, as is evident from the fairly precipitous decline in stock prices at the same time a seemingly viable earnings hedge was in place. Indeed, in 2000 Barrick began supplementing its SDC program with purchases of call options on gold, presumably to try and maintain the benefits of the SDC program from

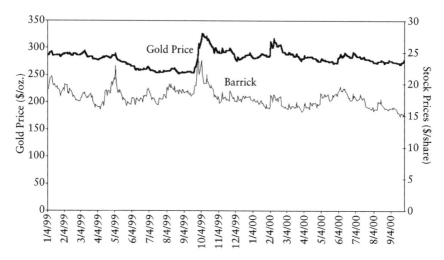

FIGURE 23.1   Gold prices and Barrick stock price, 1999–2000.

an earnings perspective but now without the *value* risk of being deprived of the benefits of gold price increases.

Changes in the Risk Tolerance of Stakeholders

Changes in the risk tolerances of security holders of firms may also precipitate divergences between actual and expected risk exposures. Tolerance is, after all, defined by stakeholders in the company who may change those tolerances over time. In the commodity sales program example discussed earlier, for example, the managers and directors might *think* they have articulated their risk tolerances properly, but when confronted with actual losses suddenly realize they are *not* prepared to deal with risks they had previously considered bearable.

The stakeholders in a company, moreover, may change over time. An old board of directors may have had a desire to hedge 100% of its jet fuel exposure, but a change in corporate control that results in the acquisition of an airline by a chemical company may result in a dramatic change in the fuel hedging goals of the firm's stakeholders.

Yet another explanation for differences between actual and target risks over time is a change in the capital structure of the firm that affects the company's potential benefits from hedging. A firm that begins as an A-rated firm with some debt may have few underinvestment problems but may still manage risk, say, to reduce the noise in its earnings signals. But if poor revenues in its primary business cause a financial deterioration in the company, underinvestment problems may begin to appear as the effective leverage of the company rises (as in Figures 6.5 and 6.6). But underinvestment problems push a firm toward *value* or *cash flow* hedging, which would represent a change from its original earnings risk management goals and could easily change a tolerable risk situation into an intolerable one.

Changes in Asymmetric Information and Conditional Expectations

Chapter 7 outlined situations in which firms might choose to hedge some risks while taking others in order to exploit perceived comparative informational advantages. This can explain some types of proprietary trading by firms. Important to remember, however, is the rather strong assumption that neither the firm's own trading nor other activities result in a correction in the information asymmetry that created that perceived profit opportunity. As discussed, the profits from some trading and hedging decisions are based on expectations *conditional on* asymmetric information.

If asymmetric information is revealed to the market *or* is revealed to the firm in a manner that suggests its initial perceived comparative informational advantage actually was not an advantage at all, the firm may suddenly find itself in a situation where it is over- or underhedged.

Changes in Market Conditions

Deviations between actual and tolerance risk levels may arise without any failure in the risk management process and without any change in stakeholder risk tolerances. Deviations between actual and desired exposures may change *purely as a result of unexpected market movements.*

One common event that can trigger a divergence between actual and desired risk exposures is a movement in the market for the firm's primary goods and services. In Chapter 12, for example, we explored the concept of a risk tolerance based on natural exposure, such as an airline that desired to bear no jet fuel price risk. To try and achieve that aim *ex ante*, the firm can take all the steps in capital allocation, performance evaluation, and internal controls. But in the end, if the airline has a wildly successful year and its jet fuel consumption demands are twice what it anticipated, *ex ante* risk controls predicated on the *original* definition of natural exposure will fall short of the mark.

Changes in financial markets can also precipitate changes in the behavior of prices, correlations, corporate credit spreads, and other variables that may cause actual market behavior to deviate from what a firm earlier *assumed* about market behavior in its risk measurement and monitoring, capital allocation, and performance evaluation processes. Long-Term Capital Management (LTCM), for example, had invested in positions that were based on correlations between interest rates and years worth of stability in spreads between those rates (e.g., government vs. mortgage). When the Russian ruble collapsed in 1998 and the Russian economy imploded, a massive flight to quality occurred that caused an unexpected and significant shift in what had previously been stable market correlations. Firms like LTCM that had been banking on those relations remaining stable for purposes of risk measurement suddenly found that capital allocated to certain risks was not enough and that risk exposures were suddenly well above worst-case levels.

THE EVOLUTION OF DERIVATIVES[4]

One means by which firms can tailor their actual risk exposures to their desired risk exposures is through the judicious use of derivatives. The basic types and building blocks of derivatives have been defined at various points in this book already, but worth a moment of time is a brief discussion of where derivatives came from—specifically, how derivatives evolve from other types of financial instruments and what the institutional marketplace for derivatives transactions looks like.

The Process of Commodization

Commentators often refer to derivatives *markets*. This is a somewhat unfortunate characterization in that it has led many to view derivatives activity as occurring in a homogenous industry with a standard set of participants. In fact, derivatives are simply contracts and, like any other contract, can be as customized as the two parties wish.

The process by which customized financial contracts evolve into homogenous markets for financial products is sometimes referred to as *commodization*. Merton (1993) defines commodization as the process by which "financial markets replace financial intermediaries as the institutional structure for performing certain [functions of the financial system]."

The process of commodization can be viewed as the process by which financial contracts evolve away from opaque bilateral negotiation between institutions like commercial banks toward transparent markets. Securitization is a good example of commodization in traditional security markets. Securitization is the process by which the liabilities or assets of an opaque institution are repackaged and transformed into securities that can be traded in a market. The principal and interest receivables on mortgage loans made by banks and thrifts, for example, are often securitized and transformed into mortgage-backed securities, now a relatively liquid and well-developed security market. Securitization is discussed again in Chapter 26 as a risk control mechanism in its own right.

Not all customized contracts evolve into standardized, traded financial instruments through the process of commodization. No market exists for homogenous financial contracts based on shoes, for example, despite the existence of long-term contracts between retailers and wholesalers to buy and sell shoe inventories in the future. Those contracts that do evolve into markets through commodization, moreover, often spawn further evolutionary changes in the process by which the *original* contracts are negotiated. Merton refers to this as the "financial-innovation spiral," which he defines as follows:

> [A]s products such as futures, options, swaps, and securitized loans become standardized and move from intermediaries to markets, the proliferation of new trading markets in those instruments makes feasible the creation of new custom-designed financial products that improve "market completeness"; to hedge their exposures on those products, their producers, financial intermediaries, trade in these new markets and volume expands; increased volume reduces the marginal transaction costs and thereby makes possible further implementation of more new products and trading strategies by intermediaries, which in turn leads to still more volume. Success of these trading markets and custom products encourages investment in creating additional markets and products, and so on it goes, spiraling toward the theoretically limiting case of zero marginal transactions costs and dynamically-complete markets.[5]

Why does commodization and the financial-innovation spiral occur? The answers to that question are many and diverse—as much in the evolution of derivatives as other financial innovations.[6] The next section summarizes the development of derivatives in the context of this process of innovation.

The Financial-Innovation Spiral in Derivatives

Derivatives have probably been around for as long as people have been trading with one another. Forward contracting dates back at least to the twelfth century, and may well have been around before then. Early forward contracts were economically no different from the ones used today. Merchants entered into contracts with one another for future delivery of specified amounts of commodities at specified prices.

A primary motivation for prearranging a buyer or seller for a stock of commodities in early forward contracts was to lessen the possibility that large price swings would inhibit marketing the commodity after a harvest. Then as now, forward contracts could be customized fully as to their material economic terms (e.g., delivery location, quality, price, time of delivery). Such was the state of affairs for a very long time, until, as discussed in Chapter 13, exchange-traded derivatives—futures—first emerged. The development of futures markets was quickly followed by the development of standardized option markets, as well. Forward contracts and off-exchange options thus underwent a textbook case of financial commodization.

As forward and off-exchange option contracts became commodized in the late 1800s and early 1900s, the demand for off-exchange contracts, however, did not subside. Exchange-traded derivatives, after all, were not *pure* substitutes for off-exchange, privately negotiated contracts. The demand for customization persisted.

Over time, off-exchange or over-the-counter derivatives began to undergo their own process of commodization. OTC derivatives became increasingly standardized *by type,* with the material terms of each particular contract remaining customized. We explained in Chapter 13, for example, that interest rate swaps can be viewed as portfolios of FRAs. Rather than being marketed and negotiated as separate forwards, these portfolios began to be bundled as single swap contracts. Many of the derivatives discussed in earlier chapters have evolved from this commodization by type of product. They include currency swaps, cross-currency swaps, commodity swaps, and collars.

One aspect of the commodization process in OTC derivatives is the evolution of transactions from *principal-principal* to *principal-agent.* In the former type of relationship, one party in an OTC derivatives transaction had to find another party with a demand for the opposite side of the contract. A farmer wishing to protect herself from falling prices, for example, had to find a counterparty with a desire for a contract providing protection from *rising* prices (e.g., a miller). In the era when users of off-exchange derivatives had to find their own counterparties, both counterparties were principals in the transaction.

Typical OTC derivatives transactions are now negotiated with one party to the contract functioning as an *agent.* Called a *dealer,* such a firm functions as an intermediary with the purpose of entering into virtually any transaction, generally on *either side* (buy or sell) of the contract. Dealers thus transact with principals, which are also called *end users,* so that principals do not need to identify a counterparty with a demand for the opposite side of the contract to enter that contract. Dealers thus can provide customized Risk Transformation services while dramatically reducing the cost of searching for counterparties in off-exchange contracting.

Why off-exchange derivatives evolved toward principal-agent or user-dealer relationships is not clear. Part of the reason must have been just an increase in the demand for off-exchange contracting, which in turn prompted users to demand a reduction in the transaction costs of searching for appropriate counterparties. On the other side of the coin, dealers may have arisen because of their comparative advantage in counterparty identification. A large bank with a large client base is already in the business of gathering client information, for example. Such a bank would seem naturally better positioned than a small regional bank to find a counterparty with a desire to take an opposite position to the small bank in an OTC derivatives contract.

The venue for negotiating OTC derivatives is today characterized in this electronic age as a forum of faxes and phones—quite the contrast to the loud pits of the futures industry. When a corporation wants to enter into a customized, bilateral derivatives contract, it generally telephones one or more dealers which offer to be the corporation's counterparty in that particular transaction. The derivatives user decides which dealer will be its counterparty in the OTC derivatives transaction (usually based on the best price quote the user receives) and then relies on faxes, messengers, or other expedients of communicating information to sign the documentation governing the execution of the derivatives contract.

Participants in Derivatives Activity

The types of institutions that participate in derivatives activity fall into several categories. Because OTC derivatives are negotiated in a relatively opaque market structure as compared to the highly transparent markets in which futures and options are traded, the participants in derivatives activity do vary somewhat depending on the type of derivatives transaction.

OTC Derivatives Participants   As noted, there are two types of participants in OTC derivatives activity: dealers and end users. Dealers are firms whose risk management business model is Risk Transformation. They act as agents for a variety of end user principals in OTC derivatives transactions that are in turn functioning in a risk control context.

Swap dealers generally run close to a matched book of derivatives, in which gross transactions net to a relatively small market risk exposure. In other words, when dealers match one counterparty to another in exchange for earning fee income, the dealers often attempt to match the terms of their transactions when feasible. When matching is not feasible, dealers typically lay off the residual market risk of their entire customer portfolio by using other low-cost OTC derivatives *and* exchange-traded derivatives. Interest rate swap dealers, for example, rely strongly on the CME Eurodollar futures contract to manage the residual risk resulting from a portfolio of end user swap transactions whose terms are not perfectly matched. This has led some to characterize the swap market as a retail market for large-dollar, customized transactions. Likewise, a function of a futures market is to provide a wholesale market in which swap dealers can manage the risks of being retailers.

Because dealers act as financial intermediaries in OTC derivatives, they typically must exhibit several characteristics to remain competitive. These characteristics include a strong credit standing, large relative capitalization, good access to information about a variety of end users, and relatively low costs of managing the residual risks of an unmatched portfolio of customer financial transactions. Firms already active as financial intermediaries are natural candidates for dealers. Most OTC derivatives dealers, in fact, are commercial banks, investment banks, and nonbank financial corporations such as trading company affiliates of insurance companies.

In the 1990s, dealers attempted to further enhance their ability to compete as agents in various swap transactions by setting up separately capitalized affiliates whose sole function is derivatives dealing. Many of these separately capitalized affiliates are affiliates of securities broker/dealers with higher credit ratings than their parent corporations. To secure such ratings, these affiliates generally have significant amounts of capital and strict policies pertaining to the use of credit enhancements like collateral in OTC derivatives.[7]

End users of derivatives, by contrast, are those institutions that engage in derivatives transactions as principals, or for a purpose other than generating fee income. They do not usually take both sides of a contract, and instead enter into derivatives to obtain or modify a particular exposure to the underlying. End users thus are typical Risk Controllers, seeking to use derivatives to close the gaps in their exposures between actual and desired risk tolerances.

End users of derivatives include commercial banks, investment banks, thrifts, insurance companies, manufacturing and other nonfinancial corporations, institutional funds (e.g., mutual funds), and government-sponsored enterprises (e.g., Federal Home Loan Banks). Dealers, moreover, may use derivatives in an end user capacity when they have their own risk control demands. Bank dealers, for example, often have a portfolio of interest rate swaps separate from their dealing portfolio in order to control the interest rate risk they incur in traditional banking.

Exchange-Traded Derivatives Participants   The dealer/user paradigm for swaps breaks down in transparent markets for exchange-traded derivatives. Perhaps the closest analogue is the relation between organized exchanges and exchange participants.

There are two primary types of organized financial exchanges in the United States—*securities exchanges* and *commodities exchanges*—with the distinction being made entirely on how they are regulated, as outlined in Chapter 19. Options on securities and foreign exchange are legally considered securities, while futures and options on futures are considered commodities. Securities exchanges, such as the Chicago Board Options Exchange, Philadelphia Stock Exchange, and American Stock Exchange thus list for trading products such as options on individual stocks, options on cash equity indexes, and options on foreign currency. Commodity exchanges, which we have called futures exchanges, allow trading in futures contracts and options on futures contracts.

Although organized financial exchanges are clearly participants in exchange-traded derivatives activity, it is incorrect to view them as analogous to swap dealers. Exchanges do maintain the trading microstructure in which prices are formed, but they merely quote prices discovered by traders. The exchanges themselves do not participate directly in the process of price formation.

Participation in trading and price formation on commodity/futures exchanges is limited to exchange members or trading participants. To become an exchange member, a firm or individual must purchase a seat on an exchange, which entitles the member to perform certain trading functions. Seats are continuously available for sale, but the number of seats on an exchange rarely changes, so that if a new firm wants to acquire a seat, it must bid one away from a current seat holder. The market for exchange seats tends to be quite competitive, and many firms hold more than one membership at any time.

In recent years, organized financial exchanges have been evolving increasingly toward demutualized, private ownership structures. Historically, futures exchange memberships were like country clubs, where the right to use the trading facility was commensurate with ownership. In the Fama and Jensen typology presented in Chapter 1, exchanges thus were like financial mutuals. Now that most exchanges are moving toward private ownership, they are evolving into open corporations where the right to trade is now sold separately from the right to invest in the exchange's capital structure.

Futures exchange trading participants may trade for their own account, for the account of another member, or for the account of an outside customer. A single firm need not be limited to any one particular use of a futures exchange. A firm might execute one transaction for an outside customer, followed immediately by a transaction made for its own account.

In practice, however, participants on futures exchanges do tend to exhibit some degree of specialization. Many firms trade solely for their own account, either to facilitate their hedging activities, to speculate, or to generate fee income by acting in a pseudo-dealer capacity. Dealers of this variety are quite unlike swap dealers, however. Whereas a swap dealer typically runs a matched book of long-dated transactions to supply liquidity to the marketplace, an organized futures exchange market maker is often called a scalper, because she essentially takes a short-term speculative position in the market in hopes of profiting from *intraday* price disparities. Scalpers rarely have open positions on their books when the market closes, but their intraday speculation does greatly enhance the liquidity of the marketplace.

Futures exchange participants that execute transactions for nonmember customers are called futures commission merchants (FCMs). FCMs are the futures industry's version of securities broker/dealers and may be either clearing or nonclearing members of a futures exchange. FCMs essentially act as brokers for outside customers, who are also participants in derivatives activity. Being neither clearing nor exchange members, outside customers face higher transaction costs, but they nonetheless are end users of exchange-traded derivatives.

THE USES AND BENEFITS OF DERIVATIVES

The degree to which firms can benefit from the use of derivatives depends on whether they are *demanders* of derivatives or *suppliers*. The former are firms in the Risk Control business model that can use derivatives to manage deviations between actual and tolerable risks, whereas the latter are in the Risk Transformation business.

Benefits to Suppliers of Derivatives Risk Transformation Products

There are several obvious benefits to being a swap dealer. First, fee income is generated whenever a dealer acts as an agent rather than a principal in a transaction. *Matching trades* allows dealers to make profits by essentially fulfilling a brokerage capacity and earning bid-offer spreads, as discussed in Chapter 17. Dealers also sometimes earn transaction fees from structuring complex products.

Second, dealers can benefit from positive clientele effects. Good reputations and competitive pricing over time will result in repeat business that benefits dealers. A related benefit is that dealers can use dealing as part of a tie-in sale. Suppose, for example, an end user brings commercial bank

Dealer A its derivatives business, such that Dealer A always acts as the firm's FCM and swap counterparty (albeit still as an agent in the latter). The end user may later decide to give Dealer A its business as a commercial bank, as well. But by then, Dealer A has gathered a great deal of information about the firm. Utilizing this *economy of scope* in information acquisition, Dealer A can offer *combined* derivatives dealing and commercial banking services to the firm at a lower marginal cost than if the two services were sold separately by that or any other dealer. Although the size of the economies of scope in banking are subject to dispute, the success of existing financial intermediaries (e.g., banks and investment banks) as derivatives dealers attests to their presence.

Finally, even if economies of scope are not present, swap dealers can derive revenues from *add-on* services, such as risk management consulting services that are provided as a related but extended dealing function.

Benefits to Risk Control Demanders of Derivatives Solutions[8]

End users of exchange-traded and OTC derivatives include commercial and investment banks, thrifts, financial corporations (e.g., insurance and finance companies), nonfinancial corporations (e.g., airlines and manufacturing firms), institutional investors (e.g., pension funds), and specialized trading firms. Corporations use derivatives in a variety of ways, some of which are explained next.

First, corporations can benefit from derivatives through lower funding costs. A U.S. corporation, for example, might borrow 75 million Deutsche marks in German capital markets, then use a currency swap to convert the Deutsche mark currency exposure to a U.S. dollar exposure. The final result could be a lower cost of funds in U.S. dollars than if the firm had sought direct financing in U.S. capital markets. Though an apparent arbitrage opportunity, international differences in taxation, regulation, and controls on capital often make these types of transactions *persistently* advantageous to some firms.

Second, derivatives allow firms to diversify their funding sources. A firm might raise capital in one market and then swap its cash flows into the currency of another market in order to diversify its creditor base. Corporations also can diversify the currency exposure of their liabilities in this manner. In today's global capital market, currency and interest rate swaps give firms the ability to borrow in the cheapest capital market, domestic or foreign, without regard either to the currency in which the debt is denominated or the nature of the interest payment. Suppose, for example, Firm Leamas is a U.S.-based firm with a large plant in Mexico. Firm Leamas might be able to reduce the costs of funding its Mexican plant by borrowing in pesos and swapping its pesos back into U.S. dollars using a peso-dollar currency swap.

Third, derivatives allow corporate institutional investors, such as pension plans, to enhance asset yields. In cases where securities trade poorly because of some undesirable feature, derivatives can be used to neutralize that feature, for example, by creating a synthetic instrument with a higher yield than a traditional instrument of the same credit quality. Asset swaps, for example, are swaps that allow firms to swap illiquid securities for similar cash flows with the same probability of default but greater liquidity.

Fourth, derivatives allow firms to expand their primary lines of business or diversify into new product and service lines. A trucking company in the primary business of supplying transportation services to a regional market might choose to expand nationally only if it can ensure that it has access to diesel fuel over time. The trucking company may choose to offset some of its price risks by using derivatives, such as entering a commodity swap to receive deliveries of diesel fuel over time at fixed prices or make (or receive) cash payments based on a floating price of diesel fuel relative to the fixed price. In this sense, the company's decision to expand is made jointly with its decision to hedge its fuel costs using the commodity swap.

Fifth, corporations may use derivatives to manage the risks of *anticipated* expansions or business investments. A corporation plagued with underinvestment problems in the sense of Froot, Scharfstein, and Stein (Chapter 7), for example, may hedge various future anticipated risk exposures by using derivatives to ensure that enough cash is available to exploit future profitable investment opportunities.

Sixth, derivatives provide an efficient method for all types of corporations to better manage the exposures to interest rate and currency risk that result from existing primary business lines. Interest rate swaps, for example, help banks of all sizes to manage better the asset/liability mismatches inherent in funding long-term assets, such as mortgages, with short-term liabilities that reprice more frequently, such as certificates of deposit. Currency forwards, options, and swaps help importers, exporters, and multinational corporations better to manage the foreign exchange risk inherent in their ordinary business operations.

Finally, derivatives provide a low-cost and effective means for both corporations and institutional investors to efficiently manage their portfolios of assets and liabilities. A fully-invested equity fund, for example, can reduce its market exposure quickly and cheaply by using futures on stock indexes instead of selling off that part of its cash equity assets that comprises the index. Corporate borrowers can also effectively manage their liability structure—fixed/floating debt ratio and currency composition—by using interest rate and currency swaps and futures.

Not all corporations find the various potential benefits of derivatives equally appealing. A firm using derivatives to reduce the expected costs of financial distress, for example, would be unlikely also to find the inventory management use of derivatives appealing. The latter use of derivatives, although beneficial to many firms, does not necessarily reduce the volatility of a firm's value or of its cash flows, both of which may be important for a financially distressed firm. In any event, a significant number of firms and organizations find that at least one of the above benefits applies to them.

THE TACTICS OF HEDGING WITH DERIVATIVES

When using derivatives to manage actual risk exposures, a firm must address several issues: what type of instrument to use (i.e., forward- or option-based derivatives); whether to use exchange-traded or OTC derivatives; and the amount to be hedged. Each of these tactical issues are explored briefly in the following sections.

As discussed in the Preface, this is not primarily a book on financial instruments. Numerous good books on derivatives review the different kinds of derivatives, their pricing, and hedging strategies. Because of the huge volume of material out there, the discussion below includes some examples but is in no way intended to be the newest best source on derivatives.

Selecting an Instrument Type

There is no hard and fast rule for how a Risk Controller should choose between forward-like and option-like risk transformation products to close an *existing* gap between actual and tolerable risks. As we saw in Chapter 3, both are fairly priced and zero NPV transactions. If the firm is cash constrained, it is *possible* that at-market forward-based derivatives will be cheaper than options because of the lack of any premium payment. But if the firm is cash constrained, it is all the more likely the Risk Transformer will demand margin or collateral that would have the same practical impact on current cash balances as a premium outlay.

Asymmetric information can have an impact on how a firm chooses to close a risk gap. Consider, for example, a firm with floating-rate debt that inherits a new board of directors that wants the firm to reduce its debt service volatility and swap into fixed-rate debt. But suppose managers and directors alike are also very bearish on interest rates. The firm might prefer to spend the money on options to protect it from rate increases but not deprive the firm of benefits from rate declines. As noted, however, the premium paid for the option will already reflect the risk-neutral probability of a rate change, so this sort of reasoning really only makes sense if the firm believes *its* view of rates is somehow better than the market view of rates reflected in current option prices and the implied volatility smile.

In general, when information is symmetric, a classical Risk Control hedger will choose the financial instrument that best offsets the exposure to be hedged—options to hedge option-like exposures, and forwards/swaps/futures to hedge forward-like exposures. Suppose, for example, a firm is concerned that jet fuel purchase demands might exceed the forecast demand level and drive its purchases above the company's natural exposure. All fuel purchases that have been forecast for the next year have been hedged with commodity swaps, as per the firm's risk policy. But if the firm is worried about unhedged amounts *above that* level, then it clearly makes sense to use options. The exposure is not firm and is an option-like exposure, and so should be the hedge.

Choosing Between Exchange-Traded and OTC Derivatives

If a company is considering derivatives as the means by which its actual risk exposure can be changed to more closely match its risk tolerance, one choice the firm must make concerns whether or not to use OTC or exchange-traded derivatives. A company's choice between the two types of derivatives depends on a variety of factors.

Customization and Basis Risk   The degree of customization that a corporation may want in a derivatives contract strongly affects the choice. If customization is less important than cost, the company might prefer to use exchange-traded derivatives because the latter *tend* to be cheaper. For cash flow and earnings risk managers, in particular, however, the customization benefits of OTC derivatives may make it easier to reduce cash flow volatility and achieve hedge accounting treatment.

If a Risk Controller considers adopting an exchange-traded derivatives solution, one issue is the degree to which the standardization creates embedded options (in the sense of those discussed in Chapter 14) and basis risk (in the context of Chapter 7) that interfere with the functioning of the hedge. In general, the less correlated the standardized product is with the asset or liability being hedged, the more problematic a risk control solution using exchange-traded derivatives. Conversely, a high and stable correlation between the futures and the asset or liability can make futures a fairly attractive solution, especially for a value hedger.

Customer Relationship Management with Risk Transformers   As discussed in Chapter 10, risk transformers leverage their product and customer relationship management processes into solutions designed to serve better their good and repeat customers. Consequently, being a risk controller on the receiving end of this can be highly attractive and can tip the scales away from standardized exchange-traded derivatives toward more customized OTC solutions.

Risk Controllers must seriously consider the benefits from any relationships they already have with OTC derivatives dealers. These dealers often are banks or investment banks, and some firms may prefer dealing with their banks when using derivatives rather than using the anonymous trading environment provided by an organized exchange. Indeed, repeat customers may even end up paying lower costs by taking all their business to an OTC derivatives dealer rather than taking some of that business to an exchange.

Credit Risk   Not all futures exchanges have strictly lower credit risk than all swap dealers. An exchange clearinghouse exposes traders to *identical* credit risks, but not necessarily *zero* credit risk—the clearinghouse, after all, might default. If the choice a firm faces is using a questionable futures exchange in a third-world country or a AAA-rated derivatives dealer, it may well opt for the latter when considering credit risk.

Regulation   As discussed in Chapter 19, OTC derivatives and exchange-traded derivatives are regulated quite differently, and differential regulation can affect the choice of product by a firm or institutional investor. A firm that has no relationship to the CFTC, for example, may prefer to avoid one, especially if the firm is already otherwise regulated (e.g., a Fed-regulated bank). In this situation, the firm may be forced to go through a FCM if it wishes to use futures, which can increase its costs and thus may prod the firm to simply opt for an OTC derivatives solution.

Risk Management Strategy and Financial Objectives   The strategic risk management objectives of the firm play a role in distinguishing between OTC derivatives and futures. Because futures are marked-to-marked at least once a day, cash flow risk managers may prefer to use swaps whose settlement dates can be structured to match the cash flow dates on the asset or liability being hedged. Unless that asset or liability also involves daily net cash flows, cash flow volatility is often heightened by a firm's use of futures.

The Cost of the Hedge   The exchange-traded/OTC derivatives tradeoff can be strongly affected by cost. On the one hand, dealers may price their services collectively and give implicit discounts for good relationship-based customers. On the other hands, dealers will pass along their costs of hedging *and* structuring. The more complex the solution, the more a Risk Controller likely must pay for the benefits of one-stop shopping.

Exchange-traded and OTC derivatives quite often are similar *enough* that multiple variations on the same risk theme can be identified to do a price comparison and back out the implied cost of customization. As discussed in Chapter 13, a swap can be represented as a portfolio of off-market, settled-in-arrears FRAs. The difference in the price of the former and the portfolio of the latter should be entirely due to the cost of *bundling*—in the former case the Risk Controller pays the Risk Transformer for packaging the FRAs, where the latter is do-it-yourself.

Another example comes from the correspondence between Eurodollar futures options, LIBOR caps, and capped loans. Eurodollar futures traded on the CME are among the most liquid and actively traded futures contracts in the world. The underlying is a 90-day hypothetical Eurodollar certificate of deposit with a face value of $1 million. The minimum price move (i.e., tick size) is $12.50 per ½ basis point, or $25 per basis point. Contracts mature in March, June, September, December, and in the spot and serial months, and maturities are available for up to 10 years.

The settlement price when a Eurodollar futures contract matures is

$$F(T, T) = 100 - R(T, T + 3)$$

where $R(T, T + 3)$ is three-month LIBOR prevailing in month T. R is annualized relative to a 360-day money market year and expressed as a *percentage* to two decimals. A futures price of 91.75 thus implies a CD rate of 8.25% per annum. To calculate the rate on which the futures contract settles—called the International Monetary Market (IMM) Eurodollar Index—the CME surveys several London banks each day to determine their quoted LIBOR rates, discards the two highest and the two lowest quotes, and takes the average of the remaining survey quotes. Prior to settlement, the futures price implies the *expected* three-month LIBOR, or the rate on a hypothetical three-month LIBOR CD expected to prevail when the futures contract matures:

$$F(t, T) = 100 - E_t[R(T, T + 3)]$$

Options on Eurodollar futures are options that give their holders the right to enter into a Eurodollar futures contract at maturity as either the long (call buyer) or short (put buyer).

The OTC derivatives analogue to a Eurodollar futures option is a LIBOR option. A LIBOR cap, for example, pays the long the difference between LIBOR and a fixed strike rate times some notional principal amount on a periodic basis. It is essentially a call option on rates. Although popular stand-alone OTC derivatives, caps are frequently embedded into loans as bundled financial instruments.

Consistent with the assumption we made in Chapter 3, suppose futures prices are uncorrelated with the IMRS stochastic discount factor. Then the future three-month rate implied by the current futures price is an unbiased expectation of the three-month spot rate when the futures contract matures. If the front-month (i.e., closest to expiration) futures price is 93.39 and the contract expires in one month, three-month LIBOR is expected to be 6.61% in a month.

Consider a firm that has two alternatives for borrowing purposes. The cost of funds for each loan is shown in Figure 23.2. One is a floating-rate loan—Loan 1—in which the firm borrows and pays a quarterly coupon of LIBOR + 50 bps on an unrestricted basis. In the other loan—Loan 2—the bank allows the firm to borrow at LIBOR + 75 bps but includes a cap that guarantees the maximum coupon rate is 7.75% per annum. On Loan 1, the firm thus expects to pay 7.11% per annum but faces a potentially unlimited increase in borrowing costs. On Loan 2, the expected interest payment next quarter is 7.36% with a maximum of 7.75%.

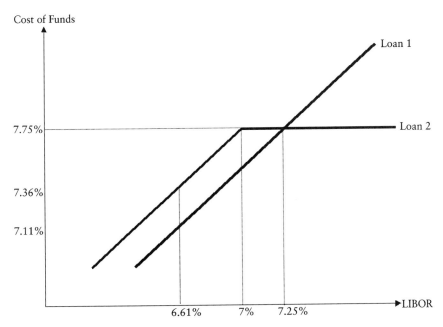

FIGURE 23.2 Cost of funds for loan 1 and loan 2.

One way that a firm can assess the cost of its alternatives—specifically, whether or not the 25 bp add on is a fair price for the cap *plus* the bank's service of embedding the cap in the loan so the firm need not worry about that—is to look at the price of a comparable LIBOR cap negotiated OTC. Alternatively, the firm can also look at the usually-cheaper Eurodollar futures market. Because Eurodollar futures are quoted in terms of prices and not rates, Figure 23.2 can be redrawn in terms of profit/loss as a function of Eurodollar price-equivalents, shown in Figure 23.3.

The break-even profit/loss on Loan 1 in Figure 23.3 occurs where rates are unchanged from their current level, 6.61% (or 93.39 in Eurodollar price-equivalents). Loan 2 has a break-even above that rate, reflecting the cost of the cap. Shown this way, in fact, it should be evident that the capped loan, Loan 2, is exposure-equivalent to a call option on Eurodollar futures. Because Loan 1 represents the exposure of the *uncapped* loan, Loan 2 can be synthetically constructed by combining the uncapped Loan 1 with a *put* on Eurodollar futures.

Once a firm recognizes the exchange-traded derivatives alternative, the cost of the do-it-yourself solution can be compared with the cost of the

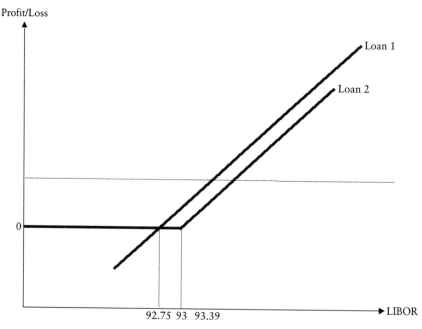

FIGURE 23.3   Loan 1 and loan 2 as Eurodollar price-equivalents.

bundled cap-and-loan. If the price of a put on front-month Eurodollar futures struck at 93 is currently 6 bps, for example, then the firm must decide whether or not the benefits of the capped loan offered by the bank are worth the 19 bps the bank is charging to bundle the cap with the loan.

Determining How Much to Hedge

The hedge ratio that a firm selects for a given exposure depends on the financial instruments used and the strategic objectives of the firm. Also important for the Risk Controller to consider are the costs of the hedge, including the costs of *rebalancing* a hedge ratio that changes over time *and* the administrative cost of recomputing hedge ratios on a regular basis. Hedges with very high administrative costs often give way to structured OTC solutions, although some firms are willing to consider a variety of intermediate alternatives first.

Principal-Matched Hedge Ratios   A principal-matched or *one-for-one* hedge ratio is the simplest hedge ratio of all. A principal-matched hedge involves the same amount hedged with derivatives that is at risk in the asset or liability being hedged on the date the hedge is initiated.

Returning to our earlier long-term commodity project hedger that is attempting to hedge catastrophic financial distress risks arising from wild swings in spot prices while simultaneously trading the basis, the optimal hedge ratio is usually one-for-one—one unit hedged for every unit sold in the long-term project. Johnson (1960) provides a sketch of the proof in his original hedging model, and Culp and Miller (1995a, c, d) provide a more contemporary discussion.[9]

Other situations in which principal-matched hedges can be attractive are situations where the firm wants to manage its risks only to a first approximation. Principal-matched hedge ratios have the weakness of being highly imperfect, but the strength of being extremely easy to both administer *and* to monitor from an internal control standpoint.

Consider a specific example of a dollar-based fund manager that operates an international equity portfolio. The investment policy allows the manager to hedge portfolio net asset value (NAV) on a discretionary basis—namely, the firm is a *value hedger.*

Suppose the manager purchases 1,000 shares of British Airways in London at £3.86 per share. At the time of the purchase, the dollar price of sterling is \$1.6805. The cost of the equity purchase *in dollars* is:

$$\$6,486.73 = £3.86 \times \$1.6805 \times 1,000$$

The manager faces two types of market risks: the risk that British Aero could perform poorly, and the risk that sterling depreciates against the dollar. Assume the manager is willing to bear the risk of declines in the value of the company given the expected return and her investment objectives but is *not* prepared to bear the exchange rate risk out of concern that it will raise the noise in the manager's performance signal one quarter hence and obscure potential investors' ability to discern her stock picking savvy.

Table 23.1 shows that the profit or loss on the position depends *both* on British Aero's performance *and* the dollar price of sterling. Table 23.1 is a type of scenario analysis as discussed in Chapter 15 where market risk is measured for nine possible combinations of exchange rate and equity price changes. The worst-case scenario is a $140.73 loss that occurs when the dollar price of sterling falls to $1.67 *and* the sterling-denominated common stock price falls by six pence per share.

Suppose the manager contemplates hedging with OTC derivatives and chooses a principal-matched hedge using a sterling *forward outright* transaction (i.e., a forward contract to sell dollars for sterling). Assume the quoted three-month outright forward purchase price for GBP is $1.6729. Because the *current* value of the position is £3,860 (i.e., £3.86/share × 1,000 shares), the manager will sell the forward with a principal amount of £3,860 at the fixed price of $1.6729/£.

Now suppose the exchange rate depreciates to $1.6700 and British Aero remains constant at the price per share of £3.86. The dollar value of the position then is:

$$\text{Net dollar profit} = (\text{Net dollar profit on naked position})$$
$$+ (\text{Net dollar profit on forward})$$

The net profit on the equity position is calculated as before—($1.67 × £3.86 × 1,000) – $6,486.73 = ($40.53). The net profit on the forward is the contract size times the difference in the forward sale price and the spot

TABLE 23.1   Scenario Analysis, British Aero—Unhedged FX Risk

$/£ Spot Rate	British Aero Price Per Share (£)		
	£3.80	£3.86	£3.90
$1.6700	($140.73)	($40.53)	$ 26.27
1.6805	(100.83)	0.00	67.22
1.6900	(64.73)	36.67	104.27

purchase price—that is, £3.86 × 1,000 × ($1.6729 − $1.6700) = $11.19. The net dollar profit/loss on the hedged position is ($29.34).

Just because the hedge plus the equity results in a loss does *not* tell us that the hedge is *a priori* a bad one. Indeed, we could have *guessed* the hedge would impose *some* loss simply because the forward price of sterling in the hedge is below the current exchange rate. Whether or not the hedge protects the manager against exchange rate *changes* cannot be determined just yet. All we know is that *if* the hedge *does* work, it will be costly because of the forward price relative to the current spot exchange rate.

To assess the quality of the hedge in protecting the manager against exchange rate *changes,* Table 23.2 repeats the scenario analysis shown in Table 23.1, but now assuming the forward hedge is in place. In fact, the hedge *does* work reasonably well. How can we tell? First, look at the value of the position *across columns*. Each column represents a different price per share of British Aero, and the position clearly still fluctuates in value for those equity price changes—just as the portfolio managers desires. Next, examine the value of the position *across rows,* each of which represents a new exchange rate. In this case, there is very little variation, indicating that the hedge is working reasonably well. The manager is protected against exchange rate *changes.*

The fact that the hedge locks in an unfavorable exchange rate is evident from examining the center box, showing a loss of $29.34 *with no change in either the equity price or the exchange rate.* Again, this simply represents the payment the manager must make to lock in a forward exchange rate at today's prevailing spot price and British-U.S. interest rate differential.

Note, however, that the hedge is *not* perfect. From row to row, there is a small amount of slippage. This occurs because the value of the equity is not constant, but the hedge chosen was principal-matched *based on the price of equity at the time the hedge was initiated.* When the price of British Aero was £3.86, the forward outright with a principal of £3,860 was just

TABLE 23.2 Scenario Analysis, British Aero—Principal-Matched FX Hedge

	British Aero Price Per Share (£)		
$/£ Spot Rate	£3.80	£3.86	£3.90
$1.6700	($129.54)	($29.34)	$37.46
1.6805	(130.17)	(29.34)	37.88
1.6900	(130.74)	(29.33)	38.27

right. But when British Aero is worth only £3.80, the forward is still based on £3,860. *The manager has become overhedged.* And conversely for equity price increases.

Because the manager chose to hedge with a forward contract, the principal cannot easily be changed. One alternative for the manager is to monitor the slippage and if the equity price moves a lot to enter into additional forwards—sterling purchase forwards to offset the sterling sales if the equity price falls and the manager becomes overhedged, or additional sterling sales to eliminate an underhedged situation if equity prices rise.

Alternatively, the manager could implement a futures hedge to help dynamically rebalance and tailor the amount hedged. Although futures might prove cheaper than new forwards, the notion that this hedge needs to be rebalanced calls into question the decision to use this hedge ratio in the first place.

Principal-matched hedges are always subject to some slippage. Either the firm is prepared to tolerate the slippage except in extremely volatile markets in order to gain the benefits of cheapness and simplicity, or the firm probably should opt for a different kind of hedge ratio altogether.

DV01, PV01, and Delta Hedge Ratios   As discussed in Chapter 15, one measure of the market risk of a position is its delta or *DV01*—dollar value of a tick or basis point. Apart from being a sensitivity measure of market risk, the *DV01* or delta is *also* a type of hedge ratio. For positions where the value of the position changes linearly with the underlying, the *DV01* can work reasonably well. For option-like exposures where gamma is significant or for exposures like fixed income instruments with a lot of convexity, the *DV01* is fairly poor.

Consider a firm with a $100 million face value loan outstanding. Suppose interest is payable quarterly and is settled in arrears, and that the next and last reset date is the third week in December—109 days from today. The loan has a floating-rate coupon of LIBOR + 50 bps, where LIBOR is defined by the bank to be the IMM Eurodollar index. Suppose the firm is a value risk manager that wants to reduce its floating-rate exposure to rising rates in December, and decides to do this by going short Eurodollar futures (i.e., long LIBOR).

Suppose the current quoted price of the December Eurodollar futures contract is 93.19. Using the assumption that the observed futures price is an unbiased predictor of future spot prices, the firm's expected interest payment to be set in December and paid three months later is 7.31% (i.e., the current futures-implied rate of 6.81% + 50 bps). Suppose the quarter following the December reset and running up to the settlement date in March has 91 days in it. So,

$$\text{Expected Dec financing cost} = (\$100\text{mm}) \times (0.0731) \times \left(\frac{91}{360}\right)$$

$$= \$1,847,806$$

As noted in Chapter 15, a DV01 or delta can be calculated either numerically or analytically. Beginning with the former approach, the firm can calculate a change in it expected financing cost if the realized 90-day LIBOR in December is 1 bp higher than implied by the current futures price:

$$+01 \text{ Dec financing cost} = (\$100\text{mm}) \times (0.0732) \times \left(\frac{91}{360}\right)$$

$$= \$1,850,333$$

The difference in the firm's expected financing cost and the +01 financing cost is clearly just $2,527, or $25.27 *per $1 million in debt*. We can interpret this as $\Delta INT/\Delta R$, or the expected change in the financing cost (INT) for a 1 bp LIBOR (R) move—that is, the delta or DV01 of the loan payment.

To calculate the DV01 hedge ratio, the firm need only *match* the delta of its loan with the delta of a Eurodollar futures contract. Happily, the DV01 of the futures contract is defined for us by the exchange when the tick size is defined. Because we know from the contract's specifications that the DV01 of a Eurodollar futures contract is $25/bp, we know that we will need to choose a hedge ratio that tries to make $\Delta INT/\Delta R$ and $\Delta ED/\Delta R$ match as closely as possible. This is $(\Delta INT/\Delta R) / (\Delta ED/\Delta R)$, or $h = \$25.27/\$25$ per million in debt, or 101.08. Because futures are only available in even lots, the firm rounds and thus goes short 101 contracts.

Even for a value hedger, however, the DV01 suffers from a problem. Suppose rates jump *immediately* by 30 bps. The firm's futures hedge of 101 short DEC Eurodollar futures yields a gain *immediately* of

$$(30\text{bps}) \times (\$25 / \text{bp}) \times (101 \text{ contracts}) = +\$75,750$$

The quoted DEC futures price is now 92.89, implying a current forward rate on three-month LIBOR expected to prevail in 109 days of 7.11%. The firm's expected financing rate is now 7.61%, and the firm's expected financing costs are now

$$(\$100\text{mm}) \times (0.761) \times \left(\frac{91}{360}\right) = \$1,923,639$$

The firm's *old* expected financing costs were $1,847,806, and its expected financing costs 200 days go up by $75,833. The futures position yielded a gain today of $75,750, so the net is a loss of $83. But is this *really* a loss?

The company's expected financing costs may have gone up 200 days hence, but you just got $75,750 in income on the hedge *today*. This money can be *invested* for the next 200 days. If we assume that the spot interest rate is 7%, the firm may invest the $75,750 for 200 days at this rate and earn $2,946 *in interest*. The firm thus actually gets $78,696 from the +30 bp change in rates relative to a change in expected financing costs of $75,833—a windfall gain of $2,863.

If rates *fall* today, however, the firm must *finance the loss* for the next 200 days. The immediate rate decline leads to an immediate variation margin call that must be funded. If the payment is funded for 200 days at the same rate as the investment rate, a 30 bp decline in rates imposes a $2,863 loss on us simply because of the need to finance the variation margin for 200 days.

This problem will arise *any time* that marked-to-market futures are used to hedge OTC derivatives or regular commercial exposures. Firms can address this problem of mismatched DV01 hedge ratios in several ways. As a simple and basic approximation, the firm can calculate a tail for the hedge, or an approximate number of contracts to subtract from the hedge to address the cash flow mistiming.[10] The number of contracts in the tail is

$$\text{Tail} = -Nr\left(\frac{d}{360}\right)$$

where N is the number of contracts in the original hedge, r is the rate at which the firm finances losses or invests gains for 200 days, and d is the number of actual financing days between the hedge initiation date and the payment of interest on the loan. In this example, the tail is as follows:

$$\text{Tail} = -101 \times 0.0731 \times \frac{200}{360} = -4.1$$

so that you reduce the original hedge of 101 short contracts by 4 contracts and go short 97 December Eurodollar futures contracts.

In general, the further away the cash flows on the asset or liability being hedged, the larger the tail and the more *overhedged* an unadjusted delta or DV01 hedge ratio will make the firm. Unfortunately, time to maturity and rates change daily, forcing the hedger to recompute the tail each day—and possibly rebalance the size of the hedge just as often.

A slightly more precise alternative to tailing the hedge is, as discussed in Chapter 15, to use a PV01, or the present value of a DV01, as the basis for the hedge ratio. This time, suppose we begin by expressing the expected financing costs in basis points:

$$INT = (\$FV) \times \left(\frac{i}{10,000} \right) \times \left(\frac{d}{360} \right)$$

where *FV* is the face value of loan, *i* is the annualized percentage 90-day rate *in basis points,* and *d* is the same as before.

In our example, $d = 91$ days, $\$FV = \$100mm$, $i = R \times 100 = 7.31\% \times 100 = 731$ bps, and $INT = \$1,847,806$. Instead of changing this number numerically as in the prior example, suppose we derive an analytical delta by differentiating *INT* with respect to *i* to find the sensitivity of the financing cost to a one bp change in rates (i.e., the basis point delta):

$$\frac{dINT}{di} = \left(\frac{\$FV}{10,000} \right) \times \left(\frac{d}{360} \right) = \$FV \times 0.0001 \times \left(\frac{d}{360} \right)$$

In our example,

$$\frac{dINT}{di} = \$100mm \times 0.0001 \times \left(\frac{91}{360} \right) = \$2,527.78$$

This is the same DV01 we found before by manually changing rates by one bp and calculating $\Delta INT/\Delta R$.

Unlike the DV01, suppose now that the firm computes the *present value* of the DV01 using the current expected financing rate and assuming it prevails over 200 days:

$$PV01 = PV(DV01) = \frac{\$2,527}{(1.0731)^{200/360}} = \$2,430.62$$

Because cash flows on the futures occur immediately, the PV01 of the Eurodollar contract is equal to the DV01— $25. Calculate the present value-matched hedge ratio as the ratio of the two PV01s:

$$h = \frac{PV01_{FRN}}{PV01_{ED}} = \frac{\$2,430.62}{\$25} = 97.22$$

So, the firm shorts 97 contracts instead of 101 as before. Now, a +30 bp rate increase yields a $72,750 gain immediately (30bp × $25/bp × 97 contracts), which can be invested at 7.31% to yield $75,698 200 days hence. This is only $175 short of the increase in expected financing costs, as compared to the $1,374 difference we saw with the DV01-matched hedge. Note, moreover, that the $PV01$ hedge ratio is the same in this example as the tailed DV01 hedge ratio.

The PV01 hedge ratio should be appealing to value hedgers and *some* earnings hedgers, provided the firms are content with a delta-based measure of risk. If there is any convexity in the position, the PV01 hedge ratio will fail to capture it, resulting again in slippage as well as the need for regular rebalancings.

The futures are still margined, however, at least daily. Whether or not a cash flow hedger will find this solution palatable thus depends more fundamentally on *why* the firm is a cash flow hedger. If the company is concerned with underinvestment in the sense of the Froot, Scharfstein, and Stein model, then this solution will not work. Although the size of the hedge has equated the present values of the cash flows, *any* cash flow volatility is undesirable in that model. But for a cash flow hedger that is concerned merely with actual cash balances on the date of its loan payment, the $PV01$ hedge will work fine.

Variance-Minimizing Hedge Ratios   What if the Risk Controller *is* concerned with convexity? One option is return to the Johnson-Stein-Ederington model presented in Chapter 2. *If* the firm is willing to assume that variance is a sufficient measure of risk for the market in question *and* variance reduction is consistent with the firm's rationale for managing risk, the variance-minimizing hedge ratio can make sense. As discussed in Chapter 2, the variance-minimizing hedge ratio is simply the OLS beta in a regression of changes in the asset or liability being hedged on the change in value of the hedge itself.

In some markets, OLS is not the best way of computing this hedge ratio. For a firm interested in using a variance-minimizing hedge of its currency risk, the fat tails of most exchange rate return distributions *and* the known serial correlation in volatility will both render a hedge ratio based on OLS beta sub-optimal. Instead, the firm can try to capture the dynamics of the market more realistically. For example, estimating a GARCH(1,1) model with errors drawn from a Student's *t* or generalized error distribution will yield a beta coefficient that outperforms OLS beta in many situations.

Other Hedge Ratios   Depending on how the firm can define and characterize its risks, other hedge ratios also can be estimated—for example, hedge ratios based on asymmetric distributions or presumed changes in vega and other risk factors that OLS beta will miss. In general, however, the more complex the hedge ratio, the more cumbersome and costly it will be for the firm to rebalance the hedge ratio.

Note also that most swaps and some forwards do not require hedge ratio estimation. Instead, the settlement dates are simply *matched,* thus eliminating the need for rebalancing. At the same time, the Risk Controller is likely to have to pay for that, because the dealer, in turn, will simply pass on *its* hedging costs to its counterparties.

CHAPTER 24

Tactical Risk Control through Actual and Synthetic Asset Divestitures

When the risk associated with an asset cannot easily be hedged with derivatives, a corporation whose tolerance for that risk is well below current or expected future exposures may have no choice but to get rid of the asset. This chapter discusses various mechanisms for such asset divestitures, both actual and synthetic, including asset sales, syndication, securitization, and synthetic securitization using derivatives.

Despite the fundamental similarity in these mechanisms for removing all or part of an asset's risk exposures from a firm's economic balance sheet, some mechanisms, as will be explained next, are more tactically oriented than others. Actual asset sales, for example, tend to be blunt and final and hence more consistent with strategic risk management decisions, whereas synthetic asset divestitures are reversible and hence more useful for tactical purposes. The particular risk control method chosen thus yet again depends strongly on the strategic risk management objectives of the firm.

ASSET SALES

When a corporation has a concern about its actual risk exposures vis-à-vis the tolerances of its stakeholders, one solution is for the company to divest itself of the asset giving rise to the unintended exposure. A Japanese firm that funds a Brazilian chemical factory with yen-denominated debt, for example, has an exchange rate risk arising from both the relative mismatch between the currency denomination of the asset (the factory) and the liability (the debt) and an absolute exposure to changes in the real/yen exchange rate arising exclusively from the asset exposure. If the risk of a devaluation becomes significant, the firm may be unwilling to tolerate the exchange rate risk.

Derivatives on the Brazilian real are notoriously hard to find outside of the United States. Consequently, the Japanese firm may not have an easily available hedging solution using derivatives. If the exchange rate risk is deemed high enough, the Japanese firm may need to sell the factory to control the risk exposure. Especially if the factory is sold at a fair price to a local firm, the resale of the asset will result in the Japanese firm bearing no exchange rate risks or costs.

Selling physical assets is not a particularly easy or low-cost way to handle the finer points of risk management tactics. On the contrary, asset divestiture is a rather blunt way of disgorging risks from a corporate balance sheet. But especially when physical assets and the real options they convey are the source of the unexpected and undesired exposure, asset divestiture may be the only solution for the firm, as in the case above.

LOAN SYNDICATION

In the early 1970s, banks began to contemplate ways of increasing their capacity to make loans in the face of uncertain economic conditions and liquidity considerations. Banks discovered that by chopping up their balance sheets into pieces and off-loading some of their loan exposures to other intermediaries, they could keep their credit and liquidity exposures manageable, their interest rate risk profiles within tolerable exposure limits, and their capital requirements down. At the same time, banks could continue earning fees on loan servicing.

Syndication in the commercial bank loan market arose in the 1970s to accommodate banks' desires to spread the risk of their commercial loans to other financial institutions. In loan syndication, a bank arranges, underwrites, and effectively sells chunks of large bank loan assets to a group of other banks or investors, called a *syndicate*.

A leveraged *commercial and industrial* (C&I) loan is a bank loan priced at LIBOR plus 150 basis points or more.[1] These noninvestment grade loans typically are senior in capital structure, collateralized, and have interest payments based on floating rates. Leveraged C&I loans may be used to finance relatively risky companies or to fund specific projects. Such loans gained popularity in the 1980s as a means of financing highly leveraged transactions (HLTs) such as LBOs, leveraged recapitalizations, and acquisitions.

Leveraged C&I loan syndication greatly increased in popularity in the mid-1980s when HLTs became popular. Aggregate liquidity was high and macroeconomic conditions were favorable, contributing to a spurt of LBOs and other HLTs and increasing corporate demands for leveraged bank financing. But still wishing to protect their balance sheets from business cycle downturns, banks became *heavily* involved in diversifying their credit and interest rate risk through leveraged loan syndication. Banks even began to establish loan distribution desks to oversee the underwriting and placement of portions of large corporate loans whose purposes were financing HLTs.

Banks continued to search for new and more efficient ways to manage their existing HLT exposures even after their actual extensions of leveraged credit had dropped off. As bank demands for risk diversification continued to grow, a secondary market for leveraged bank loans emerged around 1989. This illustrates an important distinction between asset *transformation* and *liquification*. The former is the transformation of a nonfungible asset into another, often-tradable form, whereas the latter is the development of actual trading in that asset in a semi-liquid or liquid marketplace. Many assets undergo a transformation process without ever undergoing liquification, but the converse is virtually never true.

Secondary market loan trading began with a few loan trading desks at a small group of money center banks and investment banks that wanted to alter their exposures to a few specific HLTs, such as the RJR Nabisco buyout. Since then, the market has continued to liquify. More than 30 loan trading desks specializing in leveraged loans now exist at various commercial and investment banks—all of which actively bid for chunks of loan exposures.[2]

SECURITIZATION[3]

Securitization is one of the cheapest and most popular means by which certain assets can be extracted from a firm's balance sheet and transformed into tradable securities.[4] A typical securitization usually includes seven participants. The first is the firm that has the asset on its books. In the case of a loan, for example, the loan originator and/or servicer is the owner of the asset and all the risk exposures—market, credit, liquidity, operational, and legal—that the asset creates.

A second participant in the securitization process is a trust, often called a special purpose vehicle (SPV), special purpose entity (SPE), or special purpose trust. The trust is an entity created for the sole purpose of purchasing the assets to be securitized from their owner and to issue securities using those acquired assets as collateral. Once the assets to be sold are conveyed to the SPV, it is responsible for the management of the collateral and the administration of cash receivables and payables. As part of those responsibilities, the SPV is responsible for the design of the asset-backed securities to be issued (i.e., the manner in which the cash inflows on the new assets will be transformed into new assets in the form of securities). The SPV may be an affiliate of the bank or investment bank that underwrites and/or distributes the securities based on the newly acquired assets, but the SPV typically cannot be a direct affiliate of the owner of the original assets.

A third participant in the securitization process is the underwriter(s) that prices the securities issued by the SPV. Apart from pricing, the underwriter also markets and distributes the securities to investors.

The fourth participant in the securitization process is the ultimate investor in the new paper. Without investors to purchase and hold or trade the securities issued by the SPV, the securitization process would not accomplish much more than transferring a nonfungible asset from one entity (the originator) to another (the SPV). Asset transformation does not occur until securities based on the assets are issued, sold, and bought.

The four above participants in the securitization process all play a role in the transformation of the asset from a nonfungible exposure on one firm's balance sheet into a tradable security. The remaining three participants are involved in the securitization both to try and ensure that some investor will buy the new securitized products and that a market for the trading of those products might arise. One such participant is the *credit support provider*—of which there may be more than one. A credit support provider helps ensure that the assets conveyed to the trust provide adequate collateral to back the new securities, even in the worst of times. Quite often the assets transferred to a SPV in a securitization are *not* adequate to back an issue without additional support, and that additional credit support—overcollateralization—comes from the credit support provide in the form of a letter of credit, guarantee, senior subordinated debt structure, or pledged reserve account. Sound credit support provision is necessary both to make the new securities attractive to their original holders *and* to stimulate trading in those securities.

Closely related to the role of the credit support provider(s) is the *liquidity* support provider. Whereas credit support providers commit to making up any shortfall on the assets of the trust below its liabilities, liquidity support providers commit instead to providing short-term financing for the *servicing* of the newly issued securities. Liquidity support is provided to ensure that mis-timings in cash flows do not trigger defaults on the new securities. Credit support providers guarantee the SPV against losses arising from credit risk on its new assets, but liquidity support providers do not—they guarantee *nothing* except short-term financing when required, and even then a liquidity support provider may demand proof that the funding need is *not* a result of a credit default.

The final participants in most securitizations are the rating agencies that assess the likelihood of default on the newly issued debt.[5] Apart from the quality of the collateral, the agencies also review the credit and liquidity support facilities in order to determine the appropriate rating. To encourage investors both to buy and to trade the new securities most securitization sponsors aim for double- or triple-A credit ratings.

Assets that have been securitized in the 1980s and the 1990s include:

- Mortgages.
- Home equity loans.
- Auto loans.
- C&I loans.
- Mobile home loans.
- Marine loans.
- Student loans.
- Franchise loans.
- SBA loans.
- Credit card receivables.
- Computer leases.
- Aircraft leases.
- Equipment leases.
- Variable annuity fees.
- Delinquent tax liens.
- Utility stranded costs.

Essentially anything can be securitized, provided the right legal infrastructure and contracting framework exist to permits securitization. Some more creative forms of securitization will be discussed in Chapter 26.

Examples of Securitization Initiatives

To illustrate how securitization can facilitate asset transformation and market liquification, several different examples of the securitization process are presented next. Although all have fundamentally the same structure, the commodization process in each of these three cases evolved a bit differently.

Mortgage-Backed Securities   Perhaps the most well-known class of asset-backed security is the mortgage-backed security (MBS). A MBS is created through the securitization of a pool of mortgage loans. The simplest example of a MBS is a mortgage pass-through security. Pass-throughs are created when holders of mortgages form a pool and sell shares of participation certificates in the pool. The cash flows earned by investors in pass-through securities are based on principal and interest payments on the underlying mortgages.

In the context of our earlier discussion, MBSs are examples of transformed assets—mortgage loan assets are transformed into tradeable mortgage-backed securities through securitization. The main types of pass-through securities available in the United States are those guaranteed by government-sponsored enterprises (GSEs), such as the Federal National Mortgage Association. Aside from providing guarantees that made the emergence of pass-throughs possible, these GSEs also played a significant role in *liquifying* the pass-through market in the early 1980s. By *trading* these securities, the GSEs essentially *created* a secondary market. In the process, the role of GSEs as institutions shifted away from the provision of loan guarantees toward active participation in the capital market as financial intermediaries.

MBSs also can be transformed into new assets through additional securitizations or the use of mortgage derivatives. Collateralized mortgage obligations (CMOs), for example, are securitized products based on the transformation of *mortgage-backed securities,* as opposed to the underlying mortgage assets themselves. CMOs first appeared in 1983 and gained widespread popularity by 1986.

CMOs are issued when a collateral manager acquires a portfolio of pass-through securities and repackages the cash flows from those securities into *tranches*. Various types of tranches can be created in a CMO structure. As an example, consider a CMO structure in which cash flows on the pass-throughs are allocated into tranches based on the prepayment speeds of the underlying mortgages. Specifically, suppose the collateral manager acquires a $400 million dollar pool of MBSs and allocates the cash flows from those securities into four tranches. The collateral manager then issues three classes of bonds with total face values of $100 million each and regular coupon payments. The residual $100 million defines the CMO's "equity" component. The first type of bond is a claim against the first $100 million principal repaid on the MBS portfolio and has an expected effective tenor of five to six years. The bonds issued against this fast pay tranche are called *A bonds*. Next come the types of bonds issued against the second medium pay tranche, based on the *next* $100 million in mortgage payments. The effective tenor of medium pay bonds usually is about 12 to 15 years. The last tranche would be the slow pay bonds whose term exceeds 15 years. The residual $100 million is then allocated to a specialized tranche known as the *Z tranche* which collateralizes the "equity" or Z bond issue. Z bonds combine features of zero-coupon bonds with mortgage pass-throughs, and holders of these bonds receive no payments until all earlier bond classes have been paid off.

Asset-Backed Commercial Paper Programs   Securities backed by *non*mortgage assets also are actively issued and traded today. One such security is issued through what is called an "asset-backed commercial paper program" (ABCP program).[6] An ABCP program involves the transformation of a pool of receivables into tradeable securities whose cash flows are based on the cash flows accruing to the receivables. The first asset-backed commercial paper program was sponsored by a commercial bank in 1983 and was backed by assets including computer leases, credit card receivables, auto loans, and more.[7] Since then, these programs have experienced dramatic growth. At the end of 1987, less than $10 billion was outstanding in asset-backed commercial paper programs, whereas over $145 billion was outstanding in ABCP programs by year-end 1996.[8]

ABCP programs evolved in the early 1980s as a response by commercial banks to the shift in corporate borrowing away from banks toward public commercial paper offerings, *especially* when the debt was used to finance asset purchases. Sensitive to ballooning credit risk exposures to their corporate customers, commercial banks were constrained in their ability to respond directly to this competitive threat. In addition, under the Basel Accord, banks were (and are) required to hold capital against credit-sensitive transactions such as loans. Consequently, banks were unable to stem the liquification of short-term project financing as it evolved away from direct bank loans to public debt markets.

ABCP programs provided banks with a means of arranging short-term financing for their customers *without directly extending them credit*. As such, asset-backed commercial paper programs created an innovative *conduit* for banks to participate in public securities issues without forcing them to relinquish their roles as opaque financial intermediaries. ABCP programs thus were an innovation that evolved in response to the liquification of project financing markets.

In an ABCP program, a bank wishing to help its customers in financing asset purchases without extending them direct credit sets up a SPV that is separate and apart from the bank and whose assets and liabilities are not consolidated onto the bank's balance sheet. The bank then supervises the conveyance of the receivables to be securitized to the SPV, and the SPV in turn securitizes (i.e., transforms) the receivables and issues paper against the rebundled cash flows. In addition to sponsoring ABCP programs, banks also participate in such programs by providing credit and liquidity support to the SPV for the new paper.[9]

Through ABCP structures, banks were able to meet the demands of their customers while avoiding the capital requirements associated with direct loan obligations and while generating fee income for related services (e.g., packaging and monitoring the receivables underlying the paper). So, the innovation of ABCP as a new financial product precipitated a shift in the institutional focus of banks away from short-term project financing toward other intermediation activities like receivables management and credit or liquidity support provisions.

CLOs and CBOs   The first C&I loan-based securitized products were called "collateralized loan obligations" (CLOs) and bear great resemblance to CMOs. In a typical CLO structure, a collateral manager acquires commercial loans from the originating bank(s), unbundles the cash flows on those loans, allocates them into tranches based on loan credit risk, and issues securities against those tranches.

Since their first appearance in 1988, CLOs and collateralized bond obligations (CBOs) have become increasingly popular. In 1990, only seven CBO originations occurred, but by 1996, more than 25 structures had been established.[10] A total of $11.5 billion in debt was securitized in 1996 through CBOs or CLOs, and as of August 1997, over $11.25 billion in debt was pledged as collateral in such programs. Fitch Investors Service, Inc., projected the total 1997 loan securitization volume in CBO structures to exceed $35 billion.[11]

Securities issued by CLO managers typically are issued against three types of tranches—based on credit risks rather than prepayment speeds as in CMOs. First, *senior debt* is issued against the highest-rated loans in the structure. Senior debt may be fixed- or floating-rate and typically has a lower expected return *and* volatility than the underlying loans. Credit enhancements often are added to the CLO structure to make the senior debt investment grade. Second, *senior subordinated debt* is collateralized with the medium credit risk loans owned by the CLO manager. Finally, *junior subordinated debt* or *equity* is the security class issued against the riskiest tranche. Expected returns and volatility often are *higher* than the aggregate return and risk of the underlying loans. Leverage, moreover, can be incorporated into the equity tranche fairly easily in a typical CLO, thus increasing both the expected return and risk of the equity tranche.

SYNTHETIC SECURITIZATIONS USING CREDIT DERIVATIVES

Through the creative use of credit derivatives called *total return swaps,* banks and other firms can manage their risks by getting rid of whole asset exposures in a manner that neither requires asset divestiture nor securitization. Credit derivatives enable firms to disgorge their market, credit, and liquidity risks on an asset *synthetically*—without the investor or a security issuer acquiring ownership of the original assets. All that is required to undertake a synthetic securitization through a swap is a viable underlying asset and a willing swap counterparty.

Mechanically, a total return swap allows a firm to enter into an agreement with a swap dealer or some other counterparty and periodically receive LIBOR plus some spread in exchange for paying an income stream based directly on the performance of the asset that the firm wants to rid itself of. Responsibility for originating and servicing the asset remains with the hedger, but the swap counterparty assumes all of the financial risks of the asset.

The Riverwood Term Loan B Swap

Total return swaps are perhaps best explained by example. Barnish, Miller, and Rushmore (1997) describe a AA-rated insurance company that entered into a swap with a bank to acquire a portion of a Term Loan B made to a firm called Riverwood International. Riverwood's Term Loan B had a principal amount of larger than $10 million, but the insurance company only wanted to acquire a $10 million participation in the loan. The insurance company thus entered into a swap with notional principal of $10 million whose total return was driven by the performance of the Riverwood loan.

The coupon paid by Riverwood on the original loan was LIBOR + 300 bps. Accordingly, the insurance company agreed with its swap counterparty to *receive* that Riverwood coupon payment of LIBOR + 300 bps *plus or minus* the change in the market price of the Riverwood loan, in exchange for which the insurance company periodically *paid* the Bank LIBOR + 75 bps. The 75 bps paid by the insurance company to the Bank was its financing spread x, and the 300 bps received by the insurance company—equal to the spread over LIBOR on the Bank's loan to Riverwood—was the gross loan interest income r. The *net interest income* portion of the swap's cash flow thus was 225 bps per period, and the remaining *principal* component of the swap's total return was based solely on the price change of the Riverwood loan.

Viewed another way, the insurance company engaged in two parallel loans with the Bank, both with a principal value of $10 million. On one loan, the insurance company *borrowed* $10 million from the Bank at LIBOR + 75 bps. On the other side, the insurance company *loaned* $10 million to the Bank at LIBOR + 300. The Bank thus paid to the insurance company exactly what it received from Riverwood in interest payments, getting 75 bps from the insurance company in return *plus* the knowledge that any decline in the market value of the Riverwood loan reduced the Bank's interest payment to the insurance company. From the insurance company's perspective, it received a stable 225 bps each period in the swap, representing the spread of the Riverwood coupon over its own financing rate from the Bank. In exchange for receiving 225 bps each period, the insurance company bore the risk of any principal default or price decline on the Riverwood loan.

To see the risk and return features of this swap, suppose first that the Riverwood loan price did not change. Suppose further (as was actually the case in this swap) that the Bank demanded 10% of the $10 million notional amount of the swap as collateral on the swap. The insurance company thus committed capital of $1 million in the form of Treasuries to the Bank to collateralize any potential losses on the swap. (The insurance company continued to earn interest on those Treasuries.) *With no change in the price of the Riverwood loan,* the insurance company thus would have earned a return of 22.5% per period in excess of the Treasury rate on its invested capital. To arrive at that number, recognize that in the absence of a loan price change, the *net* interest income on the swap to the insurance company was $225,000:

$$
\begin{aligned}
\text{Net income} &= \$10,000,000 \times [(\text{LIBOR} + 300 \text{ bps}) - (\text{LIBOR} + 75 \text{ bps})] \\
&= \$10,000,000 \times 225 \text{bps} \\
&= \$225,000
\end{aligned}
$$

Relative to the $1 million in collateral posted by the insurance company, the return *in excess of the Treasury rate on the collateral* was 22.5%. Because the insurance company posted only $1 million in collateral for a cash flow stream based on a $10 million principal amount, the *leverage factor* embedded in this swap was 10:1, explaining the high return on capital.

Now, suppose the Riverwood loan declined in market value because of missed interest payments or the prospect of an unrecoverable principal default. If the Riverwood loan depreciated by 10%, for example, the income to the insurance company would have been *reduced by the entire amount of the capital pledged as collateral* (i.e., a 10% market value decline on a $10mm loan would have resulted in a $1mm reduction in swap income for the insurance company).

Derivatives-Based Structured Notes

The financial innovation process does not end with derivatives. On the contrary, derivatives create demand for other derivatives, as well as other securities. In that regard, firms have begun to issue structured notes based on synthetically securitized assets. A structured note is any debt security that combines features of a straight debt instrument with a derivatives contract.[12] Structured notes based on total return swaps with bank loans behind them have been called Leveraged Loan-based Structured Notes (LLSNs) and Bank-Loan Asset-Backed Secured Note Trust Notes (BLAST Notes™).

Derivatives-based structured notes are issued in the same manner as securitized products, with the same seven types of participants involved. Instead of an asset owner that coveys assets to the SPV, however, a derivatives-based structured note involves a swap counterparty that enters into a total return swap with the SPV. The cash flows on that swap then serve as the collateral for the securities issued by the SPV to investors, which are in turn backed by credit and liquidity support providers.

Mechanically, the issuance of the structured notes can be viewed in several distinct steps. First, the issuer must decide on the leverage factor to be reflected in the note. A leverage factor of 2 : 1, for example, implies that the loan portfolio underlying the structured note is twice as large in face value as the total subscriptions to the note will be. Based on that leverage factor, the issuer then collects initial subscriptions of some amount from investors and invests those proceeds in Treasury securities. These Treasuries serve effectively to collateralize the face value of the notes and, hence, to guarantee principal repayment.

Given the subscription amount and leverage ratio, the sponsoring bank or investment manager then engages in a total return swap with the bank that originated the desired loan portfolio. As in any total return swap, the note issuer pays LIBOR plus some financing spread in exchange for receiving payments equal to the price change in the loan portfolio plus LIBOR plus the spread of the loan portfolio's yield over LIBOR. Payments to note holders are based on the income from the swap. Note that the leverage factor comes into play because the interest payments between the trust and the bank/sponsor are based on the full value of the loan portfolio, whereas the subscriptions collected by the SPV are less than that amount. A leverage factor of 2 : 1, for example, implies a loan portfolio and swap with a principal amount twice as large as the face value of the securities issued by the SPV. Coupon payments are based on the structured note's face value, but the *actual coupon yield* is twice as high.

A concrete example will help illustrate the mechanics. The Chase Secured Loan Trust Note was a derivatives-based structured note sponsored by Chase Securities. The underlying loan portfolio on which the coupon payments of the notes were based had a $150 million face value. The SPV issued the notes entered into a total return swap with Chase that had payments based on the $150 million loan portfolio and a notional principal of $150 million. The Trust periodically paid Chase LIBOR plus a financing spread of 125 bps, in return for which the Trust received periodic payments equal to LIBOR plus the coupon rate on the loan portfolio of 365 bps plus the change in the price of the loans. Chase thus paid the Trust a (possibly negative) *net* spread of 240 bps plus the loan price change.

The Trust collected $50 million from investors as an initial subscription for the notes. The ratio of this subscription amount to the notional principal of the swap (i.e., face value of the loan portfolio) thus was 3:1. After collecting its initial subscription to the notes, the trust invested the $50 million in Treasuries earning 6.4% per annum.

In return for their initial investment of $50 million, the investors in the Chase structured securities received a *leveraged* coupon payment of 13.6% plus the loan price change, computed relative to the $50 million face value of the notes. The coupon yield of 13.6% was based on the 6.4% Treasury yield *plus* the *leveraged* net spread of 7.20% on the loan portfolio embedded in the swap—that is, the 240 bps net spread times the leverage factor of 3:1.

CHAPTER 25

Strategic Risk Control with Structured Liabilities

E fficiency enhancement-oriented firms can often restructure their liabilities to accomplish risk control objectives. This type of risk control is generally much more strategic than tactical, but it can be effective for both purposes if well-crafted and properly implemented.

A structured liability or structured debt instrument can be defined as a straight debt instrument whose cash flows are linked to the value of some underlying asset, reference rate, or index. Structured debt instruments are thus debt plus derivatives. They are also sometimes called *hybrid debt*.[1] Some of the means by which firms can use these instruments—as *issuers* of them—to manage their risks both strategically and tactically are summarized in this chapter.[2]

REDUCING CREDIT RISK AND EXPANDING DEBT CAPACITY

Structured products have been used to manage credit risk stemming from changes in interest rates, foreign exchange rates, commodity prices, equity prices, the slope of the yield curve, the correlation between asset prices, and other prices and rates.[3] Smithson and Chew (1994) document an excellent example of how one firm used a structured liability to help its lenders manage their credit risk and to increase its own debt capacity.

In late 1989 Sonatrach, the state-owned hydrocarbon producer of Algeria, was having difficulty servicing a conventional floating-rate note issue held by a syndicate of banks. In 1990, the Chase Manhattan Bank led a restructuring in which Sonatrach's FRNs were retired with a series of inverse oil-indexed bonds. The transaction was structured as follows:

1. Sonatrach issued new FRNs indexed at 100 basis points over LIBOR to a group of syndicate banks.
2. Sonatrach also wrote two-year calls on oil with a strike price of $23 to Chase.
3. Chase wrote seven-year calls on oil (strike $22) and wrote seven-year puts on oil (strike $16) to the syndicate banks.

In return for being granted the oil price puts and calls by Chase, the syndicate accepted a significantly lower spread over LIBOR—by some estimates, several hundred basis points lower—than what would otherwise have been Sonatrach's floating-rate cost of funds. This reduction in interest costs in turn reduced the likelihood that Sonatrach would experience further financial trouble. The options, moreover, imposed no additional oil price risk on Sonatrach because the firm was committed to additional option payments only when the price of oil rose above $23. The company's financing burden thus increased only when it could most afford the additional interest payments.

By restructuring the notes in this fashion, Chase and its investors increased the creditworthiness of Sonatrach, thereby increasing the probability of receiving their promised payoffs. At the same time, by cutting its periodic cash flow volatility and its debt overhang, Sonatrach reduced its underinvestment costs (as discussed in *both* Chapters 6 and 7) dramatically and thus increased its debt capacity.

MANAGING LIQUIDITY AND CASH FLOW RISK

Because of the uncertain speeds at which demand deposit accounts (DDAs) will reprice, unanticipated cash flow and funding shocks can be a major risk for depository institutions that fund their assets with DDAs. One particular structured note was very popular in the early 1990s as a source of funding risk management for many cash flow-focused Risk Controllers.

Between June and December 1993, over $2 billion in accrual notes and bonds were issued by corporations, mainly financial institutions. One such institution, Paribas Capital Markets, issued a two-year accrual note in 1993 that paid 1.35% over the two-year Treasury rate for each day LIBOR remained within a specified range and *that paid nothing* for those days LIBOR fell outside the range. As shown in Table 25.1, the payoff range moved upward over time to reflect a positively-sloped forward rate yield curve.[4]

If rates remained within the reference range throughout the entire period, Paribas would end up paying exactly 1.35% over two-year Treasuries. But if rates rose more slowly than what was implied by the shape of the reference

TABLE 25.1 Reference Ranges for
Paribas' LIBOR-Linked Accrual Notes

Coupon Period	LIBOR (%)
1	3.25–4.00
2	3.50–4.5625
3	3.75–5.00
4	3.75–5.3125

Source of data: Falloon (1993).

range in Table 25.1, the accrual structure would have reduced Paribas' borrowing costs. And if rates rose and remained above the ceiling of the reference range, Paribas' borrowing costs would actually have gone down.[5]

The Paribas structured notes can be viewed as zero coupon bonds with a series of embedded digital options. Once in the money, the option payoffs did not increase with the level of interest rates. For investors, the Paribas accrual notes thus represented a combination of straight debt and a short position on interest rate volatility. In return for giving Paribas the corresponding long position on volatility, investors (who presumably view the reference range as a likely outcome) were able to obtain a higher rate of return.

Paribas was evidently willing to pay as much as 150 basis points over its normal floating-rate cost to protect itself against the funding risk of sharp increases in interest rates. Such an increase would have raised not only the interest cost of conventional floaters, but also—more importantly—Paribas' cost of attracting and even just retaining DDAs.

MANAGING THE COSTS OF ASYMMETRIC INFORMATION

Structured debt has proven especially useful in raising funds when management believes the firm's prospects are about to improve significantly but the capital market does not necessarily agree. As discussed in Chapter 7, when a firm has a lot of intangible or latent assets (e.g., R&D, patents, intellectual property, e-commerce), capital market participants may be significantly less equipped to assess the true NPVs of the firm's investment opportunities. Especially if credit and capital markets are exaggerating the firm's risk by misperceiving the noise contained in earnings announcements. In this context, structured debt can help reduce the cost of underinvestment in the sense of Froot, Scharfstein, and Stein (1993) and increase the signal to noise ratio reflected in accounting aggregates like earnings, both of which were discussed in Chapter 7.

Rating Sensitive Notes

Consider the floating-rate, rating-sensitive notes issued by Manufacturer's Hanover in February 1988. This security provided that, if Manufacturer's credit rating fell, the spread over LIBOR that was paid on the notes would increase.

Why would Manny Hanny issue such a security? Investors presumably charged a lower spread in return for this (partial) protection against a credit downgrade. But if viewed as a risk management vehicle from the issuer's point of view, such rating sensitive notes have a serious shortcoming: They would have required an *increase* in interest payments at precisely the time when the issuer was least able to afford it.

Of course, this may have been the only set of terms on which the bank's investors would have agreed to provide debt financing. But another possible explanation is that Manny Hanny's management felt that, in the bank's then-depressed circumstances, further downgrading of the firm's credit position was highly unlikely. Especially if the firm was more focused on value and earnings than cash flows, senior managers and stakeholders may well have been willing to bet their perception of the firm's growth prospects and financial condition against the credit market's skepticism by putting themselves in a position to be penalized should they be proved wrong.

Putable Bonds

The same argument can also be used to help explain why some corporations choose to issue putable notes and bonds, including Merrill Lynch's LYONs™ which are putable, callable, zero-coupon, convertible bonds. Such securities give investors the option to put the notes back to the issuer for their face value if either interest rates rise or the firm's credit rating falls. By granting such options, the issuing firm funds its operations at a lower rate—or, in the case of zero-coupon LYONs™, a lower yield to maturity.

At the same time, issuers of putable notes bear considerable interest rate and liquidity risks. They will be forced to redeem and perhaps refinance at higher interest rates if either rates rise or their own credit position weakens. As in the case of rating sensitive notes, offering such options to investors makes sense mainly in cases where management's information about the firm's financial stability and future is better quality than the market's and significantly exceeds the expectations of the market.

Convertibles

Convertible bonds, a relatively old-fashioned kind of structured liability, may be an especially useful way of resolving differences in assessments by management and investors of the firm's risk and creditworthiness. Brennan and Schwartz (1988) argue that convertibles are relatively insensitive to estimates of the issuer's credit risk because their two components—debt and an option on the firm's equity—are affected by increases in risk in totally opposite ways. An increase in or underestimation of the volatility of a company's cash flows may reduce the value of fixed debt claims, but it serves to *increase* the value of the option on the company's equity.

Largely for this reason, the use of convertibles tends to be concentrated among smaller, high-growth companies with more volatile earnings—companies that find straight debt financing prohibitively expensive. Convertibles are ideal for such issuers because the lower interest payments (LYONs™, in fact, are *zero-coupon* convertibles), reduce the risk of financial distress and reduce the Myers underinvestment problem.

REDUCING AGENCY COSTS

Chapters 5 and 6 indicated that risk management can provide an alternative to mechanisms like bond covenants for reducing the costs of conflicts between managers and security holders or amongst security holders. Structured debt can reduce such costs by addressing sources of conflict between bondholders and either the management team or shareholders. Putable bonds, for example, guard against the managerial temptation to leverage or otherwise increase the risk of the company by giving bondholders the option to put the security back to the issuer. Convertibles also help control asset substitution—as well as the inclination of management to underinvest in the sense of Myers' debt overhang—by the mere fact that the convertible holders participate in any gains created at the expense of the bondholders.

Convertible and putable LYONs™ were reportedly introduced in 1985 by Merrill Lynch White Weld Capital Markets Group in part to address the problem of asset substitution.[6] Indeed, holders of LYONs™ were *doubly* protected against any efforts by management to increase the risk of its investment projects—they could either redeem the notes if things were turning out badly, or, if the increased risk turned into the prospect of greater rewards, they could convert their claims into equity. Consistent with this argument, early issuers of LYONs™ such as Waste Management and MCI were primarily companies in risky, or at least temporarily out of favor, businesses.[7]

In addressing agency problems like those mentioned above, management can achieve the same result by issuing straight debt and then just using derivatives as discussed in Chapter 23 instead of issuing structured debt. But one advantage of structured debt in such circumstances is that it reduces the costs incurred by security holders in monitoring the borrower's hedging activity—costs that (see Chapter 5) are ultimately borne by the inside manager/equity owners.[8] Structured debt reduces monitoring costs by forcing the borrower to precommit itself to a hedging policy *as a condition of borrowing.*

To illustrate this point, suppose that the creditors of an exporter insist that the firm hedge its exposure to foreign exchange depreciation. To hedge, the firm could enter into agreements to sell foreign exchange forward. But that would require that the creditors continuously monitor the company's foreign exchange exposure to ensure that the exposure *remains* hedged.

The debt of the exporter could instead be structured such that the principal is paid either in foreign exchange or in dollars indexed to a foreign exchange rate. This would ensure that the firm hedges its currency exposure, greatly reducing the creditors' monitoring costs and thus lowering the rate of return they would require. At the same time, the structured debt holders can (and typically do) include bond covenants that prohibit the firm from undoing its embedded hedge with transactions in the derivatives markets.

CHAPTER **26**

Insurance and ART

In this chapter, we review the use of insurance contracts as both tactical and strategic risk control mechanisms. Unlike derivatives, insurance is useful primarily for situations in which a firm is concerned about a possible *future* deviation of actual risks from tolerance levels. For reasons to be explained in the first section, insuring an existing loss tends to be expensive and difficult because the firm seeking insurance usually has much better information than the insurer about the nature of the loss. This is, of course, true for *unrealized* losses, as well, leading to the well-known moral hazard and adverse selection problems that plague the design of insurance contracts.

After setting forth some of the basic economics and terminology of the insurance industry, this chapter goes on to summarize the wide—and rapidly expanding—market for classical insurance products. In addition, the booming new market for Alternative Risk Transformation (ART) products is explored. The chapter concludes with a discussion about how insurance solutions are rapidly evolving toward full integration with derivatives and securitization control solutions.

THE CLASSICAL INSURANCE MARKET

As noted in Chapter 16, classical insurance contracts are examples of commercial option-like contracts. Despite the similarities between insurance and derivatives, however, discussions of the two risk control products are often separated by a wide gulf of terminology. Typical finance books pay little attention to insurance, and typical insurance texts do not often delve deep into derivatives.[1] Nevertheless, insurance and derivatives are fundamentally more similar than different.

Relations between Insurance and Derivatives

An insurance contract is a contract in which one party purchases the right to be compensated by another party for specific losses above an agreed-upon level in a particular state of the world. The demand side of insurance consists of purchasers or end users of insurance contracts—Risk Controllers. Both individuals and organizations fall into this category. Some commonly insured risks include physical injury, death, fire, flood, earthquake, theft, vandalism, automobile accidents, business malpractice, liability arising from the disposal of dangerous wastes, liability arising from environmental pollution, and so on.

Because options and insurance both pay off only in certain states of the world, they are both types of *state-contingent claims*—contracts that pay off when some specific state of the world occurs. The payoff on a call (put) option occurs only when the underlying price or rate rises above (below) the strike price or rate. For an insurance contract, the payoff occurs only when the loss owing to a particular circumstance exceeds any deductible.

As noted in Chapter 14, traditional insurance is similar to an option contract in several ways; most obviously, both insurance and options limit liability for their purchasers. In the case of insurance, a policy *holder* never has to make a payment in excess of the premium *to the insurer*. True, the purchaser of an insurance policy may have some liability tracing to the event underlying the contract, but that is not the same as the purchaser's liability on the insurance contract itself. If an insurance purchaser partially insures its exposure, has a coparticipation provision, or has a deductible, the adverse event with which the purchaser is concerned may still impose some loss on the purchaser. That additional loss, however, does not represent a gain *for the insurer*. Likewise, options give their purchasers limited liability, as already explained.

Options and insurance also create similar credit exposures between counterparties. Because option and insurance purchasers have limited liability to the sellers of those contracts, option writers and insurance companies face no credit risk from their counterparties. The purchaser of an insurance or option contract, by contrast, does bear credit risk. This exposure is the main reason why purchasers of these contracts are concerned about the capital adequacy of sellers, but the converse is not true. Because *only* purchasers bear it, credit risk in options and insurance is one-sided.

Despite the similarities between traditional insurance and options, however, options and insurance are *not* identical. As noted in Chapter 14, an insurance contract only pays off if the purchaser has experienced a loss *and* has an insurable interest. An insurance contract purchaser cannot experience a *net* gain. Option purchasers and sellers, by contrast, need *not* have an insurable interest in the underlying to own, trade, buy, sell, or exercise an option. Their interest instead is called *optionable*.

For many types of insurance contracts, situations in which would-be purchasers do not have an interest are hard to imagine. Everyone will die, so everyone has a potential interest in life insurance. Everyone, however, does not have a direct interest in *everyone else's* life insurance. Jay Leno cannot take out a life insurance policy that pays off if David Letterman dies, for example, nor can Letterman take out such a policy on Leno.

The Design of Classical Insurance Contracts

An important practical consequence of the distinction between insurable and optionable interests is that insurance contracts, based on the former, tend to be associated with very specific assets or liabilities of the firm taking out the insurance policy. The fact that an insurance purchaser must have an insurable interest in the asset or liability for which it is seeking loss protection gives rise to two problems in the relationship between the insurer and the company seeking insurance protection. Both are a result of asymmetric information and thus are problems that do not occur in a M&M world. The first problem—moral hazard—occurs because the insurer has imperfect information about the actions taken by the insured that may affect the probability of a loss or the size of the loss. The second problem—adverse selection—occurs because the insurer likely has less information about the causes and consequences of a loss than the insured given the idiosyncratic nature of the insurable firm-specific loss.

Because derivatives are based on market risks that are *optionable* interests of the specific firm using the contracts and not necessarily *insurable* interests, they are not plagued by the moral hazard and adverse selection problems that face insurers. For insurers, however, these two problems are sufficiently significant that the design of insurance contracts must take them into consideration, else the insurance market may fail to converge to equilibrium *or* the insurer will incur unsustainable economic losses in providing risk protection.

Moral Hazard   When the purchaser of insurance can take actions that impact either the probability of incurring an insurable loss or the size of that loss, the problem of moral hazard can arise. Without fire insurance, for example, an individual may spend more on fire prevention. But with fire insurance coverage, the home owner may not pay as much attention to fire prevention issues. Similarly, a corporation that insures the full value of a shipment of cargo crossing the ocean may be less inclined to invest in the safest ship around knowing that the insurer will be there to pick up the loss.

Insurers include several common features in their contracts to mitigate moral hazard problems. One is a deductible. The higher the deductible, the more out-of-the-money the insurance option and the more cost the insured party bears before the insurance kicks in. A similar effect is achieved with co-pay provisions in which an insurer agrees to pay, say, half the loss but leaves the remainder of the loss to be retained by the insured party.

Adverse Selection The adverse selection problem was first identified by Akerlof (1970) and his "market for lemons." In the Akerlof model, used car dealers are presumed to have better information about the quality of cars they are selling than buyers. Indeed, buyers are presumed to be unable to verify the quality of the car they are buying *at any cost.* In the best case scenario, the buyer knows only the probability that the car will be bad. This leads to an *expected* price the buyer will pay that will be too high for lemons and too low for good cars. The result of the Akerlof situation is that bad cars drive good cars out of the market. Sellers will not sell good cars because they are too cheap. But buyers *know* that sellers will only sell bad cars or lemons, which means that all cars are sold at the price of lemons—and indeed, all cars sold *are* lemons.

Like Akerlof's market for auto lemons, insurance markets can encounter the same problem. Suppose we consider health insurance and imagine two types of people—sick and healthy. People buying insurance know their own state of health, but the insurance company does not. If the insurer knows only the proportion of sick people, the premium the insurer will quote will reflect the expected health of the people to be insured. As in Akerlof, however, the higher the price, the fewer healthy people will want insurance. When the price more closely approximates the true price that should be charged to the sick, the resulting equilibrium is that only the sick people will buy insurance.

To clarify the nature of the adverse selection problem, consider first a simple insurance model with no adverse selection. Suppose there are a large number of potential flood insurance purchasers and that these purchasers are risk-averse individuals with utility functions that are increasing and concave in wealth in the sense of Chapter 2. People are identical and have the same probability π of experiencing a loss L from flood damage. Assume all these individuals start with a wealth endowment W.

Figure 26.1 is a typical diagram depicting equilibrium in the insurance market. The x-axis is wealth in the state of the world in which a flood does not occur, and the y-axis is wealth in the state of the world in which a flood does occur. The point marked O represents the base *no insurance* case. At this point, individual wealth is W if no flood occurs and $W - L$ in the event of a flood. The 45° line is the *full insurance line* in which the wealth of the individuals is the same *regardless* of whether a flood occurs.

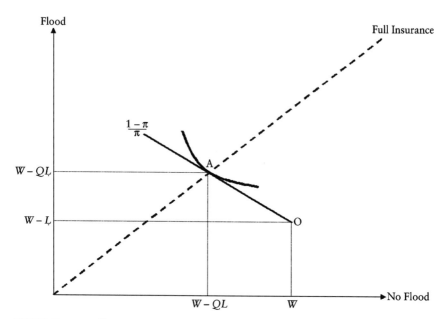

FIGURE 26.1   Full insurance with actuarially fair prices and homogeneous consumers.

The isolutility curve shown in Figure 26.1 indicates the tradeoff the individual is willing to make between wealth in the no flood state and wealth in the flood state. The slope of the indifference curve shown is negative and decreasing in wealth. The more wealth the person has, the less valuable a transfer of wealth from the no flood state to the flood state.

As discussed in Chapter 2, an insurance policy is actuarially fair or fairly priced when the premium per unit of coverage equals the probability of a loss. With no transaction costs, the insurer thus breaks even at this price. The line in Figure 26.1 from endowment point O running through point A on the full insurance line is called the *fair odds* line because the slope of the line is $(1 - \pi)/\pi$. In other words, the line shows the trade-off between wealth in one state and wealth in another such that the trade-off is equal to the ratio of the probability of one state to the probability of another. In this sense, all insurance contracts offered along this line are actuarially fair.

Now suppose an insurance company sets a single price of insurance $Q = \pi$ and lets each consumer choose her own level of coverage z at that price. When a flood does not occur, the utility of the individual will be $U(W - Qz)$, where z is the amount of coverage purchased and U is the utility function. If a flood occurs, the individual realizes utility of $U(W - L$

$-Qz+z$)—her endowment minus her loss less the price paid for insurance coverage z *plus* the coverage level z. The consumer chooses z to maximize her *expected* utility of wealth:

$$\max_z \left[(1-\pi)U(W-Qz) + \pi U(W-Qz+z-L) \right]$$

which yields the following first-order condition for optimum insurance coverage

$$\frac{U'(W-Qz+z-L)}{U'(W-Qz)} = \frac{(1-\pi)Q}{\pi(1-Q)} \qquad (24.1)$$

Because the insurance is actuarially fair and lies along line OA somewhere, $Q = \pi$ and Equation 26.1 becomes

$$U'(W-Qz+z-L) = U'(W-Qz)$$

which is true only when $z = L$.

In other words, the consumers purchase full insurance. This occurs in Figure 26.1 at the tangency point between the indifference curve and the fair odds line, point A, which also lies on the full insurance line. This situation is a general result and an extension of some of the principles developed in Chapter 2—namely, when insurance is priced to be actuarially fair, risk-averse consumers always fully insure.

In practice, insurance companies typically charge an actuarially fair price *plus* a load to reflect the insurer's cost of writing the policy, managing its own risks, and administering the accounts. The insurance contracting line is no longer line OA with slope $(1-\pi)/\pi$. As Figure 26.2 illustrates, the new insurance contract line OB has a slope $(1-Q)/Q$. When $Q > \pi$, the slope of line OB is smaller than the slope of line OA. Now the consumers' indifference curve is tangent to the insurance contracting locus at point C, which is below the full insurance line. When insurers charge a price equal to the actuarial price plus a load, equilibrium implies partial insurance.

Suppose we again ignore transaction costs but now assume the potential flood insurance purchasers are divided into two groups—high-risk and low-risk. Within each group, people are identical and have the same probability of experiencing some loss L from flood damage. The probability of realizing flood damage is denoted π_L and π_H for the low- and high-risk groups, respectively, and the insurer cannot distinguish between members of the two groups.

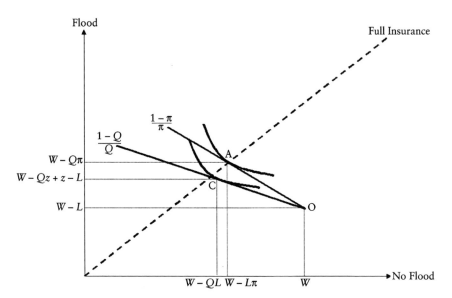

FIGURE 26.2 Insurance with actuarially unfair prices and homogeneous consumers.

Consider first an Akerlof-like model in which the insurance company sets a *single* price of insurance Q and lets each consumer choose her own level of coverage at that price. The low-risk consumer chooses z to maximize her expected utility of wealth:

$$\max{}_z\left[(1-\pi_L)U(W-Qz)+\pi_L U(W-Qz+z-L)\right]$$

which yields the following first-order condition for optimum insurance coverage

$$\frac{U'(W-Qz+z-L)}{U'(W-Qz)}=\frac{(1-\pi_L)Q}{\pi_L(1-Q)}$$

Similarly, for high-risk individual the insurance coverage purchased is the z that satisfies

$$\frac{U'(W-Qz+z-L)}{U'(W-Qz)}=\frac{(1-\pi_H)Q}{\pi_H(1-Q)}$$

Because $(1 - \pi_H)/\pi_H < (1 - \pi_L)/\pi_L$, $z_H > z_B$. This is illustrated graphically in Figure 26.3.

When the price of the insurance is set at $Q = \pi_L$, the low-risk individuals purchase full insurance at point A_L. But the high-risk consumers have indifference curves that are not as steep. The tangency between the high-risk consumer's indifference curve and the insurance contracting like at price $Q = \pi_L$ thus is point A_H. Because this point is above the full insurance line, high-risk customers buy *more* than full insurance. The insurance company breaks even on the low-risk customers but loses money on the high-risk customers.

Now consider a higher price Q such that $\pi_H > Q > \pi_L$. In this case, the low-risk customers buy less than full insurance at point B_L, which means the insurance company makes a profit on them. But high-risk customers continue to buy more than full insurance at point B_H. Whether or not the insurer makes enough on the low-risk customers to subsidize the high-risk customers is unclear.

Finally consider the price $Q = \pi_H$. In this situation, the low-risk consumers' indifference curve is never tangent to the insurance contracting line for levels of wealth below W. High-risk consumers fully insure at point C_H,

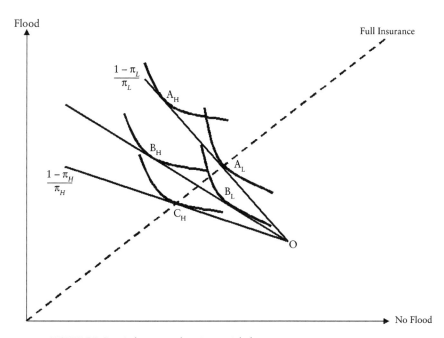

FIGURE 26.3 Adverse selection with heterogeneous consumers.

low-risk consumers purchase no insurance and remain at point O, and the insurer breaks even. Unlike the other two, this equilibrium thus is stable. Unfortunately, it also is the Akerlof outcome, as Figure 26.3 illustrates. When the insurer cannot distinguish between groups, the price will eventually be driven to the probability of flood damage being sustained by high-risk individuals, and low-risk individuals will be driven out of the market.

Rothschild and Stiglitz (1976) propose a solution to this conundrum. They argue that the key is in not offering consumers the choice of coverage. Instead, they propose a pair of insurance contracts, one of which gives high-risk individuals full insurance coverage at a high price and the other gives low-risk people *partial* coverage at a low price. The result is a separating equilibrium that causes consumers to choose the contract that also reveals their risk type to the insurer.

Figure 26.4 illustrates a classic Rothschild-Stiglitz separating equilibrium. The high-risk consumers will choose point C and fully insure, and the insurance company breaks even. The low-risk consumers will choose to insure *partially* at point E, where the indifference curve for the low-risk type is on line OA just below where the two indifference curves cross. The high-risk types prefer C to E, and the low-risk types prefer E to C.[2]

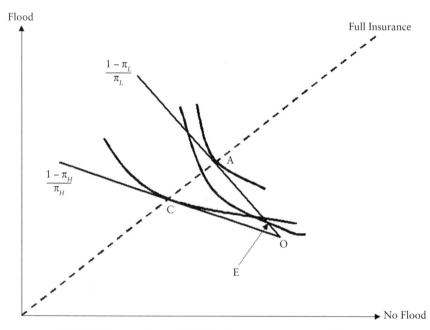

FIGURE 26.4   A Rothschild-Stiglitz separating equilibrium.

One problem with this solution to adverse selection proposed by Rothschild and Stiglitz is that theirs is a static model. Across multiple time periods, unstable behavior can result. In the first period, the high- and low-risk types reveal themselves in the separating equilibrium. In the next period, the insurer knows who is who and thus simply offers a full-priced policy with full coverage to each group. But if people know that will happen, then high-risk types might choose the low-risk policy in the hope they will be confused with the low-risk type.[3]

In a more practical context, insurers often choose a middle ground in which a multi-period contract is offered to customers based on their voluntary disclosure of whether they are a high or low risk. Over time, the insurer will gain more information about the insured parties. As a loss record accumulates, the insurer will eventually know which type the consumer is. The contract might specify that if the insurer realizes the voluntary disclosure of type was not truthful (e.g., a cancer patient pretending to be healthy), the person's policy is either dropped or the person is reclassified—perhaps also with a stiff penalty premium to pay for dishonesty.

INSURANCE COMPANIES AND RISK CULTURE

Insurance companies are Risk Transformers. Their very business is the supply of financial innovations to their customers that allow those customers to transform their risks. Nevertheless, just because a company is in the business of *supplying* risk transformation products does not mean the firm will not also *demand* risk transformation products for its own risk control purposes. On the contrary, most participants in the insurance industry do not retain all—or even most—of the risks they incur through the classical underwriting process.[4]

An insurance company's decision to manage one type of risk in a particular way does not imply the firm will seek to reduce *all* the risks to which it is exposed, nor does it imply that a risk management method chosen for one risk will be applied to all risks. As emphasized in Chapter 9, selective risk management is a commonly observed feature in well-capitalized firms whose primary business pertains in some way to financial intermediation or risk bearing. Perhaps no better example of this exists than the insurance industry.

When an insurance market participant acts as a Risk Controller and seeks to manage some of its risks, the company can be expected to focus on risk mitigation mechanisms and markets in which it perceives itself as having a comparative informational advantage. In other words, an insurance company can be expected to manage the risks arising from its insurance activities using means with which it is already familiar, already has relative expertise, and in which it already participates.

Not surprisingly, many insurance companies thus choose to control their insurance risks using private contracts negotiated *with other insurance participants.* Companies that provide insurance thus often insure the risks of insurance, or purchase reinsurance. Specifically, reinsurance is a contractual arrangement in which a *primary* insurer transfers to another company some or all of its losses on policies it has issued or will issue. The primary insurer is called the *ceding firm,* and the acquiring firm is called the *reinsurer.* The amount of risk *not* transferred by the primary insurer is called *retention.* And when a *reinsurer* purchases insurance from another reinsurer the contract between the reinsurer and the seller of the insurance policy is called *retrocession.*

By contrast, when insurance companies and reinsurers want to manage risks *not* directly related to the special information they possess from their primary business lines, they often engage in derivatives transactions as end users. Interest rate risk, for example, is a risk about which an insurer might have no special information, especially when compared to a money center commercial bank. Yet, insurers sometimes have huge asset/liability mismatches associated with their primary business lines. Insurance companies are thus active participants in interest rate derivatives, such as options on swaps and caps, that can provide insurers with attractive, low-cost ways of managing both their interest rate and liquidity risks.

THE MECHANICS OF CLASSICAL INSURANCE AND REINSURANCE[5]

The insurance industry has a language and terminology that is almost as complex as finance and derivatives. Understanding the way insurance companies do business requires some familiarity with this lexicon, as the definitions of terms often also communicate the way that insurers think about risk.

Insurance Underwriting

The basic building block in a traditional insurance contract is the concept of a risk layer. Suppose for the moment that Firm Bud Fox is concerned solely with the risk of losses arising from a single source of risk, such as operational risk—fraud, in particular. Assume that the risk of fraud can be quantified in the sense that discrete probabilities can be associated with ranges of losses that Firm Fox may incur. Whether based on *ex ante* probabilistic models or actuarial frequencies of losses, suppose Firm Fox associates its range of losses from fraud with probabilities as in Table 26.1.

TABLE 26.1   Firm Fox Loss Exposures to Fraud

Bin	Range of Loss ($)	Probability of Loss (%)
1	0–100,000	60
2	100,000–200,000	20
3	200,000–300,000	10
4	300,000–400,000	5
5	400,000–500,000	3
6	Over 500,000	2

If Firm Fox decides to retain the entire first layer of losses, any loss under $100,000 will not be covered by insurance. Specifically, if Firm Fox agrees with Insurer Gordon Gekko that $100,000 is the deductible for its fraud insurance policy, the first $100,000 loss—the first layer—is then called the self-insured retention (SIR) of the firm.

Insurer Gekko is the first source of funds to which Firm Fox has recourse in the event a fraud-related loss exceeds $100,000. Gekko is thus the *primary insurer.* As such, Insurer Gekko likely will limit its coverage of Firm Fox to a maximum amount—say, $400,000. Insurer Gekko thus agrees to cover losses in bins 2 to 4. Insurer Gekko is said to be covering $300,000 in excess of the deductible $100,000, or "300 xs 100."[6] This defines the second layer of cover, where the first layer was the SIR.

Losses above the second layer—known as the *excess layer*—are usually insured by a different insurance company from the primary insurer. Suppose Firm Fox purchases an additional 100 excess 400 cover from Insurer BlueStar. This insurer is known as the *excess carrier* or *surplus lines carrier* and will cover losses that occur between $400,000 and $500,000. Yet another excess layer of insurance can be purchased for, say, 200 excess 500 from Insurer Teldar. This layer is called the *second excess layer.*

The dividing lines between layers are called *attachment points.* In this case, Firm Fox has bought total insurance coverage such that the primary layer attaches at $100,000, the excess layer attaches at $400,000, and the second excess layer attaches at $500,000. Suppose that the third excess layer attaching at $700,000 is self-insured.

Reinsurance

Now suppose the primary insurer Gekko wishes to off-load some of the risk it has underwritten in the 300 excess 100 layer of Firm Fox's fraud-related losses. Gekko can approach Darien RE for reinsurance. Like Firm Fox,

Gekko will have a primary retention of some of the risk—say 100 excess 100, so that Gekko bears the cost of fraud-related losses above $100,000 but is seeking reinsurance for losses above $200,000.

Reinsurance comes in several varieties. First, *per-occurrence* reinsurance is an agreement in which the reinsurer assumes the total losses tracing to a single event specified in the contract when total losses exceed the primary insurer's retention. In this example Darien RE might assume all the risk of losses at Firm Fox from a single rogue trader in excess of $200,000 up to $400,000.

Second, *aggregate* reinsurance involves an agreement between insurer and reinsurer for the latter to assume the total losses of the former when the insurer's losses *over a specific period of time* exceed its retention. To continue the example, Darien RE would then assume all the risk of losses at Firm Fox in excess of $200,000 up to $400,000 arising from all acts of fraud over one calendar year.

Third, a *stop-loss agreement* involves a reinsurer's agreement to cover some percentage of the insurer's losses when the insurer's loss ratio exceeds the specified fraction of *total* premiums collected. The loss ratio is the ratio of the primary insurer's losses to total premium collected across all customers. A 20% in excess of 70% stop-loss reinsurance contract offered by Darien RE to Insurer Gekko, for example, would cover $2 million of losses in excess of $7 million if Gekko collected $10 million in total premium.

Reinsurers often engage in activities to limit their risk exposures to insurers. Reinsurers may themselves engage in reinsurance contracts, for example, called retrocession agreements. In addition, several types of provisions are commonly included in reinsurance contracts to help reinsurers attain their desired exposures to risk. Coparticipation provisions, for example, require the primary insurer to share in the excess-of-loss. Reinsurance contracts also often involve layering, whereby reinsurers agree only to provide coverage to insurers for losses between specific minimum and maximum loss levels.

Layering allows reinsurers to diversify away otherwise-correlated risks. Some reinsurers prefer low-level layering, where the frequency of their losses may be higher, but so are the premiums. Others may opt for upper layers, accepting a lower premium in exchange for a smaller probability of losses.

Horizontal versus Vertical Layer Splitting

Classical insurance described in the prior section is known as *vertical* protection or layering because each layer of protection is stacked on top of the one prior. An alternative form of protection is *horizontal* layering, in which more than one insurer divides coverage of a single layer. The two methods of layering can be combined, moreover. In our earlier example, Insurer Gekko and Insurer Douglas might split evenly the 300 excess 100 primary layer. Insurer Sheen, Insurer BlueStar, and Insurer Manheim then might split the 100 excess 400 first excess layer in thirds. And Insurer Teldar and Insurer Holbrook might split the 200 excess 500 second excess layer, with Teldar taking 80% of the losses between $500,000 and $700,000 and Holbrook taking the remaining 20%. Within each layer, the insurers split the losses *as they occur.*

GUARANTEES AND SYNTHETIC CAPITAL

One problem with traditional insurance can be disputes over the nature of the insurable interest. Was the loss that Firm Fox wants its insurance to cover fraud, or was it professional incompetence that Firm Fox is merely *claiming to be* fraud? Arguments over the actual obligation of the insurer can become quite protracted.

As an alternative, a firm seeking *unconditional* coverage can seek a *guarantee* rather than a traditional insurance policy. In a guarantee, the policy of the insurer is to pay first and ask questions later. Indeed, *so* firm are guarantees that they are often called *soft capital* facilities—because they are a close substitute for equity capital.

One area in which such facilities have become extremely popular is the provision of guarantees to financial exchange clearing houses for the purpose of covering default risk assumed by central counterparty settlement agents. Marsh Ltd., for example, has an Exchange and Clearing House group based in London whose sole function is the placement of such soft capital facilities. More than five major global futures, options, and securities exchange clearing houses now rely on such facilities to supplement their margin and/or member- and owner-backed guarantee funds. These facilities are guarantees that pay off in the event of a default, but only in the event of an actual default.

ALTERNATIVE RISK TRANSFER

The explosion over the last few years in ART is literally revolutionizing the risk transformation product market and has dramatically improved the ability for firms to obtain *total* risk control solutions from insurance companies. ART may refer to any of three recent innovations in the insurance market—the development of integrated total risk insurance solutions; the provision of liquidity and "finite risk" facilities; and the evolution of alternative sources of financing insurance risk. Each of these will be discussed in turn.

Total Risk Policies[7]

In the earlier example, Firm Fox was assumed to be facing—or interested in only insuring—fraud-driven operational risk. But suppose Firm Fox is now looking for a more comprehensive risk management solution that involves coverage for more than just fraud. Suppose Firm Fox is a grain elevator operator that is exposed to the risk of rising wheat prices and declining milled flour prices. Suppose further that Firm Fox is highly leveraged, quite conservative, and aggressively interested in protecting itself from losses arising from fraud *and* either wheat price increases or flour price declines.

Blended Layering   Because the risk of wheat price increases and flour price decreases are correlated risks, better cover and pricing can be attained by Firm Fox if it can identify an insurer that will write a *basket* policy covering some blended layer of loss across all three of these risk areas. In the extreme, Firm Fox might even want to insure a chunk of its *total earnings*.

Firm Fox can now approach Insurer Gekko and request an integrated coverage policy that has a single deductible and covers *all* losses across a range of specified products and business lines. Because the integrated cover allows Insurer Gekko to manage its exposure in a way that takes correlations across losses into account, the resulting pricing for the integrated coverage will almost certainly be more advantageous than if Firm Fox separately insured each of these individual component risks.

A very important result of the recent innovations in integrated liability policies is the ability of firms to structure market, credit, and liquidity risk management solutions *with insurers directly*. Once unavailable through one-stop shopping—if at all—total liability protection, earnings protection, and bundled market risk protection now can be obtained through insurance structures. This provides risk controllers with a powerful new tactical risk control tool that simply did not exist two decade ago.

Transaction Insurance   Another product to emerge from integrated layering total risk policies goes beyond earnings insurance and tackles risks associated with corporate actions and transactions, such as mergers and acquisitions. Suppose, for example, that Company Pressman is for sale and undergoing due diligence by Company Stone. A major shareholder in Company Pressman, Firm Kitman, is concerned that an adverse outcome in the next U.S. presidential election will scuttle the merger, resulting in a skid in

Company Pressman's stock price. Firm Kitman can seek an integrated risk transfer policy that provides insurance coverage in the event the merger breaks down and ensure that its total equity holdings do not decline below their premerger-announcement value (net of premium).

Second Risk Triggers   Especially in integrated layering policies, insurers and reinsurers have become increasingly interested in the inclusion of *second risk triggers* (SRTs) in their policies. SRTs create coverage for insurance purchasers that is conditional on certain events transpiring.

Suppose a firm purchases an integrated liability insurance policy that covers most of its market, credit, and operational risks. The premium is, say, $50,000 and the deductible is $500,000 relative to a base earnings amount of $1 million. If earnings fall to $100,000, then the deductible of $500,000 makes no sense. Consequently, the firm might include a SRT that resets the deductible to a different number for a given earnings report.

If the new deductible is based on the current level of earnings, then we say that the firm's earnings represent an internal trigger—internal because earnings are internal to and at least to some extent responsive to risk control decisions made by the firm. Alternatively, the policy could be defined relative to an external trigger, such as a $200,000 in exchange rate losses, which is not under as much control by the insurance purchaser as its own earnings are.

Liquidity Provision Facilities

An increasingly popular type of ART transaction involves the *financing* of losses rather than *payment* in the event of losses. Such transactions—sometimes called *finite risk* products—tend to resemble interest rate swaps more than options. In these products, the insurer has very little if any capital at risk. The insurer is instead leveraging its position in the financial market to assist smaller, less-capitalized firms in financing or amortizing losses over a longer horizon than might otherwise be possible in the absence of such vehicles.

Consider, for example, a firm acting as a DVP agent for securities transactions that has no responsibilities to provide trade guarantees or act as a central counterparty. Nevertheless, in some circumstances the DVP agent might wish to temporarily cover replacement cost settlement losses in order to preserve goodwill or market integrity. In this case, the DVP agent might seek a structure that does not reimburse losses, but rather helps the DVP agent leverage its, say, $25 million in capital into a broader funding cover. Specifically, a finite risk product could be offered in which an insurer accepts existing recourse capital—for example, the $25 million—as the basis for a facility that could provide up to $100 million in temporary bridge financing that would be applied to replacement cost losses incurred by the DVP agent. In the event no losses occur, the $25 million plus some investment income would be returned to the DVP agent, less any arrangement fees.

In the event of a default or a replacement cost loss that falls under the finite risk structure, however, the loss could then be funded out of the $100 million cover provided by the insurer, up to $25 million. Losses in excess of that $25 million then either could be covered by a supplemental default policy or could be turned into a low-interest loan.

To be more explicit, a traditional insurance vehicle likely would involve a deductible in which the DVP agent bears the first layer of losses. As an alternative, a finite risk vehicle seeks to leverage the DVP agent's capital into international money market opportunities. By exploiting the bid/offer spread on this lend-lease type of arrangement, income is generated that gradually adds to the fund to reduce the insurance element, or, alternatively, to self-fund the facility. The result is an income generating vehicle that also provides a levered increase in effective cover.

Developments in Financing and Controlling Insurance Risk

The explosion in the risk control and financing tools used by insurers and reinsurers in the last decade has been dramatic. What was once an industry that preferred reinsurance and retrocession above all other financing and risk transfer mechanisms is now the industry in which securitized products and derivatives are experiencing some of their most dramatic growth.[8]

Securitization   To date, insurers and reinsurers have successfully transformed their contingent liabilities into traded securities held as investments by hedge funds, mutual funds, pension plans, and the like. Life insurance companies can now offload mortality and expense fees to the capital market. Guaranteed minimum income benefit and guaranteed minimum death benefit contracts are now boilerplate product offerings. Earthquake, hurricane, and other weather risks are routinely pushed off the balance sheets of insurers and reinsurers into the bond market. And even basic property and casualty exposures are now floating around somewhere as traded debt instruments.

Probably the most dramatic developments have occurred in the area of catastrophic insurance and reinsurance. In 1999 alone, about $2 billion in insurance risk—almost all of which was catastrophic—was transferred to the bond market through approximately 12 transactions.[9]

One reason that securitization arrived at the doorstep of catastrophic insurance before other areas of the insurance industry was the sobering series of massive insurance payouts insurers had to make in a three-year period of time for Hurricane Hugo (1989), Hurricane Andrew (1992), and the Northridge earthquake (1993). One reinsurer lost about half of its capital and premium surplus on Hurricane Andrea alone.[10] In three short years, the global insurance industry recognized that it needed not only an additional source of capital, but a *diversified* source of capital. Where better to look than pension and mutual funds?

Cat bonds, as they are called, come in essentially three flavors: single-peril, multiperil, and indexed. Single-peril cat bonds are associated with a single major disaster, such as a loss incurred by a specific firm from a single major hurricane. Multiperil cat bonds typically involve exposures of a single firm to more than one disaster, often of different types—for example, East Coast hurricane and West Coast earthquake. And index cat bonds are usually single-peril events that cover losses incurred by more than one company.

A typical cat bond is issued by a SPV that collects investment proceeds from investors and premium paid on catastrophic reinsurers to the cedant. The SPV invests the combined funds—usually tax-free—and generates income and writes the reinsurance contract back to the cedant. Sometimes a portion of the proceeds generated from note issues are invested in Treasuries to guarantee a principal repayment and earn a higher credit rating.

Derivatives   As Chapter 25 illustrated in the case of total return swaps on loans, swaps can be used to facilitate synthetic securitizations. Not surprisingly, swap financing has arisen in the last few years as a substitute for cat bonds in the catastrophic insurance area. In April 1998, for example, Mitsui Marine and Fire entered into a swap with Swiss RE in which Mitsui made periodic cash payments to Swiss RE (i.e., premium) in exchange for a claim on a contingent series of cash flows based on losses incurred in the event an earthquake of greater than 7.1 magnitude on the Richter scale hit Tokyo. The swap represented a $30 million risk transfer, and Swiss RE in turn used another swap to hedge *its* exposure. Just as in the case of credit derivatives, swaps are beginning to emerge as a synthetic securitization device in insurance (i.e., as a form of both tactical risk control *and* a source of synthetic capital).

As discussed in the last two sections, catastrophic insurance bonds, derivatives, and other structures also include both integrated risk solutions *and* pure financing vehicles like finite risk and financial reinsurance.

Catastrophic risk is also one of the risks that has already made its way to the world of exchange-traded derivatives. In December 1992, the CBOT introduced catastrophe or CAT futures contracts that were based on cat losses by region. But by 1994, the volume on these contracts had fallen to nearly zero, primarily because the contract's design admitted significant basis risks for reinsurers and was subject to potential adverse selection and moral hazard problems.[11]

Rather than try to salvage CAT futures and options, the CBOT decided in 1995 to dispense with the old contracts altogether and introduce PCS Options, based on an index compiled by Property Claims Services (PCS™), one of the major industry authorities in catastrophic loss estimation. Unlike the CAT options, the newer PCS options are cash-settled options with an underlying cash value determined by a new index. PCS options do *not* call for delivery of a futures contract.

PCS provides estimates of nine catastrophic loss indexes on a daily basis. These indexes are geographical and track PCS-estimated insured catastrophe losses nationally, by region (Eastern, Northeastern, Southeastern, Midwestern, Western), and by state (Florida, Texas, and California). To arrive at catastrophic loss estimates, PCS surveys at least 70% of companies, agents, and adjusters involved with catastrophic insurance. PCS's industry loss estimates are based on this survey, adjusted for nonsurveyed market share, and adjusted again to take into account PCS's "National Insurance Risk Profile." The PCS index value for any region is PCS's loss estimate divided by $100 million.

For each of the nine PCS indexes, the CBOT lists PCS options. PCS options for each index are available in *large cap* and *small cap* forms. Large cap PCS options track estimated catastrophic losses ranging from $20 billion to $50 billion, whereas small cap PCS options track only losses of less than $20 billion.

PCS options have settlement values based on a reporting period that includes an *event period* and some lag time. In other words, PCS options are based on losses that *occur* in the event period but that are *reported* for the event period plus some lag time. All but the Western and California PCS options have quarterly event periods. Options thus are listed that correspond with the end of the four event quarters: March, June, September, and December. For the Western and California indexes, the event period is *annual*.

PCS option purchasers have a choice between two *development periods* during which losses can be reported. Option buyers can elect a 6-month or 12-month period in which losses for the event quarter are reported and revised. The options trade until the last day of the development period. Such European-style options thus can be exercised only at the end of the development period.

A popular trading strategy in many option markets is a *call spread*. A long call spread is the simultaneous purchase of a call option at one strike price and sale of an otherwise identical call option at another, *higher* strike price. A short call spread, by contrast, involves purchasing the call option with the higher strike price and selling the lower-strike call option.

The seller of a long call spread is thus the buyer of a short call spread, and vice-versa.

PCS call spreads can be attractive to insurers and reinsures because they create protection for their purchaser between a specific range of values of the underlying—that is, they are a source of synthetic vertical layering. Suppose, for example, a call spread is purchased with a lower strike price of 100 and a higher strike price of 120. The purchaser *pays* a premium to acquire the call with strike 100, thereby *limiting its downside* to 100. By simultaneously *writing* the call with strike 120, the spread purchaser *collects* premium that can be used to offset the cost of the downside protection, in exchange for which the seller gives up any upside potential on the trade for index levels above 120. If the 120 call had been written *outright*, the seller would collect premium and have practically unlimited downside liability, gaining no benefit from index increases above 120. By writing the 120 call *in conjunction with* the 100 call purchase, however, the purchaser has locked in a layer of protection between index levels of 100 and 120. This call spread is called a 100/120 call spread, reflecting the two strike prices.

If a reinsurer or insurer wants protection for its third quarter 1996 Eastern exposure to losses from hurricanes, a 60/80 call spread covers PCS estimated losses for the Eastern United States of between $6 and $8 billion for that quarter. If the premium for the 60/80 call spread is 5 points, the hedger pays $1,000 (5 × $200) for a $4,000 layer of protection [i.e., (80 − 60) × $200]. At settlement, if the PCS-estimated Eastern losses are below $6 billion, the spread expires worthless. Suppose instead losses are estimated by PCS in excess of $8 billion. In that case, the 60/80 call spread purchaser receives the maximum on the spread, or $4,000 [(80 − 60) × $200]. Having *paid* 5 points for the spread, the hedger's *net* gain is 15 points, or $3,000 ($4,000 gain − $1,000 premium paid). Finally, if losses are within the protection layer—say, $7.5 billion—the call spread purchaser has a net gain of the *actual* estimated loss less the premium paid, or $2,000, namely (75 − 60) × $200 − $1,000 = $2,000.

CONCLUDING NOTE

This is in many ways a fitting way to end this book. As this chapter has hopefully demonstrated, the conventional barriers between once-distinct financial products and industries are falling. Perhaps nowhere are the opportunities for structured risk management solutions more interesting right now than in the ART area of insurance—an area that has quite rapidly come to include total risk and integrated insurance, securitized products, and derivatives.

Nevertheless, these are all just different mechanisms for *controlling* risk. Without a sound risk management strategy, tactics are of little more than ad hoc solutions to periodic problems. But here again, the insurance industry also illustrates how risk management *strategy* can be leveraged into a significant business opportunity. Insurers have been and remain classic Risk Controllers and demanders of risk management products. At the same time, the attention of insurers to leveraging the risk management expertise into customer management and product innovation has clearly paid off. And as a result, the insurance community is rapidly overtaking the rest of the capital markets world as the source for one-stop shopping and integrated risk transformation products.

notes

Chapter 1   The Nature of Risk

1. Portions of this section borrow liberally from Smith (1988) by permission.
2. Wildavsky (1988), p. 2.
3. See Smith and Culp (1989) for a more detailed discussion of forestalling and engrossing in the *The Wealth of Nations*.
4. Astute readers might quarrel that in cases like environmental pollution, society at large bears more of the cost than the guilty polluter. Called a *negative externality*, this is true *only* in the absence of well-specified property rights, as is well demonstrated in the work of Ronald Coase, winner of the 1991 Nobel Prize in Economic Sciences.
5. In fact, a good deal of evidence suggests that more people die from good drugs being marooned in the drug approval process than from bad drugs being released to the market. For evidence and some excellent examples of this, see Kazman (1990, 1992).
6. See Global Derivatives Study Group (1993) and Gooch and Klein (1993).
7. See Cunningham and Casper (1993).
8. See Markham (1987).
9. Portions of this section draw from Culp and Mensink (1999).
10. A more detailed version of this section appeared in Culp (1995).
11. Regulatory risk is not, strictly speaking, diversifiable. But because it also does not represent a systematic risk factor, treating it as idiosyncratic purely for classification purposes is harmless enough. See the discussion in Culp (1995).

Chapter 2   Risk Aversion, Insurance, and Hedging

1. Another common assumption made about utility functions is called "additive separability," which means that the maximization of consumption/wealth

opportunities over a lifetime is equal to the sum of the period-by-period utilities of wealth, or

$$U(W_1 + W_2 + W_3 + \ldots) = U(W_1) + U(W_2) + U(W_3) + \ldots$$

This enables us to focus on a two-period model without any loss of generality.

2. Support for the Friedman-Savage proposed solution is not uncontroversial. For an alternative explanation, compare Markowitz (1952).
3. We know that $U_{www} > 0$ is required because γ can be positive or negative, but investors only like $\gamma > 0$.

Chapter 3   The Irrelevance of Corporate Financing and Risk Management Decisions

1. Unfortunately, the temptation to jump directly from the Johnson-Stein-Ederington model straight to corporations has not entirely disappeared. See the discussion in the Introduction of Culp and Miller (2000).
2. See Coase (1937), Alchian and Demsetz (1972), and Jensen and Meckling (1976).
3. Jensen and Meckling (1976), pp. 9–10.
4. This particular representation of the Modigliani-Miller assumptions is based on the analysis in Fama (1976).
5. Fama (1976) shows that this assumption can be relaxed if it is replaced with the assumptions that no firm is a monopolistic supplier of any security *and* firms all maximize their total market value at whatever prices are given from a perfectly competitive securities market. We will work with the equal access assumption for simplicity.
6. Culp and Miller (1995c).
7. See Cochrane (2000) for a detailed discussion of the correspondence between this representation of the CAPM and the traditional formulation presented in Chapter 1. Much of the analysis and presentation in this section closely follows Cochrane (2000).
8. Cochrane (2000) provides an excellent survey.
9. These terms to describe different types of derivatives were popularized by the Global Derivatives Study Group (1993) and Smithson (1998).
10. Compare Fama and French (1987, 1988).
11. Black and Scholes (1973); Merton (1973).
12. Even if the swap is off-market, the price paid can be subtracted from the NPV shown as an investment cost, in which case the total NPV would still be zero.

Chapter 4   Increasing Expected Cash Flows or Reducing the Cost of Capital by Managing Risk

1. This figure and many of the subsequent figures in this chapter are adapted from Smith and Stulz (1985) who are the original developers of these rationales for corporate hedging.

Chapter 6 Reducing Conflicts among Security Holders by Managing Risk

1. There is no economics behind this assumption; we are simply following Myers and deliberately ordering states of nature from the worst to the best in terms of their impact on the value of the new asset. We also assume the function $V_G(t + 1, s)$ is linear in s for simplicity, and again with no loss of generality.
2. The graphics and presentation of the problem and risk management solution in this section are adapted from Smith (1995).
3. Fama (1976), p. 42.
4. For an analysis of bond covenants, see Smith and Warner (1979).

Chapter 7 Controlling and Exploiting Informational Asymmetries by Managing Risk

1. See also French (1986), Fama and French (1987), and Fama and French (1988).
2. For those more formally inclined, let Ω be a finite set containing all possible states of nature and let the class $\Im$ of subsets of Ω denote a σ-algebra on Ω. P is a probability measure, such that the triple $(\Omega, \Im, P)$ forms a probability space. $\Im_1, \Im_2, \ldots$ is a sequence of σ-algebras on $\Im$, such that $\Im_i \subset \Im_j \; \forall i < j$. The sequence $(\Im_i)$ forms a filtration where $i = 0, 1, 2$. Now let Λ denote a subalgebra that is contained by $\Im$. At each period i, the partition Λ_i is the set of events observable to the marketing firm. (Λ_i) is a filtration that represents how information is revealed to the marketing firm over time, where $\Lambda_1 \subset \Lambda_2 \subset \Lambda_3$. Let Φ denote another sub-algebra that is contained by $\Im$. At each date i, the partition Φ_i is the set of events observed by all other market participants—so-called public information. The filtration (Φ_i) represents how information is revealed to other market participants over time, such that $\Phi_1 \subset \Phi_2 \subset \Phi_3$. The marketing firm's information is related to public information at any time j as follows: $\Phi_j \subset \Lambda_j \subseteq \Im_j \; \forall j$. Using our simplified notation, a time 0 conditional expectation evaluated by the marketer is a Λ_0—measurable random variable, $E_0^*(X) = E(X|\Lambda_0)$. A time 0 conditional expectation evaluated by the public is a Φ_0—measurable random variable, $E_0(X) = E(X|\Phi_0)$.
3. The analysis here closely follows Stulz (1996), but some different inferences and conclusions are drawn.

Chapter 10 Risk Culture and Risk Management Business Models

1. For a discussion of the major derivatives disasters, see Culp, Miller, and Neves (1998) and Culp, Hanke, and Neves (1999). The social costs of these and other so-called derivatives disasters are discussed in Miller (1997).
2. This is *not* an argument, however, for mandatory shareholder risk disclosures. See the discussion in Miller and Culp (1996).
3. See Culp and Neves (1998a).

Chapter 11   Integrating People, Technology, and Processes through Enterprise-Wide Risk Management

1. Compare DeLoach (2000) for a good introduction to EWRM. See also Euromoney Books (1998).
2. DeLoach (2000), p. 5.
3. The ostensible "specialness" of banks is typically regarded as a call to arms for their regulation. See Corrigan (1982). For a contrary view, see Aspinwall (1983).
4. Actually, some of these functions *are* uniquely provided by banks in some countries because of particular regulations. The U.S. payment system, for example, is completely bank-centric—final and irrevocable funds transfers can only be effected by institutions with reserve balances on deposit at the Federal Reserve, and banks are virtually the only institutions in that category. See Culp and Neves (1998c). But this unique role of banks in national payments owes *not* to some inherent comparative advantage they have in funds transfers, but rather to the *status quo* regulatory system.
5. To see why, simply consider other institutions that serve these same functions: nonbank clearing organizations participate in transaction intermediation, payments, and settlement; backup liquidity is provided routinely through nonbank entities, such as GE Capital Corp.; monetary policy is regularly implemented through nonbank primary government securities dealers and transmitted through nonbank avenues such as money market mutual fund accounts, and so on. See Aspinwall (1982).
6. See Diamond (1984, 1991).
7. See Diamond (1991).
8. See Stiglitz and Weiss (1983).
9. See Fama (1985).
10. See James (1987).
11. See note 7.
12. See Diamond (1984, 1989, 1991).
13. Recall, scale economies occur when increased output leads to lower average costs. Scope economies, by contrast, are realized when the same input (e.g., information) can be used for multiple outputs (e.g., lending and capital market intermediation), resulting in lower total costs for the multiproduct firm.
14. See, for example, Diamond (1989) and Lummer and McConnell (1989).
15. See, for example, James (1987).
16. Diamond (1984, 1989).
17. See Rajan (1992).
18. The text that follows is based on an unpublished short article written by the author jointly with Dr. Phil Pyburn. Mike Ashmore also contributed substantially to the article and the processes outlined.
19. One-on-one meetings can be very important in such situations. Because a board of directors is comprised of people who are often peers, asking questions in ALCO meetings is often viewed as inappropriate. People often do not wish to admit their ignorance in front of their peers—even if that ignorance is totally

understandable. (The farmers, after all, are *capable* of understanding all aspects of risk management. It is simply not their job and hence unnecessary for them to do so.) One-on-one meetings can greatly facilitate knowledge management by skirting this problematic element of group dynamics.

Chapter 13   Spot, Forward, and Forward-Like Exposures

1. Other reasons can include the hypothecation or rehypothecation of securities used in securities lending transactions, deliberate lags imposed because of physical safekeeping or custodial constraints, lags created at the registrar, and so forth.
2. Portions of this section are drawn from Culp and Neves (1998c).
3. This section contains excerpts from Culp (1995b).
4. Chicago Board of Trade (1997).
5. Petzel (1989), p. 6.
6. In particular, when the marginal cost of extracting oil is constant, the value of the oil in the ground is the same as the value of the oil sold in the spot market because the rate of increase in the value of the oil in the ground is equal to the discount rate used to take the present value of future oil sales. See Hotelling (1931).

Chapter 14   Identifying Option, Option-Like, and Real Option Exposures

1. This book is not intended to be the latest catalogue of option products, nor is it intended to cover the pricing of various option and option-like structures. For better sources on both counts, see Hull (2000) and Smithson (1998), on which many of the product descriptions and examples in this section are loosely-and in some cases not so loosely-based.
2. The term OTC refers here to over-the-counter derivatives, not options on OTC stocks or equity options traded on an OTC stock exchange like the Nasdaq/ Amex. For purposes of this discussion, options on any equities listed on any securities exchange—including an OTC stock exchange—are considered exchange-listed or exchange-traded and not OTC.
3. For an excellent discussion of the options embedded in bond futures, see Burghardt and Belton (1994). Much of the discussion in this chapter of bond futures and their embedded options is adapted from this book.
4. If the short is not a clearing firm, the short may be required *by its clearing firm* to give intent to deliver earlier than 8 P.M. on the Notice Day. If the short's clearing member requires notification by, say, 7 P.M. so that the clearing member has time to inform the exchange of a delivery intent by 8 P.M., the length of time governing the value of the wild card option shrinks by one hour.
5. If the option was at-the-money at issuance when the stock price was $S(t)$, then the strike price was also $S(t)$. And if the option does not allow exercise until the stock price doubles, the option only has positive value when $S(T) \geq 2S(t)$, so that *if* the option can be exercised its minimum value is $2S(t) - S(t)$ or $S(t)$.

6. In practice, *some* restrictions will be placed on delivery, such as maximums per period or minimum elapsed days between deliveries.
7. Compare Merton (1973).
8. Compare Quigg (1995).
9. For an excellent discussion of the use of real options at Airbus Industrie and one of the best real options case studies around, see Stonier (1999).
10. This example is based on Section 1.2 of Trigeorgis (1995).
11. See Micalizzi and Trigeorgis (1999).
12. This figure and the analysis is based on an example in Amram and Kulatilaka (1999).

Chapter 15   Measuring and Monitoring Market Risk

1. Special thanks to Ron Mensink of the State of Wisconsin Investment Board for granting permission to use his graphs in Figures 15.1 and 15.2 and for his more general collaboration with the author over time, which has greatly influenced the material in this chapter.
2. There is actually a trace of currency risk in this domestic equity portfolio arising from American Depository Receipts, but it is too small to see.
3. Note that $\lim_{\varepsilon \to 0} \Delta = \partial V / \partial z$.
4. Whether to divide by N or $N - 1$ is debatable. N is used here for consistency with other measures of volatility explored later.
5. A wide variety of similar models are also available, including the simple ARCH model of Engle (1982), GARCH-in-mean or GARCH-M, Exponential or EGARCH, and so forth. For a survey of these models in general, see Engle (1995) and in financial applications see Gourieroux (1997).
6. We cannot tell from the picture whether the distribution is leptokurtic or platykurtic. Because the left-hand tail is fatter than the normal but the right-hand tail is thinner, the net effect is ambiguous visually.
7. Implied volatility can be used to infer the true distribution of returns that corresponds to the observed volatility smile, and these inferences can serve as the basis for calculating probabilistic risk measures like VaR.
8. Portions of this section draw from prior published work by the author, including Culp, Mensink, and Neves (1998) and Culp, Miller, and Neves (1998). In addition, portions draw on various documents developed by the author jointly with Andrea Neves both for clients and for strategic planning purposes at CP Risk Management. For comments on various forms of earlier drafts, the author thanks Ron Mensink of the State of Wisconsin Investment Board, Kamaryn Tanner and Randy Moore of Frontier Analytics, and Chris Cockburn, Eve Kingsley, and Bill Pryor of Russell/Mellon Analytical Services.
9. For interested readers, the sample kurtosis is calculated for a time series of N historical returns r as

$$K = \frac{N(N+1)}{(N-1)(N-2)(N-3)} \sum_{j=t-N+1}^{t} \left(\frac{R_{j-1,j} - \overline{R}}{s} \right)^4 - \frac{3(N-1)^2}{(N-2)(N-3)}$$

10. The change in the volatility parameter only affects the parametric normal methodology if the one-period VaR is generalized to a multi-period VaR.

11. Picoult (1998) presents a very thorough and complete discussion of Monte Carlo methods in VaR estimation.

12. This is also a criticism sometimes leveled at VaR. If the VaR for some portfolio of exposures is $X at the 95% confidence level, the risk manager knows the loss is not expected to exceed $X more than 5% of the time. But she does not know how large the 5% of losses that *will* exceed $X are.

13. Aït-Sahalia and Lo (2000) propose an adjustment to VaR using state-price densitities that incorporates risk aversion, time preferences, and other "economically important" features of left-hand tail realizations.

14. Compare Feller (1971) and Hill (1975).

15. Nelson (1991) does much the same thing by using a Generalized Error Distribution as the foundation for his Exponential GARCH or EGARCH model.

16. For further discussion of these methods, see Derman and Kani (1994), Dupire (1994), Rubinstein (1994), Derman, Kani, and Chriss (1996), Jackwerth and Rubinstein (1996), and Chriss (1997).

17. RiskMetrics™ is not the only source for primitives. The assumption that corporate credit quality is equivalent to interbank or government credit quality is completely unique to the most basic RiskMetrics™ data set.

18. Recall we discussed a remainder term when a Taylor series was first introduced in Chapter 2. By leaving terms in the Taylor series with higher polynomial orders, the remainder term is reduced and the "fit" of the Taylor series to the actual price/value function improves. But because the Taylor series is just an approximation, adding new terms will not always solve the problem that the series itself is an approximation of the value of the function *around a specific point*. Large price moves away from current value thus simply are not covered by Taylor series in many cases.

19. This section and the next are based heavily on Culp, Miller, and Neves (1998).

20. Dembo, Aziz, Rosen, and Zerbs (2000) of the well-known risk software vendor Algorithmics outline a method they call "mark to future" that takes portfolio changes over the risk horizon into account.

21. Much of this section is a more generalized version of the discussion in Culp, Mensink, and Neves (1998).

Chapter 16   Identifying, Measuring, and Monitoring Credit Risk

1. This example is not a very good one, as both insurance companies and unregulated special purpose company affiliates of investment banks tend to be very highly capitalized-in the latter case often more than their regulated parent. See Culp (1995c).

2. The term "spread risk" that is also often used to describe this source of risk is so-named because of the potential for broad credit considerations to change the spread of certain securities over the riskless rate.

3. Compare Fama and French (1992, 1993).

4. This section is based on and closely follows Culp and Neves (1998c).
5. For transfers of funds for funds instead of funds for assets, as in currency transactions, the analogue is called the Payment-versus-Payment (PVP) principle.
6. See Bank for International Settlements (1999), Saunders (1999), and Matten (2000).
7. For a highly practical and thorough discussion of credit scoring models. See Lewis (1992). A more recent survey of internal rating systems more generally can be found in Bank for International Settlements (2000).
8. Modifications to the basic Z-score model have been made for different types of borrowers and to reflect changing market conditions. Compare Altman (1993). Other modifications are summarized in the excellent reference book Caouette, Altman, and Narayanan (1998).
9. This figure is a common one for depicting the Merton model and the KMV model that will be discussed shortly. Compare Ong (1999) and Crouhy, Galai, and Mark (2000).
10. Crouhy, Galai, and Mark (2000).
11. For firms without publicly traded equity, KMV offers the Private Firm Model®.
12. $\Gamma(r)$ is the gamma function, and $\Gamma(r) = \int_0^\infty x^{r-1} e^{-x} dx$ and $\Gamma(r + 1) = r!$ if r is an integer.
13. Compare Altman and Eberhart (1994).
14. Keenan (2000).
15. Matten (2000).
16. Ong (1999) and Shimko (1999) provide good surveys of the recent contributions, some of which are reprinted in Shimko (1999).
17. Ong (1999), Saunders (1999), Shimko (1999), Crouhy, Galai, and Mark (2000).
18. The figure presented and notation are based on Crouhy, Galai, and Mark (2000).
19. For an introduction to measure theory, see Billingsley (1995). Changes of probability measure are discussed in a fairly practical manner in Huang and Litzenberger (1988).
20. The risk-neutral valuation approach is set forth in Ross (1978) and Harrison and Kreps (1979). Cochrane (2000) provides a complete summary of the issues and a current survey of the literature.
21. In other words, the calibrated expression actually postulates T^γ rather than $T^{0.5}$ and then verifies that γ is approximately $\frac{1}{2}$. See Crouhy, Galai, and Mark (2000).
22. Stock purchases and sales are not generally described as *spot* in the United States because of the absence of single-stock forwards and futures. In other countries (e.g., Australia) that *do* have single-stock forwards and futures, however, the distinction has more meaning. The term spot is adopted here because a subsequent example will involve a single-stock forward.
23. Compare Smithson (1998) and Jorion (2000).
24. These figures are based on those presented in Smithson (1998), who in turn credits his figures to Denise Boutross. Similar figures appear in Jorion (2000) and elsewhere.

25. CreditMetrics assumes the potential exposure of a swap is calculated externally and imported into the model as an expected potential exposure, which is then treated in the same basic manner as a bond. See Crouhy, Galai, and Mark (2000).
26. Equivalently, we could assume all calculations are expressed as a percentage of PCE.
27. Compare Bank for International Settlements (1999).
28. Credit risk management is often done selectively by firms, not so much because they are selective risk managers but because some aspects of credit risk management are easier than others.

Chapter 17   Identifying, Measuring, and Monitoring Liquidity Risk

1. Net liquid assets can also be expressed as a liquid asset ratio, or the ratio of liquid assets to either volatile liabilities or total assets.
2. Uyemura and Van Deventer (1993).
3. Compare Uyemura and Van Deventer (1993).
4. Ibid.
5. Culp and Kavanagh (1994). See also "Debtors' First Amended and Restated Disclosure Statement Pursuant to Section 1125 of the Bankruptcy Code," *In re The Drexel Burnham Lambert Group, Inc., et al.,* No. 90 Civ. 6954 (S.D.N.Y. Jan. 3, 1992).
6. Culp and Kavanagh (1994).
7. For a survey of the major models and issues in market microstructure theory see Easley and O'Hara (1995). Most of the major contributions to the study of market microstructure can be found in Stoll (1999).
8. Garman (1976).
9. See Grossman and Miller (1988).
10. The core argument of Grossman and Miller (1988) is that one of the best measures of liquidity is the number of market makers. A dealer market in which firms do quote two-sided prices but are not obligated to do so thus may actually be preferable to a market where a single participant is obligated to maintain continuous two-sided quotes.
11. Demsetz (1968).
12. Both quoted and effective spreads are often divided by two to reflect the cost of a one-way trade rather than a round turn.
13. Roll (1984) suggests defining the effective spread in such markets as $2\sqrt{-\text{cov}}$ where cov is the first-order autocovariance in price changes.
14. Glosten and Milgrom (1985) argue that the bid-ask spread compensates dealers for "adverse selection"—losses that might arise when buyers and sellers have better information than the dealers.
15. This approach was proposed by Bangia, Diebold, Schuermann, and Stroughair (1999).

16. These preventive steps were suggested by Culp and Miller (1995c) in the case of MG Refining and Marketing.

17. Either form of the pure synthetic strategy would allow the firm to earn interest on its margin or margin-equivalent deposit. Thus, despite the seemingly large numbers of the *principal* values involved for a large hedging program, the total *interest* cost would only be the net difference in interest paid on the loan and the interest earned. If prices on the hedge move adversely and early in the life of the hedged program, the amount of funds on deposit earning interest will fall below the principal on the loan. In this sense, when prices fall there is an additional interest cost to the firm over and above the interest cost built into the hedging basis, but the opposite is also true when prices move in favor of the hedge.

18. Portions of the remainder of this section are based on Culp and Miller (1995b).

19. See the Culp and Miller papers reprinted in Culp and Miller (2000).

20. C & L Treuarbeit Deutsche Revision and Wollert-Elmendorff Industrie Treuhand, *Report No. 4011742 RE: The Special Audit in Accordance with Paragraph 142 Section 1 AktG of Metallgesellschaft Aktiengesellschaft Frankfurt am Main* (February 6, 1995).

Chapter 18   Identifying, Measuring, and Monitoring Operational Risk

1. ISDA/BBA/RMA (1999).

2. These examples are based on the sample data entry form for the British Bankers' Association operational risk and loss database.

3. See footnote four in ISDA (2000).

4. Bank for International Settlements (1998).

5. This discussion follows Jorion (2000).

6. This property follows from the result that the joint density of s and n divided by the marginal density of n yields the conditional density of s given n. See, for example, Mood, Graybill, and Boes (1974).

Chapter 19   Identifying and Managing Legal Risk

1. Portions of this section are based on Culp and Kavanagh (1994).

2. Compare Appendix III of Global Derivatives Study Group (1993) with Global Derivatives Study Group (1994).

3. See Global Derivatives Study Group (1993) and Gooch and Klein (1993).

4. See Patrikis (1996).

5. This has been the position of the author. Compare Culp (1991, 1995a, b, c, 1998), Culp and Hanke (1994a, b), Culp and Mackay (1994), Culp, Hanke, and Neves (1999), and Culp, Miller, and Neves (1998).

6. See 1992 ISDA Master Section 5(a)(vi). Other events of default are discussed in the 1992 ISDA Master in Section 5(a). See Global Derivatives Study Group

(1993), Appendix III, pp. 18–19 for a survey of the use of certain such clauses in master agreements by dealers.

7. Close-out netting requires the calculation of a lump-sum net payment based either on a "Market Quotation" method or a "Loss" method. In the former, the net lump-sum payment is equal to all amounts due prior to termination, plus replacement cost. In the latter, payment is equal to the non-defaulting counterparty's total net losses and costs. See 1992 ISDA Master Section 6(e)(i).

8. Compare Patrikis and Walraven (1992).

9. No. 92 Civ. 3098 (S.D.N.Y. Nov. 9, 1992).

10. See Asquith and Cunningham (1992).

11. Shirreff (1991).

12. *Brane v. Roth*, 590 N.E. 2d 587 (Ind. Ct. App. 1992).

13. For a cogent analysis of this case and the Compaq case. See Cunningham (1998).

14. *In re Compaq Securities Litigation,* No. H-91–9191 (S.D. Tex. May 16, 1991). Again, see Cunningham (1998) for a discussion.

15. This section draws heavily from Culp (1998).

16. See Culp and Mackay (1994).

17. See Markham (1987).

18. See Stein (1988).

19. A board of trade is *usually* synonymous with an organized exchange, but not always. Compare *Salomon Forex, Inc. v. Tauber,* 8 F.3d 966 (4th Cir. 1993), and *CFTC v. William C. Dunn and Delta Options,* 2 COMM. FUT.L. REP. &26,429 (2d Cir. June 23, 1995).

    Two types of products that might be deemed "futures contracts" fall outside the jurisdiction of the Commodity Futures Trading Commission. The first are products that are *excluded* from the CEA by statute, including forward delivery contracts and contracts falling under the so-called "Treasury Amendment." The second are products that the CFTC has *exempted* from the CEA by decree(usually at the behest of Congress. Exempt products include certain swaps, hybrid securities, and oil delivery contracts. Unlike *excluded* products which have been proclaimed beyond the scope of the Act by Congress, exempt products are exempted from regulation without a determination that the products are or are not futures. Also unlike excluded products, exempt products can later be determined to be nonexempt. For a good background discussion of these issues, see Young (1997).

20. 7 U.S.C. Section 6

21. "Commodities" must underlie all futures contracts. So, for a contract to be subject to CFTC regulation, the asset underlying it first must be deemed a "commodity." By broadening the definition of a commodity, the 1974 act thus also broadened the definition of a "futures contract," *de facto* if not actually *de jure.*

22. Institutions using only exempt futures contracts or contracts that resemble futures but have not been legally classified as futures are not subject to CFTC regulation. See Young (1997).

23. Securities laws not discussed here that also are relevant include the Public Utility Holding Company Act of 1935, the Trust Indenture Act of 1939, the Investment Company Act of 1940, the Investment Advisors Act of 1940, and the Securities Investor Protection Act of 1970.
24. Exempt securities are products that fall under the legal definition of securities but are exempt from regulation under the Act. A classic example are Section 144A private placements.
25. Compare Culp (1991) and Russo and Vinceguerra (1991).
26. CEA Section 2(a)(1)(A)(i)
27. See Securities Exchange Commission-Commodity Futures Trading Commission Jurisdictional Correspondence, *compiled at* [1975–1977 Transfer Binder] COMMODITY FUTURES LAW REPORTER (CCH) & 20204 (N.D. Ill. 1975), at 20829.
28. *Board of Trade of the City of Chicago v. SEC,* 677 F.2d 1137 (7th Cir.), *vacated* 459 U.S. 1026 (1982) (hereinafter *GNMA Options*).
29. *GNMA Options,* p. 1142 n.8.
30. *Chicago Mercantile Exchange v. SEC,* 883 F.2d 537 (7th Cir. 1989), at 545. (hereinafter *CME v. SEC*).

Chapter 20   Ex Ante Capital Allocation

1. Large portions of this chapter are based on Culp (2000).
2. Thanks to Barb Kavanagh for helping develop this example and the version of it that appears later in this chapter.
3. This section is drawn from Culp (1999).
4. In this article, risk-adjusted return on capital (RAROC), return on risk-adjusted capital (RORAC), and risk-adjusted return on risk-adjusted capital (RARORAC) are treated as synonymous. As long as risk is adjusted properly, the name of the measure is of secondary importance. RAROC is a specific type of risk-adjusted performance measure (RAPM). A discussion of non-RAROC RAPMs can be found in the excellent book by Matten (2000).
5. Relations between these risk measures and the traditional Sharpe ratio measure of market risk are explored in Culp and Mensink (2000) and Dowd (2000).
6. This and other methods of relating EaR to CaR are discussed in Matten (2000).
7. See Saita (1999).
8. A related hurdle rate that does not differentiate between systematic and idiosyncratic risk is the Sharpe ratio, whose classical implementation is explored in Sharpe (1994). Dowd (2000) generalizes this to a more useful measure of return per unit of risk at the margin.
9. EVA is a registered trademark of Stern Stewart & Co.
10. Problems with RAROC-like "risk budgets" are especially pronounced at institutional investors that tend to have long risk horizons and frequent changes in portfolio composition that are not reflected in most VaR or EaR measures. See Culp, Mensink, and Neves (1998).

Chapter 21   Ex Post Performance Measurement and Compensation

1. This section is taken from Culp and Mensink (2000).
2. This is also sometimes called the *Information Ratio*. Many practitioners also refer to the Modified Sharpe Ratio discussed later as the Information Ratio. To avoid any confusion, the term Information Ratio is not used to describe *any* performance measures in this book.
3. Strictly speaking, the ratio should be average excess historical returns divided by the standard deviation of the *difference* between actual portfolio returns and the T-bill rate. In doing the actual calculation, most people simply calculate the standard deviation of portfolio returns as the denominator. If the risk-free rate is truly risk-free, the variance of the risk-free rate is zero and the variance of the actual portfolio return *less* the risk-free rate should *equal* the variance of the actual return. Sometimes people actually do calculate the standard deviation of the residual because the T-bill rate does exhibit some positive variability.
4. See Sharpe (1994) and Dowd (2000).
5. See Matten (2000).
6. Compare Saita (1999).
7. Ibid.
8. See Zaik, Walter, Kelling, and James (1996).

Chapter 22   Internal Controls

1. Some of these principles are discussed in Culp, Hanke, and Neves (1999).
2. Miller (1997) explains that many of these disasters did not even really involve derivatives, much less did they precipitate any egregious social costs.
3. See Miller (1997), Culp, Miller, and Neves (1998), and Culp, Hanke, and Neves (1999).
4. Portions of this section are drawn from Culp and Mackay (1995).
5. This particular goal of front-line risk management and its framing was developed by Ken French.
6. See Global Derivative Study Group (1993).

Chapter 23   Tactical Risk Control with Derivatives

1. For more detail, see Culp, Miller, and Neves (1998) from which portions of this text are drawn. See also Culp, Hanke, and Neves (1999).
2. See Stoll (1995) and Kuprianov (1997) for more detailed discussions of Barings.
3. The parallels to Metallgesellschaft are not accidental. For yet another explanation of why such a situation might arise. See Culp and Miller (1995b, d).
4. This section is based on Culp (1995a) and Culp and Overdahl (1996).
5. Merton (1993), p. 23.
6. See, for example, Miller (1986, 1992).
7. See Culp (1995c).

8. This section is based on Culp and Mackay (1994,1995) and Culp and Overdahl (1996).
9. Several papers that disagree with Culp and Miller are reprinted in Culp and Miller (2000), as are Culp and Miller's responses to those criticisms.
10. Petzel (1989).

Chapter 24   Tactical Risk Control through Actual and Synthetic Asset Divestitures

1. See Barnish, Miller, and Rushmore (1997).
2. Ibid.
3. The remainder of this chapter is extracted with only minor modification from Culp and Neves (1998b).
4. For a good review of the issues involved in securitizations, see Kendall and Fishman (1997).
5. Securities issued by government-sponsored enterprises such as Fannie Mae often do not require ratings to be successfully placed and traded.
6. Securities issued in ABCPs are fundamentally distinct from asset-backed securities. Asset-backed commercial paper programs virtually always are sponsored by banks, whereas asset-backed securities may be issued by any intermediary or firm. Non-mortgage asset-backed securities came onto the scene in 1985 when First Boston underwrote a security issue based on computer leases held as receivables by Sperry.
7. See Kavanagh, Boemio, and Edwards (1992) for a particularly good description of the mechanics of ABCP programs.
8. Stone and Zissu (1997).
9. See note 7.
10. For these details and a useful summary generally, see Fridson (1997).
11. Ben-Amos (1997).
12. Structured notes are discussed more generally in Culp and Mackay (1997).

Chapter 25   Strategic Risk Control with Structured Liabilities

1. See Smithson and Ekew (1992) and Doherty (2000).
2. This chapter is based heavily on Culp, Furbush, and Kavanagh (1994). See also Culp and Mackay (1997).
3. See Finnerty (1988) and Smithson and Chew (1992).
4. The term *yield curve notes* was also sometimes used to describe these instruments.
5. Some of these accrual notes contained embedded barrier options, so that once a rate moved outside the range the structure knocked-out.
6. Issuers of LYONs included Waste Management, Inc., Staley Continental, Inc., G. Heileman Brewing Company, and Joseph E. Seagram & Sons, Inc. See McConnell and Schwartz (1986) and Smithson and Chew (1992).

7. See Smithson and Chew (1992).
8. See Jenson and Meckling (1976).

Chapter 26   Insurance and ART

1. Doherty (2000) is a notable exception. His book provides a truly integrated look at risk management including both insurance and derivatives. This chapter provides only an overview of insurance solutions to risk control problems, and interested readers are directed to Doherty's excellent text for a much more detailed treatment.
2. For completeness, you should also show that the separating equilibrium is not dominated by a Pooling equilibrium. Although the proof is omitted, any standard reference on the economics of uncertainty will include the proof. See, for example, Laffont (1990), chapter 8, on which the whole model in this section is loosely based.
3. See note 1.
4. See Mayers and Smith (1990).
5. This section is based largely on the excellent discussion in Doherty (2000), Chapter 14.
6. One must use caution and context in interpreting these numbers. A coverage of 50 xs 10 could mean $50 million above $10 million or $50,000 above $10,000.
7. For a more detailed discussion of ART integrated risk policies and basket insurance, see Hill (1998) and Doherty (2000).
8. Compare Bernero (1998) and Lane and Beckwith (2000).
9. Lane and Beckwith (2000).
10. Bernero (1998).
11. For a more detailed discussion, see Culp (1996).

bibliography

Aït-Sahalia, Y., and A. Lo. 2000. "Nonparametric Risk Management and Implied Risk Aversion." *Journal of Econometrics,* 94, pp. 9–51.

Akerlof, G. 1970. "The Market for 'Lemons': Qualitative Uncertainty and the Market Mechanism." *Quarterly Journal of Economics,* 43, pp. 941–973.

Alchian, A.A., and H. Demsetz. 1972, December. "Production, Information Costs, and Economic Organization." *American Economic Review,* 42, 5, pp. 777–795.

Altman, E.I. 1968, September. "Financial Ratios, Discriminant Analysis and the Prediction of Corporate Bankruptcy." *Journal of Finance,* pp. 589–609.

Altman, E.I. 1993. *Corporate Financial Distress and Bankruptcy,* 2nd ed. (New York: Wiley).

Altman, E.I., and A.C. Eberhart. 1994. "Do Seniority Provisions Protect Bondholders' Investments." *Journal of Portfolio Management,* 20, pp. 67–75.

Altman, E.I., R.G. Haldeman, and P. Narayanan. 1977. "ZETA Analysis: A New Model to Identify Bankruptcy Risk of Corporations." *Journal of Banking and Finance,* 1, pp. 29–54.

Amram, M., and N. Kulatilaka. 1999. *Real Options: Managing Strategic Investment in an Uncertain World* (Boston: Harvard Business School Press).

Aspinwall, R. 1983. "On the 'Specialness' of Banking." *Issues in Bank Regulation,* 7.

Asquith, J., and D. Cunningham. 1992, March. "Swaps and Termination Events: Legal and Business Considerations." Presented before the Annual General Meeting of the International Swap Dealers Association.

Bangia, A., F. Diebold, T. Schuermann, and J. Stroughair. 1999, June. "Liquidity on the Outside." *Risk,* 12, pp. 68–73.

Bank for International Settlements. 1998. *Operational Risk Management* (Basel, Switzerland: Basel Committee on Banking Supervision).

Bank for International Settlements. 1999. *Credit Risk Modelling: Current Practices and Applications* (Basel, Switzerland: Basel Committee on Banking Supervision).

Bank for International Settlements. 2000. *Range of Practice in Banks' Internal Ratings Systems* (Basel, Switzerland: Basel Committee on Banking Supervision).

Barnish, K., S. Miller, and M. Rushmore. 1997, spring. "The New Leveraged Loan Syndication Market." *Journal of Applied Corporate Finance*, 10, 1.

Ben-Amos, O. 1997, August 18. "Collateralized Issuance Zooming to New Heights." *American Banker*.

Bernero, R.H. 1998. "Second-Generation OTC Derivatives and Structure Products: Catastrophe Bonds, Catastrophe Swaps, and Life Insurance Securitizations." In *Securitized Insurance Risk*. Eds. M. Himick and S. Bouriaux (Chicago: Glenlake).

Best, P. 1999. *Implementing Value at Risk* (New York: Wiley).

Billingsley, P. 1995. *Probability and Measure*, 3rd ed. (New York: Wiley).

Black, F. 1976. "The Pricing of Commodity Contracts." *Journal of Financial Economics*, 3.

Black, F., and M. Scholes. 1973. "The Pricing of Options and Corporate Liabilities." *Journal of Political Economy*, 81, pp. 637–659.

Brennan, M.J. 1958. "The Supply of Storage." *American Economic Review*, 48, pp. 50–72.

Brennan, M.J., and E.S. Schwartz. 1988, summer. "The Case for Convertibles." *Journal of Applied Corporate Finance*, 2, 1.

Burghardt, G.D., and T.M. Belton. 1994. *The Treasury Bond Basis* (Chicago: Probus).

Campbell, J., A. Lo, and C. MacKinlay. 1996. *The Econometrics of Financial Markets* (Princeton, NJ: Princeton University Press).

Caouette, J.B., E.I. Altman, and P. Narayanan. 1998. *Managing Credit Risk* (New York: Wiley).

Chicago Board of Trade. 1997. *Commodity Trading Manual* (Chicago: Board of Trade of the City of Chicago).

Chriss, N. 1997. *Black-Scholes and Beyond: Option Pricing Models* (Chicago: Irwin).

Coase, R.H. 1937. "The Nature of the Firm." In *Readings in Price Theory* (Homewood, IL: Irwin).

Cochrane, J. 2000. *Asset Pricing* (Princeton, NJ: Princeton University Press).

Corrigan, E.G. 1982. "Are Banks Special?" *Federal Reserve Bank of Minneapolis Annual Report*.

Cox, J.C., and S.A. Ross. 1976. "The Valuation of Options for Alternative Stochastic Processes." *Journal of Financial Economics*, 3.

Crouhy, M., D. Galai, and R. Mark. 2000. "A Comparative Analysis of Current Credit Risk Models." *Journal of Banking & Finance*, 24, pp. 59–117.

Culp, C.L. 1991, summer. "Stock Index Futures and Financial Market Reform." *George Mason University Law Review,* 13, 3.

Culp, C.L. 1995a, July. *A Primer on Derivatives* (Chicago and Washington, DC: Board of Trade of the City of Chicago, and Competitive Enterprise Institute).

Culp, C.L. 1995b, December. "Regulatory Uncertainty and the Economics of Derivatives Regulation." *The Financier: Analysis of Capital and Money Market Transactions,* 2, 5.

Culp, C.L. 1995c, summer. "Regulation and the Growth of Derivatives in the Global Banking System." *Derivatives Quarterly,* 1, 4.

Culp, C.L. 1996. "Relations Between Insurance and Derivatives: Applications from Catastrophic Loss Insurance." *Proceedings of "Rethinking Insurance Regulation"* (Washington, DC: Competitive Enterprise Institute).

Culp, C.L. 1997, December. "The Role of Eurodeposit Futures in Swap Rate Determination: An Empirical Analysis." Working Paper, Graduate School of Business, The University of Chicago, Chicago.

Culp, C.L. 1998. "Derivatives Regulation: Problems and Prospects." *Derivatives Use, Trading & Regulation,* 4, 2.

Culp, C.L. 1999, October 15. "Wettbewerbsnachteile für Schweizer Banken? Konsultativpapier des Basler Ausschusses mit Schwächen." *Neue Zürcher Zeitung.*

Culp, C.L. 2000, March. "Revisiting RAROC." *Journal of Lending and Credit Risk Management.*

Culp, C.L., D. Furbush, and B.T. Kavanagh. 1994, fall. "Structured Debt and Corporate Risk Management." *Journal of Applied Corporate Finance,* 7, 3.

Culp, C.L., and S.H. Hanke. 1994a, July/August. "Derivatives Dingbats." *The International Economy,* 8, 4.

Culp, C.L., and S.H. Hanke. 1994b, September/October. "Pummeling Derivatives." *The International Economy,* 8, 5.

Culp, C.L., S.H. Hanke, and A.M. P. Neves. 1999, May/June. "Derivatives Diagnosis." *The International Economy,* 13, 3.

Culp, C.L., and B.T. Kavanagh. 1994, May/June. "Methods of Resolving Over-the-Counter Derivatives Contracts in Failed Depository Institutions: Restrictions on Regulators from Federal Banking Law." *Futures International Law Letter,* 14, 3–4.

Culp, C.L., and R.J. Mackay. 1994. "Regulating Derivatives: The Current System and Proposed Changes." *Regulation,* 4.

Culp, C.L., and R.J. Mackay. 1995. "Managing Derivatives Risk: A Strategic Approach." In *Handbook of Business Strategy* (New York: Faulkner & Gray).

Culp, C.L., and R.J. Mackay. 1997, March/April. "An Introduction to Structured Notes." *Derivatives*, 2, 4.

Culp, C.L., and R. Mensink. 2000, fall. "Measuring Risk for Asset Allocation, Performance Evaluation, and Risk Control: Different Problems, Different Solutions." *Journal of Performance Measurement*, 4, 1.

Culp, C.L., R. Mensink, and A.M. P. Neves. 1998, winter. "Value at Risk for Asset Managers." *Derivatives Quarterly*, 5, 2.

Culp, C.L., and M.H. Miller. 1995a, April . "Auditing the Auditors." *Risk*, 8, 4.

Culp, C.L., and M.H. Miller. 1995b, April 25. "Blame Mismanagement, Not Speculation, for Metall's Woes." *European Wall Street Journal*.

Culp, C.L., and M.H. Miller. 1995c, winter. "Metallgesellschaft and the Economics of Synthetic Storage." *Journal of Applied Corporate Finance*, 7, 4.

Culp, C.L., and M.H. Miller. 1995d, summer. "Hedging in the Theory of Corporate Finance." *Derivatives Quarterly*, 8, 1.

Culp, C.L., and M.H. Miller. 2000. *Corporate Hedging in Theory and Practice: Lessons from Metallgesellschaft* (London: Risk).

Culp, C.L., M.H. Miller, and A.M.P. Neves. 1998, winter. "Value at Risk: Uses and Abuses." *Journal of Applied Corporate Finance*, 10, 4.

Culp, C.L., and A.M. P. Neves. 1997, fall. "Risk Management by Securities Settlement Agents." *Journal of Applied Corporate Finance*, 10, 3.

Culp, C.L., and A.M. P. Neves. 1998a, summer. "Credit and Interest Rate Risk in the Business of Banking." *Derivatives Quarterly*, 4, 4.

Culp, C.L., and A.M. P. Neves. 1998b, summer. "Financial Innovations in Leveraged Commercial Loan Markets." *Journal of Applied Corporate Finance*, 11, 2.

Culp, C.L., and A.M. P. Neves. 1998c, April. *Securities and Multi-Currency Settlement Systems: Systemic Risk and Risk Management* (Washington, DC: Competitive Enterprise Institute).

Culp, C.L., and J.A. Overdahl. 1996. "An Overview of Derivatives: Their Mechanics, Participants, Scope of Activity, and Benefits." In *The Financial Services Revolution*. Ed. C. Kirsch (Chicago: Irwin).

Culp, C.L., and P. Planchat. 2000, summer. "New Risk Culture: An Opportunity for Business Growth and Innovation." *Derivatives Quarterly*, 6, 4.

Cunningham, D.P. 1998. "Do Corporations Have a Duty to Hedge?" In *Managing Financial Risk*, 3rd ed, C. Smithson (New York: McGraw-Hill).

Cunningham, D.P., and R.Y. Casper. 1993, July 9. "Over-the-Counter Derivatives Transactions: Netting Under the U.S. Bankruptcy Code, FIRREA, and FDICIA," Memorandum. (New York: Cravath, Swaine and Moore).

DeLoach, J.W. 2000. *Enterprise-Wide Risk Management* (London: Financial Times-Prentice Hall).

Dembo, R.S., A.R. Aziz, D. Rosen, and M. Zerbs. 2000, May. *Mark to Future: A Framework for Measuring Risk and Reward* (Toronto, Canada: Algorithmics).

DeMarzo, P., and D. Duffie. 1994. "Corporate Incentives for Hedging and Hedge Accounting." *Review of Financial Studies.*

Demsetz, H. 1968, February. "The Cost of Transacting." *Quarterly Journal of Economics,* 82, 1, pp. 33–53.

Derman, E., and I. Kani. 1994, February. "Riding on the Smile." *Risk,* 7, pp. 32–39.

Derman, E., I. Kani, and N. Chriss. 1996, summer. "Implied Trinomial Trees of the Volatility Smile." *Journal of Derivatives,* 3, 4, pp. 7–22.

Diamond, D. 1984. "Financial Intermediation and Delegated Monitoring." *Review of Economic Studies,* 51.

Diamond, D. 1989. "Asset Services and Financial Intermediation." In *Financial Markets and Incomplete Information: Frontiers of Modern Financial Theory,* 2. Eds. S. Bhattacharya and G. Constantinides (Savage, MD: Rowman and Littlefield).

Diamond, D. 1991. "Monitoring and Reputation: The Choice Between Bank Loans and Directly Placed Debt." *Journal of Political Economy,* 99.

Diamond, D., and R. Verrecchia. 1982. "Optimal Managerial Contracts and Equilibrium Security Prices." *Journal of Finance,* 37.

Dixit, A.K., and R.S. Pindyck. 1994. *Investment Under Uncertainty* (Princeton, NJ: Princeton University Press).

Doherty, N.A. 2000. *Integrated Risk Management* (New York: McGraw-Hill).

Dowd, K. 1998. *Beyond Value at Risk* (New York: Wiley).

Dowd, K. 2000. "Adjusting for Risk: An Improved Sharpe Ratio." *International Review of Economics and Finance,* 9, pp. 209–222.

Duffie, D. 1988. *Security Markets: Stochastic Models* (New York: Academic Press).

Duffie, D. 1996. *Dynamic Asset Pricing Theory* (Princeton, NJ: Princeton University Press).

Dupire, B. 1994, January. "Pricing with a Smile." *Risk,* 7, pp. 18–20.

Easley, D., and M. O'Hara. 1995. "Market Microstructure." In *Handbooks in OR & MS, 9: Finance.* Eds. R.A. Jarrow, V. Maksimovic, and W.T. Ziemba (Amsterdam: Elsevier).

Ederington, L.H. 1979. "The Hedging Performance of the New Futures Markets." *Journal of Finance,* 34, 1.

Engle, R. 1982. "Autoregressive Conditional Heteroskedasticity with Estimates of the Variance of United Kingdom Inflation." *Econometrica,* 50, pp. 391–407.

Engle, R. 1995. *ARCH: Selected Readings* (New York: Oxford University Press).

Euromoney Books. 1998. *The Practice of Risk Management* (London).

Falloon, W. 1993, December. "Fairway to Heaven." *Risk,* 6, 12, pp. 21–27.

Fama, E.F. 1976. "The Effects of a Firm's Investment and Financing Decisions on the Welfare of Its Security Holders." *American Economic Review,* 68, 3.

Fama, E.F. 1985. "What's Different About Banks?" *Journal of Monetary Economics,* 15.

Fama, E.F., and K.R. French. 1987, January. "Commodity Futures Prices: Some Evidence on Forecast Power, Premiums, and the Theory of Storage." *Journal of Business,* 60, pp. 55–74.

Fama, E.F., and K.R. French. 1988. "Business Cycles and the Behavior of Metals Prices." *Journal of Finance,* 43, pp. 1075–1093.

Fama, E.F., and K.R. French. 1992. "The Cross Section of Expected Stock Returns." *Journal of Finance,* 47, pp. 427–466.

Fama, E.F., and K.R. French. 1993, February. "Common Risk Factors in the Returns on Stocks and Bonds." *Journal of Financial Economics,* 33, 1, pp. 3–56.

Fama, E.F., and M.C. Jensen. 1983a. "Agency Problems and Residual Claims." *Journal of Law and Economics,* 26.

Fama, E.F., and M.C. Jensen. 1983b. "Separation of Ownership and Control." *Journal of Law and Economics,* 26.

Fama, E.F., and M.C. Jensen. 1985. "Organizational Forms and Investment Decisions." *Journal of Financial Economics,* 14.

Fama, E.F., and M.H. Miller. 1972. *The Theory of Finance* (New York: Holt, Rinehart, and Winston).

Feller, W. 1971. *An Introduction to Probability Theory and its Applications,* 2. (New York: Wiley).

Finnerty, J.D. 1988. "Financial Engineering in Corporate Finance: An Overview." *Financial Management,* 1, 4, pp. 14–33.

French, K.R. 1986. "Detecting Spot Price Forecasts in Futures Prices." *Journal of Business,* 59, pp. S39–S54.

Fridson, M.S. 1997, May 21. *A Guide to Collateralized Bond Obligations* (New York: Merrill Lynch).

Friedman, M., and L.J. Savage. 1948. "The Utility Analysis of Choices Involving Risk." *Journal of Political Economy,* 56, pp. 279–304.

Froot, K.A., D.S. Scharfstein, and J.C. Stein. 1993. "Risk Management: Coordinating Investment and Financing Policies." *Journal of Finance,* 48, 5.

Froot, K.A., D.S. Scharfstein, and J.C. Stein. 1994, November/December. "A Framework for Risk Management." *Harvard Business Review.*

Garman, M. 1976. "Market Microstructure." *Journal of Financial Economics,* 3, pp. 257–275.

Garman, M. 1996. "Improving on VAR." *Risk,* 9, 5.

Global Derivatives Study Group. 1993. *Derivatives: Practices and Principles* (Washington, DC: The Group of Thirty).

Global Derivatives Study Group. 1994. *Derivatives: Practices and Principles: Follow-up Surveys of Industry Practice* (Washington, DC: The Group of Thirty).

Glosten, L.R., and P.R. Milgrom. 1985. "Bid, Ask and Transaction Prices in a Specialist Market with Heterogeneously Informed Traders." *Journal of Financial Economics,* 14, pp. 71–100.

Gooch, A.C., and L.B. Klein. 1993. "A Review of International and U.S. Case Law Affecting Swaps and Related Derivative Products." In *Advanced Strategies in Financial Risk Management.* Eds. R.J. Schwartz and C.W. Smith, Jr. (New York: New York Institute of Finance).

Gourieroux, C. 1997. *ARCH Models in Financial Applications* (Amsterdam: Springer Verlag).

Grossman, S.J., and M.H. Miller. 1988. "Liquidity and Market Structure." *Journal of Finance,* 43, pp. 617–633.

Harrison, J.M., and D.M. Kreps. 1979. "Martingales and Arbitrage in Multiperiod Securities Markets." *Journal of Economic Theory,* 20, pp. 381–408.

Hill, B. 1975. "A Simple General Approach to Inference about the Tail of a Distribution." *Annals of Mathematical Statistics,* 3, pp. 1163–1174.

Hill, D. 1998. "Rethinking Risk: Across Traditional Boundaries." In *Securitized Insurance Risk.* Eds. M. Himick and S. Bouriaux (Chicago: Glenlake).

Hotelling, H. 1931. "The Economics of Exhaustible Resources." *Journal of Political Economy,* 39, pp. 137–175.

Huang, C., and R.H. Litzenberger. 1988. *Foundations for Financial Economics* (Amsterdam: North-Holland).

Hull, J., and A. White. 1998, spring. "Value at Risk When Daily Changes in Market Variables are Not Normally Distributed." *Journal of Derivatives,* pp. 9–19.

Hull, J.C. 2000. *Options, Futures, and Other Derivatives,* 4th ed. (Upper Saddle River, NJ: Prentice Hall).

Ingersoll, J. 1987. *Theory of Financial Decision Making* (Tottowa, NJ: Rowman and Littlefield).

Ingersoll, J., and S. Ross. 1992, January. "Waiting to Invest: Investment and Uncertainty." *Journal of Business,* 65, 1, pp. 1–29.

ISDA. 2000, September. *Operational Risk Regulatory Approach Discussion Paper* (New York: International Swaps and Derivatives Association).

ISDA/BBA/RMA. 1999, December. *Operational Risk: The Next Frontier* (New York: International Swaps and Derivatives Association., British Bankers' Association, and RMA: The Risk Management Association).

Jackwerth, J.C., and M. Rubinstein. 1996. "Recovering Probability Distributions from Option Prices." *Journal of Finance,* 51, 5, pp. 1611–1631.

James, C. 1987. "Some Evidence on the Uniqueness of Bank Loans." *Journal of Financial Economics,* 19.

Jarrow, R., and S. Turnbull. 1999. *Derivative Securities,* 2nd ed. (New York: South-Western).

Jensen, M.C., and W.H. Meckling. 1976. "Theory of the Firm: Managerial Behavior, Agency Costs and Ownership Structure." *Journal of Financial Economics,* 3, 4, pp. 305–360.

Johnson, L.L. 1960. "The Theory of Hedging and Speculation in Commodity Futures." *Review of Economic Studies,* 26.

Jorion, P. 1997, summer. "Lessons From the Orange County Bankruptcy." *Journal of Derivatives,* 4, 4, pp. 61–66.

Jorion, P. 2000. *Value at Risk,* 2nd ed. (New York: McGraw-Hill).

Kaldor, N. 1939. "Speculation and Economic Stability." *Review of Economic Studies,* 7, pp. 1–27.

Kavanagh, B., T.R. Boemio, and G.A. Edwards. 1992, February. "Asset-Backed Commercial Paper Programs." *Federal Reserve Bulletin,* 78, 2.

Kazman, S. 1990. "Deadly Overcaution: FDA's Drug Approval Process." *Journal of Regulation and Social Costs,* 1, 9.

Kazman, S. 1992. "Saying Yes To Drugs." *Journal of Regulation and Social Costs,* 2, 6.

Keenan, S.E. 2000, January. *Historical Default Rates of Corporate Bond Issuers, 1920–1999.* (New York: Moody's Investor Service Global Credit Research).

Kendall, L.T., and M.J. Fishman. 1997. *A Primer on Securitization* (Cambridge, MA: MIT Press).

Keynes, J.M. 1930. *The Theory of Money: Volume II, The Applied Theory of Money* (London: Macmillan). Reprinted 1950.

Knight, F.H. 1921. *Risk, Uncertainty, and Profit* (Boston: Houghton Mifflin).

Kuprianov, A. 1997. "Derivatives Debacles: Case Studies of Large Losses in Derivatives Markets." In *Derivatives Handbook: Risk Management and Control.* Eds. R.J. Schwartz and C.W. Smith, Jr. (New York: Wiley).

Laffont, J-J. 1990. *The Economics of Uncertainty and Information* (Cambridge, MA: MIT Press).

Lane, M.N., and R.G. Beckwith. 2000, fall. "Trends in the Insurance-Linked Securities Market." *Derivatives Quarterly,* 7, 1, pp. 26–35.

Lewis, E.M. 1992. *An Introduction to Credit Scoring* (San Rafael, CA: Fair/Isaac).

Longin, F.M. 2000. "From Value at Risk to Stress Testing: The Extreme Value Approach." *Journal of Banking & Finance,* 24, pp. 1097–1130.

Lummer, S., and J. McConnell. 1989. "Further Evidence on the Bank Lending Process and the Reaction of the Capital Market to Bank Loan Agreements." *Journal of Financial Economics,* 25.

Markham, J.W. 1987. *The History of Commodity Futures Trading and its Regulation* (New York: Praeger).

Markowitz, H. 1952. "The Utility of Wealth." *Journal of Political Economy,* 60, pp. 151–158.

Markowitz, H. 1959. *Portfolio Selection* (New York: Wiley).

Matten, C. 2000. *Managing Bank Capital,* 2nd ed. (New York: Wiley).

Mayers, D., and C.W. Smith, Jr. 1982. "On the Corporate Demand for Insurance." *Journal of Business,* 55, pp. 281–296.

Mayers, D., and C.W. Smith, Jr. 1987. "Corporate Insurance and the Underinvestment Problem." *Journal of Risk and Insurance,* 54, pp. 45–54.

Mayers, D., and C.W. Smith, Jr. 1990. "On the Corporate Demand for Insurance: Evidence from the Reinsurance Market." *Journal of Business,* 63.

McConnell, J.J., and E.S. Schwartz. 1986, July. "LYON Taming." *Journal of Finance,* 41, 3, pp. 561–577.

Merton, R.C. 1973. "The Theory of Rational Option Pricing." *Bell Journal of Economics and Management Science,* 4, pp. 141–183.

Merton, R.C. 1974. "On the Pricing of Corporate Debt: The Risk Structure of Interest Rates." *Journal of Finance,* 29, pp. 449–470.

Merton, R.C. 1992. *Continuous-Time Finance* (London: Blackwell).

Merton, R.C. 1993. "Operation and Regulation in Financial Intermediation: a Functional Perspective." Working Paper 93–020 (Harvard Business School).

Merton, R.C., and A.F. Perold. 1993, fall. "Theory of Risk Capital in Financial Firms." *Journal of Applied Corporate Finance,* 6, 3.

Micalizzi, A., and L. Trigeorgis. 1999. "Project Evaluation, Strategy and Real Options." In *Real Options and Business Strategy: Applications to Decision Making.* Ed. L. Trigeorgis (London: Risk Books).

Miller, M.H. 1986. "Financial Innovation: The Last Twenty Years and the Next." *Journal of Financial and Quantitative Analysis,* 21.

Miller, M.H. 1992, winter. "Financial Innovation: Achievements and Prospects." *Journal of Applied Corporate Finance,* 4, 4.

Miller, M.H. 1997. *Merton Miller on Derivatives* (New York: Wiley).

Miller, M.H., and C.L. Culp. 1996, June 22. "The SEC's Costly Disclosure Rules." *Wall Street Journal.*

Miller, M.H., and D.J. Ross. 1997, summer. "The Orange County Bankruptcy and its Aftermath: Some New Evidence." *Journal of Derivatives,* 4, 4, pp. 51–60.

Mood, A.M., F.A. Graybill, and D.C. Boes. 1974. *Introduction to the Theory of Statistics,* 3rd ed. (New York: McGraw-Hill).

Myers, S.C. 1977. "The Determinants of Corporate Borrowing." *Journal of Financial Economics,* 5, pp. 147–175.

Nelson, D.B. 1991. "Conditional Heteroskedasticity in Asset Returns: A New Approach." *Econometrica,* 59, pp. 347–370.

Ong, M.K. 1999. *Internal Credit Risk Models* (London: Risk Books).

Patrikis, E.T. 1996, April. "Dealer/End User Relationships: What They Are and What They Should Be." Remarks presented before the End Users of Derivatives Association (Washington, DC).

Patrikis, E.T., and K. Walraven. 1992. "The Netting Provisions of the Federal Deposit Insurance Corporation Improvement Act of 1991." *Futures International Law Letter,* 12, 1.

Petzel, T.E. 1989. *Financial Futures and Options* (New York: Greenwood Press).

Picoult, E. 1998. "Calculating Value-at-Risk with Monte Carlo Simulation." *Monte Carlo: Methodologies and Applications to Pricing and Risk Management* (London: Risk Books).

Pownall, R.A. J., and K.G. Koedijk. 1999. "Capturing Downside Risk in Financial Markets: The Case of the Asian Crisis." *Journal of Banking and Finance,* 18, pp. 853–870.

Property Claim Services. 1993. *The Catastrophe Record: 1949–1993* (Rahway, NJ).

Quigg, L. 1995. "Optimal Land Development." In *Real Options in Capital Investment: Models, Strategies, and Applications.* Ed. L. Trigeorgis (New York: Praeger).

Rajan, R.G. 1992. "Insiders and Outsiders: The Choice Between Informed and Arm's-Length Debt." *Journal of Finance,* 47.

Roll, R. 1984, September. "A Simple Implicit Measure of the Effective Bid-Ask Spread in an Efficient Market." *Journal of Finance,* 39, 4, pp. 1127–1139.

Ross, A. 1978. "A Simple Approach to the Valuation of Risky Streams." *Journal of Business,* 51, pp. 453–475.

Ross, S.A. 1989, July. "Institutional Markets, Financial Marketing, and Financial Innovation." *Journal of Finance,* 44.

Rothschild, M, and J. Stiglitz. 1976. "Equilibrium in Competitive Insurance Markets." *Quarterly Journal of Economics,* 90, pp. 629–649.

Rubinstein, M. 1994, July. "Implied Binomial Trees." *Journal of Finance,* 49, 3, pp. 771–818.

Russo, T.A., and M. Vinceguerra. 1991. "Financial Innovation and Uncertain Regulation: Selected Issues Regarding New Product Development." *Texas Law Review,* 69, 6.

Saita, Francesco. 1999, autumn. "Allocation of Risk Capital in Financial Institutions." *Financial Management*, 28, 3.

Saunders, A. 1999. *Credit Risk Measurement: New Approaches to Value at Risk and Other Paradigms* (New York: Wiley).

Sharpe, W. 1994, fall. "The Sharpe Ratio." *Journal of Portfolio Management*, pp. 49–58.

Shimko, D. 1999. *Credit Risk: Models and Management* (London: Risk Books).

Shirreff, D. 1991. "Dealing with Default." *Risk*, 4, 1.

Smith, C.W., Jr. 1995. "Corporate Risk Management: Theory and Practice." *Journal of Derivatives*, 2, 4.

Smith, C.W., Jr., and R.M. Stulz. 1985. "The Determinants of Firms' Hedging Policies." *Journal of Financial and Quantitative Analysis*, 20, 4, pp. 391–405.

Smith, C.W., Jr., and J. Warner. 1979. "On Financial Contracting: An Analysis of Bond Covenants." *Journal of Financial Economics*, 7, pp. 117–161.

Smith, F.L., Jr. 1988. "Environment Policy at the Crossroads." In *Environmental Politics: Public Costs, Private Rewards*. Eds. M. Greve and F. Smith (New York: Praeger).

Smith, F.L., Jr., and C.L. Culp. 1989. "Speculation: Adam Smith Revisited." *The Freeman*.

Smithson, C.W. 1998. *Managing Financial Risk*, 3rd ed. (New York: McGraw-Hill).

Smithson, C.W., and D.H. Chew, Jr. 1992, winter. "The Uses of Hybrid Debt in Managing Corporate Risk." *Journal of Applied Corporate Finance*, 4, 4.

Stein, J.L. 1961. "The Simultaneous Determination of Spot and Futures Prices." *American Economic Review*, 51.

Stein, W.L. 1988. "The Exchange-Trading Requirement of the Commodity Exchange Act." *Vanderbilt Law Review*, 41.

Stiglitz, J., and A. Weiss. 1983. "Incentives Effects of Terminations: Applications to Credit and Labor Markets." *American Economic Review*, 73.

Stoll, H., ed. 1999. *The International Library of Critical Writings in Financial Economics, 4: Microstructure: The Organization of Trading and Short Term Price Behavior* (Cheltenham, England: Elgar).

Stoll, H.R. 1995, fall. "Lost Barings: A Tale in Three Parts Concluding with a Lesson." *Journal of Derivatives*, 3, 1, pp. 109–115.

Stone, C.A., and A. Zissu. 1997, spring. "Asset Backed Commercial Paper: Get With the Program." *Journal of Applied Corporate Finance*, 10, 1.

Stonier, J. 1999. "Airline Long-Term Planning Under Uncertainty: The Benefits of Asset Flexibility Created Through Product Commonalty and Manufacturer Lead Time Reductions." In *Real Options and Business Strategy: Applications to Decision Making.* Ed. L. Trigeorgis (London: Risk Books).

Stulz, R.M. 1984. "Optimal Hedging Policies." *Journal of Financial and Quantitative Analysis*, 19, 2, pp. 127–140.

Stulz, R.M. 1990. "Managerial Discretion and Optimal Financing Policies." *Journal of Financial Economics,* 26, pp. 3–27.

Telser, L. 1958, June. "Futures Trading and the Storage of Cotton and Wheat." *Journal of Political Economy*, 66.

Telser, L. 1960, August. "Reply to Cootner." *Journal of Political Economy*, 68, 4.

Trigeorgis, L. 1995. "Real Options; An Overview." In *Real Options in Capital Investment: Models, Strategies, and Applications.* Ed. L. Trigeorgis (New York: Praeger).

Trigeorgis, L. 1996. *Real Options: Managerial Flexibility and Strategy in Resource Allocation* (Cambridge, MA: MIT Press).

Trigeorgis, L. 1999. *Real Options and Business Strategy* (London: Risk Books).

Tufano, P. 1996. "Who Manages Risk? An Empirical Examination of Risk Management Practices in the Gold Mining Industry." *Journal of Finance,* 51.

Uyemura, D.G., and D.R. Van Deventer. 1993. *Financial Risk Management in Banking* (New York: McGraw-Hill).

Venkataraman, S. 1997, March/April. "Value at Risk for a Mixture of Normal Distributions: The Use of Quasi-Bayesian Estimation Techniques." *Economic Perspectives* (Chicago: Federal Reserve Bank of Chicago) pp. 2–13.

Wildavsky, A. 1988. *Searching for Safety* (New Brunswick, NJ: Transaction Books).

Williams, J. 1986. *The Economic Function of Futures Markets* (New York: Cambridge University Press).

Wilson, T. 1997a, September. "Portfolio Credit Risk I." *Risk,* 10, 9.

Wilson, T. 1997b, October. "Portfolio Credit Risk II." *Risk,* 10, 10.

Working, H. 1948. "Theory of the Inverse Carrying Charge in Futures Markets." *Journal of Farm Economics,* 30.

Working, H. 1949a. "The Investigation of Economic Expectations." *American Economic Review.*

Working, H. 1949b, December. "The Theory of Price of Storage." *American Economic Review.*

Working, H. 1953, June. "Futures Trading and Hedging." *American Economic Review.*

Working, H. 1962, June. "New Concepts Concerning Futures Markets and Prices." *American Economic Review.*

Young, M.D. 1997. "The Quest for Legal Certainty: What Derivatives Are Subject to the Commodity Exchange Act?" In *The Financial Services Revolution.* Ed. C.E. Kirsch (Chicago: Irwin).

Zaik, E., J. Walter, G. Kelling, and C. James. 1996, summer. "RAROC at Bank of America: From Theory to Practice." *Journal of Applied Corporate Finance,* 9, 2.

Zangari, P. 1996, second quarter. "An Improved Methodology for Measuring VaR." *RiskMetrics™ Monitor* (New York: JP Morgan).

index

597